Monumenta Archaeologica 22

K'AXOB:
RITUAL, WORK, AND FAMILY
IN AN ANCIENT MAYA VILLAGE

EDITED BY
PATRICIA A. MCANANY

COTSEN INSTITUTE OF ARCHAEOLOGY
UNIVERSITY OF CALIFORNIA, LOS ANGELES
2004

This book is set in 10-point Janson Text, with titles in 25-point Times New Roman.
Edited by Abby Sider
Designed by William Morosi

Library of Congress Cataloging-in-Publication Data

K'axob : materiality, ritual practice, and social reproduction at a formative Maya village / edited by Patricia A. McAnany ; with contributions by Eleanor Harrison ... [et al.].
    p. cm. — (Monumenta archaeologica ; v. 22)
 Includes bibliographical references and index.
 ISBN 1-931745-09-9 (alk. paper)
 1. K'axob Site (Belize) 2. Mayas—Antiquities. 3. Excavations (Archaeology)—Belize. I. McAnany, Patricia Ann. II. Harrison, Eleanor. III. Monumenta archaeologica (Cotsen Institute of Archaeology at UCLA) ; v. 22.
 F1435.1.K35K39 2004
 972.82—dc22
                    2004005570

DEDICATION

*For Concepción Campos,
landowner of K'axob and
guardian of the ancestors.*

CONTENTS

Dedication   *iii*

Acknowledgments   *vii*

Preface to a Hybrid Publication   *ix*

1.   Situating K'axob within Formative Period Lowland Maya Archaeology   *1*
     Patricia A. McAnany

2.   Landscapes of K'axob in Deep and Current Time   *11*
     Patricia A. McAnany

PART I: The Built Environment   *19*

3.   Domiciles and Construction Histories   *23*
     Patricia A. McAnany

4.   Nourishing the Animus of Lived Space through Ritual Caching   *65*
     Eleanor Harrison-Buck

5.   Soaked and Steamed Sustenance: Evidence from Sherd-Lined Pits   *87*
     Victoria L. Bobo

PART II: Mortuary Ritual   *105*

6.   Ancestors: Bioarchaeology of the Human Remains of K'axob   *109*
     Rebecca Storey

PART III: Pottery   *139*

7.   The Potter's Choice of Clays and Crafting Technologies   *143*
     Mary Lee Bartlett

8.   Ceramic History of K'axob: The Early Years   *169*
     Sandra L. López Varela

9.   Pottery Vessels of K'axob   *193*
     Kimberly A. Berry, Sandra L. López Varela, Mary Lee Bartlett,
     Tamarra Martz, and Patricia A. McAnany

10.   Artifacts of Fired Clay   *263*
      Mary Lee Bartlett

PART IV: Stone Tools   *275*

11.   Tools of the Trade: Acquisition, Use, and Recycling of Chipped Stone   *279*
         Patricia A. McAnany and Polly A. Peterson

12.   Obsidian Blades and Source Areas   *307*
         Patricia A. McAnany

13.   Ground and Polished Stone Tools   *317*
         Patricia A. McAnany and Justin P. Ebersole

PART V: Personal Adornment and Cosmological Expression   *331*

14.   The Art of Shell Working and the Social Uses of Shell Ornaments   *335*
         Ilean Isel Isaza Aizpurúa

15.   Ornaments of Bone and Semiprecious Stone   *353*
         Mary Lee Bartlett

16.   The Quadripartite Motif and the Centralization of Power   *367*
         Annabeth Headrick

PART VI: Biological Resources   *379*

17.   Contribution of Fishing and Hunting to Subsistence and Symbolic Expression   *382*
         Marilyn A. Masson

18.   Mollusca of K'axob: For Supper and Soul   *399*
         Ryan Harrigan

PART VII: Denouement   *415*
         Patricia A. McAnany

Bibliography   *421*

Author Biographies   *443*

Glossary   *446*

Index   *448*

ACKNOWLEDGMENTS

As the K'axob Project was conceived over a decade ago and fieldwork for this publication was undertaken over the course of three years (1990-1993), many individuals have been involved and it is difficult to know where to begin to acknowledge individual contributions. Employing a tried-and-true direct historical approach, I extend my appreciation to those at the Cotsen Institute of Archaeology who bravely charted new publication terrain to bring off this hybrid publication. At the Digital Archaeology Lab, we thank the former director, Louise Krasniewicz. Without her vision, enthusiasm, and tenacity, the digital part of this publication would not have seen the light of day. Working daily in the digital lab, Tamarra Martz constructed a framework for the electronic materials and fit the pieces together. The aesthetic appeal of the digital materials is due, in part, to the artistic talent of graphic artist Judith Botsai. At the press, Marilyn Beaudry, director of publications, allowed a new kind of publication to be born—one that blended hard-copy and digital media. Anonymous reviewers provided valuable feedback on the manuscript, and this strengthened the final product. Chip Stanish, as director of the institute, provided continued and strong support for this hybrid publication and Julia Sanchez brought the project to completion.

This project took shape during my 1999-2000 leave of absence from Boston University, during which I was fortunate enough to participate in the Bunting Fellowship Program at the Radcliffe Institute for Advanced Study, Harvard University. Additional support for the publication was provided by the Radcliffe College Dean's Fund, Boston University Dean's Discretionary Fund, the Ahau Foundation, Edward Harris, and Peter D. Joyce. This funding supported Boston University graduate students Kimberly Berry and Ben Thomas, both of whom expended many hours compiling and checking data sets, generating illustrations, and working with digital photo images. The continued efforts, patience, and precision of Kimberly Berry greatly enhanced the digital component of this publication.

Field research was funded by a National Science Foundation (NSF) Grant (SBR-9112310) as well as a supplementary NSF grant, three NSF REU (Research Experience for Undergraduates) grants, and an NSF dissertation improvement grant to Mary Lee Angelini (now Mary Lee Bartlett). Undergraduate field study programs, operated during the 1990 and 1993 seasons, were funded by the Division of International Programs at Boston University; the field school students were instrumental in the collection of the data reported in this volume.

Fieldwork in Belize was conducted under permit from the Department of Archaeology, Belmopan, Belize, and permission was generously granted for temporary export of study collections to the archaeology laboratory at Boston University. Special thanks are due to the Belizean archaeological commissioners, specifically John Morris, Allen Moore, and the late Harriot Topsey. Over the years, undergraduate and graduate students as well as colleagues have worked tirelessly in the K'axob lab at Boston University to complete the analysis of this material. In addition to the contributors to this volume, Emily Hall, Cara Lonardo, Jose Aguayo, and Pia Terranova deserve special mention. Thanks to Michael Glascock and the staff of the University of Missouri Research Reactor Center for neutron activation analysis of the obsidian, and also to the staff of the Arizona AMS Facility and the Oxford AMS Laboratory for radiocarbon analyses. The fruits of these lab analyses are presented in the pages to follow.

The quality of the archaeological data presented herein is due in large part to the exemplary field efforts of undergraduate and graduate students, colleagues, volunteers, and local workers who meticulously excavated and recorded the beautifully stratified deposits of K'axob despite rainstorms and the predictable tropical malaise. Too numerous to list here, they can be viewed in action in the field setting of K'axob in the accompanying digital *Photo Database*. Peter D. Harrison introduced the site of K'axob to me in the context of the 1981 Pulltrouser Swamp Project, and I will be forever grateful to him for his generosity and encouragement. A final nod of thanks must go to land-owner Concepción Campos, who buoyed our spirits with his philosophical insights and kept me ever mindful of the profound responsibility I incurred in disturbing the many ancestors of K'axob who slept below the roots of his sugarcane plants. Telling the story of how they lived and of how they died, presenting the materiality of their existence, and chronicling their domiciles—dense with ritual as well as work-related features—represents the first step in discharging this obligation.

PREFACE TO A HYBRID PUBLICATION

Digital technology has changed the face of archaeological publishing. No longer do archaeologists need to wrangle with book editors over the number of data tables allowed in a monograph. No longer does the inquisitive student in search of comparative case material need to re-enter data print-set on the fading yellow pages of an overpriced hard-bound book. The digital medium is here to stay and is rapidly transforming the fashion in which we collect, publish, and curate our data sets. But given the built-in obsolescence of digital technology, archaeologists have been wary, and rightly so, of investing too much too quickly in the digital medium. The hybrid form of this publication represents a marriage of two kinds of media: traditional paper and twenty-first-century digital. It draws, we hope, on the strengths of both media and avoids the shortcomings of each.

During the Society for American Archaeology meetings of 2000, I began to talk seriously with Louise Krasniewicz, then of the UCLA Digital Archaeology Lab, and Marilyn Beaudry-Corbett, then director of publications at the UCLA Cotsen Institute of Archaeology, about the possibility of publishing a printed volume side by side with digital material. The printed volume would contain the narratives of K'axob and could be read at any time and any place without the need to gain access to technical equipment. Such "rocking chair" appeal, however, is offset by the fact that high publication costs preclude the inclusion of comprehensive data sets and color images in such a printed format. Even if one could publish pages of raw data (as has been done in the past), they are of limited use to other analysts, who are required to undertake the onerous task of converting paper data sets to digital ones. A digital publication, on the other hand, allows dissemination of full data sets in a readily usable format in addition to color photographic images of hundreds of artifacts—including here more than one hundred pottery vessels.

On digital media, a comprehensive rather than a selective record can be disseminated, thus enhancing the future analytical potential of any given database. For instance, in this printed book you will find a subset of construction phase and burial plans, but the comprehensive set is available on the digital medium by accessing the *Domiciles Database* and the *Burials Database*.

The more I discussed the possibility of a hybrid publication with Louise and Marilyn, the more obvious it became that we would be creating two very distinct publications. Each should be able to stand alone, and each would be enhanced immeasurably by being paired with the other. The power of the word in hard copy is well matched by the visual power and analytical potential of the digital medium. The stand-alone quality of each medium means that the hard-copy volume can be read cover to cover and fully absorbed without turning on a computer. If one desires to view more than the skeletal profiles of pottery vessels as presented in Chapter 9, then one can study full-color images (and several Quicktime® videos) by opening the digital *Pottery Vessels Database*. For nearly every chapter there is at least one digital file—containing images, text, or both—that presents the full corpus of available information. In the front of each major section of this book, a *Guide to Accompanying Digital Materials* lists and describes the relevant digital databases. The digital format provides easy access to reference material as well as the possibility of cross-indexing data files to conduct analyses that, no doubt, will reveal new patterns in the K'axob data. The color images of excavation locales and crews in the *Photo Database* and the *Tour of K'axob*, moreover, promote an experiential understanding of this archaeological project that is not easily achieved in a black-and-white print medium. In short, this hybrid publication can be read and used in a number of ways, and the hard-copy and digital presentations can be used separately or together.

CHAPTER 1

SITUATING K'AXOB WITHIN FORMATIVE PERIOD LOWLAND MAYA ARCHAEOLOGY

PATRICIA A. MCANANY

Due to its somewhat inaccessible stratigraphic placement beneath the massive building programs of the Classic period, with few exceptions Formative Maya archaeology has been glimpsed through a narrow window at the bottom of a test trench. Moreover, the limited appearance of hieroglyphs gives the impression that the Formative period was a time "before history" or at least before Classic period literati forged narratives of time in hieroglyphic texts. While, through epigraphic feats of "code-breaking," scholars of Classic Maya texts have breathed life into the political machinations of Classic period rulers, insights into the preceding period have been won using more traditional archaeological tools—trowels, shovels, picks, and screens. Three seasons of large-scale excavations deep into the Preclassic deposits of the Maya site of K'axob—situated in the New River valley of northern Belize (figure 1.1)—have yielded an informative array of archaeological material associated with ancient Maya domiciles. This information is relevant to many of the key issues of Formative archaeology, such as the circumstances and timing of the founding of Maya communities, the materialization of institutionalized authority, the role of ancestors in social reproduction, the nature and extent of artisan traditions, and the formalization of local and regional procurement networks. In this volume, these issues are examined through a case study of a village that thrived during the time before rulers were memorialized in stone as *ch'ul ajaw*, or divine lord. But this study does not simply trace the roots of the Classic period florescence; rather, it examines the Formative period on its own terms. Balancing a village-centric and a regional perspective, the chapters to follow deal with such topics as the expression of ritual and cosmology within a domestic context, the materialization of village identity through artisanship, and the extent to which K'axob interacted with and emulated larger centers both nearby and far away.

This chapter initiates the study first by examining the history of inquiry into Lowland Maya Formative archaeology and second by situating K'axob within the

Figure 1.1 Map of eastern Mesoamerica showing relevant archaeological sites. *Illustration by K'axob Project staff.*

larger issues of Formative period archaeology. Throughout this volume, the term "Formative" is used more frequently than is the term "Preclassic." The goal of this convention is to focus on the similarities (and differences) between the village tradition of the Maya Lowlands and that of the rest of Mesoamerica. The time frame indicated by the term "Formative" spans 2500 BC to AD 250. As is discussed in chapter 2, this study is most concerned with the middle and later parts of the Formative period and the early part of the Classic period, or the time between 1000 BC and AD 400.

INQUIRY INTO THE FORMATIVE PERIOD IN THE MAYA LOWLANDS

Formative period Lowland Maya archaeology arguably commenced with the Uaxactun Project undertaken by the Carnegie Institution of Washington from 1926 to 1937; this pioneer project, undertaken at a site located in what was then the extremely remote southern Petén, produced the first codification of Preclassic Maya pottery. Borrowing terms from K'iche' Mayan, Robert E. Smith (1955:3) called the earliest red pottery "Mamom" ("grandmother" in K'iche') and noted that it occurred only in the "black dirt underlying all masonry structures". Above it, a slightly different red ware that Smith called "Chicanel" ("concealer" in K'iche') was found "in the brown dirt above ash and black dirt". These red monochromes have since become markers of the geographical extent of Lowland Maya Formative, or Preclassic, populations. Mamom and Chicanel, in particular, have been generalized from Uaxactun-specific ceramic complex names to lowland-wide ceramic sphere designations.

The Uaxactun Project also uncovered a monumental construction that was assigned to the Chicanel ceramic sphere—the fabled Str. E-VII-sub (Ricketson 1937), complete with mosaic masks adorning its façades and a possible astronomical alignment (later known as the Group E assemblage). About the same time and later, Preclassic materials were excavated at several sites in what was then called British Honduras: at San Jose and at Benque Viejo, a.k.a. Xunantunich, by J. Eric Thompson (1939, 1940); at Barton Ramie by Gordon Willey (Willey et al. 1965); and at San Estevan by William Bullard (1965). All confirmed the stratigraphic priority of the plain red wares of the Preclassic ceramic spheres. In retrospect, these British Honduras projects were harbingers of what would later come to be recognized as the very heavy settlement signature of

Formative populations along the rivers and wetlands of contemporary Belize. On the opposite (western) side of the lowlands, riverine sites such as Altar de Sacrificios and Seibal also yielded early red-ware pottery, classified within the Xe and Real phase complexes, respectively, from the base of deep test excavations (Sabloff 1975; Willey 1970). To the north, field research at the Yucatec site of Dzibilchaltun revealed Formative architecture in the Mirador Group (Andrews IV and Andrews V 1980) in addition to the presence of a sizable Formative village at nearby Komchen (Andrews V et al. 1984; Ringle and Andrews V 1988). To the west, Lowe (1977) noted the presence of Late Formative Maya pottery (specifically, a type called Sierra Red) at the Grijalva valley site of Chiapa de Corzo, an area typically characterized as Mixe-Zoque rather than as Maya.

In 1955 the University of Pennsylvania initiated a long-term project at Tikal. The prevalence of Preclassic materials in burials and structures underlying the hallowed North Acropolis of Tikal (Coe 1990) hinted at the existence of a large and nonegalitarian Formative period population in the rolling hills and wetlands of the Petén. Later excavations by Juan Pedro Laporte in the vast Late Formative Mundo Perdido complex confirmed the presence of massive Late Formative architectural complexes (Laporte and Fialko 1990). At nearby Uaxactun, home of the first recognized Late Formative truncated pyramid, Juan Antonio Valdés (1993) later uncovered additional Formative period monumental architecture at Group H. Without a doubt, the gem in the crown of Preclassic Lowland Maya monumental architecture was found at the northern Petén site of El Mirador. There, Matheny (1986) and later Hansen (1998) identified the largest pyramids ever constructed in the Maya region (Danta and Tigre complexes) as dating to the Late Formative period. At Mirador towering, truncated pyramids are topped by three pyramidal shrines arranged in triangular form. This triadic structure, as well as the sculpting of stuccoed deity masks on building façades and the absence of burial tombs, have come to characterize Late Formative Lowland Maya monumental architecture.

Between 1975 and 1985 Belize once again became a focus of Formative research with the excavation of residential structures at Cuello (Hammond 1991a), the discovery of a stucco-mask-adorned pyramid (Str. 5C-2nd) at Cerros (Freidel

1979), and the exploration of a 33-meter-tall pyramid (Str. N10-43) at Lamanai (Pendergast 1981). Although the discovery of Formative period monumental architecture provided a valuable complement to previous discoveries in the Petén, it was the large-scale excavation of actual house compounds at Cuello that provided the first high-resolution, longitudinal view of the domiciles and domestic patterns of a people that Hammond (1977: 128) referred to as the "earliest Maya." Material remains interpreted as ancestral to Classic period and contemporary Maya include the following characteristics: apsidal domiciles often with subfloor burial interments and a spatial arrangement around a central patio, well-formed pottery (featuring slipped monochrome red wares), and a lithic technology based on the production of chert bifaces. The sophistication of the pottery technology became an issue when Hammond (1977:133) proposed to deepen the Formative period chronology by linking charcoal that had been radiocarbon-dated to circa 2500 BC with basal pottery identified as the Swasey complex. Subsequent assays on early charcoal from Cuello as well as other Formative deposits at Belizean sites failed to substantiate this extended chronology or to yield dates in excess of 1200 BC for pottery-bearing contexts. Currently, early radiocarbon dates (circa 1000 BC) for cultural material that is recognizably Maya have been reported from Awe's (1992) excavations at Cahal Pech in the Belize River valley and from Thomas Hester's team working on the Archaic/Formative interface at the stone-tool quarry and production site of Colha (Iceland 1997; Potter et al. 1984). Still, questions linger regarding the Cuello chronology and the lack of a recognizable phase of incipient settlement and initial pottery experimentation, elsewhere called the Early Formative period (circa 2500–1000 BC).

In the Maya Lowlands, the number of sites exhibiting Middle and Late Formative (1000 BC–AD 250) components has continued to grow, and the distribution now extends from the top of the Yucatan Peninsula to the base of the Alta Verapaz and from the Caribbean Sea west to the Grijalva River. Despite this ever-growing corpus, however, there has been no codification of a preceding Early Formative component. Numerous cores of lowland lakes and wetlands have yielded an abundance of charcoal dating to this time period (Deevey et al. 1979; Pohl et al. 1996), indicating that environmental disturbance, presumably induced by human efforts at deforestation, took place

at this time. However, a settlement signature is lacking. Pohl and others (1996) have postulated that Archaic period (6000–2500 BC) and Early Formative Maya settlements existed along the fringes of now inundated waterways and wetlands, while others see a population radiation of Maya people into the lowlands during the latter half of the Early Formative (Andrews V 1990; Clark, Hansen, and Perez 2000; McAnany and López Varela 1999). This farming population either replaced or comingled with an existing, low-density horticultural population that archaeologists have not yet been able to distinguish from the scattered remains of an Archaic population. The site of Colha, situated in the zone of a prime chert resource, represents one of the few Lowland Maya sites with a documented Preceramic to Formative period transition (Iceland 1997). The unresolved issue of the link between Archaic and Early Formative populations and later Maya settlements of the Middle Formative period remains one of the great mysteries of Maya archaeology. Data presented in this volume provide no support for substantial occupation prior to the Middle Formative period, at which time evidence suggests that there occurred a definite "founding" event. Despite extensive excavation during 1997 and 1998 along the edges and within the island fields of the K'axob wetlands (Berry and McAnany 1998), no evidence was found to support a model of a transition in settlement locale from the margins of the wetlands to higher ground. Whoever preceded the first villagers of K'axob left behind only a faint imprint on the landscape.

Currently, research into the Formative period is concerned with establishing precedents to Classic period monumental architecture (Hansen 1998); defining the earliest occurrence of recognizably Maya material culture, such as a sweat bath (Hammond and Bauer 2001); and defining the social, ritual, and economic character of Formative Maya village life (for example, McAnany and López Varela 1999; McAnany, Storey, and Lockard 1999; Isaza and McAnany 1999, among others). The latter research, which is more fully represented here, is critical to a social historical understanding of Middle and Late Formative Maya society. While publications to date have tended to emphasize either precocious monumentality or stratigraphic sequences, this volume expressly purports to re-create life in a Formative Maya village by distilling social, ritual, economic, and political information from artifacts, features, and stratigraphy.

ISSUES RELEVANT TO FORMATIVE K'AXOB

Despite earlier assertions that the Formative period should not be considered simply a "precursor to," or the "antecedent of," Classic period society, there is a strong tendency to consider the Classic period as a benchmark from which to view previous and subsequent periods (that is, the Formative and the Postclassic periods). Such comparisons can lead to tremendous insights if they are not laden with the prejudicial baggage of the civilizational "florescence" perspective; that is, the notion that, metonymically speaking, the Classic period is a flower in full bloom, which implies that the Formative period is a bud and the Postclassic period a withered bloom. Societies do transform, although not always in accordance with archaeologically established period boundaries. Some of the most compelling questions that we can pose address the transformations (or lack thereof) that separate the Classic from the Formative period. Either directly or obliquely, excavation data from K'axob can be brought to bear on a number of key issues, most of which address the question of the magnitude and quality of the differences between the Formative and Classic periods.

This many-sided question is not a simple one; even approaching it can lead one into the dangerous waters of teleology. Archaeological approaches to change tend to be polarized between those that are evolutionary, or processual, and those that are postmodernist, or postprocessualist. While the former view change as predictable and nearly universal, the latter view it as historically contingent, agent-motivated, and random. In general, the authors of this volume adopt an approach to change that embraces both social process and human agency. Rebecca Storey, who chronicles the "deathways" of K'axob inhabitants, rightly focuses on individuals and the agency implied by the manner of their interment. On the other hand, Marilyn Masson and Ryan Harrigan, presenting patterns of fauna and mollusca consumption based on remains largely retrieved from midden deposits, adopt a more processual view and examine broad data trends. Pure agency theory, born in the intellectual cauldron of Western, postindustrial society, places a premium on individual action in contexts within which individuals enjoy a level of freedom. As several scholars have noted (Barrett 2001; Dobres and Robb 2000; Gillespie 2001), in traditional group-focused village societies like K'axob, such freedom was

the exception rather than the norm. This is not to say that the chapters that follow trivialize the importance of persons; rather, it is to say that the social matrix from which change was germinated (that is, kin groups) is quite distinct from the social matrix of postindustrial society. Let us now examine some key distinctions that may or may not separate the Formative period from the Classic period.

STRUCTURES OF AUTHORITY

Did formal rulership exist during the Middle and early part of the Late Formative periods? And, if so, were the rulers divine kings? What was the nature of the larger matrix within which the village of K'axob was founded and thrived? Little is known of the early systems of governance in the Maya region, and opinions as to the origin and organization of Formative statecraft generally fall into two camps: Olmec-derived versus autochthonously Maya. Although opinions are divided as to the exact form and time span of Olmec governance (Clark 1997), those espousing Olmec derivation generally utilize arguments framed around shared iconographic elements. If Olmec rulers were divine rulers, and if Maya principles of statecraft were directly grafted from the Gulf Coast, then divine kings could have existed from the "get go" in the Mirador Basin and at other locales exhibiting early, monumental architecture. On the other hand, if rulership was reinvented in the Maya Lowlands—based on an amalgam of Olmec motifs (to establish a historical pedigree) with the Mesoamerican Middle Formative Ceremonial Complex (Reilly 1995)—then the institution of rulership could have emerged independently during the Formative period, while the institution of divine rulership could be a development of the Early Classic period. In the latter scenario, the construction of monumental architecture could precede the establishment of rulership. Annabeth Headrick's (chapter 16) observation that the iconographic motifs and structural arrangement of ritual contexts at K'axob bear strong parallels to well-established Olmec principles of canonical expression (as seen on objects such as the Humbolt Celt) highlights the fact that Formative period boundaries were quite permeable and that spheres of influence were deeply interpenetrative.

The dialogue between Clark and Hansen (2001) regarding the issue of Formative Maya rulership demonstrates that there is no straightforward answer to this question and that even the monumental Mirador Basin sites can be interpreted as deriving either from the Olmec or from the Maya. Regardless of the origin of Maya rulership, Formative village sites such as K'axob were not unaffected by the political winds of change that swept across the lowlands. In fact, material patterns reveal strong directional change in the formality of architectural differentiation and mortuary ritual, as is discussed in chapters 3 and 6. Such transformations, as opposed to stasis, suggest that villages were both responding to and playing a part in the political trends that ultimately spawned the explicitly self-recording dynasties of divine rulers.

MATERIALIZATIONS OF AUTHORITY

Is the Formative period monumental architecture of the lowlands a materialization of early systems of labor drafts (even tribute obligations)? Or does it represent cooperative community efforts, as Burger (1992) argues with regard to the massive structures of Initial period coastal Peru? If rulership existed, then could the large, Preclassic pyramids signify voluntary, royal work/royal ritual as Feeley-Harnik (1985) has noted is the case among African chiefdoms? The depersonalized iconographic programs of Formative pyramids (Freidel and Schele 1988) coupled with the absence of royal entombments (Hansen 1998) indicate that, in all probability, early pyramids were not mortuary shrines for dead dynasts. Regardless of the ritual uses of early pyramids and the rationale for their construction, the fact that they were constructed indicates concentrations of power (and resources) and the existence of hierarchies of authority necessary to planning and executing massive construction projects. Although pyramid construction does not seem to have commenced at K'axob until the onset of the Classic period, monumental building programs were executed nearby and conceivably involved the labor (voluntary or coerced) of K'axob residents. For example, Nohmul engaged in the construction of a massive Late Formative platform (Hammond et al. 1988) and certainly relied on labor from surrounding communities to quarry, transport, and set tens of thousands of soft marl blocks. Upriver, one of the largest pyramids constructed during Formative times was built at Lamanai. In chapter 7 Mary Lee Bartlett presents ceramic petrographic evidence that links K'axob with Lamanai, thus providing support for the notion that canoe traffic may have transported labor to Lamanai

and pottery or temper back to K'axob. Regardless of the manner in which K'axob residents may have become entangled in labor obligations away from their village, throughout the Formative period constructions at home remained modest, though differentiated.

HIERARCHY AND SOCIAL REPRODUCTION

Was Formative society class-divided, simply ranked, sectored into lineages (McAnany 1995a) or "houses" (Joyce and Gillespie 2000; Lévi Strauss 1982), or all of the above? These questions go to the heart of the matter, and, given the tremendous range in size and architectural elaboration of Formative sites, there may be many answers to this question rather than a single "golden rule." In reference to a class structure, Sharer (1992:134) has noted that few elite residences (or palaces) have been recorded, and this suggests that social distinctions were more relaxed during the Formative period. At K'axob architectural differentiation can be detected beginning around 200 BC, when platform construction raised certain domiciles higher than those that rested on simple low plinths. This trend is followed by protracted mortuary rituals at the locale of more elaborate architecture; that is, operation 1 (see chapters 3 and 6 as well as McAnany and López Varela 1999; and McAnany, Storey, and Lockard 1999). Greater elaboration of cache deposits and the differential presence of the painted red quadripartite motif followed suit.

The marked sequences of rebuilding that are so evident in the stratigraphy of K'axob platforms provide a strong indication that the domicile itself represented a materialization of social reproduction and the continuity of a kin group. A link between the history of a domicile's residents and the structure itself was forged through the strategic placement of burial interments within the construction mass of the platform. In this regard, the residents of K'axob can be considered a variant of the "house" society proposed by Lévi Strauss (1982), although there is little question but that more inclusive, suprahouse kin groupings existed at Formative K'axob and elsewhere in the Maya Lowlands. Regardless, the strong corporate ethic underwriting the domiciles of Formative K'axob provide a better example of the putative "house" model than do traditionally invoked examples from Maya Classic period royal compounds and dynastic burial shrines (Gillespie 2000; Joyce 2000a; see also Houston and McAnany 2003).

RITUAL PRACTICES

Ancient residential compounds are increasingly recognized as a vital focus of domestic ritual (Plunket 2002). Philip Arnold (2001:4–5), in particular, has called attention to the materiality of ritual practice, especially within cosmologies that ascribe animate status to places. If anything, this study demonstrates how, through mortuary practice and dedicatory caching, the domiciles of K'axob were both the subject and the locus of ritual performance. As Eleanor Harrison-Buck (chapter 4) notes, these highly visible domestic rituals often concerned the termination, regeneration, and nourishing of life. Highly localized and tethered to the domicile, the cosmological principles materialized in these ritual deposits amounted to much more than simple local knowledge. Headrick (chapter 16) demonstrates that K'axob ritual knowledge included a visual vocabulary generally associated with Olmec iconography. Expressed in structural arrangements that indicate a deep understanding of the symbolism of the cross, this knowledge base expressed in Formative period village contexts indicates that a significant part of Classic period royal ideology was elaborated from widely held beliefs rather than conceived in royal courts and imposed on the masses. This is most certainly the case for symbolism linked to such specific icons as the quadripartite motif, which is much in evidence within the burial and cache deposits of the most elaborated domiciles of Late Formative K'axob. The durability of Maya cosmological precepts is demonstrated by Harrison-Buck (chapter 4), who finds strongly parallel themes running between contemporary Maya ritual practice and the cache deposits of Formative K'axob.

Are directional changes in ritual practice detectable at K'axob? As the chapters to follow show, the answer to this question is an emphatic "yes!" Among other trends, the reduction of golden chert debitage over burial interments and one highly significant cache is a hallmark of the later part of the Late Formative (see chapter 11). Mortuary ritual, especially, shows pronounced directional change in burial position and in the presence of non-articulated human remains (see chapter 6). Since death ritual is primarily about the living, we can assume that these changes indicate new distinctions in social relations. Also, if ancestor interments are linked to place-making and place-claiming rituals, then it stands to reason that treatment of the dead might change as the landscape filled with farmers, and land and resources became less plentiful.

ARTISAN PRODUCTION

As Firth (1967:168) noted in reference to the economy of Polynesian Tikopia, there is a "close association between technical processes and ritual activity." That is, artisan production is ritually entangled. In the Maya region, Bishop Diego de Landa (Tozzer 1941) also notes this connection in early Colonial Yucatan—a connection that is strengthened by illustrative examples depicted in the Postclassic Codex Madrid. In the Formative deposits of K'axob, such an association may be particularly true for the shell bead production activities documented by Ilean Isaza in chapter 14. Middle Formative extramural areas contained large numbers of incomplete, locally made shell beads, a type also discovered within burials. Isaza further suggests the possibility that the incomplete shell beads found within burial fill may be the result of a scattering ritual.

In chapter 7 Bartlett examines the technological basis of pottery production at K'axob and highlights the artisan skill necessary to produce the finely detailed pottery of the Middle Formative period and the extremely large, vertical-walled bowls of the Late Formative period. Over the long term, changes in pottery technology can be detected; however, there is a remarkable intergenerational stability in the transmission of artisan skill and knowledge. In chapter 9 Kimberly Berry and others describe the vessels themselves in detail and illustrate them in profile form. Challenging the assumption of uniformity in Late Formative period pottery types such as the Sierra Red, Bartlett presents evidence that the pottery artisans of K'axob stylistically differentiated their pottery from that of neighboring communities such as Cuello, Colha, and Cerros. Taking a larger view of things, Sandra López Varela (chapter 8) characterizes the impact of macrosocial processes on K'axob pottery artisans and, in so doing, situates the Formative pottery of K'axob within the greater sphere of eastern Mesoamerica.

PROCUREMENT NETWORKS

As is discussed in chapter 2, residents of K'axob inhabited a landscape rich in biotic resources but poor in hard stone and mineralogical resources. For this reason, procurement networks were of vital concern. Intraregional networks through which durable items such as pottery, chert implements, and marine shell were circulated have been demonstrated for the Classic period (Shafer and Hester 1983; McAnany 1989; Reents-Budet et al. 1994). Interregional networks moving obsidian, greenstone, and other valuables (see McAnany 1993a for a summary of sources) were also operative. At what time were these networks formalized and how were "consumers" supplied? For instance, the flint-knappers of Colha, who supplied stone tools as well as eccentrics to northern Belize and selected items to southern Quintana Roo and the Petén, did not leave behind large debitage piles that are temporally assignable to the Middle Formative. If they did engage in large-scale tool production, then the evidence is buried beneath Classic period construction or was re-used as Classic period building material.

Several lines of evidence from K'axob indicate that, during the early facet of the Middle Formative period, access to raw materials was less restricted than it was during later times. From the founding of the village, Caribbean marine shell is present (see chapter 14). As Patricia McAnany, Polly Peterson, and Justin Ebersole discuss in chapters 11 and 13, during Middle Formative times, hard stone sought after by K'axob villagers for chipped and ground stone tools was acquired from far and wide. This situation complements that of pottery acquisition. Both López Varela (chapter 8) and Bartlett (chapter 7) report that K'axob pottery of the early facet of the Middle Formative period is highly diverse both stylistically and compositionally. This fact suggests a large, open system of pottery or temper trading. During the Late Formative period, however, both pottery and chipped stone become much more stylistically and compositionally standardized. During the Formative period, scales of artisan production do not follow a progression from local to regional. In fact, over time procurement seems to become entrenched in highly localized networks. Acquisition of distant materials such as obsidian (chapter 12) and greenstone (chapter 15), which required the maintenance of multinodal networks, played a minor role at K'axob.

CULINARY PRACTICES AND AGRICULTURAL STRATEGIES

Were the founders of K'axob culinary generalists or were they specialized maize farmers? The post-1500 BC radiation of farmers across the Maya Lowlands may have been linked to the availability of larger, more productive varieties of maize; Charles Miksicek (in Turner and Miksicek 1984) has identified maize in the lowest levels of K'axob Formative deposits. This finding is corroborated by a stable isotope analysis of a longitudinal sample of K'axob burial interments, which signaled the presence of maize in the diet of Middle Formative individuals (Henderson 1998). Although the mollisols of K'axob may be well suited to maize farming, data presented by Masson (chapter 17) and Harrigan (chapter 18) suggest that Formative occupants were just as interested in harvesting the wetlands, particularly readily available species of small fishes, turtles, and freshwater gastropods. The presence of over fifty net sinkers in the collection of fired clay artifacts (see chapter 10) suggests that net fishing was widely employed. In chapter 5 Victoria Bobo provides further support for a cuisine based on maize and wetland fauna. Sherd-lined pits, ubiquitous domestic features only of the Formative period, reveal contents and a form suggestive of soaking maize and steaming gastropods. K'axob cuisine was undoubtedly augmented by other crops as well.

Finally, were Formative Maya farmers using simple slash-and-burn techniques or were they more fully diversified, employing a weeding-and-hoeing regime and placing fields in both the uplands and the wetlands? The highly controversial raised fields of Pulltrouser Swamp (Pope et al. 1996; Turner and Harrison 1983) are located on the immediate western edge of K'axob. Data highly relevant to this question were collected during the 1997–1998 K'axob wetlands project (Berry and McAnany 1998, 2000). In this study, the issue is addressed via typological and wear-pattern analysis of bifacial tools and debitage from Formative domiciles. Results presented by McAnany and Peterson in chapter 11 indicate that use polish and the oval biface form are not a fabrication of the Classic period but enjoy a deeper antiquity at K'axob.

SETTLEMENT HIERARCHIES

Did settlement hierarchies exist in the Formative period? There are many ranking schemes for Classic period centers, but few scholars have attempted to apply them to Formative sites. There are obvious scalar differences between the great Formative capitals of the Mirador Basin (such as El Mirador and Nakbe) and small communities such as K'axob, and these indicate marked power differentials. Chapter 2 proposes a New River settlement hierarchy centered on Lamanai.

Chapter Two
Related CD Resources

Tour of K'axob

LANDSCAPES OF K'AXOB IN DEEP AND CURRENT TIME

PATRICIA A. MCANANY

WETLAND AND RIVER LANDSCAPES OF NORTHERN BELIZE

Often characterized as the lungs of an ecosystem, wetlands are now widely recognized as a valuable part of the human habitat, and conservation groups all over North America work to preserve boggy areas that, from a developmental perspective, were once considered useless tracts of land. Featuring pronounced biotic diversity, the wetland and river landscapes of northern Belize appear never to have suffered the neglect and disdain heaped upon wetlands of northern latitudes during the postindustrial age. Quite the contrary, tropical, Caribbean-watershed wetlands appear to have been a magnet to early Maya settlers and to have sustained large populations throughout the Classic period. While the rivers provided aquatic resources and a ready-made transportation corridor, the wetlands were a source of additional protein resources, hard wood and palms for construction purposes, and water that, throughout a pronounced dry season, was available for farming and household provisioning.

While the lure of fresh fish and turtle may have provided an incentive to early Maya settlers of K'axob, this small-fauna cornucopia was offset by an extremely limited local geological profile. The landscape of northern Belize is one of wetlands and low ridge lines underlain by a soft *sascab*, or marl, suitable for earthen platforms and packed floor surfaces but inadequate as building blocks for stone walls and vaulted roofs. The paucity of hard stone for construction is matched by a lack of durable stone for manos and metates, and of microcrystalline stone suitable for chipped stone tools such as oval bifaces and celts. It is probably no exaggeration to suggest that the hardest material locally available to K'axob residents was found in deciduous hard woods. The soft texture of this landscape has tremendous implications with regard to provisioning the households of K'axob. As evidence presented in this volume shows, the founders of K'axob were actively involved in networks through which hard stone was acquired, particularly for ground, polished, and chipped tools. Variety in the paste composition of the early pottery of K'axob also implicates a far-flung network for acquiring either temper or finished pottery; however, over time, clay resources closer to home were more actively exploited. Marine shell also appears in the earliest levels of K'axob, suggesting a ready connection to the Caribbean Sea; however, worked river shells of mother-of-pearl bivalves are equally well represented. One of the definitive differences between the Middle and Late Formative artifacts of K'axob is the emphatically local nature of artifacts of the latter period. Data presented in this volume indicate that, when the far-flung networks of earlier times collapsed, the residents of K'axob learned to live and thrive on resources derived from their immediate wetland and river landscape.

FORMATIVE PERIOD GEOPOLITICS IN THE NEW RIVER VALLEY

Some Lowland Maya rivers, such as the Usumacinta, are swift flowing, only partially navigable, and leave behind only limited pockets of flat, fertile floodplains on which to farm (Aliphat 1994). In contrast, the New River has a gentle current with no rapids, maintains a high level through the dry season, and is bordered by wetlands. As a natural corridor of transportation, the river provided the residents of K'axob with easy access to Caribbean shell and to mineral resources available around the New River Lagoon (see chapters 7 and 14 for more detail). Moreover, the route of the New River contains several Formative period settlements between Lamanai at the source of the river and Cerros at its mouth (see figure 1.1). Settlements in between include San Estevan, Nohmul, Cuello, Yo Tumben, Kokeal, Tibaat, Pech Titon, Chi Ak'al, and K'axob.

The political geometry of the Middle Formative is currently unknown, but by the latter half of the Late Formative period a site hierarchy had emerged in the New River valley, and Lamanai occupied the apex both politically and physiographically. Over 33 meters in height, Late Formative structure N10-43 is one of the largest pyramids built during the Late Formative period (Pendergast 1981). Cerros, located at the terminus of the New River, may have enjoyed a very close link with Lamanai and also engaged in pyramid construction during the latter part of the Late Formative (Schele and Freidel 1990: 96–129). Nohmul, straddling the divide between the drainages of the New River and

the Rio Hondo, occupies an uncertain position in this hierarchy. The spatial extent of Formative period occupation at Nohmul (Pyburn 1989a), plus the construction of a massive Late Formative platform built entirely of shaped sascab blocks (Hammond et al. 1988), indicates that a large labor force could be mustered at this locale. Based on current evidence (Bullard 1965; Hammond 1991a; Levi 1993), Cuello and San Estevan seem to have occupied the next lower tier of the hierarchy, followed by K'axob, which was one of several villages located in the New River valley. Evidence suggests that the tool-producing site of Colha, located well to the east of the New River valley, enjoyed a close interaction with most communities of northern Belize; however, locally, Colha may have been part of a separate political sphere headed by Altun Ha, its neighbor to the south.

The extent to which this site hierarchy translated into active political control of lower-order centers is far from obvious. Comparative stylistic analysis of Late Formative pottery from K'axob, Cerros, Colha, and Cuello indicates the presence of distinctive forms and methods of surface decoration beneath the surficial uniformity of the Sierra Red type (see chapter 7; also Bartlett and McAnany 2000a). Whether these localized artisan traditions served to assert community identity in the face of political control or simply represent the random drift of stylistic expression in the absence of any overarching controls is revisited later in the denouement of Part VII.

MODERN RESEARCH LANDSCAPE OF K'AXOB

Before 1981 the place now known as K'axob was a relatively undeveloped property owned by Rafael Campos and his son Concepción. Seasonally, milpa farmers from San Estevan paddled their dugout canoes across the New River to cultivate small plots of land. Airborne in the 1970s with the Royal Air Force, archaeologist Norman Hammond flew over this bit of high ground between Pulltrouser Swamp and the New River and declared that a minor ceremonial center likely existed at the locale. During the first season (1979) of the Pulltrouser Swamp project, Peter D. Harrison and B. L. Turner focused their efforts primarily on settlement and wetland features on the western side of the Y-shaped swamp, but they did reconnoiter and note settlement between the arms of the swamp and along its eastern border (Turner and Harrison 1983:Fig. 9-1). During the succeeding 1981 season, the author joined the Pulltrouser Swamp project as a graduate student and was dispatched to the eastern side of the wetlands, where two pyramid plazas surrounded by nearly a hundred satellite residences were documented. At that time, much of the site was in milpa fallow (*k'ax*, in Yucatec Mayan), so Peter D. Harrison selected a plural form of this word as the site name. During the 1981 season, K'axob was mapped with a tape and compass, and a program of test excavations was undertaken (map published in Harrison and Fry 2000). Testing revealed the presence of finely laminated Formative period deposits underlying the southern pyramid plaza. At the end of the 1981 season, Concepción Campos built a road into the site in order to develop the land for sugarcane farming, and today the site is a patchwork of sugarcane fields and low bush.

In 1990 the author returned to the site as principal investigator of the K'axob Project accompanied by a group of undergraduate students who had matriculated in a study abroad program through the Division of International Programs at Boston University. Thomas W. Killion codirected the first of three seasons of intensive fieldwork in the southern part of K'axob, the heartland of Formative period settlement. A topographic and fine-grained rectified map of K'axob was initiated during this season; work on the map continued over the next five seasons (figure 2.1). Structure numbers were retained from the 1981 map, but a new series of excavation numbers, starting with 1, was implemented. Operations 1, 7, and 8 commenced during the 1990 field season (figure 2.2). Evidence of complex mortuary rituals encountered during this field season provided the inspiration for both a National Science Foundation proposal focused on an investigation of ancestor veneration and a topical book entitled *Living with the Ancestors* (McAnany 1995a). With support from the National Science Foundation, fieldwork resumed at K'axob during the summer of 1992, with Marilyn Masson as field director. During this rainy summer season, excavation continued at operation 1, and operations 7 and 8 were completed. New excavation units were opened at operations 10, 11, 12, and 13. The final season of fieldwork to be focused on the Formative period (1993) was undertaken with the support of an NSF supplemental grant and Boston University Division of International Programs—in effect, a season of combined research and field school training. During this season, excavations were completed at operations 1, 11, and 12. Three subsequent field seasons at K'axob (1995, 1997, and 1998) focused on the Classic period and the wetlands. Analysis

of materials from these more recent excavations is ongoing (Berry 2002; Berry and McAnany 1998; Henderson 1998; McAnany 1997; McAnany 1998a; McAnany and Berry 1999).

In addition to the substantial number of scholarly publications on K'axob, three Ph.D. dissertations have been written (Angelini 1998; Henderson 1998; López Varela 1996) and one other is in progress. Three masters theses are based on K'axob material (Harrison 2001; Isaza 1997; Peterson 2001) as well as three senior theses (Ebersole 2001; Kobza 1994; Lonardo 1996). This volume stands as a tribute to the efforts and insights of the forenamed individuals as well as to those unnamed individuals whose daily efforts in the field ensured the collection of abundantly detailed information from three highly productive field seasons. The accompanying digital materials contain a *Tour of K'axob* and a *Photo Database*, both of which provide an excellent opportunity to view the location and physical surroundings of each excavation and to "meet" the individuals involved in the field research.

A CHRONOLOGY FOR K'AXOB

Due to the well-stratified deposits of Formative and Early Classic period K'axob and the long period over which domiciles were occupied, the construction of a relative chronology based on ceramic type-variety analysis could be realized. Through the combined efforts of Sandra L. López Varela and myself, ceramic complexes were established for the Formative, Classic, and Postclassic periods at K'axob (table 2.1). Employing the convention of ending each complex name with the first syllable of the site (in this case *k'ax*), López Varela and I established the following complex names for each time period: for the Middle Formative, Chaakk'ax; for the Late Formative, K'atabche'k'ax; for the Early Classic, Nohalk'ax; for the Late Classic, Witsk'ax; and for the Postclassic, Kimilk'ax. The Yucatec Mayan complex names play on a prevalent characteristic of each time period: *chaak* for the Joventud Red pottery of the Middle Formative; *k'atabche'* for the bold cross motif painted on the base of some of the operation 1 mortuary vessels; *nohal* for the spread of settlement into the northern part of K'axob during the Early Classic period; *wits* because the final version of the tallest pyramid of K'axob (structure 1, standing at 13 m) was constructed during the Late Classic; and *kimil* to signify the death of the community as it had existed during earlier times.

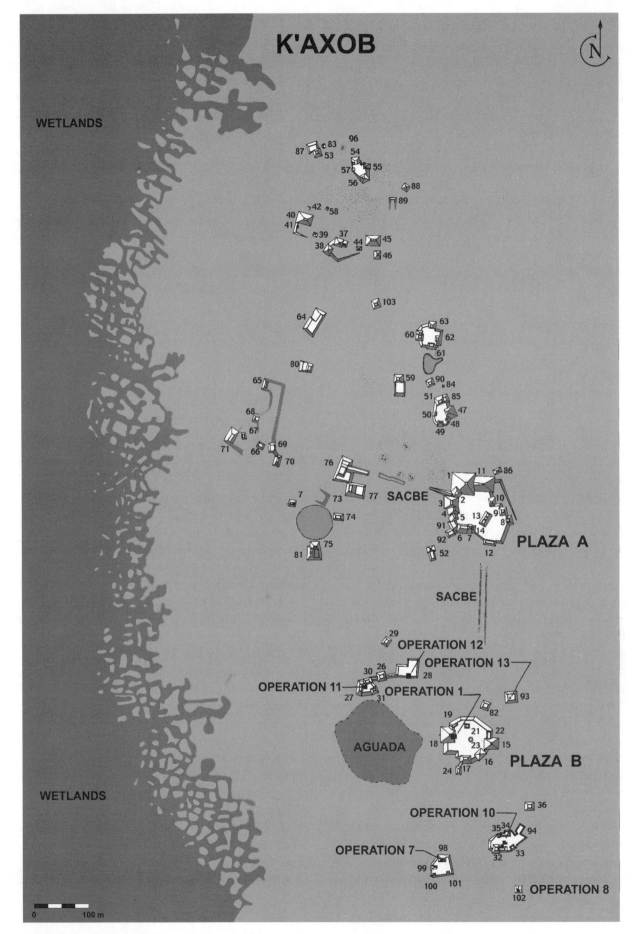

Figure 2.1 K'axob showing pyramid plazas A and B and wetland margin along western side of site. *Illustration by K'axob Project staff and staff of UCLA Cotsen Institute Digital Archaeology Laboratory*

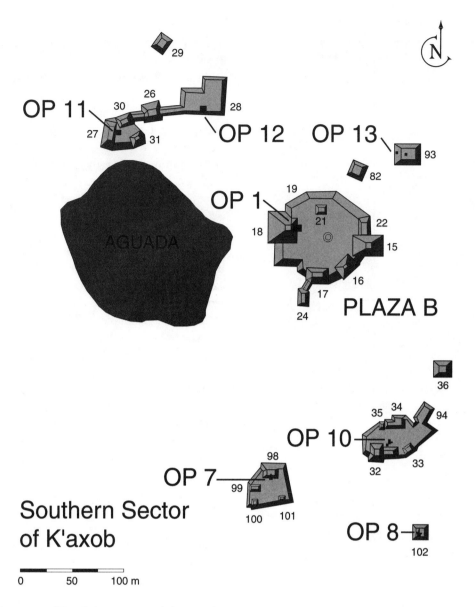

Figure 2.2 Southern sector of K'axob showing pyramid plaza B and seven operations (excavation units) upon which study is based. *Illustration by K'axob Project staff and staff of UCLA Cotsen Institute Digital Archaeology Laboratory*

After conducting a type-variety analysis of the pottery from the initial three seasons of excavation, López Varela (1996) was able to identify an early and a late facet of the Chaakk'ax complex; an early, late, and terminal facet of the K'atabche'k'ax complex (the terminal facet contains the mammiform tetrapodal forms); and an early facet of the Nohalk'ax complex (table 2.1; see also chapter 8 for additional detail). Emphasis on Classic period deposits during the 1995 season enabled refinement of the Nohalk'ax, Witsk'ax, and Kimilk'ax complexes (López Varela 1997). Twenty-five accelerator mass spectrometer dates (see McAnany and López

Varela 1999:Table 3 and Fig. 4) from Formative period contexts provide support for the following blocks of time: 800–400 BC for the Chaakk'ax complex, and 400 BC until approximately AD 250 for the K'atabche'k'ax complex. Currently, the Nohalk'ax complex is not well anchored chronometrically; consequently, the start and end dates are simply those traditionally employed in Maya studies: AD 250–550. Stylistic changes within ceramic complexes proved to be more temporally sensitive than radiocarbon dates as there are few perceptible temporal trends in the radiocarbon age of samples within each complex (see McAnany and López

Table 2.1 General chronology of K'axob

TIME	MAJOR PERIODS	K'axob	
1200	*LATE*		
1100			
1000	*EARLY*	**Kimilk'ax**	
900	*POSTCLASSIC*		
800	*TERMINAL*		
700			
600	*LATE*	**Witsk'ax**	
500			
400	*EARLY*	**Nohalk'ax**	
300			
200	*CLASSIC*		
100			*Terminal Facet*
A.D.	*PROTOCLASSIC*	**K'atabche'k'ax**	
B.C.			
100			*Late Facet*
200			
300	*LATE*		*Early Facet*
400	*FORMATIVE*		
500			*Late Facet*
600			
700		**Chaakk'ax**	
800	*MIDDLE*		*Early Facet*
900	*FORMATIVE*		
1000			
1100	*EARLY*		
1200	*FORMATIVE*		

Varela 1999:Fig. 4). As a consequence, facets have been defined on the basis of changes in pottery style. When applied to individual contexts (or zones), the resulting data set provides a temporal framework for architectural and artifact analysis, as is apparent in the following chapters.

SOUTHERN K'AXOB AND THIS VOLUME

The focus of this volume is southern K'axob and excavations undertaken between 1990 and 1993.

Architecturally, this study includes material from beneath the final plaza floor of pyramidal plaza B and six satellite residences (figure 2.2). Primarily Formative and Early Classic in date, these deposits represent the remains of domiciles that were built and rebuilt over a span of a thousand years. In the pages to come, it will become apparent that this built environment represents the materialization of social forces with a strong ritual and economic subtext. In the most elemental sense, the artifacts and structural remains of K'axob are relevant to understanding the fabric of village life before social classes became an enduring fact of life. The information provided in each chapter is augmented considerably by access to digital files containing the unabridged databases. (Readers interested in the details of an analysis can gain access to any data file directly from the opening navigation screen.) Following this chapter, the remainder of the volume is divided into six parts. At the beginning of each part, a *Guide to Accompanying Digital Materials* is presented, as is an interpretive summary of the chapters within that section of the volume. As with any comprehensive publication of an archaeological project, organizing what may appear to be disparate bits of information into a synthetic whole can be a real challenge. While many organizational schemes are possible, this book is structured by classes of material remains.

With this logic, the following section (Part I) begins with the built environment (structures and features) and provides an overview of the stratified series of excavated domiciles of southern K'axob, revealing their function as both a place of ritual and of mundane domestic activities. Ritual performance geared to nourishing the animus of lived space provides the focus of chapter 4, which examines the cache deposits placed within the built environment. Chapter 5 discusses the form and function of sherd-lined pits (intrusive features built into floors and extramural areas) and entertains important implications for changes in culinary practices near the end of the Formative period.

In Part II, emphasis shifts to the human remains interred within the built environment. The bioarchaeology of over one hundred human remains provides the focus of chapter 6, in which mortuary ritual is described within an architectural context and is supplemented with a presentation of the age, sex, and paleopathologies of the K'axob interments. This detailed analysis of the ancestral remains of K'axob serves to remind us of the close connection between people and place, and the powerful manner in which social memory was recorded through mortuary rituals followed by house occupants.

Part III deals with the most ubiquitous of artifacts, those made of fired clay. In chapter 7, the materialization of village identity through artisanship is tackled through a petrographic analysis of clays and pottery fabric, while the broader ceramic history of K'axob is presented in chapter 8. In chapter 9, the 100+ pottery vessels of K'axob are illustrated and described, and are grouped by ceramic complex and archaeological context. Small artifacts of fired clay, such as net weights and ocarinas, are presented in chapter 10.

In Part IV, the focus shifts to hard-stone materials that were chipped, ground, or polished to create tools. Mostly imported materials, chert and chalcedony, obsidian, and ground stone tools and debitage comprise the subjects of chapters 11, 12, and 13. For each raw material type, methods of procurement are discussed in light of data patterns.

Personal adornment and cosmological expression are the topics of Part V, which begins with an examination of shell working and the social uses of shell ornaments (chapter 14). A presentation of bone artifacts and semi-precious greenstone ornaments comprises the substance of chapter 15. Cosmological expression is the topic of chapter 16, in which the meaning and significance of the cross motif at K'axob is situated within a larger body of Mesoamerican beliefs.

Biological evidence relevant to both subsistence and symbolic expression is presented in Part VI, which contains analyses of fauna (chapter 17) and mollusca (chapter 18). Part VII (a denouement) contains a final synthesis and reflections on the Formative village of K'axob.

Analysis of the built environment and artifacts of K'axob are wrapped around several larger themes: emergent political authority, increasing politicization of ancestors as revealed by mortuary ritual, inequality among families as expressed architecturally, shifting networks of trading alliances, and increasingly localized resource acquisition. In the next chapter, we begin with the built environment.

PART I

THE BUILT ENVIRONMENT

Context is the most fundamental part of archaeological recording. Accordingly, Part I contains three chapters, all of which present information regarding built features within the village of K'axob. These chapters, along with chapter 6, provide key data on the contextual envelopes from which artifacts (the foci of later chapters) were retrieved. In chapter 3, Patricia A. McAnany introduces the seven excavation units upon which this volume is based. Sequential construction of domiciles and associated domestic features throughout a period spanning the Middle Formative through the early part of the Early Classic has yielded an unusually crisp series of construction phase plans, samples of which are presented in chapter 3. Evidence from the basal layers of the excavation unit that underlies plaza B suggests that a founding event occurred around 600 BC. Repeated spatial co-occurrence of ritual features (such as burials and caches) with domestic culinary features (such as sherd-lined pits) indicates the presence of a unitary cosmology that did not separate ritual and domestic labor into separate spheres.

Eleanor Harrison-Buck continues the theme of ritual expression in chapter 4 with a presentation of the twenty-two recorded cache deposits. Examining content, configuration, and context of each cache, and informed by ethnographically documented dedication and termination rituals, Harrison-Buck finds that the majority of cache deposits were established to activate or nourish the animus of a structure. The presence of fish and frog bones in a cache of four vessels arranged in a cross pattern bespeaks both the importance of wetland fauna as an indicator of seasonality in a cosmological sense and the importance of this resource to the ancient residents of K'axob.

In chapter 5 Victoria Bobo explores Formative period cuisine from the vantage of thirty-one sherd-lined pits—prominent features of Formative period domiciles. After an exhaustive examination of variability in pit location, dimensions, construction, and contents, Bobo turns to the sherds that formed the lining of the pit walls. She notes that many pits are lined with a mosaic of small, broken sherds that measure less than 5 x 5 cm. Such conservation and recycling is a prominent characteristic of the material culture of K'axob and is also discussed in Part IV—Stone Tools. Ultimately, the sherd-lined pits were not built for a single function but appear to have been used primarily (and sometimes sequentially) for three purposes: steaming molluscs, fish, or small game; lime-soaking maize; and roasting foods. Bobo links the disappearance of these features at the end of the Formative period with changes in the scale of food preparation and, notably, the appearance of large, striated jar forms capable of soaking larger quantities of maize.

GUIDE TO ACCOMPANYING DIGITAL MATERIALS.

Information presented in Part I is augmented by several types of digital resources. For visual images of the location and appearance of the seven excavation units discussed in chapter 3 ("Domiciles and Construction Histories"), view the Tour of K'axob. The stratigraphic sequences of each excavation unit (except operation 8) can be viewed in 3-D Excavations, which allows the viewer to stand in the bottom of an excavation unit and view the section walls as they appeared at the end of the excavation. The construction sequence of each excavation unit has been divided into construction phases, and most of these phases can be viewed in the Domiciles Database, which contains plan-view maps and a description of each provenience unit according to context (or zone). Many of the construction phases were also recorded photographically, and these can be viewed in the Photos Database (queried by operation and phase number). Likewise, photographic images of the cache deposits discussed in chapter 4 can be viewed in the Caches Database. Since pottery vessels constitute an important component of many of the caches, the Pottery Vessels Database is also pertinent to this chapter and can be queried using provenience information (operation and zone). More information and visual images of greenstone from caches and, specifically, of the "triadic" cache contents are available in Greenstone Database and Triadic Cache Contents Database, respectively. Finally, the information presented in chapter 5 ("Soaked and Steamed Sustenance") is complemented by photographic and textual information in the Sherd-Lined Pits Database.

Chapter 3
Related CD Resources

Domiciles
3-D Excavations
Burials
Caches
Sherd-lined Pits
Tour of K'axob

DOMICILES AND CONSTRUCTION HISTORIES

PATRICIA A. MCANANY

In modern times the term "place of residence" rings with legalistic implications while, at the same time, the physical plant itself indexes social and economic standing, as Blanton (1994:10) has discussed. The extraordinary power of residence to represent the wealth and well-being of its occupants is not confined to modern times. In fact, within traditional, corporate-based economies the house provides the organizational fulcrum of activity groups commonly recognized as a household (Netting, Wilk, and Arnould 1984). In many respects, the residence within postmodern capitalist society is but a pale shadow of its former self. Capitalism separates labor from the residence, thus reducing the centrality of the domicile in organizing labor and the value accorded to domestic tasks. On a local scale, the emergence of political hierarchies can diminish the role of the domicile as a venue for ritual activities (Marcus 1999:70). These demonstrable trends indicate that, although "a house is a house" whether it be built in the twenty-first or the first century, the significance of these shells of human habitation and the activities undertaken within their walls can differ dramatically. As Allison (1999:2) astutely observes, even within a given place and period of time, houses cannot be assumed to conform in a standardized fashion to some rigid prescriptive formula.

The central and iconic importance of domiciles in many contemporary (albeit traditional) as well as ancient cultural contexts has prompted researchers to return to Lévi-Strauss's société à maisons, or "house society," model (Carston and Hugh-Jones 1995; Joyce and Gillespie 2000). This model privileges the transgenerational flow of resources through a coresidential corporate entity and views the fetishization of the house as a means of maintaining continuity and entitlement. More traditional concerns of kinship studies, such as bloodlines and descent, are seen as ideal constructs that are so seldom realized on the ground that they are quite useless (c.f. Houston and McAnany 2003). Imagining the house in more concrete terms than did Lévi-Strauss, advocates of a house society model have emphasized the indexical power of the house to project group identity and hierarchy

(McKinnon 2000). Other house society researchers have focused on what Blanton (1994:9) characterizes as canonical communication—the house as a metaphor of cosmological principles, order, and social relations, or the house as a metaphorical body with a mouth and a need to be nourished (Carsten and Hugh-Jones 1995:2-3). These characterizations of the house as an iconic, multigenerational locale of ritual as well as economic activity accord well with the domiciles of K'axob. As presented below, many K'axob domiciles endured through several centuries, were refurbished and expanded frequently, housed the remains of ancestors, and were the recipients of offerings to nourish the animus of lived space.

The Formative and Early Classic period domiciles of K'axob were built and rebuilt between 600 BC and AD 400. Their residential function is attested to by the association of external midden areas and the interment of deceased family members under floors and within construction units. As is the case at many northern Belizean Maya sites, the platforms upon which domiciles were placed often contain tell-like stratigraphic sequences. This fact, along with the nature of the local building material (sascab, or soft marl), produces clear, layer-cake stratigraphy. The absence of hard stone in the immediate environment of K'axob also translates into a lack of freestanding walls and rubble-filled platforms, both of which tend to deconstruct explosively rather than gracefully sag as does sascab. Due to the absence of freestanding walls or vaulted roofs, the domiciles of K'axob are generally identified by packed marl or plaster floors delimited by an outline of footing stones. The walls and roofs of K'axob domiciles were presumably built of organic materials (walls of upright poles and roofs of thatch). Fragments of daub, particularly from the base of operation 1, indicate that walls were sometimes finished with a layer of plaster-like material. While some of the platform retaining walls were faced with imported hard stone, most domicile construction materials—sascab, post-and-beam timbers, wall wattle, and palm thatch—could have been procured within the local environment.

The domiciles of K'axob were substantial in size, ranging between 24 and 64 m². This fact, coupled with the detailed construction histories present at each excavation locale (ranging from three to twelve construction phases per excavation unit) and, thus, the pronounced depth of many excavations, means that no domiciles were excavated in their entirety. Excavations

can be viewed as windows on the past rather than as whole residences.

WINDOWS ON THE PAST

Within the southern sector of K'axob, there are seven excavated "windows" of varying sizes and depths (see figure 2.2 for their location; the digital *Tour of K'axob* also provides clear visual and spatial information on each excavation locale). Generally, excavations were located in the southern pyramid plaza of K'axob (operation 1) and within six satellite residential groups. As shown in figure 2.2, none of the satellite excavations is located more than 350 m from the southern pyramid plaza. Three are positioned to the south of operation 1 (operations 7, 8, and 10), two to the northwest (operations 11 and 12), and one to the northeast (operation 13).

Within each unit (*operation*), excavation was conducted in reference to cultural stratigraphy. Each individual context, whether an intrusive pit or unit of construction fill, was given a *zone* number (and sometimes subdivided into subzones). For the most part, the zone designation is the minimum unit of provenience. Zones that represented coeval building and occupational deposits were grouped into a *construction phase* and numbered in ascending order from the base of the excavation to the surface. In the accompanying digital *Domiciles Database*, a plan view of each construction phase is available for study as well as an entry for each zone number that is labeled by deposit type and ceramic complex. In this chapter, a sample of phase plans describing the major characteristics of K'axob domiciles is presented.

Many of the operations were excavated through more than one field season; excavation (or operation) directors generally produced an excavation report (table 3.1). Excavation summaries from the 1992 and 1993 seasons were compiled into interim reports that were submitted to the Department of Archaeology in Belmopan, Belize (McAnany 1993b, 1995b). In this manner, reports were generated for each operation: operation 1 (White 1990; Jackson 1993; Bobo 1995), operation 7 (McDermott 1991; Estrada Belli 1993), operation 8 (McCormack 1993), operation 10 (Henderson 1993), operation 11 (McCormack 1995), operation 12 (St. Laurent 1993; Henderson 1995), and operation 13 (Martonova 1993). Later refinement of excavation summaries make the original documents somewhat obsolete, although the insights of the

Table 3.1 Excavation units at K'axob (1990-93)

Operation	Overall Dimensions (m)*	Average Depth (m)	Approx. cu m	No. of Construction Phases	Years of Excavation	Operation Directors
1	6 x 8	2.4	115	12	1990, 1992, 1993	Patricia A. McAnany, Lorren Jackson, and Matthew Bobo
7	3 x 4 & 1 x 1	1.6	21	9	1990, 1992	Matthew McDermott, Francisco Estrada Belli
8	2 x 7, 0.5 x 2.25 & 1 x 1.5	0.9	15	3	1990, 1992	Marc Wolf, Valerie McCormack
10	2 x 7	1.3	18	6	1992	H. Hope Henderson
11	4 x 4	1.5	24	7	1992, 1993	Valerie McCormack
12	6 x 6	0.7	25	6	1992, 1993	Robert St. Laurent, H. Hope Henderson
13	2 x 4	0.4**	3	3	1992	Ingrid Martonova
Total			**221**	**46**		

*Trench dimensions grouped where necessary.
**Op. 13 not excavated to basal construction.

original excavators continue to prove invaluable. (Photographs of the operation directors can be viewed in the digital *Photo Database*.)

Overall dimensions of each operation differ markedly (table 3.1), as do the shape of the units. Differences in the average depth and stratigraphy of most units can be seen by opening the *3-D Excavation* program in the accompanying digital material. Based on approximate cubic meters of excavated fill, the seven excavations can be ranked in four groups of descending size: (1) operation 1, the largest unit with 115 cu m; (2) operations 7, 11, and 12 with 21–25 cu m; (3) operations 8 and 10 with 15 and 18 cu m, respectively; and (4) operation 13 with only 3 cu m. Differences in the cubic meters of excavated fill (table 3.1) are reflected particularly in the artifact sample from each operation. Operation 1—with the largest dimensions—yielded the largest volume of artifacts and the most complex construction history (twelve construction phases distributed among six ceramic complexes, table 3.2). Its location, on the eastern flank of pyramidal structure 18 within plaza B (figure 2.2), no doubt contributed to the high level of construction activity as did the Early Chaakk'ax-complex initiation of construction at this locale.

Operation 7, a second-tier excavation, yielded the largest sample of Early Nohalk'ax construction phases (five) and the second largest number of construction phases (nine). Situated on the northern side

of a substantial basal platform, operation 7 was excavated into structure 98 (figure 2.2), with construction activity initiated during Late K'atabche'k'ax times (table 3.2). Operation 8, in contrast, was placed within a low, single platform (structure 102) that reached its present height through three successive construction phases, which were restricted to Late and Terminal K'atabche'k'ax times (table 3.2). Third-tier in terms of the cubic mass of excavated material, operation 8 contrasts starkly with its third-tier companion, operation 10. With twice the number of construction phases, operation 10 spans the period from Early K'atabche'k'ax through Early Nohalk'ax and contains a large, distinctive fire feature at its base. Operation 10 was excavated into the middle of a basal platform (figure 2.2), which may explain its two lip-to-lip cache deposits.

Sharing the second-tier ranking with operations 7 and 12, operation 11 yielded evidence of seven construction phases spanning Early K'atabche'k'ax through Early Nohalk'ax (table 3.2). Situated on a basal platform directly to the east of structure 27, operation 11 most resembles operation 1 in containing finely laminated strata from multiple K'atabche'k'ax domestic construction events. The final operation to occupy the second tier is operation 12, which was located at the southern end of a large Formative period basal

Table 3.2 Number of construction phases by operation and ceramic complex

	CERAMIC COMPLEX AND FACET							
	Chaakk'ax		K'atabche'k'ax			Nohalk'ax		
Operation	Early	Late	Early	Late	Terminal	Early	Total	% of Total
1	2	1	4	1	3	1	12	26.1
7	0	0	0	2	2	5	9	19.6
8	0	0	0	2	1	0	3	6.5
10	0	0	2	2	1	1	6	13.0
11	0	0	3	2	1	1	7	15.2
12	0	0	0	4	1	1	6	13.0
13*	–	–	–	–	–	3	3	6.5
Total	2	1	9	13	9	12	46	
% of Total	4.3	2.2	19.6	28.3	19.6	26.1		100.0

*Op. 13 not excavated to basal construction.

platform (structure 28, see figure 2.2). The site of six construction phases that spanned Late K'atabche'k'ax through Early Nohalk'ax times, operation 12 yielded evidence of several domiciles that shifted location through time. For operation 13, only the upper Early Nohalk'ax levels were excavated. Situated on a single platform (structure 93), operation 13 yielded evidence of three construction phases and, had excavation not ceased due to time constraints, would certainly have borne K'atabche'k'ax-complex material.

CONSTRUCTING (AND RECONSTRUCTING) THE DOMICILES OF K'AXOB

The use of soft marl, or sascab, as the dominant construction material means that, in most cases, construction phases are defined by one or more units of fill topped by a floor surface. Generally, soft marl blocks were used for wall footings. Minor renovations, such as a floor resurfacing (often following a burial interment), took place between major construction events. Such activities were defined as a subphase of construction. An intrusive deposit, such as a burial or a cache, was classified with the construction phase from which it intruded. Extramural deposits, such as a midden or an exterior pit feature, were classified with a specific construction phase based on patterns of abutment as well as surface elevations.

The pottery in every zone underwent type-variety analysis by Sandra L. López Varela (1996; see also chapters 8 and 9 of this volume). Contiguous deposits with similar pottery were assigned to the same ceramic complex, and in this way a relative chronology was built. This chronology is supported by and extends the chronometric chronology discussed in chapter 2. This framework was then linked with the construction phase sequence for each operation (resulting chronology of construction phases is presented in table 3.2). Of the forty-six construction phases documented for the seven operations, only three date to Chaakk'ax times (all from operation 1). Succeeding Early K'atabche'k'ax-complex construction sequences have been documented only at operations 1, 10, and 11. In contrast, by Late K'atabche'k'ax times construction had ensued at all excavation locales except for operation 13 (which likely would have revealed Late K'atabche'k'ax construction had it been fully excavated). This pattern continues through Terminal K'atabche'k'ax and Early Nohalk'ax times, with the notable exception of operation 8, which contained no evidence of construction above its Terminal K'atabche'k'ax deposits. Operations 7 and 13, on the other hand, exhibit the highest number of construction phases during the latter complex. A cessation of construction activity after the early facet of the Early Classic period is a strong characteristic of southern K'axob. In contrast, the northern part of K'axob contains evidence of vigorous construction during the latter half of the Early Classic through the Epiclassic periods (McAnany 1997). Given the excavation data currently under consideration, however, domicile construction was most active during the K'atabche'k'ax complex (thirty-one phases, 67% of the total) and specifically during Late K'atabche'k'ax times, when thirteen construction phases are documented.

PREVAILING TRENDS IN DOMICILE CONSTRUCTION AND REFURBISHING

Although the full corpus of construction phase plans is available in the digital *Domiciles Database*, little narrative text accompanies the data presentation. Here, selected phase plans from each operation are presented and discussed in order to illustrate trends and distinctions in domicile size, construction technique, and associated features.

Operation 1. Although there are only twelve construction phases at operation 1, minor alterations within phases (entailing subphase plans) bring the total number of phase plans to twenty. Ten of these plans are featured here. For additional discussion of the construction phases of operation 1, see McAnany and López Varela (1999). Although Early Chaakk'ax phase 1a of operation 1 lacks any evidence of a prepared marl floor or a footing wall (figure 3.1), two highly significant burial interments were placed within the paleosol (burials 1-43 and 1-46). The concentration of posthole features, moreover, indicates that some type of structure once existed at this locale. There are pronounced status distinctions between the two burials. Burial 1-43—a gracile adult male and the only individual known to have been buried in a prone position at K'axob—was draped with a blanket of shell beads (see chapter 14) and two distinctive pottery vessels (see chapter 9). Burial 1-46, on the other hand, is an adult female with little in the way of burial accoutrements (see chapter 6 for additional mortuary details). This dyad, placed within two separate pits and accompanied by disparate furnishings, creates a sense of a purposeful foundation event. The size of the domicile that eventually is constructed on top of this mortuary event reinforces the impression that these two individuals represent the installation of a crafted social memory. That is, these interments appear to be a conscious attempt to mark this locale in the memory of descendants.

Shortly after these foundation burials, the area was used as a food processing locale, as witnessed by the triad of sherd-lined pit features (figure 3.2; see also chapter 5). The earliest known bona fide structure at K'axob was built during phase 2 and was renovated four times. Figure 3.3 shows the ultimate renovation phase before the structure was buried. The apsidal curve of the structure plinth can be seen, as can the chaotic pattern of postholes internal to the structure. The excavated portion of the structure covers about 32 m², and it appears to have been bisected by the excavation. Roofed-over area probably totaled around 64 m², a substantial structure for a large family or a village leader (the lack of coeval domiciles of smaller size severely limits interpretation). A full assemblage of domestic features exists in areas adjacent to the domicile, including a possible kitchen floor appended to the southwestern wall of the structure (zone 58), a midden area to the northwest of the main structure (zone 59), fire features, sherd-lined pits, and burial interments.

During succeeding Early K'atabche'k'ax times, there is active construction activity at operation 1, and the location and size of the structure changes radically. During phase 4, the edge of an apsidal structure is obvious in the northwestern corner of the excavation unit, with a floor surface extending to the south of it (figure 3.4). Burial interments both within the floor surface and in the eastern yard area (burials 1-24, 1-44, 1-31, 1-34a, and 1-34b), along with domestic pit features, reinforce the bivalent use of this area. Apparently it was perceived as both a place for the ancestors as well as a place to construct culinary features such as sherd-lined pits (zones 114 and 151). The superpositioning of the two in the northeastern portion of the unit (zones 112 and 152a) provides a clear example of this linkage. By phase 6, the location of the main domicile had shifted back to the eastern half of the excavation unit (figure 3.5); phase 6a contains one of the earliest cache deposits known from K'axob (zone 121; see chapter 4). Once again, the excavation unit nearly bisects the apsidal plinth of this domicile, which is much smaller than the underlying Chaakk'ax structure. About 12 m² of the western half of the structure was exposed, suggesting that the entire structure covered about 24 m². A floor resurfacing and a highly significant burial interment mark overlying construction in phase 6b (figure 3.6).

At this point in time, two adult males were buried in the center of the structure along its long axis. A small, shallow dish painted with a red cross on the exterior of the base was placed with each individual (see chapter 9 for description of vessels 013 and 014, chapter 16 for a discussion of cross motif, and *Pottery*

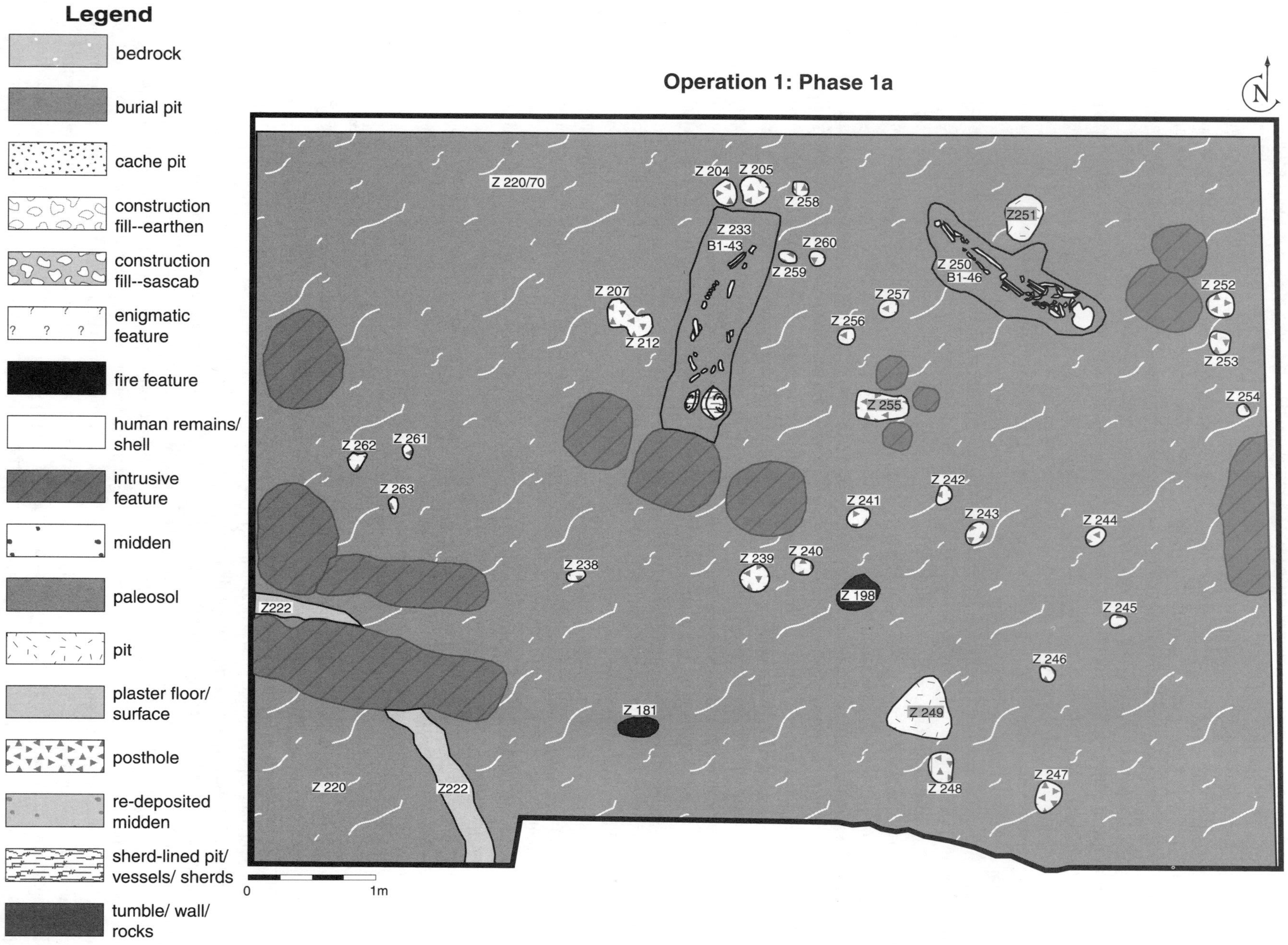

Legend

- bedrock
- burial pit
- cache pit
- construction fill–earthen
- construction fill–sascab
- enigmatic feature
- fire feature
- human remains/ shell
- intrusive feature
- midden
- paleosol
- pit
- plaster floor/ surface
- posthole
- re-deposited midden
- sherd-lined pit/ vessels/ sherds
- tumble/ wall/ rocks

Operation 1: Phase 1a

Z 222
Z 220
Z 222
Z 262
Z 263
Z 261
Z 220/70
Z 238
Z 181
Z 207
Z 212
Z 204
Z 205
B1-43
Z 233
Z 259
Z 260
Z 258
Z 239
Z 240
Z 256
Z 257
Z 198
Z 241
Z 255
Z 249
Z 248
Z 242
Z 243
Z 250
B1-46
Z 251
Z 247
Z 246
Z 244
Z 245
Z 252
Z 253
Z 254

0   1m

N

Figure 3.1 Early Chaakk'ax phase plan 1a from operation 1 with legend for all phase plans. *All illustrations prepared by K'axob Project staff and staff of UCLA Cotsen Institute Digital Archaeology Laboratory*

Operation 1: Phase 1b

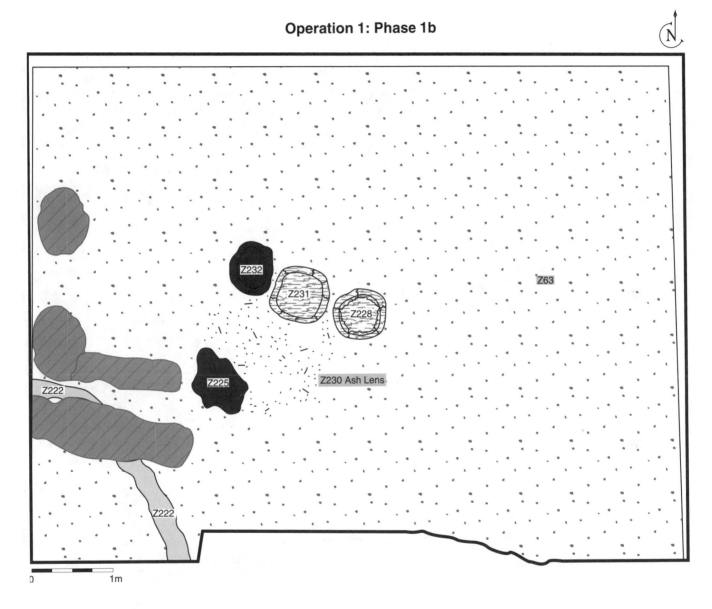

Figure 3.2 Early Chaakk'ax phase plan 1b from operation 1

Operation 1: Phase 2d

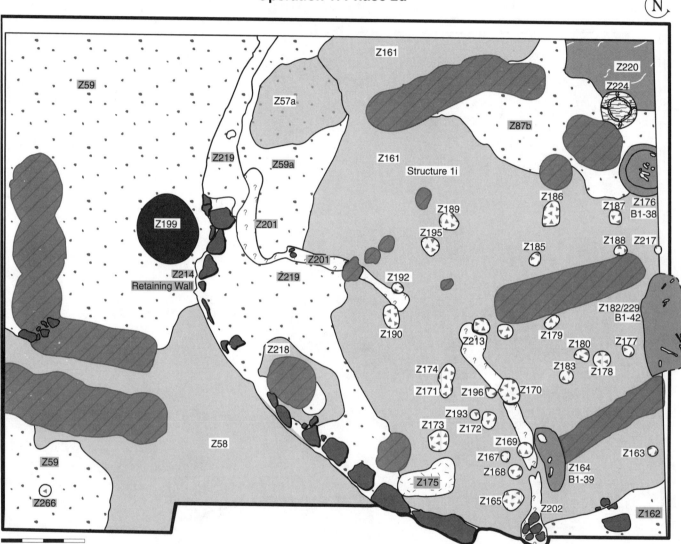

Figure 3.3 Early Chaakk'ax phase plan 2d from operation 1

Operation 1: Phase 4

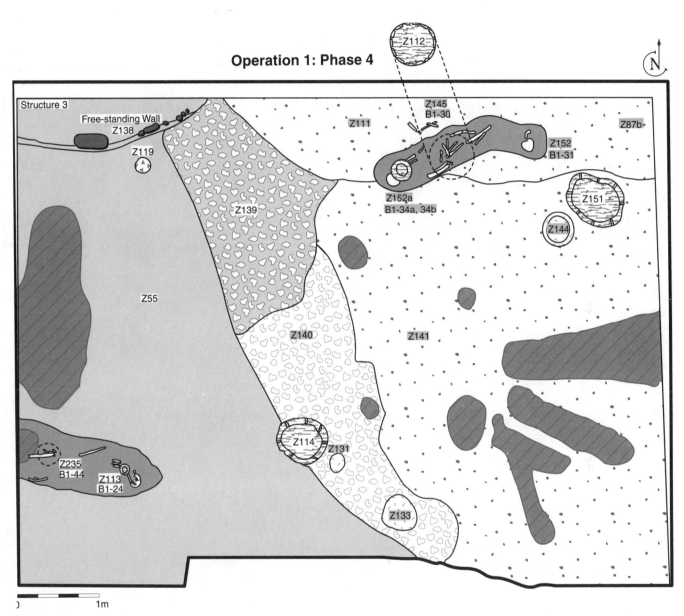

Figure 3.4 Early K'atabche'k'ax phase plan 4 from operation 1

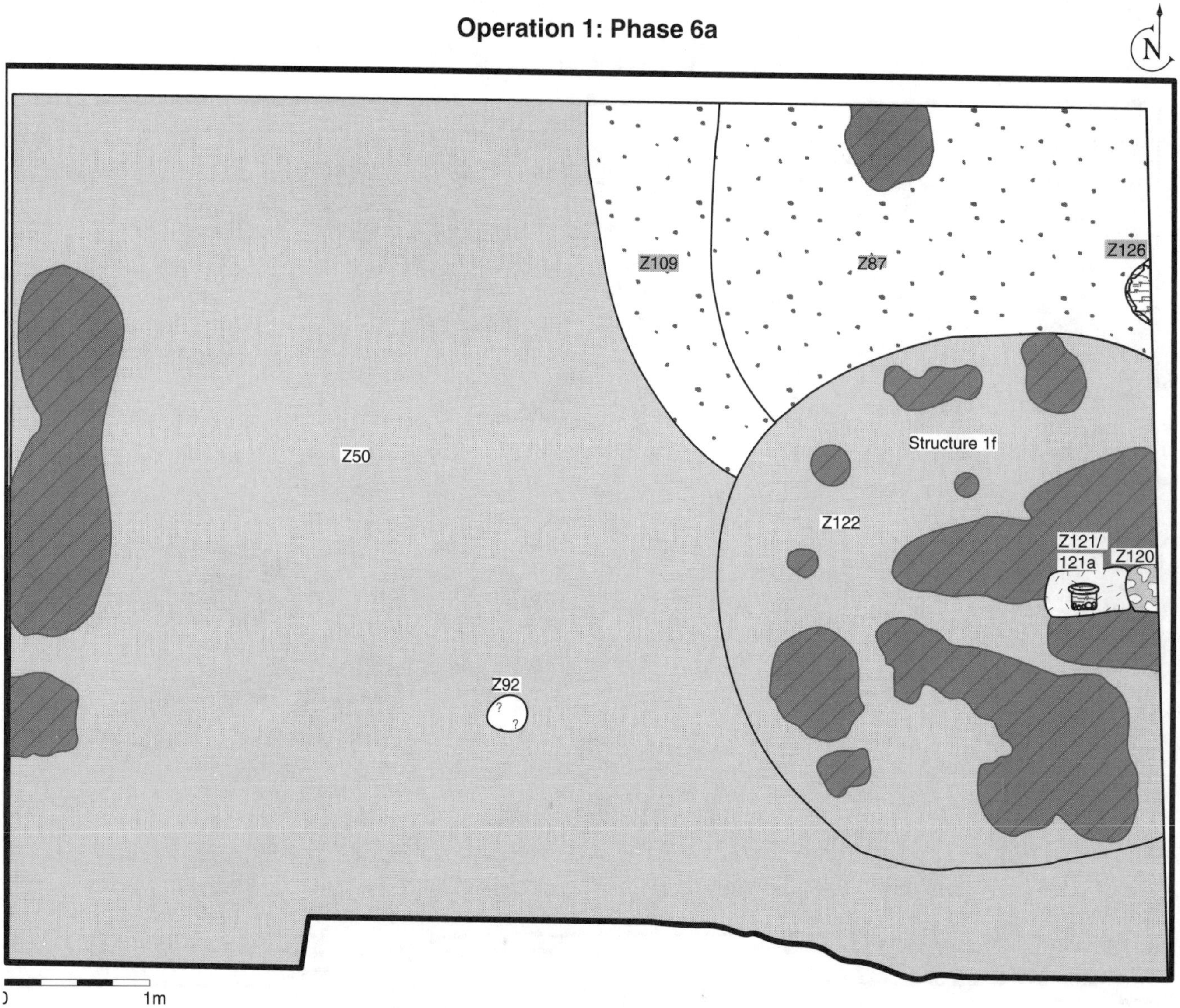

Operation 1: Phase 6a

Figure 3.5 Early K'atabche'k'ax phase plan 6a from operation 1

Operation 1: Phase 6b

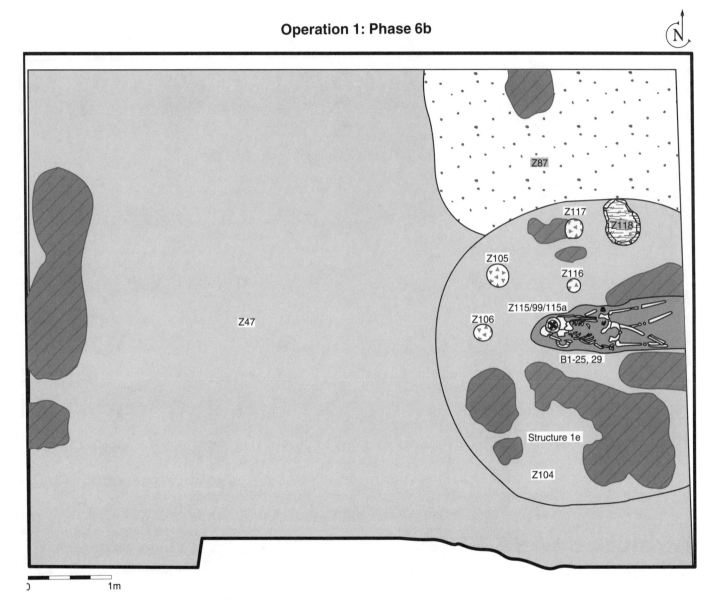

Figure 3.6 Early K'atabche'k'ax phase plan 6b from operation 1

Operation 1: Phase 7

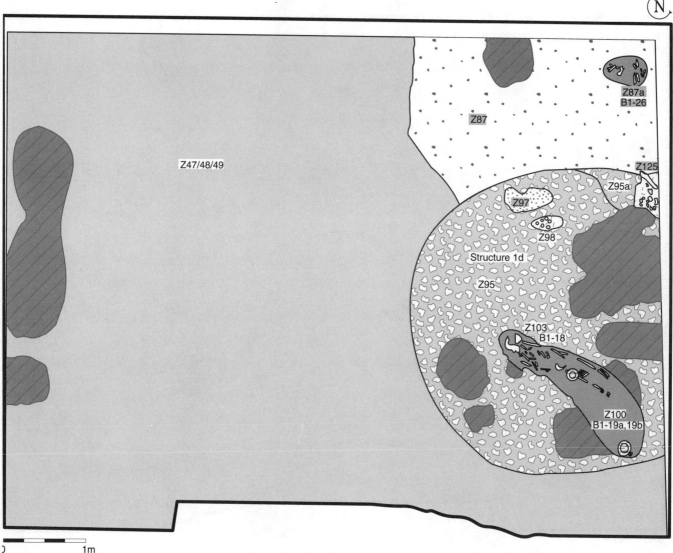

Figure 3.7 Early K'atabche'k'ax phase plan 7 from operation 1

Operation 1: Phase 8c

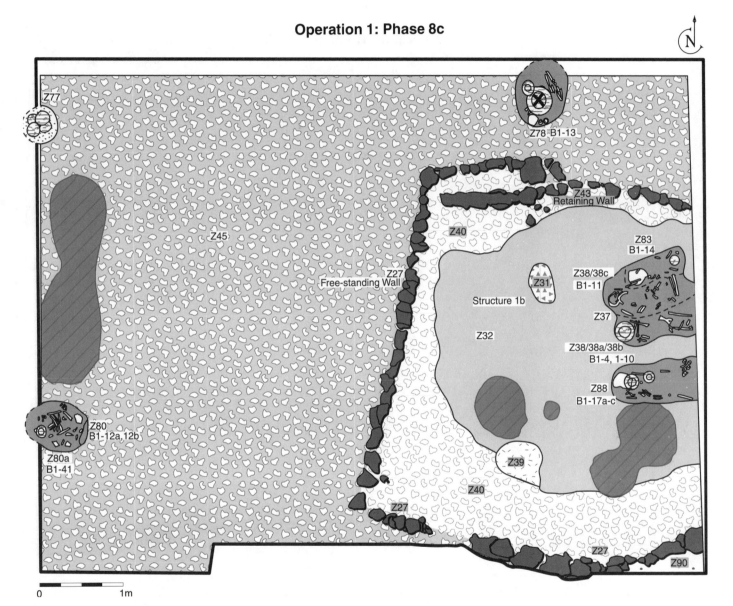

Figure 3.8 Late K'atabche'k'ax phase plan 8c from operation 1

Operation 1: Phase 9

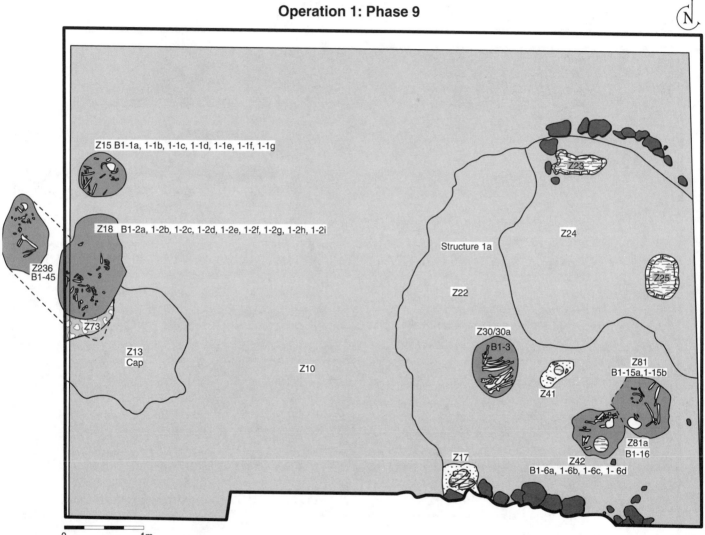

Figure 3.9 Terminal K'atabche'k'ax phase plan 9 from operation 1

Operation 1: Phase 12

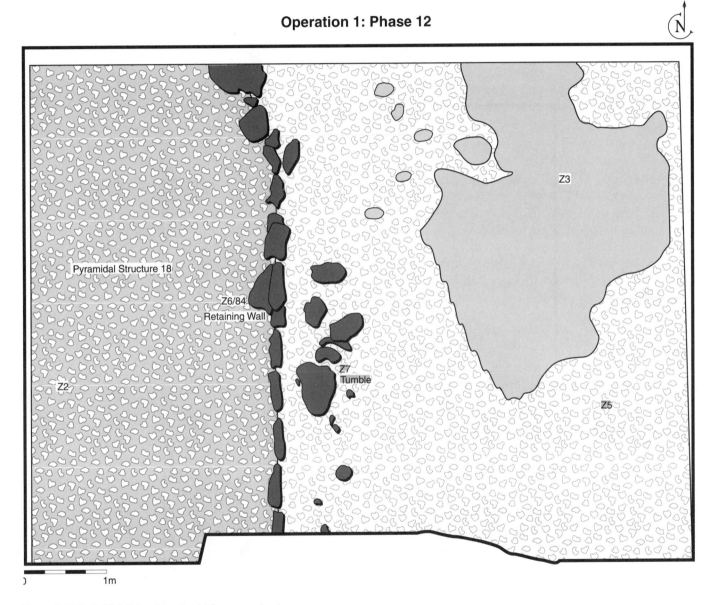

Figure 3.10 Early Nohalk'ax phase plan 12 from operation 1

Operation 7: Phase 1

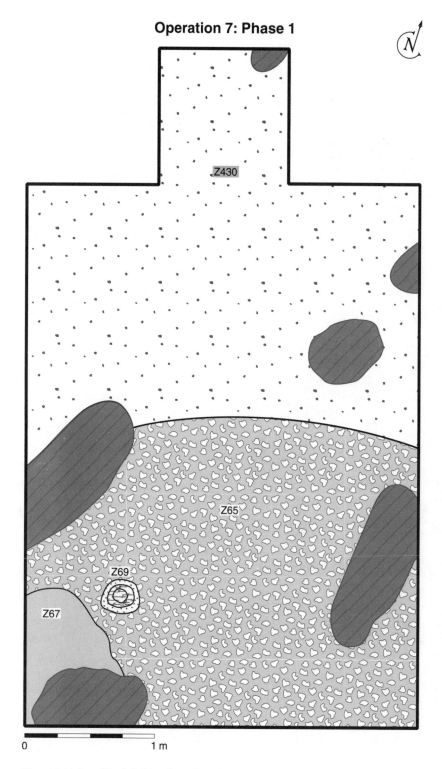

Figure 3.11 Late K'atabche'k'ax phase plan 1 from operation 7

Operation 7: Phase 3a

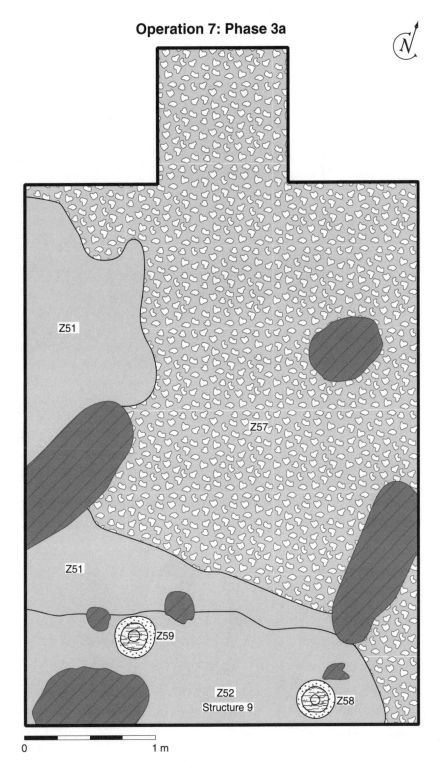

Figure 3.12 Terminal K'atabche'k'ax phase plan 3a from operation 7

Operation 7: Phase 5

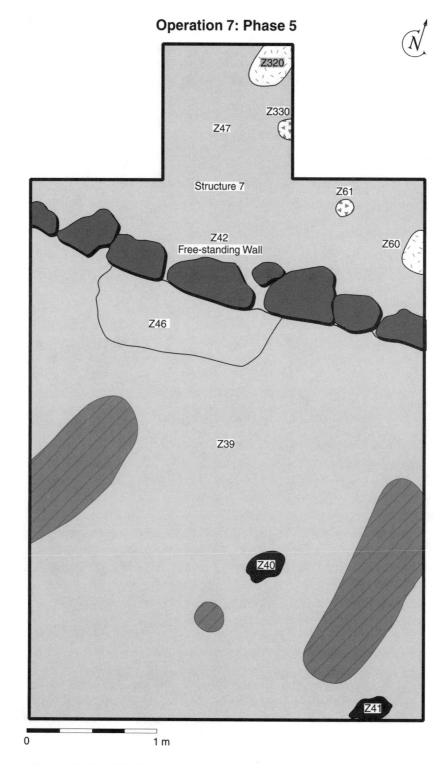

Figure 3.13 Early Nohalk'ax phase plan 5 from operation 7

Operation 7: Phase 7

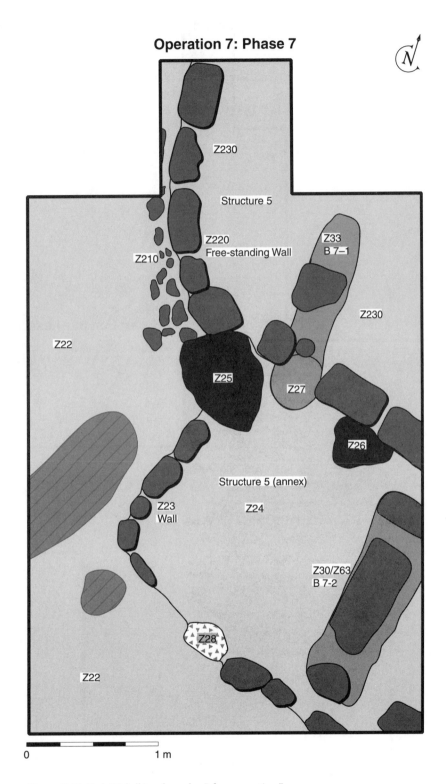

0   1 m

Figure 3.14 Early Nohalk'ax phase plan 7 from operation 7

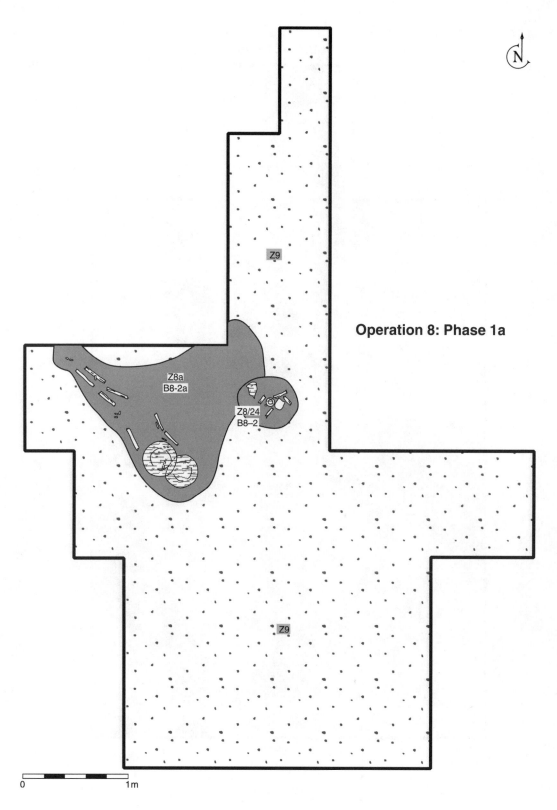

Figure 3.15 Late K'atabche'k'ax phase plan 1a from operation 8

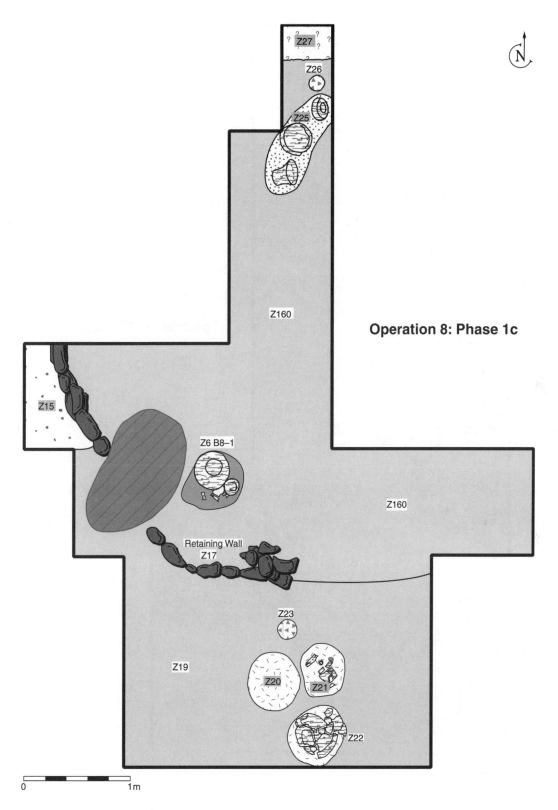

Figure 3.16 Late K'atabche'k'ax phase plan 1c from operation 8

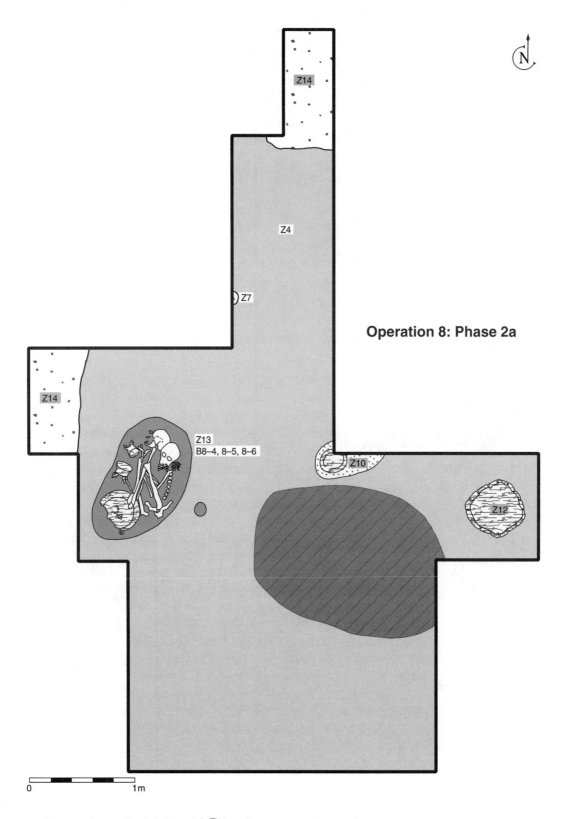

Operation 8: Phase 2a

Figure 3.17 Late K'atabche'k'ax phase plan 2a from operation 8

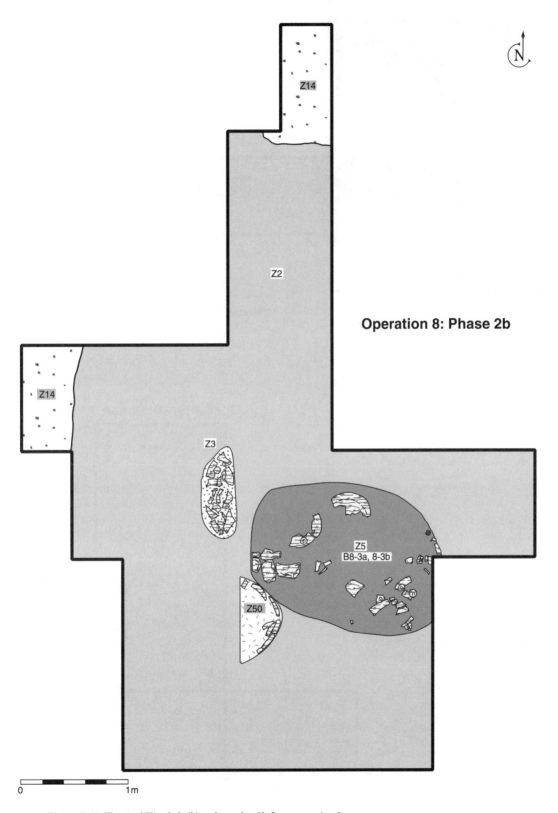

Figure 3.18 Terminal K'atabche'k'ax phase plan 2b from operation 8

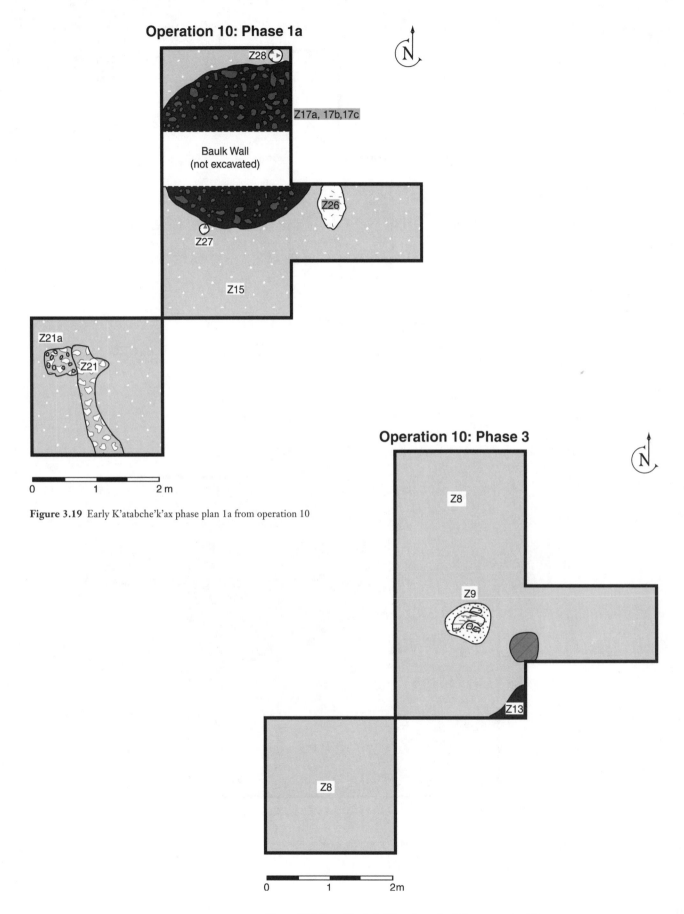

Figure 3.19 Early K'atabche'k'ax phase plan 1a from operation 10

Figure 3.20 Late K'atabche'k'ax phase plan 3 from operation 10

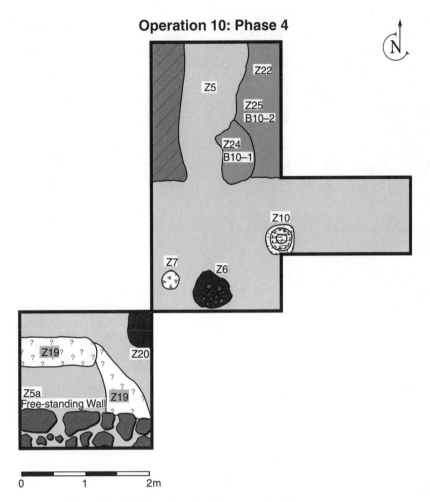

Figure 3.21 Late K'atabche'k'ax phase plan 4 from operation 10

Operation 11: Phase 1a

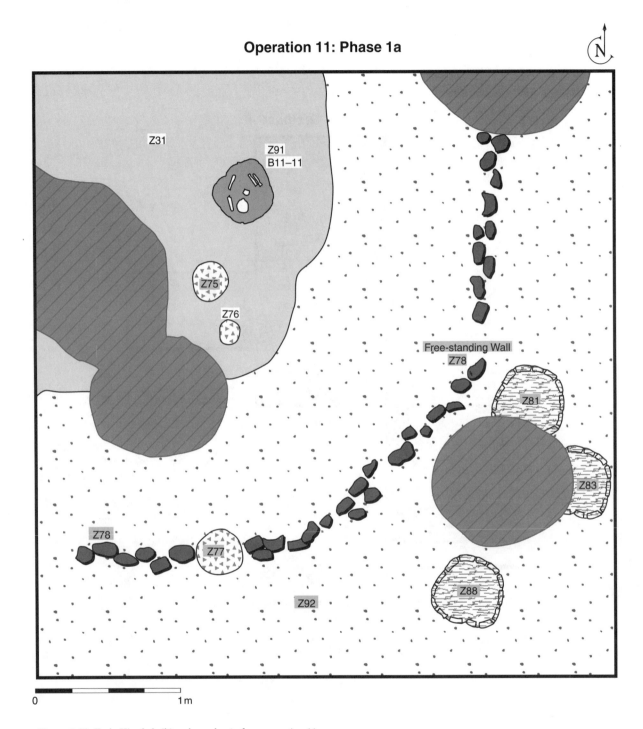

Figure 3.22 Early K'atabche'k'ax phase plan 1a from operation 11

Operation 11: Phase 4a

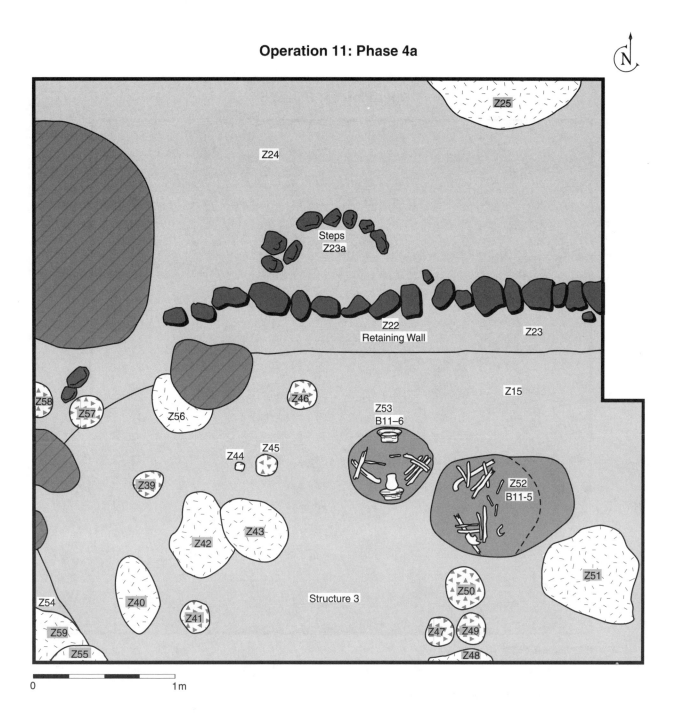

Figure 3.23 Late K'atabche'k'ax phase plan 4a from operation 11

Operation 11: Phase 5

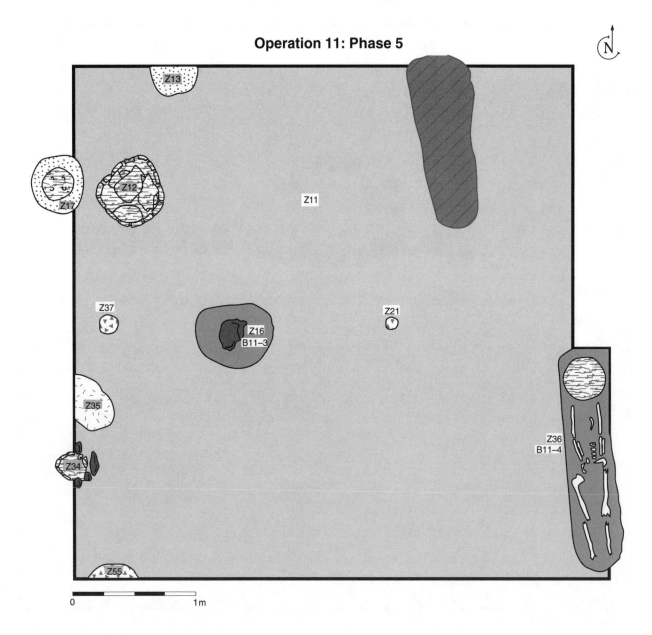

Figure 3.24 Late K'atabche'k'ax phase plan 5 from operation 11

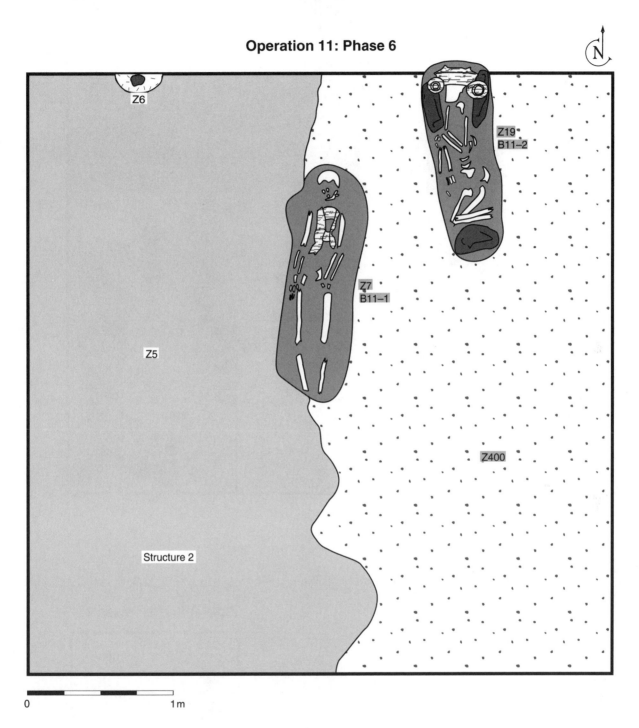

Figure 3.25 Terminal K'atabche'k'ax phase plan 6 from operation 11

Operation 12: Phase 2

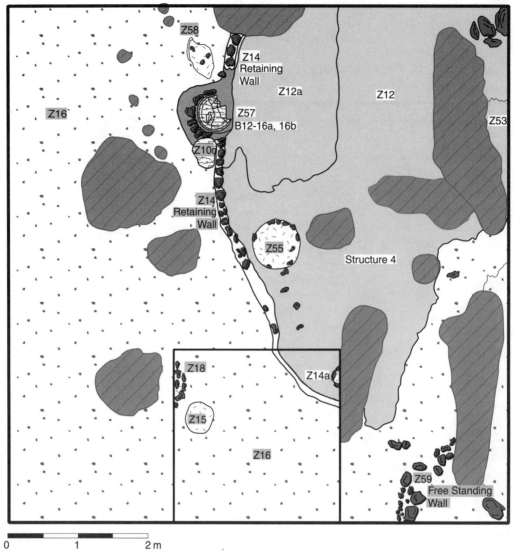

Figure 3.26 Late K'atabche'k'ax phase plan 2 from operation 12

Operation 12: Phase 2

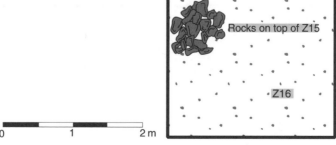

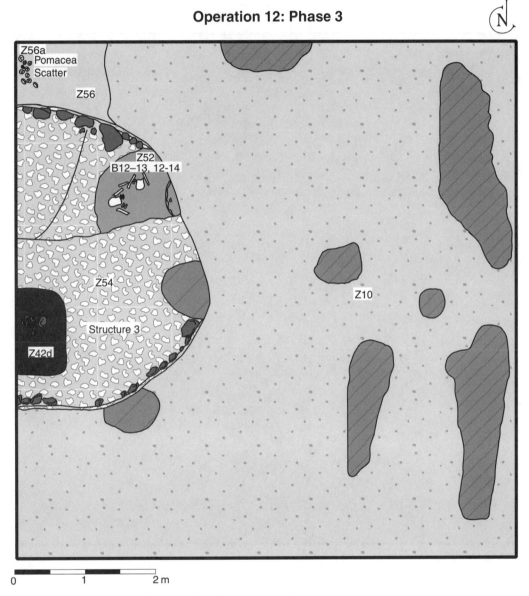

Figure 3.27 Late K'atabche'k'ax phase plan 3 from operation 12

Operation 12: Phase 5

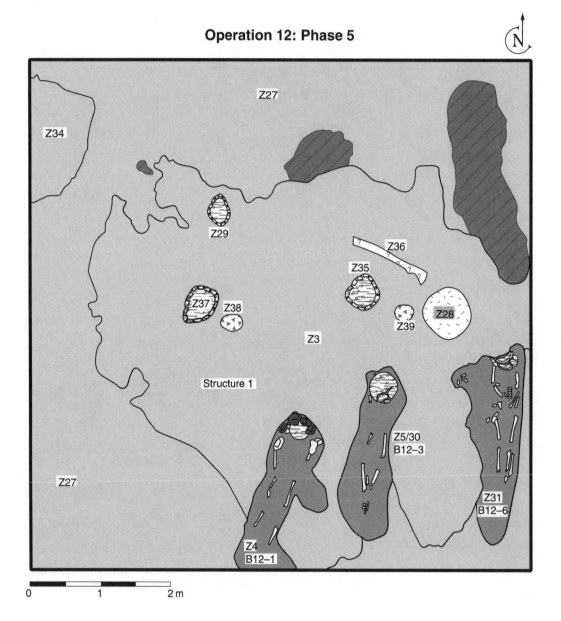

Figure 3.28 Terminal K'atabche'k'ax phase plan 5 from operation 12

Operation 13: Phase 2

A

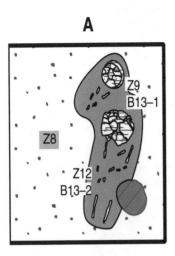

Figure 3.29 Early Nohalk'ax phase plan 2 from operation 13

B

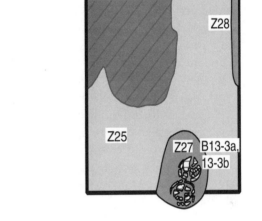

Operation 13: Phase 3

A

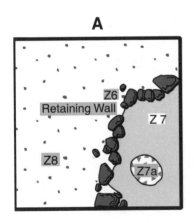

B

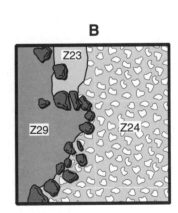

Figure 3.30 Early Nohalk'ax phase plan 3 from operation 13

Vessels Database for color images). The twinlike nature of this interment, with two individuals and two nearly identical vessels, is striking in light of the role played by twins in Maya cosmology (as heroes and founders) and the iconic significance of the quadripartite motif in centering the universe. At K'axob, this motif enjoys a highly restricted distribution, occurring in burials and caches only within operation 1 through the Terminal K'atabche'k'ax complex. The final Early K'atabche'k'ax construction phase (7, see figure 3.7) contains an early occurrence of a complete spouted vessel that was associated with the interment of an extended adult female. She was accompanied by the secondary remains of a young-to-middle-aged adult and a child (the latter placed on the pelvis of the female; more details on this possible family grouping—burials 1-18, 1-19a, and 1-19b—in chapter 6). Spouted vessel 009 had been capped with a bowl (vessel 008), indicating that the spouted jar likely once contained a beverage to nourish this important female and her associates in the afterlife.

At operation 1, Late K'atabche'k'ax times brought about the construction of a rectangular platform as the base for an apsidal domicile (figure 3.8). Construction phase 8 was modified four times; figure 3.8 shows the penultimate manifestation (phase 8c). Located once again in the eastern portion of the excavation unit and presumably bisected by the eastern section wall, the rectangular platform measures about 4 x 4 m (exposed portion). If symmetrical, the entire platform would have covered about 32 m². During this time period, the ritual significance and the perceived centrality of this locale are materialized through both ancestral interments and cache deposits. Specifically, a cache of four small bowls arranged in a cross pattern and containing seasonally specific fauna and a ritual scattering of golden chert microdebitage were intruded into the surface of zone 45 near the northwestern section wall. (For more information about this cache, see chapters 4, 11, and 17.) Less than 6 m to the east, another ritual scattering of chert took place over the flexed body of an adult covered with a large inverted bowl with a cross painted on its exterior base (figure 3.8, see also chapters 6 and 9). Additional burial interments were located both within the structure and directly to the west of it. The latter context contained a seated young adult (possibly female) adorned with greenstone as well as the secondary remains of a child and an adult (see chapter 6 for additional details regarding this possible family grouping). In comparison to the burials placed

outside of the structure, those located within the apsidal structure topping the platform were modest interments of extended individuals. The extramural plaza space of phase 8 is devoid of domestic pit features and concentrated midden areas. This suggests that the phase 8 structure may no longer have been a domicile sensu stricto but, rather, had been converted into a ritual structure within a large residential compound. Domestic features could have been relocated outside the perimeter framed by the window of operation 1.

By Terminal K'atabche'k'ax times, successive plaza resurfacing had buried the rectangular platform (figure 3.9, phase plan 9), but the presence of an apsidal plinth signals the continued existence of some type of structure at this location. Domestic features are increasingly scarce, however, and confined to a set of sherd-lined pits built inside the apsidal structure (zones 23 and 25). The southwestern perimeter of the structure is marked by the placement of a cache of three vessels ringed by small limestone spheres, or *yuntunob* (see chapters 4, 9, and 13). The basal vessel of this cache contained an assemblage of small items (figurines, beads, disks, and unworked shell) coded by color and number into groups of three (see chapters 4, 14, and 15). This so-called triadic cache marks what was to be the final apsidal structure at this location. Less than 4 m to the west, a small, low platform was built to seal a complex multiple-burial feature that intruded into a thick marl floor (zone 10). Both zone 18 (burials 1-2a through 2i) and its companion pit to the north—zone 15 containing burials 1-1a through 1g—were dedicated with a ritual scattering of golden chert microdebitage. Both mortuary facilities contained a large inverted Society Hall Red bowl prominently painted with a cross motif, final expressions of the centrality of this locale (more on these extraordinary mortuary contexts in chapters 6, 9, 11, and 16).

The final Early Nohalk'ax construction event at operation 1 sealed the underlying abodes of the ancestors by erecting pyramidal structure 18 (as shown on the surface plan of figure 2.2). Phase plan 12 (figure 3.10) indicates the line of stones remaining from the basal course of the front retaining wall. No evidence of a staircase remained; surficial debris in this area included Late Postclassic Chen Mul-style incensarios, suggesting that continued use of this area through the Classic and Postclassic periods included ritual performance as well as stone robbing.

In summary, the window to the past afforded by excavations at operation 1 spanned Early Chaakk'ax through Early Nohalk'ax times. Phase plans reveal the transformation of this locale from a large, apsidal residence bordered by domestic features and debris to a more formalized rectangular platform structure and, ultimately, to the locale of a pyramid structure. Mortuary ritual is a constant through time, although burial accoutrements increasingly carry symbolic information regarding the centrality and authority of those buried in this ancestral locale. The cache deposits, moreover, encode major principles of Maya cosmology through numerical, spatial, and color patterning.

Operation 7. In contrast with operation 1, this smaller excavation unit contained nine construction phases spanning Late K'atabche'k'ax through Early Nohalk'ax times. Including subphases, a total of eleven phase plans exist for operation 7; four are discussed here. The floor of the earliest domicile of operation 7 is poorly defined; however, it is marked symbolically by the placement of an upright San Martin Brown jar (vessel 111, see chapters 4 and 9) within an intrusive pit (figure 3.11). With an intervening construction phase, this Late K'atabche'k'ax structure is eventually capped by a Terminal K'atabche'k'ax domicile (phase plan 3a, figure 3.12) that was also marked by the inclusion of two cache deposits (see chapter 4). In this case, two small dishes were placed near the northern and eastern edges of an apsidal plinth, a placement reminiscent of the triadic cache of operation 1.

The ensuing Early Nohalk'ax complex witnessed the construction of a series of well-delineated domiciles in the northern portion of operation 7. These structures indicate the vitality of K'axob during a time period that is often underdetected outside of the Petén. Phase plan 5 (figure 3.13) shows a simple line of soft sascab stones that traverse the unit, defining an apsidal structure located to the north. More detail is available for the apsidal plinth and front porch complex of later construction phase 7 (figure 3.14). The front annex of this structure contains burial 7-2, an adolescent male interred underneath a stone-roofed pit with two distinctive polychrome vessels (see chapters 6 and 9). If this burial was placed on the midline of the annex, then the full porch probably covered 9 m². Moreover, the apsidal structure to which the porch is annexed can be estimated to have covered 24 m², yielding 33 m² for the entire complex. A second interment of a child was placed inside of the structure (burial 7-1). A similar pattern of Early Classic domicile construction featur-

ing a front annex and axial interments is recorded by Schulz (1997) at structure 54 (operation 14) in the northern extreme of K'axob. Two additional Early Nohalk'ax construction phases were built over the phase 7 structure, but neither contained burial or cache features within the perimeter of the excavation.

Operation 8. The cruciform arrangement of trenches at operation 8 yielded evidence of three construction phases and a total of five phase plans. Here four phase plans are presented: three from Late K'atabche'k'ax construction layers and one from the final construction event of Terminal K'atabche'k'ax times. In a manner reminiscent of the basal layer of operation 1, two burial interments mark the beginning of Late K'atabche'k'ax construction at operation 8 (phase plan 1a, figure 3.15). These foundation burials were capped by a large apsidal structure defined by a line of stones along the southwestern edge (phase plan 1c, figure 3.16). Inside of this 36 m² structure, an additional interment—the secondary remains of an old adult—were buried along with a cache of three vessels (see chapters 4 and 6). The southern boundary of the overlying Late K'atabche'k'ax structure (phase 2a, see figure 3.17) is not clearly defined, although the western and northern boundaries are roughly coterminous with the underlying phase 1c structure. The structure of phase 2a contained a sherd-lined pit (zone 12); a cache of two nested vessels, one of which is spouted (zone 10); and a burial feature containing two fully articulated and flexed individuals and the partial, disarticulated remains of a third (burials 8-4, 8-5, and 8-6). Another twin interment (evocative of Early K'atabche'k'ax burials 1-20 and 1-29 from operation 1), these two middle-adult males received equally auspicious treatment as they were interred with mammiform tetrapodal vessels, obsidian, and greenstone.

The significance of this locale continued to echo through the final Terminal K'atabche'k'ax construction (phase 2b, figure 3.18). Another burial feature (zone 5), possibly linked to the termination of the occupation of structure 102 (poorly defined this close to the surface), consisted of the secondary remains of two adult males and the ritual killing and scattering of several mammiform tetrapodal vessels and greenstone beads.

Operation 10. Located in the central plaza of a basal platform, this excavation yielded evidence of six construction phases and a total of seven phase plans spanning the period from Early K'atabche'k'ax through Early Nohalk'ax. Here, three phase plans are presented. The most striking feature of the basal layer of operation 10 is the presence of a large, 3 m diameter firepit (figure 3.19). This 50 cm deep feature contained poorly preserved wood fragments but few other artifacts that might indicate its specific use. The firepit was later capped by a layer of construction fill and a small apsidal structure, only part of which can be detected on phase plan 2 (see *Domiciles Database*).

Judging from the series of lip-to-lip caches (zones 9 and 10) that were placed within the plaza floor of phase 3 and phase 4 constructions (see figures 3.20 and 3.21, respectively) as well as the presence of adjacent domiciles, this area seems to have been formalized into a central patio space during Late K'atabche'k'ax times. Although lip-to-lip caches were not found within operation 1, they too mark the centrality of a location, albeit in a qualitatively different fashion. The zone 9 cache literally contains a reference to the primordial hearthstones by way of three small stones placed in an upright vessel. In upper phase plan 4 (figure 3.21), the lip-to-lip cache is closely associated with two burials (placed immediately to the north of the cache), a firepit located less than 1 m southwest of the cache, and the northern footing wall of a structure located 3 m to the southwest. Thus, in operation 10, as have been evidenced in operations 1 and 8, rituals of place-making that involve ancestor interments and activation of the soul of a residential compound go hand-in-hand with more mundane activities of firepit construction and domicile erection.

Operation 11. This 1.5 m deep, 4 x 4 m excavation uncovered seven construction phases that are recorded in ten phase plans. After operation 1, domicile construction began the earliest at operation 11 (Early K'atabche'k'ax) and continued through the Early Nohalk'ax complex. Here, a sample of four phase plans is presented. Assuredly, the earliest domicile at operation 11 was substantial and apsidal (figure 3.22). This window on the past revealed only the southeastern portion of a floor and a stone-lined plinth that probably once covered about 24 m². Just as the early layers of operation 1 featured a triad of sherd-lined pits, so too does phase 1a of operation 11 (zones 81, 83, and 88). Additionally, a sherd-lined pit (zone 91), later used as a burial interment (burial 11-11), was placed inside the phase 1a structure. In the overlying renovations of phase 1b, several burials were interred, including that of an old male who was seated and furnished with a spouted vessel shaped as a duck (see chapters 6, 8, and 9).

Late K'atabche'k'ax times witnessed dramatic restructuring in the location, shape, and height of domicile construction at operation 11. A platform, possibly apsidal, was constructed during phase 4a (figure 3.23). Only the northwestern portion of the platform was exposed in the excavation; all told, it likely measured 8 m (E-W) by 4 m (N-S) for a total area of 32 m². Within subphases a and b of construction phase 4, two individuals were interred within intrusive pits located within the domicile (burials 11-5 and 11-6), the latter seated in a bell-shaped pit and furnished with three bone needles and two pottery vessels (see chapters 6, 9, and 15). In the upper subphase, a large, deep storage pit (zone 20) was discovered. Later, this feature was filled with refuse, particularly broken fragments of ground stone. Subsequently, the platform was covered by a large unit of construction fill that created a central plaza surface (phase 5, figure 3.24). The presence of a lip-to-lip cache (zone 17) in the western section wall harkens back to the lip-to-lip caches intruded into the central plaza of operation 10 and reinforces the notion that lip-to-lip cache deposits are linked with the activation of central plaza spaces rather than with individual domiciles. As witnessed at previous operations, domestic features such as sherd-lined pits were intruded into the same plaza surface as the cache. The placement of an extended burial (11-4) on top of the phase 5 surface was one of the final events of this phase. Buried by subsequent construction during phase 6, this old adult male, whose head was protected by a large inverted bowl (vessel 106), either dedicated the ensuing construction or, perhaps, was memorialized by it.

The final two burials of operation 11 were placed in a midden area (zone 400) located to the east of a large phase 6 Terminal K'atabche'k'ax structure of unknown dimensions (figure 3.25). Possibly a male and a female, the male burial (11-2) is significantly more elaborate than that of the female. Like the Early Nohalk'ax interment of a young male in operation 7, the burial 11-2 context contained a basal-flange polychrome and a stone-roofed pit. The increasing tendency to memorialize young males in focal mortuary deposits—also evident in burials 1-1 and 1-2 of operation 1—could be interpreted in several ways, one of which points to the increasing importance of warfare at the end of the Formative period.

Operation 12. The 6 x 6 m area of operation 12 allowed almost complete exposure of the Terminal K'atabche'k'ax domicile of phase 5. Totaling six construction phases and an equal number of phase plans, three of these plans are presented here. Location of the domiciles of operation 12 varies considerably through time. The earliest documented Late K'atabche'k'ax structure occupies the eastern portion of the excavation unit (phase plan 2, figure 3.26). Only the southwestern part of this structure is exposed, but it appears to be an apsidal structure with an overall area of about 32 m². The most striking characteristic of the phase 2 structure is a burial/cache placed in the western footing wall of the structure. This feature includes a flat-bottomed bowl (vessel 088) into which was placed a stemmed macroblade, the secondary remains of an adult and a child, and a large deposit of *Pomacea* spp. shell (see chapters 4, 6, and 9). Subsequently, this structure was buried by phase 3 construction that entailed the building of another apsidal domicile directly to the west of the earlier structure (phase plan 3, figure 3.27). Slightly smaller, this apsidal plinth was defined by a line of stones that likely delimited an area of around 24 m². Although no cache deposits were explicitly recognized in this phase, two adults were buried in the northeastern part of the domicile. A final Late K'atabche'k'ax construction phase (4, see *Domiciles Database*) once again shifted the position of the domicile to the east, while the midden or yard area to the west became the focus of burial interments.

During Terminal K'atabche'k'ax construction, a domicile was built nearly in the center of the excavation unit (phase plan 5, figure 3.28). Again, the structure was a low, apsidal plinth that contained a combination of domestic and ritual features. Similar in size to the phase 3 construction, the phase 5 structure differed from it in two significant ways. In the characteristic K'axob fashion of integrating ritual with domestic economy, three sherd-lined pits were constructed inside the structure and three extended burials—oriented to the north—framed the southern boundary of the structure. Construction activity at operation 12 continued into Early Nohalk'ax times. In the final phase (6), domicile location shifted to the north, but the pattern of cardinally oriented, extended burials was maintained (see plan in *Domiciles Database*).

Operation 13. The two noncontiguous 2 x 2 m squares that comprised operation 13 yielded evidence of three Early Nohalk'ax construction phases and the same number of phase plans. Given the shallow depth of this excavation, it is unusual that it bore evidence of four burial features, three with secondary remains

and one of an extended adult male. The latter is shown in phase 2 (burial 13-2; figure 3.29) along with the secondary remains of burial 13-1, 13-3a, and 13-3b. Burials 13-1 and 13-2 were placed within a midden or extramural area, while burial 13-3 was intruded into the plaster floor of a phase 2 structure of unknown dimensions. The overlying construction phase (3, figure 3.30) contains evidence of a low retaining wall, although the small size of the exposure precludes estimation of its size.

OVERALL PATTERNS IN SIZE AND SHAPE OF DOMICILES

All told, excavations at K'axob produced evidence of approximately twenty partially excavated structures. These structures span the complexes of Early Chaakk'ax through Early Nohalk'ax and have many features in common (table 3.3). First of all, the majority of structures are low plinths or building foundations that are less than 20 cm in height. Taller platforms, per se, were encountered only in operations 1 and 11, and the only assuredly rectangular platform was built at operation 1. This location in pyramid plaza B was also the only excavation to contain a construction phase attributable to pyramid building; at all other locales, domiciles were constructed from the bottom to the top of the excavation unit. No plinths clearly deviated from an apsidal shape; the rectangular form was reserved for platforms, pyramids, and domiciles of the later Classic period. The size of structures varies both within and between excavation units (table 3.3). The 64 m² domicile at the base of operation 1 is singular in its large size: it covers almost double the area of any other domicile. The recurrence of 24 m² and 32–33 m² domiciles suggests that, among basic house sizes, there may be a larger and a smaller variant. All structures were similar proportionally; that is, they appeared to be twice as long as they were wide.

The domestic function of the majority of structures is reinforced by the presence of features such as midden areas and sherd-lined pits. The rich artifact content of the midden deposits and some of the pit features further supports the domestic nature of these structures, and the specific inclusion of pottery, chipped stone, ground stone, fauna, and mollusca provide additional corroboration (see chapters 8, 11, 13, 17, and 18 for in-depth studies). The dual domestic and ritual significance of these locales is indicated by the spatial comingling of cache deposits and burial interments with

Table 3.3. Characteristics of K'axob domiciles (dash indicates insufficient evidence for assessment)

Operation	Construction Phase & Subphase	Ceramic Complex*	Predicted Structure Area (m²)	Structure Shape	Structure Type
1	2	E. C.	64	apsidal	plinth
1	6	E. K.	24	apsidal	plinth
1	8	L. K.	32	rectangular	platform
1	8	L. K.	24	apsidal	plinth
1	9	T. K.	30	apsidal	plinth
1	12	E. N.	–	rectangular	pyramid
7	1	L. K.	–	–	plinth
7	3a	T. K.	–	apsidal	plinth
7	5	E. N.	–	apsidal?	plinth
7	7	E. N.	33	apsidal with porch	plinth
8	1b-c	L. K.	36	apsidal	plinth
8	2	L. K.	–	apsidal?	plinth
10	4	L. K.	–	–	plinth
11	1a	E. K.	24	apsidal	plinth
11	4	L. K.	32	apsidal?	platform
11	6	T. K.	–	–	plinth
12	2	L. K.	32	apsidal	plinth
12	3	L. K.	24	apsidal	plinth
12	5	T. K.	24	apsidal	plinth
13	3	E. N.	–	–	plinth

* E. C., Early Chaakk'ax, E. K., Early K'atabche'k'ax, L. K., Late K'atabche'k'ax, T. K., Terminal K'atabche'k'ax, E. N., Early Nohalk'ax.

sherd-lined pits, fire features, and midden deposits. Mortuary features within the built environment—which indicate an active concern with creating and maintaining descent narratives—are closely linked to construction events and thus to construction phases.

MORTUARY RITUAL AT K'AXOB DOMICILES

The sample of burial remains from K'axob, while tallying over one hundred individuals, nevertheless represents a very selective subset of all of the men, women, and children who lived and died there. While Storey (chapter 6) focuses on the bioarchaeology of the individuals, this section summarizes major temporal trends in the construction of sixty-three burial features. Since multiple interment is a common occurrence at K'axob, burial feature tallies necessarily diverge from counts of individuals. When burial features are tabulated by operation, ceramic complex, and construction phase, several trends emerge (table 3.4). The numerical dominance of operation 1 is clear, with 46% of all burial features excavated at this locale and 100% of all Chaakk'ax burials. Conspicuously absent from operation 1, however, are Nohalk'ax complex burial features, which are most frequent in the diminutive operation 13 (table 3.4). Operation 7 yielded burial features from Early Nohalk'ax construction only, despite the Late and Terminal K'atabche'k'ax construction phases. In

Table 3.4 Number of burial features per ceramic complex and construction phase*

| | CERAMIC COMPLEX AND FACET | | | | | | | | Ratio of Burial Features to Constr. Phases |
| | Chaakk'ax | | K'atabche'k'ax | | | Nohalk'ax | | % of Total | |
Operation	Early	Late	Early	Late	Terminal	Early	Total		
1	8	3	8	8	2	0**	29	46.0	2.4
7	_***	–	–	0	0	2	2	3.2	0.2
8	–	–	–	4	1	–	5	7.9	2
10	–	–	0	1	1	–	2	3.2	0.3
11	–	–	5	4	2	0	11	17.5	1.6
12	–	–	–	6	3	1	10	15.9	1.7
13	–	–	–	–	–	4	4	6.3	1.3
Total	8	3	13	23	9	7	63		
% of Total	12.7	4.8	20.6	36.5	14.3	11.1		100.0	

* Counts based on burial features rather than number of individuals within features.
** Zero indicates an absence of burial features within a construction phase.
*** Dash indicates the absence of a construction phase.

contrast, at operation 8 (Late and Terminal K'atabche'k'ax) burial contexts occurred in every complex during which there was construction activity. These same two complexes also represent the only time during which burial features were constructed at operation 10, even though there is earlier construction activity in the form of a large firepit. At operation 11, burial contexts are numerous but are restricted to the three facets of the K'atabche'k'ax complex. Finally, for operation 12, burial features are found in every complex during which there is construction activity.

The intensity of mortuary ritual at each of the seven excavation locales can be summarized as the ratio of burial features to construction phases (table 3.4). Not surprisingly, the construction of mortuary features relative to overall construction activity was most frequent at operation 1, followed, in order of decreasing intensity, by operations 8, 12, 11, 13, 10, and 7. Featuring a ratio of 2.4 mortuary features per construction phase, operation 1 contained almost twice the number of features recorded at other operations. The central location and seminal deposits of operation 1 mark it as a distinctive location that likely encoded a founding narrative for the village. At any rate, at this locale more energy was invested in mortuary ritual that, in conjunction with continued construction activity, created a physically stratified record of past residents.

Across the operations several qualitative differences in mortuary ritual can be identified. For instance, the cross motif as well as the practice of scattering golden chert microdebitage is restricted to operation 1, where seated burials seldom occurred before Late K'atabche'k'ax times. In operation 11, on the other hand, deep circular pits for the interment of seated individuals can be found in the Early K'atabche'k'ax complex. As Storey (chapter 6) notes, multiple interments of adults and of children are more common in operation 1 and often give the impression of family members reunited in death, although burials of co-interred males occurred at both operations 1 and 8. Storey also observes that, over time, greater care was taken with the interment of young males, revising the stereotypical pattern of mortuary ritual designed to transform elders into ancestors. The stone-roofed pits of extended Terminal K'atabche'k'ax and Early Nohalk'ax burials—found in operations 7 and 11—were built for young males. These types of interments are absent from operation 1. It must be noted, however, that in 1981 a looted Early Classic slab-lined tomb was recorded in structure 16, which is located on the southeastern side of pyramid plaza B (figure 2.2). Through time, as the scale of the constructions of the residential group occupying plaza B expanded spatially outside the window to the past that is defined as operation 1, material within the excavation unit came to reflect a smaller part of the total ritual and domestic activities of that residential group.

FINAL CONSIDERATIONS

Can the Formative domiciles of a village such as K'axob inform us about early rulership, monumental architecture, hierarchical social divisions, or ritual practice? Moreover, when K'axob is compared to Formative structures excavated elsewhere in northern Belize at sites such as Cuello (Gerhardt 1988; Hammond 1991a), Colha (Anthony 1987; Sullivan 1991), or Cerros (Cliff 1988; Cliff and Crane 1989), can any differences be discerned? The answer to both questions is "yes," and the starting point is the 64 m² domicile at the base of operation 1. The size and singularity of the Early Chaakk'ax house is evocative of a large apsidal structure discovered at Paso de la Amada on the Pacific Coast of Chiapas and dated to the Locona phase (1400– 1250 BC). Called a "chief's house" by its excavators (Blake et al. 1995:171), this construction is considerably larger than the K'axob domicile and predates it by 800 years. Nevertheless, both structures are distinctively large in comparison to overlying constructions, and both were found in the basal strata of their respective excavations. For K'axob, the interpretation of this domicile as that of a village leader, if not a chief, is bolstered by what appears to be a founding event in the form of two burials located underneath the large structure. Moreover, the construction phases built over the seminal structure serve to emphasize that the locale was maintained within the active social memory of the community. The total sacralization of this locale in the form of pyramid construction did not occur for over a thousand years. In the intervening centuries, the operation 1 locale was slowly transformed from a large residence bustling with domestic features to a well-maintained platform containing ancestors and dedicatory caches but decreasing amounts of domestic debris. If we assume a stable residential group, then we can posit that, by Late K'atabche'k'ax times, authority was increasingly institutionalized around the kin group that eventually supervised the construction of plaza B, complete with its pyramids.

The domiciles of K'axob are locally distinctive in several ways. Notable is the emphasis on wetland fauna at the expense of mammals in the midden areas adjacent to the domiciles (see chapters 17 and 18). The prominence of the quadripartite motif at K'axob also sets it apart from neighboring villages of the Formative period (see chapter 16) and suggests that the pottery artisans of K'axob crafted social identities along with pottery. The abrupt cessation of construction activity after Early Nohalk'ax times also separates the domiciles of K'axob from those of neighboring communities, where construction tended either to cease at the end of the Formative period or to continue through the Classic period.

Due to the longevity of occupation at K'axob, many domiciles were rebuilt and expanded over a thousand-year time span. This longevity would seem to accord well with a house society model, which can be further bolstered by the evidence of canonical communication in the form of offerings placed within domiciles to nourish and activate the soul of the house. The long stratigraphic sequences of mortuary interments might also be cited as evidence of a house society. On the other hand, emphasis on ancestor interments also indicates a concern with maintaining pathways to the past—or creating descent narratives—and such behaviors are devalued by proponents of a house society model.

Throughout this sample of Formative and Early Classic domiciles there is a pronounced spatial integration of ritual and domestic features; burial interments are situated side by side with sherd-lined pit features. Such integration has also been observed by Hodder (2000) at Çatalhöyük—a large neolithic village in southern Turkey—where symbolism, ritual, and household activities took place in the same room. This spatial co-occurrence likely reflects an ideology in which domestic tasks were ritualized and ritual practice was viewed as a domestic activity. To a large degree, this integrative cosmology is an enduring feature of Maya society and is not restricted to the Formative period; however, it is noteworthy that it is so clearly detected in the built environment of this early village. Overall, the Formative and Early Classic period domiciles represent a built, maintained, and renovated environment that provided a stage for the pursuit of livelihood, the storage of social memory, expressions of identity, status, and ancestry, and, as presented in the following chapter, a place to nourish the animus of lived space.

Chapter 4
Related CD Resources

Caches
Triadic Cache Content
Pottery Vessels
Domiciles

CHAPTER 4

NOURISHING THE ANIMUS OF LIVED SPACE THROUGH RITUAL CACHING

ELEANOR HARRISON-BUCK

Ancient Maya caches have an elusive quality not only in their secretive placement (sacred contents stashed beneath a floor of an exterior patio or entombed in architecture) but also in their meaning and function within society. Caching behavior is generally defined as ritual in function, a practice that spiritually binds the built environment to a supernatural realm. Recent studies of ritual activity, however, suggest that caching behavior represents far more complex ideological concerns than was previously thought (Brady and Ashmore 1999; Becker 1992; D. Chase 1988; Freidel et al. 1993; Mock 1998; Schele and Freidel 1990; among others). In light of these studies, caches cannot simply be defined as ritual in function. This definition oversimplifies their meaning and underestimates their importance to ancient Maya society.

Caches are known to play a symbolic role in Maya life, acting as a spiritual expression of a ritual event framed in space and time. Increasingly, offerings are defined as part of either a dedication or a termination ritual because they can both activate and deactivate the animus, or soul, that was believed to be housed in both objects and architecture. Formative and Early Classic period cache deposits from K'axob suggest that caches served a number of different and often overlapping ritual functions. Through an analysis of twenty-two caches, three potential functions can be discerned:

- Cyclical ordering of space: demarcating places and boundaries
- Cyclical ordering of time: marking events
- Memory and identity: venerating ancestors and gods

Although cache functions are categorized here rather rigidly, they are certainly not mutually exclusive. On the contrary, the information presented below supports the argument that caches often represent a fusion of sacred functions. Cache formations symbolize active thought and provide insight into complex ideological constructs inextricably linked to ancient Maya life. The K'axob cache data recovered from the 1990–93 seasons reflect both continuity and transformation in the social, political, economic, and ideological spheres of this ancient Maya village. The collection of caches represents a deep cultural tradition that developed early in the site's history of occupation, beginning in the early facet of the Late Formative period (ca. 400 BC). While no caches were recorded in the preceding Middle Formative period (ca. 1000–400 BC), an early occupation that dates to this period (represented in stratified deposits) was identified at plaza B in operation 1. The data indicate that this locale may have served as a founding residential unit for the site's earliest occupants and that it was an area that was in consistent use for over 800 years (McAnany and López Varela 1999). During the transition from the Terminal Formative (or Protoclassic) to the Early Classic (ca. AD 250), the first pyramidal structure was built at K'axob in plaza B. A noticeable elaboration in caching behavior accompanied the advent of public ceremonial architecture, signifying a shift toward both political hierarchy and ritual centralization.

The cache pattern, as well as the construction episodes, represents a pronounced transformation in community organization at the end of the Late Formative. Ritual no longer appears to be a solely domestic-based activity but also involved centralized public ceremony, presumably orchestrated by the long-standing lineage occupying plaza B. The site as a whole reflects a pervasive pattern in Maya settlement organization where land, dwellings, and ceremonial spaces were inextricably linked with family, kin, and community (McAnany 1995a; Ashmore and Knapp 1999:16–17; Bender 1998; Bender et al. 1997).

A CONCEPTUAL FRAMEWORK FOR THE INTERPRETATION OF CACHING BEHAVIOR

A cache deposit is a physical manifestation of an event. Patterns recognized in caching behavior reflect ideological principles present throughout the Maya region. Similar patterns, evident in the comparative analysis of Maya caches, signify a general cultural connectedness to cosmological concerns. As Mock (1998:4) notes, "the task is to merge both the cosmological structure and the internal patternings or content." By examining content as well as configuration, context, and placement of cache deposits one can achieve a more finely grained interpretation of the internal patterns and their potential meaning with regard to ritual and ideology.[1] Here, this method of examination aids in deciphering the twenty-two K'axob cache deposits found in the 1990, 1992, and 1993 excavations. The caches were placed

in various locales within the built environment, which includes dwellings, outside patio spaces, and ceremonial architecture.

As has been said, traditionally, caches are defined as part of either a "dedication" or a "termination" ritual. This is an important distinction, yet, within an archaeological context, it often remains somewhat ambiguous. Dedicatory caches mark the beginning of a new construction; they work to ensoul and ritually charge a space. A clear case of a dedicatory ritual is an interment placed directly within the construction fill of a building without intruding on any other construction phase. Termination caches, on the other hand, are usually related to the end use of a structure or patio space. Typically, scholars (for example, Becker 1992) define a termination offering as ritual contents in an uncapped pit that clearly intrude into the floor of the building being terminated, thus signifying the end of its use. Furthermore, particular cache configurations, such as an inverted or smashed vessel, are other possible indicators of termination events. For the modern-day Zinacantan Maya, different offering materials serve to open and close the spiritual channels to the underworld, and the act of inverting an object, such as a reed mat or blanket, indicates death or ritual termination (Vogt 1998:29). Like a reed mat turned upside down or a blanket turned inside out, inverted vessels found in ancient contexts are indicative of the termination of someone or something. Numerous burials from K'axob contain inverted vessels placed over the heads of the deceased, perhaps symbolically "putting out the fire" of the living soul. Inverted vessels found in caches may share a similar meaning; that is, they worked to close off the spiritual channels and to extinguish the soul of a lived space. Likewise, smashed vessels appear to represent the ritual killing of the life force inhabiting an object or a place.

Beyond simply dedicating and terminating space, however, caches express complex principles pertaining to the cosmogonic structuring of the Maya world, which is situated squarely within a time-space continuum. The offertory tradition ensures the continuance of the cosmological cycle, the essence of which is composed of gods and ancestors. Cache deposits mark regular rituals that were performed to honor world creation, the cosmos, and its powerful spirits; therefore, they serve as functional markers of space, time, memory, and identity. This basic conceptual framework, elaborated upon below, is founded upon the wealth of recent literature on Maya ritual, which enables a comprehensive interpretation of what caching behavior means and how it functioned in society.

MARKERS OF SPACE AND TIME

Schele and Freidel (1990:236) have proposed that at Cerros, another Formative Maya community in northern Belize, ancient dedicatory rituals coupled with cache deposits worked to transform parts of the built environment into sanctified space where the gods would materialize during ritual events. During the Classic period, dedicatory caches still demarcated sanctified locales, yet served to aggrandize extant political boundaries and royal kingship and effectively legitimize the powers of the elite. Diane Chase (1985a) argues that Postclassic offerings found in elite residential units at the site of Santa Rita were perhaps placed there during annual public ritual circuits in an effort to reorder space, mark important boundaries, and emphasize political unity among the populace. Vogt (1976, 1998) indicates that the contemporary Zinacantan Maya place offerings at strategic points within architectural complexes to define the parameters of sacred space and to unify household groups with the community. Clearly, while the material expressions of dedicatory rituals have changed through time, the underlying meaning of caches as mechanisms for ordering space and creating boundaries within a given area are durable concepts that have remained consistent for thousands of years.

Numerous scholars have shaped current understanding of Maya cosmology and stressed that time and space were (and continue to be) seen as a convergent, cyclical entity (D. Chase 1988; Joyce 1992; Schele and Freidel 1990). Aveni (1980) has studied time-tracking among the Maya and noted the importance of quadrilateral space as the fundamental principle for ordering their world. Coggins (1980) has suggested that directionality was based on the path of the sun rather than on the four cardinal directions as we understand them. The Maya view of the cosmos in a time-space continuum was played out in their settlement patterns, with special-purpose buildings aligned for observing the sun, moon, equinoxes, eclipses, and other planetary movements (Ashmore 1989, 1991). Like the meaningful building alignments, the placement of caches often mirrored Maya visions of the cosmos. Situated at the corners and/or along the central axes of structures, caches sometimes formed horizontal and vertical patterns that resembled a quadrangle with a center, or *axis*

mundi (centralized ritual space), that likely symbolized the Maya world and its layered universe. Other offerings were placed in stairways, doorways, and walls to mark "places of transition, where contact with the underworld, and thus with power, was strongest" (Mock 1998:6). Vogt (1976, 1998) notes the continued Maya belief in this world view. Offerings placed at the four corners and center of a Zinacantan household reinforce the importance of the quadripartite space as part of a metaphoric reenactment of world creation.

According to Freidel and Schele (1989:234–236), caches may represent specific events in the ritual calendar, possibly involving the agricultural cycles around which Maya life revolved. Glyphic inscriptions found at numerous ancient Maya sites provide scholars with more direct information about periodic ritual performances that accompanied offerings. Dedicatory rituals often correspond with important bundles of time, usually commemorating the *tun* (year) or the *k'atun* (twenty-year) period endings (see Taube 1988a and A. Chase 1991). The concepts that underlie these cyclical events, however, are part of everyday life. Nearly half a century ago, Thompson (1954:258) suggested that "every feature of Maya life had its religious aspect." In other words, ritual practice was never an isolated activity for the ancient Maya but, rather, a fundamental aspect of daily life that informed every step of production, from ensuring a fruitful harvest to making a household complete (see also Thompson 1970 and Monaghan 1998).

MARKERS OF MEMORY AND IDENTITY

Numerous studies of the built environment provide a literary foundation that aids in our conceptions of ancient lived space (Lawrence and Low 1990; Bender 1993, 1998; Houston 1998; among others), bringing to light how "undifferentiated *space* [was] transformed into marked and delimited *place*" (Pearson and Richards 1994:4). The plethora of offerings found in domestic contexts from the Formative period indicate that ritual was a critical element of household construction and production. A person's right to land was legitimized through personal offerings. Like a name bestowed on a place, caches instilled into a space both meaning and social identity. Similarly, mortuary deposits provided a household with the memory and identity of important ancestors and also served to validate the landholding of a particular lineage (McAnany 1995a; McAnany et al. 1999; Brady and Ashmore 1999).

While the significance of venerating certain ancestors appears undeniable, Becker (1992) suggests that certain problematic deposits found at Tikal, carrying portions of human skeletons, may have functioned much like caches. Such burials can consist of the partial remains of older, primary burials that were encountered during structural modifications in antiquity and were reinterred in subsequent construction phases (see Storey, chapter 6). These collections of disarticulated bone are evidence of how the meaning of material remains can change over time. Once honoring a particular ancestor, redeposited remains may have been transformed into earth offerings, feeding the gods in an effort to harness their power and to secure a safe place for the living. These actions not only altered the meaning of the deposit but may also have eventually modified the function of a lived space. The household and its accompanying ritual deposits became both the medium and outcome of social practice as the activities that constituted them changed over time (Pearson and Richards 1994).

Encapsulated within the built environment, caches appear as micro-expressions of a larger conceptualized and ideational world that Ashmore and Knapp (1999:1–30) describe as the sociosymbolic landscape. While they address ritual space on a macroscale, encompassing both the natural and built environments, this chapter deals exclusively with the latter. Nevertheless, ritual caching bears many conceptual parallels to landscape cognition, particularly in the areas of memory, identity, social order, and transformation. Anchored within this conceptual framework, the following section reviews the twenty-two cache deposits from K'axob and provides a basis from which to interpret the potential meaning or meanings each held in the ancient past.

CACHES OF K'AXOB

This chapter represents the first comprehensive analysis of the caches of K'axob. It builds on the work of Masson (1993) and McAnany and López Varela (1999). Table 4.1 provides a brief description of the twenty-two caches found during the 1990, 1992, and 1993 seasons. This table is reproduced digitally as *Caches Database* and contains photo images of many of the caches in situ. Individual cache vessels can also be viewed in color in the *Pottery Vessels Database*. Each cache is described in detail below, with special attention to content, configuration, context, and placement. This presentation is followed by a discussion of the general patterns recognized in the archaeological record. The final section reviews possible interpretations of caching behavior using comparative archaeological and ethnological studies.

The twenty-two caches are listed by operation (or unit of excavation) and by the zone (or smallest unit of provenience; table 4.1). Caches were recorded in operations 1, 7, 8, 10, 11, and 12 and were associated with either the interior floors of buildings or the exterior patio surfaces within identified architectural complexes. Associated construction phase and ceramic complex for each cache are listed in table 4.1. Construction episodes consist of bundles of zones that represent coeval construction events, labeled by phase number from the base of the excavation, and dated via a ceramic chronology. The majority of caches found date to the K'atabche'k'ax ceramic complex (ca. 400 BC to AD 250), which is divided into early and late facets and correlates to the Late Formative period. There is also a terminal facet for the K'atabche'k'ax complex that is coeval with the Protoclassic period (ca. AD 50 to AD 250).[2] Two of the twenty-two caches date to the early facet of the K'atabche'k'ax ceramic complex, fourteen date to the late facet, and six date to the terminal facet. Only one cache of lithics appears to correspond to the early facet of the Nohalk'ax, which represents the beginning of the Early Classic period.

Operation 1

One of the most extensive excavations ever performed at K'axob, operation 1 was positioned on the eastern side of a 3.5 m high pyramid within plaza B, the second largest pyramid plaza (see chapter 2, figure 2.2). Investigations of this area revealed continuous layers of stratified deposits consisting of twelve construction episodes, which span the Middle, Late, and Terminal Formative periods (ca. 800 BC to AD 250), and one phase corresponding to the early facet of the Early Classic (ca. AD 250). During Formative times, plaza B appears to have functioned as a residence for an extended family unit, based on the configuration of platforms that were constructed over time to form an enclosed, octagon-shaped plaza group.

During the Middle Formative this architectural complex housed the earliest known occupants of K'axob, who developed the first formalized offertory tradition at the site by the beginning of the Late Formative period (ca. 400 BC). Such a beginning date for offerings associated with architecture appears

Table 4.1 K'axob caches

Op	Zone	Sz	Ceramic Complex	Construction Phase	Vessel #	Description
1	9		Terminal facet K' atabche' k' ax	phase 11	020	1 upright Society Hall Red bowl
1	14		Terminal facet K' atabche' k' ax	phase 11		1 partially reconstructible flat-bottomed Sierra Red bowl and fragments of another vessel
1	17		Terminal facet K' atabche' k' ax	phase 9	024, 025, 028	"triadic cache" - 3 vessels with 7 limestone balls and shell and jade accoutrements
1	41		Late facet K' atabche' k' ax	phase 8d	044	inverted Sierra Red Gadrooned vessel with portion of human skeleton
1	77		Late facet K' atabche' k' ax	phase 8c	029, 030, 032, 035	"quadripartite cache" - 2 Society Hall Red and 2 Sierra Red vessels
1	85		Late facet K' atabche' k' ax	phase 8a		1 chipped biface celt and 1 stone
1	97		Early facet K' atabche' k' ax	phase 7		3 jade beads and snake vertebrae
1	121	a	Early facet K' atabche' k' ax	phase 6a	055	1 upright Laguna Verde Incised vessel
7	6	a	Early facet Nohalk'ax	phase 9		lithic cache of 2 macroblades and 1 broken biface
7	58		Terminal facet K' atabche' k' ax	phase 3a	059	1 inverted Sierra Red dish with an obsidian blade inside
7	59		Terminal facet K' atabche' k' ax	phase 3a	060	1 inverted Sierra Red dish
7	69		Late facet K' atabche' k' ax	phase 1	111	1 upright San Martin Variegated Brown bowl with a tubular greenstone bead inside
8	3		Terminal facet K' atabche' k' ax	phase 2b	095	1 inverted Aguacate Orange bowl with nubbin feet, covered with stones
8	10		Late facet K' atabche' k' ax	phase 2a	066, 067	2 nested Sierra Red vessels: 1 spouted jar and 1 bowl
8	25	a, b, c	Late facet K' atabche' k' ax	phase 1b	069, 070, 072	3 Sierra Red vessels: 1 flared cylinder, 2 grooved bowls (1 inverted with strap handles)
10	9	a, b, c	Late facet K' atabche' k' ax	phase 3	075, 076, 125, 126	2 "lip-to-lip" caches: upper cache (including V. 075), that contained 3 stones, & lower vessel pair (with V. 076) plus 2 vessels (V.25 & 126) found in subzone c.
10	10	a	Late facet K' atabche' k' ax	phase 4	073, 074	1 pair of "lip-to-lip" Sierra Red bowls
11	11	a	Late facet K' atabche' k' ax	phase 5		1 partially reconstructible Sierra Red vessel
11	13		Late facet K' atabche' k' ax	phase 5		a high density of Colha caramel-colored chert (n>160) and 1 netsinker
11	17		Late facet K' atabche' k' ax	phase 5	081, 082	1 pair of "lip-to-lip" Sierra Red vessels
12	8		Late facet K' atabche' k' ax	phase 4	088	1 partially reconstructible Sierra Red vessel
12	57		Late facet K' atabche' k' ax	phase 2	093	1 Sierra Red bowl with portions of 2 humans (Burial 12-16a & 12-16b) & 1 macroblade

consistent with other nearby site centers, including Lamanai (Pendergast 1998), Cerros (Walker 1998; Robertson 1983; Garber 1983a), and Cuello (Robin et al. 1991). Although the context of the earliest recorded cache at K'axob (operation 1, zone 121a) was somewhat disturbed by a number of intrusive features, the partial remains of a pit dug into an interior household floor were discernible. The cache pit intruded into the primary floor of phase 6a and terminated on the preceding floor. A complete Laguna Verde Incised ceramic vessel (vessel 055, see chapter 9) was placed upright on a flat stone that had been placed at the base of a pit on an earlier floor (figure 3.5). Perhaps when the pit was filled the vessel tilted to one side, the position in which it was found during excavation. The elevation of the surrounding floor indicates that the vessel was positioned beneath the surface of the floor; however, the edges of the pit were difficult to define due to innumerable surrounding intrusive features, and it was unclear whether the pit was subsequently capped with plaster. Nonetheless, the upright position of the vessel, its exclusive association with structure 1-f, and its possible position on the structure's central axis seemingly confirm its function as a dedicatory cache, acting as the spiritual animus, or ensoulment, of structure 1-f.

Structure 1-e was built directly on top of the floor remains of structure 1-f and appears identical in floor plan. Although no caches were found in association with structure 1-e (phase 6b), two burials (1-29 and 1-20/25) containing extended individuals were found in two overlapping trenches, coincidentally located directly above the zone 121a cache of phase 6a (figures 3.5 and 3.6; see Storey, chapter 6). The superimposed position of the ritual deposits emphasizes the importance of this particular spot, perhaps seen for generations as the center of the building, where communication with the otherworld could be conducted. Furthermore, the two vessels that accompanied the mortuary remains each contained the earliest occurrence of the painted cross motifs, symbolic of the Maya quadripartite world view (see Headrick, chapter 16). Together, the cache and the twin burials strongly support the notion of the center, or navel, of a household as a focal point for ritual activity in Formative times.

The subsequent construction of structure 1-d mirrors the apsidal floor plans of structures 1-f and 1-e. The structure contains another significant burial of several individuals, including a female and child who were likely family members (see chapter 6 for further

discussion of burials 1-18, 1-19a, and 1-19b). As new family members took on the roles of their deceased ancestors, a dedicatory ritual was performed along the northern end of this new floor, an event that appears to have held a very different meaning from the earlier zone 121a cache. During this final Early K'atabche'k'ax construction phase (7), a pit was dug into the interior household floor and a deposit (zone 97) of three jade beads and several snake vertebrae was placed inside (figure 3.7). These sacred items, charged with symbolic meaning, are reflective of a cosmology that is documented in other comparative contexts; namely, in numerous iconographic references. "For the ancient Maya ... serpents were symbols of the path along which supernaturals traveled on their way to being manifested in this world ... [and] were also the path of the sun and the planets as they moved through their heavenly cycles" (Freidel et al. 1993:196). The serpent, a recurring motif codified through time and space, was a fundamental element associated with ancient Maya myths of creation and the primordial ancestral lineage. Powerful vision serpents acted as vehicles of transformation and conduits to and from the underworld, believed to be accessible through sanctified bodies of water. Steeped with cosmological metaphor, snake remains appear particularly fitting for a dedicatory cache, a dynamic symbol linking an earthly place to the underworld of gods and ancestors. Snake vertebrae have been found in other ritual contexts, including a Late Classic cache at Uaxactun (Smith 1950) and a Terminal Classic burial at Seibal (Olsen 1978). Pohl (1981:78–79) suggests that ritual deposits containing snake vertebrae remains may represent the ancient *cuch* ceremony, a year renewal celebration honoring the agricultural cycles (see also Taube 1988a). The inclusion of three jade beads, possible symbols of fertility, may represent the "seeds" of agricultural productivity that the ritual hoped to secure (see section below on the quadripartite cache [zone 77] for further discussion of the cuch ceremony).

The following construction phase (8a) in operation 1 initiates the late facet of the K'atabche'k'ax complex, which consisted of prominent modifications to both the living space and surrounding outside patio space. The household space was enlarged and elevated above the surrounding patio space with a three-course building platform. Into this new and improved structure 1-c, a burial (1-23) was interred in roughly the same centrally located position and orientation (head toward the west) as those found in structure 1-e. While no caches were reported inside the household, one dedicatory deposit was found in the new outside patio space just to the north of the exposed western half of the structure. Here, a pit feature was dug, and the zone 85 cache containing a single stone and a bifacial tool was placed inside. Recalling Monaghan's (1998:47–52) recent studies of ritual and production as conjoined activities, which expand on Thompson's (1954, 1970) ideas, a simple cache of utilitarian debris (materials perhaps used in the new building project) seems appropriate for the dedication of this outside patio space.

Another construction episode (phase 8c) modified the residence only slightly to form structure 1-b, and a new patio floor was built. One of the most elaborate caches (zone 77), found in the section wall of the northwestern corner of the excavation unit, was interred within the outside space (figure 4.1; see also figure 3.8). Limited exposure to the west of the cache hinders a comprehensive reconstruction of the cache context, but possibly it was placed in what was once the center of a residential plaza circumscribed by a series of structures, including structure 1-b. Placed within an intrusive pit, the zone 77, or "quadripartite" cache, contained four bowls that were stacked in two layers to form a cross (figure 4.1). The upper two vessels, both Society Hall Red, were oriented in a north-south line, and the lower set of Sierra Red, Grooved variety bowls was aligned in an east-west line. The quadripartite configuration may be a reflection of cosmological ordering, likely representing the sacred four directions and the ritual partitioning of the Maya world (McAnany 1995a; Bassie-Sweet 1996; Masson 1993; Vogt 1976). Cross motifs found painted on the base of several vessels interred as grave goods in earlier and later burial contexts from Operation 1 are perhaps different expressions of the same concept (McAnany and López Varela 1999; see Headrick, chapter 16, for an expanded discussion of the cross motif).

Each of the shallow, straight-sided bowls in the quadripartite cache held various collections of faunal remains (see also chapter 17). The east vessel contained frog bones, a fish maxilla or premaxilla, rodent teeth, and a high density of microdebitage (n > 100). The north vessel contained a marine shell, frog bones and all of the vessels held fetal deer teeth. Masson (chapter 17) notes that the west vessel contained the most intact rows of fetal deer teeth. The west vessel also contained frog bones and a light density of microdebitage. The contents of this cache are clearly as significant as is the configuration of the four vessels. The abundance of fauna from this complex deposit may shed light on the accompanying ritual. Both Edmonson (1971) and Pohl (1983) note that Tohil, one of the principal gods of the K'iche' Maya, took the form of a deer and demanded offerings of young deer. The Postclassic Yucatec Maya were also known to sacrifice small deer to their god Tabay, perhaps a female fertility deity, on specific ritual occasions (Tozzer 1941; Pohl 1981, 1983). Tracing the imagery found on painted ceramics from the Late Classic, and on codices from the Postclassic (Madrid and Dresden), Pohl (1983:62–70) concludes that "the deer was a primary player in the most important ritual drama of the Maya ceremonial cycle, the *cuch* rite marking year renewal." Masson (chapter 17) notes the continued practice of these protohistoric fertility

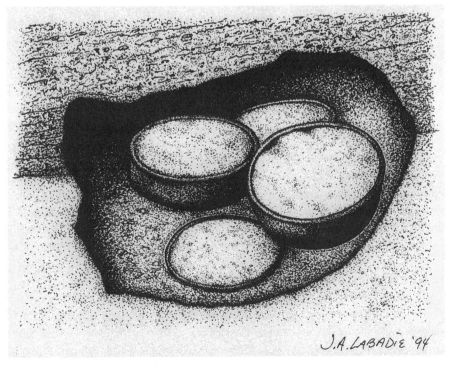

Figure 4.1 Quadripartite cache (zone 77) found in an outside patio space, excavated in operation 1. *Illustration by Antoine John Labadie*

rituals that today are referred to as the Ch'a-Chak ceremony (Freidel et al. 1993:2). Evidence of fetal deer remains, specifically whole mandibles, in both the quadripartite cache from K'axob and two caches from Cuello (Robin et al. 1991) lends further support to the notion that, during Formative times, the cuch ceremony, or some variant thereof, was possibly performed annually and/or at significant period endings. Landa documents that, during the month of Zip, the cuch ceremony involved not only the sacrifice of young deer in an outside courtyard (also the performance area for the quadripartite cache) but also communal fishing parties (Tozzer 1941:155–156). Pulltrouser Swamp, immediately to the west of K'axob, still holds a wealth of fish that locals line and net. The fish remains from the quadripartite cache suggest that, during annual celebration in antiquity, these fresh waters were a fundamental part of ritual space. The wetlands also provide a habitat for frogs, whose remains were found within the east, west, and north vessels of the quadripartite cache. Pohl (1983) notes that frogs were also important species in fertility rituals such as the cuch ceremony. Frogs are representative of standing water, the coming rainy season, moisture, and fertility, and they are fitting symbols for a year renewal ceremony that asked the gods for good rains and a prosperous agricultural yield in the coming year.

McAnany (chapter 3) and McAnany and Peterson (chapter 11) note the selective use of golden chert microdebitage, scattered over the quadripartite cache, and suggest that it was a significant aspect of ritual behavior. Evidence of scattered golden chert debitage was also found in several burials in operation 1, exclusively in contexts where vessels with the quadripartite or cross motif were present. As a symbol of completion, the cross motif not only appears as a representation of the axis mundi, but it may also have had ties to fertility ritual and annual completion cycles as early as the Late Formative. Scattering events are known to correspond with important completion events or period endings in calendar-related rituals of the Classic period, and the evidence presented here suggests that this ritual tradition originated in the Formative period.

At operation 1, structure 1-a, built over the top of structure 1-b, ends the series of residential construction episodes dating to the Late Formative period. The form of structure 1-a was only slightly modified and held several burials, along with a problematic deposit (zone 41) that contained only a small portion of human

skeletal remains, found underneath an inverted gadrooned vessel (figure 3.9). The bone, highly disarticulated and fragmentary, is likely the remains of an earlier burial that was encountered during activities of phase 8d construction and was reinterred in a small, isolated pit. The zone 41 deposit is interpreted as an offering, resembling the problematic deposits that Becker (1992) describes from Tikal. As intrinsic components of a spiritual realm, these problematic deposits are expressions of the ever-changing sociosymbolic landscape, for they "embody multiple times as well as multiple places, [and] thereby materialize not only continuity and sequence, but potentially change and transformation as well" (Ashmore and Knapp 1999:18). Zone 41 is an example of a deposit whose meaning transformed within a new context. Although the bones were no longer a venerated ancestor, the inhabitants apparently recognized that the remains were not without ritual significance; they reinterred them in a newly constructed pit. The dynamism of social space becomes evident as the spiritual essence of the deposit is recycled in this secondary state, possibly functioning as an earth offering for the gods who made the household safe and prosperous for the living.

Construction phase (9) appears to straddle the divide between the terminal facet of the K'atabche'k'ax (Terminal Formative period) and early facet of the Nohalk'ax (Early Classic period), marked by several deposits significantly more elaborate than those previously found at K'axob. The overall design of the apsidal-shaped house and outdoor plaza space further defined by an important cache that was placed in the wall of what appears to be the southwest perimeter of structure 1-a (figure 4.2; see also figure 3.9). This offering (zone 17) appears to dedicate the structure and mark a powerful transitional space. Marking the boundary between interior and exterior space, the cache perhaps functioned as a means of opening up powerful channels to the otherworld, which was thought to exist in these liminal spaces within the household (Mock 1998:6).

The contents of the cache appear as meaningful as does the deposit's placement. There were three vessels stacked on top of each other, with the middle dish apparently serving as a lid for the bottom vessel. Surrounding the top vessel were seven limestone spheres, commonly called *yuntunob*, or slingshot stones. The offering is called the "triadic cache" due to the provocative contents that appear in sets of three inside the bottom vessel (figure 4.3, see also chapter 15, figure

a)

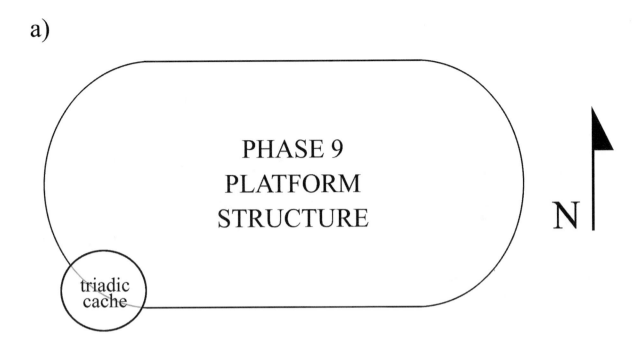

b)

Figure 4.2 (a) Diagrammatic planview of phase 9 apsidal platform structure showing location of triadic cache (zone 17) found in operation 1; (b) reconstruction drawing of triadic cache placed within low wall of structure. *Both illustrations by Eleanor Harrison-Buck*

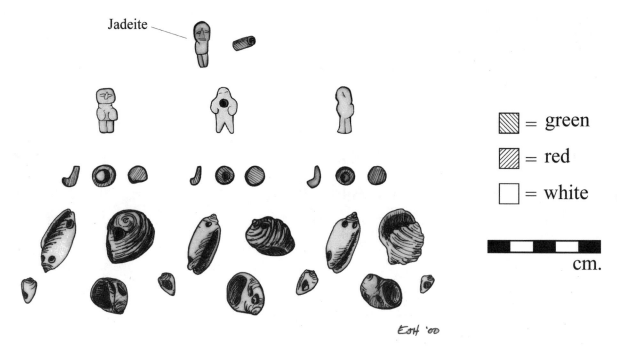

Figure 4.3 Contents from triadic cache (zone 17). Note overt triadic structure and color coding of objects as well as possible male and female attributes on top four figurines. *Illustration by Eleanor Harrison-Buck*

15.9). McAnany and López Varela (1999:162) note the overt triadic structure, color coding, and possible significance of the vessel's contents:

> The central figure is a small, flat, "mother-of-pearl" humanoid shell figurine with a perforated chest cavity. A sole tubular jadeite bead may be associated with this individual. A triad of figurines accompany this central character: two flat figures made from red *Spondylus* sp. shell with lightly carved facial and body features and a third green jadeite figurine carved into more of a three dimensional form. These three carvings may represent supernaturals, although they possess human features. Each of the three is associated with highly patterned, color-coded accoutrements. Specifically, there are three sets of the following: a perforated bead, a disk, and a comma-shaped element. Two of the sets were crafted from shell, whereas the third was carved from jadeite. The triadic structure of the cache continues with three tinklers and three sets of perforated marine gastropods of decreasing size (that is, three large shells, three medium shells and three small shells). The symbolic nature of these carefully chosen elements displays a concern with triads,

the colors of red, green, and white, and the primordial fertility of shell and jadeite, and perhaps sacrifice—if the void in the chest of the central individual is meant to imply heart excision.

Upon close inspection, the humanoid figures have facial features—eyes, nose, and mouth. Also, arms, or possibly breasts, were lightly incised into all three shell figurines, including the individual with a perforated chest cavity (see figure 4.3). The jadeite figure, on the other hand, does not display these features but appears more phallic in shape. The variation of the materials and the differences in form suggest that perhaps a male and three females are represented. The Maya often imposed gender onto things and represented the two sexes as complementary beings (for example, the moon is frequently associated with a female god, while the sun is associated with a male god). Both shell and jade were seen as fertility symbols; notions of reproduction and the life cycle, being fundamental aspects of agricultural rituals, would be further illustrated by the juxtaposition of male and female attributes.

The red, green, and white objects found in the triadic cache may be another expression of the quadripartite world view, for these colors (as well as black) are known to represent the four cardinal directions. The overt triadic structure may reflect the vertical, threefold partitioning of the universe marked by the celestial, earth, and underworld layers, which were then further subdivided. Clearly, the color-coded objects with discrete numerical configurations were purposefully placed in the deposit, perhaps by a community leader or shaman honoring the Maya creation myth. These details remain speculative, but an examination of the composition, content, context, and placement of this deposit allows one to begin to reconstruct a ritual event that may express a fusion of ideational concepts, including the cyclical ordering of the cosmos in space and time.

A nearly identical assemblage of offerings dating to the same time period (ca. Terminal Formative-Early Classic) was found inside two vessels that accompanied the burial of a single individual at the site of Las Ruinas de Arenal, located in the western Belize Valley (Taschek and Ball 1999). The authors note that the vessels and their contents more closely resembled the configuration of caches than that of burial accompaniments, apparently a pattern typical of the Terminal Formative-Early Classic Belize Valley interments (Taschek and Ball 1999:220). Two vessels, one placed at the northern end and another at the southern end of the body, held small figurines that are strikingly similar to those found in the triadic cache, especially those placed in the southern vessel (figure 4.4). Both burial vessels appear to include four figures "individually cut or carved from a raw material naturally colored the appropriate one of the hues symbolically associated with the cardinal directions in Maya lore at which it was placed" (Taschek and Ball 1999:221), including red (*Spondylus* shell), white (nacreous shell), black (obsidian),

and yellow (*Spondylus* shell). The four figurines in each vessel were properly positioned in terms of the cardinal direction they represented, with a carved greenstone (albite) figurine positioned in the center. In addition, several comma- and disc-shaped pieces of shell accompany the five figurines in the southern vessel and are nearly identical in both number and form to those found in the triadic cache. Interestingly, these elements have been interpreted as "remnants of a disintegrated mosaic *Tlaloc* (rain god) war emblem" (Taschek and Ball 1999:221; see also Freidel et al. 1993:301, Fig. 7:8). Like the triadic cache, the contents and composition of these offerings appear to reflect the Maya world view, the ritual partitioning of the cosmos, and early renderings of the dualism of war and fertility-related ritual (assuming that their assessment of the Tlaloc deity is correct). According to Taschek and Ball (1999:221), the miniature figurines, sometimes referred to as "Charlie Chaplin" offerings, "have an extensive Terminal Preclassic-Early Classic distribution in the

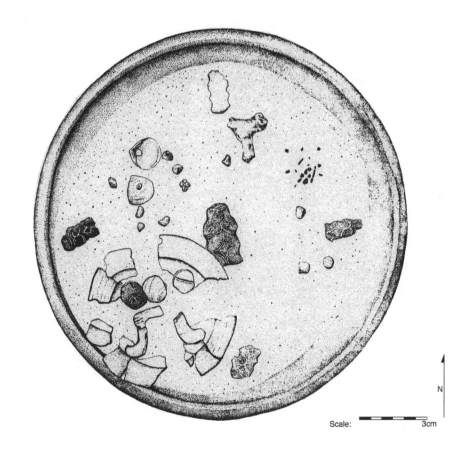

Scale: 3cm

N

Figure 4.4 South offering in burial 91B-1 at Las Ruinas de Arenal, Belize (Taschek and Ball 1999:Fig. 11b). Note striking similarities between contents of deposit and triadic cache (zone 17) of operation 1 at K'axob, especially four miniature shell figurines and comma- and disc-shaped elements. Both deposits date to the Terminal Formative-Early Classic period. *Reproduced courtesy of Joseph Ball*

central western Belize-eastern Petén zone," including sites such as Buena Vista del Cayo, San Jose, Uaxactun, and Caracol, among others. The strikingly similar deposits from such distant polities shed light on the degree of widespread interregional interactions taking place during Formative times and the general connectedness and concern with cosmological principles involving numerical, spatial, and color patterning.

During phase 9 a new outside patio space was built and two elaborate burials were interred to the west of structure 1-a, just south of the earlier deposit of the quadripartite cache. The mortuary deposits (burials 1-1 and 1-2, see chapter 6) consisted of both primary and secondary individuals and were laden with rich grave goods, including greenstone, marine shell, hematite, and several ceramic vessels (figure 3.9). One of the burials (burial 1-2) was evidently reopened several times in order to inter more individuals, apparently functioning as an ancestral shrine for important family members of plaza B (McAnany and López Varela 1999; see also Storey, chapter 6). The deposit created a centralized locale where bundles of ancestral bones were placed, perhaps brought together not only to create a ritually charged space but also to honor an important lineage. Furthermore, the purposeful selection of vessels painted with the cross motif reinforces the notion that this locale was an important cosmic center within plaza B and the site as a whole.

Pyramidal structure 18 was positioned directly above this sacred locale and was imbued with power through hundreds of years of continuous domestic ritual activity. A set of cache deposits (zones 9 and 14), placed beneath the central axis of structure 18 in an east-west alignment, signals the pyramid's imminent construction. At Cuello, the first pyramidal form was dedicated with two caches, each consisting of a single vessel (Robin et al. 1991:229). Additionally, mass burials were introduced at Cuello around the same time as monumental architectural construction and reflect the beginnings of political centralization as early as 400 BC (Robin et al. 1991:224). These deposits are reminiscent of K'axob, where a mass burial, a group of caches, and the subsequent construction of a pyramidal platform appear to have been purposefully placed directly above an accumulated and ritually charged mass of long-standing residential space, raised by hundreds of years of continuous occupation.

The two caches (zones 9 and 14), found beneath structure 18 at K'axob, work to further delineate plaza B as an axis mundi at the dawn of the Early Classic period. A flat-bottomed bowl (zone 14) was left partially intact and was inverted directly on the remains of a living surface positioned over the series of previous household structures, terminating what appears to be the final floor before the construction of the pyramid. A collection of smashed ceramic vessels in this same area, approximately 1 m to the northeast of the zone 14 cache, lends further support to the notion of ritual termination. Meanwhile, 4 m directly to the west of zone 14 a dedicatory cache consisting of a Society Hall Red, flared, cylinder-like vessel (zone 9) was placed upright in the construction fill of the new pyramidal platform of structure 18. Both caches mark an important functional transition occurring within plaza B. The monumental construction signifies not only a transformation in architectural style but also the emergence of centralized power within the community. The data suggest that the long-standing lineage occupying plaza B developed and prospered during the Formative period, and that its power was politically centralized and publicly announced by the end of the Late Formative period.

Operation 7

About 200 m directly south of plaza B there stands a small plaza group where operation 7 was positioned, in the center of structure 98, its largest building platform (see chapter 2, figure 2.2). Excavations revealed that occupation spanned the late facet of the K'atabche'k'ax to the early facet of the Nohalk'ax (Late Formative to Early Classic periods). The earliest cache deposit (zone 69) was found in the first phase of occupation; an eroded plaster floor is what remains of this initial residence (figure 3.11). A complete San Martin Brown jar from the late facet of the K'atabche'k'ax complex was placed upright in an intrusive pit. A tubular greenstone bead was placed inside the vessel. Greenstone is an exotic item not found in abundance at K'axob and was perhaps a symbol of fertility that served as an earth offering to the gods during ceremonies honoring the agricultural cycles.

Two floors with thick layers of construction fill were laid on top of this first floor. Two separate caches were associated with the third household floor surface, which dates to the Terminal K'atabche'k'ax, both apparently functioning as termination offerings but with markedly different intent (figure 4.5; see also figure 3.12). One cache (zone 58)—found in a shallow, uncapped pit that was dug into the floor—consisted of an obsidian blade

Figure 4.5 Plaster floor of operation 7 with two caches of inverted dishes, zones 58 and 59. *Photo from K'axob Project archives*

placed underneath an inverted Sierra Red vessel. Iconography often depicts the Classic period elite using obsidian blades and other instruments for ritual bloodletting. Diane Chase (1985a) suggests that the Postclassic Maya used obsidian to let blood onto paper, which was then offered to the gods. This obsidian blade was likely used in similar ritual celebrations during Formative times as well. No nearby obsidian sources exist around K'axob, and sourcing by INAA (instrumental neutron activation analysis) indicates the volcanic material came from the Ixtepeque source (see McAnany, chapter 12), found approximately 50 km southeast of Guatemala City, near the modern town and ancient site of Asunción Mita. A limited accessibility to this resource is reflected in the overall low densities of obsidian recovered from excavations at K'axob. This suggests that the material was a particularly coveted resource that, at least in this context, was used for domestic ritual activity occurring within the largest household of a small residential compound.

The second cache (zone 59), another small Sierra Red dish, was inverted on the surface of the same floor (figure 4.5; see also figure 3.12). The inverted position of both vessels, left in place as the floor was covered by the construction fill of the subsequent household floor, is suggestive of death or the extinguishing of the proverbial flame. As Stuart (1998) has noted, the fire, however, enters not only the house but also the object. Thus, while the zone 59 cache may have terminated the spirit dwelling within the house, the zone 58 cache

seemingly killed the spirit residing in an implement used for ritual purposes. Perhaps after the head of the household repeatedly used it in ritual bloodletting, the object simply could not be discarded. By placing it under an inverted vessel, the life force was reversed and the spiritual flame was extinguished.

During a subsequent architectural modification, dating to the early facet of the Nohalk'ax, the zone 6a cache (consisting of two complete macroblades and a broken bifacial tool) was deposited in the fill of construction phase 9 (see chapter 11, figure 11.16). The two macroblades are particularly intriguing, for not only were they made of a distinctive honey-colored chert from the nearby Colha source but they were also made from raw material with distinctive bands of color, likely preselected for a ritual purpose. The tips of both blades have a pronounced, deep reddish-brown color and are similar to five macroblades currently on display in the Peabody Museum at Harvard University. Though the provenience is apparently unpublished, the five blades are reportedly from a Late Classic cache from the site of Tayasal in Guatemala. With the exception of those from K'axob, the author knows of no other comparable specimens. In both cases the raw material for each flint blade appears to have been chosen for the natural color distribution and knapped so as to retain what looks like blood on the tips of the tools. Little to no utilization was found on the blades (see McAnany and Peterson, chapter 11), and it is quite possible that they were used solely for a ritual event, perhaps bloodletting or animal sacrifice, which then ritually charged the materials and made them a fine candidate for the dedicatory cache of this Early Classic structure.

Operation 8

Structure 102, a single, low platform, is located about 150 m to the east of operation 7. Operation 8 was positioned in the center of this platform (see chapter 2, figure 2.2). The structure was occupied only from the Late to Terminal K'atabche'k'ax, with three successive phases of construction. Three cache deposits were recovered from excavations, the earliest of which was found in the compact marl construction fill of the initial structure. The zone 25 cache consists of three complete vessels placed in the fill of the platform during construction, clearly acting as a dedicatory cache for this initial Late Formative building (figure 3.16). Two burials (8-2 and 8-2a) were also recovered from this preliminary stage of occupation, yet they were found in the underlying paleosol, which was mixed with midden material (figure 3.15). Together, these ritual deposits were critical for the founding of this household; they sanctified the new residential locale and instilled a sense of spiritual connectedness and belonging. The deceased individuals were likely members of the family constructing the home and provided this initial residence with meaning and social identity.

The zone 25 cache deposit consisted of three vessels, including a Sierra Red cylinder with outcurved sides and a gadrooned Sierra Red bowl, both of which were placed upright and contained several pieces of chert debitage. The third vessel, a grooved Sierra Red bowl with strap handles, was inverted and devoid of artifacts. The cache of three vessels was perhaps an abstract cosmological expression relating to the three-fold universe, with the one inverted vessel symbolizing the underworld of the dead. Together, they ritually charged the space and spiritually bound the earthly with the underworld. The traditional Zinacantan Maya would say that, as the earth god had been appeased, the household was now complete and ready to be inhabited.

Following resurfacing, a new building dating to the Terminal K'atabche'k'ax complex was constructed over the south side of the old structure. A dedicatory cache (zone 10) was placed within this construction fill and deposited in a pit that intruded into the new household floor (figure 3.17). A Sierra Red spouted jar with a vertical neck was placed inside a large Sierra Red bowl with flaring sides. These nested vessels may have been meant to embrace the spirit ensouling the new construction and to open the channels of supernatural communication.

A burial pit with three individuals (8-4, 8-5, and 8-6) was intruded into the same household floor and appears to have terminated the use of this space (see Storey, chapter 6). A large stone capped the burial pit and protruded above the floor, which was then subsequently resurfaced. Although this upper floor surface was severely disturbed by plowing, an intrusive pit with a cache (zone 3) of an inverted Aguacate Orange vessel with nubbin feet was identified. The cache pit was capped with stones that protruded into the subsequent construction (figure 3.18). The rough covering of stones and inverted position of the vessel suggest that it served as a termination cache for this final phase of construction. Also intruding into this last floor was a burial (8-3) containing the disarticulated remains of a young and a middle adult male, along with several vessels that were ceremonially killed, further suggesting that this final floor surface was systematically terminated at the time of abandonment. Although this last floor was highly disturbed by recent plowing, it is clear that no occupation resumed at structure 102 until the Postclassic, when artifacts suggest that the area was used for short-term procurement activities.

Operation 10

Operation 10 is positioned in the central patio of a basal platform group located less than 200 m southeast of plaza B (see chapter 2, figure 2.2). The excavation provides insight into communal use of outside patio space, household growth, and community interaction from the Early K'atabche'k'ax to the Early Nohalk'ax (Henderson 1998). Hearths, storage areas, dedicatory caches, and burials were revealed, and these deposits shed light on the integration of production and ritual behavior in a shared public space.

The first formalized patio space appears to have been terminated with a cache (zones 9a, 9b, and 9c) of at least two smashed miniature vessels and two identical Society Hall Red vessels placed lip-to-lip; that is, one is inverted and stacked directly on top of the other (figure 3.20 collapsed in plan view as zone 9). The zone 9 cache deposit of two miniature vessels and two lip-to-lip bowls was placed in the base of a pit that was lined with stones. A plaster capped surface sealed this deposit and served to support a second set of lip-to-lip vessels. In this upper deposit, the base of the top inverted vessel was purposefully cut out and placed to the side, like a lid that had just been removed. The vessel was perhaps left open so as to welcome the spiritual essence that was believed to enter the home during the dedication ceremony. Inside the lower bowl were three stones, perhaps symbolic of the first mythic act of creation documented in the Popol Vuh (Tedlock 1985:261). The three stones of the cosmic hearth (also known as the three stars of Orion), used by the primordial ancestors, are believed to have been placed in the sky in order to create the initial centering of the world (Freidel et al. 1993: 67, 79, and 127). I have observed Kekchi Maya living in southern Belize still building their hearths with three stones indicating the durability of Maya tradition. The vessels of orange-paste were subsequently buried by the construction fill and sealed by the plaster surface of the following plaza floor. The transitional positioning of the complex offering, placed in between floors, suggests that the bottom deposit was meant to ritually terminate the use of the earlier construction while the top set of vessels served to dedicate the use of the new floor. Sometimes referred to as a valedictory cache (Hammond 1991a:227–228), this type of offering placement was perhaps meant to simultaneously kill the spirit of the old lived space and to ensoul the new one.

The lip-to-lip vessel configuration is a pervasive pattern in the Maya offertory tradition and is found at various Maya sites, including Lamanai (Pendergast 1998), Cuello (Robin et al. 1991), and Uaxactun (Smith 1950), among others. Landa (Tozzer 1941:143) noted that the Postclassic Maya placed both human and animal hearts, as well as gifts of food, in lip-to-lip caches and offered them to the gods and ancestors at Year Ending celebrations. These Uayeb ceremonies occurred during the last five days of the solar year. It is possible that this ceremonial tradition has a strong cultural continuity as evidence indicates that it dates back to the Late Formative.

Toward the end of the Late Formative period, a residential structure was built on a low basal platform over a portion of the plaza floor which was not resurfaced at this time and was well worn, presumably because of prolonged use. Another lip-to-lip dedicatory cache (zone 10), dating to the late facet of the K'atabche'k'ax complex, was found within a pit that intruded about a meter into the patio floor (figure 3.21). Again, the base of the top inverted vessel was

removed, shifted to one side, and seemingly left open after its burial for the gods. Two mortuary deposits (10-1 and 10-2) were also recovered from intrusive pits in this outside patio floor but appear to have been interred at the end of the floor's use. One burial (10-2) contained an adult individual, possibly male, in an extended position with smashed vessels lining portions of the pit. Two vessels, one inside the other, were inverted over the head of the deceased. Another burial (10-1) was a primary interment of a female individual in the flexed position. Similar to the other burial, a number of whole and smashed vessels were present, covering parts of the torso and also lining portions of the pit. In addition, large portions of smashed flared bowl fragments were found on the floor surface that capped the burial cut. The bowls had been ceremonially killed as though to release the spirit and ritually terminate the living space.

Operation 11

Operation 11 straddles the patio surface and eastern edge of a long platform (structure 27) that forms part of a raised patio, located approximately 200 m northwest of plaza B (see chapter 2, figure 2.2). Excavations revealed an occupation that spans the early facet of the K'atabche'k'ax complex to the early facet of the Nohalk'ax complex. The three caches that were recovered from operation 11 are associated with the same construction phase (5) and date to the Late Formative, which corresponds to the late facet of the K'atabche'k'ax ceramic complex.

Phase 5 construction consisted of a poorly preserved floor that covered an elaborate platform construction (structure 3) and its accompanying patio space (figure 3.24). The lack of a structure (combined with the lack of postmolds and the presence of a *chultun*, or storage area, and several stone- and sherd-lined pits) supports the notion that this area was an outside patio space during phase 5. The three caches were intermingled with these utilitarian deposits. The first cache (zone 11a) was deposited within the fill of the patio to dedicate the new building project (and therefore is not shown on figure 3.24). A Sierra Red vessel, found partially intact in the fill, appears to have ritually charged and ensouled the new outside space. This pattern of vessels found floating in construction fill with no intrusive pits is common throughout the Maya area. Similar dedicatory caches have been noted at Cuello (Hammond 1991a), Cerros (Freidel and Schele 1989),

Seibal, and Uaxactun (Smith 1950, 1982), among others, not to mention the previously discussed contexts at K'axob in operations 1, 7, and 8.

The second cache (zone 13) was placed in a pit that intruded into the patio floor (figure 3.24). The cache consists of a netsinker and a high density of northern Belize Colha chert (n>160), primarily sharp flakes of microdebitage, indicative of a single reduction event (see chapter 11). Eight of the twenty-two cache deposits reported from K'axob contained lithic material, although not all of them contained the highest quality golden chert mentioned above for operation 1. Excavation reports from sites such as Uaxactun (Smith 1950) and Piedras Negras (Coe 1959) report an extraordinarily large number of caches with associated chert debris. The pattern indicates that chert, used in the act of flint knapping, was an important element of ritual behavior. Garber and colleagues (1998) note several sites in the Maya area, including Blackman Eddy in western Belize, where lithic tools and/or debitage flakes deposited in caches form potentially important numerical configurations. They postulate that both the configuration of the lithic contents and the number of pieces may relate to the layered cosmos and the gods of the underworld. It is possible that the common presence of microdebitage in caches indicates that lithic reduction events regularly accompanied ritual activity. Lithic reduction and, perhaps more important, the scattering of the microdebitage debris appear to be important ritual behaviors at K'axob and elsewhere in the Maya area. As noted earlier, the evidence in operation 1 suggests a strong connection between the scattering of high-quality golden chert microdebitage and special purpose deposits consisting of the cross motif, which allude to Maya world view, creation, calendrical completion cycles, and agrarian fertility. Perhaps the debitage from zone 13 is wastage from the fabrication of a tool that was made for ritual sacrifices in honor of a god such as Chac, who brought about the fertile rains and was known for wielding his stone ax. Alternatively, the debris could be the remains of ritual destruction, terminating the use of a ceremonial instrument. Whatever the case, scattering the microdebitage debris appears to have been a meaningful part of the ritual event.

The third cache (zone 17) was another dedicatory offering that consisted of a pair of vessels in a lip-to-lip configuration. The cache, perhaps offered to the gods in one of the annual agricultural celebrations, was partially disturbed by looters between the 1992 and 1993 seasons. Unfortunately, no sediment or cultural material was found inside the pair of vessels; therefore, it is unclear whether the deposit once contained any other sacred contents. The two vessels are both of a Sierra Red type with nubbin teats on their bases, dating this intrusive deposit to the terminal facet of the Late Formative period.

Operation 12

Operation 12 was placed along the southern edge of a wide platform, known as structure 28 (see figure 2.2). The unit of excavation is situated approximately 30 m north and 100 m east of operation 11 and is part of the same residential compound, forming an eastern platform extension. Temporally, construction activity spans the late facet of the K'atabche'k'ax complex through the early facet of the Nohalk'ax complex.

Along the western edge of the earliest structure exposed in operation 12, an elaborate and unique deposit (zone 57) was placed within a shallow pit lined with stones and sherds (figure 3.26). A shallow Sierra Red dish contained the partial remains of two skulls and a complete macroblade. Covering this were roughly 100 *Pomacea* spp. shells and freshwater bivalves that were found spilling over the vessel. The ritual deposit protruded into the construction fill of the subsequent floor, perhaps functioning as a valedictory offering for two construction phases. The special selection of skulls, with no other apparent body parts, and the rich offerings found in the deposit marked this as more of an offering than a burial. The skulls do not show signs of decapitation; rather, Storey (chapter 6) concludes that they were reinterred from an unknown burial context. She argues, however, that the portions of skeletal remains were carefully selected to serve a symbolic role, helping to communicate the ritual death of a living surface. The transitional positioning of the deposit, associated with two consecutive construction phases, is suggestive of a valedictory offering, simultaneously terminating an old structure and dedicating a new one.

A new outside patio was subsequently laid down and contained an intrusive pit with what appears to be a dedicatory cache deposit (zone 8) of a partially reconstructable Sierra Red vase. In comparison to other plaza groups on the site, evidence of a series of thick midden deposits pre- and postdating this floor suggests an accumulation of trash far exceeding normal domicile use for this particular area.

Table 4.2 Patterns of K'axob cache deposits

PROVENIENCE		SUGGESTED FUNCTION			ARCHITECTURAL CONTEXT		PLACEMENT OF CACHE	
Operation	Zone/ subzone	Dedication	Termination	Valedictory	Interior Space	Exterior Space	Within Intrusive Pit	Within Construction Fill
1	121a	X			X		X	
1	97	X			X		X	
1	85	X				X	X	
1	77	X				X	X	
1	41	X			X		X	
1	17	X			X		X	
1	14		X			X?	X	
1	9	X			X			X
7	69	X			X		X	
7	59		X		X			
7	58		X		X		X	
7	6a	X			X			X
8	25a,b,c	X			X			X
8	10	X			X		X	
8	3		X		X		X	
10	10a	X				X	X	
10	9a,b,c			X		X	X	
11	17	X				X	X	
11	13	X				X	X	
11	11a	X				X		X
12	57			X	X		X	
12	8	X				X	X	

Although the accumulation of debris ultimately functioned as fill for the series of floor constructions, the high density of refuse and the large number of stone-lined pits containing mostly Chicago Orange vessel fragments suggest that structure 28 was an area used, at least in part, for production activities that may have serviced intra- and intersite needs. Project ceramicist López Varela observed that some of the Chicago Orange ceramics could represent a stage in pottery production, perhaps one of a number of production activities that took place at this locale.

GENERAL PATTERNS NOTED IN THE RITUAL CACHES OF K'AXOB

Distinct patterns noted in the cache deposits of K'axob are charted in table 4.2. Two of the twenty-two caches may represent valedictory caches, four are interpreted as termination caches, and the rest (sixteen) appear to have functioned as dedicatory offerings. The discrepancies are perhaps due, in part, to our limited terminology, which tends to lump activities rather than to split things into more finely grained explanations. It seems certain, however, that at least four deposits (including operation 1, zone 9; operation 7, zone 6; operation 8, zones 25a, 25b, 25c; and operation 11, zone 11a) found exclusively within construction fill without any associated pits functioned as dedicatory offerings for a new building project. In operation 7, zone 59, an inverted dish found on the surface of a floor is the one cache without an intrusive pit that has been defined as part of a termination rather than as a dedication ritual. All other caches (n = 12) lumped under the category "dedication" may represent specific events in the ritual calendar and perhaps should be categorized otherwise. However, our lack of certainty fails us in this respect, and our clear-cut terminology may, in fact, hinder rather than help our assessment of cache function. Given these limitations, as well as the restricted exposure of excavations, it cannot be said with certainty that dedicatory caches were more prevalent than termination offerings. Ethnohistoric literature credits both activities as being equally important in terms of household ritual (Tozzer 1941).

Only three caches were found within single platform mounds; the other nineteen caches were recovered from multiplatform architectural complexes. While the percentage of single mounds tested was substantially lower, the low number of recovered caches indicates that isolated individual mounds may not have been the primary locus of domestic ritual (for an alternative explanation see Henderson 1998:97). Single platforms are often interpreted as developmentally young or as the visible remains of new family house lots, perhaps of younger siblings or newcomers (Robin 1997:2). McAnany (1995a) describes these isolated structures as tied economically to larger compounds of extended or more heterogeneous family groupings. Ethnographic data from Maya communities in Chiapas suggests that older male members of the community were held in greater esteem than younger male members and that ritual responsibilities were earned through seniority and rank (Vogt 1998; Gossen 1999). Evidence of more elaborate caches found within the older, more developed platform groups, especially plaza B, suggest that the same was true in Formative times; that is, that the focus of domestic ritual activity was led primarily by the most established inhabitants of the community.

Vogt (1976:179) states that ethnographic ceremonies, such as the Year Ending/Renewal ritual, "express the unity of the hamlet and symbolize its relation to the ceremonial center." The cache data from K'axob suggest that Vogt's testimony may be applicable to the Formative Maya. Caches found in outside patio spaces represent the remains of more public ritual events within a domestic setting, as opposed to ritual events taking place within the confines of a single household, and may reflect attempts to promote a sense of unity and solidarity within the developing community of K'axob. The nine cache deposits found in outside patio spaces support the idea of a gathering together of different family groups, probably not only to perform ritual events but also to create work parties for larger residential construction projects that would necessitate more than a single family unit.

During these ritual events, new plaza floors were built and caches were deposited, perhaps in an attempt to ritually purify and reaffirm to the community the boundaries of a lineage's residential space. Hence, the development of the offertory tradition during the Late Formative may have marked increased efforts by the inhabitants of plaza B, as well as the community as a whole, to legitimize their landholdings and to centralize a workforce, which, in turn, promoted public ceremony and exercised extant lineage power. This communal effort resembles what Clark and Blake (1994) call "competitive feasting," where different lineage heads host communal feasts in exchange for labor. These types of ritual activities spawn new power relationships between household units. As a result, wealthy kin groups can gain more power and centralize authority. Rank also becomes more pronounced within a community system. Arguably, this mechanism could have enabled a lineage head residing at plaza B to build the first public ceremonial center for the community and to emerge as the dominant lineage of K'axob.

INTERPRETING ANCIENT CACHING BEHAVIOR USING ETHNOGRAPHIC AND ARCHAEOLOGICAL COMPARISONS

At K'axob, evidence of caching behavior during the Late Formative and Early Classic periods sheds light on the importance of establishing one's household and ties to land, still a critical aspect of modern Maya ritual behavior. When the Zinacantan Maya build a house, they realize they are taking materials owned by the earth lord, who must be appeased through offerings. Only then is the household complete and ready to be inhabited (Vogt 1970, 1976, and 1998). Like the Maya, the modern Mixtec say that "not making an offering [in a household] would be like putting down roof shingles without nailing them to the cross-beams" (Monaghan 1998:48). The four caches from K'axob that were placed within the fill of household floors during the construction process substantiate the longevity of the belief in household dedication ceremonies, perhaps offered to Cauac, the ancient equivalent of the Zinacantan earth god.

Vogt (1976:55) indicates that household ritual for the Zinacantan is a delicate process analogous to the ensoulment and nourishment of a human being:

> For the next three days [after the initial house ritual] the house must be carefully attended for it now possesses an innate soul and requires special care, "just as a sick person" following a curing ceremony. In the days following the ritual the family members remain at home and begin to place their hair combings in the cracks of the walls, signifying their occupancy and symbolizing their belonging.

In various Mayan languages the terms for parts of the body are also used to describe parts of the house, indicating that the household is seen as a living soul that must be cared for both in life and in death. This belief likely goes back to the time of the ancient Maya, where we find abundant evidence to suggest that structures were considered living entities. At Cerros, caches sanctified lived space while smashed deposits and the act of ritual destruction served to deactivate the built environment. Purposeful defacement of plaster masks found on an earlier construction phase of Cerros structure 5c accents the need for formal termination of architecture. It appears that this sanctified building ultimately functioned as an offering itself and, presumably, was given over to the gods and the ancestors when it was ceremonially buried (Freidel and Schele 1989:239). At around the same time, or just slightly later, a similar, albeit smaller-scale, version of building termination occurred at Seibal. The Late Formative Structure 4E-10 appears to have been partially demolished, terminated with two ritual vessels, and carefully buried under several layers of different types of construction fill (construction phases III–V). A final layer of stone-filled soil was "dumped over the entire pyramid as the culmination of a multi-step valedictory ritual or structure entombment" (Tourtellot 1988:148).

Like structures, inanimate objects were also believed to retain a spiritual essence. The ritual performed by a shaman or ruler spiritually charged the material item in question. Utilizing recent epigraphic decipherments, Stuart (1996) suggests that this ritual interaction was a principal focus of ancient Maya ceremony. Once sanctified with sacred power, an object was given a name, at which time it was perceived as being spiritually alive and in ongoing communication with supernaturals. The act of opening and closing portals to the underworld through material media is still found among contemporary Lacandon Maya of northern Chiapas, Mexico, who annually create and destroy incensarios representing gods in the Incense Burner Renewal Ceremony (McGee 1998). Similarly, ancient vessels found smashed on floors of buildings at K'axob and elsewhere in the Maya area indicate a long-held belief that the spirit living inside an object must undergo ritual death when no longer needed.

This type of ritual termination is suggested for the obsidian blade that was found beneath a vessel in the zone 58 cache of operation 7. The reverse effect may have been intended for the objects in the triadic cache of operation 1, thus imbuing them with the kind of ritually charged power that Stuart (1996) describes. Depictions of gods or rulers impersonating or representing the "spirit" of a god on Classic period stone monuments and other objects may have been perceived as animate entities serving as sources of religious meditation, much like Christian icons. Arguably, Postclassic effigy censers representing deities, found in the context of ceremonial caches at the site of Santa Rita Corozal (D. Chase 1985b), may have been viewed in a similar way. These effigies, as well as the more abstract forms found in the triadic cache, may have been seen as vessels housing the spirits of supernatural beings.

Caching behavior at K'axob reflects the Maya world view both horizontally (in the form of the quincunx, or cross pattern) and vertically (in the form of the threefold universe). Moreover, cache rituals indicate that cyclical ordering of places and events in a time-space continuum was as important to the Maya then as it is now. For the Zinacantecos, wooden crosses function as both physical and spiritual markers of sacred locales, acting as the ritual partitions of the cosmos. The wooden crosses, often covered with pine branches, mark entranceways to the underworld and are portals for communicating with powerful deities and ancestors. The underlying concepts of cosmological ordering found in the modern cross shrine rituals allude to the significance not only of certain offerings at K'axob, such as the quadripartite and triadic caches, but also to the physical partitioning of space within the ancient community.

Contemporary cross shrines also are reminiscent of the dedication of stelae or "world trees" that served to mark a location as an axis mundi, a tradition that began in the Maya area during the Late Formative period. Like wooden crosses, stelae were placed at chosen sanctified locations within the built environment (such as an outside plaza space in front of a pyramidal structure or around the edges of a ceremonial center). In addition to these sacred locales, contemporary Zinacantan Maya often situate their cross shrines at the foot or summit of mountains. Both contemporary and ancient Maya believe that the gods and ancestors were housed in the mountains. Thus, *wits* (the Mayan word for mountains and also pyramids) were and continue to be focal points of religious activity. Perceived as the home of the ancestors, artificial wits were constructed by the Classic Maya to house important ancestors (Stuart 1987:16–24; Schele and Freidel 1990:233). According to Vogt (1976:44), the various sacred locales marked by crosses are "extremely important to Zinacanteco ritual life and receive frequent attention in offerings that relate living Zinacantecos to their deities and to the dead." Similarly, iconography and texts found on ancient stelae frequently honor events involving gods and ancestors of the royal elite, and the stelae are often accompanied by dedicatory offerings. The striking similarities between cross shrines and stelae dedication indicate the strong cultural continuity in Maya tradition, one that was arguably present during Formative times.

Epigraphers have deciphered a set of verbs pertaining to the dedication and erection of sculptural and architectural monuments from ancient Maya centers such as Copan. Examples of verbs include "to perforate" and "to pierce the earth for planting" (Freidel and Schele 1989:234–236). The recent flood of epigraphic insights provides a better understanding of rituals accompanying caching behavior and offers potential parallels with the archaeological record, where textual evidence is limited or non-existent. At Cerros, offerings that include lip-to-lip vessels were found in association with specific architectural modifications to structure 5c, and they may correspond with a series of ritual events occurring before and after an important period ending (Freidel and Schele 1989). Like K'axob, the offerings are placed at certain spots within this ceremonial structure (that is, on the central axis of rooms, doorways, and stairs), which may represent important thresholds between the earthly and spiritual realms. Clearly, rituals were not singular events but parts of more extensive ceremonies pertaining to celestial movements and agricultural cycles.

At K'axob we are without monuments and inscriptions; we have only the abstract expressions of the ritual deposit. Nevertheless, complex cache deposits, such as the two pairs of lip-to-lip caches found in zone 9 of operation 10, may represent a series of ritual deposits that "spanned multiple discrete, but sequentially integrated events over periods of time" (Freidel and Schele 1989:234). The zone 9 cache, along with two other lip-to-lip caches, suggests that ritual cycles corresponding to the seasonal round and year-ending celebrations were also acknowledged at the agricultural village of K'axob. When examined carefully and compared with that of other sites, such as Cerros, the data set of cache deposits from K'axob offers a window into the development of a complex ideological and cosmological infrastructure. This tradition began in Formative domestic contexts and was ultimately played out in high ritual performance during the Classic period.

At K'axob, the role of caches in domestic ritual transformed as did concepts of ancestral veneration during the Late Formative period. Ritual deposits containing portions of human skeletons, including the zone 41 cache and the elaborate ancestral shrine in operation 1 (along with the zone 57 cache from operation 12), epitomize the concept of ideological evolution. The introduction of multiple, disarticulated interments suggests the growing importance of collective lineage power, perhaps introduced as a result of increasing competition between lineages. Robin and Hammond (1991:224) note that secondary human interments were most common in public contexts at Cuello and that bundled remains were unique to mass burials, which were introduced around 400 BC. They suggest that these disarticulated remains "lost not only their identity as individuals, but their social identities as well, and can be interpreted as human grave goods" (224). Moving the remains of sacred ancestors and redepositing them in a centralized locale effectively de-emphasized the individual and produced an effect similar to caching. Secondary deposits appear as both the medium and outcome of changing social practice. Like caches, these multiple burials offered a new space a sacred demarcation and activation and, in essence, suggest a greater reliance on collective lineage power and affiliation than previously existed.

Utilizing genealogical ties as a tactical key for maneuvering into a position of political power becomes increasingly evident during the Classic period and is vividly illustrated in various iconographic media, including stelae, murals, and painted ceramics. Scholars have argued that a lineage-based succession or descent system developed at the end of the Late Formative, which facilitated the introduction of royal kingship in the Classic period (Gossen 1999). While a more acute sense of hierarchy and a greater emphasis on lineage affiliation appears to materialize at this time (see Freidel and Schele 1988), social organization manifest through descent and kinship alliance was probably well established at K'axob and elsewhere in the Maya area and simply became more formalized with changes in political organization. More elaborate ritual events noted at K'axob during the Late Formative were likely organized by lineage heads vying for control over communal work parties, thus creating more formalized leadership and the need to forge stronger lineage ties than before. The evidence for caching behavior reflects a long tradition of religious worship deeply nested in the fabric of family, kin, and community—a network that developed concomitantly with the political regime that emerged at K'axob by the end of the Late Formative.

ENDNOTES

1. For purposes of clarification, *content* refers to the specific artifacts that make up a cache and *configuration* indicates the way in which the contents were laid out within a deposit. The *context* of a cache refers to the exact placement of the deposit and any contemporaneous relationships to other features in that same context. Finally, the *placement* of an offering signifies the more general locale of the deposit, for instance, whether it was interred within or on top of the construction of an interior or exterior space.

2. The present volume focuses on the Formative period Maya of K'axob; therefore, the following analysis does not include several Classic period caches found during the 1995 and 1997 field seasons at K'axob.

Chapter 5
Related CD Resources

Sherd-lined Pits
Domiciles

SOAKED AND STEAMED SUSTENANCE: EVIDENCE FROM SHERD-LINED PITS

VICTORIA L. BOBO

INTRODUCTION

In recent years archaeologists have intensely studied the lowland area of the Yucatan Peninsula, bringing to light a variety of data concerning domestic activities practiced by the ancient Maya. Excavations during the 1990, 1992, and 1993 field seasons at K'axob in northern Belize have revealed the presence of many intrusive features lined with ceramics. These sherd-lined pits have been found in association with ancient residences across the site, and they resemble similar features at nearby sites such as Colha, Cuello, and Nohmul. In this chapter, the morphology of sherd-lined pits and possible functions of these features are addressed, and the sherd-lined pits of K'axob are compared to those of other Maya sites. These features are primarily related to Formative period household activities because the features diminish in number as the Protoclassic and Classic periods approach. There also appears to be variance in pit size, depth, linings, and artifactual contents, revealing a suite of functions for these domestic features. Domestic activity studies, such as the following investigation of sherd-lined pits among the Lowland Maya, are significant in that they not only provide data about Formative period household organization but also contribute to our knowledge of the practices that built and held together Maya civilization over its 3,000-year history.

DEFINING SHERD-LINED FACILITIES

Sherd-lined pit features were first exposed at the site of K'axob in 1990. As additional facilities were uncovered in 1992 and 1993, a literature review revealed that there had been no detailed discussion of sherd-lined pits in Mesoamerican archaeological studies. Their specific functions and morphological characteristics were not well known across the Maya area, and although they appeared to relate to Formative Maya domestic activities and possibly to ceremonial undertakings at K'axob, this idea remained untested. It was recognized that, if properly studied, these features could be linked to understanding the rise of social complexity among the ancient Maya and that such a study would be invaluable for future researchers.

Sherd-lined features at K'axob were noted to have slight variances in their morphology and artifactual contents. A definitive function for the features was not clear, however. They seemed relatively simple in design, consisting of small pits (as opposed to a larger basin such as a *chultun*) lined with sherds (and often with additional linings). They tended to be located outside dwelling structures. The morphological variation and differing artifactual contents in the facilities indicated the possibility of multiple functions. In addition, there were no known ceramic firing pits at the site of K'axob at that time (the 1993 field season), and some of the sherd-lined facilities did provide evidence of burning residues. Thus, it was conceivable that such features could have been used as ceramic firing pits during at least one use phase. With a substantial database accumulating by the 1993 field season, it became increasingly clear that an in-depth study of the form, constitution, and function of sherd-lined facilities from K'axob could produce interesting information about early Maya domestic activities.

COMPARATIVE MATERIALS

In order to investigate the characteristics of sherd-lined pits, comparative data on similar features throughout the Maya Lowlands were amassed. Within the archaeological literature, several different terms have been used to describe such features. They have been mentioned as "firepits" (Gerhardt 1988; Hammond 1991a) and/or "hearths" (Pyburn 1989b), thus complicating the search for comparative data. The data set used in this study was extracted from available data in published monographs, unpublished site reports, and theses. Features with morphological similarities to those defined at K'axob as "sherd-lined pits" were compiled into a comparative database. It should be noted that domestic pit features sometimes included stone-lined as well as ceramic-lined pits. In addition to data from K'axob, two nearby Maya sites (Cuello and Colha) contained what could be defined as sherd- or stone-lined pits. Published morphological and temporal information was also available (Anthony 1987; Gerhardt 1988; Hester et al. 1981; Sullivan 1991). These two sites yielded a total of thirty-one lined domestic features for comparative analysis.

When available, the following relevant variables were recorded: linings, firing evidence, artifactual remains within pits, numbers of vessels in primary sherd linings, diameter, depth, time period, and location (table 5.1). Gaps in the data set reflect the lack of pertinent information rather than a definitive absence of a characteristic.

Distinct patterns were noted in the statistical analysis of several variables in the comparanda. These patterns include pit linings, firing evidence, ceramic types, chronological designations, and construction techniques (morphology, depth, and diameter). The analytical results of studying each of these variables in the comparanda materials are discussed below.

PIT LININGS

Out of thirty-one total pit features, twenty-three lined features had been recorded. At least twelve of the thirty-one pit features from Colha and Cuello are noted to be lined with sherds; the remaining nineteen are not specifically documented as sherd-lined. Thirty-nine percent of the "other" linings consisted of clay, whereas stone linings comprised 26% of the sample. Just over 17% of pits in the comparanda were lined with both clay and stone, and these clay and stone linings were sometimes accompanied by a double layering of ceramics. The high percentages of clay and stone linings are important to note as they appear to form a significant variant of lined-pit constructions at the sites of Colha and Cuello.

FIRING INDICATORS

Various firing indicators were also noted in the published data for sherd- and stone-lined facilities. Out of a total of fifteen lined pits with firing evidence, 27% contained ash in some form. Unspecified firing evidence noted simply as "present" in the literature occurred in 33% of this subsample of pits. The remaining pits contained a burned surface. These findings indicate that fifteen of the thirty-one pits in the comparanda showed evidence of firing, primarily in the form of burned linings or an ashy matrix.

CERAMIC TYPES AND VESSEL FRAGMENTS

The ceramic types that comprised the lining material in these facilities may have been purposely selected either for their ability to retain heat (for example, for steaming activities) or for their ability to withstand repeated firing or cooking episodes. In conjunction, the

Table 5.1 Comparanda of sherd-lined pits from Colha and Cuello, Belize

Number	Site	Feature No.	Lining	Firing Evidence	Artifacts/Other	Characteristics of Sherd Lining	Diameter (cm)	Depth (cm)	Period	Construction Phase
1	Colha	1981-2	Marl	Present	Charcoal, fishbone	Large vessel fragment			Middle Formative	
2	Colha	1979-3 Op. 2006	Clay	Ash present	Flakes, chert core	One vessel	40	130		
3	Colha	1979-3 Op. 2006	Clay	Ash present	Flakes	One vessel	40	130		
4	Colha	1981-27 Subop. 5	Marl, plaster	Burned surface	Flakes, microfaunal		70		Middle Formative	
5	Colha	1981-28	Soil	Burned surface			30			
6	Cuello		Clay	Present		Vessel base	42	17	Early Middle Formative	Phase IA
7	Cuello		Clay	Present		Vessel base	42	17	Early Middle Formative	Phase IA
8	Cuello		Clay	Present		Vessel base	42	17	Early Middle Formative	Phase IA
9	Cuello		Clay	Present		Vessel base	42	17	Early Middle Formative	Phase IA
10	Cuello	52	Stone		Daub		47	12	Early Middle Formative	Phase IA
11	Cuello	53	Stone				47	12	Early Middle Formative	Phase IA
12	Cuello						40	20	Early Middle Formative	Phase II
13	Cuello						40	20	Early Middle Formative	Phase II
14	Cuello	241	Double layer of ceramics			Two vessels	40	20	Early Middle Formative	Phase II
15	Cuello	255							Early Middle Formative	Phase II
16	Cuello						45	20	Early Middle Formative	Phase III
17	Cuello						45	20	Early Middle Formative	Phase III
18	Cuello						45	20	Early Middle Formative	Phase III
19	Cuello						45	20	Early Middle Formative	Phase III
20	Cuello	42	Clay	Ashy soil		Vessel base	48	24	Formative	Phase IIIA
21	Cuello	44	Stone				56	20	Late Formative	Floor 502
22	Cuello		Clay	Burnt lining, ashy soil			43	12	Late Formative	Phase V, west of chultun
23	Cuello			Ashy soil			43	12	Late Formative	Phase V, west of chultun
24	Cuello		Clay	Burnt lining, ashy soil			43	12	Late Formative	Phase V, west of chultun
25	Cuello		Clay, stone	Burnt lining, ashy soil			43	12	Late Formative	Phase V, west of chultun
26	Cuello		Clay, stone	Burnt lining, ashy soil			43	12	Late Formative	Phase V, west of chultun
27	Cuello	22	Clay, stone, double layer of ceramics				70	40	Late Formative	Phase VIII
28	Cuello	17	Stone				70	40	Late Formative	Phase VIII
29	Cuello	214	Clay, stone, double layer of ceramics				70	40	Late Formative	Phase VIII
30	Cuello	267	Stone				70	40	Late Formative	Phase VIII
31	Cuello	145	Stone			Vessel base	70	40	Late Formative	Phase VI

approximate numbers of vessels comprising a pit's lining could also reveal distinct ceramic selection choices. For example, specific vessels may have been intentionally broken for pit construction. In contrast, previously broken fragments from multiple vessels may have been used. The former situation could signify a special importance associated with particular ceramic types as opposed to a more utilitarian, grab-bag construction technique.

At Cuello, the most prevalent ceramic used for sherd linings was Chicago Orange. Sierra Red ceramic fragments were infrequently found in lined pit facilities at this site. During the Late Formative, however, a significant number of Society Hall fragments are detected (Hammond, personal communication, 1994).[1] Based on ten sherd-lined pits from Cuello for which vessel part was documented, 60% are vessel base sherds (the number of vessels represented by these sherds is not documented), whereas 30% are either one large fragment or multiple fragments from a single vessel. Linings built of multiple vessels compose only 10% of the cases. One facility from Cuello not listed in the data set of published material was made up of fragments from approximately seven vessels (Hammond, personal communication, 1994).

Although the pattern of sherd linings composed of low vessel numbers is provocative, it should be remembered that this subset of the database contains only ten cases. The number of vessels constituting the remaining twenty-one cases is not documented. The scant notation of vessel numbers in the comparanda precludes general inferences as to pit construction techniques.

CHRONOLOGICAL DESIGNATIONS

Chronological placement of sherd-lined pits was determined either by relative dating methods (such as ceramic typology) or absolute chronology (usually radiocarbon assays; see Anthony 1987; Gerhardt 1988; Hester et al. 1981; Sullivan 1991). Upon examination, the range of dates of pits from Colha and Cuello is quite early in terms of Maya chronology. Results from both absolute and relative dating techniques reveal that lined pits from Colha and Cuello fall within the Formative period (1200 BC to AD 50/100).

CONSTRUCTION TECHNIQUES

Construction methods employed when building sherd-lined facilities may be detected through the various dimensions of the pits. Two measurements regularly reported in the literature and worthy of note are pit diameter and depth. These variables are important when studying the standardization of pit construction methods and possible differences in function between pits of varying sizes. The distribution of diameter measurements takes a bimodal shape when plotted in histogram form (figure 5.1). A quasinormal distribution of values in the first mode suggests some standardization in the diameters of sherd-lined pits. The presence of a second mode, however, indicates that there are some pits with exceptionally large diameters. What may be implied from the larger measurements is that the majority of these facilities from Colha and Cuello are approximately 43 cm in diameter (the median diameter of the thirty measured pits) with a few larger exceptions. These exceptions may indicate special uses of particular lined pits. Features with greater diameters could provide more volume for use and therefore may have been useful for large-scale activities.

Volume may also be affected by a feature's depth, however (figure 5.1). Shape of the depth histogram is skewed to the right, suggesting variability in desired depth and, therefore, possibly different volume requirements. As with diameter values, extreme depth values are present at or beyond double those of most sherd-lined features. The mean and median depth values are 29.5 cm and 20 cm, respectively, and the entire range extends from 12 cm to 130 cm in depth.

In sum, the Maya appear to have constructed wider pits in some instances and deeper pits in others, presumably due to functional variation or differences in the scale of activities. Different functions cannot be inferred directly from dimensions alone, however. To detect functional variability, pit contents, location, and morphology must be analyzed together. Such fine-grained data are available for the sherd-lined pits of K'axob.

SHERD-LINED PITS OF K'AXOB

This chapter builds on senior thesis research (Kobza 1994) on the form and function of thirty sherd-lined pits of K'axob (table 5.2). The complete data set of these features is available in digital form in the accompanying *Sherd-lined Pits Database*, which includes many in situ color photos of these features.

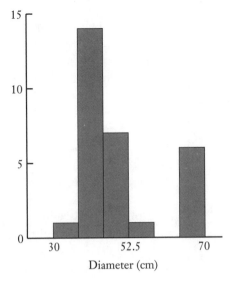

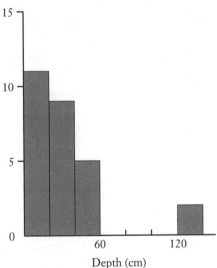

Figure 5.1 Histograms of diameters and depths of lined pits within comparanda data set (measurements in cm).

SPATIAL LOCATIONS

The positioning of domestic features at any archaeological site is particularly important as it can often indicate specific activity areas and distinguish between ceremonial and day-to-day events. The location of pit features is examined below, both by excavation area and by specific structure; this analysis is followed by an intrasite comparison of artifactual contents.

Excavation areas. During the course of archaeological investigations at K'axob, excavation units (operations) were positioned within plaza areas as well as peripheral structures to document architectural and domestic sequences. When encountered, sherd-lined pits were identified as intrusive pits either partially or completely lined with vessel fragments. A total of thirty such pits was identified within five excavation units: operations 1, 7, 8, 11, and 12 (for location of excavation units, see figure 2.2). Only operation 10 lacked any sherd-lined pits, although it did contain an immense, charcoal-filled pit as the basic construction phase.

During excavations, such pits were often uncovered as single features intruded into a prepared surface or an extramural yard area. There were instances, however, when two or more sherd-lined pits were found in close proximity. This pit clustering is intriguing as the alignment of pits suggests that a sequence of related tasks was undertaken within a sharply delimited area. For instance, one can imagine that preparation for a large feast might necessitate the construction of several lined features in order to soak, steam, or roast foods such as maize and mollusca. At three excavation units (operations 1, 11, and 12) clusters of sherd-lined pits assignable to a single construction phase were found. Of the thirty pits from K'axob, over one-third (n = 13) were intruded into structures and middens within operation 1. Of the thirteen pits at operation 1, five form two distinct clusters. The first grouping occurs during phase 1 construction, which involved use of paleosol as a living surface and the formation of a midden near the northwest corner of operation 1 (figure 3.2). Two sherd-lined pits (zones 228 and 231) are clustered together with a firepit (zone 232) along a northwest-southeast alignment (figure 5.2). These features date to the Middle Formative (or early facet of the Chaakk'ax complex). The second grouping of sherd-lined features at operation 1 occurs within phase 9 construction during the terminal facet of the K'atabche'k'ax complex. The two features (zones 23 and 25) were intruded into a single floor (zone 24) and thus occupy the same activity space (figure 3.9). Zone 25 itself is made up of two sherd-lined basins of unequal size that were built adjacent to one another and may have been used at the same time.

The adjacent positioning of sherd-lined pits is relatively rare at K'axob. The remaining nine pits in operation 1 (zones 93, 114, 112, 118, 136, 126, 151, 208, and 224) are not associated with other lined features inside or outside structures. Sherd-lined pits are far more frequently associated with other types of intrusive features (such as burials) than they are with other pits. The defined pattern of sherd-lined pits in operation 1 reveals that they were frequently intruded into floors that also contained intrusive burial features. Thus, there is minimal clustering of pits as

Table 5.2 K'axob sherd-lined pit provenience at indoor versus outdoor locations

Operation	Zone	Feature Into Which it Intrudes	Location
1	23	Floor	Inside
1	25	Floor	Inside
1	93	Floor	Inside
1	112	Midden	Outside
1	114	Midden	Outside
1	118	Midden	Outside
1	126	Floor	Inside
1	136	Patio Floor	Outside
1	151	Midden	Outside
1	208	Patio Floor	Outside
1	224	Midden	Outside
1	228	Midden	Outside
1	231	Midden	Outside
7	53	Patio Floor	Outside
7	270	Floor	Inside
8	12	Floor	Inside
11	12	Midden	Outside
11	34	Patio Floor	Outside
11	81	Midden	Inside
11	83	Midden	Outside
11	85	Midden	Outside
11	88	Midden	Outside
11	89	Midden	Outside
12	10	Midden	Outside
12	20	Midden	Outside
12	29	Floor	Inside
12	35	Floor	Inside
12	37	Floor	Inside
12	44	Patio Floor	Outside
12	9/27	Patio Floor	Outside

opposed to their more frequent presence as individual features in the domestic activity space.

As previously noted, operation 11 also contains a cluster of sherd-lined pits in a domestic area. Two features (zones 85 and 89) were intruded into a midden (zone 72) dating to the early facet of the K'atabche'k'ax complex. These two pits are aligned east-west. Two additional sherd-lined pits also date to this construction phase, although they were built during an earlier subphase: zones 83 and 88. The particular positions of these four features seem to indicate a wider distribution of such pits across a work area.

The fact that four of the seven sherd-lined pits in operation 11 (specifically, zones 85, 89, 83, and 88) were constructed during one phase indicates a significant emphasis on the activities undertaken at these features during the initial construction phase. Dating to the early facet of the K'atabche'k'ax complex, the cluster may represent four one-time use events or continuous use of these four pits over an extended period of time. The remaining pits from operation 11 represent single intrusive features (zones 12, 34, and 81).

The only other excavated area that included a substantial number of sherd-lined pits is operation 12. This operation yielded seven such features, including a clustering of sherd-lined pits within two construction phases. Three associated but not cardinally aligned pits (zones 29, 35, and 37) were found intruding into a floor of phase 5 construction that dates to the terminal facet of the K'atabche'k'ax complex. This cluster of three facilities represents another occupational phase with intensified single-event or multiple-use domestic activities. Two pits in this cluster (zones 29 and 35) were notably constructed with atypical, sloping sidewalls, producing

Figure 5.2 Triad of pits located at base of operation 1, showing two unexcavated sherd-lined pits (zones 228 and 231) and an excavated fire pit (zone 232). Vessel from burial 1-43 shown in foreground. *Photo from K'axob Project archives.*

unusual pit shapes when compared to similar features elsewhere at K'axob. Zones 29, 35, and 37 are also notable in that only their bases were lined with sherds.

The next example of pit clustering is similar to one noted from operation 1. Zone 10c in operation 12 is made up of two adjacent and differentially sized basins. These basins intrude into a midden area located next to structure 4, which contained a burial/cache deposit very close to the sherd-lined pit locations. Whether these pits were multi-use or single-event features is not known. The remaining three sherd-lined pits in operation 12 are single features not associated with other pits (zones 9/27, 20, and 44).

The remaining sherd-lined pits were excavated in operations 7 and 8. Two single pits were uncovered at operation 7 and one at operation 8. There are smaller numbers of sherd-lined facilities at these operations, and clustering is absent. Within operation 7, a sherd-lined feature (zone 270) was cut into the zone 26 floor; zone 53 was intruded into the floor (zone 43) of an earlier structure. The only additional pit under investigation

(zone 12) was found in operation 8; here, zone 12 dates to the K'atabche'k'ax complex and intrudes into a floor of phase 2a construction. Operation 7 revealed fewer pit constructions within an area that was occupied for a shorter period of time than operations 1, 11, and 12. Zone 270 of operation 7, in particular, dates to the early Nohalk'ax complex, a time of limited pit construction. In accordance with what has been revealed at operation 7, the limited construction span of operation 8 also shows little use of sherd-lined pit features.

Based on these data, it appears that early households in proximity to the center of K'axob were involved in the most frequent facility construction. The clustering of sherd-lined pits, whether for single- or multiuse events, occurs in association with plaza B and in association with the activities at nearby structures investigated through excavations at operations 11 and 12. Sherd-lined basins exhibit a tendency to cluster within these three excavations, but there are also examples of single sherd-lined pits that intruded into domestic floors and outside work spaces. It may be that clustering of basins within an area signifies either their simultaneous use or successive use phases in which one pit was abandoned and another was built to replace the abandoned, neighboring feature. In contrast, at operation 11 there is a more dispersed distribution of sherd-lined pits in the domestic workspace of each phase, and this may indicate a difference in domestic activities at this particular location during construction phases 1 through 5.

Structural associations. Workspace is linked to pit functions and the ways in which K'axob's inhabitants conceptualized domestic space. K'axob inhabitants not only engaged in craft production, constructed innumerable platforms topped by dwellings, and buried their dead in a manner suggestive of an elaborate belief system, but they also conducted these activities within a domestic environment. Accordingly, the spatial relationship of pit features to interior, as opposed to exterior, domestic spaces was investigated (table 5.2). Seventy percent of sherd-lined pits were located in outdoor workspaces. Most instances of outdoor placement were described as intrusions into midden deposits, with patio floors composing the remainder of exterior locations. The remaining sherd-lined features were intruded into floors that constituted indoor living and workspace. The placement of pits inside household areas is significant when compared to the locations of similar features from nearby Nohmul. Pyburn (1989b) describes nine sherd-lined pits at Nohmul, all of which were located in outdoor contexts. Based on published excavation data to date, the contrast between sherd-lined pit use at K'axob and Nohmul may indicate different organization of domestic workspace.

Regardless, both K'axob and Nohmul reveal a tendency to place such features in outdoor workspaces, an important fact when attempting to reconstruct activities conducted within and near residences. The activities for which sherd-lined pits were constructed likely necessitated outdoor locations for ventilation, increased lighting, and/or other external conditions. Outdoor placement of these features may also inform us about cultural proxemics. Outdoor patios and other workspaces are public in nature. Thus, the tendency to situate a sherd-lined facility in an outdoor setting may indicate a communal or even ceremonial function rather than a private activity.

The complexity of spatial and temporal trends in both outdoor and indoor areas is also of interest. In particular, temporal changes in the spatial location of such basins can be detected at Cuello, where sherd-lined facilities are increasingly constructed away from the patio area of Phases II–IV, resulting in increased formality of the outdoor area (Hammond and Gerhardt 1990). This pattern is not detected at K'axob, as sherd-lined facilities are consistently constructed in areas that directly surround domestic structures during all construction phases.

Spatial location and artifactual remains. Even with the large number of outside intrusions, a few sherd-lined pits were intruded into the floors of house structures at K'axob (table 5.2). Placement of these features indoors may relate to the different function of indoor as opposed to outdoor sherd-lined pits. For example, indoor pits may have been used for boiling procedures or food storage, whereas steam baking may have taken place in outdoor pits. To test for a relationship between the artifactual contents of pits and their location, a series of chi-square tests were conducted. Analyses were performed for types of artifactual materials found within sherd-lined pits (namely, charcoal, ash, and shell) that were presumably from the pit's use rather than from its construction or from activities that occurred after it was no longer in use. Interestingly, chi-square tests revealed no relationship between charcoal remains and pit location. However, further examination of specific counts of charcoal fragments reveals a different picture. The bulk of charcoal fragments, when separated by their placement inside or outside domestic structures, do tend to occur in outdoor sherd-lined pit locations. Ten pits located outside domestic structures yielded either high- or low-density charcoal remains, whereas only four indoor pits contained any charcoal at all.

When evidence of ash was examined in light of pit locations, a significant relationship was noted. The calculated chi-square value (7.659) was significant at the 0.05 level. Although a phi-square analysis of the same variables revealed a weak relationship (a value of 0.247), important information is obtained through a count breakdown of sherd-lined pits with noted ash remains. A total of nine such features have ash remains, and in each of these cases, the sherd-lined pits are intruded into areas outside structures. These data lend plausibility to the theory that outdoor locations were often chosen for pit construction because these features were designed to contain fires that burned at a heat intense enough to deposit a layer of ash.

The last chi-square tests examine the relationship between sherd-lined pit location and dietary remains within the features. One of the theories regarding the functions of pit features is that they were used to steam-

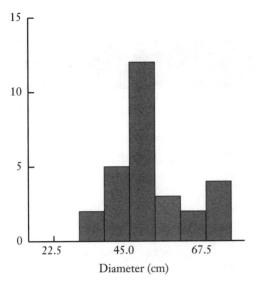

Figure 5.3 Distribution of diameter measurements of K'axob sherd-lined pits.

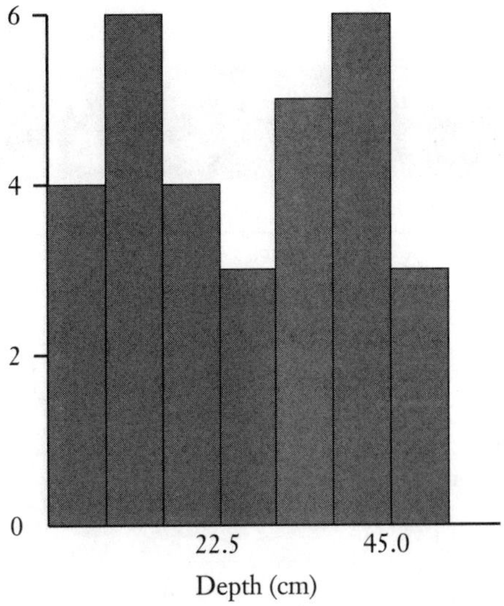

Figure 5.4 Distribution of depth measurements of K'axob sherd-lined pits.

bake *Pomacea flagellata* (an edible, freshwater gastropod; see chapter 18). A statistically insignificant chi-square value is reported for tests of both complete *Pomacea* and shell fragments for the two pit locations. It must be noted, however, that more numerous examples of shell-filled pits exist in outdoor locations. Of the ten pit facilities containing complete *Pomacea flagellata* remains, seven were in outdoor contexts.

The knowledge gained here regarding pit content versus placement can aid in deciphering functional tendencies evident for sherd-lined facilities. In addition, the spatial tendencies identified above facilitate understanding of how such features were incorporated into the domestic setting.

CONSTRUCTION AND MORPHOLOGY OF SHERD-LINED FACILITIES

Since sherd-lined pits appear as part of the domestic environment created by K'axob's early inhabitants, it is useful to know not only where they were placed but also how they were constructed and whether they changed over time. Summary statistics for pit features, presented below, shed light on construction techniques and provide substantial comparative data for future study at K'axob and other Maya sites.

Depth and diameter. Of the thirty sherd-lined pits excavated to date at K'axob, twenty-eight have recorded diameter measurements. These diameter data indicate a wide range of sizes, from 30 cm to 74 cm (the mean value is 51.1 cm, and the median value is 47 cm).

A histogram of diameter values reveals a weak bimodal tendency (figure 5.3). The greatest number of pits (n = 12) fall in the first mode, implying that most pits required a diameter of approximately 50 cm for a specific purpose or a group of related activities. The larger mode of diameter measurements may represent a different pit function from that detected in the first mode. The minimum depth for sherd-lined pits from K'axob is 6 cm, whereas the maximum depth is 50 cm. Most depths fall into one of two modes (between 7 and 14 cm and between 37 and 45 cm; figure 5.4). As previously suggested, clustering of data into two or more modes may represent multiple functions. When examined together, sherd-lined pit diameter and depth dimensions seem to discount theories of singular function over time and/or in different locations.

Dimensional variance over time. The bimodality represented in each pit dimension could result from changes in pit construction over time rather than from differing functions. To compare diameter measurements with recorded temporal information, the diameter variable was transformed from a ratio to an ordinal scale. Categories of small, medium, large, extra large, and extra extra large include the following dimensions: 30–40 cm, 41–50 cm, 51–60 cm, 61–70 cm, and 71+ cm. If bimodality were a function of diameter variance over time, then it would be expected that clusters of diameter sizes would occur in certain time periods. Breakdowns of sherd-lined pits from ceramic complex into their respective diameter classes, however, show no correlation between diameter and

Table 5.3 Distribution of K'axob sherd-lined pits by temporal designation and size

CERAMIC COMPLEX	RANKED SIZE					
	Extra Extra Large	Extra Large	Large	Medium	Small	Total
Chaakk'ax	1	1	0	4	1	7
Chaakk'ax/K'atabche'k'ax	1	0	0	2	1	4
Early & Late K'atabche'k'ax	1	1	3	5	2	12
Terminal K'atabche'k'ax	0	0	2	1	2	5
Total	3	3	5	11	6	28
Note: Two sherd-lined pits have undetermined diameter measurements (operation 1, zone 23 and operation 8, zone 12).						

time (see table 5.3). Clustering of both medium (n = 5) and large sized (n = 3) sherd-lined pits, for example, occurs during the K'atabche'k'ax complex. In the Terminal K'atabche'k'ax, however, another cluster of large sized pits (n = 2) is detected.

Diameter and depth of K'axob sherd-lined pits in perspective. As previously discussed, the distribution of diameter measurements of sherd-lined pits from Cuello and Colha also forms a bimodal shape indicative of two distinct designs at all three sites. Thus, taken together, the diameter data from Colha, Cuello, and K'axob discount notions of a single function for these pits.

On the other hand, examination of depth values for both the comparanda and K'axob data sets does not reveal a consistent bimodal tendency. As discussed above, the depths of lined pits from Colha and Cuello form a normal distribution. Depth data under investigation from K'axob, however, show a distinctly bimodal shape. Possibly, the sherd-lined pits at K'axob were more substantially modified for one or more purposes.

Sherd characteristics. Sherd linings themselves also preserve information relating to the construction design of the facilities. Some notable characteristics include the numbers of ceramic fragments composing each lining, sherd size, thickness, form, and type. A sample of twenty-two sherd-lined facilities was selected for individual sherd analysis based on distinctive morphology, spatial and temporal location, and detail of field documentation.

One interesting trend in pit construction comes from the number of vessels represented in each sherd-lined basin. Sherd linings from Colha and Cuello, for example, appear to include a maximum of two vessels in any given basin. The range of vessel numbers at

K'axob, however, extends from a minimum of two vessels to a maximum of thirty-nine vessels used to line a single pit. In the subsample examined, only five pits contained fewer than five vessels in their linings. Assuming that the vessel counts from Colha and Cuello are accurate, this contrast reveals that a substantially more diverse population of ceramic fragments was used in the construction of sherd linings at K'axob. These pits appear more likely to have been constructed of sherds from previously broken vessels set into a prepared depression. At K'axob, sherd linings evidence preconstruction vessel breakage in nineteen pits. The Colha and Cuello examples seem to be made up of sherds from a single vessel set into a prepared pit and positioned in the shape of the original vessel. The large number of recycled sherds set into the walls of K'axob pits is also revealed by an analysis of sherd size measured in four increments. Small sherds are those less than 5 x 5 cm in size; medium are those between 5 x 5 cm and 10 x 10 cm; large are those between 10 x 10 cm and 15 x 15 cm; and extra large are those greater than 15 x 15 cm.

Of the 951 sherds analyzed from twenty-two sherd-lined pits, 58 percent were classified as small. Due to the possibility of postconstruction breakage, small sherds were analyzed for fresh breaks, and, when possible, all sherds were refitted for greater accuracy in size estimations. The substantial percentage of small sherds used to line the pits reinforces the mosaic quality of pit construction at K'axob. Medium-sized fragments comprise nearly 33 percent of the sample, whereas large and extra large sherds comprise a negligible 8 percent. Larger sherd sizes are indicative of pit construction involving the placement of whole vessels, yet at K'axob such large fragments are rare, especially when

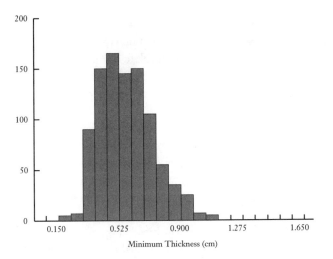

Figure 5.5 Distribution of minimum sherd thickness values (cm) for ceramic linings.

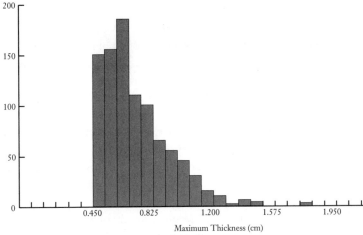

Figure 5.6 Distribution of maximum sherd thickness values (cm) for ceramic linings.

compared to Colha and Cuello. These findings indicate that, primarily, most sherd linings were constructed of small and medium-sized sherds, often from numerous vessels. K'axob Maya constructed sherd linings by creating a contoured mosaic surface composed of previously broken pottery rather than by employing entire vessels.

Sherd thickness can indicate conscious selection in the design and construction of sherd-lined pits for specific thermal properties. Rice (1987a:364) has discussed the link between thickness and thermal conduction as well as durability:

> Different degrees of thermal conductivity are desirable for different purposes; refractory bricks, for example, should have low thermal conductivity, to provide better insulation in kilns and not lose heat, whereas saggars and cooking pots should have high conductivity to transmit heat rapidly to their contents.

In the K'axob sample, minimum and maximum thickness was measured for each sherd (see figures 5.5 and 5.6). The thickness of sherds composing ceramic linings range from 0.55 to 0.67 cm. Due to the extreme variance of wall thickness within a single sherd, it is difficult to detect any change in vessel types over time. The skewed patterning detected in the distribution of both minimum and maximum sherd thickness does indicate that thicker sherds predominate. The thermal implications of generally thicker sherds will be discussed below when we consider the function of sherd-lined pits.

Ceramic forms and types. The use of sherds from cooking/storing wares as opposed to serving vessels can be distinguished by reference to the Type:Variety ceramic classification system (see chapter 8).

The most frequently encountered ceramic type in K'axob's sherd-lined pits is Chicago Orange (77% of 923 sherds). The remaining 23% include the following types: Sierra Red (n = 119 sherds), Joventud Red (n = 20), eroded nondiagnostic sherds (n = 18), and Monkey Falls sherds (n = 14). Chicago Orange and Monkey Falls are two ceramic types typical of cooking/storing vessels. Ritual, serving, and drinking vessels are represented by Sierra Red and Joventud Red types (see chapter 8 and López Varela 1996). At K'axob, linings were composed of a mixture of heterogeneous types of ceramics. This pattern suggests that broken vessels from cooking pots and serving bowls were not segregated as they were provisionally discarded or stored for possible recycling. Reuse of ceramics as viewed through sherd linings is an example of what Schiffer (1987) describes as "secondary use." Artifacts or features involved in secondary use need not require extensive modification in order to be incorporated into a different activity. Sherd linings, therefore, exhibit secondary use through the incorporation of broken cooking/storage and serving vessels that were presumably discarded into nonsegregated piles.

Closely connected to ceramic type is the portion of the vessel selected for the lining. Categories of vessel parts include rim sherds, base sherds, and body sherds. Most of the sherds fall into the body sherd category. This dominance may result partly from the fact that rim and base fragments are limited in number when compared to the possible number of body fragments resulting from vessel breakage. Substantial numbers of body sherds could also be due to their generally small size; they may have been chosen for their ability to conform to the shape of pit walls much in the form of a mosaic inlay. These sherds could also be fit closely together, limiting the spaces between vessel fragments and creating a more uniform lining.

Termination of sherd-lined pit use. So far, the discussion of pit construction has concentrated on the morphology of these features. An effective way of studying sherd-lined pit termination involves examining the materials recovered during flotation of fill samples. Rather than attempting to differentiate between fill inclusions and artifacts associated with pit function (as opposed to termination), fill contexts are approached as primarily relating to termination activities. As previously noted, sherd-lined pits are prevalent in outdoor areas and tend to intrude into midden deposits. Not surprisingly, the dense concentration of artifacts recovered from many fill matrices resembles what is found in midden deposits. If K'axob's residents wanted to fill the basins in order to prevent problems in high-traffic areas, midden-like soil would have been easy to obtain from surrounding areas. It is also conceivable that pits were left open for some time after their use, accumulating soil and debris in the same manner as the surrounding midden.

Artifacts recovered from the bases of sherd-lined pits or attached in some fashion to their sidewalls also provide tantalizing evidence of the final uses of these features. A significant number of sherd-lined pits contained a bifacially worked stone tool fragment and/or a mano or metate fragment at their bases or in their sidewalls. Others contained debitage within the bulk of the fill, which parallels data from Cuello; however, instances of stone tool or mano/metate inclusions from K'axob number only six. These cases are noted to come from deep stratigraphic locations within pits and yet are included within the fill context. It is also interesting that all five sherd-lined features containing a worked stone artifact within their basal fill are found at operation 1, an area of significant domestic activity in its earliest levels and intense ceremonial activity later in time. A number of disparate activities could have resulted in the deposition of these artifacts: random discard, a dedicatory closure of the pit, or discard of a tool used in conjunction with sherd-lined pit function. If these artifacts were part of a dedication ritual, then the artifacts themselves may be representative of the types of activities undertaken in each pit (for instance, a mano or metate inclusion could relate to maize processing). For a comparable example of an offering of utilitarian tools, see the discussion of the operation 1, zone 85 cache in chapter 4.

Function of sherd-lined pits. Having reviewed the morphology and termination of pit features at K'axob and the recorded characteristics of similar features at other Maya sites, we are still faced with the question of how these features were used. As suggested above, there may have been a suite of functions associated with these features. Their morphological characteristics show two modal tendencies with regard to depth and diameter, and two primary artifact types are included in the fill matrix of the pits (bifaces and manos/metates). Such bimodality suggests that there was more than one reason to construct a sherd-lined pit.

In order to appropriately address the functional nature of these facilities, several hypothetical functions are investigated below. Not all functions may apply to K'axob's sherd-lined features; thus, the goal here is to find the evidentiary limits for the interpretation of pit function. The following three functions for sherd-lined pits are investigated: (1) cooking facilities, (2) features constructed for the preparation and processing of maize, and (3) small kilns for pottery production. All three hypotheses have relatively strong supporting data from K'axob and/or other nearby Maya sites.

Cooking features. Due to the morphological characteristics of these facilities and the artifacts associated with the pits, boiling and steam baking of foods are primary considerations. If sherd-lined pits were used in cooking, then the thermal properties of the sherd linings become important, and an analysis of these properties may allow their function to be discerned with greater accuracy. First, in terms of intrinsic ceramic properties, ceramic vessels in general are poor conductors of heat. Due to this fact, potters producing cooking vessels try to gain as much control over the thermal conductivity of the clay fabric as is possible. This is accomplished by adjusting a vessel's porosity (Rice 1987a:367). The greater the porosity in a ceramic, the better its thermal conductivity and the smaller the chance that it will crack as a result of thermal stress. Another major property to consider in the study of a vessel's resistance to thermal stress is temperature (Rice 1987a:367). When a ceramic is heated, it responds to the increase in temperature by expanding. If a vessel expands beyond the boundaries of its microstructural pores, cracks will develop. The size

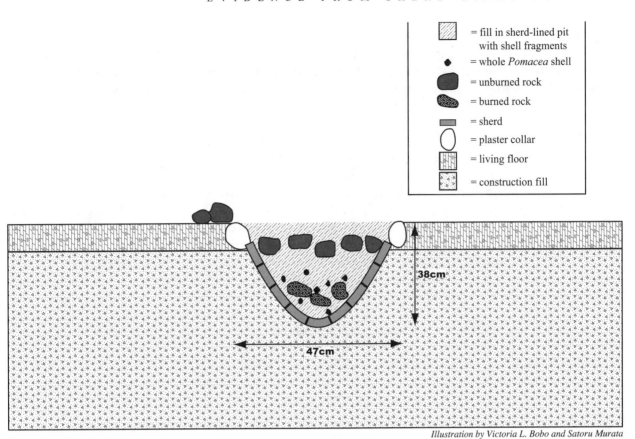

Illustration by Victoria L. Bobo and Satoru Murata

Legend:
= fill in sherd-lined pit with shell fragments
= whole *Pomacea* shell
= unburned rock
= burned rock
= sherd
= plaster collar
= living floor
= construction fill

Figure 5.7 Idealized cross-section of sherd-lined pit from operation 12 (zone 37).

of pore spaces is also important in terms of a vessel's insulation abilities. Large pore spaces in a ceramic will result in low insulation ability for that particular vessel. Small-pored vessels will be good insulators of heat because they conduct heat slowly, thereby retaining it within their walls for longer periods of time. Therefore, vessels with a coarse-grained temper would be desirable for use in boiling or baking of foods, whereas vessels with a fine-grained temper would be useful for steaming food. Due to the fragmentary nature of sherds used to line pits, a sherds' resistance to thermal stress may have been inconsequential whereas its thermal conductivity may have been of great importance. Vessel fragments that were either good insulators of heat (for example, sherds with fine-grained tempers) or that were good conductors of heat (for example, highly porous sherds) could presumably have been used in steam baking and/or boiling of foods, respectively.

Analysis of sherd-lined pits at K'axob reveals evidence of steaming or other cooking activities in the form of additional clay or plaster linings that may have increased the insulation ability of these features. These additional linings exist directly below sherd linings in ten of the

thirty examples. Six pits contained multiple layers of ceramics that may have increased heat retention. Another distinguishing attribute of sherd-lined pits that suggests steam cooking is the presence of *Pomacea flagellata* shells or bone directly above the base of the pits. Provenience is important here as artifacts and soil at base locations are more likely to be associated with the pit's function or an intermediate use stage than with fill deposits. *Pomacea flagellata*, turtles, fish, or small mammals common in K'axob faunal assemblage could have been placed in sherd-lined pits for steam cooking. Analyses of fauna from pit contexts reveals the presence of deer, turtle, fish, rodent, and dog remains from a total of six facilities (zones 27 and 81 from operation 11 and zones 9/27, 29, 35, and 37 from operation 12). The desired temperature could be reached by placing heated stones in a pit or by heating stones with a small fire within the pit itself. Once the stones were heated, food items could be placed in the feature, and the sherd lining would provide enhanced insulation for steaming or baking. Zone 37 of operation 12 is an example of a sherd-lined pit that shows evidence of steaming activity from heated stones (figure 5.7). Here, the rocks filling the pit are not burned; fire-altered rocks are only seen near the bottom of the pit. Layering of the fill therefore suggests removal of some stones during or after cooking, with termination of the pit's use indicated by the upper layer of unburned materials and soil, either intentional fill or gradual accumulation in the pit after abandonment. Other evidence from zone 37 lends credibility to a steam-baking process. The lower stratum contains a low density of charcoal and a high density of shell fragments, including complete *Pomacea flagellata*. Inclusion of whole *Pomacea* spp. discounts the idea that shell is simply part of fill used to close this feature, as shell included within fill tends to be purely fragmentary.

Another possible example of a steam-cooking feature is found at an early facet K'atabche'k'ax pit feature (zone 114) from operation 1 (see figure 5.8). Here, the basin is filled with ash, charcoal, and silty clay at its base. A uniform layer of 110 *Pomacea flagellata* shells, some of which are burned, tops this lower burned layer. A compact burned layer of clay caps this stratum. A dense charcoal layer, followed by a dark gray, silty clay further covers the burned clay. Stratigraphy within the pit reveals a sequence of two use stages separated by two burned layers. The basal sequence of ash and charcoal followed by a dense layer of *Pomacea* spp. shells indicates one cooking event. The *Pomacea* spp. do not seem to be intrinsically dedicatory in nature as they are sometimes burned yet very uniformly spaced at the bottom level (as would occur in a cooking process). Steaming is likely to have occurred during the first use stage as evidence of direct fire at the base is slight (that is, sparse remains of charcoal and ash). Heated stones could have been used during this early process.

The second use stage probably involved a fire within the feature. Compact clay between the two stages forms a base for the pit's next function. Burning evidence in the clay itself probably resulted from the firing activity that created the dense charcoal layer directly above it. Finally, a layer of silty soil sealed the feature. Alternatively, the two stages indicated in this feature's fill may have been part of a single event. The upper burned clay layer may have served to seal food items in the basal portion of the feature, at which point a fire was lit above the food cache to fuel or enhance steaming. Why the *Pomacea flagellata* shells were never removed from the feature is a bit of a mystery. Possibly, they remained in situ due to the symbolic or dedicatory nature of the cooking process itself, or they may represent excess food that spoiled or was never consumed. Rather than cleaning out the feature for subsequent use, the contents were simply covered and sealed. It is also possible that freshwater gastropods were consumed and the shells returned to the pit for disposal.

Maize soaking features. In contrast to the idea that sherd-lined pits functioned as basins for cooking food, some may have played a role in processing food, especially maize. The soil of K'axob is a rich mollisol, and the wetland to the west of the site center is bordered by many island fields; both these features were integral to agricultural production in antiquity. Recent pollen cores from interisland canals have yielded evidence of maize, cotton, and other economic cultigens (Jones 1999). Maize itself was used to produce both food and drink, and as population in the Maya region grew, maize took on increasing importance as a food staple. In order to prepare maize for consumption as tamales or a corn drink (such as *atole* and *posole*), the kernels are often steamed or boiled in limewater to soften them (Sharer 1983:240). This maize-soaking process has been documented both historically and ethnographically. Flannery (1976:33) notes the connection of maize to lime as revealed by artifacts from the site of Salinas La Blanca in Guatemala:

> A fourth feature of the Salinas La Blanca household cluster would be the sherd or sherd-and-shell midden ... Thousands of the sherds were from neckless jars or *tecomates*, and hundreds of these had a limey crust on the interior, which suggests they were used for boiling or steaming maize in lime water.

> Maize may have been prepared in limewater as a stage in corn drink production—one of the plant's early uses (Sharer 1983:241).

Sherds encrusted with lime deposits are present in ten cases and are not restricted to one ceramic type. In six of the lime-corroded, sherd-lined pits, deposits of lime have formed on more than one sherd type. On the other hand, lime deposits solely on fragments from one vessel of one ceramic type are far less common.

Lime, or calcium carbonate, buildup is a chemical reaction associated with the pH of contact materials and the release of carbon dioxide into those materials. The chemical reaction involved in the formation of calcium carbonate is linked to temperature and/or salinity increases that result in subsequent pH alteration. In features containing high temperatures, lime deposits are more likely to accumulate. An example of this in modern households is rapid lime buildup in warm humidifiers. As water is heated and dispersed about a room, lime accumulates on the inside walls of a humidifier.

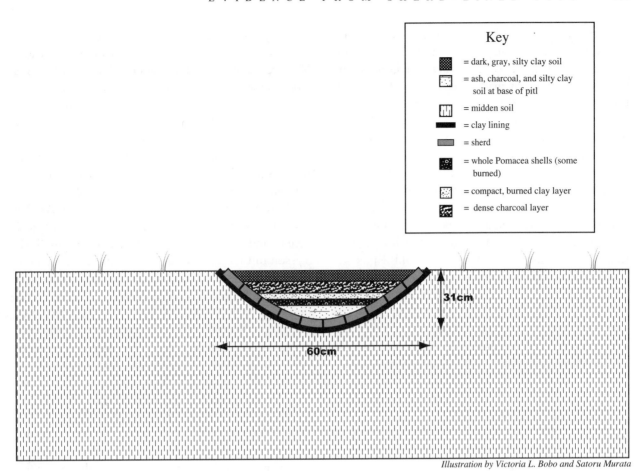

Key

= dark, gray, silty clay soil

= ash, charcoal, and silty clay soil at base of pitl

= midden soil

= clay lining

= sherd

= whole Pomacea shells (some burned)

= compact, burned clay layer

= dense charcoal layer

31cm

60cm

Illustration by Victoria L. Bobo and Satoru Murata

Figure 5.8 Idealized cross-section of sherd-lined pit from operation 1 (zone 114).

The same method of lime buildup may apply to ancient features in which heat was a factor. Frequent soaking of a heated limewater mixture in a sherd-lined facility would produce a situation similar to that produced by a heated humidifier. The following pits contain exaggerated amounts of lime residue: zones 25, 151, 208, 224, and 228 from operation 1; zones 12, 83, 88, 89 from operation 11; and zone 27 from operation 7. It is thus possible to infer lime-soaking activities in instances where lime corrosion is substantial.

It is possible, however, that a combination of soil pH, sherd pH, and the high temperatures sustained within pits during their use may have caused lime corrosion after pits were no longer used. Notably, only 33% of K'axob's sherd-lined pits contain extreme lime corrosion. Sherds from utilitarian vessels excavated from other contexts sometimes reveal fine, lacy calcium carbonate buildup on their interior and exterior surfaces. Lime accumulation in these instances appears linked to natural agents.

In order to address the possibility of natural lime accumulation on sherds in pits, soil pH was considered. For example, Graham (1985:215) has noted leaching of calcite from sherds in acidic soils of the Stann Creek District of Belize. The soils of K'axob, however, have neutral pH values ranging from six to eight (Darch 1983:63). The more acidic values of six come from soil near the surface, whereas deeper soils have more alkaline pH values. Thus, substantial amounts of lime accumulation on excavated sherds from deeply buried sherd-lined pits are more likely the result of activities connected to lime use in the past than of natural buildup.

In the maize-soaking process, boiled maize mixture is allowed to sit overnight and is rinsed the following morning (the softened form is referred to as *kuum*; Sharer 1983:240). Most sherd-lined pits could hold substantial amounts of maize suspended in limewater and may have been constructed when large quantities of maize were processed for special feasts. (The average pit could hold 27 liters.) In this way sherd-lined pits could serve as short-term storage pits for a maize mixture and, therefore, would be useful as secondary features in a boiling process.

If the sherd-lined pits were used as containers for a limewater solution, then leakage prevention would have been a likely issue. As already noted, many pits had a clay, plaster, or marl lining at their base. Such linings are not remarkably permeable and would curtail leakage over the course of one night. Only 50% of the pits with lime encrustation contain secondary linings. Thus, lime-soaking activities in sherd-lined pits may have been limited to only a small number of selected pits, or lime encrustation may have been removed through postexcavation laboratory techniques. The extreme calcium carbonate accumulation, however, suggests that lime-soaking activities constituted a likely function for at least some of the pits.

Pottery production features. The discussion so far has concentrated on functional interpretations focused on cuisine and cooking. An altogether different hypothesis contends that sherd-lined pits may have been used to manufacture ceramics. Studies at Cuello have led Hammond and others (1991) to assert that ceramic-lined pits may have been used as kilns for pottery production. This idea prompts further scrutiny of the sherd-lined pits of K'axob.

Rye (1981:98) has noted that the earliest forms of ceramics were probably manufactured in open fires or pit hearths. If sherd-lined pits were used as firing areas for pottery manufacture, then it is significant to note that at K'axob most pits have been found within Formative levels. During a pit-firing procedure an area is chosen for firing and a hole is dug for placement of fuel and control of the firing space. Ethnographic studies have shown that low mudbrick walls (or baffles) are often constructed around the excavated area, sometimes using the wall of a house as one boundary (Rice 1987a:158). Fuel is placed inside the base of the pit and pots are placed on top of the fuel; more fuel is interspersed around the vessels.

Although open fires often leave little artifactual evidence of pottery firing, pit hearths would be more likely to retain evidence of their use as pottery kilns. As Sinopoli (1991:103) notes, "In household production, firing usually takes place in the open without permanent facilities and leaves little easily identifiable trace in the archaeological record." But when permanent facilities such as sherd-lined pits are constructed, evidence of their use as kilns should be present. This is precisely what has been argued for ceramic-lined basins at Cuello. Features 119 and 87 at Cuello (a ceramic-lined pit and a chultun, respectively) have been cited as possible production areas: "In Bruhn's opinion

... [F87] has yielded wasters, large sherds for protective baffles (such as those found in [F119]), and low-fired sludge which are good evidence of the area from which the chultun contents derived having been used for pottery manufacture" (Hammond and Kosakowsky 1991:174). Thus, elements of a pottery production area that may be found in a pit kiln include wasters, baffles, and hard, baked clay linings that would have resulted from the intense kiln heat. Unfortunately, ceramic pieces that can be positively identified as wasters have not yet been recovered at K'axob. As Rye (1981:8) notes, "Wasters occur wherever pottery was made," and thus their absence at K'axob is more likely a result of their absence at excavated locales. In addition to lack of waster evidence, remains of what could be termed baffles is scant at K'axob. Only six sherd-lined pits bear evidence of what could be interpreted as baffles surrounding one or more sides. Zone 9/27 at operation 12 was defined along one edge by limestone rocks up to 10 cm in diameter. Zone 151b at operation 1 contained rocks around its northwest perimeter, and zone 224 had a limestone rock 13 cm in length excavated from its plaster collar. Operation 12's zone 37 contained two burnt rocks that lined the pit's western side. Zone 34 from operation 11 contained several rocks outlining the feature. Finally, operation 11's zone 83 had five stones forming a semicircle on the northeast side of the pit. At best, these examples are circumstantial and incomplete evidence for baffles at K'axob. Rocks located near the outside of a pit's edge do not directly imply baffles. Perhaps in the future well-preserved baffles will be excavated at the site; however, as yet that evidence is not present.

The evidence for pottery firing in sherd-lined pits at Cuello is hard, clay-baked linings—evidence that high-temperature fires once burned in those features. A bonfire or pit-firing facility may have been the function of several of Cuello's pit features (Hammond, personal communication, 1993). This same evidence of hard-baked pit linings is present at K'axob. Zone 126 of operation 1 featured a plaster lining burned in places, and zone 112 of the same operation was lined with burned plaster as well. However, not all sherd-lined pits from K'axob or Cuello contain burned or baked clay, plaster, or limestone linings. In fact, there are only two examples of burned lining material at K'axob. Several sherd-lined pits were lined with a material that remained unbaked and was sometimes associated with ash or charcoal, implying a function more closely tied to cooking than to pottery production.

Table 5.4 Proposed functions for sherd-lined pits of K'axob (X = definite; P = probable)

| SHERD-LINED PIT PROVENIENCE | | | | | POSSIBLE USES | | |
Operation	Zone	Period	Ceramic Complex	Facet	Steaming	Soaking	Burning
1	208	Middle Formative	Chaakkax	Early			X
1	224	Middle Formative	Chaakkax	Early			P
1	228	Middle Formative	Chaakkax	Early	X	X	X
1	231	Middle Formative	Chaakkax	Early	X	X	X
1	112	Late Formative	K'atabche'kax	Early	X		X
1	114	Late Formative	K'atabche'kax	Early	X		X
1	118	Late Formative	K'atabche'kax	Early	P		P
1	126	Late Formative	K'atabche'kax	Early	X		P
1	136	Late Formative	K'atabche'kax	Early	X		P
1	151	Late Formative	K'atabche'kax	Early	X		P
11	81	Late Formative	K'atabche'kax	Early			X
11	83	Late Formative	K'atabche'kax	Early		X	P
11	85	Late Formative	K'atabche'kax	Early	X		
11	88	Late Formative	K'atabche'kax	Early		X	P
11	89	Late Formative	K'atabche'kax	Early		P	
12	20	Late Formative	K'atabche'kax	Late	P		
1	93	Late Formative	K'atabche'kax	Late			X
7	270	Late Formative	K'atabche'kax	Late	P	P	X
8	12	Late Formative	K'atabche'kax	Late	P		
11	12	Late Formative	K'atabche'kax	Late		X	X
12	9/27	Late Formative	K'atabche'kax	Late	X		P
11	34	Late Formative	K'atabche'kax	Late		P	P
12	10	Late Formative	K'atabche'kax	Late	X		
12	44	Late Formative	K'atabche'kax	Late	X		
1	23	Late Formative	K'atabche'kax	Terminal	P		
1	25	Late Formative	K'atabche'kax	Terminal		X	
7	53	Late Formative	K'atabche'kax	Terminal	X		
12	29	Late Formative	K'atabche'kax	Terminal	X		
12	35	Late Formative	K'atabche'kax	Terminal			
12	37	Late Formative	K'atabche'kax	Terminal	X		P

In sum, the sherd-lined facilities of K'axob appear to have been involved in multiple functions involving steaming, soaking, and burning (table 5.4). As a sample of the pits contained evidence supporting more than one function, it is likely that use regimes varied through time. Early pit uses may have been targeted at one specific activity, and later uses on another. This pattern of change may be particularly relevant to maize processing, which, later on, likely became a more significant part of the diet than is detected in Formative deposits. Ironically, the demise of sherd-lined pits may be linked to the rise of maize as a major staple and the concomitant increase in the scale of maize processing. Just as large striated jars suitable for maize soaking become common at K'axob (McAnany and López Varela 1999), sherd-lined pits disappear as a domestic facility.

Early sherd-lined pits have notable attributes that distinguish them from later examples. For instance, during the Chaakk'ax complex, two sherd-lined pits and one fire pit were constructed in alignment. Aligned sherd-lined pits do not occur during K'axob's later construction phases. Sherd-lined basins from the late facet of the K'atabche'k'ax complex are found as isolated features.

Different cooking methods, such as direct firing versus steam baking, may account for some of the variation between excavated materials in the pits. In addition, various methods of food preparation are suggested by the sherds themselves. In particular, lime soaking seems to have occurred in several pit features throughout the Formative occupation at K'axob.

It is also interesting that sherd-lined features follow a detectable pattern that is seen in several types of excavated features at K'axob and other Maya sites. As constructed facilities, pits were used beyond their original function. For example, zone 16 at operation 11 is a chultun originally constructed as a storage pit that was used as a burial in its last use stage. The same postuse pit function is seen in zone 91 of operation 11, a sherd-lined pit. Burial 11, a seated child, was interred in zone 91 as the final use stage. Burial 11 implies that K'axob Maya used their intrusive features for various activities and ritual interments, and these pits were no exception to such multiple functions. Their use as burial pits may also indicate their importance; mortuary ritual played an important role at K'axob, and it does not seem likely that residents would inter a loved one in a previously used feature that had particularly negative or unimportant connotations.

CONCLUSIONS

The archaeological investigation of sherd-lined intrusions reveals much about Maya history at K'axob and Formative period cuisine in general. What K'axob's sherd-lined intrusions reveal of Maya history is even more enlightening when it is realized that, in general, these facilities are infrequently documented in the archaeological literature. This study of sherd-lined pit characteristics and morphology provides an understanding of the basic procedures behind the formation of sherd linings and the functional tendencies of these features. For example, bimodality of dimensions suggests two standard measurements for both diameter and depth, indicating two size classes for different needs. Artifactual remains within sherd-lined basins also imply multiple functions: lime residue seems to indicate maize preparation, and burnt *Pomacea flagellata* remains signify cooking activity. Linings of clay, plaster, or marl are burned in numerous examples and yet are unaltered in others, adding further testimony to the idea of multiple sherd-lined pit functions. Analyses of morphology, construction, contents, and function of these features ultimately contribute to our knowledge of ancient Maya domestic activities.

Some of the most fundamental knowledge of past civilizations has been acquired through ceramic studies. The research presented herein has shown the value of ceramic fragments in unraveling thoughts and activities of the ancient Maya. In particular, such pits reveal pottery use beyond what is traditionally assigned to whole vessel forms. Maya residents at K'axob chose to line pits with ceramic fragments for cooking procedures. Sherd-lined pits therefore reveal not only domestic activities but also the ingenuity of Maya household strategies of resource use. Continued excavation and research at sites discussed in this study and at other areas of the Maya Lowlands promise to document additional examples of sherd-lined facilities. It is hoped that future research into these distinctive features will further elaborate Maya domestic activities and Formative period cuisine.

ENDNOTE

1. All personal communications with Norman Hammond took place between September of 1993 and April of 1994 in the form of conversations between Hammond and the author regarding the Independent Work for Distinction (Kobza 1994) undertaken at that time by the author.

PART II

MORTUARY RITUAL

Singular both in importance and in chapter number, this part builds on the contextual information presented in Part I by examining another type of pit feature—the mortuary context. Rebecca Storey provides a discussion of 107 ancestors of K'axob, placing each interment within its architectural context. In linking burial features to new construction events or the termination of older domiciles, she provides insight into the larger meaning behind death ritual. In the process, she chronicles broad trends in the position and completeness of skeletons as the complexity of mortuary ritual amplifies, particularly during Terminal K'atabche'k'ax times. Storey discusses the possible family linkages suggested by the many multiple interments of individuals of all ages and both sexes, particularly at the excavation unit (operation 1) placed within plaza B. The repeated presence of a single primary interment surrounded by the secondary remains of at least another adult and a child reinforces this interpretation.

The human remains of K'axob are striking in their inclusion of females and children. The earliest spouted vessel was placed with a female and, overall, three of six such vessels recovered from burial contexts were found with females. On the other hand, one of the earliest and most lavishly adorned burials recovered from K'axob—burial 1-43—is male, as are all identified individuals buried with a vessel upon which the cross motif was painted. If anything, burial rituals of the more populous Terminal K'atabche'k'ax complex demonstrate a trend toward greater elaboration in the interment of young males, a pattern also noted at nearby Cuello. Given the relatively low indices of paleopathologies charted by Storey, this drop in age of death may be attributable to political factors such as increased warfare.

GUIDE TO ACCOMPANYING DIGITAL MATERIALS.

Broad contextual information regarding the location of each burial can be gleaned by referring to the construction phase plans available in the *Domiciles Database*. More specific information regarding each individual interment and associated artifacts can be found in the *Burial Database*, which includes a line drawing of nearly every interment. A record of skeletal elements present in each interment can be examined in the *Skeletal Elements Database*. Associated data sets present detailed information on burial accoutrements and can be queried by provenience or by burial number. These include the following databases: *Pottery Vessels* (which includes color photographic images and some quick-time video images), *Cross Motif Vessels, Obsidian, Worked Shell, Worked Shell from Burial 1-43, Greenstone,* and *Carved Bone*.

Chapter 6
Related CD Resources

Burials
Skeletal Elements
Pottery Vessels
Greenstone
Carved Bone
Worked Shell
Burial 1–43 Worked Shell
Cross Motif Vessels

ANCESTORS: BIOARCHAEOLOGY OF THE HUMAN REMAINS OF K'AXOB

REBECCA STOREY

INTRODUCTION

Burial underneath or near the residence was a common practice among pre-Columbian societies of Central and North America. The dead were not feared, nor were they necessarily placed in a special cemetery away from living residences. This pattern is well discussed for the Maya in McAnany (1995a) and for K'axob specifically in McAnany, Storey, and Lockard (1999). During pre-Columbian times, Maya families often resided in platform mound groups corresponding to kin groups. The disruption of life by death and interment in such contexts would only be expected where family members were transformed into the ancestors who were an integral part of Maya cosmology (see McAnany 1995a; Schele and Friedel 1990). As will be seen at K'axob, burials were placed into functioning use spaces and were also incorporated into construction episodes. The reconstruction of residences and patios among the Maya may be timed to the occurrence of death (Robin 1989).

At K'axob, 107 individuals were recorded within a mortuary context in a domestic setting (see *Burials Database*). Mortuary behavior at K'axob shows variability both within and across the Formative and Early Classic. This behavior reflected increasing elaboration and varying treatment of apparent family members, and it affords insight into the relationships between the living and the dead. A drawback to a full understanding of these relationships is the fact that excavations at K'axob opened only a portion of the residences. Thus, the individuals in this study consist of a sample of those who were buried in and around these residences.

There are two basic types of interment. A primary interment is one in which the individual is placed soon after death, and the skeleton retains its original articulation and reflects its original placement. A secondary interment is one in which the individual is represented by a partial, disarticulated skeleton. Such disarticulation can result from several behaviors, such as reburial of a disturbed primary inhumation, interment of chopped bits of a sacrificed individual, or a process of treatment that reduces a body to skeletonized elements before inhumation. Archaeological context often serves to distinguish among these possibilities, but it is not always possible to discern how a skeleton came to be a secondary interment. Some researchers have considered Maya secondary interments as evidence of sacrifice (see Welsh 1988; Robin 1989). In many cultures, however, secondary interment is part of an important and protracted funerary ritual that can serve a wide range of functions with regard to transferring the honored dead from among the living and reconstituting relationships among the living (Hertz 1960). Sacrificed individuals, on the other hand, usually have marks of defleshing or cutting that indicate dismemberment. A secondary burial is usually incomplete because of the accidental loss, or lack of preservation, of all skeletal elements when the individual was moved from his/her original burial place or place of treatment. A variety of bones seem to be included among K'axob secondary interments, as would be the case if these items had been recovered as carefully as possible. This does not seem to indicate the ritual interment of a recently sacrificed person. However, it is also possible that, in the case of a secondary interment, preferred bones were recovered and considered sufficient to represent the individual. One of the patterns currently under investigation is the differential presence of K'axob skeletal elements according to type of interment. This analysis will allow for greater discrimination between preservation biases and intentional selection of elements for reburial (see *Skeletal Elements Database*). At K'axob there are scattered and bundled secondary interments, and there is no clear evidence that any individuals were defleshed or cut before interment.

At this point, sex and age determinations are somewhat preliminary. Because of the humid burial environment, K'axob skeletons are fragmentary and eroded. Standard osteological techniques were applied (Buikstra and Ubelaker 1994), and sex was determined by morphological differences (mostly of the skull). A preliminary division of males and females was based on robusticity of long bones. Age was determined for juveniles by tooth formation and eruption standards. For adults, age was estimated within broad age categories based on a preliminary ranking of tooth wear. Young adults would be in their twenties, while older adults would be over fifty at death. All age and sex determinations are tentative, pending the results of ongoing analyses. The same caveat pertains to paleopathological indicators of health, such as childhood anemia, infectious conditions, and stresses during growth. When appropriate, age and sex patterns, health indicators, and mortuary behavior are compared with the contemporary site of Cuello.

The available skeletons provide a window into the ritual behavior and living conditions of the people of K'axob. Accordingly, the discussion of burial ritual is organized chronologically, beginning with the earliest known interments of the Chaakk'ax complex and ending with early facet Nohalk'ax burials. The discussion of individuals within their architectural context is followed by an examination of health indicators for this sample of Formative Maya villagers.

MORTUARY PATTERNS OF K'AXOB BURIALS

Early facet, Chaakk'ax ceramic complex

There were eight interments, comprising nine individuals, in this ceramic complex. All were from the operation 1 trench, representing the earliest known inhabitants of the village of K'axob. The dominant mode was extended, primary inhumation of a single individual in simple earthen pits, with minor use of secondary interments. All appeared to be buried underneath a domestic structure and were probably members of the main kin group of the household. There were four adults and five juveniles.

The very earliest construction at K'axob was built directly on the paleosol. It consisted of a perishable structure recognizable from postholes cut into the paleosol. Two single, extended primary inhumations, cut into the paleosol, were associated with this first structure (burials 1-43 and 1-46). Already, at this early point, there were differences in the mortuary treatment of different individuals. Burial 1-46 is a middle-aged adult female, an extended, primary interment lying partially on her right side, with the head to the southeast. Her only accompaniment was a very small shell bead found in the pelvic area. Burial 1-43, on the other hand, is one of the most richly accompanied burials at Formative K'axob (figure 6.1). More robust than burial 1-46, this young/middle-aged adult would have been a gracile male. He was accompanied by two inverted vessels (one over the head and the other near the head); two shell-bead bracelets; two shell-bead armbands; and many beads that were clustered near the head, torso, and pelvic areas (and probably had been embroidered onto a robe or shroud). He was also adorned with a

Burial 1-43

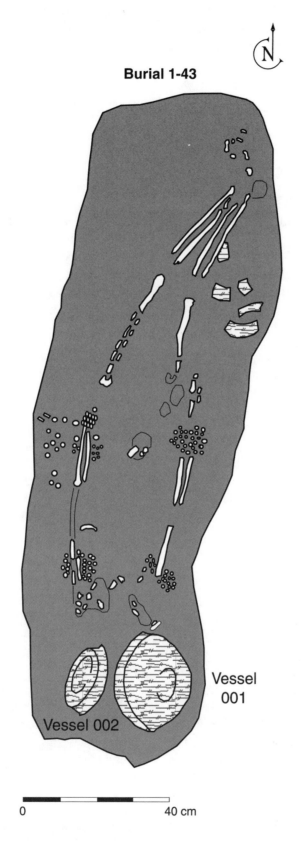

0   40 cm

Figure 6.1 Burial 1-43. *All illustrations prepared by K'axob Project staff and staff of UCLA Cotsen Institute Digital Archaeology Laboratory*

tubular bead of jadeite. His feet pointed north and, interestingly, his body lay in a prone position (determined because the identifiable right side bones were on the left side of the body). The direction of the face is not accurately reconstructable but was probably toward the earth (given the lower position of the teeth). Vessels covering the head are a common pattern among Maya burials, but here they were probably not placed directly over the face. The prone position is uncommon among extended burials, which are generally placed on the back or side, and this may be an indication of the special status of this individual.

The priority and characteristics of these burials make it seem as though these individuals were one of the founding couples of K'axob. Burial 1-43 certainly seems to fit such a description; he had a special status during life, and this is commemorated by the shell adornment, ceramics, and the expense of an article of clothing embellished with shell beads. Burial 1-46 may be burial 1-43's spouse, dying at a different time and meriting no special accompaniments.

Sometime after these burials, a more substantial dwelling was built here, the first of a series of structures. Six interments were associated with structure 1i, with two burials (1-37 and 1-39) apparently being the termination events, as a new floor and structure were constructed shortly after the placement of these two individuals. Four interment episodes preceded them. Burial 1-40 was apparently placed into a subfloor/midden area of the structure. This single, extended, primary inhumation was partially disturbed some time after burial. A child of about five to seven years of age, the head was outlined with a semicircle of limestone rocks. Three freshwater *Pomacea* shells were placed around the feet. Part of this individual's skeleton was interred with burial 1-38, which consisted of the teeth and part of the humerus of a young adult male. Placed in a collared, partially sherd-lined pit, burial 1-38 is definitely a secondary interment of a very partial skeleton, although it had been placed with some care. The teeth were found all together, including some of those of burial 1-40; other bones were scattered nearby but were not bundled. There was one shell bead with this secondary interment. The pit was probably used for culinary purposes and, when abandoned, served as a receptacle for disturbed burials 1-38 and 1-40. This multiple secondary interment probably resulted from the expedient reburial of skeletons that had been accidentally disturbed, most probably by construction activities.

Burial 1-42 was placed in a pit dug through the plaster floor of the structure, which was later partially repaired. This burial is that of an adult male, accompanied by two shell beads, a bone bead, and a piece of hematite. Finer aging is not possible because only long bones were present and only part of the legs were recovered. The burial position and type for this individual are difficult to determine. The right leg appears to have been articulated but, by its position in the pit, cannot be from either an extended or flexed burial (see illustration in *Burials Database*). The length and depth of the pit, 1.1 x 1 m, was not large enough for either a semiflexed burial with bent knees or a seated burial with bent, crossed legs. The spread of bones in the pit indicated a scattered secondary interment, with partial articulation of some elements maintained.

Burial 1-35, placed in a simple pit under a work area inside the structure, was also a secondary interment. This skeleton consisted of just the skull and teeth of a child who was two to three years old at death. It was accompanied by three shell beads and eleven small shell tinklers. Robin (1989) and others have suggested that such a burial (parts of a child placed in a pit sprinkled with shell) might be evidence of child sacrifice. It is arguable that burial 1-35 could be a dedicatory sacrifice for a new structure. The bone is too deteriorated to detect evidence of cutting or other modifications that might clearly indicate sacrifice. As discussed above, burials 1-38 and 1-42 are composed of pieces of previous burials that were disturbed or moved (from where is unknown but probably nearby). Both were placed with some care in a new place, possibly with some of their original offerings or with new shell beads. Even the burial 1-40 child had its disturbed parts reburied with burial 1-38, but the rest of that skeleton remained unaffected. The child of burial 1-35 could also be a redeposited disturbed interment with original or new offerings to accompany the cranium.

Burials 1-37 and 1-39 represent individuals whose deaths either initiated a rebuilding of the structure or coincided with a decision to rebuild. Their situation does not indicate which of these scenarios might be more reasonable. Burial 1-39 is an extended primary interment bisected by a later interment. This infant, around nine months of age at death, was accompanied by no offerings. Burial 1-37 actually contained two individuals, but the main individual was placed as an extended, primary inhumation. There was a whole marine shell over the heart and a shell bead near the right hand. This juvenile, eleven to thirteen years of age at death, was found with the skeletal parts of a perinate, a possible newborn. Because the excavators were not aware that these bones belonged to a second individual, it is not known where the baby was placed in relation to the main interment. This does hamper interpretation as the perinate was very fragmentary and small. This kind of mortuary context brings the past alive with a particular poignancy. It is, of course, possible that this is not a case of a mother and baby dying in childbirth but of two deaths within a residential group occurring at about the same time and receiving a dual interment. The juvenile (given preservation conditions sex cannot even be hinted at) seems to be young for motherhood, but it is certainly biologically possible. For a young adolescent, the prognosis for a successful pregnancy would not have been good and thus death in childbirth may be indicated. If the baby had still been inside the mother, then the case would have been strengthened, but we shall probably never know. It is possible that the proximate deaths of an older baby of the family and a young mother-to-be (recently married into the family?) spurred the closure of this first structure and the construction of a new residence.

Summary. Primary, extended interment of a single individual in an earthen pit was the most frequent burial treatment, but there were variations. Of the two multiple interments, one is a possible mother and child, and the other is the secondary interment of two individuals. Only three of nine individuals were secondary. Two individuals apparently had no offerings, while all the others were at least accompanied by shell beads. The richest burial was that of a primary adult, while the second richest was the secondary interment of a child. The multiple secondary interment was in a collared, partially sherd-lined pit, and one child had a partial cist about the head. The secondary interments were of partial skeletons, with the bones scattered in a pit and at least one shell bead included.

During the early facet, four adults and five juveniles were interred under an active residence, a pattern expected for a prehistoric household in which juvenile mortality would be likely to predominate. There were three males and at least one (and possibly two) females present. None of the adults was old. The death age of the three juveniles place them in a high-risk category. The older child and young adolescent are from an age range whose mortality rate is usually dramatically less than that of young children. Their loss would have been keenly felt by the household. In short, six out of nine individuals (67%) of this facet who were buried

under the structure died while still in their prime. The demographic and mortuary characteristics of this sample are consistent with deaths and interments that might occur within a family group.

Late facet, Chaakk'ax complex

During this period, structure 1 was rebuilt and resurfaced; the new structure, 1h, was shifted slightly to the east. Three interments of single individuals were associated with this facet. Burial 1-28 was placed inside the southern edge of the structure; the individual was extended and slightly rotated to her right side. The young/middle-aged female had a vessel covering her head and was accompanied by another vessel and thirty-two shell beads. Burial 1-33 was cut into the structure floor and placed in a small, shallow pit. Although excavators noted that burial 1-33 might be the remains of a disturbed primary extended burial, with the lower legs extending beyond the excavation, the few bones present and the shallowness of the pit indicate a probable secondary bundle of femora, teeth, and phalanges. This young adult male was accompanied by no offerings. Again, as in the earlier facet, this context seems to represent the expedient reburial of a disturbed individual. Both of these burials were probably interred only at the end of the use life of structure 1h. It may be that the death of an important female (burial 1-28) initiated a termination of this structure.

Burial 1-30a was also an extended primary burial, with lower legs cut by a later interment. This individual was placed outside the structure, under the midden/activity surface west of it. Badly deteriorated, this young adult, sex indeterminate, was accompanied by two vessels (one covering the head) and fourteen shell beads. This was the earliest interment outside of a residential structure and was probably placed during a time when the area was in use. Very similar in burial accoutrements to those of interments placed inside the structure, this interment seems to indicate that no particular stigma was attached to the extramural placement of this individual. Later facets feature both elaborate and simply adorned burials inside and outside of structures, so that the whole of the domestic space was seen as proper for burial.

Summary. Only prime-age adults were recovered from this facet. In general, the primary burials were more richly endowed than were earlier burials (except for burial 1-43), while the secondary interment had no offerings (all secondary remains from the early facet contained shell offerings). There were no multiple interments, and all were placed within simple pits. This summarizes the differences between the two facets of this complex. It is a small sample, thus making it difficult to form generalizations, especially as later periods display a more inclusive age range. This sample contains too few burials to represent all the deaths that must have occurred within a couple of household generations, so many of the deceased must have been interred in areas that were not excavated. One pattern that contrasts with that of later interments is that both primary interments were buried with more shell beads than were found in any subsequent interments.

THE MIDDLE FORMATIVE (800–400 BC) BURIALS OF K'AXOB IN COMPARATIVE CONTEXT

Establishment of the village of K'axob yielded a family interment pattern of twelve individuals, presumably kin members, buried in simple pits under and around a functioning domestic residence. Single, extended interments predominated, but there are four secondary interments as well. All but one were placed inside of structures. All but three included grave offerings, and two of the unadorned were juveniles. The offerings consisted of shell and ceramics, usually only a couple of shell beads. The heads of three adults had been covered with a vessel; these interments also contained more shell artifacts than did those without head coverings (except for the secondary interment of a child with fourteen shell ornaments). Thus, from the beginning there were differences in mortuary elaboration, and this probably reflected social distinctions among members of the kin group. Adults appear to have been buried with more offerings than children.

Comparison with the nearby contemporary, but somewhat more precocious, Cuello site is instructive. The Middle Formative begins a bit earlier at Cuello but bears architectural similarities to K'axob (Hammond et al. 1995). Again, the burials were associated with functioning residences and are considered family burials (Robin and Hammond 1991). Comprising fifty-five individuals (Saul and Saul 1997), the Cuello Middle Formative sample is considerably larger than that at K'axob; the Bladen and Mamom phases provide temporal equivalents to the K'axob Chaakk'ax complex. The six individuals of the Swasey phase (1200-900 BC) likely predate any recovered burials at K'axob. The Swasey burials—both primary extended and flexed interments—generally lacked grave goods

(Hammond et al. 1995). Grave goods appeared during the transition to the Bladen phase (900-650 BC). The eighteen individuals of the Bladen phase probably overlapped with the early facet of the Chaakk'ax, while the thirty-one Mamom (650-400 BC) interments spanned both facets of the Chaakk'ax complex.

The Bladen and Mamom burials (compiled from Robin and Hammond 1991; Hammond et al. 1991; Hammond et al. 1992; Hammond et al. 1995) include more adults (thirty-two) than juveniles (seventeen), and the sexes are unequally represented: twenty adult males, ten adult females, and four undetermined. Most were placed in simple pits, and all but one appear to have been placed inside structures. All were single interments and, at Cuello, head-covering vessels were more common (found with twenty-four of forty-nine interments).

There are two salient differences between Cuello and K'axob burials from this time. The first distinction lies in the greater variety in Cuello burial positions, which include flexed burials and possibly an early seated burial (Robin and Hammond 1991:207). However, the putative seated individual, burial 9, has cut marks on several bones and red ocher on others. Robin (1989) comments that this individual was defleshed before burial. This context was not completely excavated, but a seated position does not seem likely. The description is more consistent with a probable secondary bundle, with the cranium placed on top. With its four vessels and jade ornaments, the painted skeleton could be an early example of mortuary behavior that was common in the Late Formative at K'axob—the curation and careful bundling of an important person who was reburied with some pomp and wealth in the patio of the residence. At Cuello, by Mamom times 81% of the interments were extended, and flexed burials had become less common. The second difference between Cuello and K'axob lies in the greater variety and wealth of burial goods at Cuello and the clear access to jade, which is found with twelve individuals. All juveniles had grave goods and five of them were adorned with jade, which stands in stark contrast to K'axob. Thus, as at K'axob, mortuary treatment gives evidence of social differentiation; however, wealth crosscuts age and sex more emphatically at Cuello than at K'axob.

Summary. During the Middle Formative period, certain patterns were present at both K'axob and Cuello. Single interments were common, and most primary interments were extended and supine. Simple pits predominated, and all ages and both sexes received burial, primarily inside residences. Most individuals were buried with shell as a grave offering, while ceramic vessels were the next most common grave good. A pattern of a head-covering vessel was present, although more common at Cuello than at K'axob. Secondary interments were present but not common. Some burials were richly endowed, especially at Cuello, while others were not. In short, both sites exhibit a clear domestic, family-member pattern of interment, with some indications of social differentiation.

Early facet, K'atabche'k'ax complex

This facet marked a transitional time, when the Middle Formative burial patterns of K'axob were transformed into the strikingly different mortuary traditions of the Late Formative period. During this time, residential construction and interment was detected beyond operation 1, resulting in a burial population of twenty-one individuals: fourteen from operation 1 and seven from operation 11. The characteristics of the burials still reflect primarily residential contexts, but expansion and increasing social differentiation within the village are also evident in this larger sample of twenty-one skeletons.

At operation 1, the plaza activity area became an important locus for burials, as seven individuals (burials 1-24, 1-44, 1-30, 1-31, 1-34a, 1-34b, and 1-26) were placed beneath plaza floors. An additional seven individuals (burials 1-27, 1-32, 1-25, 1-29, 1-18, 1-19a, and 1-19b) were associated with construction phases 5 to 7 of structure 1, which underwent several rebuilding episodes and floor raisings during the early facet.

The activity area of the plaza appeared to have been the locus of the earliest interments. Burial 1-24, a probable older female, was a primary burial that had been disturbed and subsequently partially bundled. Several parts of the skeleton were apparently reconstituted as a bundle in one part of the original pit, with a vessel head covering and two shell beads. Parts of the skeleton—including pieces of vertebrae, the hands, and some long bones—were found in the disturbed portion of the pit along with a piece of jade. Burial 1-24 seems to have been disturbed and then respectfully reinterred, although no effort seems to have been made to recover all of the skeleton for repositioning as a bundle. As no new interment was placed here at this time, the reason for the disturbance is unknown.

Interestingly, under burial 1-24, there was a thin plaster cap below which a few long bones (burial 1-44) had been placed. These bones were poorly preserved, but by size and position this appears to be the secondary interment of a child (finer aging may not be possible). How much time elapsed between this secondary interment and the overlying burial 1-24 is unknown, but they are presently considered to be two separate interment episodes.

Structure 1g represents the next rebuilding of the domestic structure, although the white plaster and clay floor (zone 134) did not cover all of it. Two burials (an adolescent and a child) were placed close together within this floor. Burial 1-32 was first, an extended supine primary interment accompanied by a *yuntun* (limestone sphere, today used as slingshot ammunition), a shell bead, and three *Pomacea* shells positioned along the head of the pit. The burial was disturbed (the skeleton is only partial) and the lower legs are missing, possibly due to the disturbance caused by placement of overlying burial 1-27. The skull of burial 1-32 is also missing, although teeth are present, which likely indicates poor preservation rather than removal of the head. This adolescent was twelve to thirteen years old, sex undetermined. The interment of burial 1-27 was the last event of this structure. This primary, extended, supine interment of a five- to six-year-old child was poorly preserved. The interment was accompanied by two ceramic vessels (not covering the head), a worked shell pendant, and a *Pomacea* shell near the knee. It was the death and interment of a child that marked the end of the use of this structure, a pattern also seen in the Early Chaakk'ax facet.

Nearly contemporary with structure 1g was structure 2, to the west, a short-term or temporary apsidal structure with a plaster floor. Two burial pits were prepared under this structure, but their context indicates that they were placed before the structure was built, probably when the area was part of the activity/work area of the plaza. Burial 1-30 was a deposit of solely lower legs and feet, with a probable secondary interment placed without any offerings or particular care. Most likely a young/middle-aged male is represented by these bones. As before, this deposit may represent a convenient reburial of an individual from elsewhere. Burials 1-31 and 1-34, however, represented an intentional multiple burial, the first at K'axob (figure 6.2). The two multiple interments of the Early Chaakk'ax facet may be regarded as expedient—two disturbed burials in one case and a probable mother and unborn baby in the other. In this case, burial 1-34a was the main interment, consisting of a primary, extended,

Burials 1-31, 1-34a, and 1-34b

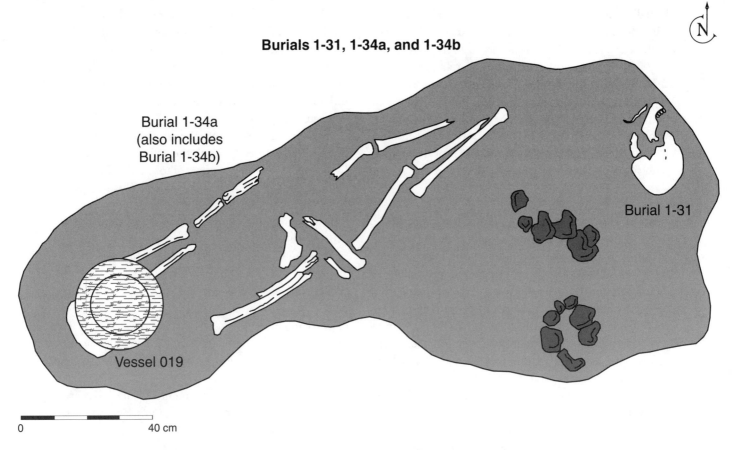

Figure 6.2 Burials 1-34 and 31

supine individual with slightly flexed legs. A middle-aged/older female, she was interred with a head-covering vessel and four shell beads (probably a necklace). Burial 1-31 was placed to the east of burial 34a and appears to be a secondary bundle interment containing a complete cranium and a few other skeletal parts. This old adult male was interred with one shell bead and a *Pomacea* shell. Mixed with the burial 1-34a bones, and not observed by the excavators in the field, were pieces of a two- to three-year-old child, burial 1-34b. Thus, while one cannot be sure, the child's bones seem to indicate a probable secondary interment, likely moved here for final interment. It is tempting to define this as a family group, a prominent husband and wife with an offspring who died young, all brought together when the last one (the woman) died. They were buried within an activity area and not beneath the floor of the residence.

After several construction episodes at structure 1, during which no interment took place, burials 1-25 and 1-29 were placed within the eroded floor of structure

1e (figure 6.3). These were two separate burial events, both placed into the same pit, the latter positioned so as not to disturb the former. Burial 1-29 was the first, a primary, extended, supine interment of a middle-aged adult male. This interment included one dish under the right humerus and two shell beads. Burial 1-25, an extended, primary, supine interment, was placed above the other, although the burial cut was slightly different. The time lag between the two episodes was probably fairly short as the position of the earlier burial seems to have been known and followed during the placement of the new grave cut. Burial 1-25 is an older adult male, accompanied by an inverted vessel found above the head, a piece of jade, and four shell beads. The two vessels with these males are interesting as their exterior bases are painted with the earliest manifestations of a quadripartite or cross motif (see chapter 16). This important Maya motif appears in selected burial contexts at structure 1 but is not found at any other residences. It may indicate the centrality of this residence (McAnany and López Varela 1999) and, perhaps, the power and prestige of the

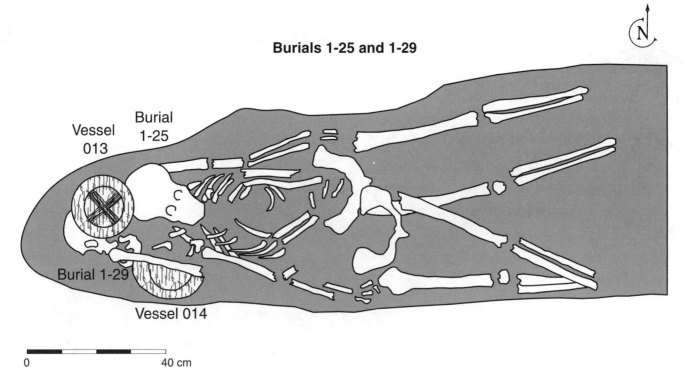

Burials 1-25 and 1-29

Figure 6.3 Burials 1-25 and 1-29

lineage. These individuals were the first to have their burial locale marked with this motif. The floor was eroded, but apparently the last of these interments did not mark a termination of this phase of structure 1. These burials were apparently intruded through the floor, the pits refilled, and the residence reoccupied.

The final construction phase of this facet resulted in structure 1d, a small circular platform into the floor of which another multiple interment was placed (figure 6.4). Burial 1-19a was the main interment, a primary, extended, supine skeleton of a middle-aged/older adult female. She was accompanied by two ceramic containers (including the earliest spouted vessel at K'axob), a piece of worked shell, and some *Pomacea*. Burial 1-18, a child of four to five years, was placed in the pit at the same time. Interestingly, this individual was placed in the lap of the primary interment. The child is represented by a complete skull that was covered by a dish, which also contained five shell beads that may originally have been part of a headdress. This secondary interment only consisted of a skull, a few teeth, pieces of mandible, and a few fragments of the upper torso. Another secondary individual (burial 1-19b), a young/middle-aged adult of indeterminate sex, was also present in this pit. This individual was not recognized in the excavation because the bones were intermingled with the main interment. There are only a few parts of this individual who, like burial 1-18, was secondarily interred at this location. The death and interment of the 1-19a female seems to have provided the opportunity to place with her these other two individuals, most likely to reunite some sort of family group. Certainly, the close physical proximity of the three individuals would seem to indicate this. This important burial context was marked by the distinctive accoutrements of the child and female and by the fact that the burial pit was sprinkled with hematite, the earliest mortuary receptacle to receive this treatment. This ceremony may have been a termination event for this particular structure.

Burial 1-26 was placed in the plaza area and was clearly mixed with midden material. This was the secondary interment of a probable middle/older adult male. The bones appear to have been scattered (some were upright) and had a shell bead and *Pomacea* shell placed with them; they were not arranged in a well-defined bundle. Thus, this secondary interment harkens back to the Chaakk'ax pattern. It appears to be an easily accomplished reinterment of a disturbed skeleton.

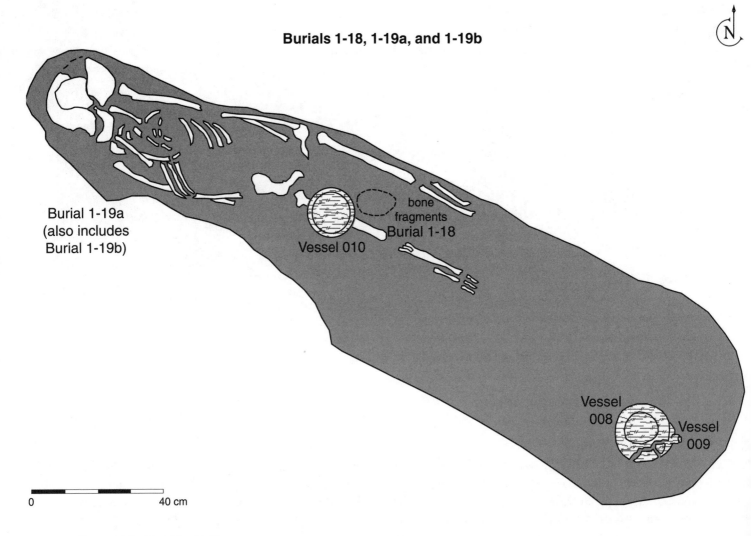

Figure 6.4 Burials 1-18 and 1-19

During the early facet of the K'atabche'k'ax complex, other residential groups were functioning and burials were interred at operation 11 (see figure 2.2 for location of operation). This patio group containing structure 27 is located on a topographic rise approximately 200 m northwest of structure 1. The operation 11 excavation was positioned on the eastern side of the mound in order to avoid disturbing later deposits and to maximize access to Formative period construction. The earliest deposits here are domestic and are similar to those of operation 1, with floors and domestic refuse. Seven individuals were interred in five burial pits.

The earliest domicile is structure 6, with a partially preserved sascab floor. Two burial pits (containing burials 11-11, 11-12a, and 11-12b) were placed within this structure. Burial 11-11 was an infant (six to twelve

months) who was interred in a pit with a sherd-lined collar that had been built into the floor of structure 6. Apparently, the body was seated but accompanied by no offerings and may have been associated with the termination of this structure. Burial 11-12a, an extended and supine interment, was placed within the walls rather than into the structure floor. Part of a multiple interment, this middle-aged female was buried with the bones of a perinate (or newborn), burial 11-12b. Again, this interment is probably a mother and child who died during childbirth or shortly thereafter (although the female should be considered to have been near the end of her childbearing years). The female had a vessel inverted over her chest and some *Pomacea* shells around her feet. This represents the earliest recovered interment of operation 11.

Burial 11-10

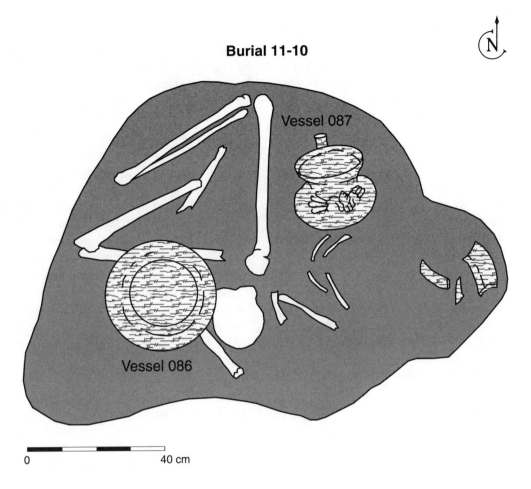

Vessel 087

Vessel 086

0   40 cm

Figure 6.5 Burial 11-10

Structure 5 was apparently constructed only slightly later than structure 6 and was finished with a plaster floor. A large pit intrudes into the floor and contains burial 11-10 (figure 6.5), a seated old adult male. He was facing toward the northwest although his head was turned to the east. Two vessels were set on either side of his body, one of which was a spouted jar (vessel 087) with a duck-effigy design (see chapter 9). *Pomacea* shells were scattered around the body. In light of the ritual and circumstances of burial, during the early occupation of the patio group this individual probably held an important leadership position. This interment may indicate the termination of structure 5.

Structure 4 was constructed some time later. Intruded into its poorly preserved floor was a shallow pit containing burial 11-9. This primary, flexed interment of an infant, six to twelve months old at death, was accompanied by the sherds of half a vessel. The construction of a new building platform of structure 3

on top of structure 4 yielded, in the construction fill, the multiple interment of burials 11-7 and 11-8. Both were seated with crossed legs, facing different directions. Burial 11-7 is a five- to eight-year-old child accompanied by half of a pottery vessel and two pieces of worked shell. Burial 11-8 is an infant around six months of age, with no offerings. It is possible that the coeval deaths of two children in the family motivated the termination of one structure and the construction of another, as was also seen in operation 1.

Summary of operations 1 and 11. In operation 1, the fourteen individuals of this facet can be divided equally into two categories. Seven were buried in the plaza/activity area and seven within the structure. Seven were primary, extended, supine burials and seven were secondary. There are five subadults and eight adults; of the adults, three are female, four are male, and one is undetermined. Three were older adults (two males, one female), three were middle-aged to old (one male, two females), and two were young to middle-aged adults (one male, one undetermined). All primary interments were extended, supine, and accompanied by offerings. Two were subadults; of the adults, three were female and two were male. Among the seven secondary interments, there were both scattered and carefully bundled ones. Four of these had no offerings, but the other three, two bundled and one scattered, certainly did. Three subadults were secondary, while only males, plus the unknown adult, were secondary. All interments were placed in simple pits, although burial 1-44 had a thin plaster cap over it.

While there were obviously many continuities in the mortuary patterns from the Chaakk'ax complex, several of these interments display patterns not previously seen. Burial 1-24 was disturbed after placement but partly reconstituted as a bundle, and part of the skeleton was apparently left disturbed and unrecovered. This is similar to Early Chaakk'ax burial 1-40. The sequential interments of burial 1-25 and 1-29, in which the later burial was placed almost on top of the earlier one, could indicate that the placement of the earlier burial was remembered and respected.

The two multiple interments of three individuals each seem to indicate a new mortuary pattern. In both cases, a primary interment's death triggered a reburial of two other individuals with the main interment. The patterns are such that a family group may be reconstituted, in each case including a child and another adult. In both cases the main interment is a female and, at least in one case, the bundle placed by the head of the female contained the bones of an adult male. The reburial of children is particularly compelling. Children certainly were buried in their own right in this residential group, but long-term curation was involved in the burial of a child elsewhere, with later exhumation and reunification with the parents after what could have been many years. The poor preservation of the skeletons at K'axob means that it may not be possible to test relationships, but it is an avenue of inquiry that will be pursued in the future.

The offerings for this facet suggest some measure of wealth. Shell is ubiquitous, as are fine pottery vessels. Jade is found with one male and one probable female, and one multiple interment had hematite sprinkled over it. Only four of the individuals had a head-covering vessel, and they included the two adults with jade. It seems that males and females were fairly equally treated, as was the case in the very small sample of the Late Chaakk'ax. Both sexes were interred within

structures as well as plaza areas. Children are also found in both locations, although they generally have fewer offerings than do adults. One child (burial 1-18) had a head-covering vessel and beads; it appeared as though the head and vessel had been carefully moved when the child was reburied. So far, this individual is the youngest at K'axob to be distinguished by a head covering. Children are usually considered to be too young to have the respect of their society, so their lavish treatment in death is likely to be a reflection of the wealth and importance of their family. Certainly, most of the children interred here reflect the wealth and influence of the family that lived in this residential group.

It may be rash to distinguish any of the burials as being more important than others. Nevertheless, burial 1-25—an old adult male with a cross-motif vessel covering his head, a piece of jadeite, and four shell beads—may have been an important leader in K'axob society. Burial 1-29, which preceded burial 1-25, also had a cross-motif vessel, but it lacked jade and received only two shell beads. The vessel was not covering the head, although it is possible that it had slipped. Since these are sequential interments within the same place in the structure, it may be that this was how leaders were memorialized at this time. Interestingly, these burials are the first since burial 1-43 whose characteristics might indicate office or position. During this facet, the burial pattern is generally primary extended or secondary with burial offerings, usually including pottery and shell of some sort, although the amount of shell diminished over time (see chapter 14). The family grouping of burials 1-18 and 1-19 might also be distinguished by virtue of the juvenile with a head covering, the sprinkling of hematite on the interments, and the earliest spouted vessel with the female.

In this facet, the ages at death of the individuals of structure 1 are notable in that the adults are mostly older, with only two (burials 1-30 and 1-19b) being prime age and dying prematurely. Of the five subadults, two (burials 1-44 and 1-34b) are young enough to have died during the most risky years for juveniles. The other subadults are either older children or young adolescents whose deaths might have been unexpected and thus more shocking. These are the subadults with offerings. The burial complement does appear to reflect a domestic residence with family members and deaths that might be expected through several generations, although to reflect actual mortality one would expect more infants and young children. It could be that such individuals either were no longer carefully interred around the residence or were placed in a location that was not excavated.

In the satellite group, the earliest structures contained interments. There were two adults (a male and a female), a child, and four infants. The seated and flexed positions appeared, and none of the individuals had a vessel inverted over his/her head. These are different interments from those of operation 1, which had no seated burials at this time. The adults had offerings, and the juveniles had very little. Except for burial 11-10, these burials are impoverished compared to the primary interments of operation 1, possibly indicating the subordinate status of the residents of this group. The death of a female in childbirth and the deaths of four children (although neither uncommon nor totally unexpected) represent deaths that could jeopardize the continued reproduction of a village. Burial of the old male (burial 11-10) was somewhat different. A large intrusive pit was constructed for his interment, and the circumstances of his offerings and position indicate planning, care, and respect. This was probably the commemoration of an important family leader, with his interment marking the termination of use of the structure.

Late facet, K'atabche'k'ax complex

During this facet there was an increasing number of burials and increasing mortuary elaboration (McAnany and López Varela 1999; McAnany, Storey, and Lockard 1999). Twenty individuals were interred at operation 1, six at operation 8, two at operation 10, four at operation 11, and eight at operation 12. Within operation 1, structure 1 became a rectangular platform with a stone retaining wall and plaster surface. The debris indicates that this building remained a multiuse structure incorporating both quotidian and ritual activities.

The first interment in this reformulated structure 1 was burial 1-23—an extended, supine primary interment—which was placed into a pit cut into the first floor. This middle-aged adult, probably a male, was accompanied by a bowl positioned near the left humerus, three shell beads, and a cache of *Pomacea* shells around the legs. Shortly after he was interred, there was a resurfacing of the structure; thus, this individual was the terminating event for the earlier floor. With the resurfacing of the structure, there were several interments associated with the new floor, two multiple and one single. The single interment (burial 1-14) is a supine child who was around two years old at death and who

was buried in an extended position with bent legs. The child had moderately rich offerings of a ceramic vessel (between the legs), two shell beads, a shell pendant figurine carved into a death's head (possibly part of a pubic shield), and a marine bivalve. The vessel contained six shark vertebrae. The elaborate treatment of this young child, who died during the most vulnerable years, must reflect the status of the parents or the household. This single interment was proximate to a slightly later group interment, burials 1-4, 1-10, and 1-11.

The three individuals in this latter interment were positioned close together but, in keeping with the pattern of earlier multiple interments, were probably buried sequentially rather than all at once. The burial pits overlapped, and that is why this can be considered a multiple interment. The closest analogue in this plaza is burials 1-25 and 1-29 of the previous facet. In this case, the two main interments shared part of a burial pit, and the later one slightly displaced the arm of the earlier one. The first interment was burial 1-10, a primary, extended, supine interment of a middle-aged female. She was accompanied by a ceramic vessel covering her head and a cache of *Pomacea* shells under her knees. Some time later, after burial 1-10 had been reduced to a skeleton, burial 1-11 was interred slightly to the north. This is a primary, semi-flexed interment of a middle-aged to older adult female with no associated grave goods. A slightly different pit was dug to bury this individual, but the body was allowed to overlap with the earlier one. Then, probably at a later time, a third individual (burial 1-4) was interred as a secondary bundle above the legs of 1-10, within the 1-10 burial pit. This individual was an older child/young adolescent who was accompanied by a sharply incurving bowl that resembles a tecomate (vessel 042). There was no attempt to put burials 1-10 and 1-11 in the same pit, but there was also no attempt to separate them.

The multiple interment of burial 1-17 was roughly contemporaneous with burials 1-4, 1-10, and 1-11 and was located immediately to the south. A true multiple interment, this pit contained three individuals who had been buried at the same time. Also a termination event for this floor, the main interment (burial 1-17a) was a primary, extended, supine, old adult, sex indeterminate. This individual received two ceramic vessels (one covering the head), one shell bead, one piece of worked shell, and some *Pomacea* scattered around the body. There were also parts of two juveniles who were not recognized in the field and thus their position and placement is unknown. Because of the very

Burials 1-12 and 1-41

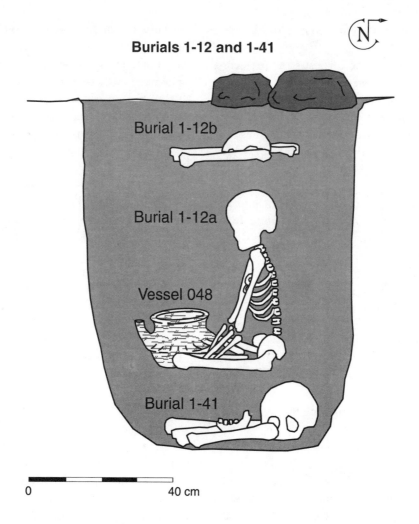

0   40 cm

Figure 6.6 Burials 1-41 and 1-12

fragmentary nature of the juvenile remains, it is likely that they were both secondary interments consisting mostly of crania. One (burial 1-17b) was a child of three to four years, and the other (burial 1-17c) was around one year old. Again, this deposit probably represents the posthumous gathering of a family group. All of the interments within this floor were clustered close together and did not by any means fill all of the available space. Thus, burial was limited to a particular part of the structure and may have been marked in some fashion on the overlying floor.

The exterior plaza floor area contemporaneous with the above burials also contained interments. Burial 1-13 was a single interment of a primary, flexed old adult, probably male, placed just off the northwest corner of structure 1. A bowl (vessel 046) with a quadripartite motif painted on the exterior base was placed

over the head, and a spouted effigy vessel (vessel 047, see chapter 9) was placed next to the body. In addition, eleven *Pomacea* shells were placed around the head, and a portion of a golden chert biface was reduced over the body (see chapter 11). The circumstances of this burial plus the presence of the cross motif suggests that this individual was moderately important. It is significant that he was buried in the more public plaza, close to the structure, rather than within it, as would have been the case earlier.

The plaza was the locale of a multiple interment (figure 6.6) that is similar in some ways to the grouping of burials 1-4, 1-10, and 1-11 inside the structure. Near the west wall of the excavation unit a pit was prepared for the bundled secondary remains of burial 1-41, an old adult, probably male. This individual consisted only of the upper body and cranium. A shell necklace consisting of a carved frog pendant bracketed by two rectangular shell beads was placed under the cranium. The placement of the grave goods on this individual is an indication of his being carefully bundled when moved to this new location. Above this bundle, the pit was expanded and partially stone-lined. Burial 1-12a (a primary seated, cross-legged interment) was separated from the cranium of the old adult male by about 7–10 cm of fill (figure 6.6). This overlying young and probably female adult was accompanied by a spouted jar (vessel 048), part of a bowl, two jade beads, and some bird bones. Above this individual and separated by about 20 cm of fill, the secondary bundled remains of a five- to seven-year-old child (burial 1-12b) were placed. At the top of the pit, the excavator noted the presence of charcoal and burnt limestone blocks, indicating a burning ritual as the pit was closed. While these three interments were grouped in one pit, they represent three separate interment episodes. Thus, at this time in the plaza B group, there appeared a pattern of placing individuals together (but as separate interment events rather than as a single interment episode that brought together primary and secondary interments). Some of the separate interment episodes involve secondary interments, individuals curated at another locale and brought to rest with possible kin.

The next resurfacing of structure 1 was more of a midden-like floor than the earlier ones, indicating probable intensive use of the surface. This is the last occupation of this facet in this operation. All interments were placed within the structure; there are none in the exterior plaza floor. There was one single interment, burial 1-3, in a bell-shaped pit. This primary, flexed interment of a probable female, middle-aged adult, was accompanied by two ceramic vessels and a shell bead. One of the vessels may have been covering the head. Nearby was the distinctive multiple interment of burial 1-6. The individuals of this interment do seem to have been placed at the same time in the same pit, but the context is distinctive as it is composed solely of the secondary bundled interment of four individuals. There was one ceramic vessel by the side of the bundle. Burial 1-6a, a middle-aged adult female, represents the most complete remains. Accompanying her were the fragmentary remains of three juveniles: burial 1-6b, a one- to two-year-old child; burial 1-6c, a three- to five-year-old child; and burial 1-6d, a newborn infant. This is certainly suggestive of a mother and her children. It is possible that the adult female died in childbirth or

soon after. However, it is also possible that all three were her children who had died very young and were later gathered together. The curation of these children and a female, and reburial as a group within the structure, is in keeping with the predominance of females and juveniles buried within the construction mass of this operation.

Also located nearby is the multiple interment of 1-15a, 1-15b, and 1-16, which is another three-individual interment that may have involved separate interment episodes. At the bottom of the pit was burial 1-16, a secondary, bundled old adult male. This individual was accompanied by a shell bead; the ritual of his reinterment included a scattering of hematite over the skeleton. Positioned slightly above the bundle was the primary, seated burial of 1-15a, a tightly flexed skeleton. This old adult, probably female, had a head-covering vessel, three other vessels, and one shell bead. This seated individual was probably placed some time after the bundle. In the upper part of the pit was the secondary interment, probably bundled, of a two- to three-year-old child (burial 1-15b) with two shell beads. The remains are mostly of the cranium. Again, there is some space between this child and the primary adult. While all these interments could have been made at the same time, the separations suggest that the location was known and individuals placed sequentially some time apart, as in the slightly earlier groupings discussed above.

This is the third case during this facet of a sequential multiple interment, and in all cases the last burial is that of a secondary bundle of a juvenile. The closure of these pits does not seem to have occurred until a suitable juvenile was reburied with the adults. While it is difficult to know the precise relationship among individuals in these interments, they could represent a gathering of a family group. During this facet, however, the death ritual was not timed to the death of a primary interment. The secondary juvenile could be a sacrifice to the others, but the separation of time and the processing of the corpse lessen the force of this explanation. It is more likely that survivors had planned to bury the second individual with the first interment even before death. The final relocation of remains of a son or daughter who had died some time earlier marked the termination of the burial pit and may have been timed to a calendrical commemoration of days elapsed since the death of the initial or primary interment. In any case, this facet witnesses the initiation of a mortuary pattern of protracted interments in the same location, a possible gathering of ancestors.

During this facet the excavations within the patio group of operation 11 continued to yield burials in what was clearly a domestic residence. During the use life of structure 3, two burials were interred. One, zone 48, was not excavated but only noted in the excavation wall. Burial 11-6, a middle-aged male, was placed in a bell-shaped pit in a seated, crossed-legged position. One ceramic vessel covered the head and another contained three *Pomacea* spp. shells; two bone needles were found near the left hand. At the termination of the structure, burial 11-5 was interred in the floor and the succeeding construction fill. This was a primary seated individual with crossed legs. A middle-aged to older adult male, this burial had no offerings. It is uncommon at K'axob for single interments to contain no grave goods, yet this individual's death seems to have occasioned abandonment of the structure.

In the succeeding construction, an exterior patio floor was constructed over structure 3. Burial 11-3 was placed in an abandoned chultun associated with this floor. This young male is notable because he was placed in an inverted seated, cross-legged position with a bowl in the lap. His head was down and his legs were up; in other words, he was upside down. This may or may not indicate some disrespect, but more likely, as burials were wrapped, his position was an accident or the result of the slumping of the body after it had been placed. The other aspects of the burial do not indicate anything that would particularly mark this individual. Burial 11-4, a middle-aged to older adult male, was probably placed during the construction of this exterior surface. This individual was an extended, supine, primary interment with just a ceramic vessel covering the head.

Within operation 11, the four burials of this facet consisted of four adult males, all likely members of the family or the residential group. All seem to have died during their prime. Three of the interments (including one not recovered) were buried during the use life of a structure, while two were termination/initiation events for new construction.

Within this facet, expansion of residential construction, as indicated by excavations, yielded additional burials. Structures were built or expanded at operations 8, 10, and 12 (see figure 2.2 for locations). These structures are considered satellite residences of the operation 1 platform group and consisted of more modest structures (see chapter 3). Satellite excavations exposed a smaller area; thus the sample represents only a fraction of the individuals who would have been interred during this period.

Operation 8 was located in a modest single platform south of plaza B. With the phase 1 construction of structure 1, two individuals, burials 8-2 and 8-2a, were placed in the construction fill under the floor, apparently as the structure was being built. These are interpreted as dedicatory interments of the structure, the placing of ancestors in a newly occupied residence. While the two were probably placed at nearly the same time, they were clearly spatially separated and thus provide an example of yet another variation on multiple interments. As one of the interments was a secondary bundle, if the intent had been to place both together it certainly could have been done. Thus, this is not a gathering of family members but, rather, two separate interments of individuals who may be more distantly related.

The central individual of this set is burial 8-2a—a primary, supine, extended interment—around whom the construction appears to have been timed. This young adult, probably male, was accompanied by two ceramic vessels, one covering the head. Some time later, burial 8-1 was intruded from the floor near burial 8-2a as a termination event for that first structure. Burial 8-1, a secondary bundled burial with a ceramic vessel covering the cranium, was accompanied by another vessel, a piece of jadeite, and two shell beads. This middle-aged to older adult was likely female, as was burial 8-2, another secondary bundled burial with a spouted vessel placed in the middle of a cluster of the bones of an old adult. The careful placing of these secondary interments with offerings is notable. One young male and an older female compose the probable dedicatory ancestors. The females, including burial 8-1, were curated here and placed as founder and termination interments. Given that this was a new residence, it would not be surprising if young males were among its founders, and burial 8-2a would be a fit founder of the new residence. One can only speculate as to why this individual would be buried here during construction.

After some time, structure 2 was built. A multiple interment—burials 8-4, 8-5, and 8-6—was placed in an intrusive pit that had been dug through the floor, likely as a termination event. All three were placed in the same pit on top of each other. First, burial 8-5, a primary, semi-flexed interment (knees bent in praying position), was placed within the pit. A large jade bead and obsidian blade were positioned in the mouth of this old adult male, and he held a tetrapodal vessel (vessel 101) inscribed with a woven mat design. This vessel also contained a small jade bead. Burial 8-6, a secondary bundle interment of a young male, was placed in the lap of burial 8-5. Last to be added was the tightly flexed interment of burial 8-4, a young to middle-aged male. Placed around the upper part of the pit were two vessels (vessels 110 and 112). Last, a large slab capped the pit and intruded above the floor surface. The upper vessels were likely meant as offerings to accompany all three individuals.

All six of the Late K'atabche'k'ax burials of operation 8 are of adults: four males and two probable females. There are only two old adults; all others may be considered to have been in their prime at the time of their death. Offerings are placed with all interment events, but there is no shell, which is unusual (although there is some jade).

Operation 10 was located in another satellite platform to the south of plaza B. The excavation was placed in the central patio area of the domestic group. Two burials were interred in the second earliest patio floor. The first burial was probably 10-2, a primary, extended interment of a middle-aged adult, possibly male. This individual was accompanied by two vessels, one covering the head. Burial 10-1 intruded partly into the previous interment pit. This primary, flexed interment with part of a vessel covering the head is a female, but, due to lack of preservation, age is not clear. The best estimate is young adult or late adolescent.

The operation 12 excavation was located just to the east of operation 11 and seems to be of a group of informally arranged households lacking a plastered central patio surface. The earliest recorded mortuary activity was associated with the termination of structure 4, the phase 2 occupation. A shallow bowl containing the fragmentary remains of the heads of two individuals (burials 12-16a and 12-16b) was placed inside a partially sherd-and-rock-lined pit. A cache of whole *Pomacea* shells was included, and a macroblade was placed inside the bowl. Burial 12-16a is the fragmentary cranium of a middle-aged male; burial 12-16b included most of the teeth of a seven- to nine-year-old juvenile. The whole context, including charcoal from a burning ritual, suggests more than just reburial. This deposit may very well be a termination cache, into which pieces of some individuals were incorporated.

The subsequent phase 3 involved the construction of structure 3. Placed in the construction fill of this structure during its use was the multiple interment of burials 12-13 and 12-14. These were seated interments. Burial 12-13 is a middle-aged to older adult, possibly female, placed in the western area of the pit. Her bones were covered by a partial ceramic vessel, and there were three shell beads as well as a piece of chert near her mouth. Burial 12-14, situated in the northern and eastern part of the pit, was completely covered by large sherds. This adult (a finer determination is not possible), probably a male, was seated and disturbed later, with his remains being partly bundled under a piece of vessel. These interments were made at the same time, although the structure itself was not long-lasting.

In the following phase of construction at operation 12, structure 2 was built over the foundation of the earlier structure 4. Four burials are associated with this phase, three of which were placed outside the structure in the midden. Three are clearly termination burials as they are interred in a seated position and covered by the subsequent construction of structure 1 and its outside surface. Burial 12-9 (figure 6.7) was cut into the structure. A seated, cross-legged primary interment with a vessel in the lap and three shell beads, burial 12-9 is a middle-aged to older adult, sex indeterminate. This was the terminating burial for this structure.

Burials 12-10, 12-11, and 12-12 were single interments located outside the structure. Burial 12-10 was placed on the edge of the structure. The lower body of a seated, cross-legged interment was found in a pit with one complete and one partial vessel by the legs, along with two shell beads. This is an adult, but no finer age or sex determination is possible. It could be that later construction removed the upper portion of the body. Burial 12-11 is a primary, flexed interment with a partial vessel as a head covering, three shell beads, and one piece of worked shell. This individual, a middle-aged to older adult of indeterminate sex, might have been interred during the use of this area. Burial 12-12, who was also buried on the edge of the structure, was a primary seated, tightly flexed interment. The head of this old female was covered with a bowl, and she was adorned with a fragment of a jade bead. These two seated ancestors were also termination burials for this occupation. In spite of the less formal layout of this residence, the burials were accompanied by shell and jade.

Summary. At operation 1, the twenty individuals of this facet are divided between adults (eleven) and juveniles (nine) nearly equally. There are five males and five females, and primary and secondary interments total ten and eleven, respectively. In fact, operation 1 is notable, compared with the satellite residences, for the representation of all ages and both sexes. There were four extended, three flexed, and two seated primary interments, the latter two positions appearing for

**Burial 12-9
upper view**

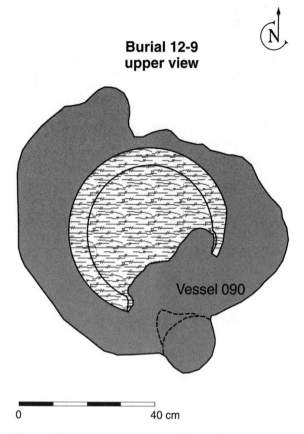

Vessel 090

0   40 cm

Figure 6.7a Burial 12-9 showing covering vessel

**Burial 12-9
lower view**

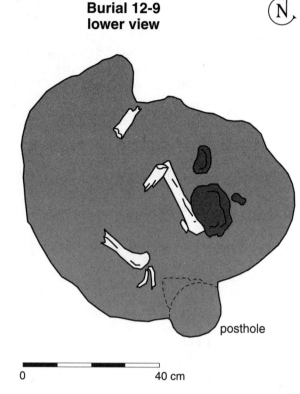

posthole

0   40 cm

Figure 6.7b Burial 12-9 showing skeletal material

the first time in this plaza. Eight of nine juveniles were secondary interments coupled with adults and bore no associated offerings. Five adults had a vessel as a head covering. Thus there are definite differences between mortuary patterns in this facet and those in earlier facets. Generally, single interment was reserved for adults, as were offerings. For the first time, multiple interments outnumbered single ones, which numbered only four. This is further evidence of a trend toward gathering individuals together for interment. This pattern is continued in the next facet.

As seems to be common in all satellite structures, adults dominated juveniles nineteen to one. There were primary interments in extended, flexed, and seated positions; and there were secondary interments as well. There were five females and eleven males. In contrast to the Late K'atabche'k'ax mortuary rituals of operation 1, burial in the satellite residences did not include the sequential multiple interments that signal a more prolonged mortuary ritual. Nevertheless, satellite mortuary treatment included both secondary scattered and secondary bundled interments. The individuals

composing all four multiple interments appeared to have been placed within the burial pit at the same time.

Terminal facet, K'atabche'k'ax complex

Mortuary ritual occurs throughout the excavation during this facet. The practice of secondary interment peaks in operation 1, with seventeen individuals placed within two pit features. While operation 10 contained only one burial, operations 8 and 11 yielded two interments apiece. Operation 12 contained three individuals. The area of operation 1 became the plaza of an expanded multidwelling group, a pattern that becomes more elaborate in the subsequent Early Classic period. During this facet, operation 1 was the locus of a very important mortuary complex which, in many ways, represents the culmination of the patterns seen in the previous facets of the Late Formative period. For operation 1, there are only two mortuary complexes within this facet, and they are on the same axis as the slightly earlier burial 1-12 and 1-41 multiple interment and a quadripartite cache (see chapter 5).

Burial 1-1

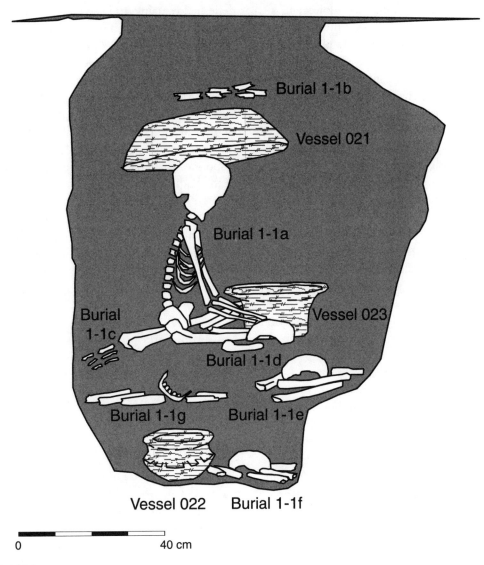

Figure 6.8 Burial 1-1

All were located underneath an exterior plaza surface to the west of the remnant structure 1. Both mortuary complexes involved multiple interments, but the number of individuals in each is distinctly higher than that found in any previous example. This Terminal Formative pattern of large numbers of both primary and secondary interments in one large burial pit is found in other sites in Belize, notably Cuello (Robin and Hammond 1991; Saul and Saul 1991) and Altun Ha (Pendergast 1982a).

Burial 1-1 is a circular pit intruded through the plaza floor (figure 6.8). There is a central figure in this deep pit consisting of a primary, seated individual with crossed legs and a head-covering vessel (burial 1-1a). A quadripartite design had been painted on the exterior of the base of head-covering vessel 021. The other six individuals are fragmentary secondary bundles placed below and above this individual. While all individuals were placed at the same time, they were placed with some spatial separation, and ceramic vessels appear to have been placed with certain of them. Five pieces of worked shell were scattered throughout the deposit. The first individual placed within the pit was burial 1-1f, the secondary bundle of a middle-aged male who was found next to a ceramic vessel. Next were the secondary interments of two fragmentary individuals, burials 1-1e and 1-1g. Burial 1-1e is a fragmentary scatter of the skeletal elements of a young adult/older adolescent, sex indeterminate, while burial 1-1g is a more compact bundle of a middle-aged to older male placed in the southern part of the pit. Directly above burials 1-1e and 1-1g are the legs of the primary interment, 1-1a, with a scattering of skeletal elements of burial 1-1d to the eastern side. Burial 1-1d is a young female. Another vessel with a cross painted on its exterior base (vessel 023) had been positioned upright by the feet of the primary interment. The very fragmentary remains of burial 1-1c were probably placed at the side of the torso and legs of the primary interment, above burial 1-1d. Consisting of a bit of a cranium, this is another young adult, sex indeterminate. Above, and placed last in the pit (clearly separate from burial 1-1a), is burial 1-1b, a secondary bundle of an old adult, sex unknown. The central seated individual, burial 1-1a, is a young/middle-aged adult, probably male. This individual has dental filing of the upper central incisors, a practice not otherwise found during the Formative at K'axob but one that became more common during the succeeding Classic period.

Thus, to summarize the situation of burial 1-1, it consists of the remains of seven individuals. Three individuals cannot be sexed at this point, but there were three males and one female. None of the individuals was clearly juvenile. There was one adolescent/young adult, two young adults, one young/middle-aged, one middle-aged, one middle-aged/old, and one old adult. Overall, this deposit yielded an age profile of prime-age individuals. The crucial event was the death of burial 1-1a, whose interment was accompanied by curated human remains. The cross motif on the ceramic vessels may be an indication of office, as this was also found with earlier males. While there are bundles, some secondary individuals seem to be more scattered (although within a delimited area of the pit). This scattering is different from the expedient secondary burial in abandoned pits seen earlier. During the Late Formative period, careful bundling and wrapping of skeletal elements characterized secondary interments. The scattered individuals were placed at the same time as burial 1-1a, and their treatment may have been part of a ritual surrounding the interment of the seated individual. While most of the individuals probably represent curated, bundled remains of important family members, this may not be the case for the young female and adolescent/young adult. Their differential

treatment suggests that they may have been sacrificed to the primary interment, although the scatter of ribs, vertebrae, and phalanges indicates careful recovery of defleshed remains, and the bones bear no evidence of cutmarks or violence. These individuals may have been interred in this context only because of their relationship to the main interment. The death of burial 1-1a necessitated no curation because this mortuary facility was quickly made available. This facility postdates burial 1-2 as it partly cuts into its fill.

The other Terminal K'atabche'k'ax operation 1 mortuary context, burial 1-2 (figure 6.9), is more elaborate, with distinct differences in the placement of the bodies. This particular complex was clearly re-entered several times, and a small low platform altar was sealed after the final entry. This feature consisted of an oblong trench with a sascab collar. A layer of marl separated the upper interments from the root interment, burial 1-45. The latter was a primary, tightly flexed middle-aged to older adult male. He was accompanied by two ceramic vessels, one containing a fragment of coral. This first individual was followed some time later with nine secondary interments placed in the slightly larger overlying pit. This individual was clearly separate from yet linked to the interments above.

The first individual placed within the burial pit was burial 1-2i, a bundle found near the southern perimeter. The bundle was composed of cranial fragments and some postcranial elements, mainly hands and feet. This was a young adult, sex unknown, with no apparent grave goods. Shortly afterward, three separate individuals were placed in the pit at about the same time, burial 1-2h to the northwest, burial 1-2g to the east, and burial 1-2f to the south (over burial 1-2i). Burial 1-2h is a very fragmentary secondary burial of a young adult, probably a male. The remains were fragmentary and scattered within a delimited area. Burial 1-2g is a bundled interment of a middle-aged/older adult, probably male. The remains had been sprinkled with hematite and were accompanied by a small spouted vessel and a jade bead (although the bead could have been a general offering to the individuals in this level of the pit). Burial 1-2f, also bundled and buried with carved bone tubes and a shell pendant, is another young adult, probably male, lying on a bed of hematite as well.

Just above these individuals and toward the center of the pit, another bundled individual was placed beneath a large, inverted Society Hall bowl with a cross painted on the interior base and side walls (vessel 034).

Burials 1-2 and 1-45

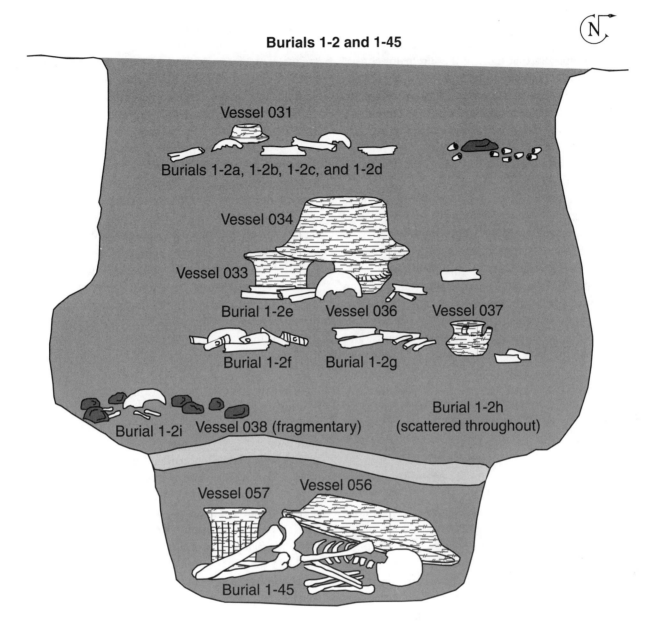

Figure 6.9 Burials 1-2 and 1-45

This individual, burial 1-2e, whose bones were covered with hematite, seems to be a young adult, probably male. This bundle was placed between two upright bowls, one of which was decorated with two monkey face appliques (vessel 036) while the other flared cylinder (vessel 033) featured a painted cross on its base. The large inverted Society Hall bowl covered both of the vessels and the bundled remains. Some shell tinklers were sprinkled in the north end of the pit. Near the top of the pit a small inverted bowl partially cov-

ered the remains of four fragmentary individuals who had been scattered around it. A jade bead was also associated with this group of four. These individuals, burials 1-2a to 1-2d, were the last to be deposited within this mortuary facility. Among these final four, burial 1-2a contained the most complete set of skeletal elements and can be identified as a young adult male. Burial 1-2b and burial 1-2d were both young adults, sex unknown. Burial 1-2c was a juvenile between seven and ten years old. This level contained broken pieces of long bone that probably belong to these individuals, but it is hard to tell one individual from another. It appears that most of these remains consist of cranial and long bone fragments.

Thus, the most formal mortuary facility known within the K'axob excavations contained the remains of ten individuals: nine adults and one child. There are six males; no females can be identified. Two middle-aged to older adults were placed near the bottom of the facility; all others were young adults. Again, these are all prime-age individuals. The preponderance of young adults could indicate sacrificial individuals, as has been suggested for the similar Cuello mass burials (see Robin and Hammond 1991), that may have been captured in warfare. However, the presence of valuable grave goods and the quadripartite motif supports the notion of an elaborate curation and gathering of important family members (see McAnany 1995a). This interpretation is reinforced by the close proximity and partial overlap of the burial 1-1 multiple interments. Thus, in this facet of operation 1, there are seventeen individuals gathered together in two deep mortuary facilities. The burial 1-2 individuals with hematite, jade, carved bone, forty-one pieces of worked shell (including pendants and tinklers), and ceramic vessels with the quadripartite motif indicate the centrality of a shrine for probable ancestors. Their presence reinforces the continued importance of plaza B during the Formative period. The wealth of grave goods and the elaborate curation and interment of mostly secondary bundles at this culminating point in the plaza is a public demonstration of the importance and centrality of this locale. In the terminal facet, the preponderance of young individuals may reflect the status of their family. This could explain why these individuals might have been leaders and worthy of elaborate mortuary treatment at ages much younger than has been recorded earlier in this group and in its satellite groups. Their age could also indicate the increasing importance and prestige of warfare, reinforcing their family status.

In the satellite groups, this facet continued to see mortuary activity at all excavations that yielded burials during the earlier Late K'atabche'k'ax facet. Interestingly, all were single interments, except for operation 8, where a multiple burial reminiscent of earlier patterns was recovered. In operation 8, a single basal platform mound, an intrusive pit cut into the floor of structure 3, contained the remains of two individuals (figure 6.10). These were both secondary scattered interments with five fragments of jade scattered over the bodies, three ceramic vessels that were apparently "killed," and a piece of worked shell. Both individuals are male: one is young (burial 8-3a) and one is middle-aged (burial 8-3b). While most of the bone was scattered within a delimited area of the pit, two bones of burial 8-3b were somewhat separated.

This appears to be a termination ritual for this area, and, as there is no further domestic activity after this facet, it may be a termination rite for the mound. As this mound began with an interment of probable ancestors, so it ended with the final scattering of curated remains and some valuable, broken offerings. Multiple, secondary interments with a scattering of accompaniments were seen in the operation 1 mortuary facilities for this facet, but this is the only similar example from a satellite group (and a small group at that).

In operations 10 and 12, the interments were very similar in that they consisted of only single, extended, supine primary interments with a vessel covering the head (this was the only grave good for each). With one from operation 10 and three from operation 12, single interment was always one of the more common modes of interment at Formative K'axob. Burial 10-3, placed under an exterior patio surface, was a middle-aged adult, sex indeterminate.

The operation 12 interments are similar in that the head area of all three was protected by either a partial cist or a stone covering. While partial cists were noted for earlier burials, this was the first time that this particular pattern defined the mortuary ritual of a domestic group, as if providing further protection for the head than that provided by a ceramic vessel. Because these individuals were placed under the floor of apsidal structure 1, these head coverings may have been very practical, since the floor was in active domestic use. Burial 12-6, a young to middle-aged adult male, and burial 12-3, a middle-aged adult, sex presently indeterminate, were buried totally within the structure and thus probably preceded burial 12-1. This latter individual, an old adult male, had both a cist and a stone cap. He appears to have been the terminal interment for this facet as his burial pit spans the structure and the outside ground surface. Given this, the pit was probably dug during the demolition of structure 1.

For operation 11, the satellite group with the greatest time depth, there were two individuals associated with this facet. They were buried under prepared exterior surfaces. Burial 11-1—a primary, extended, supine interment of a middle-aged/older adult—was probably female. This individual had a

Burials 8-3a and 8-3b
(contains fragmentary
Vessels 096, 097, and 098)

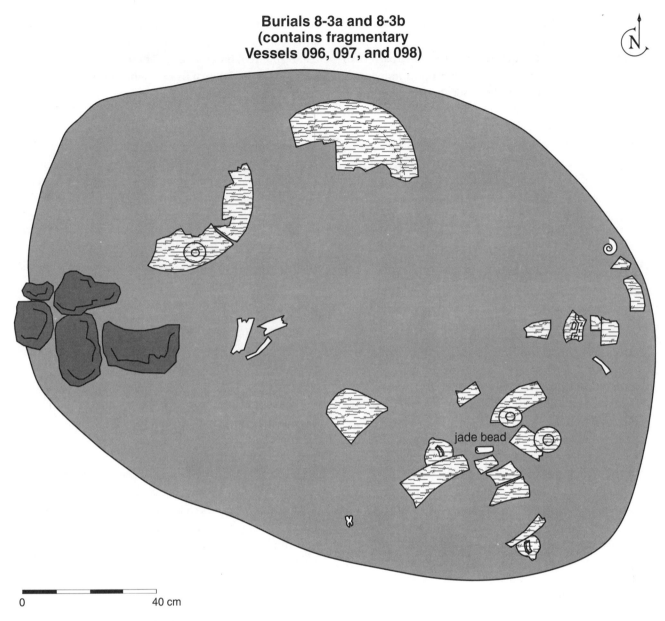

0   40 cm

Figure 6.10 Burials 8-3a and 8-3b

broken vessel placed as a kind of shield over the chest; the interment was placed near the sidewall of the structure. Burial 11-2, a little farther to the east, was associated with two layers of stones along and above the body. Two of the stones were positioned on either side of the skull, perhaps as a partial cist. The interment was a primary, flexed young adult male, with three ceramic vessels. One covered the head and is notable as it is a polychrome marked with a Kan cross (vessel 102). The other two flanked the head. Both of these interments probably occurred during the use of

this living floor, although burial 11-2 could be the termination burial for this phase of construction. After this mortuary interment, additional construction occurred at this domestic group but there was no further mortuary activity.

Summary. This facet reveals quite a divide in mortuary behavior among the K'axob platform groups. Operation 1 displayed a very distinctive "gathering of the ancestors" along with the construction of specialized facilities and a shrine for these individuals. This mortuary behavior clearly marks off the inhabitants of plaza B from other satellite residents and sets the stage for the further elaboration of plaza B during the Classic period. The termination of the occupation of operation 8 was marked by a scattering of individuals and valuable artifacts. In the other three groups, interments were clearly domestic in origin. All were adults, and all but one were males. The one distinguished individual is burial 11-2, whose grave accoutrements, specifically a polychrome bowl with a Kan cross motif (vessel 102) and the burial cist, mark this individual as a harbinger of the Early Classic pattern. The presence of cists and head-covering vessels in operation 12 also has similarities to the patterns of the following period.

LATE AND TERMINAL FORMATIVE BURIALS (400 BC–AD 250) OF K'AXOB IN COMPARATIVE CONTEXT

At eighty-six individuals, the K'atabche'k'ax sample is far larger than that of the Chaakk'ax Middle Formative period. Clearly, the size of the village of K'axob had increased. Mortuary practices, moreover, contained new dimensions, although extended primary interments and secondary interments certainly continued. Notable changes include the addition of seated and flexed primary interments for adults, an increase in the number of individuals included in multiple interments, and the combination of primary and secondary interments in both single and sequential interment events. There is a general increase in the complexity of interment events, although overall the wealth of individual burials is less than it was during the Middle Formative period. There is more variety of items (including jadeite and hematite) included as grave goods. Forty-three individuals can be classified as secondary interments and another forty-three can be classified as primary; it was not until the terminal facet that secondary interments outnumbered primary interments. The trend to reunite what appear to be kin groups culminated in more protracted gatherings of curated and recently deceased individuals in operation 1. While there are some complex interment rituals preserved in the satellite platform groups, the burials generally appear to have followed quickly upon individual deaths without protracted curation of human remains for later multiple interments.

The Late Formative interments at Cuello can be compared with those of K'axob. There are 111 interments during this period, the bulk of the skeletal sample (as at K'axob). There are only sixteen juveniles,

and there are sixty-five males to fifteen females (Saul and Saul 1997), so there is also a bias toward adult males (the K'axob sample is not quite so skewed). The Cuello sample is drawn from a public plaza area, which seems to have been the focus of much mortuary activity, and residential platforms (Robin and Hammond 1991). The former included mostly adult males, while females and children were found primarily in the residences. There are two mass burials in the public plaza area (Robin 1989; Saul and Saul 1997) that are definitely reminiscent of burials 1-1 and 1-2 at K'axob. Cuello Mass Burial I, the earlier of the two, contained thirty-two individuals. There were two primary, seated males, with other secondary bundles placed in their laps or near their feet; an additional twenty-one bundles were placed around the central burials. Mass Burial II also contained two primary males with body bundles (containing eight individuals in two bundles) plus the remains of five others. These burials were originally interpreted as sacrificial (Robin and Hammond 1991) and the secondary individuals as mutilated bodies. Presumably, the youths of the primary burials were sacrificed as a dedicatory offering to the pyramid that was constructed at this time. These are mostly young to middle-aged males, as was true of the K'axob context. The similar K'axob interments are not interpreted as sacrifices but as a gathering of the ancestors. There are also seven other interments at Cuello that are interpreted as sacrifices (Saul and Saul 1997), including burial 10, which was an extended primary interment with the head set to the side, as though the body had been decapitated (Robin 1989). There is no burial at K'axob that provides as good a context for a sacrificed individual as burial 10. Thus, while the Mass Burials at Cuello may possibly be reinterpreted in the future as more similar in their purpose to those at K'axob, there is some evidence of sacrifice at Cuello, which may have been more affected by warfare than was K'axob.

Early facet, Nohalk'ax complex (from AD 250)

With this period there are some shifts in the mortuary patterns, yet continuities with previous practices are definitely visible. Within the window afforded by the excavation units, only the satellite group of operation 12 continued to perform mortuary rituals (two interments) and thus made the transition from the Terminal Formative to the Early Classic period. Two additional satellite groups, operation 7 and operation 13, interred two and five individuals, respectively, during this facet.

Burials 13-3a and 13-3b

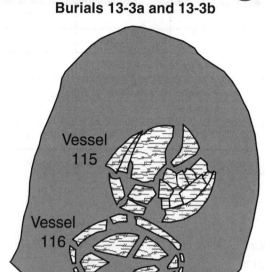

Vessel
115

Vessel
116

0   40 cm

Figure 6.11 Burials 13-3a and 13-3b

Unfortunately, the burials from this facet were very fragmentary and highly eroded, probably because they were found so near the surface. During this time, platform construction did seem to slow down, but the occupation of platforms did not (see chapter 3).

In operation 12, mortuary ritual included a sequential multiple burial in a partial stone-lined cist that was used to hold two individuals, most definitely with some time separating the interments. The first interment, a middle-aged male called burial 12-4, was placed in an extended, supine position with one ceramic vessel covering the head. During a later interment episode, the right leg of this individual was disturbed and displaced to the north at a slightly lower level. For this to occur, the burial probably still retained some articulation, as the leg was moved as a unit; thus the time between interments was probably not very long. It is also possible that the leg slipped to a lower level due to natural taphonomic processes, although this is not very likely. In preparation for the second, upper interment (burial 12-2), there was a slight redefinition of the burial cist; a circular extension was placed at the northern end and

a cap of stones was placed over the upper interment. Burial 12-2 was a young adult male buried with a "killed" polychrome vessel protecting the head and a shell pendant and shell bead adorning the body. He was primary and flexed. This pit intruded into the floor of the structure, and the capstones were level with the floor surface. Thus, the placement of this double burial was clearly marked. The deceased were obviously important members of the residing kin group.

Operation 7 contained only two single interments during this facet, both placed under the floor of a structure. Burial 7-1, interred in an irregular pit cut into the floor, consisted solely of the fragmentary cranium of a six- to seven-year-old child. Two shell beads were placed with this apparent secondary burial. This interment may have been a termination event, although the fragmentary nature of the remains and the fact that this individual was a juvenile distinguish it from previous examples of such behavior. Burial 7-2, in contrast, was buried while the floor was still in use, as the stone cist was capped by finishing plaster. This primary, extended, supine interment of a young/middle-aged adult (sex indeterminate) was well furnished with an inverted flanged polychrome bowl covering the head (vessel 109). Another distinctive polychrome bowl with peccary-shaped feet (vessel 110; see chapter 9) had been placed upright near the side of the body. Such burial accoutrements suggest that this young deceased person was an important family member.

In operation 13, four interments were uncovered, one single and two multiple. Burial 13-1 was placed in a deposit just outside the wall of structure 1. Part of a vessel covered fragments of a cranium and some other skeletal elements. This appears to be a secondary bundle of an adult; due to the fragmentary nature of the remains, no further determination of age or sex is possible. Burial 13-2 and 13-4 were placed in close proximity and at about the same time. Both were placed in construction fill along the edge of structure 1. The head of burial 13-2—a primary, extended, supine interment of a young adult male—was covered with a vessel. Under the legs of this individual there were fragments of an inverted vessel and a few scattered bones. This secondary interment, burial 13-4, was a seven- to eight-year-old child. These two secondary and one primary interments may very well have been part of dedicatory events placed as the residential space was under construction. In contrast, burial 13-3 was placed in an intrusive pit cut through the floor of the structure and may represent a

Table 6.1 Demographic characteristics of the K'axob sample by facet

Facet	Juveniles	Adult Males	Adult Females	Adults	Totals
Early Chaakk' ax	5	3	1		9
Late Chaakk' ax		1	1	1	3
Early K'atabche'k' ax	10	6	4	1	21
Late K'atabche'k' ax	10	15	11	4	40
Terminal K'atabche'k' ax	1	14	2	8	25
Nohalk' ax	3	4		2	9
Totals	**29**	**43**	**19**	**16**	**107**

termination event (figure 6.11). This burial is composed of the conjoined, bundled secondary remains of two individuals placed under two inverted ceramic vessels. Burial 13-3a is an eight- to ten-year-old child, while burial 13-3b is an adult male (no finer age determination is possible). Parts of both individuals were found under both vessels.

The Nohalk'ax sample here reported upon is small (although later excavations at K'axob have added to it). Analysis of skeletal material from the 1995 field season will add to an understanding of Early Classic mortuary behavior that can only be sketched here. The interments reveal continuities with earlier patterns and retain a familial flavor. During Nohalk'ax times it was more common to construct stone-lined cists and to utilize capstones. The extended position is the most popular for primary interments (there is only one Nohalk'ax flexed interment), and seven out of nine had a head-covering vessel. Five out of nine individuals were secondary interments, three of these being found in multiple interments. There are six adults (four are male) and three juveniles (no females yet identified). The children were found solely in secondary contexts. The trend previously identified for the Late Formative period of more adults—especially males—and fewer children and females continues in the sample presently available for the Early Classic period.

DEMOGRAPHY AND HEALTH INDICATORS IN THE K'AXOB SKELETAL SAMPLE

At present, ninety-eight individuals from the Formative period and nine from the Early Classic period have been identified through osteological analysis (see

Skeletal Elements Database). Table 6.1 lists the demographic breakdown of the sample by facet. The bulk of the sample dates to the Late Formative K'atabche'k'ax complex, with fewer individuals from the Middle Formative Chaakk'ax complex. This undoubtedly reflects the expansion of the village during the Late Formative period, but it is probable that the earlier period is somewhat underrepresented. There are twenty-nine juveniles and seventy-eight adults. Of the latter, there are forty-three males, nineteen females, and sixteen indeterminate adults. The table clearly reveals the trend toward fewer juveniles and females after the Late K'atabche'k'ax facet. As is common among ancient Maya burial samples, males are favored (Haviland 1997). Here the trend may be exacerbated by excavation favoring the centers of platform groups, where the most important family members would tend to be interred. Table 6.2 compares the demographic breakdown between operation 1 and the satellite groups. The concentration of adults, particularly adult males, is evident in the satellite groups, whereas juveniles are almost as common as adult males in operation 1. The sex ratio of males to females is also more balanced in operation 1. The status and prestige of the individuals residing at plaza B was apparently such that children and females (probably marrying in from other important families outside of K'axob) could also be interred inside structures and in central patios. For the other residences, males are definitely favored with interment in central locations.

In this sample, locational preference favored the inside of structures, with sixty-five inside to forty-two outside (table 6.3). In operation 1, only the Terminal K'atabche'k'ax contained only individuals placed

Table 6.2 Comparison of demography of operation 1 skeletal sample with satellite platform groups

Facet	Juveniles	Adult Males	Adult Females	Adults	Totals
Operation 1					
Early Chaakk' ax	5	3	1		9
Late Chaakk' ax		1	1	1	3
Early K'atabche'k' ax	5	5	3	1	14
Late K'atabche'k' ax	9	4	6	1	20
Terminal K'atabche'k' ax	1	9	1	6	17
Nohalk' ax					0
Totals	**20**	**23**	**12**	**9**	**63**
All Other Operations					
Early Chaakk' ax					0
Late Chaakk' ax					0
Early K'atabche'k' ax	5	1	1		7
Late K'atabche'k' ax	1	11	5	3	20
Terminal K'atabche'k' ax		5	1	2	8
Nohalk' ax	3	4		2	9
Totals	**9**	**21**	**7**	**7**	**44**

Table 6.3 Age and sex of interments by burial location and facet

Facet	Inside Structures	Exterior Surfaces
Early Chaakk' ax	3 males, 1 female, 5 children	
Late Chaakk' ax	1 male, 1 female	1 adult
Early K'atabche'k' ax	4 males, 3 females, 8 children	2 males, 2 females, 2 children
Late K'atabche'k' ax	10 males, 8 females, 2 adult, 9 children	5 males, 3 females, 2 adults, 1 child
Terminal K'atabche'k' ax	4 males, 1 adult	10 males, 2 females, 7 adults, 1 child
Nohalk' ax	3 males, 1 adult, 2 children	1 male, 1 adult, 1 child

Table 6.4 Burial position by ceramic complex and facet

Facet	Extended	Seated	Flexed	Primary Unknown	Secondary Scattered	Secondary Bundled	Secondary Unknown
Early Chaakk' ax	5			1	4		
Late Chaakk' ax	2					1	
Early K'atabche'k' ax	7	4	1	2	2	4	2
Late K'atabche'k' ax	7	10	7			15	2
Terminal K'atabche'k' ax	5	1	2		9	8	
Nohalk' ax	3		1			5	
Totals	**29**	**15**	**11**	**3**	**15**	**33**	**4**

Note: The Early Chaakk'ax, Early & Late K'atabche'k'ax complexes contain individuals found in two different burial positions, thus the inflated total.

Table 6.5 Frequency of health indicators among juveniles at K'axob

Facet	HYPOPLASIAS		POROTIC HYPEROSTOSIS		INFECTION	
	Present	Absent	Present	Absent	Present	Absent
Early Chaakk' ax	3	1	1	1	1	1
Late Chaakk' ax						
Early K'atabche'k' ax	2	4		3	3	1
Late K'atabche'k' ax	4	3		1		1
Terminal K'atabche'k' ax	1					
Nohalk' ax	2					
Totals	12	8	1	5	4	3

outside of structures. The special mortuary facilities of operation 1 provide the explanation for this pattern. Otherwise, all ages and both sexes are found both inside and outside, and inside outnumber outside in both operation 1 and the satellite groups. Children are much more likely to be buried inside structures.

Children were also more likely to be secondary interments, usually with adults. There are twelve primary juvenile interments to seventeen secondary ones. Nine males and five females are secondary, and secondary and multiple interments were common both in operation 1 and in the satellite groups. Table 6.4 lists the pattern of burial positions by facet. Extended burials are found at all times. Seated and flexed burials are present during the Late Formative, but only during the Late K'atabche'k'ax does this position outnumber extended burials. Eight males were seated as opposed to only two females and three children. In the flexed position there are five males, one female, and one child. Thus, seated and flexed positions characterized mostly males.

Several patterns in mortuary behavior are noteworthy. Only twenty-six individuals were buried with no grave goods. Of these, seven were single interments: three juveniles, three males, and one female. The other nineteen were part of multiple interments. Of these, thirteen are juveniles, probably buried with other family members. The other six adults, all in operation 1, were placed either in burial 1-1 or burial 1-2, large multiple interments. Thus, grave furnishings were the normative pattern.

As discussed under each facet, some burials appear to be termination events for structures. As all ages, single and multiple interments, and rich and not-so-rich burials are involved, it is probable that the death of family members near the time of planned construction may have affected the timing of structure expansion and thus the placement of termination burials. Only in a few of the instances discussed do the ritual and situation of the interment seem to indicate that a special termination event was practiced.

The pattern of a vessel covering the head, as extra protection for that part of the body, was common practice among the ancient Maya. While this pattern is present from the earliest facet, it is not the most common pattern until Nohalk'ax times, when the crania of seven out of nine interments were covered with a vessel. Otherwise, it was found mostly in primary burials and also with secondary bundles. There are thirty-three individuals involved, two of which were secondary child burials. Eight females were so treated as compared to seventeen males. The remainder can only be classified as indeterminate adults. Thus, head coverings were favored for males, and young to old ones were so honored. The proportion of individuals treated in this way at Cuello was greater for both the Middle and Late Formative, whereas at K'axob it is a minor mortuary pattern.

The pattern of health indicators on the skeletons at K'axob can also be compared with that found at Cuello. While poor preservation will underestimate the proportions of individuals affected in a skeletal sample, the K'axob sample in general has slight manifestations of chronic health problems. The skeletons were scored for the presence of linear enamel hypoplasias on the teeth, porotic hyperostosis on the cranium, and infection on the long bones of the leg. These are indicators of

Table 6.6 Frequency of linear enamel hypoplasias in susceptible teeth among adults

Facet	PRESENT			ABSENT		
	Males	Females	Adults	Males	Females	Adults
Early Chaakk' ax	1	1				
Late Chaakk' ax		1				
Early K'atabche'k' ax	4	2		1	1	
Late K'atabche'k' ax	9	8	1	2	2	2
Terminal K'atabche'k' ax	11	1	4	2	1	1
Nohalk' ax	1		1	1		
Totals	**26**	**13**	**6**	**6**	**4**	**3**

Table 6.7 Frequency of infection and porotic hyperostosis among adults

Facet	PRESENT			ABSENT		
	Males	Females	Adults	Males	Females	Adults
Infection						
Early Chaakk' ax	1	1		1		
Late Chaakk' ax		1				
Early K'atabche'k' ax	3	3		2	1	
Late K'atabche'k' ax	8	6	1	5	3	2
Terminal K'atabche'k' ax	2	1	4	7		
Nohalk' ax	2			1		
Totals	**16**	**12**	**5**	**16**	**4**	**2**
Porotic Hyperostosis						
Early Chaakk' ax				1	1	
Late Chaakk' ax					1	
Early K'atabche'k' ax				4	4	
Late K'atabche'k' ax	2	1		12	6	1
Terminal K'atabche'k' ax	4			2	2	1
Nohalk' ax	1		1	1		
Totals	**7**	**1**	**1**	**20**	**14**	**2**

chronic problems; the first two occur during childhood but are preserved to be scored in adulthood. Infection can occur at any age and is seen as an indicator of the hygenic environment and the strength of disease resistance among a population. Childhood problems are indicators of serious morbidity; obviously, the fewer occurrences in a population, the better the childhood environment and the better the chances for surviving to adulthood. Linear enamel hypoplasias reflect a period of growth arrest during the time of tooth formation caused by malnutrition, infectious disease, or both. Of course, the individual recovers as, if he/she did not, there would be no line to score. The frequency of these hypoplasias reflects the risks of serious morbidity during childhood within a population. Porotic hyperostosis is an indicator of iron-deficiency anemia during childhood, usually precipitated by some combination of a lack of sufficient dietary iron, the prevalence of infection, and parasites.

The indicators on juveniles are listed separately from those of adults. As these individuals did not survive to become adults, they often represent more frail individuals. Table 6.5 lists the pathologies present among twenty-two of the individuals aged fifteen and younger. Individuals are scored only if they contained susceptible teeth and diagnostic skeletal elements; seven were too fragmentary to score. Infection and linear enamel hypoplasias are the more common indicators, although sample sizes are very small at present. Porotic hyperostosis is rare, with only one case out of six scorable. These indicator patterns are similar to those of the adults, where linear enamel hypoplasia is by far the most common indicator, followed by infection (Tables 6.6 and 6.7). Porotic hyperostosis is rare and does not appear until the Late K'atabche'k'ax. The juveniles actually have slightly fewer prevalences than the adults. Among the juveniles, 60% displayed evidence of hypoplasias, 17% of porotic hyperostosis, and 57% of infection. Among adults, signs of paleopathologies were slightly greater: 78% with hypoplasias, 20% with porotic hyperostosis, and 60% with infection.

Interestingly, the Cuello population displayed patterns similar to those at K'axob (Saul and Saul 1997). Linear enamel hypoplasias were common, present in 59% of the scorable dentitions, with a trend of increasing prevalence through time. At K'axob more of the scorable adults had hypoplasia (78%), and the proportion remained high during all periods. Porotic hyperostosis was quite rare at Cuello (4%), lower than at K'axob. Infection of the tibia affected 69% of the scorable individuals, which was comparable to K'axob.

While there are definitely skeletal indicators of stress present at K'axob and, as Saul and Saul (1997) point out, also at Cuello, these proportions are less than have been reported for many Maya sites, especially those of the Classic period. As indicators are slight, morbidity may not have been a heavy burden for the population, and most individuals seem to have survived health stresses. At both sites the low incidence of porotic hyperostosis, the indicator of iron-deficiency anemia, is particularly interesting. An environment with sufficient dietary iron and a low incidence of parasites may be indicated. Such a situation would be an important factor in making K'axob a thriving village during the Formative period.

CONCLUSIONS

The K'axob skeletal population contains all ages and both sexes, indicating that all family members were potentially entitled to interment in and around the domestic residences (see *Burials Database* for more detail on all individuals). Adult males did dominate in numbers, in certain burial positions, and in richness of grave offerings. However, females, especially in the important plaza B group, were found in equivalent locations, were curated as secondary bundles, and sometimes had rich furnishings. Through time, children tended to become less evident in the sample and also to be curated and buried with adults. Clearly, the Formative pattern of mortuary behavior was one of increasing elaboration and variety. This behavior became more restrictive through time in that males became prevalent and fewer interments displayed rich grave goods. The overall pattern is congruent with ritual that surrounds the interment (and reinterment) of family members who were commemorated and transformed into ancestors rather than with sacrificial victims who dedicated and terminated structures or accompanied local inhabitants. The confusion for Mayanists may arise because ancestors apparently included more than adult males.

While there were minor health problems, at this level of analysis the burden of morbidity does not seem to have been sufficient to have prevented the people of K'axob from successfully adapting to their environments, both natural and cultural. The care and ritual with which many of the inhabitants were placed after death—the curation and reburial of grouped individuals—linked the living with the dead at Formative K'axob. Analysis of their remains and architectural context allows a twenty-first-century glimpse into the rich web of relationships and cosmology within which the people of K'axob passed their daily lives.

PART III

POTTERY

Clay was a basic yet crucial resource for the pottery-crafting artisans of K'axob. Artifacts fabricated primarily from locally available clays compose the substance of Part III. In the first of four chapters, Mary Lee Bartlett examines the physical properties of northern Belizean clays available within this wetland and river landscape and presents the results of a large-scale clay characterization program. Using petrographic and instrumental neutron activation analysis, the mineralogical and chemical composition of clays and temper materials is then compared to the pottery fabric of a sample of Formative period sherds. Bartlett finds that, although some "exotic" vessels are present during all facets of the Formative period, there is a decided trend toward the use of local clays (available within 7 km) by Terminal K'atabche'k'ax times. The concomitant rise of vessel forms and decorative styles unique to K'axob and distinct from Cuello, Colha, and Cerros served to imbue the vessels with a local identity. Bartlett notes that these long-term trends were balanced by a remarkably stable tradition of pottery production in which paste recipes (which varied by vessel form and function) and crafting technologies were handed down, relatively unchanged, through many generations.

In chapter 8 Sandra López Varela situates the pottery of K'axob within the larger Maya world of the Formative and Early Classic periods. Through the analytical lens of type-variety ceramic classification, López Varela notes the cosmopolitan nature of the heterogeneous types present in the early facet Chaakk'ax deposits of operation 1. She traces stylistic influences on the earliest K'axob pottery back to Chiapas and the Gulf Coast and reexamines the affiliation between Xe pottery of the Pasión region and Early Chaakk'ax material. She constructively reviews the current, difficult taxonomic situation of Formative period pottery in northern Belize, where a proliferation of type names followed on the heels of the now discarded Cuello "long" chronology. The disappearance of Early Chaakk'ax type diversity in favor of the more standardized reds and bichromes of Late Chaakk'ax and Early K'atabche'k'ax times signaled the onset of more intensive local production (as Bartlett also notes). Taking a close look at the intrasite distribution of types and decorative motifs, López Varela intimates that the making of hierarchies within K'axob may not have been focused exclusively on plaza B.

In chapter 9 Kimberly Berry and others present the corpus of K'axob vessels for study. An image (photo or line drawing) is available for nearly every one of the 114 complete or partially/totally reconstructable vessels. Primarily red monochromatic bowls and deep dishes, the slipped pottery of the K'axob Formative period is characterized by clean, simple lines with a clear tendency for vessel volume to increase through time. In many respects, this trend culminates in the large vertical-walled, wide-flared rim Society Hall Red bowls (sometimes bearing a basal decoration of a painted cross). These bowls, as well as the overall majority of vessels, were encountered in burial contexts. Cache contexts yielded the second highest number of vessels. With these contexts in mind, chapter 9 presents artifacts that, without a doubt, were cosmologically charged and many of which were ritually "killed." The visual richness of this chapter and the presentation of vessels grouped by context provide a superb complement to the contextual information presented in chapters 4 (caches) and 6 (mortuary ritual) as well as the stylistic discussions of chapter 8. Designed to facilitate easy cross-referencing and contextual analysis, the chapter is organized by ceramic complex and facet, provenience, and individual context.

In chapter 10 Bartlett presents an analysis of artifacts (other than pottery vessels) made of fired clay. Although the sample totals only 120 artifacts, these "small finds" hold a potency that belies their size. The fired clay artifacts are referable to a range of activities that include gaming, fishing, weaving, ritual practice, music making, personal adornment, and the decoration of cloth and paper. Although encompassing a wide range of artifact types, from ocarinas to roller stamps, the majority of fired clay objects were fishing gear, specifically weights or sinkers for fishing nets. Net weights were fabricated both from raw clay and from recycled sherds. Due to the high frequency of artifacts crafted from sherds, Bartlett devotes the second half of her chapter to this class of artifacts. Chapter 10 echoes the themes of material conservation and recycling introduced earlier by Bobo (chapter 5) in reference to sherd-lined pit facilities, and it foreshadows a discussion in Part IV of the curation of hard stone used for chipped and ground tools. Both chapters 5 and 10 remind us that excavated extramural areas with high densities of large pottery sherds should be perceived as resource stockpiles rather than as dumps.

GUIDE TO ACCOMPANYING DIGITAL MATERIALS.

Each chapter of Part III considers artifacts made of clay. The petrographic analysis undertaken by Bartlett is presented in two digital databases: *Clay Petrography* and *Ceramic Petrography*. The ceramic history of K'axob as presented by López Varela is based on analysis of both the *Pottery Sherds Database* and the *Pottery Vessels Database*. Each can be viewed separately. Text information and images of complete and reconstructable vessels presented by Berry and others in chapter 9 is expanded in the *Pottery Vessels Database*, which also contains color photographic images and quick-time videos for a selection of vessels. Finally, the digital database of *Fired Clay Artifacts* contains comprehensive textual data as well as photographic images of selected artifacts.

Chapter 7
Related CD Resources

Clay Petrography
Ceramic Petrography

CHAPTER 7

THE POTTER'S CHOICE OF CLAYS AND CRAFTING TECHNOLOGIES

MARY LEE BARTLETT

The earliest known pottery from K'axob is both sophisticated and well made. Apparently the artisans who produced these ceramics were cognizant of the variety of clay resources present in northern Belize and knew how to apply differing strategies both to render them workable and to ensure firing success. Analysis of the technological choices made by these Formative Maya potters in terms of resource choices and formation techniques provides evidence of localization of resource exploitation over time and, by the end of the period, the development of unique stylistic markers for the village of K'axob. Further, such analyses provide evidence of trade networks, interaction spheres, and the responses of people from small villages to evolving social complexity.

In this chapter I investigate the choices made by village potters in terms of (1) resource procurement strategies, (2) paste preparation approaches, (3) forming techniques and stylistic attributes, and (4) firing methods. A variety of analytical techniques were employed to study these ceramic production methods, specifically, petrographic analysis, instrumental neutron activation analysis (INAA), xeroradiography, and visual analysis of stylistic attributes. The results indicate that, during the course of the Preclassic period, potters increasingly chose to use local resources (within 7 km of K'axob) to produce pottery vessels with unique stylistic markers identifying their community membership.

Mineral data from petrography and chemical data provided by neutron activation suggest that the K'axob community was linked to other areas along the New River through networks of trade involving both vessels and raw materials. During the course of the Formative period, clay preparation techniques became increasingly related to potential vessel use. Almost exclusively, the utilitarian, unslipped wares were made with the addition of calcite temper, while the techniques employed to form slipped vessels became more variable. These changes, including the development of community stylistic markers, occurred as the society at large increased in complexity; this suggests that community affiliation and an identification with place can be an important concomitant of complexity.

143

SAMPLING METHODS

To determine resource exploitation strategies, clay samples from northern Belize were compared with ceramics from K'axob. The specific study area is the Belizean portion of the northern Coastal Plain (shown in figures 7.1 and 7.2).[1] A total of 143 samples were collected, of which 108 were analyzed using petrographic analysis and INAA.[2]

In order to compare clays to ceramic samples from K'axob, the samples were first levigated to remove the largest inclusions.[3] Bricks were formed, allowed to dry, and then fired to 600°C in a kiln. This process was adopted to approximate as closely as possible the firing temperatures used by the Preclassic Maya in the production of ceramics. A portion of each sample was thin-sectioned and studied under a petrographic microscope, while a second portion was sent to the Missouri University Research Reactor (MURR) facility for INAA under the direction of Dr. Michael Glascock and Dr. Hector Neff. The digital *Clay Petrography Database* presents the information gleaned from this mineralogical analysis.

The 108 prepared clay samples were then compared to 300 ceramic samples. Ceramics were chosen from well-controlled stratified contexts and selectively sampled based on the type-variety classification system (see chapter 8). A large sample was selected to mitigate the inherent bias in the sampling process. The sample was taken from three distinct periods of occupation based on ceramic and architectural data: (1) the earliest residential occupation, dating to the Middle and Late Middle Preclassic period and represented by the early and late facets of the Chaakk'ax ceramic complex; (2) the transitional period of the beginning of the Late Preclassic period represented by the early facet of the K'atabche'k'ax ceramic complex; and (3) the end of the Late Preclassic, which in this study includes the late and terminal facets of the K'atabche'k'ax ceramic complex.

Attempts were made to sample at least twenty-five specimens from each ceramic type (as classified by López Varela 1996). Within each of the three temporal groupings, samples were drawn from five excavation units (operations 1, 7, 8, 11, and 12). The largest sample derived from operation 1, a 6 x 8 trench in pyramid plaza B. As noted in chapter 2, this unit contained the only stratified sequence of materials from the onset of occupation during the middle phase of the Middle Preclassic through the end of the Preclassic period.

Initial analysis included the recording of Munsell coloration of surface and paste, measurement of rim and base diameter (when possible), height, thickness, and (when applicable) determination of breakage pattern. Form designation was based on the descriptions by Gifford (1976) and Sabloff (1975) and determined by López Varela (1996). Forms include plates, dishes, bowls, vases, jars, and tecomates. This information can be viewed in the *Ceramic Petrography Database*.

GEOLOGICAL RESOURCES

The soils of northern Belize are predominantly calcareous, formed primarily from the chemical and mechanical breakdown of limestone. These soils and the underlying limestone bedrock provided a rich agricultural base as well as the resources necessary for construction and crafts such as ceramic manufacture. Although the area has been defined as a uniform limestone plain (Wright et al. 1959), soil formation processes have resulted in an observable diversity in color, texture, and composition (Darch 1983; King et al. 1992; Angelini 1998; Bartlett, Neff, and McAnany 2000). At K'axob, soil differentiation is due, for the most part, to the processes of alluviation and the wet conditions inherent in a low-lying swamp environment adjacent to a river.

The northern Coastal Plain, which extends from the Yucatan Peninsula of Mexico in the north to the Belize River in the south, is composed primarily of carbonate sedimentary rocks that are Cretaceous and Tertiary in origin (Johnson 1983:12). This marine shelf emerged during the Oligocene and Miocene (Flores 1952; Johnson 1983) and tilted northerly during the Pleistocene (West 1964; Johnson 1983). Much of the area proximate to K'axob is composed of a thick layer of alluvium that has been deposited primarily as the result of erosion from the Maya Mountains. This mountain range formed sometime earlier in the Cenozoic (Wright et al. 1959:23).

During one of the warming intervals of the Pleistocene, sea level rose to the 55 m contour, creating a bay immediately north of the Maya Mountains (Wright et al. 1959:25). Subsequently, this level receded to the 15 m contour forming modern Chetumal Bay. Two rivers, the Rio Hondo and the New River, flow north to the bay, following a fault system that runs northeast-southwest from the Maya Mountains. Tectonic activity along this fault system created scarp and swampy swale topography between the two rivers (Wright et al.

1959:25; Johnson 1983:17). Pulltrouser Swamp is one example of this scarp and swale topography. K'axob is located on the eastern side of the depression formed by the southern arm of this swamp complex.

To the west of Pulltrouser Swamp, two limestone ridges—the San Pablo Ridge extending southward into Guatemala at 40 m above sea level and the Rio Hondo Ridge at the 200 m contour extending northeast along the Rio Bravo and west of the Rio Hondo into Mexico (McDonald and Hammond 1985:13)—provide the highest relief in the northern region. Quarries or outcrops along these two ridges are a likely source for the limestone used for Maya construction in the alluvial plain between the two rivers. Analysis of rocks collected from a modern quarry along the San Pablo Ridge contiguous to the ancient Maya site of Lamanai suggests that this is the source for the rock used as temper for some of the ceramics excavated at K'axob.

The underlying bedrock of the alluvial plain of northern Belize is weathered limestone, referred to by the local name of *sascab* (Darch 1983; Darch and Furley 1983). This chalky, crumbly marl is composed primarily of pure calcium carbonate. Clay minerals and quartz sand are present in varying degrees. Sascab is used today to build roads, much as it was in the past. A soil profile observed in a bulldozer trench located approximately half a kilometer west of Pulltrouser Swamp is described as follows: (1) an A horizon consisting of dark organic, clayey topsoil; (2) an underlying layer with high clay content beginning at 35 cm and terminating at approximately 86 cm; and (3) a thick layer of sascab beginning at 86 cm and extending to the bottom of the trench at 210 cm.[4]

The combination of carbonate bedrock and erosion from the Maya Mountains within a subtropical climate has produced the noticeable variability in soils. This variability and the definition of specific regional soil suites and subsuites are described in detail by Wright et al. (1959) and, more recently, by King et al. (1992). For this study, these suites are identified in terms of land systems; clay sampling locales were chosen based on the distribution of these soil suites (figures 7.1, 7.2).

Differentiation based on the characteristics of soil suites enables the delineation of three broad zones, defined primarily by the presence or absence of sand-sized or smaller mineral grains of either monocrystalline quartz, chert, or calcite (figure 7.3). Specifically, the zones are: (1) a quartz belt bordered by the Belize River to the south and the Northern Highway to the east; (2) an alluvial area present to the north of the Old Northern Highway and east of the Rio Hondo; and (3) a chert zone located north of the Belize River and east of the Northern Highway. This last area is the source for chert tools found throughout northern Belize, beginning in Formative times (Shafer and Hester 1991).

CLAY MINERAL CONTENT OF SOILS

Clay minerals are ubiquitous in northern Belizean soils. Based on data from X-ray defraction, previous studies in the Pulltrouser Swamp environs indicate that the predominant clay mineral is smectite, which has a two-lattice structure joined in loose bonds (Darch 1983; Darch and Furley 1983). This structure enables water and other elements to penetrate between the layers, accounting for the high shrinkage and expansion characteristic of this type of clay mineral (Rice 1987a:48–49).

To counteract this shrinkage potential, smectite clays require the addition of temper, aplastic inclusions (typically with an identical or lower thermal expansion characteristic), or the mixing of clays with less shrinkage (Rice 1987a:407). Maya potters using this type of clay added crushed calcite or grog (crushed ceramics) to the paste to ensure firing success. In addition, one ceramic sample showed evidence of clay mixing, indicating that this technique was also employed. Kaolinite, which is used in porcelain production, is a mineral forming stronger bonds with less elasticity. This type and illite, which is a three-layer clay with less expansion than smectite clays, are also present in measurable percentages in the Pulltrouser Swamp environs (Darch 1983) and would produce ceramics requiring less temper. The mixing of clays composed of different clay minerals would enhance the likelihood of successful pottery manufacture. The K'axob potters apparently had both the close knowledge of their resources and the skill to manipulate them to suit their needs.

APLASTIC MINERAL COMPOSITION OF SOILS

Mineral grains observed petrographically further define soil variability in northern Belize and validate the delineation of the three zones discussed above (figure 7.3). I employed petrographic analysis to validate the differences in soils. The results provide a comprehensive database of high clay content soils in the study area (see *Clay Petrography Database*).

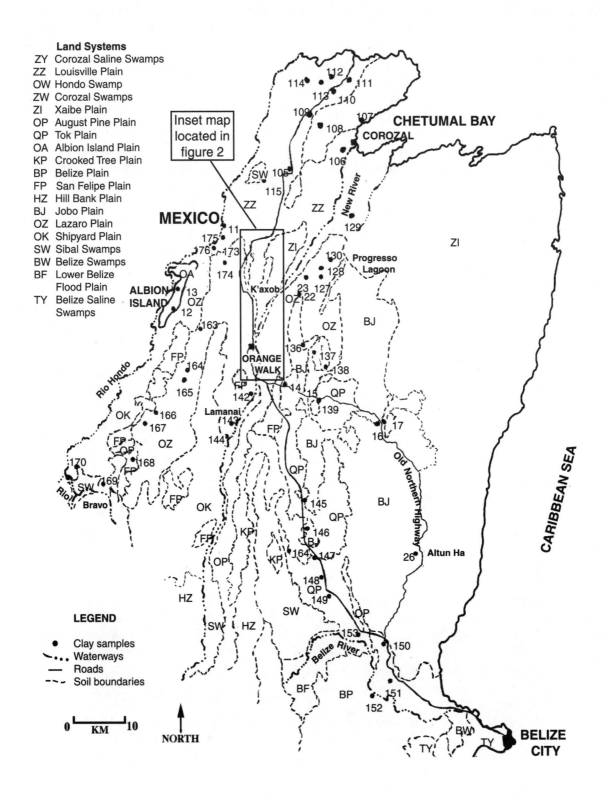

Land Systems
ZY Corozal Saline Swamps
ZZ Louisville Plain
OW Hondo Swamp
ZW Corozal Swamps
ZI   Xaibe Plain
OP August Pine Plain
QP Tok Plain
OA Albion Island Plain
KP Crooked Tree Plain
BP Belize Plain
FP San Felipe Plain
HZ Hill Bank Plain
BJ Jobo Plain
OZ Lazaro Plain
OK Shipyard Plain
SW Sibal Swamps
BW Belize Swamps
BF Lower Belize
     Flood Plain
TY Belize Saline
     Swamps

LEGEND
●   Clay samples
∙∙∙∙ Waterways
——   Roads
– – – Soil boundaries

0   KM   10

NORTH

Figure 7.1 Northern Belize, indicating soil suites defined by King et al. (1992) and soil and core sampling areas. *Illustration by Mary Lee Bartlett*

The two most prevalent mineral grains are quartz and calcite ($CACO_3$). Quartz grains, which are either of marine origin or have been transported from the Maya Mountains, are particularly resistant to physical and chemical weathering because of their strong chemical bonds. Calcite is present from the breakdown of the underlying carbonate bedrock. Other mineral grains that define soil areas include chert (which includes chalcedonic quartz), shell, and gypsum (table 7.1).

Calcite can be found in three distinct forms: (1) microcrystalline calcite or calcite mud (micrite) in which the calcite crystals are between 1 and 5 microns (figure 7.4a); (2) carbonate grains composed primarily of fossilized shell remains (figure 7.4b, labeled as calcite with oolites; and (3) sparitic calcite, which is composed of coarse-grained calcite crystals from 0.02 to 0.1 mm in size (figure 7.4c). Quartz is also found in three forms: (1) chalcedony or chalcedonic quartz (figure 7.4d); (2) monocrystalline quartz (figure 7.4e, labeled simply as quartz); and (3) polycrystalline quartz (figure 7.4f). Occurring in variable percentages, monocrystalline quartz, mostly sand size, is the most prevalent.

Quartz is most abundant along the Pine Ridge areas, which extend north and southwest of the Northern Highway and in two core samples.[5] Chalcedonic quartz (figure 7.4d) is present to a limited extent and only in the eastern part of the study area, where it occurs with chert grains. Polycrystalline quartz is present as the result of plastic deformation caused by stress on rock during tectonic uplift (Blatt 1992:85). Polycrystalline quartz is widely distributed in the soil and is also present in rocks analyzed from the limestone quarry near Lamanai. The ubiquity of this mineral throughout the study region suggests that it is not a good predictor of soil provenience.

On the other hand, chert is one of the primary predictors of soil provenience since it occurs only in the zone located east of the Northern Highway (figure 7.5a). This rock is the basis for the toolmaking industry established at Colha during Formative times (Shafer and Hester 1983, 1991; Shafer 1994). Chert formation processes can either be primary (occurring directly from chemical processes acting upon siliceous organisms such as diatoms) or secondary (occurring through the replacement of limestone; Adams et al. 1984:82). In thin-section, chert was present only in samples taken along the Old Northern Highway (figure 7.1). Darch and Furley (1983) report chert nodules found randomly in core samples in northern Belize. One suspects that these are random occurrences as the result of past depositional activity rather than a primary formation area.

Gypsum ($CaSO_4 2H_2O$) is an evaporite believed to be formed from the precipitation of seawater (Carozzi 1993). This mineral was used by the ancient Maya in the formation of plaster. Soils containing gypsum (figure 7.5b) are found in Pulltrouser Swamp, along the three rivers, and in one core sample. Gypsum may provide a characteristic to differentiate soil areas, but the sample is too small in the present study to make this determination.[6] This mineral is not found in ceramic pastes.

Table 7.1 Inclusions found in clay sediments from northern Belize

Inclusions	Number of Samples	Size (mm)	Shape	Point Count	Boundaries
Sparitic calcite	29	.15-.35	Subangular	10-24%	Diffusing
Calcite with fossils	4	.16-.40	Round	5%	Clear/diffusing
Micrite	21	1.7-.05	Subround/ subangular	10%	Diffusing
Quartz	97	1.2-.01	Subround/round	.02-66%	Clear
Polycrystalline quartz	6	1.6	Subangular	9%	Clear
Chert	4	.30-.65	Subangular	1%	Clear
Gypsum	15	1.2-.25	Subangular	25%-50%	Clear/diffusing
Shell	17			5%	Diffusing
Iron oxides	46	.05	Subround/round	5%	Diffusing

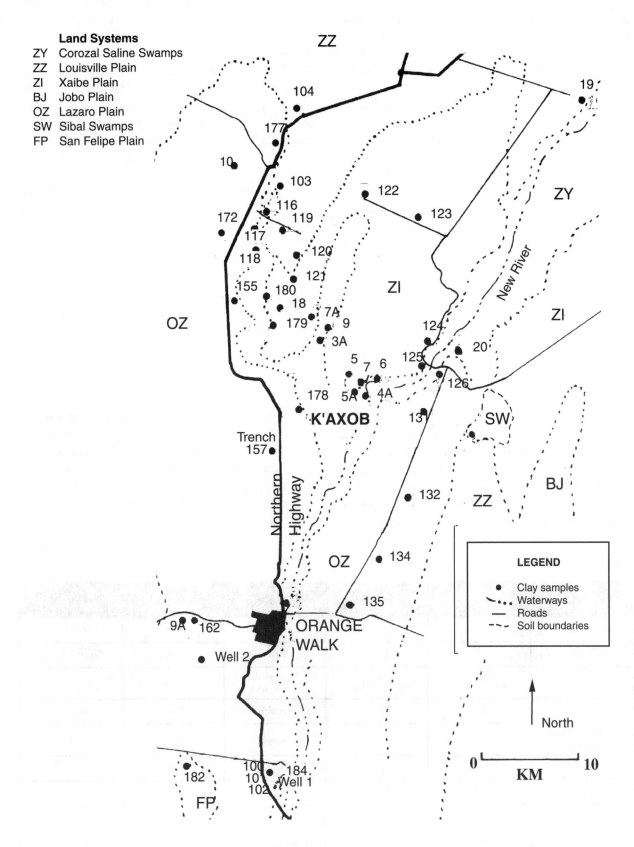

Figure 7.2 Soil suites and sampling locales around K'axob. *Illustration by Mary Lee Bartlett*

Shell is present in clays from freshwater lagoons and along the Rio Hondo and the New River, those areas that contain modern, small molluscs. In thin-section, the shell boundaries are observable, but in others the shell is decomposing, leaving a brown stain in the clay (figure 7.5c). Shell is present primarily in Mamom (Middle Preclassic) ceramics and then only to a limited extent (three samples).[7]

Iron oxides also occur in a variety of samples (figure 7.5d). This mineral grain is usually silt-size, below .05 mm. Like polycrystalline quartz, iron oxides are prevalent in clay samples throughout the region, and a chi-square analysis reinforces the lack of distribution patterning.[8]

SOIL MATRIX

Soil matrix, or groundmass—all material below silt-size—provides another attribute that differentiates soils. The soil matrices identified petrographically are characterized by three different types (table 7.2). Type 1 contains few, if any, silt-sized inclusions; the few that are present are always quartz (figure 7.4e). Round to subround quartz occurs in sand size also. Iron oxides may or may not be present but no calcite minerals are observable. In this type, the clay platelets are observable, suggesting the presence of kaolinite clay minerals. Shrinkage tends to be lower than in other samples, although statistically this difference is not significant.

Type 2 has observable silt-size calcite, usually sparitic calcite, but the boundaries of the minerals are diffused or merged (figures 7.4c and 7.4d). The size of these calcitic areas is below .01 mm, and they are highly birefringent; that is, they display high interference colors in cross-polarized light. Although some of the diffusing character of the calcite may be due to changes

from firing, in most cases this mineral decomposition is a result of weathering.

Type 3 contains tiny, round, silt-size sparitic calcite grains less than 0.01 mm in size. The completely round calcite grains are cemented together by a small quantity of clay minerals.

The distribution of these three matrix types is as follows: Type 1 is most prevalent in the chert and quartz zones (zones 1 and 3). Type 2 is the most evenly distributed and is found not only in the northern alluvial zone (zone 2) but also along alluvial and swamp deposits in the other two zones. Type 3 appears to be present only in the northern alluvial zone 2, although further testing is needed in order to validate this.[9] Soil matrix type appears to be related to depositional and soil formation processes. The underlying sascab seems to have less impact in the chert and quartz zones than in the northern alluvial area. These three soil matrix types can be used to assess provenience for soils and, with a more fine-grained sampling, can help define possible resources for clays used to produce ceramics in the past.

In summary, petrographic analysis of soils validates the conclusions of Wright et al. (1959) and King et al. (1992), who contend that three broad-based zones exist in northern Belize. Chert is found in areas east of the Northern Highway; monocrystalline quartz is present to the west. The northern area is primarily an alluvial zone high in organics, with an underlying layer of sascab affecting the development of soil suites. These three zones can be further subdivided based on soil matrix type. These findings are supported by INAA discussed below. The results suggest that fine-grained sampling using multiple analytical approaches can refine resource exploitation even in a relatively uniform limestone plain (Bartlett et al. 2000).

Table 7.2 Three groundmass types visible in soil sediments in northern Belize

Type	Defining Characteristic	Predominant Inclusions	Zones Present*	Ceramic Group
Type 1	Few silt-sized quartz inclusions	Quartz or chert with quartz	1, 3	Grog group; quartz group
Type 2	Diffusing silt-sized sparitic calcite, tempered quartz rare or absent	Calcite	1, 2, 3	Predominantly calcite group
Type 3	Round sparitic calcite tempered grains less than 0.01 mm in size and uniform in appearance; quartz rare or absent	Few large sparitic calcite	2	Calcite group
*Refers to zones delineated in figure 7.3.				

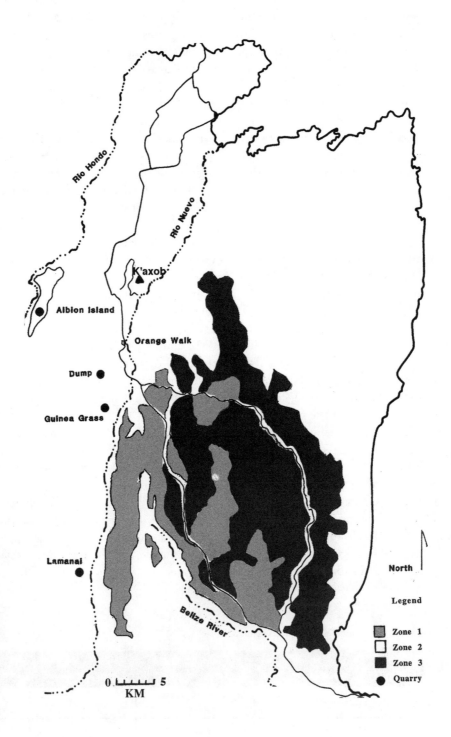

Figure 7.3 Soil zones (adapted from King et al. 1992) and quarry sites discussed in text. *Illustration by Mary Lee Bartlett*

CHEMICAL CHARACTERIZATION OF SOILS

Instrumental neutron activation analysis reveals a north-south distribution of chemical elements. The difference is most marked within those sediments found in the northern areas near the town of Corozal as compared to those found in the southern quartz and chert zones. Those samples from the center of the study area—K'axob—represent an area of overlap between the more northern soils and those further to the south. The differentiation among areas seems most pronounced in the percentage of calcium (Ca) present in the soil.

The samples were prepared using the protocol of the Missouri University Reactor Facility (see Glascock 1992).[10] Results indicate that clay samples do not form into distinct groups; rather, the differentiation is loosely overlapping (figure 7.6). Graphic representation in which the distribution of the element calcium is compared to hafnium illustrates the overlap. The enriched calcium present in some soils is the result of the decomposition of the underlying bedrock, while hafnium is a replacement for zirconium in zircon grains. These higher concentrations of hafnium will generally occur in older sediments within concentrations of very fine sand or silt.[11] The difference between deposits resulting from erosion of the Maya Mountains in the south and the marine environment of the north probably account for the differentiation of these two elements.

Variability in chemical composition determines agricultural potential for these soils. The area around Pulltrouser Swamp and, indeed, much of the northern zone 2 region is classified as the Louisville subsuite (King et al. 1992). Soils of this type are fertile and important areas for the growth of sugarcane and, in the past, maize (216–217). The sandy soils of the pine ridge, on the other hand, are generally low in nutrients, are covered with natural vegetation (242–243), and lack evidence of substantial ancient settlement. Clays in these sandy areas, however, require little potter intervention to promote workability and insure firing success.

ROCKS

Consolidated surface rocks are found in few places in northern Belize. Small outcrops of weathered limestone can be found along lagoons such as Honey Camp, and chert nodules are present in the chert zone to the south of Pulltrouser Swamp. Tectonic activity has resulted in ridges and scarps, which are the location of modern quarries (figure 7.3). As a part of the K'axob project, forty-four rock samples were collected from surface areas around lagoons, near archaeological sites (where they were probably transported from other regions), and from three quarry sites and one rockface with observable fossilized shell. Samples of known geological provenience were analyzed petrographically. Most of the rocks from lagoons are relatively soft, weathered limestone, which, in thin-section, are difficult to differentiate from one another.

The following modern quarry locations were tested: (1) Albion Island; (2) the cliff face on the road to Guinea Grass; (3) the local dump southwest of Orange Walk Town (Tower Hill); and (4) along the San Pablo Ridge two miles north of the central precinct of the Maya site of Lamanai (figure 7.3). The rocks most similar to the calcite in ceramic pastes came from Albion Island and the Lamanai quarry. These findings are discussed more extensively in the section on paste preparation techniques.

In summary, soils are noticeably different throughout northern Belize in spite of the marine origin of the underlying bedrock. These differences are manifest in the color and texture of samples as well as in mineral and chemical characterization. This variability permits the investigation of resource procurement strategies for crafts such as ceramic production, and it also had a profound influence on agricultural potential and possible trade networks.

CERAMIC PASTE DESCRIPTION

In this section I discuss the ceramic pastes from Formative K'axob ceramics. These data provide a basis for the grouping of ceramics into distinct sets. In petrographic analysis, three groups can be defined. Membership is characterized either by clay matrix or aplastic inclusions, the sand-size material that is either naturally occurring or deliberately added by the potter. According to INAA of pottery samples, four distinct groups are indicated based on the variability of elemental concentrations (figure 7.7). The data from these two avenues of inquiry can be compared to the data from clay sediment analysis to ascertain resource exploitation strategies as well as production methods (see chapter 8 for a further discussion).

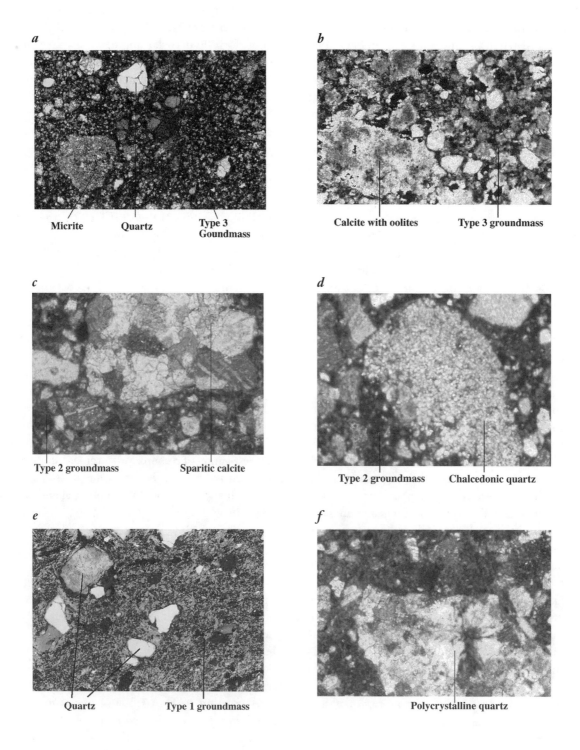

a.

Micrite   Quartz   Type 3 Goundmass

b.

Calcite with oolites   Type 3 groundmass

c.

Type 2 groundmass   Sparitic calcite

d.

Type 2 groundmass   Chalcedonic quartz

e.

Quartz   Type 1 groundmass

f.

Polycrystalline quartz

Figure 7.4 Examples of quartz and calcite mineral grains discussed in text. Photographs taken in cross-polarized light. Field of view is 2.00 mm in width at 10X.
a. Micrite and monocrystalline quartz in type 3 groundmass
b. Fossils within a calcite grain in type 3 groundmass
c. Sparitic calcite grain in type 2 groundmass
d. Chalcedonic quartz grain (chalcedony) in type 2 groundmass
e. Monocrystalline quartz grain in type 1 groundmass
f. Polycrystalline quartz forming within a sparitic calcite grain in type 2 groundmass. *Photos by Mary Lee Bartlett*

PETROGRAPHIC GROUPS BASED ON GROUNDMASS

The groundmass types present in ceramics are the same as the three types present in clay samples, indicating that they were rarely mixed prior to pottery fabrication. They are represented in the ceramic sample in the following percentages: (1) type 1 comprises 20% of the sample; (2) type 2 is present in 50% of the sample; and (3) type 3 comprises the remaining 30% of the sample. As noted above, among the clay samples type 1 is primarily found in zones 1 and 3, the quartz and chert belts south of K'axob. Type 2 and type 3 can be found in clays closer to K'axob, so 80% of the pottery thin-sections contained a groundmass characteristic of clays proximate to K'axob.

To further illustrate the variability in the presence of calcium carbonate in these three groundmass types, representative petrographic slides of ceramics were dipped in hydrochloric acid, which will dissolve all calcium carbonate (figures 7.8a and 7.8b). After treatment, type 2 and type 3 groundmass indicated the presence of a high percentage of $CaCO_3$ (figure 7.8a) and the lowest percentage of clay minerals, while type 1 was least affected by the treatment because it is predominantly composed of clay minerals and quartz (figure 7.8b). Type 1 is most likely the noncalcareous paste type discussed in chapter 8.

PETROGRAPHIC GROUPINGS BASED ON APLASTIC OR MINERAL GRAIN INCLUSIONS

Aplastic inclusions either reflect potter intervention or the naturally occurring material in sediment used to produce the pottery. As noted above, the inclusions naturally present in northern Belizean clays include: iron oxides, quartz, calcite (fossilized, micritic, and sparitic), chert, gypsum (in some cases), shell (occasionally), and mudstones. With the exception of gypsum, which is not found in pottery, ceramics from K'axob have the same inclusions and groundmass types as soil sediments.

Quartz is present in 82% of ceramic samples and is similar in appearance and in frequency of occurrence to that found in clay-based soil samples, particularly those found in the quartz and chert zones in the southern part of the sample region.[12] Quartz occurs with or without grog and calcite. Only 7% of the ceramic samples contain only quartz with no evidence of either calcite or grog temper. The quartz in ceramics is similar in appearance and frequency of occurrence to that of clay samples, particularly those collected near the site of Colha (samples 15, 16, 17) and the Black Creek area (samples 148, 149; see figure 7.1).

Iron oxides are dense, dark red inclusions of amorphous, rounded shape. They are present in 222 ceramic samples. Most are silt-size and, therefore, may not be reflected in point count data. The presence of iron oxides accounts for the red coloration of the pastes of some ceramic samples. This color is intensified if the firing temperature exceeds 650°C. Use of clays high in oxides increases over time.[13] Although the sample size is too small to be statistically significant, Chaakk'ax complex types such as Tierra Mojada, Timax Incised, and Toribio Red-on-Cream all contain oxides. K'atabche'k'ax types, such as Sapote Striated (81%) and Hillbank Red (84%), were constructed primarily from iron oxide–bearing clays. These percentages probably reflect the ubiquity of iron oxides in soils around K'axob. Only a more fine-grained sampling of sediments in the study region could determine if any patterning of resources is actually represented.

Chert is present in 10% of the ceramic sample but, based on point count data, occupies only 1% of the field of view. In angularity, appearance, and size, the chert in ceramics and clays is similar. Chert is present in all ceramic types except the resist wares from the Early Chaakk'ax period. This finding suggests that this type of decorated ceramic was not being traded from Colha. Petrographic analysis of Colha resist-decorated vessels is necessary in order to determine if they might have been traded to Colha from elsewhere during this early period.

Dolomite, $CaMg(CO3)2$, is present in ceramics embedded within sparitic rock fragments and, in two cases, appears as an individual mineral grain (figures 7.9a and 7.9b). None of the clay samples studied contained dolomite, although Darch (1983) reports dolomite in samples from Pulltrouser Swamp; furthermore, D. King (1996) states that it is present in sediments from Albion Island. The rock from Albion Island did contain a dolomite grain surrounded by sparitic calcite, suggesting that if dolomite is found within a larger rock fragment in the ceramic paste, then it is probably temper and the source of the rock was probably Albion Island.

Grog, crushed ceramics that appear as angular fired particles with clear boundaries between the inclusion and the clay matrix, is also present in some ceramics

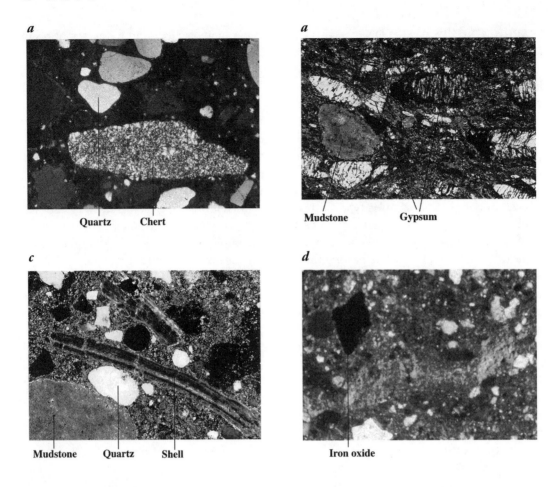

a

Quartz   Chert

a

Mudstone   Gypsum

c

Mudstone   Quartz   Shell

d

Iron oxide

Figure 7.5 Examples of mineral grains in clays discussed in text. Photographs are taken in cross-polarized light. Field of view is 2.00 mm in width at 10X.
a. Chert grain with quartz
b. Gypsum and mudstone fragment
c. Shell with mudstone fragment and quartz
d. Iron oxide. *Photos by Mary Lee Bartlett*

(figure 7.9c).[14] The definitive marker for grog is the presence of slip (a coloidal suspension of clay applied to the vessel wall) on an angular inclusion. Clay pellets, or even sand-sized particles of ceramics, can be added inadvertently to ceramics, but these are rarely found in ceramic pastes and are generally not slipped. Grog is usually present with round to subround quartz or, more occasionally, with both quartz and calcite. If calcite is present, it generally represents only 1 to 2% of the field of view. The groundmass tends to be type 1 with the least silt-sized inclusions.

Calcite also occurs in ceramics. The three mineral types present are the same as those that appear in clay sediments, specifically sparitic calcite, micrite (mud), and calcite with fossils. These inclusions may have been added by potters, based on the following criteria: angu-

larity of inclusions, percentage present in comparison with that found to be naturally occurring in clays, clear boundaries between the inclusion and the groundmass, and the uneven size differential among inclusions (that is, poor sorting). For the naturally occurring clay sediments, the percentage of calcite present did not exceed 24% of the field of view. Leaching, due to the high rainfall in northern Belize, contributes to the rapid breakdown of calcite and accounts for the absence of a high percentage of distinct calcite grains.

In ceramics suspected of having had calcite added as temper, the inclusion occupies 30 to 60% of the field of view based on point count data. Over half of the ceramic sample had high frequencies of calcite. For these ceramics, the calcite was angular to subangular and the boundaries tended to be clear.

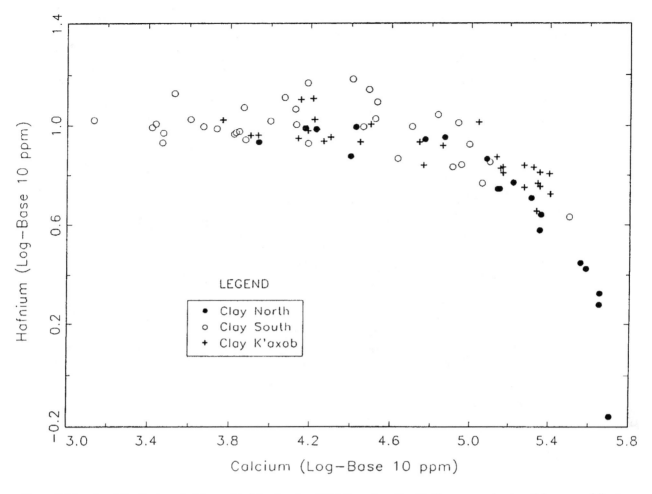

Figure 7.6 Log-based distribution of calcium and hafnium based on INAA from clays. Graphic illustrates overlapping of clay groups following a south to north distribution. *Illustration by Mary Lee Bartlett*

Boundaries between inclusions and groundmass are dependent in part on the temperature at which a ceramic was fired and on the weathering of the clay sediment. Clear boundaries suggest that firing temperature was low and that the inclusions were added. For clays, calcite was subangular with diffusing or merging boundaries with an uneven size differential.

Based on aplastic inclusions, the three groupings are: (1) ceramics with grog tempering, (2) ceramics with calcite tempering, and (3) ceramics from naturally occurring clay with no evidence of tempering. The grog group tends to have a type 1 groundmass, while all three groundmass groups are represented in the calcite group. The group containing no temper is composed only of the type 1 groundmass. These more workable clays, requiring the least potter intervention, are found predominantly in the quartz and chert belts south of the K'axob site.

CERAMICS GROUPS BASED ON INAA DATA

Samples were prepared and irradiated using the same procedure as that used for clays (see Glascock 1992). Numerous factors can affect the reliability of INAA. Elements can vary within a clay bed. The action of the potter in mixing clays, levigating, and adding temper can affect element data. Postdepositional leaching or crystallization of secondary minerals can alter the ceramic paste (Arnold et al. 1991; Bishop 1992; Neff 1992). Arnold (1992) suggests that a large sample size both of ceramics and of a wide variety of clay resources within the study area addresses many of these concerns. The strength of the findings can be enhanced when this method is combined with petrography (Bartlett, Neff, and McAnany 2000).

As mentioned above, the final result of statistical calculations of the INAA sherd data indicates the presence of four separate groups (figure 7.7). Ninety

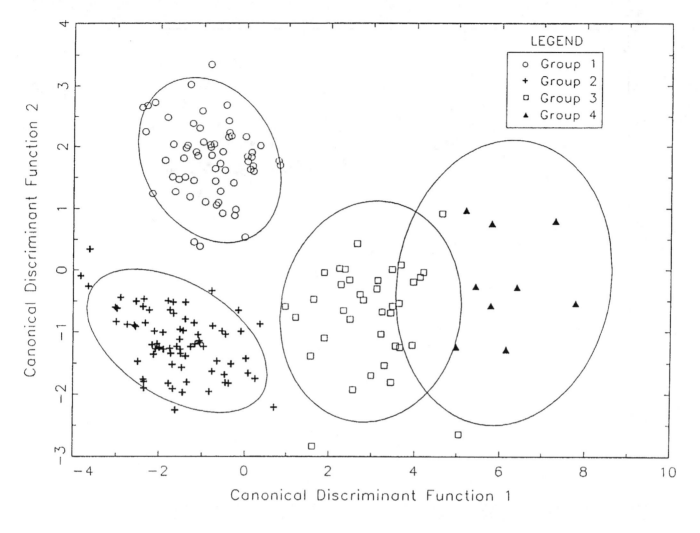

Figure 7.7 Canonical discriminant analysis of elemental concentrations from INAA illustrating separation of ceramics into four groups. *Illustration by Mary Lee Bartlett*

percent of the sample can be assigned to these four categories, with the remainder overlapping between the two largest groups. When compared to petrographic determination and type-variety designation, the groups tend to separate by time period and whether the vessel was slipped or unslipped. The four groups delineated by the canonical discriminant analysis shown in figure 7.7 are as follows: group 1 is composed of ceramics that contain grog, quartz, and a few calcite minerals. Petrographically these sherds have inclusions that occupy 20 to 30% of the slide and a type 1 groundmass. The majority of the sherds date to Late K'atabche'k'ax times, and 99% are slipped. These are probably the noncalcareous paste vessels identified by their refiring experiments on sherds from K'axob (see chapter 8; Daszkiewicz, Schneider, and Bobryk 1999). The second group is predominantly composed of

vessels with a high percentage (30 to 60%) of calcite. Seventy percent of these cases are ceramic types assumed to have been utilitarian. These include Chicago Orange vessels and the unslipped Monkey Falls and Sapote Striated types. This group contains approximately equal numbers of vessels from the three time periods, suggesting that technology did not change over time in the production of utilitarian wares. The groundmass present in group 2 is as follows: type 1 is present in 12% of cases; type 2 represents 48% of the sample; and type 3 is present 40% of the time. Group 3 is composed of vessels with high percentages of all three types of calcite; sparitic, calcite with fossils, and micritic. Eighty-five percent of vessels are slipped and the majority date to the Chaakk'ax complex. Group 4 is composed of only nine cases of variable types. Half of this group contains high percentages of calcite, and

a

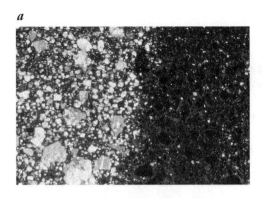

b

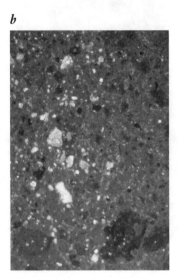

Figure 7.8 a. Petrographic thin-section of calcite-tempered ceramic manufactured from type 3 groundmass after application of HCl to the right side.
b. Petrographic thin-section of grog-tempered ceramic manufactured from type 1 groundmass after application of HCl to the right side. *Photos by Mary Lee Bartlett*

the other half contains grog with either quartz or quartz and calcite. In two cases chert is present. All of the samples are slipped vessels: six from the Chaakk'ax complex, two from the early facet of the K'atabche'k'ax complex, and one from the late facet of the K'atabche'k'ax complex.

Comparison of INAA groups with those from petrographic analysis indicates that grog-tempered, slipped ceramics have a different elemental signature from types with calcite temper and from ceramics of the Chaakk'ax complex (Angelini 1998).

In conclusion, the clay paste present in ceramics is sufficiently variable both chemically and petrographically to suggest separate groups. These groups are based both on the type of clay exploited and potter intervention. When the three possible clay resources found in this study are compared to ceramic pastes, changes in resource exploitation strategies over time and paste preparation techniques can be suggested. The changes indicate a slowly evolving tradition of ceramic production in which there is increased localization of clay resource extraction and a differentiation in the formation techniques used for utilitarian versus nonutilitarian wares. These results are discussed below in terms of the steps of production.

RESOURCE PROCUREMENT

Determination of possible procurement locales is predicated on the tenets that soils are sufficiently variable to make comparison possible and that soils are being formed today under conditions similar to those of 2,000 years ago. Both of these conditions seem to be present in northern Belize. Petrography points out visual variability in groundmass and aplastic inclusions in soils, and INAA validates elemental variability. Johnson (1983:20) notes that soils buried under the raised fields built in Pulltrouser Swamp during Maya occupation of nearby K'axob "are characteristic of those which develop under the present climate and hydrological regime." King et al. (1992) note that some of the soils in northern Belize are young in geological terms and are still in the process of formation. Two thousand years is a short period in geological time, and there is no evidence that conditions of today are markedly changed from those of the geological near past. Since the goal of this study was never to pinpoint particular clay sources but, rather, to investigate the possibility of localized use of resources and any changes over time, comparison between clay sediments and ceramics was determined to be feasible. Localized production was concluded if clay resources were found within 7 km of the site, a distance based on Arnold's (1989:50) statistical study of the resource procurement strategies of modern potters.

TEMPORAL CHANGE IN USAGE

Among the three types of groundmass, the most commonly used clay sediment is type 2 with diffusing calcite minerals. Although its usage does decrease slightly over time, throughout the Preclassic period it remains the preferred type. Utilization of the type 1 groundmass with no apparent calcite inclusions increases from the Middle Preclassic to the Late Preclassic period. Finally, use of the type 3 with the highest percentage of round sparitic calcite decreases over time.[15]

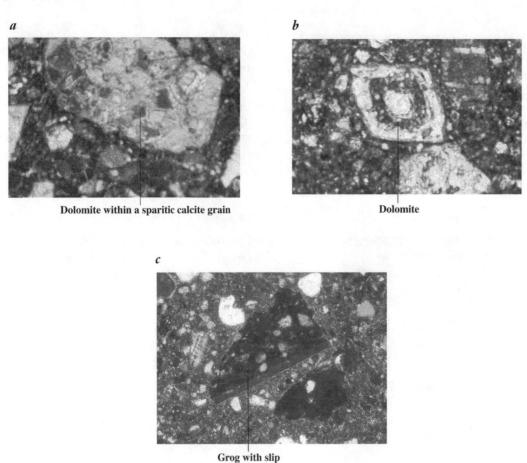

a

Dolomite within a sparitic calcite grain

b

Dolomite

c

Grog with slip

Figure 7.9 Examples of two types of aplastic inclusions present in ceramic samples but not found in clay samples. Photographs taken in cross-polarized light. Field of view is 2.00 mm in width at 10X.
a. Example of dolomitization within sparitic calcite grain.
b. Example of single grain of dolomite.
c. Two examples of grog. One has obvious slip and other does not. *Photos by Mary Lee Bartlett*

The clays that are most similar to the ceramics with a type 1 groundmass are found along the sandy pine ridge area southwest of K'axob (clay samples 147 and 148, see figure 7.1). The other two groundmass types are found in samples proximate to K'axob. The INAA data, discussed below, supports the idea that clay usage observed petrographically does shift over time.

Principal components analysis was employed to compare the elemental data from clays, ceramics, and rocks to determine the overall resemblance of the clays to the pottery and to identify elements that show divergence (see Bartlett, Neff, and McAnany 2000:Fig. 12). The results indicate that barium concentrations in the pottery are acting to separate the ceramics from the clays on component 2. The rocks, which are almost pure $CaCO_3$, also form a distinct group. Since the clays and ceramics were fired, driving off CO_2 and creating

a relative increase in other elements, this factor may account for the separation of the rocks from the clay and ceramic samples.

When these same data are compared using principal components analysis based on a correlation matrix, the dilution of elements by the high percentages of calcium is less apparent, suggesting that clays and ceramics can be compared. When principal component 1 was compared with principal component 3, based on a correlation matrix, it appeared that barium—with some contribution from calcium, potassium, and sodium—was separating the pottery from the clays (see Angelini 1998). When barium is compared to calcium, the data demonstrate that barium concentrations, not calcium (either naturally occurring or temper), separate the ceramics from clays. Calcite temper, therefore, cannot be the source of enriched barium (Angelini 1998);

rather, postdepositonal alteration may have affected the barium content in ceramics. Eliminating barium from the data set should enhance the comparison. This approach was successful for groups 1 and 3, but some other element, which could not be determined, prohibited comparisons in group 2. If further clay sourcing is performed in northern Belize, then this problem will have to be addressed, particularly considering that the calcite-rich ceramics are (predominantly) the utilitarian wares that are assumed to be produced locally.

Once comparison was deemed to be feasible for groups 1 and 3, Mahalanobis distance calculation was used to compare the raw elemental concentrations from the three discrete ceramic groups with the raw elements present in clay samples. (Group 4 has too few cases to be considered in this calculation.) The results of the comparison suggest that the ceramics from these two groups have similarities with several clay samples (see Angelini 1998 for the probabilities of matches with Ni, Ba, and Ca eliminated). Group 1 ceramics dating predominantly to the Late Preclassic period appear similar to a clay sample from the wetland and a trench sample from K'axob (samples 119 and 258). Group 3, which is composed primarily of Mamom sphere ceramics, is more variable and includes local and nonlocal possibilities. Matching clays are found at Sapote Lagoon, the Rio Hondo, the Rio Bravo, the road to the ferry at San Estevan, and the bedrock sample from operation 7.

A canonical discriminant analysis was performed on the four ceramic groups, and discriminant function scores were calculated for the clays as well as for the four pottery groups. Using the discriminant scores, mahalanobis distance to the centroids of the pottery groups was then calculated for all the clays. The results indicate that, during the late and terminal facet of the K'atabche'k'ax complex, group 1 ceramics, representing primarily slipped vessels with grog tempering, most resemble the clays found near the site of K'axob. The most similar clays to these ceramics are: sample 007, an aguada (seasonally inundated depression) at K'axob; sample 100, adjacent to the New River south of Orange Walk Town (based on petrographic analysis, this clay is the most visibly similar to the pebbly based clays found in some ceramics); sample 116, near the modern town of San Jose, 5 km north of K'axob; sample 155, a seasonal stream near K'axob; sample 179 from the site of K'axob; and sample 177, the sample most distant to K'axob—namely, a sandy area near San Pablo to the west (figure 7.10). All of these areas are within the 7 km catchment area suggested by Arnold (1989)

for resource procurement. In contrast, groups 3 and 4, those ceramics dating predominantly to the Middle Preclassic period, seem to be most similar to clays sampled at a distance from K'axob. These samples include: samples 122, 113, and 114, all from northwest of K'axob toward the Rio Hondo near Chan Chen; sample 013, on the banks of the Rio Hondo at San Antonio; sample 183, a stream near the rock quarry at Lamanai; and sample 171, from the banks of the Rio Bravo. The only sample from K'axob with similarities to the Chaakk'ax ceramics was taken from bedrock exposed beneath operation 7. The other bedrock samples were not matches. Petrographically, these ceramics frequently contain calcite with fossils, a mineral not present in the clays around K'axob and not represented in K'atabche'k'ax ceramics.

These results indicate that the potters of the Preclassic period exploited many of the clay sediments present in northern Belize. Utilization of these clay pastes did change with time. During Chaakk'ax times, the closest match between clays and Mamom-sphere ceramics are found in samples from the Rio Hondo area, near Lamanai, and by the Rio Bravo. By the K'atabche'k'ax complex, increased use of local clays to produce Chicanel-sphere (Late Preclassic) ceramics is apparent. Further testing than was possible in this research could help to pinpoint these resources more precisely. Finding the source of calcite temper is a logical place to begin. Temper sources are limited in northern Belize. The closest match to the sparitic calcite inclusions identified in ceramics comes from a quarry near Lamanai at the southern end of the New River. Interestingly, one of the clay sources possibly exploited to manufacture the earliest ceramics is from this area also. Dolomite is present in a rock from Albion Island, which is an area that is a clay match with ceramics also dating to the earliest period. These data indicate that resource exploitation was confined to a limestone-based area. Further testing of areas beyond northern Belize, such as in the lowlands of Guatemala and the northern Yucatan, would have to be undertaken to eliminate the possibility of trade from other limestone areas.

PASTE PREPARATION

Petrographic analysis indicates that two strategies of clay preparation were employed by Maya potters: (1) addition of temper and (2) clay mixing. Clay mixing was apparent only in one sample, suggesting that it was either not a prevalent practice or that potters mixed clays so well that it is undetectable. As noted in the section describing the appearance of ceramics in thin-section, Maya potters added calcite or grog as temper to clays, depending on the intended use of the vessel. Unslipped wares, assumed to be utilitarian, were invariably made with clays tempered with calcite. These include the plain and striated wares that tend to show evidence of burning on both the inner and outer surfaces. Burning could occur postdepositionally, but ethnographic evidence suggests that these were the types of vessels generally used for cooking and water storage (Reina and Hill 1978). The preparation techniques for slipped vessels is more variable and includes those made with addition of calcite or grog or with no alteration to the clays. Based on refiring experiments, López Varela (chapter 8) notes a difference in groundmass among utilitarian wares. She suggests that these differences may be predicated on intended vessel usage, an observation that certainly warrants further investigation.

Temper choice does change over time. The use of calcite temper decreases (chi square probability value of .0014 [X^2 =16.76 with 4 df]), while the use of grog for temper and the use of clays with a type 1 paste composition increases. Sixty-four percent of slipped pottery from the late facet of the K'atabche'k'ax complex were made from type 1 clays as compared with 9% of ceramics from the earlier Chaakk'ax complex.

The addition of temper increases vessel porosity and decreases the impact of clay expansion and shrinkage during drying and firing. Calcite temper increases the thermal shock value of a ceramic because calcite has a lower coefficient of thermal expansion than the clay body (Rye 1981; Rice 1987a). Historically, modern potters in the Yucatan manufacture vessels with calcite for this purpose (Thompson 1958). On the other hand, grog temper is readily available and easy to crush, although its thermal shock value would not be different from that of the clay body. The increased use of this type of temper for serving vessels may have been an expedient choice or it might reflect ideology. In Africa, the Sirak Bulahay make some grog-tempered vessels as a means of including the ancestors at meals, and others use it as protection against powerful spirits (Sterner 1989). When a vessel linked to an ancestor is broken, a new vessel is created using the crushed particles in the ceramic paste (Sterner 1989:458).

The calcite used as temper is predominantly sparitic calcite. As noted above, rocks of this type are not locally available around K'axob. The two sites with rocks that appear similar petrographically to the temper are found

in a quarry near Lamanai and on Albion Island (figures 7.11a and 7.11b). Certainly trade from Lamanai is possible along the New River, which is slow-moving and permits easy access along its length. The similarity among clays and temper with K'axob pottery suggests a possible trade network in either raw materials or in finished ceramics. That most of these vessels were utilitarian suggests that the raw materials rather than the finished vessels were traded.

The presence of dolomite surrounded by sparitic calcite in a rock sample from Albion Island suggests that this may also have been a source for temper in ceramics. Further testing of the quarry site on the island could assess the variability of rock from the area. Again the distances are not great, suggesting that either the resource or the finished vessel may have been imported to K'axob.

Maya potters were skilled in working with all types of readily available clays. They possessed a thorough knowledge of a number of paste preparation methods and seemed to employ specific techniques in response to potential usage and to the particular clay resource used. These abilities were passed down through the centuries of the Formative period with remarkably little change.

FORMATION TECHNIQUES

Previous researchers have suggested that a variety of methods were utilized to produce Formative Maya pottery. Anna Shepard (1939) suggested that the large vessels present during the Late Formative period required support and were perhaps made from molds. Coil-building has also been suggested as a forming technique (Kosakowsky and Hammond 1991:174). Coiling is a technique in which rolled lengths of clay are joined to each other to form a vessel. One small Chicago Orange jar from Cuello (examined by the author in the course of comparative stylistic research) does show evidence of incomplete smoothing of coils present on the inside of the vessel. Robertson-Freidel (1980) states that incomplete smoothing of unslipped, utilitarian wares left evidence of coils on the pottery from Cerros. Rye (1981:67) suggests that vessels made from coils will show variation in wall thickness. For the K'axob pottery, this type of variation is not obvious, suggesting that the potters were either very good at evening walls or that other techniques were used. Rye notes that vessel form dictates the formation technique utilized in production (63). For example, vessels with a flat base can be made on any horizontal surface, while incurved bases, which are present in a few of the predominantly Society Hall Red bowls dating to the Late K'atabche'k'ax complex at K'axob, required a mold to hold the shape until the clay hardened. In this study, evidence of forming techniques was obtained through the analysis of form, breakage patterns, petrographic analysis, and xeroradiography.

BREAKAGE PATTERNS

Breaks generally occur in areas of greatest weakness. In most instances, this weakness is present at joins, such as those that occur between the walls and base. Rye (1981:67–68) suggests that meandering and irregular breaks occur most frequently in coil-made ceramics.

The following breakage points were identified on K'axob pottery: (1) the necks of jars tend to break at the place of join to the body; (2) bowls or dishes break at the join between the body and rim and vertically along the wall (these forms generally remain intact from the rim to the inside of the angle creating the base); (3) vessels with a direct rim tend to break horizontally within the body of the vessel, perhaps along the join of two coils (Rye [1981:68] notes that this will occur if the vessel was too dry when the coils were joined); (4) for some intact rims, breaks slant down the walls to a point creating a triangular shaped piece. The break at the base includes either one to two centimeters of the base or begins one to two centimeters up the wall of the vessel and includes no base. This suggests that flat-bottomed vessels are formed in at least two steps, with the base made separately and joined to the body of the vessel either at a point inside the base or along the outer wall of the vessel. No weakness is apparent in the wall itself.

PETROGRAPHIC ANALYSIS

The alignment of voids in ceramic samples provides evidence of forming behaviors. In all instances, observations of voids were made from a thin-section of a vertical cut of the ceramic wall, and, when possible, only thin-sections of rims and bases were analyzed. Thirty-nine percent of the sample had voids oriented parallel to the wall. Theoretically, this type of orientation occurs (1) in pinch pots when the vessel is drawn, (2) in flattening and forming coil-made vessels, and (3) when the vessel is beaten into shape (Rye 1981).

An additional void pattern present in K'axob vessels includes alignments parallel to the inner and outer edge of the vessel walls with random patterning in the center. The exact percentage of this type of pattern was not noted. According to Rye (1981), this pattern is consistent with mold-made vessels. Perpendicular voids would suggest joins of coils. In no case was perpendicular alignment identified, except at the base join and the outflaring of the rim. Random patterning of voids is also suggestive of coil-making. In this study, the pattern is referred to as cross-hatching and is apparent in fifty-four samples (18% of the total). Thirty-nine percent of the sample have voids parallel to the walls, 18% show cross-hatching, 18% have no discernible pattern, and 9% of the voids were aligned diagonal to the wall.

The alignment of voids does not appear to be related to time periods, suggesting that the technological knowledge of a variety of forming techniques was present at the time of earliest settlement of K'axob. This knowledge enabled the successful manufacture of the small vessels of the Chaakk'ax complex and the large Sierra Red and Society Hall Red vessels that appear in the late and terminal facets of the K'atabche'k'ax complex.

XERORADIOGRAPHY

The technique of xeroradiography enables the visualization of patterns in the ceramic body through the use of a high magnification X-ray machine. X-rays are passed through an object and the image is photographed on negative film. The image can then be studied through a light box. Differentiation in densities present within the object will be apparent, for light and dark areas on the film provide evidence of the formation techniques employed (Carr 1990; Rice 1987a:403–404).

Ten sherds, each representative of a different ceramic type and collectively of a variety of forms, were X-rayed at the Medical Center of Central Massachusetts in Worcester, Massachusetts. The criteria for selection were based on sherd size, form, and type. The sherds were placed vertically on a plate and X-rayed; the X-rayed images were then studied through a light box (Angelini 1998).

Analysis of the X-rays indicates that, although some vessels were coil-made, other methods of construction were also part of the repertoire of techniques employed by the Formative Maya. The sample is not sufficiently

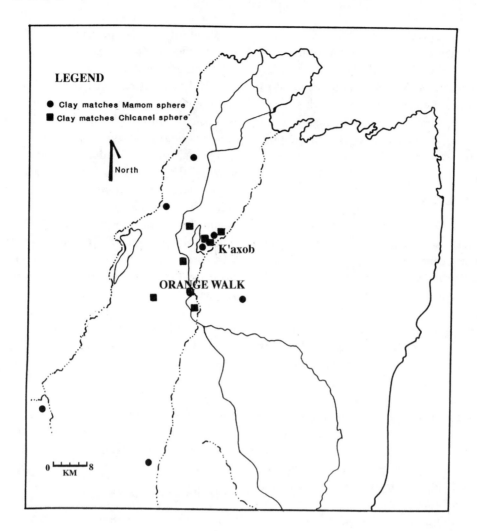

Figure 7.10 Clay sampling areas that match most closely with ceramics. *Illustration by Mary Lee Bartlett*

large to suggest definitively that different forming techniques were used to produce specific vessel forms. The evidence does indicate that dishes were not made by the coiling technique and that bowls were made using a variety of forming techniques.

The three avenues of evidence assessing possible formation techniques indicate that the Maya were skilled in the use of a variety of approaches and that they applied these different techniques depending upon the vessel form desired. The larger vessels, particularly those with incurving bases, were made from molds, as is suggested by Shepard (1939). Use of the paddle and anvil technique is suggested for the very thin-walled Hillbank Red types. Small bowls were made from either coils or a pinching technique. Dishes and some bowls appear to be mold-made. Jars were probably made by coiling. Again, Maya potters demonstrate

their flexibility and expertise in the techniques of pottery manufacture.

STYLISTIC ATTRIBUTES UNIQUE TO K'AXOB

The evidence of site-specific ceramic design and form is apparent at K'axob by the K'atabche'k'ax complex. The particular design pattern unique to the village of K'axob is the cross motif, a quadripartite pattern slipped on the outer and/or inner surface of the base of two Sierra Red vessels in the early facet and a number of Society Hall Red vessels dating to the Late and Terminal K'atabche'k'ax facets (see chapter 16). The cross is wiped onto the vessel, creating a streaky pattern diagnostic of Society Hall Red vessels. The middle vessel in the drawing (figure 7.12a) was excavated from an elaborate secondary burial context

a

b

Figure 7.11 Examples of two rocks with sparitic calcite. Photographs taken in cross-polarized light. Field of view is 2.00 mm in width at 10X.
a. Sparitic calcite rock from Albion Island.
b. Sparitic calcite from Lamanai quarry. *Photos by Mary Lee Bartlett*

consisting of four other vessels, shell bracelets, and pendants. Skeletal evidence indicates that the burial contained the remains of more than five individuals. This exact design pattern is not reported for Colha, Cuello, or Cerros.

Another apparently site-specific variety at K'axob is the Sierra Red: Gadrooned variety (figure 7.12b) established by López Varela (1996; see also chapter 8). The primary feature of these vessels is incised horizontal ribbings that are from 1 to 1.5 cm in width and are separated by 0.5 to 1 cm of encircling indentation. This pattern apparently was formed by incising and smoothing vessel walls during the leather-hard stage of production. López Varela (1996) notes that the slip appears mottled and is similar to the lighter slip color of Society Hall Red vessels. Paste is variable and can consist of grog temper or calcite tempering. Quartz is present in the majority of sherds analyzed but always co-occurs with either calcite or grog.

Society Hall Red vessels were an important part of ritual practice at K'axob primarily during the late and terminal facets of K'atabche'k'ax times. This type of vessel was first described by Smith (1955) for Uaxactun and has been reported from Cerros (but earlier and only in domestic contexts; Robertson-Freidel 1980) and at Cuello (but with more variable shapes; Kosakowsky 1987). At K'axob, these vessels appear predominantly in burial contexts. López Varela (chapter 8) reports that Society Hall Red vessels compose only 6% of the red wares. Rim diameters vary from 19 to 54 cm and represent some of the largest vessels at K'axob. These vessels appear fairly standardized, with thick vertical walls, everted rims, and flat or incurved

bases (with a sharp-angled bend forming the base), and, frequently, with a slipped quadripartite pattern on the base (see chapter 16).

The absence of certain types and forms is also noteworthy. Tecomates, never very frequent, all but disappear at K'axob by Chicanel times (see chapter 8). The only utilitarian ware present in the Chaakk'ax complex is Chicago Orange. Monkey Falls and Sapote Striated types appear in the early facet of the K'atabche'k'ax complex. The observed variation of utilitarian wares present at sites such as Cerros (Robertson-Freidel 1980) is absent at K'axob. Black-slipped wares are represented by only two sherds of Polvero Black (López Varela 1996). Cream-slipped vessels are present at K'axob but only in limited numbers (Flor Cream sherds compose 0.16%). White slip is present on only one sherd dating to the Chaakk'ax period. These rare vessel types were probably not produced at K'axob.

FIRING

To determine firing temperatures, the clays sampled from northern Belize and sherds from archaeological contexts were refired to varying temperatures and subjected to varying firing regimes (see chapter 8 for a discussion of refiring experiments). The results were thin-sectioned and analyzed petrographically. Three sherds with variable paste composition were selected for this experiment. Specifically, these were (1) a sherd with a high percentage of sparitic calcite (sample 277), (2) a sherd with grog and quartz (sample 278), and (3) a sherd composed of grog and calcite (sample 275). The

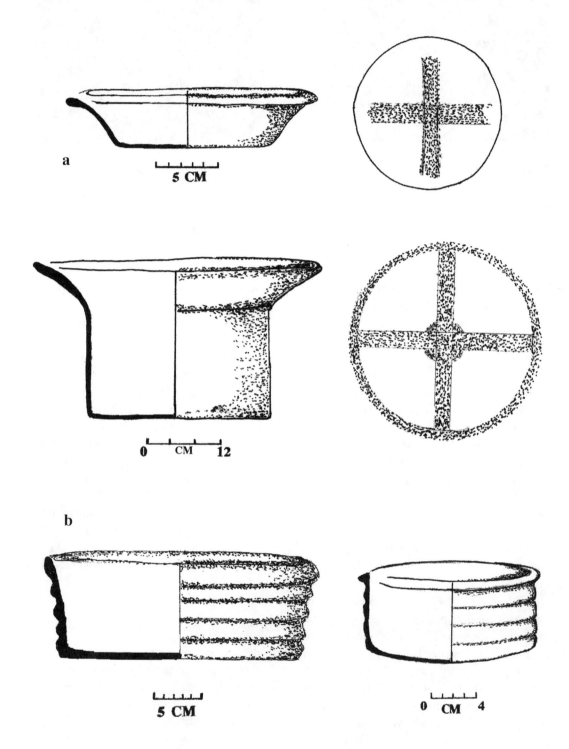

Figure 7.12 Illustration of unique stylistic markers from vessels at K'axob.
a. Two examples of cross motif painted on exterior (upper dish) and interior (lower bowl).
b. Gadrooned vessel from K'axob. *Illustration by Mary Lee Bartlett*

samples were all drawn from an operation 1 sherd-lined pit dating to the late facet of the K'atabche'k'ax.

The calcite-tempered Chicago Orange bowl sherd evinced no change at 650°C (sample 277). The calcite was clear and highly birefringent with no evidence of chemical decomposition of the paste or mineral inclusions. Firing to 800°C did produce marked change. The sparitic calcite chemically altered dramatically. No birefringent colors were evident. Voids around inclusions increased and the calcite and paste were disintegrating. The paste color also became redder as further oxidation of iron oxides occurred. This test indicates that original firing temperature was between 650°C and 800°C.

The second sample (sample 278), which contained rounded quartz and grog with quartz inclusions, had yellow clay bands and a micritic area with no birefringence at 650°C, indicating no change from the original sample. At 800°C the sherd had begun to disintegrate. Voids were apparent and particularly wide around inclusions. The micritic areas were no longer apparent. The paste had assumed a dark red color as the iron oxides were further oxidized. Firing temperature must have been well below 800°C.

The third sample (sample 275) containing rounded quartz and grog with calcite inclusions evinced changes by 650°C. The grog temper had begun to disintegrate, and micrite, apparent in the original sherd, was no longer evident. At 800°C the grog had altered to a gray color with no birefringence, and the paste was very red. Original firing temperature was below 650°C.

In contrast, clay samples tended to spall at 600°C. Carbon was trapped within the paste and, in combination with other chemicals, formed a hard, black vitrified area. The occurrence of vitrification was decreased when the clays were preheated and then the heat was raised slowly. If clays high in organics, such as the zone 2 clays, were utilized, then some form of preheating was probably employed and firing likely did not exceed 600°C. Most sherds have a darkened interior, indicating that the organics were not completely oxidized. Complete oxidation would occur if firing temperature exceeded 600°C.

Previous research on firing temperature in calcite-tempered sherds indicates that temperature must remain below 750°C for the calcite to remain stable (Rye 1981). Rice (1987a) suggests that the firing temperature should not exceed 850°C. Refiring of sherds from K'axob indicates that firing temperatures probably did not exceed 800°C and often remained below 650°C. The experiments by Daszkiewicz, Scheider, and Bobryk (1999) suggest the same findings. Experiments with clays suggest that firing temperatures may be lower than expected because of the high organic content of many clays. Rye (1981) observes that clays may contain 10 to 20% organics and that these will be indicated by a black or gray core of incompletely oxidized carbon. In many Formative Maya ceramics, this darkened core is evident.

A final note on firing techniques involves the type of facility utilized to fire the ceramics. The assumption is that pottery was fired using an open firing method. Fireclouding on the inner and outer surface of vessels produced by drafts or contact with fuels is suggestive of open firing. Fireclouding is common on slipped vessels from the Maya Preclassic period. There is no evidence that firing temperature changed over time. In the Middle Preclassic period, vessels have fireclouding and darkened cores similar to those found in Late Preclassic vessels.

SUMMARY

Preclassic Maya potters were skilled artisans who were able to produce vessels from a variety of clay types using a number of different preparation and formation techniques, depending on the form and use of the proposed vessel. These technological approaches remained a part of their repertoire throughout the Formative period. Subtle technological change is observable in terms of the degree that a particular clay resource was exploited or the frequency with which a particular preparation technique was employed. Localization of production is apparent by the end of the K'atabche'k'ax complex. The variations in soil formation processes in the region allow for this determination. Alluvial deposition, erosion from the Maya Mountains, progressive and trangressive sequences as the oceans rose and fell are some of the factors contributing to this variability. Maya potters were cognizant of the differences in clays and developed techniques to render them workable. Over time, they increased the usage of those techniques that were most effective with local clays.

The presence of unique community markers by the end of the Late Preclassic period also indicates the development of a community identity linked to place. A unique marker for K'axob is the quadripartite pattern slipped on the inner or outer base of some vessels. Gadrooned vessels also seem to be an innovation unique to K'axob. The presence of stylistic differences among northern Belizean sites by the Late Preclassic period suggests the presence of a localized potting tradition within an overarching sphere (Bartlett and McAnany 2000a).

Resource procurement and the variability in clay usage from the Middle to the Late Preclassic period provide evidence of trade networks. The links between rocks from the Lamanai area and Albion Island should be investigated further. Both the resource and the pottery could have been easily transported. Intensive testing of clays in both areas might help to pinpoint whether the temper or the finished vessel was being traded.

Potters made vessels in a variety of forms, depending upon intended use. The forming techniques employed were variable. The coiling method was probably the most prevalent, but mold-making and the use of a paddle and anvil were also common, especially by the end of the Preclassic period. These methods would have increased the speed of production and (possibly) efficiency of production, suggestive of craft specialization. Paste preparation techniques were predicated on vessel use. Utilitarian, unslipped vessels were made with calcite temper, while slipped vessels were more variable. Use of grog temper or the addition of no temper increased throughout the Preclassic period. Grog is easier to crush and more readily accessible than calcite, which is made from crushed limestone that had to be imported. These factors may account for the increased use of grog, or perhaps, as with the Sirak Bulahay, grog from broken heirlooms facilitated communication with the ancestors. This ideological explanation may be a contributing factor in the increased occurrence of grog usage for ceremonial vessels.

K'axob operated within a network of larger centers; nevertheless, potters were able to localize production and to develop unique style markers for their community. These markers provided a separate identity for this village within a larger society, suggesting that K'axob developed as a relatively self-sufficient community while surrounded by larger, presumably dominant, centers.

NOTES

1. The specific study area is bounded to the north by the town of Corozal and Chetumal Bay, to the northwest by the Río Hondo, to the southwest by the site of Lamanai along the New River, to the east by Progresso Lagoon and the archaeological site of Altun Ha on the Old Northern Highway, and to the south by the Belize River (figures 7.1, 7.2).

2. Soil samples with a high clay content were collected with a posthole digger at an approximate depth of 30 to 40 cm.

3. In-depth discussion of the preparation methods used can be found in Angelini (1998) and Bartlett et al. (2000).

4. Darch and Furley (1983:184) report core samples in the Orange Walk area, with an A horizon of generally less than 40 cm. In all of their samples, the underlying layer of sascab extended to the depth of the core (2 m). Additional bore hole data from northern Belize record a depth of sascab extending to 20 m or more (Darch and Furley 1983:189).

5. In the alluvial deposits along the two rivers, quartz occupies only 10 to 20% of the field of view, based on point count data, and is present only as small grains (below .05 mm at 10X). In samples along the pine ridge (zone 1), quartz occupies 30 to 60% of the field of view and varies in size from .01 mm to 1.05 mm at 10X. Quartz along the pine ridge can be subangular in appearance, indicating less physical weathering. In contrast, quartz grains found in the alluvial zone (zone 2) are round, indicating either increased physical abrasion that occurred in a marine environment or that the grains had been rounded in the course of transport from a source area, likely the Maya Mountains. Quartz found in zone 3 (the chert belt) is similar to that found in zone 1.

6. When present, gypsum occupies between 20 to 40% of the field of view based on point count data.

7. When present, shell occupies 1 to 10% of the field of view.

8. A soil region (Xaibe subsuite) west of Corozal has distinctly red-brown soil (5YR 3/2) and several samples fired red (2.5YR 2/6), which is indicative of iron oxides and smectite clay minerals.

9. A chi-square test indicates that the probability that distribution among these three zones would occur by chance is .008 (chi square is 13.78 with 4 degrees of freedom).

10. INAA involves the bombardment of incident nucleus with neutrons, producing radioactive isotopes exhibiting unique measurable gamma rays that serve to identify and quantify them (Glascock 1992:12). Once the elemental data are collected, they are transformed into log base 10 values to decrease the differences among the major elements and the trace elements and to utilize the normal distribution, which is more apparent when based on logarithms. Ni and Sr were eliminated from the

thirty-five-element data set because they contained missing values that could affect the calculations. When gamma ray peaks are below detection, missing data can occur. Once the data were transformed the results were compared using principal components analysis. Group membership was tested using Mahalanobis distance calculation (Angelini 1998; Bartlett et al. 2000).

11. A t-test determined that the probability that the Ha-Ca distribution is random is .0001.

12. Generally quartz is round to subround and occupies from 15 to 20% of the field of view.

13. Fourteen percent of ceramics from the Chaakk'ax complex contain oxides, as compared with 36% by the late facet of the K'atabche'k'ax complex.

14. Based on point count data, grog can represent from 3 to 26% of the field of view.

15. The probability that these changes would occur by chance alone, based on chi square, is .006 ($X^2 = 14.22$ with 4df).

Chapter 8
Related CD Resources

Pottery Vessels
Pottery Sherds
Cross Motif Vessels

CERAMIC HISTORY OF K'AXOB: THE EARLY YEARS

SANDRA L. LÓPEZ VARELA

Si los tepalcates hablaran qué no nos dirían.
(If sherds could talk, the stories they would tell us.)

Since the 1960s, Maya ceramic research has used the type-variety system as a principal tool of classification. The potential of this method relies on its inner capacity to provide a chronological and spatial framework from which to interpret Maya society. Critical to ceramic research and central to the type-variety system is the process of inter- and intrasite comparisons that enables a researcher to appraise the significance of a particular ceramic collection. To appraise the meaning of a ceramic sample and to define intersite ceramic relations, comparisons of attributes are made with available collections. The procedure provides a setting for understanding pottery network distributions or long-standing social interactions that are also addressed from the perspective of mineralogical and elemental studies of sherd composition (for example, Angelini 1998; Ball 1983; Gifford 1976; Jones 1986; Neff, Bishop, and Arnold 1988; Rice 1987a, 1991).

The type-variety system has proved to be a fine descriptive tool when combined with characterization and provenience studies, but has provided only limited knowledge about the social and physical variables affecting Maya pottery production and technology. Like our colleagues in northern Belize (Pring 1977a; Kosakowsky 1987; Fry 1983; Valdez 1987; Reese and Valdez 1987; Meskill 1992; Robertson 1986), we selected the type-variety system as a first step to classifying pottery from K'axob because it provided the required chronological framework. The K'axob relative ceramic sequence is anchored chronometrically by a series of twenty-five radiocarbon assays analyzed at the University of Arizona and Oxford Laboratories (Hedges et al. 1992:337–338) and is further supported by stratigraphic data (López Varela 1996; McAnany and López Varela 1999). According to these results, the founding of K'axob occurred shortly after 800 BC, during the Middle Formative (800–400 BC).

To further understand the K'axob ceramic sample and to evaluate intersite ceramic relations, I studied the sherd collections available at the Department of Archaeology (Belmopan), the Centro-INAH (Yucatan), the Peabody Museum (Harvard University), the University of Texas (Austin), and the Museé de l'Homme (Paris). This classic type-variety study, which has resulted in the classification and the seriation of pottery from K'axob, was based purely on stylistic and macroscopic fabric differences. For a complementary approach to classification based on the chemical and mineralogical analysis of pottery fabric, see Bartlett (chapter 7; see also Bartlett, Neff, and McAnany 2000). Here the comprehensive program of analysis undertaken by Bartlett (352 ceramic samples and 143 soil samples) is further augmented by the analysis of an additional seventy-one sherd samples of selected types and varieties from the Middle Formative to the Late Postclassic periods (Daszkiewicz, Schneider, and Bobryk 1999). The samples analyzed by Daszkiewicz, Schneider, and Bobryk in the laboratory at Freie Universität Berlin provide information on several problematic issues related to the type-variety classification of the pottery of K'axob. Results of their analysis serve as an analytical guide to exploring these issues and emphasize the need to expand this program of study to other sites. Full results of this suite of analyses will be published elsewhere. In this chapter, only results relevant to the Middle Formative through the Early Classic periods are presented.

Here, I discuss the pottery of each ceramic complex from the Middle Formative through the transition to the Early Classic period, noting evidence of local production and importation. This ceramic history is based on the analysis of the pottery sherds and vessels from the 1990–1993 excavations, the full corpus of which can be examined in the accompanying *Pottery Sherds Database* and *Pottery Vessels Database*. More information and images of specific vessels (identified by number) are available in the following chapter as well as in the *Pottery Vessels Database*. Throughout this chapter, the mortuary and cache vessels of K'axob are referenced by vessel number and ceramic complex. Images of these vessels can be found in chapter 9, which is arranged by ceramic complex. A thumbnail sketch of the relevant K'axob ceramic complexes is provided in table 8.1. The earliest, Middle Formative pottery of K'axob (800–400 BC) has been divided into an early and late facet of the Chaakk'ax ceramic complex. The Late Formative (400 BC to AD 250) pottery of the K'atabche'k'ax complex can be subdivided into early, late, and terminal facets; the last facet

contains a significant admixture of Protoclassic material. Several of the excavations conducted in the southern portion of K'axob yielded an uppermost Early Classic component (Nohalk'ax complex) that is introduced toward the end of this chapter. This complex will be examined in further detail in later publications, which will include a larger corpus of Early Classic material from the 1995 field season.

In addition to presenting the early ceramic complexes of K'axob, I examine regional evidence of the earliest Lowland Maya pottery and its implications for understanding the founding of K'axob. I discuss the confounding effects of the variable application of the type-variety system to the Formative period of northern Belize.

FIRST VILLAGERS OF THE CHAAKK'AX CERAMIC COMPLEX (800–400 BC)

Ceramics from the Chaakk'ax ceramic complex originated from excavations at operations 1 and 11. Chaakk'ax occupation levels consisted primarily of apsidal structures with middens, sherd-lined pits, patches of burned floors, and extended burials (see chapter 3; Henderson 1998; McAnany and López Varela 1999). The Chaakk'ax ceramic complex is defined by a suite of eight radiocarbon AMS assays from construction phases 1–3 of operation 1 (McAnany and López Varela 1999:154). Phase 1, the paleosol occupation, included the oldest Formative ceramics found at K'axob and defines the beginning of a Middle Formative ceramic complex. Phases 1 and 2 contained Xe, Real, and Mamom ceramics and are followed by Phase 3, which included only Mamom ceramics, supporting the establishment of an early and late facet for this ceramic complex (López Varela 1996). An early facet of the Mamom ceramic complex was established (rather than a late facet of the Xe ceramic complex) because, quantitatively, most of the types correspond to the Mamom ceramic sphere (table 8.2). The presence of Xe and Real ceramic material, along with the stratigraphy, supports the integrity of an early facet of the Chaakk'ax ceramic complex. The diversity and richness of early facet Chaakk'ax with regard not only to the ceramic material but also to the entire artifact assemblage, suggest an early village with established agricultural and ritual practices and far-flung trading networks (McAnany and López Varela 1999).

Table 8.1. Prevalent characteristics of the early ceramic complexes of K'axob

Complex/Period/Sphere	Facet/Time range	Characteristics
Nohalk' ax Early Classic Tzakol	Early AD 250 - ?	Gradual replacement of the earlier dominant red-slipped surfaces with glossy orange slip (2.5 YR 5/8), polychrome painting (Actuncan and Dos Arroyos groups), and variegated colors with continuation of waxy wares. Painted motifs include the Kan Cross, a shell motif and an undulating jaguar. Vessel feet were sometimes modeled to form animal features, for example, peccary heads Dishes with rounded sides and ring bases dominate in the Aguila ceramic group, together with bowls with basal breaks or Z-angles and jars with vertical necks. Vessel rim diameters diminished during this period, ranging between 17 and 26 cm, in contrast to the larger bowls of the earlier K'atabche'k'ax ceramic complex with diameters of 22 to 46 cm.
K' atabche' k' ax Late Formative Chicanel	Terminal 50 BC – AD 250	Red wares dominated the terminal facet and Sierra Red: Sierra Variety was the preferred type. Pottery of Chicago Orange was discontinued in favor of striated wares. Modes added to the late facet include the Holmul polychrome tradition (Guacamallo Red-on-Orange and Ixcanrio Orange polychrome), and large Aguacate Orange serving bowls with mammiform tetrapods as well as outflaring bowls with basal flanges. Geometric motifs and wavy and straight lines continued to emulate the Usulutan tradition in dichrome pottery. Vessels were decorated with crosses, monkey-face applications, and half-moon incisions.
	Late 200 - 50 BC	Jar forms were modified through application of continuous striations to the vessel body. Jars feature short, outcurved necks with a direct rim and rounded lip in three main ceramic types: Chicago Orange: Chucun Variety; Monkey Falls Striated: Monkey Falls Variety; and Sapote Striated: Unspecified Variety. Jar necks of the Sierra Group increased in height and vessel capacity expanded from the early facet. Pottery samples of Monkey Falls Striated, Chicago Orange, and Sierra Red with a non-calcareous matrix and temper of coarse crystalline calcite probably were built for cooking or boiling water. Jars with application of button appliques or nail impressions to the neck juncture and a calcareous matrix were probably used for storage. Strap handles with small apertures were attached to jars to facilitate hanging with a cord. Bowls exhibit vertical walls and *tecomate* forms completely disappeared. Vessels from the Sierra Group sometimes were decorated with appliques, fluting, gadrooning, impressing, incising, modeling and punctates. Less significant were the black, cream, red-on-cream, and red-on-orange wares. Society Hall Red: Society Hall Variety bowls were characterized by outcurved sides, an outflared everted rim and a rounded lip, often with a painted quadripartite motif across the base. Hillbank Red (a Gale Creek Red ware) was introduced. Also present are an Unnamed Red-on-Orange and Unnamed Orange-on-Cream, both Usulutan related types.
	Early 400 - 200 BC	The *tecomate* was replaced by jars (with a short neck, a direct rim with a rounded lip) and bowls with incurved sides. Spouted jars, some with handles, were introduced. The Sierra Group occurred intermittently in ritual and domestic contexts. The burgundy slip of the Joventud group disappeared in favor of the red of the Sierra group. There was an abundance of new types and varieties with dichrome decoration and appliqued bands. Incised lines formed geometric motifs such as half circles, diagonal or rectilinear-curvilinear patterns (revealing a lingering pre-Mamom tradition). Effigy vessels appeared for the first time.
Chaak' k' ax Middle Formative Mamom	Late 600 - 400 BC	Pre-Mamom component disappeared and was replaced by Mamom ceramics. There was a dramatic decrease in the diversity and frequency of ceramic types in comparison with the earlier facet. Primary types include Joventud Red, Guitara Incised: Guitara Variety, Muxanal Red-on-cream: Unspecified Variety, and Chicago Orange. Orange mottled pottery disappeared in favor of red-slipped ceramics. Decoration, mainly circumferential lines, was incised on flat-bottomed, flaring-walled bowls with wide everted rims. There was a gradual replacement of *tecomates* with jars during the Middle to Late Formative transition at K'axob. Sierra Red first appeared in a Middle Formative interment (Burial 1-30a).
	Early 800-600 BC	Pottery types of the early facet that were imported to K'axob include Abelino Red, Pital Cream, Joventud Red, and Muxanal Red-on-Cream. Local ceramics are represented by Chicago Orange which accounts for over two-thirds of the total sherd count. Most pottery made from calcareous clays, some tempered with calcite. Forms include thin-walled bowls, dishes, and a few tecomates; there is a relative absence of jars. All wares were slipped with orange slip predominating (80%) followed by dark red (24%) and smaller percentages of red-on-cream, black, resist, and cream slips. Incising with one to three lines was a favored decorative featured in Guitara Incised: Guitara Variety and Muxanal Red-on-Cream: Unspecified Variety. The characteristic dark red slip of Joventud Red and Abelino Red produced distinctive surface decoration. Pre-slip incised circumferential lines occur near the rim on the exterior part of vessels, on the horizontal everted rims, or as incised-bottom lines. Chamfering was an important technique used to decorate the *tecomate* form.

Table 8.2 Types and varieties of the Chaakk'ax ceramic complex

Ceramic Type: Variety	Total Number of Sherds	Percentage of Total Number of Sherds
Xe and Real Ceramic Types		
Abelino Red: Abelino Variety (early facet)	23	0.21
Toribio Red-on-cream: Toribio Variety (early facet)	35	0.31
Mamom Ceramic Types		
Chicago Orange: Chucun Variety (early and late facets)	7, 801	70.19
Chunhinta Black: Unspecified Variety (early facet)	25	0.22
Desvario Chamfered: Unspecified Variety (early facet)	1	1.01
Joventud Red: Jolote Variety (early facet)	170	1.53
Joventud Red: Unspecified Variety (early and late facets)	2, 087	18.78
Guitara Incised: Guitara Variety (early and late facets)	452	4.07
Muxanal Red-on-cream: Unspecified Variety (early and late facets)	195	1.75
Pital Cream: Pital Variety (early facet)	137	1.23
Pital Cream: Red Slipped Variety (early facet)	61	0.55
Tierra Mojada Resist: Tierra Mojada Variety (early facet)	112	1.01
Timax Incised: Timax Variety (early facet)	12	0.11
Unnamed Resist Orange (early facet)	3	0.03
TOTAL	**11,114**	**100.00%**

EARLY FACET OF THE CHAAKK'AX CERAMIC COMPLEX

Pottery from the early facet of the Chaakk'ax ceramic complex comprises types and varieties produced mostly outside of K'axob (Angelini 1998; Bartlett, Neff, and McAnany 2000; Daszkiewicz, Schneider, and Bobryk 1999; see chapter 7). The local aspect of Chaakk'ax ceramics is seen in the vessels of Chicago Orange, which are covered with a thin orange wash (López Varela 1996). Vessels classified as Chicago Orange predominate in the Chaakk'ax ceramic complex and account for 71% of the total sherd count. The early facet of the Chaakk'ax ceramic complex includes distinctive thin-walled bowls, dishes, and a few tecomates; there is a relative absence of jars (López Varela 1996; McAnany and López Varela 1999; figure 8.1). The few jars that existed in the early facet of the Chaakk'ax ceramic complex correspond to those of Chicago Orange and Joventud Red. The relative absence of jars until the end of the late facet suggests the changes in the scale and character of domestic cook-ing and storage that took place on the brink of the Late Formative period. Deposits so far excavated have yielded only decorated ceramics with monochrome and bichrome slips; there is an absence of unslipped vessels.

Chaakk'ax pottery bears modal similarities to pottery from sites such as Altar de Sacrificios, Seibal, Tikal, Uaxactun, El Mirador, Piedras Negras, Yaxha-Sacnab Lake Basin, Tayasal-Paxcaman zone, Barton Ramie, Colha, Cuello, Kichpanha, Becan, Komchen, Acachen, Chan Chen, Caledonia, the Guatemala Highlands, and Mayapan. Chemical and mineralogical results support the argument that Mamom ceramics from K'axob combine local expressions with external stylistic and formal influences that originated during pre-Mamom times. These external stylistic and formal influences may have originated from the Pacific Coast of Chiapas, Honduras, and El Salvador and are represented in modes of skillfully executed pottery. Some vessels exhibit incisions and groovings that reflect the inheritance of the earlier ceramic complexes of Mesoamerica, mainly Cuadros and Jocotal phase ceramics (Clark and Blake 1994; Blake et

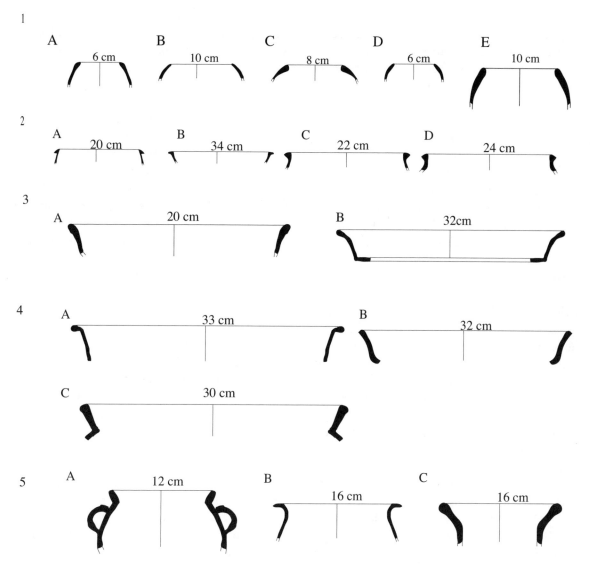

Figure 8.1 Type and forms of early and late facet Chaakk'ax ceramic complex; *Row 1 Tecomates*: (A) Chunhinta Black, (B) Pital Cream, (C-D) Chicago Orange, (E) Joventud Red; *Row 2 Bowls*: (A) Chunhinta Black, (B) Tierra Mojada Resist, (C-D) Chicago Orange; *Row 3 Dishes*: (A) Abelino Red, (B) Pital Cream; *Row 4 Bowls*: (A) Guitara Incised, (B) Muxanal Red-on-Cream, (C) Tierra Mojada Resist; *Row 5 Jars of Chicago Orange with* (A) outcurved neck and direct rim, (B) outcurved neck and horizontal everted rim, and (C) outcurved neck and direct rim. *Illustration by Sandra L. López Varela*

al. 1995). The beveled outflaring rims in some dishes and bowls of Abelino Red, Guitara Incised, and Muxanal Red-on-Cream are reminiscent of Cuadros ceramics from the Pacific coast of Chiapas (Blake et al. 1995).

The chemical and mineralogical signature of some types and varieties of the Middle Formative period indicates that they are likely imports to K'axob; that is, their paste composition deviates from the local signature of calcareous clays (Angelini 1998; Bartlett, Neff, and McAnany 2000; Daszkiewicz, Schneider, and Bobryk 1999). Six samples, in particular, deviate to such an extent that they may be regarded as imports from a

region with geochemically differing clays or carbonates. These samples include the Xe type, Abelino Red, which is associated with the early pottery-using group that entered the Maya Lowlands by 1000 BC.

One sample of Abelino Red (Y715; samples analyzed by Daszkiewicz, Schneider, and Bobryk in the laboratory at Freie Universität Berlin are referenced by their "Y" series number) and one of Joventud Red (Y716) belong to this group of proposed imports. Chemical and mineralogical characterization of Joventud Red (Y715), Abelino Red (Y716), and Pital Cream (Y713) reveal cryptocrystalline and sparitic aggregates of carbonates as well as grog temper. One of the grog particles in Abelino Red (Y716) is from a sherd full of the boomerang-shaped volcanic glass that clearly marks this "sherd-within-a-sherd" as a foreign import. Samples of Muxanal Red-on-Cream (Y714), Joventud Red (Y715), and Abelino Red (Y716) contain higher concentrations of potassium (Daszkiewicz, Schneider, and Bobryk 1999) than was observed in local types such as Chicago Orange. In Muxanal Red-on-Cream (Y714), the grain sizes above 0.5 mm are from crushed coarse crystalline calcite and cryptocrystalline, and sparitic aggregates of carbonates. In her survey of rock types local to K'axob, Bartlett (chapter 7) found no sparitic carbonates, providing conclusive evidence that this inclusion was imported (either as temper or as already incorporated into vessels).

The presence at K'axob of Tierra Mojada Resist, Timax Incised, and a few Unnamed Resist Orange sherds confirms the extended spatial distribution of coeval ceramic traditions of El Salvador. Besides the stylistic and modal influences received from the Pasión and El Salvador at the end of the early Middle Formative, there is another independent line of ceramic development that probably links northern Belize to the Yucatan Peninsula. Expressed in the spatial distribution of the Muxanal group, this type is restricted to a region encompassing northern Belize north to Rio Bec (Ball 1977:152). It appears only in minor quantities at Altar de Sacrificios (Adams 1971:27), Uaxactun (Ball 1977:151), Yaxha-Sacnab Lake Basin (Rice 1979:22), and El Mirador (Forsyth 1989:125). The poor representation of Muxanal Red-on-Cream in the Petén and its absence at Barton Ramie support the idea that northern Belize participated in different ceramic networks—networks that did not necessarily include its Belize River Valley neighbors. However, without the wider application of archaeometric and provenience studies, we are unable to detect the one or the many workshops that could be producing such pottery in order to establish firm intersite distributions.

LATE FACET OF THE CHAAKK'AX CERAMIC COMPLEX

During the late facet of the Chaakk'ax ceramic complex (600–400 BC), the pre-Mamom component disappeared and was replaced by Mamom ceramics. A similar replacement occurred at Colha and Kichpanha (Valdez 1987; Reese and Valdez 1987), where the Joventud group and the Richardson Peak Unslipped type substitute for the Consejo group and the Copetilla Unslipped types. The late facet of the Chaakk'ax ceramic complex also experienced a dramatic decrease in the diversity and frequency of ceramic types in comparison with the earlier facet. Only three types of monochrome and bichrome serving bowls continue in production through this facet: Joventud Red, Guitara Incised, and Muxanal Red-on-Cream (see *Pottery Sherds Database*). The same scarcity of ceramic types was also detected at Colha (Valdez 1987), El Mirador (Forsyth 1989), and Becan (Ball 1977). At these sites, ceramic production concentrated only on the making of red, black, and cream monochromes and red-on-cream pottery. The wide distribution of essentially the same pottery styles suggests closely connected communities (Clark, Hansen, and Pérez 2000). Precisely at this time, El Mirador, located to the west near the Guatemala-Mexico border, became a powerful site in the Maya region (Clark, Hansen, and Pérez 2000). The relative decline in ceramic variety might be related to the profound political changes that occurred in eastern Mesoamerica as the powerful Olmec realm headed for collapse (Clark, Hansen, and Pérez 2000).

Stylistically, late facet Chaakk'ax is more closely related to El Mirador Basin and the Pasión and Petén regions. Incised decoration, mainly a circumferential line near the rim of flared bowls, is a diagnostic trait at K'axob and El Mirador. The orange mottled pottery that linked K'axob to the southern Maya Lowlands disappeared in favor of red-slipped ceramics. The only evidence of orange ceramics in the assemblage occurs in Chicago Orange.

The late facet is dominated by flat-bottomed, flaring-walled vessels with wide everted rims, which are important forms during Mamom times at K'axob, Colha (Valdez 1987), Kichpanha (Reese and Valdez 1987), the Pasión (Adams 1971), and El Mirador Basin regions. The jar form still constitutes a minor percentage of the assemblage as the thin-slipped Chicago Orange bowls outnumber jars by two to one (McAnany and López Varela 1999:158). The gradual replacement of tecomates with jars during the Middle to Late Formative transition at K'axob may be a response to new food products and new forms of cooking (see chapter 5). Thus, the appearance of jars in Mesoamerica may be related to intensification of agriculture and the role of maize within the diet. This could explain why ceramic forms of earlier Mesoamerican peoples—for example, those of earlier

Barra and Locona phases (Clark and Blake 1994:27)—were not designed for cooking but, rather, for serving food and beverages.

The striated vessels and the unslipped pottery of the Late Formative period are also absent at this time. Signaling the advent of the Late Formative, two vessels, one a Matamore Dichrome and the other a Sierra Red, were deposited in the Middle Formative interment of an individual (burial 1-30a; vessels 017 and 018). Hereafter, the Sierra Red Ceramic group constitutes the dominant monochrome red ware of the Late Formative period.

GRAPPLING WITH MULTIPLE CLASSIFICATION SCHEMES FOR THE MIDDLE FORMATIVE PERIOD

Since type-variety classification is a tried-and-true method of establishing a relative chronology for both sites and regions, the nomenclature of classification, as well as supporting radiocarbon assays, are often subjected to intense critical scrutiny. Nowhere is this more evident than in northern Belize, where claims for the "earliest Maya" have sparked a lively debate over both pottery nomenclature and associated chronometric dates. Original placement of the Swasey complex of Cuello within a time range of 2600 to 1200 BC (Hammond et al. 1976; Pring 1977a) radically "drew down" all Lowland Maya Formative chronologies. Although this complex has since been recalibrated to 1200 to 900/800 BC, the Swasey and the Bladen complexes (800–600 BC) still pose taxonomic difficulties (Andrews V and Hammond 1990). After the chronology was shortened, Kosakowsky and Pring (1998) attempted to revise the Cuello ceramic classification, but the origins, singularity, and taxonomy of Swasey and Bladen ceramics continue to be debated (López Varela 1996; Joyce and Henderson 2001). The lingering chronological and typological problems for the application of the type-variety system to northern Belize prompted me to examine the correspondence between northern Belize ceramics and those of the rest of the Maya Lowlands. I found that many of the new type names established for Cuello already existed in the published literature of the Petén. In defining Swasey and Bladen ceramics, chronological criteria had been given priority over similarities in slip, form, and decoration.

In effect, the early radiocarbon dating of the Swasey complex was employed as a criterion to establish the Swasey and Bladen types (Pring 1977a; Kosakowsky 1983, 1987) as, at the time, the newer and more recent dates were not available to Pring (1977a) and Kosakowsky (1983, 1987a). A good example is the establishment of Patchchacan Pattern-Burnished: Patchchacan Variety by Kosakowsky (1987:14–15), originally identified by Pring (1977a) as an Unspecified Variety of Yotolin Pattern-Burnished type at Maní Cenote. In 1987 Kosakowsky chose to classify the Cuello pattern-burnished pottery as a new type because the Cuello sherds predated the presence of Yotolin Pattern-Burnished type by more than 1,000 years. Kosakowsky and Pring followed a similar path in establishing most Swasey and Bladen types (see López Varela 1996 for further discussion).

Pring (1977a) and Kosakowksy (1987) argued rightly, and within the logic of the type-variety system, that the new ceramic types predated established types in other areas regardless of their similarities; so new names were given to already established types or varieties. With the adoption of a shorter chronology for Cuello (Andrews V and Hammond 1990), there is no longer any chronological disparity among the types. The establishment of a new type called Consejo Red: Consejo Variety is a critical example since this type has similar ceramic attributes in form and slip to Abelino Red: Abelino Variety, a Xe type from Altar de Sacrificios (compare Kosakowsky 1987:16 to Adams 1971:20). The reassessment of the Cuello chronology renders Consejo Red: Consejo Variety coeval with Abelino Red: Abelino Variety. Clarifying this taxonomic problem is relevant to understanding the genesis of Maya ceramics and colonization of Belize, for Abelino Red may be informing us of the distribution of a pre-Mamom Pasión-derived ceramic component.

With this example, one can question whether geographical distance justifies the creation of a type or simply of a variety—Abelino Red: Consejo Red Variety. Certainly, for the later Late Formative and Classic periods, pottery with such closely matched slips and forms are not given different type names. In the Maya area it is widely accepted that the paste, waxiness, and color of a type such as Sierra Red vary from zone to zone. In Yucatan, Sierra Red is less waxy and is made of a more compact paste than it is in the Petén-Pasión regions. Regardless of the differences, ceramicists type both as Sierra Red with respective varieties. Sierra Red is a good example of the flexibility of the type-variety system. This type may constitute an example of a cultural type or mental template spanning several regions, with paste and slip difference imposed by available raw materials (Flannery and Marcus 1994:3).

In the ceramic literature of northern Belize, it is common to find a proliferation of new and redundant types and varieties. Valdez (1987:51) noticed that one type at Colha might be nearly identical to two or more types present elsewhere. The proliferation of type names makes it difficult to assign a single name as an equivalent to those from other sites (Valdez 1987:51). Valdez appreciated the problem and made an effort to fit Colha ceramics to existing types or varieties. For ceramic identifications, Valdez (1987:52) ultimately decided to use the name of the type from the site physically closest to Colha to avoid further confusion (see Valdez 1987). Unfortunately, when nonceramic researchers in the Maya area seek a comprehensive guide to the types of northern Belize, they are faced with the arduous task of figuring out why the same types have more than one name. Certainly, this was not the original purpose of the type-variety system (Smith and Gifford 1966). As Forsyth (1989:7) has suggested, we must revise "the received classification" to better reflect actual similarities in Maya Lowland pottery. Unfortunately, basing our observations on stylistic or macroscopic grounds will rarely solve the typological problems. In order to determine whether a type is local or imported we need not only INAA but also fine-grained technological analysis.

At K'axob the original type names are employed as a means to emphasize the problematic issues of classification nomenclature (López Varela 1996). For example, I report the Cuello type Consejo Red as Abelino Red: Abelino Variety because its characterization signature is foreign to K'axob. If ceramicists can agree on the reestablishment of this type as a variant of Abelino Red, based on stronger analytical methods, then it could be classified as Abelino Red: Consejo Variety. In the meantime, a revision of the Swasey and Bladen ceramic names could resolve what falsely appears to be a lack of ceramic ties between northern Belize and the rest of the Maya Lowlands during the early Middle Formative period. A revised classification would also mitigate the arduous task of figuring out why types in northern Belize carry so many pseudonyms.

A shortened chronology for Cuello brings the Swasey and Bladen types closer in time to the Xe ceramic tradition (Pring 1977a:362; Marcus 1984:830; Hammond 1991b:6). The different type names, however, make Belizean Formative pottery technology appear to have been more insular than it actually was. Consequently, I disagree with Hammond's view that the modal links and the few closer type-level parallels between Bladen and the Xe sphere, demonstrated by Kosakowsky, make Bladen separable from Swasey at slightly more than the facet level (Andrews V and Hammond 1990:575). I support Andrews' observation that Swasey and Bladen ceramics are not sufficiently different to warrant separation into two complexes (Andrews V and Hammond 1990:579); rather, Swasey and Bladen ceramics appear to constitute an early and late facet of a single ceramic complex that includes significant local ceramic expression (Andrews V and Hammond 1990:579). The minor differences between Swasey and Bladen likely constitute a transitional stage between Xe and Mamom ceramic spheres.

ON THE ORIGINS OF THE CHAAKK'AX CERAMIC COMPLEX

The adoption of ceramic technology in present-day Belize occurred around 1000–900 BC, at least 200 years after the Gulf Coast Olmec had become a powerful influential polity in Mesoamerica (Clark 1997:213). Although Archaic populations existed in northern Belize around 1400 BC (Iceland 1997), the populations that eventually became sedentary adopted ceramic technology later in time. Recent archaeological evidence found in the Maya Lowlands indicates the presence of semi-sedentary bands at the beginning of the Early Formative period (Cheetham 1990:19). Evidence tends to support the notion that Middle Formative sedentary populations in the Maya Lowlands incorporated ideas originating on the Pacific coast of southeastern Mesoamerica during the second millennium BC (see Clark, Hansen, and Pérez 2000; Viel 1993). Even Cunil pottery from the Belize Valley site of Cahal Pech (Cheetham 1990; Awe 1992), dated to circa 950 BC, suggests close links with the Pacific and Gulf coasts. In the Cunil assemblage, the presence of rounded bowls with short solid legs is reminiscent of the earlier Locona to Ocos incurved-sided bowl with restricted orifice and solid legs (see Cheetham 1990). In addition, the Chitam subcomplex at Cahal Pech is charged with Olmec-like symbolism (Cheetham 1990:51).

Around 900 BC sedentary villages appear to have been rapidly established in the central Maya Lowlands (Cheetham 1990; Clark, Hansen, and Pérez 2000). Outside this area, village life and pottery production had already existed for several centuries (Cheetham 1990:24). The earliest Maya pottery in the Pasión is attributed to a ceramic complex called Xe at Altar de Sacrificios (Adams 1971) and Real at Seibal (Sabloff 1975). The Xe ceramic complex is composed of emergent Maya characteristics blended with stylistically foreign components that are closer to Mixe-Zoque (Andrews V 1990; Clark, Hansen, and Pérez 2000) than to El Salvador (Sharer and Gifford 1970).

Differences in ceramic assemblages between Altar de Sacrificios and Seibal suggest the existence of independent lines of local ceramic production or acquisition at both sites. The ceramic assemblages of Seibal and Altar de Sacrificios share the following Xe types: Abelino Red, Achiotes Unslipped, Baldizon Punctated, Chompipi Incised, Crisanto Black, Huetche White, and Pico de Oro Incised. Several Xe types identified at Altar de Sacrificios, such as Yaltata Orange, Datile Red-on-Black, and Uzbaldo Daub-on-Buff (Adams 1971:80), never made their way to Seibal. Characteristic Seibal types of the Real-Xe ceramic complex (such as Yalmanach Impressed, Edmundo Fluted, and Valdemar Fluted) are not represented at Altar de Sacrificios.

The fluted tradition, notable at Seibal (Sabloff 1975) during the Real-Xe ceramic complex, is not a significant component of the ceramic assemblage of Altar de Sacrificios (Adams 1971). Large bolstered-rim tecomates and the white slipped Huetche group, for example, are more significant at Seibal than at Altar de Sacrificios (Sabloff 1975:229), suggesting that Seibal enjoyed more intense contacts with the Gulf coast than did Altar de Sacrificios (Sabloff 1975:230). The fact that Xe pastes at Altar de Sacrificios present closer affinities to an Isthmian source than pastes at Seibal (Andrews V 1990) further supports the premise that Xe pottery was intrusive into the Pasión River drainage from Chiapas and that it was not an autochthonous Maya development (Andrews V 1990). Based on attribute analysis, the major types of slipped Xe ceramics (such as Abelino Red, Huetche White, and Crisanto Black) indicate strong affiliation with earlier ceramic complexes. This earlier southern Mesoamerican tradition includes Duende, Conchas I, Dili (Chiapa II), and Escalera (Chiapa III) phases within Chiapas (Adams 1971:153). Vessel forms, as noted by Andrews (1990:7), are closely related to ceramic traditions in Chiapas and Tabasco (such as Puente ceramics from Chontalpa) (Willey 1977:400).

Xe ceramics from Altar de Sacrificios are stylistically close to those used by the Mixe-Zoque peoples who inhabited central Chiapas to the west (Andrews V 1990; Clark, Hansen, and Pérez 2000). This observation runs contrary to the notion that Xe inhabitants arrived from El Salvador (Gifford 1976:61). Sharer and Gifford (1970:446–454) associated the Xe group with the making of unslipped Jocote Orange Brown pottery, a type characteristic of El Salvador. However, this Xe type has not been reported for Altar de Sacrificios (Adams 1971) or Seibal (Sabloff 1975). Simply put, one would expect to find earlier variants of the Altar de Sacrificios or Seibal Xe types at sites such as Chalchuapa in El Salvador, and these types are missing in the ceramic assemblage of this site. Besides, types of the Jocote Brown group (such as Palma Daub) are relatively rare in the Pasión region; rather, they are distributed in central and northern Petén as well as Belize (Foias 1996:215; López Varela 1996; Lee 1996).

The identity of Jocote Orange Brown, first established at Uaxactun (Smith and Gifford 1966), is not clear. Adams (1971:119) reports that Jocote Brown corresponds completely to Achiote Unslipped: Raudal Variety. This is the only observation that may affiliate Jocote Orange Brown with Xe ceramics. However, Sabloff (1975:230) is not convinced that the Jocote group material at Chalchuapa and Barton Ramie and the Real pottery of Seibal are the same. Jocote Brown coexists with the following Mamom pottery types in the Jenney Creek ceramic complex: Joventud Red, Chunhinta Black, Pital Cream, Deprecio Incised, and Paso Dante Incised (Gifford 1976).

For Cahal Pech, Lee (1996:85) reports a ceramic assemblage similar to that of Barton Ramie, in which Jocote Brown and Savana Orange coexist with Mamom ceramics such as Joventud Red, Pital Cream, and Chunhinta Black. These Mamom types are identified for Altar de Sacrificios and Seibal (Sabloff 1975; Adams 1971) but in isolation from Xe or Real pottery. Even at Colha (Valdez 1987), Jocote Brown occurs with Mamom ceramics. The coexistence of Jocote Brown with Mamom ceramics implies a later temporality for this type, in which case Jocote Brown cannot be associated with Xe populations. Jocote Orange Brown may be considered one of the earliest ceramic types traded from El Salvador into the Belize Valley and northern Belize. Together with other lines of ceramic diagnostics (such as Palma Daub and Savana Orange), Jocote Orange Brown is also found in central and northern Petén regions during Mamom times. At Chalchuapa, Sharer (1978:125) suggests that the Colos complex represents the first indication of linkages to the Maya Lowlands, a notion that I support. However, I would like to suggest that the stylistic and modal influences from El Salvador into the Pasión and the Belize Valley arrived at the beginning of the Middle Formative, signaling the onset of Mamom times.

Savana Orange, also from El Salvador, later developed into important Usulutan types and monochrome and grooved pottery types that bear an orange slip (Sharer 1978). Ceramic links with El Salvador were not recognized in the lowlands until defined at Seibal (Sabloff 1975) as the Tierra Mojada group. Tierra Mojada Resist is associated with one of the earliest blotchy Usulutan ceramics, the Puxtla group from Chalchuapa (Sharer and Sedat 1987), and is present both at K'axob (López Varela 1996) and in the Pasión (Foias 1996:228). According to Andrews V (1990:14), Tierra Mojada Resist represents continued interaction among the southern Maya Lowlands, the Maya Highlands, and probably the Mixe-Zoquean areas to the west and the south. Lowe believes that the "cloudy resist" ware is the type fossil for the Escalera Phase sphere in Central Chiapas (Lowe 1978:366). The Tierra Mojada group includes an incised type, Timax Incised (see vessel 001, chapter 9), that corresponds closely with common decorative modes in the southeastern highlands (Sharer and Sedat 1987:308).

Orange-brown and resist-technique pottery, on the other hand, is part of the ceramic influence coming from El Salvador at the end of the early Middle Formative period. Presence of Chunhinta Black, Pital Cream, and Tierra Mojada Resist supports participation of K'axob, the Petén, the Pasión, and the Belize Valley sites within the same sphere of pottery distribution (Gifford 1976; Hohmann and Powis 1996; Sabloff 1975; Foias 1996). Ceramic influences at K'axob deriving from western El Salvador can be perceived in the presence of orange sherds very similar to Savana Orange, which are key to the beginning of the Mamom horizon (Gifford 1976:61) in the upper Belize River Valley.

Populations around Copan, the Belize Valley, and the Pasión River acquired ideas originating on the Gulf and Pacific coasts and subsequently incorporated them into their local ceramic assemblages. Differences among Rayo, Cunil, and Xe pottery suggest the entrance of several populations into the Maya Lowlands between 1400 and 800 BC. Sharer and Gifford's (1970) earlier hypothesis regarding the origins of Xe can now be dismissed since the Jenney Creek ceramic complex postdates earlier pottery and, thus, does not bear any similarity to what was originally defined as Xe pottery. As for K'axob,

the early facet Chaakk'ax reflects the establishment of a village during the Middle Formative period. Apparently the founding of K'axob was undertaken by established farmers who maintained interregional contacts with the Pasión and the Belize Valleys as well as their far-flung El Salvador neighbors. Ironically, the origins of the Chaakk'ax ceramic complex appear to be more closely related to the Pasión region than to the Belize Valley. Chaakk'ax ceramics do not integrate with the Belize Valley until the later part of the Cunil phase. Thus, it comes as no surprise to see a Xe and Real component in K'axob ceramics associated with Mamom pottery, although this constituent disappeared by the late facet of the Chaakk'ax ceramic complex.

One final question—when and how did Xe ceramics enter northern Belize—remains difficult to answer. Precise dating of the early Middle Formative in the Maya area has been hampered by the difficulty of obtaining reliable radiocarbon samples. The midden deposits from which most samples are obtained, although stratified, often include older charcoal (see Hammond 1991a; Clark and Gosser 1995; Blake et al. 1995). According to radiocarbon dates and the spatial distribution of Xe ceramics, early Xe farmers entered the Pasión region between 930 and 560 BC and established Altar de Sacrificios. Xe occupation in the Pasión is supported at Altar de Sacrificios with a radiocarbon sample (Gx-172) taken from human bone, which yielded a date in the broad range of 930–560 BC (Adams 1971:146). The Gx-172 sample is in certain association with Xe ceramics because it was found in a burial. Dating of the Xe complex at Altar de Sacrificios also relies on its overlapping correspondence with Dili and Escalera complexes at Chiapa de Corzo (Adams 1971:146). The context of Formative pottery at Seibal is largely that of refuse deposits excavated beneath the A Group plaza (Willey 1970:320–321). The only radiocarbon date for Seibal was obtained from organic material within one of the five Real ceramic complex jars associated with a cache (Sabloff 1975:229). The Real ceramic complex is dated between 800 and 600 BC. Xe ceramics are present within the early facet of the Chaakk'ax ceramic complex, dated to approximately 800–600 BC, and occur within sherd-lined pits and burials.

Until 1979 the ceramic literature of Colha (Adams and Valdez 1979:74) included a handful of Xe type names; in this report Adams and Valdez presented their Mamom complex as an extension of the Pasión region. Almost ten years later, the Colha ceramic assemblage

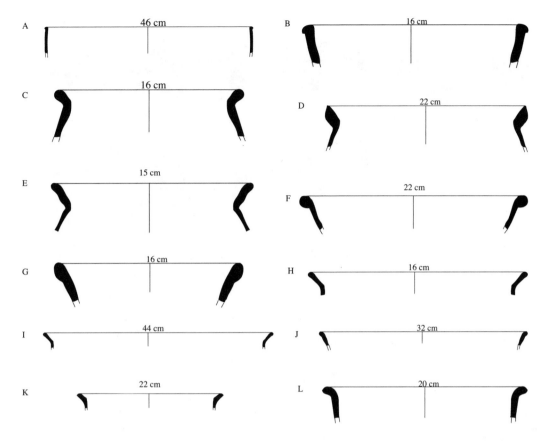

Figure 8.2 Types and forms of cooking and storage vessels of the K'atabche'k'ax ceramic complex: (A-B) Chicago Orange bowls; (C) Sapote Striated bowl; (D-E) Monkey Falls striated bowls; (F-G) Sapote Striated jars; (H-J) Chicago Orange jars; (K-L) Monkey Falls striated jars. *Illustration by Sandra L. López Varela*

bore different type-variety names, only some of which could be associated with Petén types (Valdez 1987). Since the 1980s Xe or Real types have been removed from the ceramic literature of northern Belize. Quite likely, this absence is a result of the apocryphal early Cuello dates and their subsequent effect on ceramic classification. Therefore, the current ceramic taxonomy of northern Belize prevents a clear understanding of the colonization process. A critical understanding of this time and process can be achieved, however, with a reevaluation of the presence of Xe and Real types within the Cuello and Colha samples.

THE ADVENT OF THE LATE FORMATIVE K'ATABCHE'K'AX CERAMIC COMPLEX (400 BC–AD 250)

The break with the Middle Formative village pattern of K'axob occurred around 200 BC (between the early and the late facets of the K'atabche'k'ax complex) when Mamom ceramics were entirely replaced by Chicanel

pottery. In terms of ceramics, the change was gradual, but the revolutionary social and political change expressed in the material culture indicates that it was a time of profound transformation. Widespread construction activity, the erection of a multicourse limestone retaining wall within the core of the site (figure 3.8), the occurrence of disarticulated burials (chapter 6; McAnany, Storey, and Lockard 1999), and the appearance of striated wares define the late facet of the K'atabche'k'ax ceramic complex. The appearance of striated jars represents an important technical and social change in terms of food consumption (figure 8.2) and the ceramic assemblage reflects the creativity and the needs of this new Chicanel stage (figure 8.3).

The K'atabche'k'ax complex appears to begin around 400 BC (McAnany and López Varela 1999:158). This complex (which continues until about AD 250) is defined by a collection of fourteen radiocarbon AMS assays originating from operations 1, 10, 11, and 12 (McAnany and López Varela 1999:154). The ceramic material and the stratigraphy permit a division of this

Figure 8.3 Ceramic assemblage of K'atabche'k'ax complex. *Illustration by Sandra L. López Varela*

complex into three facets: early, late, and terminal (López Varela 1996). The early facet was a transitional stage to the Chicanel ceramic sphere, as phases 4 to 7 at operation 1 contained both Mamom and Chicanel ceramics (see *Pottery Sherds Database*).

THE EARLY FACET PERIOD OF TRANSITION (400–200 BC)

Several technological innovations separate the early facet of the K'atabche'k'ax ceramic complex from earlier, Middle Formative times. Significant among the many changes taking place in the village was the replacement of the tecomate form with both a jar form and a bowl with incurved sides. In contrast to Chaakk'ax times, the bowl-to-jar ratio dropped to 1.3:1 (López Varela 1996; McAnany and López Varela 1999:159). The replacement suggests a change in terms of processing and cooking food or liquids. The new jar form has a short neck and a direct rim with a rounded lip. A few exceptions to this form exhibit a rim with a pointed lip reminiscent of the earlier pre-Mamom rim of outflared sides dishes and bowls (compare figure 8.2 with figure 8.1). The introduction of spouted jars, some with handles, is clear evidence of these new changes (see vessels 009 and 087, chapter 9).

The red, black, and red-on-cream pottery from earlier Chaakk'ax times continued to be acquired during early facet K'atabche'k'ax. Throughout this facet, the Sierra group (first introduced in burial 1-30a at operation 1) occurs intermittently in ritual and domestic contexts. This facet represents the final presence of the burgundy color (dark reddish brown 2.5YR3/3) of the

Joventud group at K'axob. As the preferred monochrome of Chaakk'ax times, the deep red of Joventud contrasts strongly with the lighter red (10R5/6, 10R 5/8) of the Sierra group.

The early facet corresponds to a transitional stage between Mamom and Chicanel that was coincident with trends at other sites in northern Belize (Valdez 1987:238; Reese and Valdez 1987:39) and Chiapa de Corzo (Dixon 1959:45). Mamom types that linger through the early facet are the same as those for the previous late facet of the Chaakk'ax ceramic complex (compare table 8.3 with table 8.2). The abundance of new Chicanel types and varieties, however, provides a point of contrast to the early facet. Some of the earliest Chicanel types in our sample include Matamore Dichrome: Matamore Variety, Puletan Red-and-Unslipped: Puletan Variety, Union Apppliqué: Unspecified Variety, Lagartos Punctated: Lagartos Variety. Decoration on these early Chicanel types, mainly dichrome painting and applique bands, follows the preexisting Mamom tradition. This trend is best illustrated by the incised decoration of Guitara Incised: Pollo Desnudo Variety, Sierra Red: Unspecified Variety, and Laguna Verde Incised: Laguna Variety (see vessels 005, 086, and 055, chapter 9). Incised lines, usually one to three, were traced on the horizontal everted part of the rim, harkening back to the earlier Mazatán pottery of the Pacific coast (Blake et al. 1995:Fig. 16). Incised lines form geometric motifs, such as half circles or diagonal or rectilinear-curvilinear patterns, some recalling the eyebrow motif or the double-line break of Olmec iconography (Clark and Pye 2000; see vessel 005, chapter 9).

Table 8.3 Types and varieties of the early facet of the K'atabche'k'ax ceramic complex

Ceramic Type: Variety	Total Number of Sherds	Percentage of Total Number of Sherds
Mamom Ceramic Types		
Chicago Orange: Chucun Variety	6291	74.91
Guitara Incised: Guitara Variety	71	0.85
Joventud Red: Unspecified Variety	778	9.26
Muxanal Red-on-cream: Unspecified Variety	111	1.32
Chicanel Ceramic Types		
Black Rock Red: Black Rock Variety	56	0.67
Flor Cream: Unspecified Variety	2	0.02
Lagartos Punctated: Lagartos Variety	1	0.01
Laguna Verde Incised: Laguna VerdeVariety	6	0.07
Sierra Red: Sierra Variety	1048	12.48
Sierra Red: Unspecified Variety	4	0.05
Society Hall Red: Society Hall	28	0.33
Puletan Red-and-unslipped: Puletan Variety	1	0.01
Union Appliqué : Unspecified Variety	1	0.01
TOTAL	8, 398	100.00%

Early facet pottery recalls not only ceramic traditions of the Chiapas region but also those of the Guatemala Highlands and the southern lowlands. A duck effigy vessel, found in burial 11-6 (see vessel 087, chapter 9), is evocative of "la pichinga," a duck effigy vessel which is still made in San Luis Jilotepeque in the Guatemalan Highlands. These K'axob vessels expressed the powerful nature of the Olmec realm in the Maya Lowlands at the end of the Middle Formative period. Soon after, Olmec culture collapsed and was replaced by narrative Izapan and Maya styles (Clark, Hansen, and Pérez 2000). Most significantly, La Venta as well as several Middle Preclassic centers of Chiapas were abandoned around 400 BC (Clark, Hansen, and Pérez 2000).

MAYA REGIONAL INTERACTION OF THE LATE FACET K'ATABCHE'K'AX (200 BC–AD 100)

The late facet of the K'atabche'k'ax can be characterized as a period of widespread construction that transformed the settlement pattern of the village in a manner that hints at a new hierarchy. Household activities changed and food-preparation areas were moved farther away from raised platforms within operation 1 (McAnany and López Varela 1999:160). The significant spatial separation of food-preparation areas was accompanied by a change in the pottery inventory. Once more, the jar form was modified through the application of continuous striations to the body of the vessel.

For a variety of reasons, this group of cooking vessels seems to have replaced older roasting or stone boiling technologies (see discussion in chapter 5). In contrast to the late facet of the Chaakk'ax complex, when the bowl-to-jar ratio stood at 11:1, by late facet K'atabche'k'ax times the ratio had dropped to 0.7:1. During this facet, jars display an increased variety of forms and can be classified into three main types: Chicago Orange: Chucun Variety, Monkey Falls Striated: Monkey Falls Variety, and Sapote Striated: Unspecified Variety (figure 8.2). Within the Sierra group, jar necks increased in height, and the vessel capacity expanded from the early facet (López Varela 1996;

Angelini 1998). Along with the expansion in formal variability, spouted jars became more abundant.

Change is also apparent in the clays used for making striated jars. Daszkiewicz, Schneider, and Bobryk (1999) subjected a small sample of these new jars to thin-sections and refiring studies in order to explore their function. Jars of the same type could exhibit either a calcareous or noncalcareous matrix. As Bartlett (see chapter 7) had extensively analyzed those jars with a calcareous matrix, subsequent analysis focused on explaining the presence of a noncalcareous matrix. In other parts of the ancient world, cooking pots generally exhibit a noncalcareous matrix with calcite temper (Daszkiewicz, Schneider, and Bobryk 1999). Pottery samples of Monkey Falls Striated or Triunfo Striated with a noncalcareous matrix and temper of coarse crystalline calcite were probably designed for cooking or boiling water (Daszkiewicz, Schneider, and Bobryk 1999). Jars of Chicago Orange and Sierra Red are characterized either by a noncalcareous matrix or a high content of crushed coarse crystalline calcite temper (Angelini 1998; Daszkiewicz, Schneider, and Bobryk 1999). Quite possibly, the jars with a calcareous matrix were used for storage (Daszkiewicz, Schneider, and Bobryk 1999). Further analysis of residues and functional properties, such as thermal shock resistance, will help to determine which of the two matrix groups would be better suited for cooking.

How was a potter or consumer to distinguish a storage vessel from one made for cooking? At K'axob, this distinction was highlighted by the application of button appliques or nail impressions to the neck juncture of storage vessels. In the case of Monkey Falls, Gifford (1976:145) perceived the difference and established the Unspecified Brown Variety for this type. In studying Classic period ceramics from Yaxchilan and Pomoná (López Varela 1989, 1995), I noticed that some striated jars were decorated with applications and/or painted with Maya Blue. The added marker may have allowed one to distinguish among cooking, storage, and possibly ritual vessels.

Ceramic production appears to have been thriving during the late facet, when many types were locally produced. Many new types were introduced (table 8.4), and striated jars were not the only innovation of the late facet. Responding to new social and economic needs, the bowl form exhibits a variety of shapes (figure 8.4). Bowls continued to be produced with flared or outcurved sides but were increasingly made with vertical walls. This development includes the fabrication of a tall bowl with vertical sides—the vase or cylindrical form. Less abundant were bowls with rounded sides. Strap handles with small apertures were attached to jars to facilitate hanging with a cord. While new forms appeared at K'axob (like the vase with slightly vertical walls), other forms completely disappeared (like the tecomate), and still others (like the bowl with rounded sides), ceased to be a common form. However, monochrome pottery continued to be dominated by the Sierra group, followed by striated and orange wares. Vessels from the Sierra group were sometimes decorated with appliques, fluting, gadrooning, impressing, incising, modeling, and punctation. Less significant are the black, cream, red-on-cream, and red-on-orange wares.

Changes in pottery technology are significant because production seems to have become highly specialized. Potters are certainly responding to new social needs during the late facet. Certain forms, for example, are made exclusively for one particular type. Such is the case for Society Hall Red: Society Hall Variety, a type known for bowls with outcurved sides, an outflared everted rim, and a rounded lip. The quadripartite motif, painted with streaky brushstrokes across the base of some Society Hall Red vessels, is found in this form (see chapter 16 and vessels 021, 023, 033, 034, 046, chapter 9). Society Hall Red bowls also exhibited mending or suspension holes, suggesting that they were used for storage or, more likely, for serving. This idea is reinforced by the fact that the paste composition of Society Hall Red bowls generally features a calcareous matrix, indicating that these forms were not used for cooking. Two samples of one of the new Chicanel types (Hillbank Red) together with four samples of Monkey Falls belong to a homogeneous subgroup with very low magnesium and very high calcium. Coarse crystalline carbonates with few well-rounded grains of quartz predominate in the samples of Hillbank Red. Ceramic fragments of Hillbank Red were rarely burned, so these jars were likely used for storage, as might also have been the case for Society Hall Red and Sierra Red jars that contained a calcareous fabric. Six analyzed samples of Hillbank Red exhibit a high content of magnesium. Quite possibly, the difference in chemical content is related to the function of the vessel.

The continuities and innovations in pottery production, detected for the late facet of the K'atabche'k'ax ceramic complex, are distinctive markers of the cultural homogeneity of the Late Formative in the Maya Lowlands. K'axob pottery of the late facet is formally and stylistically similar to ceramic traditions reported at

Table 8.4 Types and varieties of the late facet of the K'atabche'k'ax ceramic complex

Ceramic Type: Variety	Total Number of Sherds	Percentage of Total Number of Sherds
Mamom Ceramic Types		
Chicago Orange: Chucun Variety	5,349	56.34
Guitara Incised: Guitara Variety	32	0.34
Joventud Red: Jolote Variety	103	1.08
Joventud Red: Unspecified Variety	465	4.90
Muxanal Red-on-cream: Unspecified Variety	10	0.11
Chicanel Ceramic Types		
Flor Cream: Unspecified Variety	7	0.07
Hillbank Red: Hillbank Variety	62	0.65
Laguna Verde Incised: Grooved Variety	2	0.02
Monkey Falls Striated: Monkey Falls Variety	424	4.47
Monkey Falls Striated: Unspecified (Brown) Variety	5	0.05
Repollo Impressed: Unspecified Variety	3	0.03
Sapote Striated: Unspecified Variety	41	0.43
Sierra Red: Gadrooned Variety	37	0.39
Sierra Red: Sierra Variety	2, 259	23.79
Society Hall Red: Society Hall Variety	689	7.26
Society Hall Red: Impressed Variety	2	0.02
Union Appliqué : Unspecified Variety	2	0.02
Unnamed Red-on-Orange	1	0.01
TOTAL	**9, 494**	**100.00%**

other sites in northern Belize (Reese and Valdez 1987; Valdez 1987; Kosakowksy 1987), the Belize River valley (Gifford 1976), the Petén (Sabloff 1975), the Pasión (Adams 1971; Foias 1996), El Mirador Basin (Forsyth 1989), and the Yucatan (Ball 1977). The late facet is also accompanied by the presence of the Unnamed group: Unnamed Red-on-Orange and Unnamed Orange-on-Cream Usulutan-related types, characteristic of El Salvador. Usulutan sherds do not occur in high frequencies at K'axob, but their identification is significant to understanding the ensuing terminal facet of the K'atabche'k'ax ceramic complex.

Pottery of the late facet also provided a medium for expressing the prevailing beliefs of Chicanel times. The placing of lip-to-lip caches within operations 10 and 11 was likely associated with calendric ritual or agricultural metaphors of cyclic death and rebirth (chapter 4; Masson 1993). At some point during Late K'atabche'k'ax times, K'axob leaders commissioned the production of four vessels (see vessels 029, 030, 032, and 035, chapter 9) to commemorate the construction of a new plaza surface within operation 1. The four vessels were arranged spatially so as to form a cross when viewed from above: two Society Hall Red vessels were placed along the upper north-south axis, and two Sierra Red: Gadrooned Variety vessels were positioned along a lower east-west axis. The elaborate nature of this ritual is indicated by the fact that the vessels were made specifically for this offering,

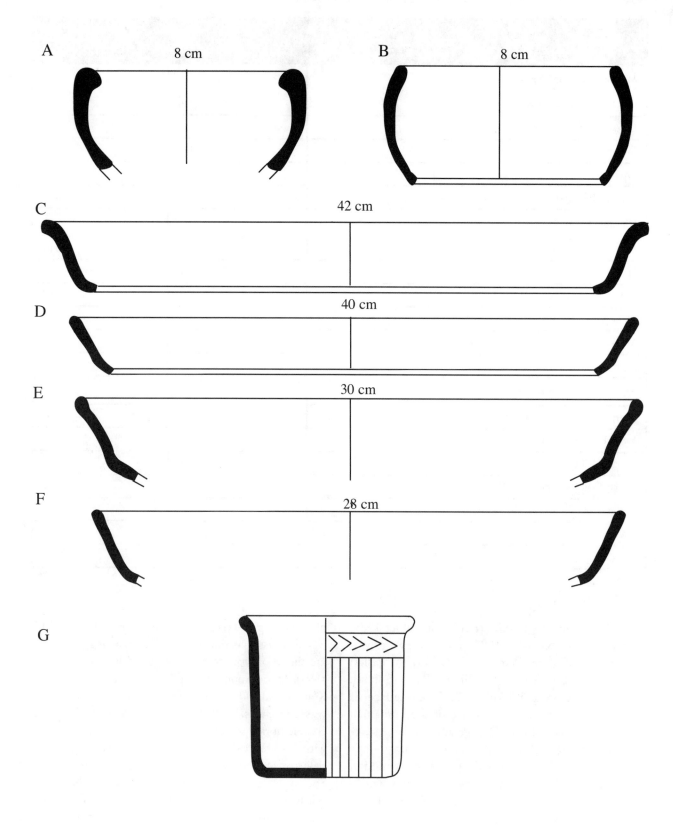

Figure 8.4 Types and forms of serving wares of K'atabche'k'ax ceramic complex: (A-B) Sierra Red incurving bowls; (C-D) Sierra Red outcurving dishes; (E) Sierra Red outcurving bowl; (F) Sierra Red flared bowl; (G) Laguna Verde Incised vase or cylinder form. *Illustration by Sandra L. López Varela*

as is suggested by the standardization in weight, form, and measurements. At K'axob the cross motif was not only reproduced spatially but the quadripartite motif was also painted on the base of several Sierra Red and Society Hall Red vessels. At this time, large-scale architecture is not present at K'axob, and neither are the deity masks that decorated the pyramids of Lamanai and Cerros. Also absent were the triadic buildings with stucco façades that possibly symbolized the beginning of a new year or a new agricultural cycle (Pohl 1983). Despite the lack of hard stone resources at K'axob, dwellers found different ways of materializing Maya beliefs and numerology.

During the Late Formative period, boulder sculptures executed in the potbelly style are found distributed within a Pacific-side region, including Tonala, Kaminaljuyu, Palo Gordo, Monte Alto, Izapa, and Chalchuapa (Demarest 1986). Potbellied sculptures portray fat, heavy-shouldered figures with arms clasping bloated bellies (Demarest, Switsur, and Berger 1982). In an attempt to participate in this widespread representation, potters from K'axob fashioned an effigy spouted jar (see vessel 047, chapter 9) that resembles these monumental boulder sculptures. This wide-faced human effigy jar from K'axob also resembles an effigy globular bowl modeled in high relief from the Comayagua Valley (Stone 1957:Fig. 10.12). Finally, new styles of painting and new forms are evident in burials 8-3 and 8-5. The polychrome painting on two Ixcanrio Orange tetrapods (see vessels 097 and 098, chapter 9) expressed a radical departure from the previous Late Formative monochromatic legless tradition. An Aguacate Orange: Aguacate Variety bowl (see vessel 095, chapter 9) in burial 8-3 indicates that, by the end of the Late K'atabche'k'ax complex, pottery already encoded new elements that come to characterize Terminal K'atabche'k'ax as well as the Early Classic period.

PERSISTENCE AND INNOVATION DURING TERMINAL FACET K'ATABCHE'K'AX (AD 100–250)

During the Terminal Formative, the community of K'axob increased in population and there was significant change in residential and burial patterns. In terms of the ceramic assemblage, pottery types of the terminal facet reflect both continuity and innovation (table 8.5). The innovative changes in the pottery assemblage generally ascribed to a Protoclassic component were gradually introduced (beginning in the late facet) and some characteristics can even be traced back to Middle

Formative times (López Varela 1996; see Brady et al. 1998). These additional modes, considered part of the Protoclassic inventory, include the polychrome tradition, orange-slipped ceramics, Usulutan designs, large serving bowls with mammiform tetrapods, and outflaring bowls with basal flanges (Adams 1971:4). Sites throughout northern Belize (Reese and Valdez 1987:41; Meskill 1992:112) and the Yucatan Peninsula (Ball 1977) contain Protoclassic pottery. Other sites, such as Chiapa de Corzo (Horcones Phase, see Peterson 1963:123) and Becan (Ball 1972:35), define the Protoclassic in terms of tetrapod mammiform pottery and Usulutan ceramics.

Despite the introduction of new modes, red wares continue to dominate the terminal facet, and Sierra Red: Sierra Variety is the preferred type. Domestic ceramics include the still fashionable types of Monkey Falls Striated: Monkey Falls, Unspecified (Brown) Varieties, Sapote Striated: Unspecified Variety, and the Lagartos Punctated: Lagartos Variety. During this facet, pottery of the Chicago Orange: Chucun Variety is discontinued in favor of the striated wares that will persist throughout the Classic and Postclassic periods. For most jar forms of the terminal facet, the neck increased in diameter (López Varela 1996; Angelini 1998), although the short outcurved neck with a direct rim and rounded lip remains in vogue.

One of the so-called new trends includes dichrome pottery within the Usulutan tradition. During the terminal facet at K'axob, Unnamed Red-on-Orange and Unnamed Orange-on-Cream pottery were decorated with geometric motifs, including wavy and straight lines, thus emulating the Usulutan ceramic tradition. The type Unnamed Red-on-Orange identified at K'axob was recognized by Sabloff (1975:197) as part of the Usulutan group at Seibal. Other sites in the Maya region report a similar type. For example, Caramba Red-on-Orange of El Mirador consists of multiple wavy and straight lines painted with a red pigment on a reddish orange background in an attempt to imitate the Usulutan types of El Salvador region (Forsyth 1989:125). Usulutan pottery, and imitations of this style, had appeared in the Maya region during Middle Formative times. Quite possibly, as I suggested earlier in this chapter, the presence of resist pottery and the corresponding imitations in the Pasión and Belize Valleys are an indication of the long-standing interaction with El Salvador. The nature of such interaction is still under discussion, specifically for the end of the Formative period.

In 1977 Pring stylistically and formally expanded the diagnostic modes and spatial distribution of what

Table 8.5 Types and varieties of the terminal facet of the K'atabche'k'ax ceramic complex

Ceramic Type: Variety	Total Number of Sherds	Percentage of Total Number of Sherds
Mamom Ceramic Types		
Chicago Orange: Chucun Variety	2,677	21.94
Chicanel Ceramic Types		
Aguacate Orange: Aguacate Variety	26	0.21
Flor Cream: Unspecified Variety	39	0.32
Guacamallo Red-on-orange: Guacamallo Variety	21	0.17
Hillbank Red: Hillbank Variety	448	3.67
Ixcanrio Orange Polychrome: Ixcanrio Variety	75	0.61
Laguna Verde Incised: Grooved Variety	1	0.01
Laguna Verde Incised: Laguna Verde Variety	10	0.08
Monkey Falls Striated: Monkey Falls Variety	4, 232	34.68
Monkey Falls Striated: Unspecified (Brown) Variety	17	0.14
Sierra Red: Gadrooned Variety	15	0.12
Sierra Red: Sierra Variety	2, 797	22.92
Society Hall Red: Impressed Variety	1	0.01
Society Hall Red: Society Hall Variety	657	5.38
Union Appliqué : Unspecified Variety	7	0.06
Polvero Black: Unspecified Variety	1	0.01
Unnamed Orange-on-Cream	29	0.24
Unnamed Red-on-Orange	5	0.04
Tzakol Ceramic Types		
Aguila Orange: Aguila Variety	573	4.70
Balanza Black Unspecified Variety	8	0.07
Lucha Incised: Unspecified Variety	9	0.07
Pita Incised: Unspecified Variety	1	0.01
San Martin Brown: San Martin Variety	2	0.02
Triunfo Striated: Unspecified Variety	133	1.09
Pucte Brown: Pucte Variety	1	0.01
Santa Teresa Incised: Santa Teresa Variety	4	0.03
TOTAL	**12, 753**	**100.00%**

Gifford (1965, 1976) had called Floral Park ceramics. The typological assemblage present at Barton Ramie was attributed to the invasion of peoples from the southeastern highlands (see Gifford 1965). Gifford established a connection with the southeastern highlands because he observed the similarities between Aguacate Orange from Barton Ramie and that of Chalchuapa. A later study by Sharer cast doubt on the relationship between Aguacate Orange from these two sites, but the invasion or contact hypothesis remained an alternative explanation for the presence of this new pottery assemblage (Demarest and Sharer 1982). Brady and colleagues (1998) reconsidered the nature and significance of the Protoclassic, employing a study of macroscopic traits to question the assumption that Floral Park ceramics comprised a discrete phase or complex.

At K'axob, dichrome pottery—mainly Unnamed Red-on-Orange and Unnamed Orange-on-Cream—is present in terminal facet K'atabche'k'ax deposits at operations 7, 8, and 11. Aguacate Orange is another addition to the pottery inventory. However, other Holmul Orange–associated types, such as Guacamallo Red-on-Orange and Ixcanrio Orange Polychrome, are present in operation 10 in contexts dating to terminal facet K'atabche'k'ax. To approach some of the problems with the chronological and typological classification of polychrome pottery, samples of Guacamallo Red-on-Orange and Ixcanrio Orange Polychrome were subjected to chemical and mineralogical analyses. All samples were found to contain a calcareous matrix. (As discussed earlier, pottery with a calcareous matrix is not suitable for cooking.) Samples of Guacamallo Red-on-Orange (Y708) and Ixcanrio Orange Polychrome (Y709) were grouped together, and results revealed that these vessels were made of a very fine fabric of silty, sandy, clayey marl. Grain sizes of coarse crystalline carbonates and very rare quartz measure from 0.01 to 0.15 mm (Daszkiewicz, Schneider, and Bobryk 1999). A second generation of grain sizes, ranging from 0.25/0.5 to 1.0/1.5 mm, consists of clay and a few aggregates of sparitic or coarse crystalline carbonates. This chemical characterization is similar to that of foreign ceramics of the early facet of the Chaakk'ax ceramic complex.

At the end of the late facet, Gale Creek red ware was introduced to K'axob in the form of a Hillbank Red type that is strongly associated with new Protoclassic modes found in operations 7, 8, 10, and 11. At Barton Ramie, Gifford (1976) noted that Sierra Red was not present in contexts with Hillbank Red: Hillbank Variety. In general, the persistence of Chicanel traits within the K'axob assemblage coeval with the introduction of new ceramic modes recalls a pattern that is similar to that described for the Grijalva region at the end of the Late Formative (Bryant and Clark 1983). For instance, Bryant and Clark (1983) report that at El Cerrito the serving wares were produced in a Maya style, but storage jars and incense burners were produced in the old Zoque style found at La Libertad. The changes suggest an influx of Maya people into the upper Grijalva River Valley by 200 BC (Bryant and Clark 1983). There, earlier inhabitants retained remnants of their Zoque identity in the plain and ritual pottery. The evidence suggests a significant intrusion of Lowland Maya people into the Grijalva River Valley and the incorporation and acculturation of earlier Zoque inhabitants into newly founded Maya communities (Clark, Hansen, and Pèrez 2000). Foreign stylistic influences can be detected on the Sierra Red group of K'axob. In an attempt to emulate the new modes, potters added a basal flange to a Sierra Red outflaring bowl (see vessel 073, chapter 9). At the same time, bases of bowls, plates, and vases were painted with an overall red slip or with a cross, suggesting a new use for these vessels and possibly new ritual purposes (see vessel 021, chapter 9).

At K'axob, the area of structure 18 (operation 1) was the center of the Formative village for almost 800 years. This fact may explain the reluctance of its dwellers, like those of Barton Ramie, to adopt new ceramic styles such as Aguacate Orange. In contrast, an Aguacate Orange vessel was placed in burial 8-3 (operation 8) of the terminal facet K'atabche'k'ax as part of a termination ritual. Another Aguacate Orange vessel was found at operation 11 in a redeposited midden of terminal facet K'atabche'k'ax. Thereafter, Aguacate Orange is present in terminal facet contexts at operations 7 and 10. Given its restricted distribution, this type seems most likely to have been imported; however, without widespread characterization and provenience studies, we are unable to assign it to a particular workshop area. The single Aguacate Orange sherd (Y710) analyzed by Daszkiewicz, Schneider, and Bobryk (1999) bore a very distinctive calcareous matrix, suggesting that it might be an import. The sample also contains high concentrations of silica and aluminum, a matrix of small carbonates grains (up to 0.01 mm), inclusions of well-rounded quartz and cryptocrystalline carbonates (up to 1.2 mm), and rare K-feldspars, hornblende, and calcareous bioclasts.

Hollow mammiform vessels were already present at K'axob prior to the terminal facet. As noted by Brady et al. (1998:22), the form persisted and evolved over several centuries from small solid nubbins or conical supports to large bulbous mammiform and conventionalized "tapir head" supports. In the same way that potters at K'axob added basal flanges to bowls finished with a traditional Sierra Red slip, tetrapod supports can be found on the monochromes of the Terminal Formative types. In other parts of the lowlands, mammiform supports were added to vessels of the Sierra Red, Quacco Creek Red, and San Felipe Brown ceramic groups (Brady et al. 1998:22).

Burials of the terminal facet are of chronological interest to our discussion because their associated accoutrements include pottery assigned to the Chicanel ceramic sphere, the Protoclassic period, and/or to Early Classic times. At operation 1, where the secondary remains of nine individuals were interred (see chapter 6), K'axob inhabitants excavated a pit down to Early Chaakk'ax levels and placed several complete Chicanel vessels (see vessels 033, 034, 036, and 037, chapter 9) amongst the human remains. Vessels were decorated with a variety of designs, including the quadripartite motif (see chapter 16), monkey-face applications, and half-moon incisions. Monkey faces (see vessel 036, chapter 9), in particular, can be associated with renewal ceremonies (Pohl 1983:66). Burial 11-2 was interred with vessels of Actuncan Orange Polychrome, Aguila Orange, and Yaloche Cream Polychrome (see vessels 102, 103, 104, chapter 9), all of which were considered Early Classic ceramics. An early occurrence of Aguila Orange also has been detected for the Cimi ceramic complex at Tikal (Culbert 1993) and for Protoclassic times in the Stann Creek District (Graham 1994:204). Compositionally, Actuncan Orange Polychrome (Y645) and Palmar Orange Polychrome (Y651) differ from earlier polychromes. Coarse crystalline carbonates and a matrix of clayey marl characterize both types, which also contain rare aggregates of sparitic carbonates, clay lumps, and, in Actuncan Orange Polychrome, a few grog particles.

Microprobe analysis conducted by Daszkiewicz, Schneider, and Bobryk (1999) on a sample of polychrome sherds supports Bishop's findings (cited in Brady et al. 1998:28) regarding strong temporal trends in the technology of polychrome pottery. For example, in cases where red and black colors were used on the same sherd (such as Actuncan sample Y646), the black paint contained both manganese and iron in contrast to the red part,

which contained only iron. Manganese was also detected in the black paint of Ixcanrio Orange Polychrome (Y649) and later Saxche Orange Polychrome (Y650).

Protoclassic ceramics show much continuity with earlier Formative styles, as has been appreciated by many authors (Gifford 1976; Hammond 1984; Graham 1994; López Varela 1996; Brady et al. 1998); therefore, the occurrence of Protoclassic pottery cannot be the result of a population intrusion from El Salvador. New evidence, proposed by several researchers (Pring 1977b; Adams and Hammond 1982; Demarest and Sharer 1982; Hammond 1984; Demarest 1986; Graham 1994; López Varela 1996), negates earlier hypotheses of intrusion or migration (Willey and Gifford 1961). Protoclassic pottery from K'axob does contain new elements, but the introduction of new modes can be found as far back as the Middle Formative period. The widespread distribution of Protoclassic pottery argues for various centers of production (Graham 1994; López Varela 1996), which need to be located and investigated. The locations of these pottery communities have yet to be identified, although so far evidence points to the El Salvador region as the ultimate and original source of production. Why this type of pottery became so prestigious at the end of the Formative period is a question that deserves further investigation. Protoclassic modes have been identified in the Petén (Culbert 1963) and in the Petexbatun regions (Foias 1996). However, so far Ixcanrio Orange Polychrome is absent from the ceramic assemblages of these two regions, suggesting that not all Maya communities had a long-term interaction with the area of Protoclassic pottery production. At Seibal, for example, Protoclassic pottery was not as significant as it was in the Salinas complex of Altar de Sacrificios or the Floral Park complex of Barton Ramie (Sabloff 1975:231).

Obviously, the end of the Formative period at other Mesoamerican sites is not associated only with the presence of Protoclassic ceramics. At sites such as Chiapa de Corzo, use of elite Maya pottery ceased and inhabitants returned to old Zoque cultural patterns (Clark, Hansen, and Pérez 2000). Foreign ceramics restricted to elite tombs came from Oaxaca, the Gulf Coast, and El Salvador (Clark, Hansen, and Pérez 2000) rather than from the Maya Lowlands. The sites of La Venta and La Libertad were abandoned, and others, like El Mirador and Kaminaljuyu, lost their hegemony. While many other sites experienced a decline, sites in northern Belize, such as Kichpanha (Reese and Valdez 1987:41) and K'axob (see McAnany, chapter 3), intensified construction activities. Even Chiapa de Corzo (Lowe 1962) participated in this renaissance (Clark, Hansen, and Pérez 2000) by building Mound 5.

Clark, Hansen, and Pérez (2000) maintain that, by 200 BC, there is clear evidence of human sacrifice as a ritual component of elite burial and building dedications in the Maya Lowlands. At Chiapa de Corzo they interpret the presence of human sacrifices in elite burials as evidence of warfare and war captives. Their presence immediately precedes the Maya incursion into the central area of Chiapas. According to Clark, Hansen, and Pérez, this was a period of unsuccessful invasion by a population yet to be identified. Through war, conflict, or some other mechanism, Maya beliefs certainly spread to these far western regions. Ritual offerings of the Horcones phase of Chiapa de Corzo (Peterson 1963:123) are similar to those of Terminal K'atabche'k'ax K'axob. Both sites shared the placing of stones in their burials and caches (see Lowe and Agrinier 1960:97, Plates 31f, 37e), a possible reference to the "three stones of creation." At K'axob, three roughly shaped chunks of limestone were found in a lip-to-lip cache in operation 10 (see chapter 4). During the Horcones phase at Chiapa de Corzo, a new style is detected in some vessels associated with Teotihuacan (see Lowe 1962).

CLASSIC PERIOD K'AXOB: EARLY FACET NOHALK'AX CERAMIC COMPLEX (FROM AD 250)

Certainly, the transition from Formative period to Classic period is poorly understood as it is anything but uniform throughout the Maya area. At the beginning of the Early Classic period, K'axob exhibits evidence of an unusually vigorous Formative to Early Classic transition that was marked by continued residential construction, burial interment, and pyramid building (see chapter 3). Pottery of this period belongs primarily to the Tzakol ceramic sphere (table 8.6). At K'axob, significant architectural changes can be detected at operations 7, 11, and 13. Most Nohalk'ax burials were placed in a cist (see chapter 6). Around Pulltrouser Swamp, the Tibaat and Kokeal settlements supported Early Classic occupation (Harrison 1983, 1989). The site of San Estevan (Levi 1993), for example, showed its greatest expansion during the Early Classic period. Altun Ha sees significant activity during both the Early and Late Classic periods (Pendergast 1979, 1982a, 1982b). The same generalization can be extended to northern Belizean sites such as Caledonia and Aventura

(Ball 1983; Sidrys 1983). In contrast, other sites in northern Belize and the Petén show only moderate occupation (see Sabloff 1975; Forsyth 1989; Foias 1996; Valdez 1987). Traditionally, weak Early Classic ceramic development in the Usumacinta and the Pasión regions had been explained in terms of the political and economic situation in the Petén, where Tikal had established its supremacy (Sabloff 1975).

Nohalk'ax pottery was concentrated in the uppermost floors of Formative house-mounds. In general, formally and stylistically Nohalk'ax pottery is very close to the following coeval complexes: Tzakol at Uaxactun (Smith 1955), Manik at Tikal (Culbert 1993), Hermitage at Barton Ramie (Gifford 1976), Acropolis at El Mirador (Forsyth 1989), Kaynikte at Calakmul (Dominguez Carrasco 1994), and Yaxcab at Yaxchilan (López Varela 1989). Noticeable among the changes introduced during the Nohalk'ax ceramic complex is the gradual replacement of the earlier dominant red-slipped surfaces with glossy orange slip (2.5 YR 5/8), polychrome painting, and variegated colors. Continuation of waxy wares into the Early Classic is a characteristic of K'axob as well as of Tikal (Laporte 1995) and Pomoná (López Varela 1995). As noted by Lincoln (1985), the endurance of the waxy wares reflects the disparity with which sites acquired the markers of Classic Maya society. In the Usumacinta and the Pasión regions, glossy ceramics are not a strong component of the pottery assemblage (Sabloff 1975; López Varela 1995; Foias 1996).

The archetypal Early Classic Aguila group is well represented at K'axob. Dishes with rounded sides and ring bases dominate in the Aguila ceramic group, together with bowls with basal breaks or Z-angles and jars with vertical necks (see vessel 103, chapter 9). In general, vessel diameters diminished during this period, ranging only between 17 and 26 cm, in contrast to the large bowls of the earlier K'atabche'k'ax ceramic complex, with diameters of 22 to 46 cm. The distribution of the Aguila group could be tracking a network related to the rising supremacy of Tikal. Aguila Orange is not reported for Seibal, a long-time competitor of Tikal, but it is found in the Petexbatun region (Foias 1996) and along the Usumacinta (López Varela 1989), where sites enjoyed strong political links to Tikal. Aguila Orange is also reported for Altar de Sacrificios (Adams 1971), Barton Ramie (Gifford 1976), and Colha (Valdez 1987).

Ceramic groups found at operations 7, 11, and 13 consist of Balanza, San Martin, Pucte, and Dos Arroyos. A dish with flared sides, direct rim, and a rounded lip is characteristic of these groups. Bowls with

Table 8.6 Types and varieties of the early facet of the Nohalk'ax ceramic complex

Ceramic Type: Variety	Total Number of Sherds	Percentage of Total Number of Sherds
Mamom Ceramic Types		
Chicago Orange: Chucun Variety	598	9.95
Joventud Red: Jolote Variety	6	0.10
Joventud Red: Unspecified Variety	57	0.95
Chicanel Ceramic Types		
Aguacate Orange: Aguacate Variety	19	0.32
Flor Cream: Unspecified Variety	11	0.18
Guacamallo Red-on-orange: Guacamallo Variety	11	0.18
Hillbank Red: Hillbank Variety	71	1.18
Ixcanrio Orange Polychrome: Ixcanrio Variety	19	0.32
Laguna Verde Incised: Laguna Verde Variety	4	0.07
Monkey Falls Striated: Monkey Falls Variety	2, 328	38.73
Monkey Falls Striated: Unspecified (Brown) Variety	6	0.10
Sapote Striated: Unspecified Variety	215	3.58
Sierra Red: Sierra Variety	1, 137	18.92
Sierra Red: Gadrooned Variety	13	0.22
Society Hall Red: Society Hall Variety	255	4.24
Union Appliqué : Unspecified Variety	1	0.02
Unnamed Orange-on-Cream	1	0.02
Unnamed Red-on-Orange	1	0.02
Tzakol Ceramic Types		
Actuncan Orange Polychrome: Actuncan Variety	14	0.23
Aguila Orange: Aguila Variety	717	11.93
Balanza Black Unspecified Variety	11	0.18
Dos Arroyos Orange Polychrome: Dos Arroyos Variety	5	0.08
Lucha Incised: Unspecified Variety	1	0.02
Pita Incised: Unspecified Variety	20	0.33
Pucte Brown: Pucte Variety	10	0.17
San Martin Brown: San Martin Variety	3	0.05
Santa Teresa Incised: Santa Teresa Variety	6	0.1
Triunfo Striated: Unspecified Variety	471	7.84
TOTAL	**6, 011**	**100.00%**

flared sides occur in the Santa Teresa Incised group. At K'axob, black slipping is represented in the Balanza group. Bowls with incurved-recurved sides and a collared neck are common for San Martin Variegated Brown (see vessel 111, chapter 9), a common type at Seibal (Sabloff 1975:102) but absent in the Petexbatun region (Foias 1996). The paste of Pucte Brown (Y653), however, forms a homogeneous group with Guacamallo Red-on-Orange (Y708) and Ixcanrio Orange Polychrome (Y709). These results invite reconsideration of Pucte Brown as part of the Peten gloss wares of the Early Classic period. This type, at least at K'axob, is part of the Holmul ware that was distributed from early facet K'atabche'k'ax to early facet Nohalk'ax times.

Polychrome decoration is best expressed in the Actuncan (see vessels 102, 109, and 110, chapter 9) and Dos Arroyos groups (see vessel 116, chapter 9) that are found all over the Maya Lowlands. Polychrome pottery is also represented in a bowl with incurved sides that is characteristic of the Yaloche Cream Polychrome (see vessel 104, chapter 9). Designs painted on K'axob polychromes include a Kan cross, a shell motif, and an undulating jaguar. Feet were sometimes modeled to form animal features, as in the four peccary heads of an Actuncan Orange Polychrome vessel (see vessel 110, chapter 9). Stratigraphically, the peccary supports can

be placed in early facet Nohalk'ax, lending credence to Brady et al.'s (1998:31) observation that tapir heads are part of the early Tzakol horizon.

In the future, interpretation of this complex may be modified as pottery from the 1995 field season, currently under study, is integrated with this preliminary view of the earliest facet of the Early Classic of K'axob. It is interesting to note that striated pottery of the Early Classic, such as Triunfo Striated, is not present in the Early Classic deposits of group B and its satellite residences but is common in the satellite compounds of group A. In group B and its surroundings, Early Classic pottery is restricted to a few serving or ritual wares, while the full complex is represented in structures surrounding group A. Likewise, differences among ceramic complexes of Early Classic sites suggest the likelihood of discrete distribution networks (López Varela 1995, 1998) that may have been coterminous with the two most influential polities of the Early Classic period— Tikal and Calakmul (Grube and Martin 1998). In future publications, the Classic period ceramic history of K'axob will continue. *Los tepalcates siguen hablando*. The sherds continue to talk, so to speak. K'axob inhabitants pursued their long-established interaction with their old neighbors and opened new arteries of communication to the Yucatan Peninsula, foreshadowing strong Terminal and Postclassic associations with the north.

Chapter 9
Related CD Resources

Pottery Vessels
Burials
Caches
Cross Motif Vessels

POTTERY VESSELS OF K'AXOB

KIMBERLY A. BERRY, SANDRA L. LÓPEZ VARELA, MARY LEE BARTLETT,
TAMARRA MARTZ, AND PATRICIA A. MCANANY

This chapter serves as a compendium of the whole and reconstructible vessels that were excavated from the site of K'axob during the 1990–1993 field seasons. The vessels span the time period of the Middle Formative (Early Chaakk'ax complex) through the early part of the Early Classic (Nohalk'ax complex). The following preamble is designed to orient the reader to the terminology and organization of this chapter. For a discussion of paste characteristics, see Bartlett (chapter 7), and for an explanation of the type-variety system, see López Varela (chapter 8).

Formative excavations at K'axob yielded 114 vessels, a few of which were unbroken while the bulk were either partially or totally reconstructible. During excavation and preliminary laboratory processing, large sherds that seemed to originate from a single vessel were assigned a unique identification number. Some 126 numbers were assigned; however, later examination of the vessels revealed that twelve were too fragmentary to be characterized as a vessel. These were demoted to sherd status, but their numbers were not

reassigned. Thus, on the pages to follow, the vessel number series extends from 001 to 126, with a few intended omissions.

The 114 vessels come from five types of cultural contexts. By far, most derive from burials (n = 80), but there are many from cache contexts (n = 28). Two were found in pit features and two formed the lining of sherd-lined pits. The remaining pair co-occurred in an Early Chaakk'ax construction fill layer. Within the overall assemblage, López Varela has identified eighteen ceramic types and numerous varieties; however, six types encompass 86% of the vessels. Sierra Red (n = 62) and Society Hall Red (n = 16) make up a disproportionate share of the group. These are followed by Aguacate Orange (n = 8), Actuncan Orange Polychrome (n = 4), Guitara Incised (n = 4), and Ixcanrio Orange Polychrome (n = 4). All other types are represented by only one or two vessels. Due to the prevalence of burial contexts, it is not surprising that most vessels were found in such features. Two patterns are of interest, though. First, all four Actuncan vessels were placed in association with human

Table 9.1. K'axob ceramic sequence in the Maya area

CORRELATION	TIME (A.D./B.C.)	MAJOR PERIODS	K'axob	Altar de Sacrificios	Barton Ramie	Seibal	Tikal	Uaxactun	Cuello	Colha	El Mirador	Chiapa de Corzo	Chalchuapa
11.0.0.0 – 10.10.0.0.0	1200–1000	LATE / EARLY POSTCLASSIC	Kimilk'ax	Jimba	New Town	Bayal	Caban / Eznab	Tepeu 3		Masson			Ahal
10.0.0.0.0	1000–800	TERMINAL CLASSIC	Kimilk'ax	Boca (Late Facet / Early Facet)	Spanish Lookout	Transition Tepejilote	Imix	Tepeu 2		Bomba		Paredon	Matzin
9.10.0.0.0	800–600	LATE CLASSIC	Witsk'ax	Pasion (Late Facet / Early Facet)	Tiger Run	Junco	Ik	Tepeu 1		Lac Na		Maravilla	Payu
9.0.0.0 – 8.10.0.0.0	600–300	EARLY CLASSIC	Witsk'ax / Nohalk'ax (Late Facet)	Chixoy / Veremos / Salinas	Hermitage	Junco	Manik	Tzakol 3 / Tzakol 2 / Tzakol 1		Post Lac Na / Canos / Ranas / Yalam		Laguna / Jiquilpas	Vec
8.0.0.0.0	300–100	PROTOCLASSIC	Nohalk'ax (Early Facet)	Ayn	Floral Park	Cantutse	Cimi	Chicanel	Cocos	Cobweb	Acropolis	Istmo	Caynac (Late Facet)
7.10.0.0.0 – 7.0.0.0.0	100 B.C. – A.D. 100	LATE FORMATIVE	K'atabche'k'ax (Terminal Facet / Late Facet / Early Facet)		Mount Hope / Barton Creek	Cantutse	Cauac / Chuen	Chicanel	Cocos	Blossom Bank	Paixbancito / Cascabel	Horcones	Caynac (Early Facet)
6.10.0.0.0 – 6.0.0.0.0	300–900 B.C.	MIDDLE FORMATIVE	Chaakk'ax (Late Facet / Early Facet)	Late Facet / San Felix (Early Facet) / Xe	Late Facet / Jenney Creek (Early Facet?)	Escoba / Real	Tzec / Eb	Mamom	Lopez / Bladen	Onecimo / Chiwa	Monos	Guanacaste / Francesca (Late Facet / Early Facet)	Chul / Kal / Colos
5.10.0.0.0 – 5.0.0.0.0	900–1200 B.C.	EARLY FORMATIVE					?		Swasey	Bolay			Tok

Table 9.2 Number of vessels arranged by ceramic complex and excavation unit (op. no.)

	CERAMIC COMPLEXES						
op. no.	Early · Chaakk'ax	Late Chaakk'ax	Early K'atabche'k'ax	Late K'atabche'k'ax	Terminal K'atabche'k'ax	Early Nohalk'ax	Totals
1	5	4	11	20	15		55
7					2	3	5
8				13	5		18
10				8		1	9
11			3	7	4		14
12				5	4	1	10
13						3	3
Totals	5	4	14	53	30	8	114

remains. Second, in contrast, only one Guitara Incised vessel was uncovered within a burial; the other three originated in construction fill (n = 2) or within a sherd-lined pit (n = 1).

Further examination of the vessels of K'axob is possible through use of the digital *Pottery Vessels Database*. Full color images, close-ups of vessel features and decoration, QuickTime video of selected vessels, and extensive documentation for each vessel aid both visualization and interpretation of the K'axob assemblage.

For the purpose of this chapter, the vessels have been organized chronologically and grouped by their context. At the top of the left-hand pages that follow, the ceramic complex is represented in large font. The complexes have been arranged sequentially and correspond to periods of time shown in table 9.1. The complex names were established by López Varela and McAnany and allude (in Yucatec Mayan) to important markers in the deep history of K'axob. Chaakk'ax refers to the red coloration of early K'axob vessels from the Middle Formative, while K'atabche'k'ax alludes to the cross motif that appears on seven vessels during the Late Formative period. A few Early Classic vessels were found in the terminal, upper levels of several operations, and these compose the early facet of the Nohalk'ax complex. While this ceramic complex represents the growth of K'axob, it also represents the final, uppermost constructions found within the seven excavations documented in this monograph. The number of vessels within each facet of each complex is enumerated in table 9.2.

Within each complex, the operation and zone numbers that contain vessels are listed in numerical order. Each provenience is defined by its cultural context (that is, burial or cache, among others) followed by a unique vessel number and description. Vessels are grouped specifically by context so that the reader can peruse the full corpus of vessels associated with a context such as a burial feature. Four vessels derive from transitional contexts, and these have been placed on a separate page between the relevant complexes. The descriptions that follow are focused on the form and surface treatment of vessels; for extensive descriptions of context or associated artifacts, the reader should reference relevant chapters and digital data sets. For burial contexts, the vessels are ascribed to specific individuals when possible, otherwise all associated individuals are listed (burial number includes the operation number followed by a number for each individual). For additional explanations of the interments, see Storey (chapter 6). Similarly, for a more complete description of vessel caches, particularly those with accompanying objects, see Harrison-Buck (chapter 4).

The vessel descriptions are formatted in the following manner: the **vessel number** in boldface print, the *Type: Variety* identification in italics, followed by vessel form and characteristic attributes in plain print. The second line describes the condition of the vessel and provides its measurements using the following abbreviations: RD for rim diameter, HT for height, and WT for weight. When a vessel was too fragmentary to measure, we entered "nmp" (no measurement possible) after the applicable parameter. The subsequent lines present additional measurements as well as a brief description of vessel shape, appliques, and other decorative elements. This paragraph often provides information about the paste and Munsell color associations (listed in parenthetical codes directly following a color: for example, reddish yellow as 7.5YR 6/6). Evidence for burning or fire treatment of the vessel is also noted. Fourteen of the most complete vessels have been accessioned into the holdings of the Department of Archaeology in Belmopan, Belize. For those vessels, the DOA No. is listed prominently at the beginning of the paragraph.

The right-hand pages that follow contain scaled images of the vessels described on the left. Vessels that were greater than 50% complete are represented either by full profile drawings or photographs. Despite the aforementioned elimination of twelve fragmentary vessels, even the 114 that have been selected for depiction represent highly variable states of preservation. Criteria for inclusion in this chapter were generous. Vessels were admitted if they permitted a full rim-to-base profile or if they derived from significant contexts. When less than 50% of a vessel exists, we left the image incomplete by drawing only the left half of the rim profile. In a few instances, no illustration was possible, and we include a note to that effect in place of the vessel. In one instance (vessel 101), a schematic representation of the vessel was used to more clearly exemplify features from the text description. Vessel images were created by photographers Michael Hamilton and Mary Lee Bartlett, and illustrators Tamarra Martz, Lorren Jackson, Eleanor Harrison-Buck, and Kimberly Berry. Vessel descriptions were written by Sandra López Varela, Mary Lee Bartlett, Patricia A. McAnany, and Kimberly Berry.

The vessels in this chapter are indicative of Formative and Early Classic wares from the agricultural village of K'axob but do not necessarily represent the full corpus of ceramic forms. Whole and reconstructible vessels at the site were usually recovered from contexts charged with significant ceremonial and ritualistic overtones. Conversely, most domestic and utilitarian wares are represented by highly fragmented and dispersed sherds. For the purposes of this chapter, we did not analyze undifferentiated sherd lots or include their hypothetical reconstructed forms. The vessels on the following pages embody the ceramic types that a Maya villager deemed appropriate to use as offerings for deceased family members or to the gods.

Please note: all vessels are reproduced at 1/3 (33.3%) of their actual size.

EARLY CHAAKK'AX COMPLEX

Operation 1, Zone 208

Sherd-Lined Pit

Vessel 121 *Joventud Red: Unspecified Variety*, bowl
Able to be Reconstructed; RD: 38 cm, HT: 5.5 cm, WT: 1335 g

A Joventud Red bowl with outcurving walls and an everted rim with a rounded lip. The base is slightly incurved and has a diameter of 32 cm.

Operation 1, Zone 210
Construction Fill

Vessel 006 *Guitara Incised: Guitara Variety*, bowl
Not Reconstructible; RD: 38 cm, HT: 6.5 cm, WT: 496 g

This bowl features outcurved sides, a direct rounded lip with a groove on both the interior and exterior, and a burned interior. A groove is incised on the interior 1 cm below the rim and 1.5 cm below the rim on the exterior. The groove width is 0.2 cm. A red (2.5YR 4/6) slip was applied to the interior and exterior surface areas, except on the grooves. The paste, which is very friable, is reddish yellow (5YR 6/8) and has large round inclusions.

Vessel 007 *Guitara Incised: Guitara Variety*, bowl
Not Reconstructible; RD: 29 cm, HT: 5 cm, WT: 133.5 g

This flat-bottomed, outcurved bowl was decorated with an incised rim line. The base diameter is 24 cm.

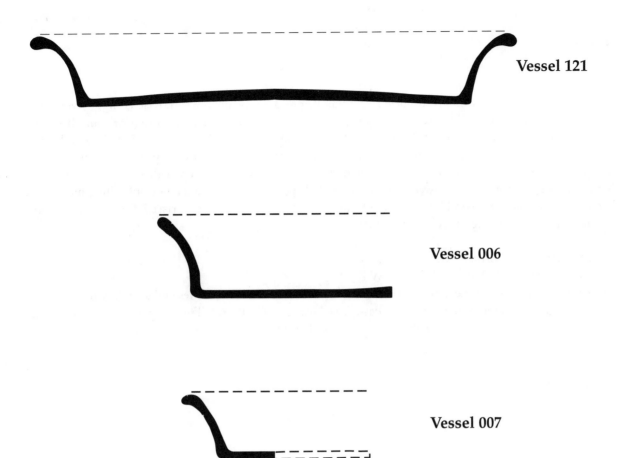

Vessel 121

Vessel 006

Vessel 007

EARLY CHAAKK'AX COMPLEX

Operation 1, Zone 233

Burial 1-43

Vessel 001 *Timax Incised: Timax Variety*, bowl
Reconstructed; RD: 32 cm, HT: 8.4 cm, WT: 981.5 g
   This bowl exhibits incurved-recurved sides. Recurving begins 3 cm below the rim. Base is slightly rounded. Texture of the paste is fine and is a reddish yellow (7.5YR 6/6) color. There was no core formation. It is covered with an orange or red (2.5YR 4/8) slip but also has a pinkish gray (7.5YR 7/2 or 7.5YR 7/3) underslip. The rim is decorated with red spots, which create separate domains of color. Red slipped trefoil decorations were added to the interior bottom of the vessel and also to the walls. Areas of color that are not distinguishable in form are also found on the exterior. Incisions include prefired, broad, round bottomed lines measuring 0.3 to 0.4 cm in width. A second line is 1.2 cm from the first one. A third line starts 1.2 cm from the second one, almost at the beginning of the recurved sides.

Vessel 002 *Toribio Red-on-Cream: Toribio Variety*, bowl
Able to be reconstructed; RD: nmp, HT: nmp, WT: 702 g
   Base diameter is 14 cm and there are no rim sherds. It is a bowl with flared sides and a slightly domed base. Thickness of the vessel wall is 0.5 to 0.7 cm. Paste is reddish gray (5YR 5/2). There are three vertical decorative bars of red paint spaced fairly evenly around the vessel. A circumferential band at the bottom of the vessel wall anchors the vertical bands.

Vessel 001

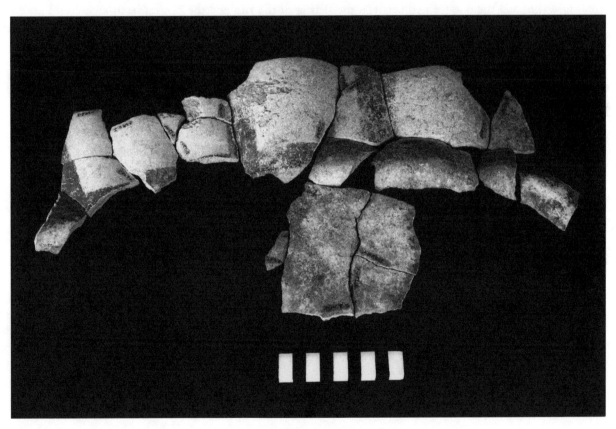

Vessel 002

LATE CHAAKK'AX COMPLEX

Operation 1, Zone 137

Burial 1-28

Vessel 003 *Joventud Red: Unspecified Variety*, tecomate
Reconstructed; RD: 10 cm, HT: 8 cm, WT: 508 g

> This tecomate is decorated with prefired incisions that start below a circumferential line surrounding the rim, which has been thickened on the interior side. These lines run vertical to the base, in a manner representative of a squash. The exterior surfaces and the base are slipped with Joventud Red. Differential firing occurs in a black (2.5YR 2.5/0) color. Thickness of the walls is 4.5 cm. This vessel was found beneath a larger vessel in burial 1-28.

Vessel 004 *Guitara Incised: Guitara Variety*, bowl
Able to be reconstructed; RD: 28 cm, HT: 10.9 cm, WT: 1532.5 g

> An incised bowl with outcurved sides, an everted rim, and a rounded lip. In comparison with other Guitara vessels from K'axob, this one was not skillfully made; the modeled and incised bands traced before firing the vessel do not run perfectly horizontally. The central band measures 3 cm in width, the one near the base 1.6 cm in width, and the one formed between the flaring of the rim and the central band measures 3 cm. The potter tried to drill in several places near the rim but did not complete the process. Drilling proceeded from both the exterior and the interior sides in pairs, but some holes never punctured the vessel.

Operation 1, Zone 143

Burial 1-30a

Vessel 017 *Sierra Red: Sierra Variety*, dish
Reconstructed; RD: 31.2 cm, HT: 5.5 cm, WT: 1572.2 g

> This flared dish has an everted rim and an almost horizontal and rounded lip. The base is slightly incurved and has a diameter of 21.5 cm. The form of this bowl is closely related to Mamom tradition. The vessel was decorated with two wavy lines on the interior walls. This decoration, although similar in appearance to resist treatment, was obtained through firing. The dish, along with an inverted bowl, was inverted over the skull of an extended interment.

Vessel 018 *Matamore Dichrome: Matamore Variety*, bowl
Reconstructed; RD: 18 cm, HT: 9.6 cm, WT: 840 g

> This bowl has incurved sides and a flat base—a form closely related to other Mamom types. The rim has a prefired incision and resembles tecomates of the Mamom sphere. The diameter of the base is 8.5 cm. The vessel was inverted with another vessel (V. 017) over the skull.

Vessel 003

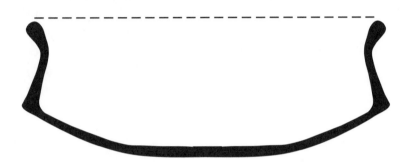

Vessel 004

Vessel 017

Vessel 018

EARLY K'ATABCHE'K'AX COMPLEX

Operation 1, Zone 100

Burial 1-19a

Vessel 008 *Sierra Red: Sierra Variety*, bowl
Able to be reconstructed; RD: 21 cm, HT: 7.5 cm, WT: 524.6 g
  The form of this bowl features incurved sides and horizontal everted rim with a rounded lip. Slipped on the interior and the exterior, the base diameter measures 12.8 cm. It served as a lid for the bottom vessel (spouted jar).

Vessel 009 *Sierra Red: Sierra Variety*, jar with spout
Reconstructed; RD: 12.5 cm, HT: 10.7 cm, WT: 931.4 g
  This spouted jar has incurved sides, a flaring neck, and an exterior thickened rim with rounded lip. The interior of the neck and the exterior walls are slipped in a color similar to other vessels of this variety. The spout is 8 cm in height and its orifice is 1.8 cm in diameter. The base is slightly incurved and measures approximately 9 cm in diameter. In situ the jar's spout pointed to the east.

Operation 1, Zone 103

Burial 1-18

Vessel 010 *Sierra Red: Sierra Variety*, bowl
Whole; RD: 15 cm, HT: 10 cm, WT: 715 g
  DOA No: 33/200-5:3 This Sierra Red bowl has rounded sides, an interior thickened rim, and an incurved base. The surface on both exterior and interior is reddish yellow (5YR 5/6) to red (10R 5/8). Fire clouding on the exterior is very dark gray (2.5YR 3/0) or black (2.5Y 2/0). The diameter of the base is 4.5 cm. Shell beads and the remains of a child's skull were found inside the inverted bowl.

Operation 1, Zone 113b

Burial 1-24

Vessel 012 *Sierra Red: Sierra Variety*, bowl
Whole; RD: 15.5 cm, HT: 8.5 cm, WT: 517 g
  DOA No: 33/200-5:5 This bowl has incurved-recurved sides, an exterior thickened rim, and a partially square lip. The base is flat with a 5 cm diameter. In the interior, though, the vessel bottom appears rounded. Surface color is reddish-yellow (5YR 5/6) to red (10R 5/8). The bowl was found upright over the head and shoulder area of an old, adult female.

Vessel 008

Vessel 009

Vessel 010

Vessel 012

EARLY K'ATABCHE'K'AX COMPLEX

Operation 1, Zone 115

Burial 1-25

Vessel 013 *Sierra Red: Sierra Variety*, dish
Reconstructed; RD: 22 cm, HT: 4 cm, WT: 488.5 g
   This dish is similar to vessel 014. Walls are outcurving with a slightly everted rim and rounded lip. Two intentional holes were drilled into the wall of the dish. These holes caused uneven breakage. A cross motif was slipped on the base of the vessel. Slip is red (10R 4/8). The paste has few inclusions and is yellowish red (5YR 5/6) with a dark gray (5YR 4/1) core. The base is slightly incurved and measures 12 cm in diameter. The vessel was found in close proximity to the skull of an adult male.

Operation 1, Zone 115a

Burial 1-29

Vessel 014 *Sierra Red: Sierra Variety*, dish
Reconstructed; RD: 20 cm, HT: 4.2 cm, WT: 544.1 g
   This Sierra Red dish is slipped on the exterior and interior. The red (10R 4/8) slip is partially eroded. A streaky cross was painted on the exterior of the base. Walls are outcurved and rim is everted with a rounded lip. Base is slightly incurved and is 12 cm in diameter. The dish was found near the right humerus of an adult male.

Operation 1, Zone 118

Sherd-Lined Pit

Vessel 005 *Guitara Incised: Pollo Desnudo Variety*, bowl
Not reconstructible; RD: 32 cm, HT: 5.5 cm, WT: 694.2 g
   This bowl with outcurved wall, everted rim with rounded lip, has an eyebrow motif incised on the rim. There are ten eyebrow motifs on rim sherds belonging to this vessel, but there were probably eleven prefired incisions with an average spacing of 4.5 to 5.5 cm. The paste has a fine compact texture and contains probable carbonate particles. Color of the paste is reddish yellow (5YR 6/8). The core has a width of 0.4 cm and a very dark gray (7.5YR 3/0) or black (7.5Y 2/0) color. Slip is a light red (10R 4/0, 10R 5/8). Rim everts 3 cm. The half circles are very similar to the unusual decoration reported for this variety at the site of Altar de Sacrificios (Adams 1971).

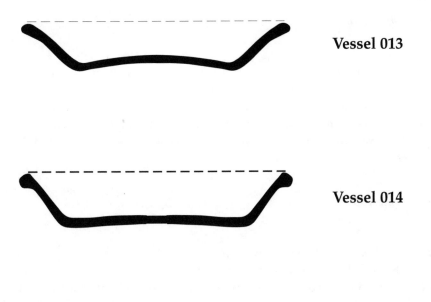

Vessel 013

Vessel 014

Vessel 005

EARLY K'ATABCHE'K'AX COMPLEX

Operation 1, Zone 121a

Cache

Vessel 055 *Laguna Verde Incised: Laguna Verde Variety*, cylinder with incisions decorating exterior
Reconstructed; RD: 21 cm, HT: 16 cm, WT: 1236 g
> A slightly flaring cylinder with an everted rim and fourteen chevrons inscribed around the body below the rim. A lower register contains design elements in the shape of an inverted "U" that measure 9 cm in height and have widths of 3 to 4 cm. Fireclouding has blackened the rim and marred the finish of the red slip. The basal diameter is 13 cm.

Operation 1, Zone 135

Burial 1-27

Vessel 015 *Sierra Red: Sierra Variety*, bowl
Whole; RD: 8.8 cm, HT: 8.3 cm, WT: 336.3 g
> DOA No: 33/200-5:8 This bowl has incurved sides, a restricted orifice with an interiorly thickened rim, and a flat base. Surface color on the exterior and interior is reddish yellow (5YR 5/6) or red (10R 5/8). Fireclouding occurs on the exterior. The diameter of the base is 5.5 cm. The vessel was found over the chest of an extended child burial.

Vessel 016 *Sierra Red: Sierra Variety*, cylinder
Not reconstructible; RD: nmp, HT: nmp, WT: 370 g
> This partial vessel lacks a rim. There is slip on the exterior and the interior of the vessel and a drill hole in the side wall. The base diameter measures 12 cm; other measurements were not possible to collect. Paste color is red (2.5YR 5/8). It was positioned over the pelvis of an extended child burial.

Operation 1, Zone 152a

Burial 1-34a

Vessel 019 *Sierra Red: Sierra Variety*, dish
Reconstructed; RD: 26 cm, HT: 4.7 cm, WT: 1034.8 g
> This dish has flaring sides and an almost horizontal everted rim. Base diameter is 20 cm. The dish was found inverted over the head of burial 1-34a.

Vessel 055

Vessel 015

No rim sherds and fragmentary base.
Rim diameter is unknown.

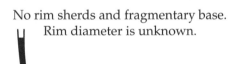

Vessel 016

Vessel 019

EARLY K'ATABCHE'K'AX COMPLEX

Operation 11, Zone 90a

Burial 11-10

Vessel 086 *Sierra Red: Unspecified Variety*, bowl
Able to be reconstructed; RD: 18 cm, HT: 14.2 cm, WT: 2167 g
> A bowl with incurved sides, slightly concave base (13.5 cm diameter), direct rim, and rounded lip. The vessel has pronounced circumferential angular ridges of 3 cm. There are two chamfers that begin at the rim. The first measures 2 cm in width, the second 3 cm. Slip is present on both the exterior and interior in a typical Sierra Red hue (2.5YR 4/8). Fireclouding occurs in gray (2.5YR 6/0) and light gray (5YR 7/1). The paste has a fine texture and a reddish yellow (7.5YR 6/6) color.

Vessel 087 *Sierra Red: Unspecified Variety*, jar with duck effigy and spout
Reconstructed; RD: 21 cm, HT: 20 cm, WT: 1325.5 g
> A Sierra Red effigy jar with incurved-outcurved sides, a long neck, and an unsupported spout. The spout is located opposite the modeled duck head effigy. There are incised lines representing the wings of the duck on either side of the vessel. The height of the vessel neck is 7.5 cm and the rim is horizontal and slightly everted. The spout measures 13.5 cm in height and its orifice is 0.7 cm in diameter. The color of the surface falls within the Sierra Red color attributes (2.5YR 4/8). Fireclouding is either gray (2.5YR 6/0) or light gray (5YR 7/1). A reddish yellow (7.5YR 6/6) color characterizes the finely textured paste.

Operation 11, Zone 93c

Burial 11-12a

Vessel 122 *Sierra Red: Sierra Variety*, bowl
Whole; RD: 22.5 cm, HT: 7.2 cm, WT: 1014 g
> DOA No: 33/200-5:14 A Sierra Red bowl that has outcurved walls, an everted rim thickened on the exterior, and a rounded lip. The diameter of the base is 14.5 cm. The bowl was inverted and placed over the chest of an adult female.

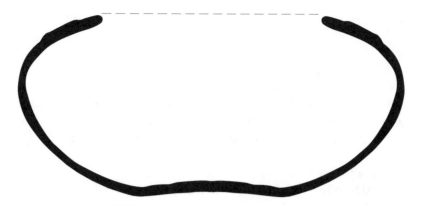

Vessel 086

Vessel 087

Vessel 122

LATE K'ATABCHE'K'AX COMPLEX

Operation 1, Zone 30a

Burial 1-3

Vessel 039 *Sierra Red: Sierra Variety*, bowl
Reconstructed; RD: 30 cm, HT: 10.5 cm, WT: 1640.7 g
  This outcurved bowl with exteriorly thickened rim and rounded lip exhibits paste and color within the characteristic attributes of the Sierra Red type. The base is flat and has a diameter of 22 cm. Wall thickness is 0.8 cm. Fragmented into sherds, the vessel was found in the western portion of a cist containing a flexed adult.

Vessel 040 *Sierra Red: Sierra Variety*, bowl
Able to be reconstructed; RD: 54 cm, HT: 7.5 cm, WT: 4624 g
  A badly eroded bowl with outcurved sides, an outflared rim, and a rounded lip. Wall thickness is 0.7 cm.

Operation 1, Zone 38

Burial 1-4

Vessel 042 *Sierra Red: Sierra Variety*, bowl
Whole; RD: 10.2 cm, HT: 8.7 cm, WT: 479 g
  This bowl has markedly incurved sides, a restricted orifice, and a double-collar neck. Paste and color are characteristic of Sierra Red. The diameter of the base is 6 cm. The bowl was associated with the secondary bundled remains of an older child or young adolescent.

Operation 1, Zone 38a

Burial 1-10

Vessel 043 *Sierra Red: Sierra Variety*, dish
Reconstructed; RD: 28 cm, HT: 7 cm, WT: 1193 g
  A dish with outcurved sides and a flat base as well as an outflaring everted rim with a rounded lip. The rim begins to flare by 3.3 cm up the wall of the vessel and becomes everted at a height of 4.6 cm. The paste and color attributes fall within Sierra Red, although the slip was probably exposed to fire. It is a darker yellowish red (5YR 4/6). The diameter of the base is 21 cm.

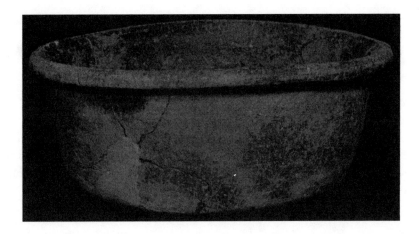

Vessel 039

Vessel 040

Vessel 042

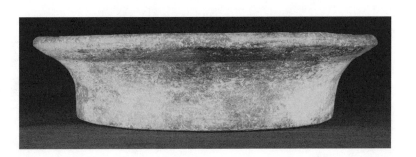

Vessel 043

LATE K'ATABCHE'K'AX COMPLEX

Operation 1, Zone 41

Cache

Vessel 044 *Sierra Red: Gadrooned Variety*, bowl
Reconstructed; RD: 16 cm, HT: 7 cm, WT: 648 g

A Sierra Red bowl with straight, vertically grooved walls and a slightly squared direct lip. Grooves are shallow and originate 1 cm below the lip. The vessel slip is red (2.5YR 4/8) and is eroded on both the interior and exterior. The paste has a gray core (2.5YR 4/1) with a few inclusions. The base is flat and has a diameter of 16 cm.

Operation 1, Zone 42

Burial 1-6a

Vessel 045 *Sierra Red: Gadrooned Variety*, bowl
Able to be reconstructed; RD: 21 cm, HT: 8.4 cm, WT: 838 g

An eroded bowl with horizontal grooves and a beveled rim. The paste and color render this vessel within the Sierra Red type, as do the decorations, though the grooves do not protrude as much as those of some of the other type vessels. Each groove is 1 cm wide. The flat base has a diameter of 16 cm.

Vessel 044

Vessel 045

LATE K'ATABCHE'K'AX COMPLEX

Operation 1, Zone 77

Cache

Vessel 029 *Society Hall Red: Society Hall Variety*, bowl
Not reconstructible; RD: 18.7 cm, HT: 7.5 cm, WT: 647.5 g

Partially reconstructible bowl with nearly vertical sides, rounded lip, exterior fireclouding, and a streaky slip on the interior. The base is slightly convex with a diameter of 14.6 cm. The color of the slip in the interior is red (2.5YR 5/6) and light red (2.5YR 6/8). The exterior color is reddish yellow (5YR 6/6) or very dark gray (7.5YR 3/0). The paste is extremely porous due to its poor preservation. This is the north vessel of the quadripartite cache.

Vessel 030 *Society Hall Red: Society Hall Variety*, bowl
Whole; RD: 18.7 cm, HT: 7.5 cm, WT: 0 g

DOA No: 33/200-5:1 This bowl has nearly vertical sides, a direct rim, a rounded lip, and a flat base. Slip color on the interior of the vessel is light yellowish brown (2.5Y 6/4) or reddish yellow (7.5YR 6/6). The predominant color on the exterior of the vessel is gray (5Y 6/1), but a red (2.5YR 5/6) or reddish brown (2.5YR 5/4) color is also present. Thickness of the walls varies between 0.4 and 0.8 cm, and the diameter of the base is 15 cm. This bowl is the south vessel of the quadripartite cache.

Vessel 032 *Sierra Red: Gadrooned Variety*, bowl
Whole; RD: 16.6 cm, HT: 5.5 cm, WT: 487 g

DOA No: 33/200-5:11 This bowl has nearly vertical walls and a flat base. It probably had been exposed to fire. The interior and exterior of the vessel have a red (10R 5/6, 10R 5/8) slip that was applied with a mottled effect. The red tends to degrade into a strong brown (7.5YR 5/6). Fireclouding is present on only one area of the exterior part of the vessel. The color varies between very dark gray (7.5YR 3/0) and red (10R 5/8). It is decorated with five circumferential grooves that were formed before firing. The uppermost groove forms the rim, which is exterior and thickened with a rounded lip. Grooves are irregular in shape and width but basically measure 0.8 to 1 cm and are separated irregularly by a 5 cm span. Thickness of the wall is 0.8 cm. This is the west vessel of the quadripartite cache.

Vessel 035 *Sierra Red: Gadrooned Variety*, bowl
Whole; RD: 16.6 cm, HT: 5.5 cm, WT: 487 g

DOA No: 33/200-5:12 This bowl has the same characteristics as the western cache vessel (V. 032) described above, except that differential firing is more frequent and the slip is better preserved. Thickness of the walls is 0.8 cm. Diameter of the flat base is 14.6 cm. This is the east vessel of the quadripartite cache.

Vessel 029

Vessel 030

Vessel 032

Vessel 035 has not been illustrated.
It is most similar to Vessel 032.

LATE K'ATABCHE'K'AX COMPLEX

Operation 1, Zone 78

Burial 1-13

Vessel 046 *Society Hall Red: Society Hall Variety*, bowl
Reconstructed; RD: 37.5 cm, HT: 16 cm, WT: 437.7 g

This bowl features flared sides, a flat base, an outflared, everted rim, and a rounded lip. The total height of the vessel is 16 cm, but the rim begins to project at a height of 11 cm and extends another 9 cm at a 45° angle. The paste color is pink (5YR 7/3) or very pale brown (10YR 7/3). The paste is fine-textured and no core was formed. A thin, pale red (2.5YR 6/8) slip was applied over the interior and exterior, but its preservation is poor. The slip is very thin and flakes easily. A distinctive feature of this vessel is the streaky painted cross-band on the exterior of the flat base, which has a diameter of 26.3 cm. The painted bands are of unequal dimensions: the larger one 23 x 2.5 cm, the smaller 20 x 2.5 cm. The smaller band does not evenly bisect the larger one. Near the rim, three attempts were made to perforate the vessel. Two drill holes were completed 11 cm apart, but the third, situated close to one of the other two, never pierced the vessel. The bowl was inverted over the head and upper torso of a flexed adult.

Vessel 047 *Sierra Red: Unspecified Variety*, jar with face effigy, spout, and handles
Whole; RD: 11 cm, HT: 13.5 cm, WT: 780.5 g

DOA No: 33/200-5:7 Because of its unique modeled decoration, this Sierra Red spouted jar effigy is not classified within any Sierra Red varieties. No such decoration has ever been reported for any of the varieties. The jar itself has a slightly everted rim, square lip, two small strap handles, a spout, and a concave base. The slip color is yellowish red (5YR 5/8) to light red (2.5YR 6/8), and the interior of the neck is slipped with the latter color. Fireclouding is also present. The paste is pink (5YR 7/3) to gray (7.5YR 6/0) and has a medium texture. Opposite the spout, there is an effigy-modeled face that covers the body of the vessel. The two strap handles vary in size. One is 1.5–2 cm in width, while the larger one is 2–2.5 cm. Each has a height of 3.6 cm. The spout measures 3.5 cm in height and its orifice is 2 cm in diameter. The height of the vessel's neck is 1.6 cm. The diameter of the base is 14 cm.

Operation 1, Zone 80

Burial 1-12a

Vessel 048 *Sierra Red: Sierra Variety*, jar with spout
Reconstructed; RD: 17.5 cm, HT: 13.9 cm, WT: 991 g

A spouted jar with incurved-recurved sides. Incurved side is gadrooned and was probably formed by pressing a finger continuously around the vessel. The neck is slightly outcurved and is 8.4 cm high. The rim is thickened on the exterior and has a rounded lip. The spout is located 4.9 cm from the rim and is 8.5 cm high. Diameter of the spout orifice is 1.4 cm. The diameter of the base is 10 cm. The slip on the vessel is red (10R 5/8) and light red (10R 6/8) and was applied to the exterior and to the interior of the neck. There are no traces of slip on the flat base, but this could be due to erosion. Fireclouding is present near the base and ranges in color from gray (7.5R 5/0) to dark gray (2.5YR 4/8).

Vessel 046

Vessel 047

Vessel 048

LATE K'ATABCHE'K'AX COMPLEX

Operation 1, Zone 81

Burial 1-15a

Vessel 049 *Chicago Orange: Chucun Variety*, jar with handles
Whole; RD: 10 cm, HT: 12.2 cm, WT: 648 g

DOA No: 33/200-5:6 A jar with incurved-recurved sides, strap handles, a slightly rounded base, and an exterior folded rim with a rounded lip. The color of the slip is the same as the paste: a light red (2.5YR 6/6). The interior of the neck was slipped with the same color. Erosion has led to smoothing marks. The basal diameter measures 6.5 cm, and the handles are 1.3 cm in width and 4 cm in height. The jar abutted the northern wall of the burial pit and was positioned on the deceased's left side.

Vessel 050 *Sierra Red: Gadrooned Variety*, cylinder
Reconstructed; RD: 20.5 cm, HT: 18.6 cm, WT: 1253 g

Cylinder with nearly vertical sides, a rim thickened on the exterior, and a slightly squared lip. A significant feature is the fluting decoration inscribed onto the sides. A circumferential line demarcates the extent of the flutes at 4.7 cm from the rim, and a second one parallels it down near the base. The flutes are irregular, varying in width from 0.7 to 1.2 cm. The decoration is reminiscent of that on a cylinder reported by Adams (1971) from the Plancha Complex at Altar de Sacrificios. The K'axob vessel has a light reddish brown (5YR 6/4) paste of a fine to medium texture and possible carbonate and iron inclusions. The exterior and interior are slipped in red (10R 5/8). Fireclouding occurs on the exterior near the rim and is variably white (5Y 8/1), dark olive gray (5Y 3/2), and very dark gray (10YR 3/1). The slip is crackled on most of the vessel, presumably because of the accumulation of carbonates. The base of the cylinder is slipped in the same color and measures 14.1 cm in diameter. The vessel was placed upright next to a seated, old adult female.

Vessel 051 *Sierra Red: Sierra Variety*, bowl
Reconstructed; RD: nmp, HT: 9 cm, WT: 2118.7 g

An extremely eroded bowl with characteristics indicating its inclusion within the Sierra Red type. The vessel has outcurved walls and remnants of a horizontal everted rim that seems to have been intentionally broken. The interior of the base is a very dark gray (10YR 3/1), the result of fire exposure. The basal diameter is 26 cm, while the rimless aperture has a diameter of 28.5 cm. The vessel was found inverted over the skull of a seated, old adult female.

Vessel 049

Vessel 050

Vessel 051

LATE K'ATABCHE'K'AX COMPLEX

Operatioxn 1, Zone 83

Burial 1-14

Vessel 054 *Sierra Red: Sierra Variety*, bowl
Whole; RD: 18 cm, HT: 9.8 cm, WT: 920 g
DOA No: 33/200-5:2 A Sierra Red bowl with incurved sides, an everted rim, rounded lip, and a flat base. The exterior and interior are slipped with a color that varies between a reddish yellow (5YR 5/6) and red (10R 5/8). Fireclouding on the exterior has produced patches of a very dark gray (2.5YR 3/0) or black (2.5Y 2/0). The diameter of the base is 14 cm.

Operation 1, Zone 88

Burial 1-17a

Vessel 052 *Sierra Red: Sierra Variety*, bowl
Reconstructed; RD: 21.3 cm, HT: 6.3 cm, WT: 739 g
Bowl with outcurved sides, rounded lip, and a flat base. The everted lip has a depression in it, which creates a "gutter" effect. Though fairly eroded, the vessel's remaining slip is a reddish yellow (5YR 6/6). Fireclouding is present on the exterior and is black (7.5YR 5/0). The diameter of the base is 13.8 cm. The vessel was positioned over the deceased's left shoulder. An associated vessel (V. 053) was inverted over the skull.

Vessel 053 *Sierra Red: Sierra Variety*, bowl
Reconstructed; RD: 35 cm, HT: 8.5 cm, WT: 1895 g
Outcurved sides characterize this flat-bottomed bowl (22 cm diameter) with an everted rim and rounded lip. The vessel is slipped on both the interior and exterior surfaces but exhibits differential firing patterns on the outside and crazing on the inside. The rim begins 6 cm up the vessel wall. This bowl was inverted and placed over the skull of an adult.

Operation 1, Zone 107

Burial 1-23

Vessel 011 *Sierra Red: Sierra Variety*, bowl
Whole; RD: 24 cm, HT: 10 cm, WT: 3116 g
DOA No: 33/200-5:9 This bowl has incurved-recurved sides, an interior thickened rim, and a slightly incurved base. The surface on both exterior and interior is reddish yellow (5YR 5/6) to red (10R 5/8). Fireclouding on this vessel obscures much of the red slip. The fireclouding is a very dark gray (2.5YR 3/0) or black (2.5Y 2/0). Rootlet marks are visible on the exterior surface. The diameter of the base is 7 cm. The bowl was found resting on the left humerus of an extended, adult burial.

Vessel 054

Vessel 052

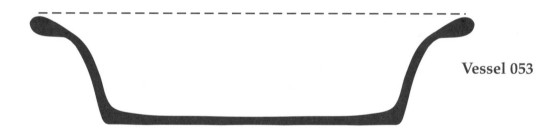

Vessel 053

Vessel 011

LATE K'ATABCHE'K'AX COMPLEX

Operation 8, Zone 6

Burial 8-1

Vessel 061 *Society Hall Red: Society Hall Variety*, bowl
Able to be reconstructed; RD: 42 cm, HT: 14.5 cm, WT: 3729 g
   A bowl with outcurved sides, a flaring everted rim, and a rounded lip. The diameter of the base is 28 cm and the height to the rim is 7.5 cm. Wall thickness varies between 0.8 and 1 cm.

Vessel 062 *Sierra Red: Gadrooned Variety*, bowl
Able to be reconstructed; RD: 17.5 cm, HT: 5.4 cm, WT: 481 g
   An eroded rounded bowl with a direct rim and rounded lip. The flat base has a diameter of 15 cm. Paste and slip color fall within the characteristic attributes of Sierra Red. The gadroon decoration is subtle, not protruding to the extent of others within this type. Each groove is 1 cm in width. The vessel walls are 0.5 to 0.7 cm thick.

Operation 8, Zone 8

Burial 8-2

Vessel 063 *Sierra Red: Sierra Variety*, jar with spout
Reconstructed; RD: 12.3 cm, HT: 11 cm, WT: 495 g
   A spouted jar with a vertical neck, exteriorly thickened rim, and rounded lip. The height of the neck measures 1.8 cm, and the spout is 4.9 cm tall with an aperture of 1.3 cm. Opposite the spout is a poorly preserved applique. The paste and color characteristics of the vessel place it within the Sierra Red type.

Operation 8, Zone 8a

Burial 8-2a

Vessel 064 *Sierra Red: Sierra Variety*, bowl
Not reconstructible; RD: 30 cm, HT: 7.7 cm, WT: 1216 g
   Only partially complete, this bowl has outcurving sides, an everted rim, and a direct rounded lip. It has been slipped on the exterior and interior, and fireclouding is present. Wall thickness is 1 cm and the base diameter is 20 cm.

Vessel 065 *Sierra Red: Sierra Variety*, bowl
Reconstructed; RD: 35 cm, HT: 8.3 cm, WT: 2004 g
   Bowl with flaring sides, an incurved base, horizontally everted rim, and rounded lip. The rim flares 7 cm from the base and has a beveled aspect. The red coloration of the vessel places it within the Sierra Red type, and there is fireclouding on the surface. The wall thickness is 1 cm and the base diameter is 21.5 cm. It was found inverted over the skull of the individual.

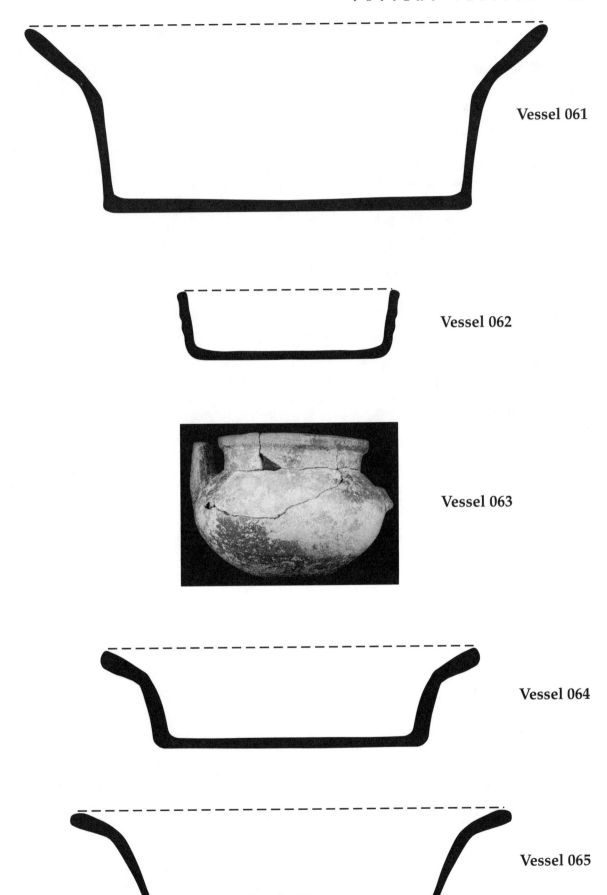

Vessel 061

Vessel 062

Vessel 063

Vessel 064

Vessel 065

LATE K'ATABCHE'K'AX COMPLEX

Operation 8, Zone 10

Cache

Vessel 066 *Sierra Red: Sierra Variety*, jar with spout
Partially reconstructible; RD: 10 cm, HT: 12.6 cm, WT: 403 g

A Sierra Red spouted jar with a vertical neck, exteriorly thickened rim, and rounded lip. The vessel is too fragmentary to determine the height or characteristics of the spout. The flat base has a diameter of 6.5 cm. This vessel was nested within another (V. 067) to form part of a cache.

Vessel 067 *Sierra Red: Sierra Variety*, bowl
Not reconstructible; RD: 32 cm, HT: 9 cm, WT: 425.5 g

A bowl with flared sides and a horizontally everted rim. The slip is highly eroded. Wall thickness measures 0.5 to 0.7 cm. Within the cache, a small jar (V. 066) had been placed inside this bowl.

Operation 8, Zone 22

Pit

Vessel 068 *Society Hall Red: Society Hall Variety*, bowl
Able to be reconstructed; RD: 49 cm, HT: 13.8 cm, WT: 4605 g

A bowl with outcurved sides, an everted rim, and a direct ovoid lip. The rim is 5.5 cm in width. Vessel paste is reddish yellow (5YR 6/8) and the slip is red (2.5YR 5/8). The base diameter is 35 cm.

Vessel 066

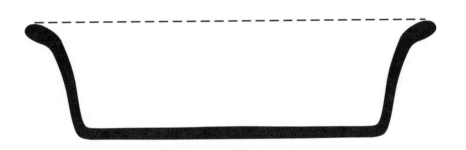

Vessel 067

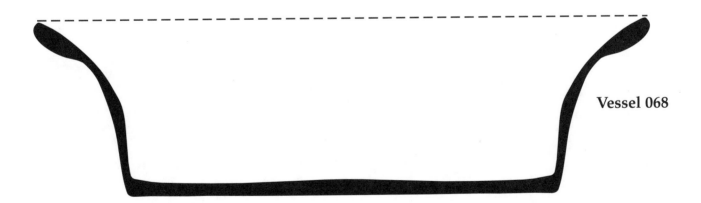

Vessel 068

LATE K'ATABCHE'K'AX COMPLEX

Operation 8, Zone 25a, 25b, and 25c

Cache

Vessel 069 *Sierra Red: Sierra Variety*, cylinder
Reconstructed; RD: 17 cm, HT: 14 cm, WT: 663.5 g

This cylinder with outcurved sides and an exteriorly thickened rim and rounded lip is extremely eroded, and it reveals a light reddish brown (2.5YR 6/4) paste under the surface. The overall slip color is dark red (2.5YR 4/8), but some fireclouding occurs and can range between a light olive brown (2.5Y 5/4), brownish yellow (10YR 6/6), and yellowish brown (10YR 5/6). The diameter of the base is 10 cm. Two pieces of chert were found inside the vessel.

Vessel 070 *Sierra Red: Gadrooned Variety*, bowl
Reconstructed; RD: 26 cm, HT: 8.5 cm, WT: 1576.8 g

This bowl has almost vertical sides. The color and paste are within the characteristic attributes of the Sierra Red type, gadrooned variety. The decoration consists of shallow grooves, measuring 1 cm in width, carved into the exterior. The grooves are not as deep as those of other Sierra Red types, possibly due to erosional processes. The diameter of the incurved base is 23.5 cm. The bowl was deposited as a cache in the subfloor of zone 16 and contained one piece of chert debitage.

Vessel 072 *Sierra Red: Gadrooned Variety*, bowl with handles
Reconstructed; RD: 16 cm, HT: 12 cm, WT: 930 g

This bowl has incurved walls, a direct rim, and a slightly squared lip. It is decorated with four circumferential grooves on the upper part of the body. Each groove is of variable width (0.5 to 0.75 cm) and the uppermost one helps to form the rim. Two strap handles attach to the rim and measure 3 cm in length. The slip is eroded and found only on the exterior, as is fireclouding. The base is rounded and curves up to a maximum vessel diameter of 22 cm. The walls vary in thickness between 0.3 and 0.7 cm. The vessel was found in an inverted position.

Vessel 069

Vessel 070

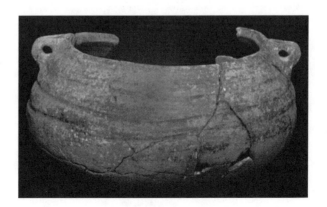

Vessel 072

LATE K'ATABCHE'K'AX COMPLEX

Operation 10, Zone 9a

Cache

Vessel 075 *Society Hall Red: Society Hall Variety*, bowl
Able to be reconstructed; RD: 42 cm, HT: 11.4 cm, WT: 2245 g

A bowl with flaring sides, a direct rim, and round lip. The basal diameter is 16 cm. The vessel was extremely eroded, so the red (2.5YR 5/8) color of the paste predominates. A very pale brown (10YR 7/3) color also occurs. The vessel was subject to carbonate accumulations. The thickness of the walls varies from 0.7 to 0.9 cm within which there is a 0.5 cm wide core of grayish brown (2.5Y 5/2). The bowl was the upright bottom vessel within the upper set of two lip-to-lip cache deposits.

Operation 10, Zone 9c

Cache

Vessel 076 *Society Hall Red: Society Hall Variety*, bowl
Able to be reconstructed; RD: 26 cm, HT: 6 cm, WT: 551 g

An eroded Society Hall bowl with outcurving sides. The base diameter is 14 cm. This was the upright bottom vessel of the lower lip-to-lip cache deposit.

Vessel 125 *Sierra Red: Sierra Variety*, jar (miniature)
Partially reconstructible; RD: 4.4 cm, HT: 6.9 cm, WT: 88.4 g

Part of a miniature jar with a basal diameter of 3.3 cm. One of two miniatures found near the base of two lip-to-lip cache deposits.

Vessel 126 *Sierra Red: Sierra Variety*, jar (miniature)
Partially reconstructible; RD: 4.3 cm, HT: 5.9 cm, WT: 77.3 g

One of two fragmentary miniature jars found near the base of two lip-to-lip cache deposits.

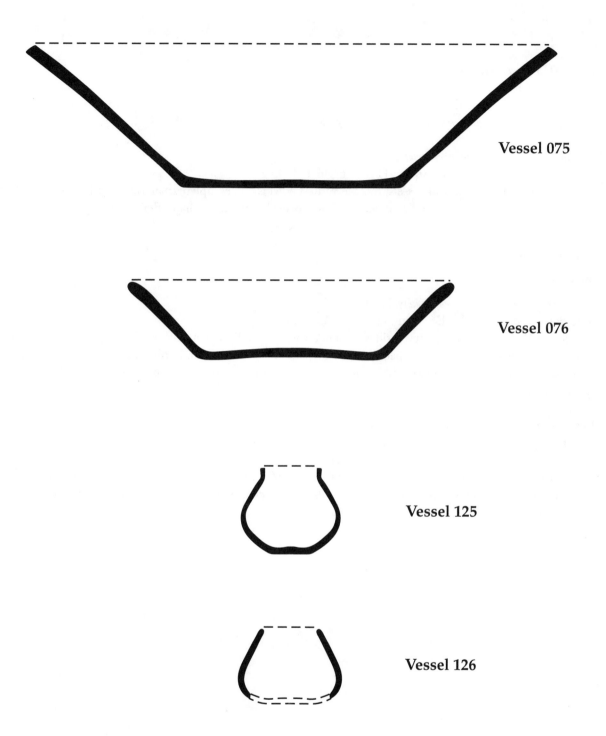

Vessel 075

Vessel 076

Vessel 125

Vessel 126

LATE K'ATABCHE'K'AX COMPLEX

Operation 10, Zone 10 and 10a

Cache

Vessel 073 *Sierra Red: Sierra Variety*, bowl
Reconstructed; RD: 36 cm, HT: 9 cm, WT: 2193 g
> A Sierra Red bowl with outcurved sides, medial flange, everted rim, and rounded lip. The base is rounded. One of two identical vessels, it was the upper half of a lip-to-lip cache with V. 074.

Vessel 074 *Sierra Red: Sierra Variety*, bowl
Able to be reconstructed; RD: 36 cm, HT: 9 cm, WT: 1943 g
> The second of two identical vessels, this Sierra Red bowl is less complete than V. 073. It has outcurved sides, medial flange, everted rim, and rounded lip. It was placed as the lower half offering in a lip-to-lip cache.

Operation 10, Zone 25

Burial 10-2

Vessel 077 *Sierra Red: Sierra Variety*, bowl
Able to be reconstructed; RD: 38 cm, HT: nmp, WT: 1395.7 g
> A Sierra Red bowl with outcurved sides, rounded base, and a direct rim with rounded lip. The interior of the vessel was burned. The slip has been burned to black but is eroded, and only small areas are apparent. The paste is a yellowish brown (10YR 5/8) color. The bowl was one of two found inverted over the head of a (possibly) male adult.

Vessel 078 *Sierra Red: Sierra Variety*, bowl
Able to be reconstructed; RD: 35 cm, HT: 12 cm, WT: 1920 g
Slightly eroded, this bowl has a straight direct rim and a square lip. The basal diameter is 18 cm, and the thickness of the wall ranges from 0.9 to 1.2 cm. Red (2.5YR 5/8) slip has been applied to the interior and exterior, while the paste is a pale brown (10YR 6/3). The vessel was one of two found inverted over the skull.

Vessel 073

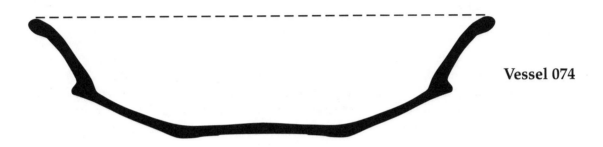

Vessel 074

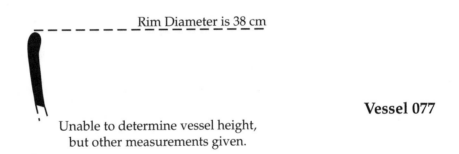

Rim Diameter is 38 cm

Vessel 077

Unable to determine vessel height,
but other measurements given.

Basal Diameter is 9 cm

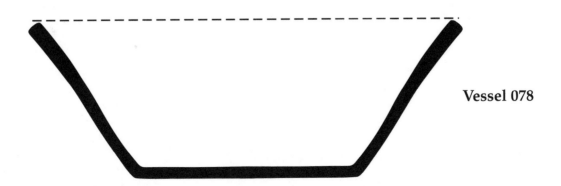

Vessel 078

LATE K'ATABCHE'K'AX COMPLEX

Operation 11, Zone 7

Burial 11-1

Vessel 079 *Sierra Red: Sierra Variety*, jar
Not reconstructible; RD: nmp, HT: nmp, WT: 2492 g

A very fragmentary Sierra Red jar with a slightly rounded base (18 cm diameter) and no rim sherds. The slip is a reddish yellow (5YR 7/8), as is the coarse paste (5YR 6/8) that contains large inclusions and a blackened core. The vessel wall is 1.2 cm thick. The jar was apparently purposefully broken during deposition to form a shield over the chest of the individual. This vessel is apparently an heirloom Late K'atabche'k'ax piece found in a Terminal K'atabche'k'ax context.

Operation 11, Zone 16c

Burial 11-3

Vessel 080 *Sierra Red: Sierra Variety*, bowl
Able to be reconstructed; RD: 36 cm, HT: 8.4 cm, WT: 1780 g

A flat-bottomed bowl (24 cm diameter) with outcurved walls and an everted, direct rim. Fireclouding is present on both the interior and exterior of the lip of the vessel. The vessel is also slipped on the interior and exterior. The paste is a reddish brown (2.5YR 4/8), and vessel thickness is 0.7 cm. This bowl was placed in the lap of a seated young adult male.

Operation 11, Zone 17

Cache

Vessel 081 *Sierra Red: Sierra Variety*, bowl with nubbin feet
Reconstructed; RD: 29.5 cm, HT: 7.5 cm, WT: 1071.5 g

One of two similar vessels (with V. 082), the bowl has round incurving sides, a round base, and a direct round lip. Four nubbin feet were added after the vessel was formed and provide support (unlike V. 082). The nubbins are each 1.5 cm in height. Red (2.5YR 5/8) slip covers interior and exterior surfaces, and the paste is a yellowish red (7.5R 5/8). The bowl was the upper vessel in a lip-to-lip cache.

Vessel 082 *Sierra Red: Sierra Variety*, bowl with nubbin feet
Reconstructed; RD: 28 cm, HT: 7 cm, WT: 1220.5 g

The second of two similar vessels (with V. 081), it is a rounded bowl with a slightly incurved rim and four nubbin feet. The feet (0.8 in height) were added after the vessel was formed and do not support the body. Red (2.5YR 4/8) slip covers the interior and half of the vessel's exterior. The paste is gray (10YR 5/1). This bowl was the bottom vessel of a lip-to-lip cache.

Vessel 079 is too fragmentary to illustrate.

Vessel 080

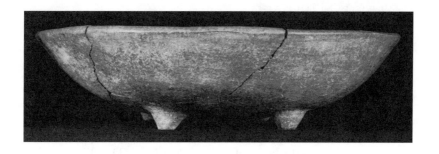

Vessel 081

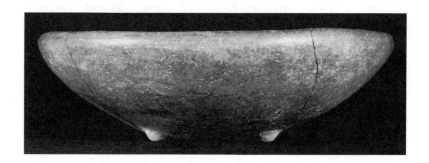

Vessel 082

LATE K'ATABCHE'K'AX COMPLEX

Operation 11, Zone 20c

Pit

Vessel 083 *Sierra Red: Sierra Variety*, dish
Reconstructed; RD: 16 cm, HT: 3.5 cm, WT: 140.5 g
    Dish with outcurving walls and a direct rounded lip. Eroded red (10R 4/8) slip is present on the interior, and the paste has a dark gray (2.5YR 4/0) core. The flat base measures 10 cm in diameter. Wall thickness is 0.3 cm but widens to 0.7 at the rim.

Operation 11, Zone 53

Burial 11-6

Vessel 084 *Sierra Red: Sierra Variety*, dish
Reconstructed; RD: 26.5 cm, HT: 8 cm, WT: 1402 g
    A dish with outcurving sides and a flared, everted rim. The flat base is 18.5 cm in diameter. The paste is finely textured with a 1 cm thick blackened core. Fireclouding occurs on the surface in variable colors: a very pale brown (10YR 7/3), dark gray (2.5Y 4/0), black (2.5Y 2/0), and red (2.5YR 5/6).

Vessel 085 *Sierra Red: Sierra Variety*, bowl
Able to be reconstructed; RD: 22 cm, HT: 13 cm, WT: 972.2 g
    Slightly flaring, this bowl has an everted rim and a rounded lip. It is slipped on the interior and exterior in red (2.5YR 4/8), but fireclouding occurs on the exterior. The paste is red (2.5YR 5/6) and has large white inclusions. The base has a diameter of 10 cm.

Operation 12, Zone 8

Cache

Vessel 088 *Sierra Red: Sierra Variety*, cylinder
Reconstructed; RD: nmp, HT: nmp, WT: 567.3 g
    A cylinder form with slightly incurved-outcurved walls at both the base and top. No rim sherds were found. The flat base is 12 cm in diameter and the thickness of the wall is 0.5 cm. The slip is eroded and blackened. This vessel is so fragmentary, accurate dimensions are not possible. The height of the largest sherd is 17.5 cm.

Vessel 083

Vessel 084

Vessel 085

Vessel 088

LATE K'ATABCHE'K'AX COMPLEX

Operation 12, Zone 40

Burial 12-9

Vessel 090 *Sierra Red: Sierra Variety*, dish
Not reconstructible; RD: 40 cm, HT: approximately 4.5 cm, WT: 900.5 g
   Very friable and in numerous pieces, this dish has outcurved, rounded walls and a direct but rounded lip. It is slipped in red (2.5YR 4/8) on the interior and exterior. The paste is moderately coarse with a yellowish red (5YR 5/8) exterior and a very dark gray (5YR 3/0) core. The thickness of the base is 1.5 cm. This dish was found upright in the lap of a seated individual.

Operation 12, Zone 42a

Burial 12-10

Vessel 091 *Sierra Red: Sierra Variety*, bowl
Whole; RD: 25.5 cm, HT: 8.9 cm, WT: 3154 g
   DOA No: 33/200-5:15 A Sierra Red bowl with flared walls, an outcurved, everted rim, and a rounded lip. The bowl has a flat base of 18.3 cm diameter and wall thickness is 1.2 cm. The paste is very fine. Fireclouding occurs on the surface of the vessel in the following colors: very pale brown (10YR 7/3), dark gray (2.5Y 4/0), black (2.5Y 2/0), and red (2.5YR 5/6).

Operation 12, Zone 42b

Burial 12-12

Vessel 092 *Sierra Red: Sierra Variety*, bowl
Able to be reconstructed; RD: 37 cm, HT: 9.7 cm, WT: 706 g
   Eroded and very fragmentary, this Sierra Red bowl flares from a flat base of 24 cm diameter. The paste and color are characteristic of Sierra Red. The vessel was found inverted over the head and torso of a seated, old adult female.

Operation 12, Zone 57

Burial 12-16a

Vessel 093 *Sierra Red: Sierra Variety*, dish
Reconstructed; RD: 40 cm, HT: 6.5 cm, WT: 1928.1 g
   A dish with flaring sides, an outflared, everted rim, and a rounded lip. The base is slightly incurved and measures 33 cm.

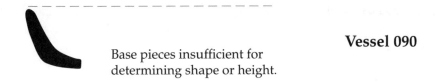

Base pieces insufficient for
determining shape or height.

Vessel 090

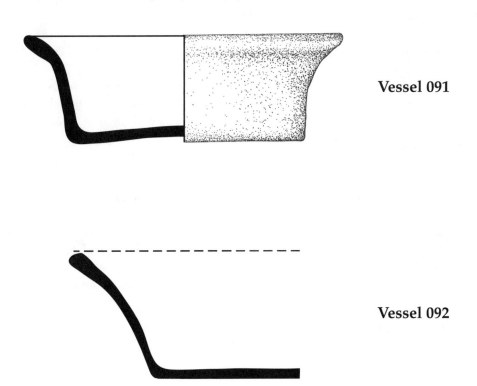

Vessel 091

Vessel 092

Vessel 093

LATE TO TERMINAL K'ATABCHE'K'AX COMPLEX

Operation 8, Zone 13a and 13b

Burial 8-4, 8-5, and 8-6

Vessel 112 *Ixcanrio Orange Polychrome: Ixcanrio Variety*, bowl with tetrapod feet
Able to be reconstructed; RD: 19 cm, HT: 11.5 cm, WT: 666.7 g

A very eroded polychrome tetrapod bowl with a painted geometric pattern. The bowl has a rounded base with a 15 cm basal diameter, slanted walls, and a direct rim with a rounded lip. The wall height of the bowl is 5.5 cm and each foot is 6.7 high. The feet have two slits (3 cm long) and a 1 cm round hole, then terminate in nubbins. Decoration is on the exterior of the vessel and consists of an orange circumferential line, double brown lines, and brown slip around the rim. The tetrapod feet are slipped on the outside. One of two vessels associated with burials 8-4, 8-5, and 8-6.

Vessel 100 *Aguacate Orange: Aguacate Variety*, bowl with mammiform tetrapod and nubbin feet
Not reconstructible; RD: 32, HT: nmp, WT: 1684.3 g

An eroded tetrapod bowl with hollow mammiform feet terminated by nubbins. The height of the feet is 8.3 cm and the diameter is 7.1 cm. This is one of two vessels associated with burials 8-4, 8-5, and 8-6.

Operation 8, Zone 13c

Burial 8-5

Vessel 101 *Eroded Polychrome*, bowl with mammiform tetrapod and nubbin feet
Not reconstructible; RD: 14 cm, HT: nmp, WT: 619.9 g

Very friable and eroded, this fragmentary mammiform tetrapod has a flared shape, ovoid feet, a direct rim, and rounded lip. The feet are 8 cm in height and have five round vent holes. Each foot terminates in a slightly rounded nubbin tip. The base of the deep bowl is also slightly rounded. The vessel's exterior is decorated with an incised mat design that is terminated near the rim by two circumferential incisions that frame a zigzag pattern.

Operation 11, Zone 36b

Burial 11-4

Vessel 106 *Aguacate Orange: Aguacate Variety*, bowl
Reconstructed; RD: 34 cm, HT: 8.2 cm, WT: 1285.3 g

A rounded bowl with a curved base. The rim is direct and the lip round. An interior incised groove, 3.7 cm below the lip, stylistically separates the rim from the body of the vessel. The interior is slipped and the paste is yellowish red (5YR 5/8) with black and white inclusions. The walls are 1 cm thick. This bowl was inverted over the head of an adult.

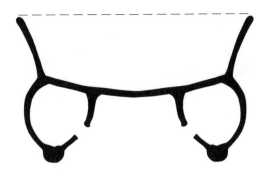

Vessel 112

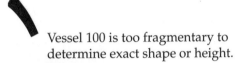

Vessel 100 is too fragmentary to determine exact shape or height.

Vessel 100

Vessel 101

Vessel 106

TERMINAL K'ATABCHE'K'AX COMPLEX

Operation 1, Zone 9

Cache

Vessel 020 *Society Hall Red: Society Hall Variety*, bowl
Reconstructed; RD: 23.7 cm, HT: 11.9 cm, WT: 1115.5 g

This outcurving bowl has an outflared, everted rim with a rounded lip. The outflaring begins 8 cm above the base and extends 4.7 cm from the walls. Base is flat and measures 14.5 cm in diameter. Color and paste are within the characteristic attributes of Society Hall Red. Vessel found upright on floor.

Operation 1, Zone 15c and 15e

Burial 1-1a

Vessel 021 *Society Hall Red: Society Hall Variety*, bowl
Able to be reconstructed; RD: 50 cm, HT: 11.1 cm, WT: 5039.6 g

This vessel is a bowl with flared sides, direct rim, round lip, and incurved base. The thickness of the walls is between 1 and 1.5 cm. Color and paste are within the Society Hall Red variety and the base diameter is 31 cm. There is a cross on the exterior base that spans the whole surface and, where the base meets the wall of the vessel, there is a circumferential band in the same color as the cross and the interior of the vessel.

Vessel 023 *Society Hall Red: Society Hall Variety*, bowl
Able to be reconstructed; RD: 30 cm, HT: 14.7 cm, WT: 2382 g

This outcurved bowl has an outflared, everted rim and a rounded lip. The outflaring rim begins at 10.3 cm from the base and is 5.5 cm in width. The base is flat and measures 16 cm. Color and paste are within the characteristics of the Society Hall variety. A cross was painted on the exterior base.

Operation 1, Zone 15g

Burial 1-1f

Vessel 022 *Society Hall Red: Society Hall Variety*, bowl
Able to be reconstructed; RD: 22.3 cm, HT: 10.4 cm, WT: 757.2 g

Bowl with shallow flange and incurved-recurved sides, everted horizontal rim, and round lip. A double line break occurs on the rim and flange. The rim extends 1.8 cm. One incised line is 1 mm and the second one, closest to the lip, measures 0.5 mm.

Vessel 020

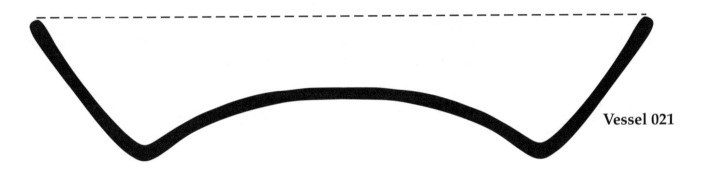

Vessel 021

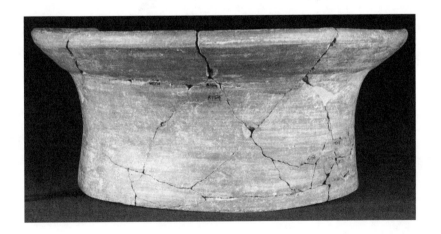

Vessel 023

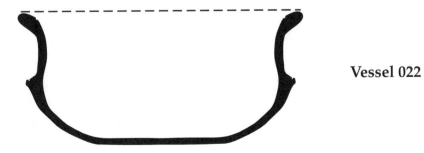

Vessel 022

TERMINAL K'ATABCHE'K'AX COMPLEX

Operation 1, Zone 17

Cache

Vessel 024 *Sierra Red: Sierra Variety*, plate
Reconstructed; RD: 14 cm, HT: 2.7 cm, WT: 223 g
This highly eroded plate contains flared sides. The slightly rounded base has a direct rim and rounded lip. Paste color is within the characteristic attributes of the Sierra Red type: a light gray (2.5Y 7/2). Although the slip has not been well preserved, remnants suggest it belongs to the Sierra Red group. Wall thickness of the vessel is 0.7 to 1 cm. One of three vessels of the triadic cache, the plate was found inside the V. 025 cylinder.

Vessel 025 *Sierra Red: Sierra Variety*, cylinder
Not reconstructible; RD: 13 cm, HT: nmp, WT: 1086 g
This eroded, rounded cylinder with a direct rim and a rounded lip has a slightly incurved base with a diameter of 16 cm. The cylinder was found beneath an upright bowl: V. 028 of the triadic cache.

Vessel 028 *Ixcanrio Orange Polychrome: Ixcanrio Variety*, bowl
Reconstructed; RD: 24 cm, HT: 6.6 cm, WT: 1122 g
This bowl features flared sides, a Z-angle flange, and an eroded slightly rounded base. The height of the wall above the basal flange is 2.8 cm. This was the uppermost vessel of the triadic cache.

Operation 1, Zone 18

Burial 1-2a, 1-2b, 1-2c, and 1-2d

Vessel 031 *Society Hall Red: Society Hall Variety*, bowl
Reconstructed; RD: 13.5 cm, HT: 4.5 cm, WT: 236.7 g
This bowl has flared sides, a direct rim, and rounded lip. Paste and color are within the characteristic attributes of Society Hall variety. The diameter of the flat base measures 10.8 cm.

Vessel 024

Rim Diameter is unknown.
Base diameter is 16 cm.

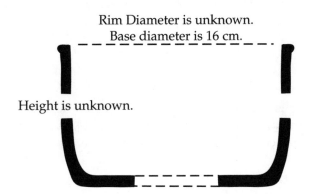

Height is unknown.

Vessel 025

Vessel 028

Vessel 031

TERMINAL K'ATABCHE'K'AX COMPLEX

Operation 1, Zone 18

Burial 1-2e

Vessel 034 *Society Hall Red: Society Hall Variety*, bowl
Reconstructed; RD: 43.2 cm, HT: 17.7 cm, WT: 4410 g

This outcurved bowl has an outflared everted rim with a rounded lip. The outflaring rim begins 8.5 cm from the base and is 7.4 cm in width. The base is flat and measures 31 cm. Color and paste composition is within the characteristics of the Society Hall variety. Slip was applied to the interior of the vessel and to the exterior of the lip, but the exterior walls are unslipped. A cross was slipped onto the interior base. The arms of the cross continue onto the walls. At the center of the cross a circle was painted and outlined by four dots, which form a quadrangle. The outflared everted rim was decorated by three incised elements that resemble eyebrows or half moons.

Vessel 033 *Society Hall Red: Society Hall Variety*, bowl
Able to be reconstructed; RD: 23.5 cm, HT: 13 cm, WT: 1267 g

This outcurved bowl has an outflared everted rim with a rounded lip. The outflaring begins 8.5 cm from the base and extends 5.5 cm from the wall. The base is flat and measures 14.5 cm in diameter. Color and paste are within the characteristics of the Society Hall variety. A cross motif was slipped on the exterior base.

Vessel 036 *Society Hall Red: Society Hall Variety*, bowl with monkey face effigy
Able to be reconstructed; RD: 20 cm, HT: 13.6 cm, WT: 1013.8 g

This bowl with incurved sides features an outflared neck, a horizontal everted rim, and a rounded lip. The base of the vessel is flat with a diameter of 9.5 cm. The base has a stroke of slip across it (not a cross). Two monkey faces were applied to the sides of the vessel. Each measures 2.5 cm across. The eyes and mouth were formed with impressed reeds. The height of the neck is 4 cm.

Operation 1, Zone 18

Burial 1-2g

Vessel 037 *Sierra Red: Unspecified Variety*, jar (miniature) with spout and 2 handles
Whole; RD: 10.6 cm, HT: 8.1 cm, WT: 371.2 g

This miniature spouted jar has incurved-recurved sides, an outcurved neck, exterior thickened rim, a rounded lip, and two handles. The vessel has paste characteristics and color of the Sierra Red type. Diameter of the flat base is 5 cm. Height of the neck is 2.4 cm; height of the spout is 5.4 cm; diameter of the spout is 1.5 cm.

Vessel 034

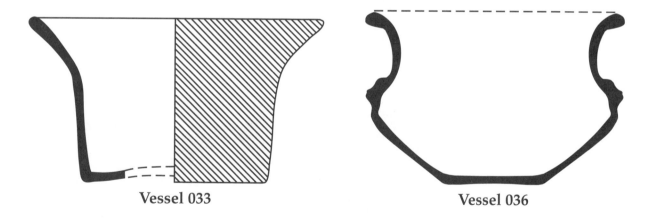

Vessel 033

Vessel 036

Vessel 037

TERMINAL K'ATABCHE'K'AX COMPLEX

Operation 1, Zone 18

Burial 1-2i

Vessel 038 *Society Hall Red: Society Hall Variety*, bowl
Not reconstructible; RD: 52 cm, HT: nmp, WT: 602.4 g
   A fragmentary bowl with flared sides, a direct rim, and a rounded lip. Society Hall slip is present on the interior and exterior portions of the lip, but exterior walls are unslipped.

Operation 1, Zone 236b

Burial 1-45

Vessel 056 *Sierra Red: Sierra Variety*, bowl
Able to be reconstructed; RD: 52 cm, HT: 9 cm, WT: 0 g
   This large bowl has outcurving walls, an everted rim, and a 40 cm diameter base. The vessel is slipped in red (10R 4/8) on both the interior and exterior. The paste has a core of yellowish red (5YR 5/8) and very dark gray (2.5YR 3/0). Wall thickness is 0.9 cm.

Vessel 057 *Laguna Verde Incised: Laguna Verde Variety*, cylinder
Reconstructed; RD: 19.5 cm, HT: 16.5 cm, WT: 1160 g
   A cylinder that has slightly incurving walls and an everted rim with a direct rounded lip. Vertical gadroons decorate the body but terminate 4 cm below the rim. Each gadroon is 3 cm in width. Two circumferential lines form a 2 cm wide band beneath the rim. Within this band, incised elements create an open chevron design. The vessel's slip, while damaged, appears as an orange-red (2.5YR 5/8) on the exterior and interior. Fireclouding is present on the exterior. The external lip exhibits a brown (5YR 4/6) coloration and the general paste color is yellow (10YR 7/6). The paste has large inclusions and a strong brown (7.5YR 4/8) core. The base diameter is 15 cm.

Vessel 038 is too fragmentary to illustrate.

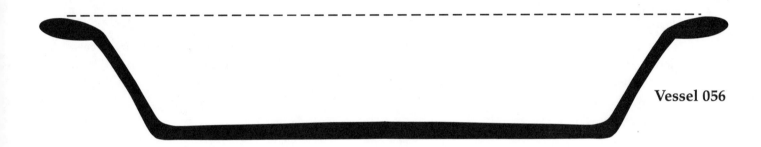

Vessel 056

Vessel 057

TERMINAL K'ATABCHE'K'AX COMPLEX

Operation 7, Zone 58

Cache

Vessel 059 *Sierra Red: Sierra Variety*, dish
Reconstructed; RD: 16 cm, HT: 3.9 cm, WT: 198.5 g
 This dish has a slightly rounded base (9 cm diameter), flaring sides, and a flared rim with a slightly squared lip.

Operation 7, Zone 59

Cache

Vessel 060 *Sierra Red: Sierra Variety*, dish
Not reconstructible; RD: 18 cm, HT: nmp, WT: 230 g
 This dish has friable outcurving walls, a direct rim, and a rounded lip. It is slipped on the interior with a yellowish red (5YR 5/8). The paste has a blackened core (10YR 4/1) and an outer color of yellow (10YR 7/6). The diameter of the base is 9 cm with a thickness of 0.5 cm.

Operation 8, Zone 3

Cache

Vessel 095 *Aguacate Orange: Aguacate Variety*, bowl with 4 solid conical feet
Able to be reconstructed; RD: 42 cm, HT: nmp, WT: 1780.9 g
 An Aguacate Orange bowl with four solid conical feet. Each foot is 2 cm in height and 0.5 to 0.7 cm thick. The rim is thickened on the interior side.

Vessel 059

Vessel 060

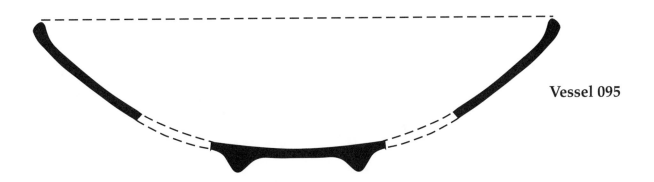

Vessel 095

TERMINAL K'ATABCHE'K'AX COMPLEX

Operation 8, Zone 5

Burial 8-3a and 8-3b

Vessel 096 *Aguacate Orange: Aguacate Variety*, bowl with mammiform feet
Able to be reconstructed; RD: 44 cm, HT: 13.5 cm, WT: 3052.7 g

The bowl has four mammiform feet and a rounded base. The feet are 7 cm in height with 3 cm diagonal slots. Wall thickness varies between 0.6 and 1.2 cm. The vessel was ritually broken at deposition and, when uncovered, contained fragments of human bone.

Vessel 097 *Ixcanrio Orange Polychrome: Ixcanrio Variety*, dish with mammiform tetrapod feet
Able to be reconstructed; RD: 34 cm, HT: 12.2 cm, WT: 907.5 g

A tetrapod dish with flared sides, direct rim, and rounded lip. The mammiform feet are hollow with a flat nubbin base. The feet are approximately 9 cm in height and 8 cm in diameter, while the nubbins have a diameter of 2 cm. Each foot has three slots (4.5 cm long and 1 cm wide). The height of the dish itself is 4.5 cm at its maximum, with walls of 3.3 cm above the feet. The vessel and feet are slipped in red (2.5YR 5/8). The interior is decorated with three circumferential lines. The first line at the rim is red (10R 4/8) and measures 0.5 cm in width. The other two are narrower bands (0.3 cm) of very dark brown (10YR 2/2). The exterior is decorated with bands of the same color. Wide circumferential strips of red extend around the rim and base of the wall. Within these, thin brown lines demarcate a 2 cm wide band around the vessel. This band is broken up by vertical groupings of five thick brown lines that alternate with rectangles of unaltered slip.

Vessel 098 *Ixcanrio Orange Polychrome: Ixcanrio Variety*, dish with mammiform tetrapod feet
Able to be reconstructed; RD: 34 cm, HT: 12.5 cm, WT: 1342 g

A highly eroded tetrapod dish with flared sides, a direct rim, a rounded lip, and mammiform feet. The hollow feet are 10 cm high and have a diameter of 8 cm. Each foot terminates in a flat nubbin base and has slots measuring 3 x 1.5 cm. The height of the dish is 3 cm at its maximum.

Vessel 096

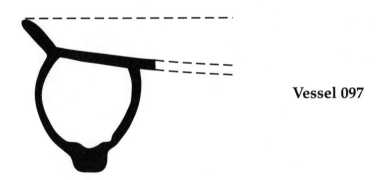

Vessel 097

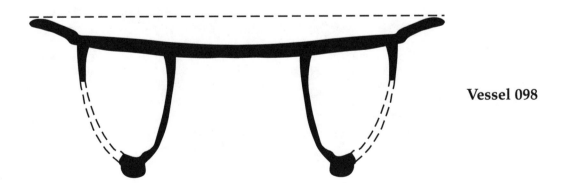

Vessel 098

TERMINAL K'ATABCHE'K'AX COMPLEX

Operation 11, Zone 19

Burial 11-2

Vessel 102 *Actuncan Orange Polychrome: Actuncan Variety*, bowl with ring base and basal flange
Reconstructed; RD: 32 cm, HT: 11.5 cm, WT: 2065.8 g

An Actuncan bowl with flared sides, basal flange, ring base, direct rim, and rounded lip. A polychrome design of two serpentine, well-endowed jaguars alternate with two large Kan crosses in a band above the flange. The basal flange itself (3.5 cm in width) is decorated with seven bisected Kan crosses, or portal motifs, arranged in alternating orientations. These motifs are red (10R 4/8) and are outlined in black (7.5R 2.5/0). The vessel was inverted over the skull of the individual.

Vessel 103 *Aguila Orange: Aguila Variety*, jar with ring base
Reconstructed; RD: 9 cm, HT: 13 cm, WT: 503 g

Jar with a vertical neck, direct rim, rounded lip, and ring base. The height of the neck is 3.5 cm. The ring base is 1.5 cm high and has a diameter of 8 cm. The slip is red (2.5YR 4/8; 2.5YR 5/8) and was applied to the exterior and also to the interior of the neck. The medium-textured paste is a very pale brown (10YR 7/3) or grayish brown (10YR 5/2) with a 0.4 cm wide core.

Vessel 104 *Yaloche Cream Polychrome: Unspecified Variety*, bowl
Reconstructed; RD: 16.2 cm, HT: 6.8 cm, WT: 435.6 g

Eroded and basically stripped to the paste, the vessel now appears as a cream colored bowl with incurved sides, a flat base, and a direct rim with a rounded lip. The color is light gray (10YR 7/2), light brown (10YR 6/3), and gray (10YR 6/1). The thickness of the walls is 0.5 cm.

Vessel 102

Vessel 103

Vessel 104

TERMINAL K'ATABCHE'K'AX COMPLEX

Operation 12, Zone 4

Burial 12-1

Vessel 118 *Aguacate Orange: Aguacate Variety*, bowl
Able to be reconstructed; RD: 41 cm, HT: nmp, WT: 1382.6 g
 A very shallow bowl with incurving walls, a direct rim, and flat lip. The dimensions are difficult to ascertain because most of the base is missing. The vessel was inverted over the head of an old adult male.

Operation 12, Zone 30b

Burial 12-3

Vessel 107 *Aguacate Orange: Aguacate Variety*, bowl
Reconstructed; RD: 36 cm, HT: 10.1 cm, WT: 1616.2 g
 A bowl with rounded sides and a direct, slightly folded rim. The interior was slipped in red (2.5YR 5/8), but none existed on the exterior surface. Wall thickness ranges between 0.5 and 0.8 cm. The bowl was inverted and placed over the head of an extended, adult burial.

Operation 12, Zone 31

Burial 12-6

Vessel 108 *Aguacate Orange: Aguacate Variety*, bowl
Reconstructed; RD: 40 cm, HT: 8.4 cm, WT: 1409.8 g
 A bowl with a rounded base and a shallow medial flange. The flange has a groove on the inside. The vessel is slipped in red (2.5YR 5/8) on the interior and has some fireclouding. Wall thickness is 0.5 to 0.7 cm and the rim is slightly folded. The vessel was found inverted over the head of an extended adult.

Operation 12, Zone 33

Burial 12-4

Vessel 114 *Aguacate Orange: Aguacate Variety*, flanged bowl
Able to be reconstructed; RD: 40 cm, HT: 8 cm, WT: 1630 g
 A very eroded and friable bowl with a rounded base, small flange, outflaring rim, and direct rounded lip. The thickness of the base is 0.68 cm. The slip is a light red (2.5YR 6/8) that coats a paste with small white inclusions and a very dark gray (2.5YR 3/0) core. The bowl was inverted over the head of an extended adult. This vessel appears to be an heirloom Terminal K'atabche'k'ax piece found in an Early Nohalk'ax context.

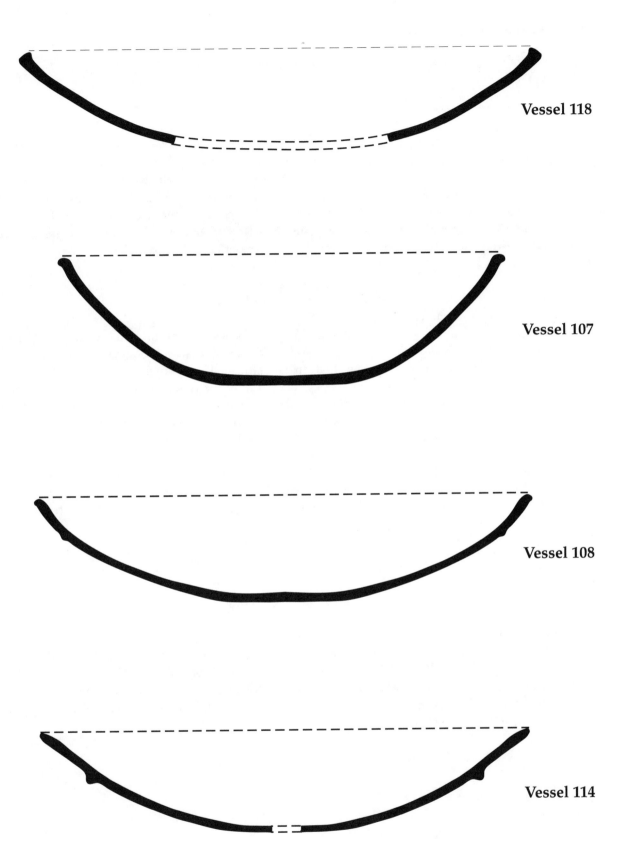

Vessel 118

Vessel 107

Vessel 108

Vessel 114

EARLY NOHALK'AX COMPLEX

Operation 7, Zone 63

Burial 7-2

Vessel 109 *Actuncan Orange Polychrome: Actuncan Variety*, bowl with basal flange
Whole; RD: 33.5 cm, HT: 11 cm, WT: 1512 g

DOA No: 33/200-5:10 An Actuncan polychrome bowl with outcurved sides and a basal flange. It has a ring base, direct rim, and rounded lip. The ring base is 4 cm in height and 7.2 cm in diameter. Decoration of the vessel body consists of two red and black hummingbird designs alternating with two framed serpent head profiles on an orange base. The flange is 2.7 cm wide and is painted with stepped forms that most likely represent half of a portal motif. These are arranged in alternating orientations. Inside the vessel there are red (1.4 cm wide) and black (0.3 cm) circumferential lines. The paste is pinkish gray and has a fine texture with some iron particles permeating the surface. There is some evidence for smoothing of the base. The vessel was inverted over the skull.

Vessel 110 *Actuncan Orange Polychrome: Actuncan Variety*, bowl with tetrapod feet
Reconstructed; RD: 17.5 cm, HT: 11.7 cm, WT: 773 g

The tetrapod bowl has hollow conical feet, slightly incurved sides, a direct rim, and rounded lip. The feet are 7.3 cm in height and are modeled and painted to represent peccary heads. The orange eyes of the peccary are outlined in red and have a very dark brown line separating them. The tips of the feet are modeled to form the mouth and were probably painted in red. The exterior rim of the vessel is decorated with a red (10R 4/8) circumferential band 0.8 to 0.9 cm wide. The middle register consists of black (7.5R 2.5/0) rectangles alternating with red (10R 4/8) ones. All rectangles measure 3 cm high, but the three black ones are shorter (averaging 7 cm) than the three red panels (averaging 9 cm). Beneath this design, a very dark brown (10YR 2/2) line and a red (10R 4/8) 0.6 cm wide circumferential band encircle the vessel near the incurved base. The interior of the bowl has a highly glossy reddish yellow (5YR 6/8) surface. The interior rim is a continuation of the external decoration with a red (10R 4/8) circumferential band that is 1 cm wide and bordered by a very dark brown (10YR 2/2) line that is 0.2 cm wide. The paste of the vessel has a fine texture and may be ash tempered.

Operation 7, Zone 69

Cache

Vessel 111 *San Martin Variegated Brown: San Martin Variety*, bowl
Whole; RD: 15 cm, HT: 13 cm, WT: 1003 g

DOA No: 33/200-5:4 A well-preserved bowl with incurved-recurved sides, a collared neck, and a flat base. The basal diameter is 7.8 cm, as is the height of the neck. The vessel is a brownish yellow (10YR 7/4). The paste is a yellowish red (5YR 5/6) and has a fine texture with probable calcite and iron particles. This vessel belongs to the basal Late K'atabche'k'ax construction phase in operation 7 but is a type that didn't become popular until the Early Nohalk'ax. The vessel represents an example of precocious craftsmanship and was, most likely, an import to K'axob.

Vessel 109

Vessel 110

Vessel 111

EARLY NOHALK'AX COMPLEX

Operation 10, Zone 23

Burial 10-3

Vessel 124 *Aguila Orange: Aguila Variety*, bowl
Able to be reconstructed; RD: 28 cm, HT: 6.1 cm, WT: 820.6 g

A flanged Aguila Orange bowl with slip on both the interior and exterior surfaces. The base diameter is 7 cm. The vessel was found inverted over the skull of an adult, extended burial. The interment occurred on the cusp of the Terminal K'atabche'k'ax to Early Nohalk'ax transition.

Operation 12, Zone 32

Burial 12-2

Vessel 113 *Actuncan Orange Polychrome: Actuncan Variety*, bowl with ring base
Whole; RD: 18 cm, HT: 8.9 cm, WT: 503 g

An Actuncan polychrome bowl that remains whole, though cracks have almost fissured the vessel. The bowl has round sides, a ring base, and a direct rim with a rounded lip. The base has a diameter of 12 cm. Overall, the interior and exterior of the vessel is slipped in a light red (2.5YR 6/8) color, which provides the base coat. Decoration consists of a circumferential band near the rim in a weak red (10R 5/4) color: 0.8 cm wide on the interior, 1.5 cm on the exterior. Motifs appear as angular, serpentine scroll designs in the same color. The bowl was inverted over the skull.

Operation 13, Zone 12

Burial 13-2

Vessel 117 *Dos Arroyos Orange Polychrome: Dos Arroyos Variety*, bowl with circumferential lines
Reconstructed; RD: 42 cm, HT: 8.4 cm, WT: 1865.2 g

Bowl with rounded and incurved sides, a ring base with a drill hole, and a direct, rounded rim. The bowl is slipped on the interior. There is a dark red circumferential line and seven eroded circles painted around the rim. Lines are painted below the rim in 0.4 cm widths and 1 cm separation. The paste is brownish yellow (10YR 6/6) and has large rounded inclusions. The vessel was inverted over the cranium of a young adult burial.

Vessel 124

Vessel 113

Vessel 117

EARLY NOHALK'AX COMPLEX

Operation 13, Zone 27

Burial 13-3a and 13-3b

Vessel 115 *Balanza Black: Unspecified Variety*, flanged bowl
Able to be reconstructed; RD: 26 cm, HT: 9.1 cm, WT: 1057.9 g
   A flanged bowl with a rounded base and eroded slip. The vessel has a dull dark gray (10YR 3/1) wash on the interior and exterior. The paste is olive brown (2.5Y 4/3) with white inclusions. Wall thickness is 0.4–0.7 cm.

Vessel 116 *Dos Arroyos Orange Polychrome: Dos Arroyos Variety*, flanged bowl
Reconstructed; RD: 31 cm, HT: 8.4 cm, WT: 1512 g
   A flanged bowl with a rounded base, flared sides, a direct rim, and rounded lip. The thickness of the walls is 0.5 cm. The paste has a fine texture and finely crushed calcite shows through the surface. The color of the paste is yellowish red (5YR 5/6). These surfaces are smoothed and covered with a yellowish red (5YR 7/8) slip color. The base of the vessel is unslipped and bears evidence of smoothing marks. The decoration on the exterior consists of red (2.5YR 5/8) or yellowish red (5YR 7/8) bands near the rim. Below these are red (10R 4/3) bands of 1.5 cm width. Vertical lines run from these horizontal bands down to the flange in a weak red (10R 4/3) color. On the flange, red (7.5R 4/8) dots were painted and encircled by "U"-shaped red (10R 4/3) motifs. On the interior, there is a red (7.5R 4/8) band near the rim that measures 1.5 cm in width. A second band in a weak red (10R 4/3) color runs beneath the first and is 0.5 cm in width. Fugitive interior paint seems to depict a seated figure wearing some sort of bird mask or headdress. Rays swirling around the interior could represent a large shell motif, from which the figure is emerging.

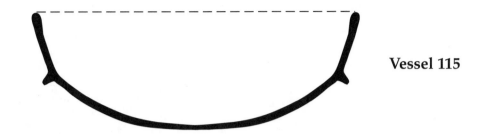

Vessel 115

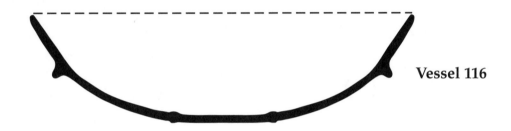

Vessel 116

Chapter 10
Related CD Resources

Fired Clay Artifacts

CHAPTER 10

ARTIFACTS OF FIRED CLAY

MARY LEE BARTLETT

The small ceramic objects excavated at K'axob were produced to meet many differing needs. Analysis of these artifacts provides evidence of subsistence strategies, ceramic manufacturing techniques, recycling, personal adornment, and ideology. The objects fall into two categories: those made from the reworking of ceramic sherds and those made directly as fired objects. Although surface artifacts dating to periods as recent as the Late Postclassic are included here, the focus is on those objects from secure, stratified Formative deposits. Each of the different residential areas—including operation 1, which evolved into a ceremonial precinct, as well as basal platform groups (operations 7, 10, 11, and 12) and the single platform residence (operation 8)—is represented in the assemblage, thus providing evidence of universality of usage across residential units.

A total of 120 small ceramic artifacts were excavated during the 1990, 1992, and 1993 field seasons at K'axob. The full data set, including many photographic images, is available in digital form as *Fired Clay Artifacts Database*. Objects similar to those reported herein have been recorded for other sites in northern Belize (Valdez and Gillis 1980; Gillis 1982; Garber 1986, 1988, 1989; Hammond 1991c; Buttles 1992, 1994; and McGregor 1994), suggesting similarities in subsistence and the presence of strong interaction spheres.

This chapter is divided into two sections: fired objects made directly from worked clay and objects made from reworked sherds. This same division is used to describe similar objects excavated at other sites, such as Colha (Buttles 1992), Cerros (Garber 1986, 1989), and Cuello (Hammond 1991c). Keeping these divisions should facilitate comparison of data. Similarly shaped artifacts, such as net sinkers, are grouped together and are assumed to represent similar functional categories.

SHAPED AND FIRED CLAY ARTIFACTS

Preformed and fired clay objects were fabricated to serve a variety of purposes. Seven artifact types are present in the K'axob assemblage, including ocarinas,

263

a spindle whorl, a roller stamp, beads, and notched net sinkers. They attest to the personal adornments, entertainment, decoration, and subsistence strategies employed during the period of occupation at K'axob.

MUSICAL INSTRUMENTS

Whistles or ocarinas. Two whistles or ocarinas were excavated from K'axob. The first was recovered from the surface of operation 1 (figure 10.1a). This zoomorphic figurine resembles a bat or, more likely, a stylized stingray. Wings are present on either side of the round hollow center section, and two small protuberances resembling horns or antennae are present on the underside. An appendage, probably a tail, was broken from the basal end. This appendage was not recovered. An air hole (diameter = 1.42 cm), probably used for blowing, is located at one end with an additional smaller hole (diameter = .82 cm), for establishing a beat, at the top. Both holes were made prior to firing of the object. The surface of the object is unsmoothed but finished with an orange wash. The paste appears to have calcite tempering and to be of moderate coarseness. The presence of this object on the surface suggests a Postclassic date for manufacture.

The second ocarina (figure 10.1b) was excavated from a Late K'atabche'k'ax living surface in operation 12. The face is human with a wide vertical indent incised in the middle of the nose and two others diagonally across the middle of each cheek, large protruding lips, and earflares. The impression created by the stylized facial features is that of a mask. The figure wears a helmet or headdress with a pattern of round punctates on the left half, while the right half is smooth. Two air holes are located on either side of the helmet. These holes would permit the escape of air during the firing of the piece and were probably used as stops when the instrument was played. The holes resemble eyes, creating a lizard-like appearance on the pockmarked side of the helmet and that of a bird on the smooth side. Observed from one view the figure has a benevolent expression, but by changing the lighting and direction the figure can become a fierce warrior.

The symbolic meaning of this piece is unknown. Anthropomorphism is a common theme in Maya iconography, and bird, toads, and reptiles are commonly represented. Humans, particularly males, are almost always depicted with some type of headgear. Long noses and protruding lips are Maya representations of

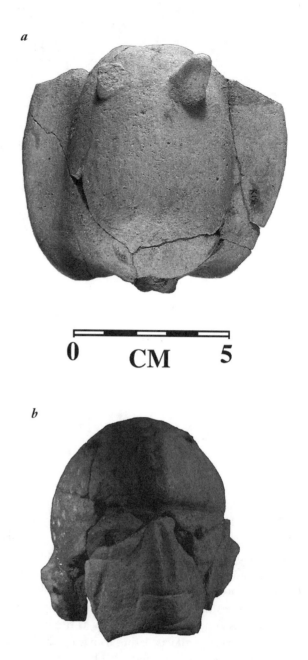

a

b

Figure 10.1 Two ocarinas, or whistles: (a) clay whistle found near the surface of operation 1; (b) ocarina with a human face from a Late K'atabche'k'ax living surface (operation 12, zone 17). *All photographs by Mary Lee Bartlett*

beauty and high rank. Whether this is meant to be a stylized portrait or a representation of a masked figure is difficult to discern.

The importance of music at ceremonial occasions is affirmed by painted murals, such as the musicians' mural at Bonampak (Miller 1988:96–97) and the painting of a procession preceded by flutes at Tonina. Ocarinas are commonly found in such Formative Maya contexts as Cuello (Hammond 1991c:177–178), Cahal Pech (Awe 1992), and Colha (Buttles 1992, 1994). Awe (1992) reports numerous figurines at Cahal Pech, noting that these predate the ceramic vessels found at the site. Most are of ritual significance. At Jaina, ocarinas shaped like human figures are commonly associated with burials dating to the Late Classic period (see Morley, Brainerd, and Sharer 1983:382). The presence of a broken whistle on the surface of operation 1, the smaller of the two pyramids in plaza B, suggests a termination ritual involving music, perhaps followed by the breaking of the instrument.

CLOTH PRODUCTION

Spindle whorl. One definitive fired clay spindle whorl (figure 10.2a) was excavated from the plowzone in operation 10, a basal platform group with deposits dating from the Preclassic to Early Classic periods and a likely Postclassic surface deposit. The whorl is well made, slightly rounded on one side with a conical rounded center. The clay composition is fine paste with some observable calcite inclusions, probably temper. The walls were smoothed and molded into a round shape with a hole punched in the center during the leather hard stage. Willey (1972:84–86) suggests that these types of whorls may have been made in a mold, and the symmetry of this specimen suggests that this may be the case. Comparable spindle whorls have been reported at a number of sites, including Mayapan (Proskouriakoff 1962), Altar de Sacrificios (Willey 1972), and Colha (Valdez and Gillis 1980; McGregor 1994). Most date to the Late Classic to Postclassic periods, although no date is given for the Colha object. Phillips (1979:64) suggests that the small size of this type of whorl would preclude it from being used for fibers larger than cotton because the torque would not have been adequate.

Roller stamp. A deeply incised cylinder (figure 10.2b) was excavated from a midden dating to Early K'atabche'k'ax times. The object appears to have been discarded after a crack formed, or perhaps it had become too worn to produce a crisp pattern. The stamp measures 6.5 cm in length with an outer diameter of 1.8 cm, an inner diameter of 1.45 cm, and a wall thickness of 1.04 cm. When rolled, the stamp creates an interlocking pattern of eights with center dots at the point of the interlock. Cylinder stamps are presumed to have been used for the decoration of textiles (Longyear 1952).

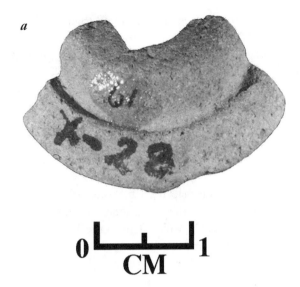

Figure 10.2 Shaped clay artifacts: (a) broken spindle whorl, possibly made in a mold, from plowzone of operation 10; (b) roller stamp excavated from midden (operation 1, zone 87) dating to the Early K'atabche'k'ax complex.

The K'axob example was manufactured from coarse paste with calcite temper. The design appears to have been molded into the clay or possibly incised and smoothed during the leather hard stage. This object is similar to one dating to the Bladen phase at Cuello (Hammond 1991c:180, Fig. 8.23a), attesting to long-term usage of this method of decoration from the onset of the Preclassic period.

PERSONAL ADORNMENT

Ceramic beads. Three types of clay beads were excavated at K'axob: round, shell-shaped, and tubular. The round beads are marble-sized (length = 1.5 to 1.8 cm; width = 1.5 cm; weight = 2.8 to 3.5 g) and were excavated from the surface of operation 8 (two are shown in figure 10.3a). All three of those excavated were recovered from the plowzone, making dating problematic. The beads were made from rolled balls of clay that were pierced with a hole prior to firing. No external decoration or slip is apparent. A mark of the string or cord (presumably to suspend the bead) is present on one. These beads may have been made to mimic large jadeite (greenstone) beads found at other sites (Coe 1959:72).

Six smaller beads shaped like tiny shells (figure 10.3b) were excavated from the construction fill of operation 12. The small beads, which date to the Early Classic period, are irregularly shaped and pierced with a small hole for stringing. These beads were found with the inner ear bone of a medium-sized mammal, possibly a raccoon. This bone also had a natural hole, so it could have been strung with the beads. The bead size suggests use as a necklace or bracelet, but they could also have been attached to clothing as additional decoration.

The final clay bead is a small, round, and finely wrought tubular bead. It was excavated from burial 11-2, a chultun dating to the late facet of the K'atabche'k'ax complex. The bead is smoothed and unslipped.

Bead adornment is present in depictions of elites on ceramics dating to the Classic period (Reents-Budet 1994:94–95, 152; and others) and can be seen on figurines, including a Postclassic incensario fragment found at K'axob (figure 10.4). Hammond (1991c, Fig. 8.25) reports clay beads from Preclassic deposits at Cuello, but these are more ornate than those found at K'axob. Beads similar to the large round beads, but with a stucco coating, are reported from Late Classic burial contexts at Altar de Sacrificios (Willey 1972:87–88). The irregularity of the K'axob beads, both large and small, suggests that these were made by hand and not

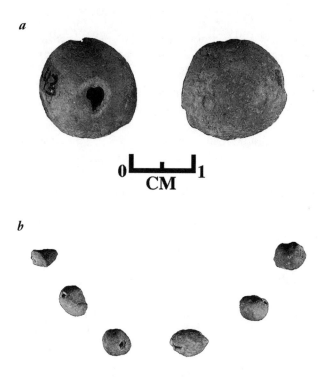

a

b

Figure 10.3 Personal adornment made of fired clay: (a) two large rounded clay beads from plowzone of operation 8; (b) six small shell-shaped clay beads, Nohalk'ax complex (operation 12).

in a mold. They were probably fashioned from locally available clay, although the beads have not been examined petrographically. The technology involved is fairly simple and requires little time and effort. Clay beads provided a readily accessible alternative to scarce jadeite and fragile shell beads.

Earflares. Two broken earflares were excavated at K'axob. One, made of bone, is discussed in chapter 15;

Figure 10.4 Examples of Postclassic Chen Mul–style incensario fragments from surface of operation 1. Photograph shows arm with beaded bracelet (left) and pectoral that would have been affixed to the front of figure (right).

Figure 10.5 Portion of incised ear flare from burial in operation 10 dating to Early Nohalk'ax times.

the other is made of clay (figure 10.5) and was excavated from a burial of Early Classic date in operation 10. This earflare is quite thin (0.2 cm thick) and is composed of a very fine paste. The diameter is 2 cm at the widest point. Firing in a reducing atmosphere resulted in a black unpolished surface finish. Postfiring, two circumferential lines were incised, each .3 cm from the outer edges. Three slanted vertical lines, 0.2 cm apart, were incised to connect the circumferential lines after firing. Similar artifacts are reported at Altar de Sacrificios (Willey 1972:89–93; Fig. 74), Piedras Negras (Coe 1959:70–71; Fig. 59), Copan (Longyear 1952:102–103; Fig. 82) and Uaxactun (Ricketson and Ricketson 1937: Plate 69). Most date to the Late Classic period, although the Uaxactun example is from a Preclassic context. These clay earflares seem to be replicas of jade and shell adornment depicted in Classic period sculpture from Palenque and other major sites. The object from K'axob was finely made by a skilled craftsperson.

INCENSARIOS

Several incensario fragments (two are shown in figure 10.4) were discovered near the surface of operation 1. Broken incensarios are found frequently on the top of structures as part of termination rituals. Many date to the Postclassic period, as do these fragments from K'axob. The pieces recovered include: (1) a human arm with a bracelet of round beads (length = 7.5 cm; diameter = 4 cm); (2) a broken half of what was probably a pectoral, a flat piece with three finger-like protrusions on the end (width = 4.6 cm; length = 5.5 cm); (3) a short strand of twisted clay rope (length = 2.2 cm; width = 1.1 cm); (4) a very eroded square sherd with button and rod-like decorations (length = 3.9 cm; width = 2.8 cm); and (5) a round tail-like piece (length = 5.4 cm). A rounded vessel foot was also found with these pieces.

The size of the fragments suggests that the incensario could have been approximately 40 cm or more in height. The surfaces of the pieces are unsmoothed, with no evidence of paint or slip. The clay paste is coarse with obvious inclusions of calcite. The figure was fashioned during the leather hard stage of the forming process, with the rounded beads of the arm and other decoration pressed on before firing.

Large Chen Mul–style incensarios are found in Postclassic assemblages, with the largest provenienced collection coming from Mayapan (Smith 1971:102–103). During rituals, copal incense was burned within the image and holes, often at the mouth, emitted the burning smoke. The flat finger-like piece, probably representing a butterfly, would have been part of the chest pectoral. Butterflies are common on incensarios from the highland Mexican center of Teotihuacan and represent fire and war (Miller and Taube 1993:48). These representations are also found in Classic Maya art. The twisted rope is commonly seen in Maya iconography depicting elites. Even during the Postclassic period, when the settlement of K'axob was much diminished, villagers were apparently participating in rituals similar to those found at the larger centers of the Maya world.

UTILITARIAN OBJECTS

Net sinkers. Thirty-four small spherical notched ceramic pieces resembling modern lead-line weights were found in varying contexts at the site (figure 10.6). These objects are made of round or oblong fired clay with notches incised into either end. Two surface clusters found in the plowzone of operation 10 probably date to the Postclassic period. These weights vary in length from 0.9 cm to 1.5 cm. The pieces were used to weight a net in much the same way as fishers use lead sinkers today. An additional notched artifact made from an Aquila Orange sherd (length = 2.4 cm; width = 1.3 cm) was found with these molded pieces, attesting to

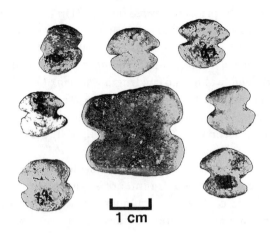

1 cm

Figure 10.6 Seven small spherical net sinkers shaped and notched before firing and large net sinker shaped from sherd; all excavated from plowzone of operation 10.

contemporaneous usage of sinkers shaped and fired for fishing as well as of those simply fashioned as sinkers from broken pottery (see large net sinker in center of figure 10.6). Only one weight was oval in shape and, at 3.7 g, was heavier than any of the other sinkers. This object was long, wider, and thicker than any of the others, suggesting that it may have been used as an end-weight on a net or as a very heavy line weight.

Sinkers of the molded type have been reported at the sites of Colha and Cerros in northern Belize (Buttles 1992, 1994; Garber 1988; and Valdez and Gillis 1980). Noting that the notched, molded objects are lighter than those formed from reworked sherds, Phillips (1979) suggests that molded weights were best suited to weight a net, while the heavier reworked sherds may have been used on lines. This technology was present at K'axob throughout the Preclassic period, beginning in Early Chaakk'ax times. Most molded pieces were found in fills, including pits and burial fill that date to the Terminal K'atabche'k'ax complex. As noted by Masson in chapter 17, the subsistence strategies of the earliest occupants of K'axob continued to be viable, with little change, throughout every period of occupation.

Miscellaneous, unclassified ceramic pieces. A Polvero Black ceramic foot was excavated from a Late K'atabche'k'ax child burial (1-14) (figure 10.7a). López Varela (1996) reports only two additional Polvero Black sherds excavated in all three seasons at K'axob. This type is identified by a waxy, predominantly black slip, often with red tinges (Kosakowsky 1987:76–78). The foot appears to represent a monkey with earflares and a protuberance in the middle of the forehead. Two lines

(width = 0. 2 cm; length = 1.8 cm) were incised on either side of the protuberance. Two additional incised marks, 1 cm in length, are present on each cheek. The nose and lips were modeled and then incised to represent the mouth and chin. After firing, holes were drilled from both sides of each ear to represent earflares, and an attempt was made to drill eyeholes, but only one was successful. Finger impressions on the hollow interior surface of the foot suggest that the clay may have been pressed into a mold to create the shape and then incised during the leather hard stage.

The limited presence of the Polvero Black type at K'axob and the singular nature of this ceramic foot suggest that the vessel may have been a trade item or a gift from elsewhere. Polvero Black vessels are more common at sites such as Colha (Valdez 1987), Cuello (Kosakowsky 1987), and Yo Tumben (Bartlett and McAnany, 2000b).

A rod-shaped ceramic piece that resembles a cylindrical bead without the hole was excavated from an Early Chaakk'ax midden in operation 1. Beads of this shape are reported at Cuello (Hammond 1991c) and Colha (Buttles 1992). In the example from K'axob, one end is broken and so the actual length of the object is not known. This piece is the earliest clay bead excavated from K'axob and is contemporary with the thousands of shell beads recorded from Chaakk'ax contexts (see chapter 14).

An applique fragment from a pottery vessel was excavated from operation 7 (figure 10.7b). This anthropomorphic shape has two indentations for eyes and a rounded protuberance that represents the nose and mouth. The exterior is smooth but unslipped and was fired black. The clay paste is red (2.5YR 5/8). The face forms a handle that is located .03 cm below a square-shaped direct rim. This applique is decorative only and could not have been used as a handle.

An additional handle similar to the L-shape of modern cups was excavated from operation 1, zone 59 (figure 10.7c). This rather fancy object was excavated from a midden dating to Early Chaakk'ax times. The handle was not slipped, and there is no evidence of the application of a wash. The earliest potters at K'axob were skilled artisans, and the examples of Early Chaakk'ax ritual ceramics are quite sophisticated.

A possible figurine fragment with a medallion or a shield with radial incised lines was excavated from a midden dating to Early K'atabche'k'ax times in operation 1, zone 87 (figure 10.7d). Although eroded, it appears to be Chicago Orange type. All these examples

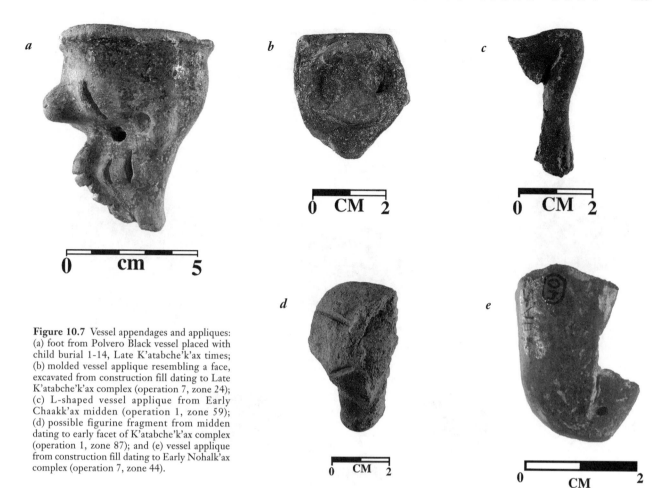

Figure 10.7 Vessel appendages and appliques: (a) foot from Polvero Black vessel placed with child burial 1-14, Late K'atabche'k'ax times; (b) molded vessel applique resembling a face, excavated from construction fill dating to Late K'atabche'k'ax complex (operation 7, zone 24); (c) L-shaped vessel applique from Early Chaakk'ax midden (operation 1, zone 59); (d) possible figurine fragment from midden dating to early facet of K'atabche'k'ax complex (operation 1, zone 87); and (e) vessel applique from construction fill dating to Early Nohalk'ax complex (operation 7, zone 44).

attest to the skill of early K'axob potters. A final applique fragment that might be a vessel foot was excavated from an Early Nohalk'ax context in operation 7 (figure 10.7e). The bottom is worn, suggesting that the piece had rested on a surface. The object is slipped and was polished to a high gloss of brown/black coloration similar to the color found on the differential streaking of Society Hall Red vessels.

REWORKED CERAMICS

Several types of reworked sherds provide evidence of recycling of materials for a variety of uses since the earliest occupation of K'axob. Four principal classes are distinguished here: net sinkers, unperforated disks, drilled disks, and miscellaneous drilled sherds. For many of these objects exact usage is debatable, although most are presumed to be utilitarian. Usage includes fishing, gaming, and personal adornment.

TYPES OF REWORKED SHERDS

Net sinkers. Bow-shaped objects (n = 29) sometimes referred to as *mariposas* (Spanish for butterflies) were produced from the reworking of sherds (figure 10.8). These recycled objects occur in a range of sizes and weights. The shape tends to be rectangular, although five are approximately square. Notches forming either a V- or U-shape were ground into the sides or ends of these sherds. The majority of artifacts have these notches incised on opposite sides of the longest dimension. Eight examples have notches incised on the shortest side of the object. In two instances, marks of lines or strings can be seen cutting through the surface finish. Some of the pieces have been rounded and ground smooth along all edges, indicating a time investment in the formation of the pieces. Others are more roughly formed, with little evidence of shaping and smoothing, and are either unfinished or simply did not require smoothing and

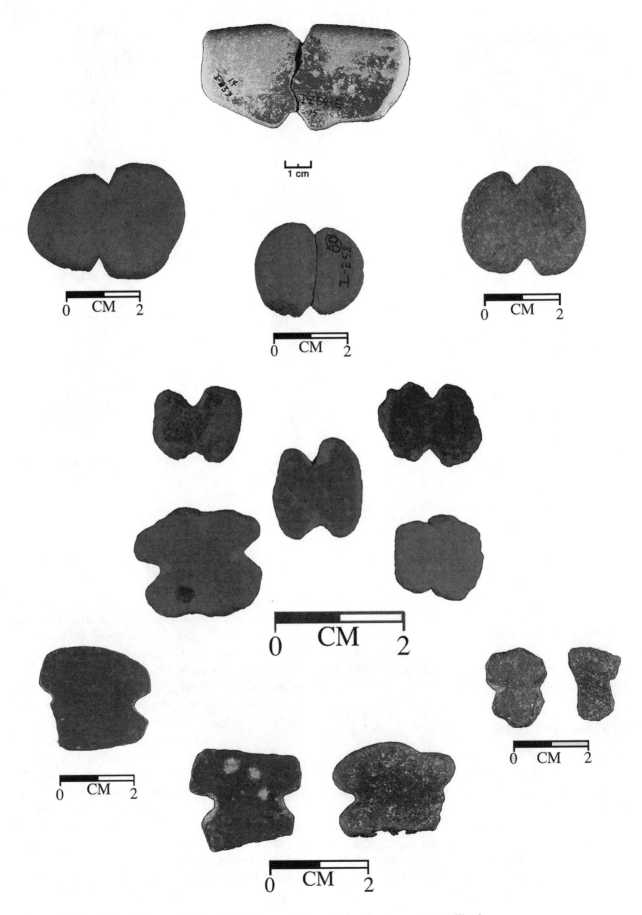

Figure 10.8 Notched net sinkers crafted from sherds from several time periods and various contexts at K'axob.

rounding. Several are quite eroded either from depositional factors or as the result of use, while others show no evidence of wear and either were used for activities that did not produce edge damage or were never used.

Excavation contexts include construction fill, middens, burials, and mixed deposits. Most were found singly, except the one excavated with the spherical weights noted above. Ceramic types, when possible to determine, represent Middle to Late Preclassic types. Size and weight are quite variable—a characteristic noted at Cozumel as well (Phillips 1979:84). Garber (1986, 1988, and 1989) suggests that this variability is related to the type of fish that was being sought. Bottom dwellers would require a larger, heavier weight, particularly in the river. Fish inhabiting the shallow swamp ponds do not necessarily require the same line depth. The smaller weights might have been used for nets or lines, although no fishhooks have been recovered. Small nets can be used to trap minnows either for bait or as a food source. Masson (chapter 17) notes the predominance of small fish in the K'axob faunal assemblage.

These notched net sinkers tend to fall into three categories based on length of the longest side: small = 1.4 to 1.6 cm; medium = 1.6 to 2.5 cm; and large = over 2.5 cm. The largest notched piece, manufactured from the rim of a Joventud Red type, weighs 30 g, is 4 cm wide, and is 7 cm long; one of the smallest weighs 0.7 g, is 1.1 cm wide, and is 1.4 cm long.

Several of the mid-sized objects were smoothed and rounded on all edges. The difference in labor investment may be related to the purpose of the artifact. Ethnographic studies reported by Kent and Nelson (1976) suggest some of these objects may have been used as weft weights for weaving. They noted that weavers in eastern Asian sites used notched stone pieces. Ethnographic studies of Ainu women in Japan report the use of stones shaped like the ceramic pieces of K'axob well into modern times (Kent and Nelson 1976). Whatever the use, their ubiquity through time and at most sites attests to the universality of subsistence and manufacturing strategies.

Net weights shaped from sherds are more common at K'axob than molded net sinkers. Like the molded variety, this type of reworked ceramic is present from Early Chaakk'ax times. Most were recovered from middens, although two were excavated from burial fill. The sample is too small to discern whether technology changed over time, although the largest examples date to Late Chaakk'ax times.

Disks. This type of reworked ceramic can be separated into three main categories: (1) small, round, reworked sherds less than 2.1 cm in diameter; (2) round, generally more finished disks between 2.6 cm and 4.2 cm; and (3) disks of varying sizes with a central perforation. These objects are made from ceramics of various types, representing time periods from the Middle Preclassic through the Early Classic. They are found in mixed surface contexts, middens, construction fill, and paleosol. Evidence of smoothing and finishing is present on some sherds but not on others. The size difference and manufacturing techniques suggest various uses.

Small disks (n = 6), found in operations 1, 10, 11, and 12, are generally round with slightly smoothed edges (figures 10.9a, 10.9b). All are eroded, with only one identifiable as to ceramic type, an Aguacate Orange from operation 12. Small disks are generally considered to be gaming pieces (Garber 1986, 1989). If this is the case, then games involving the use of disks were played from earliest times. Indeed, many cultures around the world present evidence of the use of such games. The Aztecs played a game called patolli, which is similar to the modern Indian game of parchesi (Miller and Taube 1993). This game is depicted on folio 20 of the Mixtec Codex Vindobonensis and is reported by Durán (1964) in his history of the Aztecs. Pueblo peoples of the American Southwest continue to play a modern form of this type of game. Games involving disks or markers were probably pan-Mesoamerican, and the Maya had apparently developed their own variation by the period of earliest settlement.

Large, round, unperforated disks have been excavated at a number of sites. Possible usages include pendants, beehive covers, jar lids, and large gaming pieces (Garber 1986, 1988; Hammond 1991c; and Buttles 1992). The disks vary in size from a diameter of 2.7 cm to 5.21 cm and were recovered from middens, pits, and floors (figure 10.9c). These disks are approximately round to oblong in shape, with evidence of edge smoothing and rounding on four of the pieces. Three were made from Hillbank Red sherds, one is an Aguila Orange, and the remainder are too eroded to be identified. All show some surface erosion and one is slightly notched on the end.

Drilled, shaped, and unshaped disks and broken sherds (broken probably as the result of failed perforation) were excavated from operations 1, 8, 10, and 11 (figures 10.9d, 10.9e, 10.9f, and 10.9g). Four are approximately round and have smooth finished edges. An additional one is the size and shape of a life-

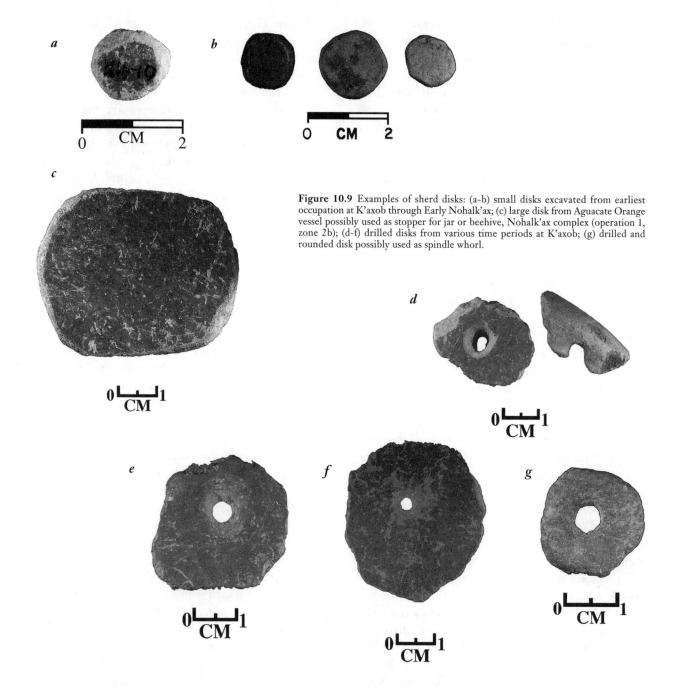

Figure 10.9 Examples of sherd disks: (a-b) small disks excavated from earliest occupation at K'axob through Early Nohalk'ax; (c) large disk from Aguacate Orange vessel possibly used as stopper for jar or beehive, Nohalk'ax complex (operation 1, zone 2b); (d-f) drilled disks from various time periods at K'axob; (g) drilled and rounded disk possibly used as spindle whorl.

saver and may have been used as a spindle whorl (figure 10.9g). Four others are roughly shaped with the perforation slightly off-center. Again the usage of these objects is speculative and varied. They may have served as crude spindle whorls, weft weights, or even pendants. Round objects with holes can be suspended from a cord and, when spun, can serve as a toy for a child. This type of object is reported at most other Maya sites, again suggesting the universality of reworked sherds for a variety of purposes.

The remainder of the shaped sherds and an effigy disk deserve mention. This disk consists of drilled holes for eyes and an incised slash to represent a mouth (figure 10.10a). Whether this piece was made simply to amuse the maker (like today's graffiti) or for adornment is unknown. The sherd was found in an Early Classic midden in operation 7. A similar jade piece with a simply carved smiling face was excavated from burial 1-25 (see chapter 15).

Three additional sherds feature drilled holes (figures 10.10b, 10.10c, and 10.10d). One is an Aquila

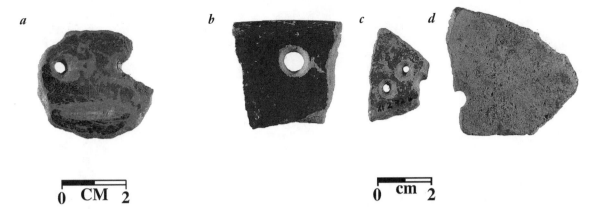

Figure 10.10 Drilled and incised sherds: (a) effigy disk from Early Nohalk'ax construction fill (operation 7, zone 4); (b-d) perforated sherds from variety of contexts.

Orange sherd with two holes. The shape is indistinct. The second is a square Guitara Incised rim sherd with a large center hole. The sides have not been worked. Several vessels from K'axob have perforated holes below the rim perhaps for the placement of a string for suspension or mending. This piece may be a broken part of a similar vessel. One oblong Joventud Red sherd with a central hole mark at the break appears to have been broken while it was being drilled.

A final example of a shaped sherd comes from operation 10. This broken piece resembles a star. The ceramic is an eroded rim sherd that cannot be typed. There are two carved points at one end, but the rest appears to have been broken. The piece dates to the Terminal K'atabche'k'ax complex and was found on a floor surface.

SUMMARY

The diversity of small objects made from clay attest to the innovative manner in which materials readily at hand were utilized. The objects at K'axob are no different in appearance than those found at much larger sites as far distant as Mayapan in the Yucatan. These similarities suggest strategies shared within an overarching sphere of interaction within which ideas and objects were traded over long distances. The proximity of K'axob to the coast via the New River provides one avenue along which these objects and ideas could have been passed.

Clay objects were important to subsistence strategies, particularly in reference to aquatic resource exploitation, and they were also used in the manufacture and decoration of cloth. The skill of the producers and the plasticity of clay meant that objects could be fashioned into very delicate and beautiful adornments (like the exquisite earspool found in operation 10) or formed into simple net sinkers (for use in the river and numerous ponds and waterways of the wetlands). The various gaming pieces found in a variety of contexts suggest a recreational facet to Maya life. Maya potters could produce intricate figurines and large incensarios. Obviously, the use of ceramic objects was not limited to the production of vessels, and recycling was an important aspect of everyday life.

PART IV

STONE TOOLS

While the resource diversity of the wetland-riverine environments of northern Belize may have been attractive to Middle Formative farmers-fishers-foragers, the bountiful food available in this landscape came with a price—the lack of hard stone. The plentiful supplies of hard building stone that existed to the north in the Yucatan and to the south in the Maya Mountains were nonexistent around K'axob, where anything harder than a soft, marl block had to be imported. This lack of hard stone meant that procurement networks had to be established for metates and manos and for chipped stone tools. Obsidian blades were also imported to K'axob, as they were to all Lowland Maya sites.

Part IV contains the stories of the hard stone tools of K'axob: what they look like; how they were made, used, and reused; and how they might have been procured in the first place. Divided into three chapters, Part IV begins with a consideration of the chipped stone (chert and chalcedony) technologies of K'axob. McAnany and Peterson (chapter 11) present the results of a comprehensive analysis of 433 formally shaped tools and 11,718 pieces of debitage (including cores). The K'axob tools are composed primarily of large bifaces (suitable for hafting as an ax or adze) and macroblades (used for cutting, among other tasks, and twice deposited as offerings in caches). Although temporal variability is indicated for a few select tool forms, the oval biface agricultural tool—often with distal use-polish—displays a remarkably stable presence through time. In terms of raw material, tool form, and technology of production, the majority of chert tools bear a strong resemblance to tools produced in the workshops of Colha, which is less than 40 km to the south of K'axob. Results of debitage analysis reinforce this linkage, as few chert cores or initial reduction debris were recorded.

In contrast, primary reduction of local chalcedony and the fashioning of expedient tools are well documented in the assemblage. During the Early Chaakk'ax complex, however, a higher diversity of raw material types is observed in both the chert debitage and tools, indicating the presence of a larger sphere of acquisition (or the mining of chert beds that were later exhausted). By the late facet of the K'atabche'k'ax complex, northern Belizean chert—a type present in the Colha workshops—begins to dominate the K'axob assemblage. This transition is taken to indicate the formalization of an exchange relationship between K'axob and Colha.

Apparently, the exchanged product held considerable value as there is ample evidence that biface tool edges were resharpened until the tool was exhausted and that broken tool fragments were recycled as core resources. Northern Belizean chert of a golden-yellow hue appears to have been particularly prized, as select burials and the single cache at which lithic reduction events occurred contained microdebitage of unburned, golden chert. The smooth articulation of agricultural labor with ritual practice, moreover, is indicated by the fact that many flakes bore evidence of wear polish on their dorsal surfaces and platforms, a characteristic that indicates detachment from a biface.

In chapter 12, McAnany turns to a type of chipped stone—obsidian—that is frequently associated with ritual activity. Clearly a long-distance import, the small sample of smoky gray volcanic glass (143 pieces) found in Formative and Early Classic deposits of southern K'axob is probably a good indicator of the difficulty of its procurement. A rather attenuated long-distance procurement network is also suggested for another import from the southern highlands—greenstone—that is present in very modest frequencies in the early deposits of K'axob (see chapter 15). Despite this relatively small sample, which is composed predominantly of prismatic blade fragments, trends in procurement by source area support the prevailing model of Middle Formative acquisition of obsidian from San Martín Jilotepeque, followed by the source at El Chayal, during the Late Formative and Classic periods. Low levels of obsidian from Ixtepeque, however, are present from Late Formative times onward. The small size of the fragmentary prismatic blades present at K'axob indicate that this material was highly curated and seldom discarded before its use life was exhausted. Perhaps due to its relative inaccessibility, the proportion of volcanic glass in overtly ritual deposits—burials and caches—never climbs above 3% of the sample.

The final consideration of hard stone tools focuses on ground and polished stone tools (chapter 13). McAnany and Ebersole find additional support for protracted patterns of usage, particularly for metates, some of which were recycled as hearth stones. Geological source materials used for ground stone are divided into three zones of acquisition: zone 1 (present in northern Belize), zone 2 (available in the Maya Mountains of southern Belize), and zone 3 (present only in the southern highlands of Guatemala). As might be expected, a significant portion of ground stone was acquired from the Maya Mountains (zone 2) during Early Chaakk'ax times. Locally available raw materials such as limestone and silcrete, however, tend to dominate the assemblage overall, and the very distant zone 3 materials (primarily basalt and greenstone) are severely underrepresented. Insights into the performative aspects of Formative period ritual are deepened by a consideration of the deposition of limestone spheres, or *yuntunob* (ancient *bola* stones), in a cache and a burial context and the discovery of two partial bark beaters in the Early Chaakk'ax midden of operation 1.

In general, Part IV provides additional support for a trend noted in Part III; namely, that Early Chaakk'ax pottery evinces greater variety than that observed during later Chaakk'ax and K'atabche'k'ax times in both paste characteristics and stylistic modes. The inference that this pattern refers to a large-scale open network of exchange or population movement is strengthened by similar trends in the procurement of hard stone.

GUIDE TO ACCOMPANYING DIGITAL MATERIALS.

The hard stone artifacts that provide the substance of Part IV are available in five digital databases. The chert and chalcedony *Chipped Stone Tools Database* contains a comprehensive textual database with select images; it can be viewed either as columnar data or by individual record. The debitage is separated into two databases, both of which are available in columnar view. *Itemized Debitage Database* contains line-item coding of artifacts from operations 1, 7, 8, 10, 13, and a portion of the debitage from operation 11. The *Grouped Debitage Database* includes debitage from the remaining portion of operation 11 and all of operation 12. In the grouped database, each line contains tallies of debitage characteristics presented by zone. The *Obsidian Database*, like that for stone tools, can be viewed in columnar or individual-record format and also contains images of selected obsidian pieces, often grouped by context or ceramic complex. The final database, that of *Ground and Polished Tools*, contains photos of selected tools and can be viewed in either columnar or individual record views.

Chapter 11
Related CD Resources

Chipped Stone Tools
Itemized Debitage
Grouped Debitage

TOOLS OF THE TRADE: ACQUISITION, USE, AND RECYCLING OF CHIPPED STONE

PATRICIA A. MCANANY AND POLLY A. PETERSON

Although rapid progress on hieroglyphic decipherment is often cited as a key development of late-twentieth-century Maya archaeology, two other developments directly relevant to a social historical understanding of Maya society deserve equal attention: the recognition of wetland reclamation and the recognition of a specialized production locale for chert tools in northern Belize. Neither discovery has been accepted uncritically but both have fundamentally changed our approach to understanding ancient Maya farming techniques and household provisioning. And these are significant developments within a field that, historically, has been characterized as one with limited interest in social history.

These topics of provisioning and wetland reclamation are directly relevant to K'axob for two reasons. First, K'axob sits astride Pulltrouser Swamp, ground zero in the controversy over the antiquity and duration of wetland reclamation (Berry and McAnany 2000; Pohl and Bloom 1996; Pohl et al. 1990, 1996; Pope and Dahlin 1989; Pope et al. 1996; Turner and Harrison 1981, 1983). Many of the stone tools discussed in this chapter may have been used in the cultivation of wetland fields. Second, the proximity of K'axob to low-lying wetlands translates into a resource deficit in terms of local sources of hard stone, both for flint-knapping and for the fabrication of manos and metates (see chapter 13). Understanding the means by which householders of K'axob provisioned themselves is a central part of building a narrative for this site. For these reasons, we provide a detailed discussion of the relevance of wetland reclamation and household provisioning to the lithics of K'axob before providing a formal introduction of the chipped stone (433 formal tools and 11,718 pieces of debitage). We combine this presentation of the data with a discussion of our methods of analysis. This section is followed by an examination of spatial, temporal, and contextual trends.

WETLAND RECLAMATION/FARMING: WHEN? FOR HOW LONG? WITH WHAT TOOLS?

As originally formulated by Turner and Harrison (1983:266), the transformation of wetlands into fertile field plots was a Boserupian-style response to the burgeoning population of the Classic period. Since calculations of wetland field production (under a double cropping regime) at Pulltrouser Swamp, Belize, far outweighed the subsistence needs of the population occupying the immediate environs of the wetlands, production was thought to be geared to export or trade (Turner and Harrison 1983:262). This formulation was later challenged by Pope, Pohl, and Jacob (1996:165–176), who questioned whether the processes involved in creating a ground pattern of island fields were entirely cultural. Evidence of Early Formative canals deeply buried beneath such surface patterns near Albion Island further suggested that wetland transformation in the form of ditching and draining wetlands may have its origins deeper in Maya antiquity (Pohl et al. 1996).

When Harry J. Shafer analyzed the chipped stone collected during the seminal 1979 field season of the Pulltrouser Swamp Project (359 lithics from surface collection and excavations at the site of Kokeal and two wetland contexts), he made several key observations. First, in terms of morphology and raw material, Shafer (1983a:214, 225–226, 240) noted that the formal tools (mostly oval bifaces) were identical to those produced at the site of Colha, about 30 km to the south of Pulltrouser Swamp (further discussion below). Second, he commented on the lack of any debitage that could be construed as production debris and the overwhelming preponderance of debitage attributable to edge refurbishing and the reuse of broken biface fragments. Third, he suggested that the frequent occurrence of a dull sheen on the distal tip of oval bifaces and the dorsal face of small, thin flakes (which often also bore a remnant of a biface edge on the platform facet) was a type of "earth polish" produced by repeated contact with silica-rich, stone-free, clay-rich soils, such as those of the wetlands (226). In this fashion, the oval biface with its pattern of use-polish was linked with the intensification of farming activities around Pulltrouser Swamp. The fortuitous discovery by Dennis Puleston of an oval biface hafted in the fashion of a modern ax and placed in a canal near San Antonio (Shafer and Hester 1986a) further strengthened the spatial linkage between the wetlands and this tool form.[1]

During the second and final season of the Pulltrouser Swamp Project (conducted in 1981), four additional circumwetland settlements were identified, mapped, and tested (Tibaat, K'axob, Pech Titon, and Chi Ak'al; see Harrison 1996; Harrison and Fry 2000). Chipped stone collected during this season greatly expanded the sample size (1,143 stone tools and 4,799 pieces of debitage), although the bulk of the material was recovered from Late Formative and Classic period contexts (McAnany 1986, 1989). The patterns first noted by Shafer reverberated throughout the larger sample. However, in the absence of a sample of Middle Formative lithics, the question of the antiquity of wetland reclamation (vis-à-vis the three-way linkage of oval bifaces, use-polish, and canal and field building activities) could not be addressed.

This problem was remedied during the following 1990–1993 field seasons at K'axob, when the Middle Formative deposits underlying plaza B (operation 1) were exhaustively investigated. In this chapter we present the sample resulting from excavations at operation 1 as well as those in the satellite Late Formative and Early Classic residences. The 12,151 pieces of chipped stone minimally allow evaluation of the presence and frequency of the oval biface and its associated use-polish during the Middle Formative, a period of pronounced settlement expansion (if not outright colonization) throughout northern Belize. A later program of intensive excavation of island fields and associated vacant terrain on the western edge of K'axob (Berry and McAnany 2000; Berry forthcoming) will further clarify the spatial association between these wetland landforms and chipped stone.

PROVISIONING K'AXOB HOUSEHOLDS WITH STONE TOOLS

Clarifying the local texture of a landscape is key to understanding the provisioning of both the household and the larger community. For instance, the wetland location of K'axob provided its inhabitants with a varied diet and the opportunity for dry-season farming which, no doubt, contributed to the low index of nutritional deficiencies within the skeletal population (see chapter 6). On the other hand, proximity to wetlands distanced the community from readily available sources of hard stone for fabricating both chipped and ground tools. Given that village landscapes tend to feature well-demarcated boundaries and that northern Belize was heavily populated during the

Table 11.1 K'axob classes of raw material and types of chipped stone

| | CLASSES OF RAW MATERIAL | | | | | | | | | | | |
| Types of Chipped Stone | Unknown, due to alteration | | N. Belizean Chert | | Chalcedony | | Other Chert | | Other Material | | Total | % of Total |
	n	Col. %	n	Col. %	n	Col. %	n	Col. %	n	Col. %	N	
Formal Tool	34	1.6	350	5.1	30	1.4	19	1.8	0	0.0	433	3.6
Flake & Flake Fragment	867	41.5	5813	85.0	1525	72.2	963	90.8	35	71.4	9203	75.7
Fire Shatter & Angular Debris	1173	56.2	646	9.4	456	21.6	61	5.7	9	18.4	2345	19.3
Quarry blank, core, or cobble	15	0.7	28	0.4	102	4.8	18	1.7	5	10.2	168	1.4
Tranchet flake	0	0.0	2	0.0	0	0.0	0	0.0	0	0.0	2	0.0
Total	2089	100.0	6839	100.0	2113	100.0	1061	100.0	49	100.0	12151	100.0
% of Total	17.2		56.3		17.4		8.7		0.4		100.0	

Formative period, this need for hard stone must have been negotiated through sanctioned access to quarry locales, participation in exchange networks, or some combination of the two.

The majority of chipped stone associated with the domiciles of Formative and Early Classic K'axob fall into the following four categories of raw material: (1) northern Belizean chert (NBC), (2) chalcedony, (3) other chert, and (4) other material (such as limestone or serpentinite as well as unknown; table 11.1). A fifth chipped stone material class—obsidian—is handled separately because of the standardization of prismatic core-blade technology, the great distance across which it was transported, and its limited frequency (n = 143 pieces, see chapter 12). Northern Belizean chert, constituting over 56% of the sample in the categories of both tools and debitage (table 11.1), was procured from a distance of about 30 km. Golden to light gray in color and evenly fine-grained in texture, the quality of NBC as a raw material is unparalleled in the Maya Lowlands. The golden chert is particularly fine-grained and, as discussed below, was used selectively at K'axob in the ritual reduction of bifaces over important burials and cache deposits. The mechanisms by which this raw material (and the highly patterned tool forms) circulated has been subject to a significant amount of debate within Maya archaeology, much of which has centered on the role of Colha, a demonstrable stone tool production locale located at the northern end of the

chert-bearing zone (Hester and Shafer 1984, 1987; Mallory 1986; Shafer 1985; Shafer and Hester 1983, 1986b, 1991; Tobey 1986).

Originally identified in 1973 by Norman Hammond and others during a survey of northern Belizean sites (Hester and Hammond 1979:v), Colha has been the site of multiple seasons of field investigation directed by Thomas Hester and Harry Shafer. This research has revealed the presence of over one hundred concentrated deposits of lithic workshop debris (some over 3 m in depth) spanning the Late Formative through the Early Postclassic periods (Masson 2001; Shafer and Hester 1991:81). Tools produced in the workshops exhibit a pronounced technological standardization and the northern Belize chert-bearing zone, as a whole, is chemically homogeneous (Cackler et al. 1999:396). During the Formative and Early Classic periods, common tool forms included an oval biface (up to 20 cm in length); a large, plano-convex tool with a tranchet bit; and macroblades (both stemmed and unstemmed; see Hester and Shafer 1984:Fig. 5). Domestic features and chipped stone tools (particularly a T-shaped adze) were recovered from Middle Formative deposits at Colha, but no concentrated deposits of workshop debris were encountered. Shafer and Hester (1991:82) suggest that production-for-exchange occurred at a low level of intensity during this early time period. On the other hand, the massive overburden of later deposits may be effectively obscuring Middle Formative debitage piles. Investigation of Archaic and Early Formative deposits at Colha indicates technological continuity in lithic reduction strategies from the Middle Formative back to the Archaic period (Iceland 1997:276–280).[2] The low incidence of NBC production materials such as blanks, cores, and cobbles in the K'axob sample (1.4%; table 11.1) suggests that limited NBC tool production transpired near the residences of K'axob.

In contrast to northern Belizean chert, chalcedony is available within 5 km of K'axob. Large nodules can be procured from the eastern side of the New River. On the interfluve between the New River and Freshwater Creek drainages, there is a belt of chalcedony that extends to the south and grades into high-quality, northern Belizean chert (Shafer and Hester 1983:Fig. 1; McAnany 1989). Variable in color and texture but often milky-white and coarse-grained, chalcedony nodules were rarely used for the fabrication of formal tools such as oval bifaces and macroblades. Often, they were introduced into the household as cores for the production of flake tools, as is shown by the fact that almost 5% of chalcedony debitage was classified as quarry blank, core, or cobble material (table 11.1).

Nearly 9% of the sample consisted of fine-grained cherts that did not fall within the range of color, texture, and inclusions exhibited by northern Belizean chert (see other chert in table 11.1). Often exhibiting inclusions of red speckles, this material was concentrated in the lower levels (Early Chaakk'ax complex) of operation 1 excavations. In fact, over 70% of this raw material come from Middle Formative contexts, suggesting that access to multiple sources of chert existed during this early time period. A pattern of high resource diversity within the Chaakk'ax complex is also noted for the ground stone (chapter 13) and for pottery paste composition (chapter 7). The raw material class labeled "other material" was limited to less than 1% of the total sample (table 11.1) and represents an occasional flake from a greenstone celt or a flake struck from a limestone mass. The final raw material category, unknown due to alteration, composes 17% of the K'axob sample. The bulk of these artifacts were burned, thus obscuring the raw material type. A smaller fraction exhibited patinated surfaces from long-term surface exposure, and some exhibited both burning and patination.

Together, these raw materials represent long-term efforts to provision households with chipped stone tools. The circumstances under which these raw materials or finished tools were acquired have engendered a lively debate within Maya archaeology. In reference to NBC, the volume of workshop debris at the Colha site strongly suggests that some of the fabricated tools were traded elsewhere. Regardless of whether the concentrated debitage deposits of Colha represent workshop locales or transported debris in situ (Hester and Shafer 1992; Moholy Nagy 1990), the intensity of production and the singularity of the site (Shafer and Hester 1991:81) suggest that it was a production center linked to consumers through a web of exchange networks or marketplaces (McAnany 1986, 1991). At Colha the chert appears to have been quarried as large nodules from shallow pits in the immediate environs of Colha's 6 sq km settlement (Shafer and Hester 1991:81). The possibility that the flint-knappers of Colha provided tools to the chert-impoverished communities to the north has been corroborated by the presence of "signature" tools fabricated of NBC as well as the underrepresentation of production debris at Cerros (Lewenstein 1987:77–78, 140; Mitchum 1994:133); Cuello (McSwain 1991:338); Santa Rita (Dockall and Shafer 1993:171); and El Pozito (Hester et al. 1991). The assumption of exclusive access to NBC on the part of Colha residents has been questioned by McSwain (1991:344–345) on the basis of the presence of cortex-bearing flakes and tools, as well as a high frequency of flakes with plain-faceted platforms, on NBC from the Middle and Late Formative deposits of Cuello. While access to NBC outside of the sprawling community of Colha is certainly conceivable, there is little doubt that the site itself was situated on top of the finest quality and most accessible chert. Debris piles composed of debitage from the final stage of tool production found among and adjacent to residences further enforces the perception of this tool-producing craft as one in which site inhabitants engaged close to their homes. In other words, the location of debitage deposits does not support a model of open access to this prime hard-stone resource. The question of export can be independently evaluated by reference to the NBC tools and debris of K'axob, which could yield evidence of local production, particularly from the Middle Formative period, a time during which large-scale tool production has not been detected at Colha. These and other issues are examined in the analysis below.

CHIPPED STONE TOOLS AND DEBITAGE OF K'AXOB

The lithic sample was recovered from the seven excavations described in chapter 3 (operations 1, 7, 8, 10, 11, 12, and 13). While the bulk of stone tools were associated with Late Formative ceramics, there is also a large collection of Middle Formative debitage (from the base of operation 1) and a sizable collection of Early Classic tools (from the upper construction phases of operations 1, 7, 10, 11, 12, and 13). The chipped stone from operations 1, 11, and 12 was analyzed and coded by Patricia A. McAnany; that of operations 7, 8, and 13 by Polly Ann Peterson; and that of operation 10 by Leanne Stowe. Formal tools were individually coded using variables described below (see *Chipped Stone Tools Database* for a complete listing). (The term "formal tool" is used to separate standardized tool forms—whether complete or fragmentary—from ad hoc or expedient tools fabricated from flakes, broken fragments of formal tools, or exhausted cores.) The debitage from operations 1, 7, 8, 10, 13, and a sample of the debitage from operation 11 were individually coded and can be found in the *Itemized Debitage Database*. Time constraints limited the itemized coding of the debitage to only a sample of operation 11. The remainder of operation 11 and all of operation 12 were coded employing an abbreviated procedure based on the grouping of debitage by minimal provenience unit, specifically zone and square (see *Grouped Debitage Database*). In total, 433 formal tools and 11,718 pieces of debitage (flakes as well as cores) were analyzed. In weight, tools sum to 16,455 g and debitage to 41,445 g. Since none of the material was available in the immediate environs of K'axob, this sample represents a total sum of 57,900 g transported, probably by tumpline, over a period of 800 to 1,000 years.

Itemized coding of the formal tools included thirteen variables (in addition to provenience, context, and ceramic complex). The following attributes were monitored: type of tool, raw material class, type of fragment, condition, presence of cortex, pattern of flake scars, presence and direction of use-polish, presence of other types of use-wear, length, width, thickness, and weight. In all cases use-wear was observed with a 5-6X hand lens. In contrast to high-powered microscopic techniques employed by Aoyama (1999:33–47) and others, this study presents observations of use-wear based on low-power magnification. A similar procedure was followed for the itemized debitage analysis, with the

Figure 11.1 Oval biface from operation 7, zone 6, square. *All photos by K'axob Project staff*

exception that the debitage was weighed by provenience unit (zone and square if so designated). Debitage variables included the following: type of debitage, raw material class, condition, presence of cortex, number of dorsal scars, platform characteristics, presence of polish, presence of striated polish, presence of marginal retouch, length, width, thickness, and grouped weight. The abbreviated coding of part of operation 11 and all of operation 12 consisted of a three-stage sort of debitage into the following groups: (1) raw material class, (2) type of debitage, and (3) for the flakes and flake fragments only, separate counts for those with and without cortex. Below, these variables and their variates are defined and discussed, and general sitewide patterns for each are presented via tables.

TOOLS OF K'AXOB

In total, nineteen different tool types were identified among the 433 formal tools of K'axob (table 11.2). The bulk of these tools (92%) were fragmentary; thirty-five complete tools were recorded (table 11.2). The tool

Table 11.2 Frequency of K'axob tool and fragment types

| Types of Tool | CLASSES OF RAW MATERIAL | | | | TYPE OF FRAGMENT | | | | | | |
	Unknown	N. Belizean Chert	Chalcedony	Other Chert	Nondiagnostic	Complete	Proximal	Medial	Distal	Total	% of Total
Nondiagnostic	1	14	2	4	15	–	4	–	2	21	4.8
Preform	–	1	–	–	–	–	1	–	–	1	0.2
Oval Biface	6	64	–	3	4	5	18	21	25	73	16.9
Chunky Biface	1	12	3	1	4	–	2	3	8	17	3.9
Nondiagnostic Biface	16	96	10	8	67	–	35	7	21	130	30.0
Reworked Biface	1	19	1	1	14	2	–	6	–	22	5.1
Blade	2	14	–	1	1	–	3	7	6	17	3.9
Stemmed Macroblade	2	31	–	–	1	3	18	8	3	33	7.6
Nondiagnostic Blade	1	4	1	–	2	–	–	2	2	6	1.4
Reworked Blade	–	3	–	–	2	1	–	–	–	3	0.7
Tranchet-bit	–	4	–	–	–	2	1	–	1	4	0.9
Hammerstone	–	2	10	1	6	7	–	–	–	13	3.0
Sidescraper	–	1	–	–	–	1	–	–	–	1	0.2
Projectile Point	–	7	1	–	–	7	–	1	–	8	1.8
Unstemmed Macroblade	3	70	2	–	13	1	7	34	20	75	17.3
Triangular Biface	–	1	–	–	–	1	–	–	–	1	0.2
End Scraper	–	1	–	–	–	1	–	–	–	1	0.2
T-shaped Uniface	–	4	–	–	–	3	1	–	–	4	0.9
Uniface	1	2	–	–	1	1	–	–	1	3	0.7
Total	34	350	30	19	130	35	90	89	89	433	
% of Total	7.9	80.8	6.9	4.4	30.0	8.1	20.8	20.6	20.6		100.0

category includes standardized types such as oval bifaces and stemmed macroblades as well as less standardized types such as unifaces and endscrapers that may be indicative of recycling activities. If a piece of chipped stone had clearly been shaped but could not be classified as a biface, blade, plano-convex tool, or any variation thereof, it was simply listed as a nondiagnostic tool (table 11.2). *Preforms*, on the other hand, are flakes that have been systematically thinned and regularized into a standard shape. They can be roughed-out bifaces or any preliminary form of the standard tool types listed below.

Oval bifaces (figure 11.1) represent one of the most common tool forms at K'axob (n = 73; see table 11.2) and throughout the Maya Lowlands. Generally lenticular in cross-section and tear-drop in shape, the oval bifaces of K'axob taper toward the hafted, proximal end. Oval bifaces were probably hafted in wooden

Figure 11.2 Reworked biface from operation 8, zone 1, square G

Figure 11.3 Macroblade from operation 8, zone 1, square F

handles like the so-called Puleston ax recovered from a canal near Albion Island (Shafer and Hester 1986a). The five complete specimens in the K'axob sample are somewhat variable in dimensions but average 132 mm in length, 61 mm in width, and 23 mm in thickness.

Chunky bifaces, or *celts*, are similar to oval bifaces, although they are not lenticular in cross-section and have less tapering at the proximal end. They tend to be thicker and rounder in cross-section. Chunky bifaces were sometimes made from chalcedony (n = 3), although they were more often crafted out of chert (n = 13). In addition to chipped stone celts, ground and polished celts made from chert, chalcedony, and greenstone were also used at K'axob (see chapter 13). Often only a small fragment of a biface survived. In such a case, the tool was simply coded as a *nondiagnostic biface*. This category was the most ubiquitous at K'axob (n = 130). Often broken bifaces retained a pattern of shallow flake scars (often with ridges polished from use-wear) and an original tool edge but had been otherwise reshaped and used as a core or modified into a new tool type. Two "complete" specimens—exhibiting no broken edges—of *reworked bifaces* (see figure 11.2)

were identified within the total sample (n = 22).

Several types of blades were identified in the K'axob sample of tools, and all more or less conform to the basic definition of a blade as a flake with parallel edges and straight, parallel dorsal ridges that are at least twice as long as they are wide. Blade forms may be triangular or trapezoidal in cross-section, and generally blades lie flat on a surface. Two size classes of blades were recorded: *blade* (less than 10 cm in length when complete), and the longer, broader *macroblade* (figure 11.3). The shorter blades are more commonly found in later Classic period deposits; only seventeen were recorded at K'axob and none was complete. These blade fragments could originally have been parts of macroblades, but their small, fragmentary size rendered it difficult for analysts to code them as such. Three reworked blades were identified (modification similar to that described above for bifaces), one of which was considered complete and exhibited dimensions of 82 mm in length, 51 mm in width, and 19 mm in length (table 11.3). *Macroblades* are considered tools in themselves; however, they can also serve as blanks for the production of wedge-shaped and T-shaped adzes as well as for

Table 11.3 Summary statistics for dimensions and weight of complete tools

Type of Tool	n	Length (mm)			Width (mm)			Thickness (mm)			Weight (grams)		
		average	S.D.*	C.V.**	average	S.D.	C.V.	average	S.D.	C.V.	average	S.D.	C.V.
Oval Biface	5	132.3	31.85	0.241	61.4	9.01	0.147	23.1	4.79	0.207	202.5	84.41	0.417
Reworked Biface	2	71.8	8.75	0.122	39.2	5.87	0.150	20.4	3.69	0.181	72.8	16.40	0.225
Stemmed Macroblade	3	147.5	18.14	0.123	59.3	17.30	0.292	13.1	3.19	0.244	98.0	20.90	0.213
Reworked Blade	1	82.0	–	–	51.0	–	–	19.0	–	–	100.6	–	–
Tranchet-bit	2	78.5	6.36	0.081	46.0	16.97	0.369	21.0	9.90	0.471	77.4	104.16	1.347
Hammerstone	7	67.3	13.73	0.204	53.1	9.08	0.171	44.3	9.20	0.208	213.5	89.21	0.418
Sidescraper	1	76.7	–	–	32.7	–	–	27.0	–	–	53.0	–	–
Projectile Point	7	36.0	6.95	0.193	12.1	1.73	0.143	2.9	0.41	0.141	1.5	0.54	0.360
Unstemmed Macroblade	1	141.6	–	–	44.7	–	–	14.1	–	–	118.0	–	–
Triangular Biface	1	66.0	–	–	45.0	–	–	10.0	–	–	51.3	–	–
End Scraper	1	41.2	–	–	38.8	–	–	13.5	–	–	28.4	–	–
T-shaped Uniface	3	80.7	8.14	0.101	38.7	9.02	0.233	16.0	1.73	0.108	53.4	17.68	0.331
Uniface	1	81.7	–	–	55.1	–	–	27.4	–	–	131.0	–	–
Total	**35**												

*S.D., Standard Deviation
**C.V., Coefficient of Variation

bifaces (Potter 1991:24). Fragments of straight-sided macroblades are common in the Formative deposits of K'axob (n = 75); however, only one unbroken specimen was recovered (see table 11.3 for dimensions). Maya flint-knappers sometimes created a bifacially worked stem on the proximal end of a triangular macroblade. *Stemmed macroblades* (figure 11.4) have distinct dorsal ridges that are the result of striking the macroblade off of the corner of a core (Gibson 1989:122). The resulting form resembles a dagger with a triangular distal end. A bifacially worked stem forms the proximal end. Of the thirty-three stemmed macroblades from K'axob, only three complete examples were found (see table 11.3), and they derive exclusively from ritual cache contexts. Bend breaks on stems from nonritual contexts, however, indicate that macroblades were used as knives (Peterson 2001:21). Broken stems were distinguished from the proximal end of an oval biface by the fact that they tend to be thinner in width and flatter on the ven-

tral face, creating a triangular cross-section. The distal portion of stemmed blades is less easily recognized because it often was reused as a core resource and so reduced that it could only be classified as a flake fragment. Note that eighteen proximal fragments of stemmed macroblades were identified but only three distal fragments (table 11.2). Although the shorter stemmed blade is known from Colha Classic period debris piles, none was recorded in the K'axob contexts under discussion. If a blade (or macroblade) fragment was too fragmentary to determine any of the aforementioned attributes, then it was simply classified as a *nondiagnostic blade* (n = 6).

Tranchet-bit tools are plano-convex in cross-section, feature a snub nose, and were probably used as adzes. A single transverse flake creates the distal bit end. When a tranchet flake is discovered, it is evidence of one completed or edge-refurbished tool. When broken or recycled, tranchet tools can be very difficult to

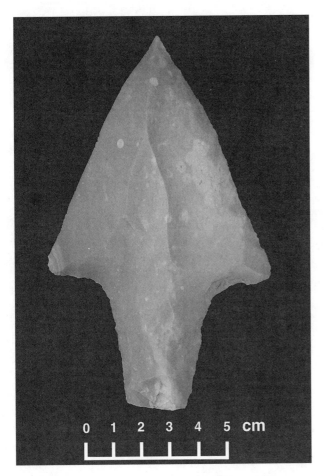

Figure 11.4 Stemmed macroblade from operation 12, zone 57, square G

Figure 11.5 Tranchet-bit tool from operation 12, zone 57, square G

recognize because their diagnostic bit is obscured. On the other hand, they are highly visible at the place of manufacture as one "orange-peel" tranchet flake equals one tranchet tool. Four tranchet-bit tools, all produced from NBC, were identified at K'axob; two of the complete tools (one of which is shown in figure 11.5) were of dramatically varying sizes, thus the large coefficient of variation for the tool class (table 11.3).

Hammerstones (figure 11.6) are nodules with hemispherical battering and crushing. The thirteen examples from K'axob are well rounded from use and often do not exhibit sharp edges unless flakes have been removed or percussion spalling has occurred. Frequently made of chalcedony (ten out of thirteen), seven complete hammerstones were found (see table 11.3 for dimensions). Wear patterns typified by battering and crushing distinguish hammerstones from cores.

Five carefully shaped unifaces were recorded; these artifacts may represent tools fabricated from broken fragments of more formal tools such as blades or bifaces, but they are more deliberately shaped than most ad hoc tools and thus are grouped with the tools rather than the debitage. This category includes one *sidescraper*, one *endscraper*, and three *unifaces* (see table 11.3 for dimensions). All scrapers exhibit at least one steep unifacial edge. The placement of this wide-angled edge determines whether a tool is classified as a sidescraper (figure 11.7a) or an endscraper (figure 11.7b). Endscrapers are usually sized to fit between the thumb and the index finger.

A more formal type of uniface is the *wedge-shaped*, or *T-shaped*, uniface, a Middle Preclassic precursor to tranchet bits (Shafer 1983b:61). Made on a macroblade with one large flake taken off of the distal edge, these tools are fairly standardized in size (table 11.3). T-shaped unifaces were found only in the Chaakk'ax layers of operation 1 (figure 11.8).

The remaining two tool types are generally associated with the Epiclassic or Postclassic periods and were recovered from the surface layers of excavation units.

Figure 11.6 Hammerstone (chert) from operation 12, zone 28

They are small projectile points and a triangular biface. The eight *projectile points* (seven were complete) are small darts that were probably hafted on the tip of an arrow and propelled by a bow. In contrast to the tools described above, the projectiles were pressure flaked; most feature side-notching and fairly standardized dimensions (see table 11.3 and figure 11.9). The *triangular biface*, another late tool form, is distinguished by a shape close to an equilateral triangle and a slender, lenticular cross-section (table 11.3). Only a single complete specimen of this tool type was recovered.

When the formal tools are arrayed against the four raw material classes, it is clear that the preponderance of formal tools (almost 81%) were made of NBC (table 11.2). Nearly 8% cannot be assigned a material class because of alteration; a meager 7% were fabricated of chalcedony; and over 4% were made of chert that was not identifiable as NBC. Within each tool class, NBC is clearly the preferred material for tools (the sole exception being hammerstones, which were made predominantly of chalcedony). The fragmentary condition of the K'axob tools is shown by the fact that only 8% of them are complete and that 92% of them are represented by proximal, medial, distal, or

a

b

Figure 11.7 Scrapers: (a) sidescraper from operation 8, zone 15; (b) endscraper from operation 7, zone 4, square A

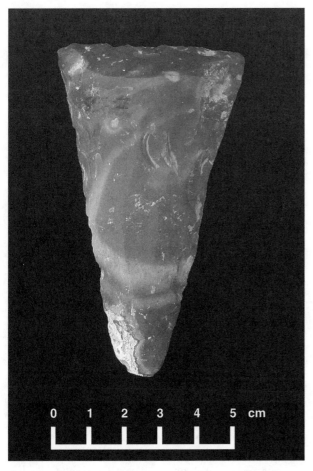

Figure 11.8 T-shaped uniface from the Chaakk'ax midden of operation 1, zone 160, square G

Figure 11.9 Side-notched projectile points from operation 8

nondiagnostic fragments of tools (the final category constituted 30% of the total; table 11.2). Proportional representation within each type of tool varies; given the heavy recycling evidenced by the K'axob tools, to a certain extent these proportions may reflect the relative usefulness of tool fragments as core masses. In other words, medial sections of bifaces represent ideal core material and their underrepresentation relative to proximal and distal fragments may reflect the fact that medial sections were not discarded until exhaustively reworked. Broken distal fragments of stemmed macroblades, as discussed above, also represent a ready-made plano-convex tool, and their lower frequencies relative to proximal stems may reflect their more protracted use lives.

Cortex was recorded for both tools and debitage. Four simple categories were noted: absent, less than 50%, greater than 50% but less than 90%, and greater than 90%. McSwain (1989:166) has noted the presence of cortex on Cuello debitage and tools and suggests that

this characteristic indicates local production. Potter (1991:27), however, notes that even at Colha finished tools frequently bear cortex. For instance, unstemmed macroblades often retain cortex on one of the dorsal facets, perhaps to provide a natural backing. Oval bifaces also feature a small area of cortex at the proximal end (see figure 11.1) that is probably a remnant of the cortical platform of the macroflake from which they were crafted (Potter 1991:27). Of the 433 tools from K'axob, 83% bore no cortex whatsoever, 16% contained cortex on less than half of their surface area, and the remaining 1% (exclusively hammerstones and backed macroblades) were covered with cortex on over 50% of their surface. As might be predicted, of the sixty-eight tools bearing cortex on less than half of their surface area, 50% were bifaces, 31% were blades (including macroblades), and 9% were hammerstones. The bulk of the hammerstones were made from local chalcedony. Given the production techniques utilized at Colha, small amounts of cortex on blades and bifaces do not provide strong evidence of local production.

Two consistent features of K'axob tool fragments are superimposed scar patterns and polish from use-wear. Biface fragments often exhibited a pattern of shallow flake scars (often with polished ridges) topped by a series of deeper flake scars. Such clear truncation was sometimes also visible on blades where shallow, multidirectional flake scars were superimposed over the original, deep, parallel scars. Another indication of the long use life of K'axob tools, this variable was coded (as a type of flake scar) in an effort to quantify the incidence of edge resharpening and of recycling. Of the 433 complete and fragmentary tools, 45% showed evidence of a superimposed pattern of flake scars. Notable tool types within this category include oval bifaces (of which 44% bore truncated scar patterns) and macroblades (of which 45% showed superimposed flake patterns).

For K'axob tools and debitage, the incidence of polish from use-wear is so clear that it can be observed without recourse to a microscope. As Shafer (1983a:242) has discussed, the dorsal surface of some flakes and distal portions of many oval bifaces exhibit a dull, silicate polish characteristic of continual contact with local mollisols that are rich in organic content and sand grains and devoid of percussive rocks. Sometimes the silicate polish is striated with fine lines that indicate the direction of tool use. Striations perpendicular to the distal edge of a tool may indicate tool use in a chopping motion, whereas oblique striations over a large surface area may be characteristic of field mulching activities (McAnany 1989:339–340; McAnany 1992:196). Although silica polish is the primary type of gloss present on K'axob tools and flakes, woodworking also creates a gloss on lithics (Lewenstein 1991); however, this gloss is a much brighter, more reflective polish than is generally observed on K'axob tools and debitage. Each tool was examined under a 5-6X hand lens, and one of four categories of polish was noted: (1) absent, (2) present only in flake troughs, (3) present only on flake ridges, and (4) present in ridges and troughs. Additionally, each tool was examined for the presence of striated polish, for which five categories were employed: (1) absent, (2) present but direction not discernable, (3) striations perpendicular to the edge of tool, (4) striations parallel to the edge of tool, and (5) oblique striations. Within the sample of tools, 44% exhibited no polish whatsoever, 1% had polish only in flake troughs, 32% showed polished ridges, and 24% exhibited surface areas that were covered with a thick

polish, both on the ridges and in the troughs. Of the 102 heavily polished tools, oval bifaces comprised 36%, nondiagnostic bifaces another 34%, with the remaining 30% scattered across the rest of the tool types. Ridge polish, which tended to exhibit greater brightness, was quite frequent along the working edges of macroblades (21% of the 138 tools exhibiting ridge polish) and on the proximal fragments of oval and nondiagnostic bifaces, which together comprised 46% of the ridge-polished tools. This latter category of polish may have been the result of the long-term wear of a haft binding against the biface.

A smaller subset of tools exhibited striated polish (only 10%). Of the forty-five tools with striated polish, 84% are bifaces. Within the nineteen oval bifaces, eight showed striated polish with no clearly discernible direction while another seven distal fragments were coated with striated polish oriented perpendicular to the tool edge (suggesting that the tools were used in a chopping motion). Among the seventeen nondiagnostic bifaces with striated polish, use-polish on the majority (n = 11) of the specimens could not be oriented. Interestingly, one tranchet-bit tool and one uniface exhibited polish with striations running perpendicular to the tool edge, a pattern consonant with adze use. One macroblade, moreover, displayed a pattern of striated polish oriented parallel to the tool edge (indicating the mechanics of knife use), which may have been the result of repeated cutting of a high-silica substance. Another blade fragment showed a pattern of striated polish oriented perpendicular to the edge.

In addition to polish, other types of use-wear were noted. Combinations and permutations were built around the following seven categories of use-wear (which include types of breakage): (1) bend break, (2) end shock, (3) battering, (4) crushing, (5) step flaking, (6) edge rounding, and (7) microflaking. For instance, the distal end of an oval biface may show edge rounding and step flaking from use. A broken fragment might exhibit the characteristic lip-and-hinge fracture of a bend break that resulted from bending or prying a tool beyond its tensile strength (such as might occur if the tool was caught in the infamous mud of Pulltrouser Swamp). Only 8% of the 433 tools exhibited none of the seven types of use-wear, while values for the remaining 92% were distributed across sixteen different permutations of the use-wear categories. The four most common types of use-wear consisted of step flaking (20%); step flaking with rounded edges (13%); a bend break with marginal step flaking (12%); and a

Table 11.4 Summary statistics for dimensions of each type of debitage in itemized analysis

Type of Debitage	n	% of Total	Length (mm) average	Length (mm) S.D.	Length (mm) C.V.	Width (mm) average	Width (mm) S.D.	Width (mm) C.V.	Thickness (mm) average	Thickness (mm) S.D.	Thickness (mm) C.V.
Quarry Blank	1	0.0	32	–	–	18	–	–	3	–	–
Core	122	1.3	39.4	11.88	0.302	31.6	8.67	0.274	19.4	6.45	0.332
Core Tool	16	0.2	51.9	13.98	0.269	42.8	14.74	0.344	21.8	10.76	0.494
Flake	4634	50.5	18.1	10.55	0.583	16.9	9.71	0.575	3.5	3.17	0.906
Flake Fragment	2629	28.7	15.3	10.2	0.667	14.5	8.86	0.611	3.4	3.2	0.941
Fire Shatter	1467	16.0	19.1	10.02	0.525	13	7.55	0.581	5.8	4.31	0.743
Angular Debris	296	3.2	20.7	10.99	0.531	13.4	7.54	0.563	7.8	4.9	0.628
Tranchet Flake	2	0.0	65.5	12.02	0.184	37	14.14	0.382	17.5	7.78	0.445
Cobble	2	0.0	44.5	0.71	0.016	33	12.73	0.386	19	15.56	0.819
Total	**9169**	**100.0**									

combination of a bend break, step flaking, rounded edges, and microflaking (9%).

The accumulation of use-wear on many of the K'axob tools and, particularly, the detection of polish (thick and striated on 10% of the tools) together with the presence of superimposed patterns of flake scars on 45% of the tool fragments, suggests an assemblage that was heavily used and reused over long periods of time. The concepts of tool curation and recycling (Binford 1979; McAnany 1988) are highly relevant to the K'axob tools and, in light of the paucity of high-quality local stone, are not surprising.

DEBITAGE OF K'AXOB

Separated into nine different types and five different raw materials, debris from flint-knapping activity is well represented at K'axob. As mentioned above, two distinct types of debitage analyses were conducted: an itemized analysis of 9,169 pieces and a grouped analysis of the remaining 2,549 artifacts. Because of time constraints, the grouped analysis was implemented for a portion of the debitage from operation 11 and all of operation 12. Temporally, this material derives primarily from Late and Terminal K'atabche'k'ax deposits, a time period that otherwise is well represented in the debitage sample. However, the spatially skewed sample of itemized debitage limits the comparison of debitage between operations. Below, each type is discussed and summary statistics for the dimensions of debitage types from the itemized analysis are presented (table 11.4). Dimensions were measured in the following fashion: length of item was measured from the proximal to distal end (or maximum length if no orientation was possible); width was measured perpendicular to the length; and thickness was measured below the bulb of percussion on flakes and at a location of average thickness for all other types. Additionally, the combined weight of all pieces of debitage from a minimum provenience unit was recorded.

A *quarry blank*, or *macroflake*, exhibited a length in excess of 10 cm (figure 11.10). Rare at K'axob, these flakes indicate access to quarries or, minimally, to primary debitage; only one macroflake was encountered in the itemized analysis, and its length (32 mm) is almost twice the average of all other flakes (18 mm). A core generally exhibits only negative flake scars, and those found at K'axob are spherical cores with multidirectional flakes removed (figure 11.11). A core tool differs from a core in that it shows marked marginal or hemispherical use-wear (figure 11.12) and a tendency toward larger dimensions (table 11.4). Given the paucity of knappable stone, unworked cobbles of chert and chalcedony (potential core material) were also re-

Figure 11.10 Rare quarry blank, or macroflake, from operation 11, zone 93, square C

Figure 11.11 Cores from operation 1, zone 33

corded. Altogether, a combined total of 168 quarry blanks, cores, core tools, and cobbles were recovered from excavations at K'axob (table 11.1).

A *flake* was so defined if it possessed a platform and/or bulb of percussion and most of its distal portion. The itemized analysis contained 4,634 flakes, over 50% of the total debitage collection that was individually analyzed. K'axob flakes average under 2 cm in length and width, although the high coefficients of variation (over 50%) indicate a large spread of values around that central tendency (table 11.4). Much of this variation is a function of raw material class (discussed in detail below). Nonetheless, the small size of the flakes indicates the tertiary character of the K'axob debitage sample. A *flake fragment* lacks a platform and/or bulb of percussion. As expected, dimensional variates are slightly lower for flake fragments (table 11.4), although the coefficients of variation are equal to or greater than that of flakes. Numerically, flakes and flake fragments dominate the debitage assemblage, constituting around 79% of both the total debitage (table 11.1) as well as the itemized debitage (table 11.4).

Just as many of the K'axob tools were burned, so was a large percentage of the debitage. Called *fire shatter*, all of this debris exhibits some combination of burning, crazing, spalling, or pot-lidding that has obscured recognizable debitage attributes such as flake scars, a bulb of percussion, or a platform surface (figure 11.13). A total of 1,467 pieces of fire shatter (16% of the total) were individually analyzed. On average, a piece of fire shatter tends to be thicker than a flake (5.8 mm as opposed to 3.5 mm), suggesting that much of it represents shattered cores or tools rather than badly burned flakes. As with the flake category, however, there is tremendous internal variability within the categories of length, width, and thickness (table 11.4). *Angular debris*, while not necessarily burned, lacks recognizable flake scars and a bulb of percussion and tends to be even thicker than fire shatter (table 11.4). Together fire shatter and angular debris compose almost 20% of both the total and the itemized debitage (tables 11.1 and 11.4).

The final debitage type, *tranchet flake*, is composed of the diagnostic "orange peel" flake that represents the ultimate step in creating or re-creating the steep-angled nose of a plano-convex tranchet-bit tool (figure 11.14). As described by Shafer (1976), an orange-peel flake is removed by a side blow to the bit end of a carefully prepared tool edge. The sample contains two tranchet flakes, both of NBC chert; on average, their dimensions are 65.5 mm in length, 37 mm in width, and 17.5 mm in width. Given the fact that there are only four tranchet-bit tools in the K'axob sample, the presence of two tranchet flakes (from operations 1 and 11) is enigmatic. Two possibilities could explain their presence relative to the paucity of tranchet-bit tools. The tremendous amount of tool recycling that took place at K'axob has obscured the numerical frequency of tranchet-bit tools which, in a recycled state, may have been classified as cores more readily than were bifaces since the latter retain a lenticular cross-section well into the recycling process. Alternatively or additionally, the orange-peel flakes may not have been produced at K'axob but could have been traded from Colha as ready-made flake tools suitable for use as, among other things, a graver.

Combined tallies of the itemized and grouped debitage analyses are presented in table 11.1, where the debitage has been collapsed into four categories: (1) flakes and flake fragments, (2) fire shatter and angular debris, (3) quarry blanks, cores, and cobbles, and (4) tranchet flakes. The combined tally of 11,718 pieces of debitage, when examined against the five raw material classes, reveals several trends. First, the assemblage is dominated by flakes and flake fragments (78.6%). Fire shatter and angular debris comprise the second most ubiquitous category (20%); quarry blanks, cores, and cobbles add only an additional 1.4%. The two tranchet flakes form a negligible percentage. As expected, over 50% of the fire shatter and angular debris were classified as unknown in terms of raw material. Of the debitage classified as northern Belizean chert, 85% consisted of flakes and flake fragments, a percentage that is similar to that of other chert. In contrast, only 73% of the chalcedony artifacts were classified as complete or partial flakes; 22% were either angular debris or fire shatter; and a full 5% were either cores, quarry blanks, or cobbles. The distribution of types within other material is proportionally similar to that of chalcedony. When the 4,634 flakes from the itemized sample are arrayed against raw material class, even starker

Figure 11.12 Core tool from operation 1, zone 219

Figure 11.13 Fire shatter from operation 13, zone 8

0 1 2 cm

Figure 11.14 Tranchet flake from operation 11, zone 4

sources in which procurement patterns were similar to those of NBC. The distribution of debitage types across the final category of other material is closest to that of chalcedony, suggesting that material falling into this residual category may also have been reduced from a primary state near the residence.

The dorsal surface of debitage was recorded by two variables. Cortex was observed using the categories described above and, additionally, dorsal scars were counted for flakes and flake fragments. Two kinds of flake scars were excluded from this count: (1) small flakes located along the dorsal face of the platform and produced during platform preparation, and (2) flakes from marginal retouch (that clearly postdate flake detachment). By raw material type, average dorsal scar count (5.3) is highest among flakes of other chert (perhaps because these flakes also tend to be larger), followed by NBC (4.9) and then chalcedony (4.2, see table 11.5). For presentation in table 11.5, cortex categories are reduced to three: absent, less than 50%, and greater than 50%. Over 90% of the NBC flakes have no cortex whatsoever, and less than 2% show cortex on over half of their dorsal surface. Flakes of other chert show slightly higher percentages of cortex (over 5% of the flakes bear cortex on over half of their dorsal surface), and cortex is completely absent in only 81% of the flakes (table 11.5). Chalcedony flakes, on the other hand, lack cortex on only 65% of the sample, with 27% displaying cortex on less than half of their dorsal face and about 8% displaying cortex covering over half of the dorsal surface. These patterns indicate, again, the more tertiary state of both the NBC and other chert flakes and the primary state of the chalcedony flakes.

Three conditions of the variable platform were recorded: (1) absent; (2) presence of a peaked, multifaceted platform (dubbed a complex striking platform by Andrefsky 1998:Fig. 5c) likely detached from a biface; and (3) presence of a plain platform likely not from a biface. Again, flakes within each raw material class display different proportions of the three platform states although, within all classes, at least 72% of the flakes displayed a simple platform (table 11.5). The primary differences occur within the relative percentage of bifacial platforms: almost 20% for NBC flakes, 21% for other chert flakes, and only 3% for chalcedony flakes (90% of which were simple platforms). The small size of the NBC flakes in addition to the high frequency of bifacial platforms hints at the central role of edge refurbishing and (possibly) recycling within this raw material class.

differences emerge (table 11.5). Specifically, chalcedony flakes are longer, wider, and nearly twice as thick as NBC flakes. Flakes of other chert are situated dimensionally between NBC and chalcedony flakes.

To summarize the raw material classes, even though NBC represents the largest percentage of debitage, there is more production debris in the chalcedony class than in any other class of raw material. This pattern supports the notion that chalcedony was acquired as nodules, reduced near the residence for flake tools, and occasionally used to fabricate a formal tool. In contrast, NBC appears to have undergone more processing prior to lithic reduction near K'axob domiciles. The distribution of values for the raw material class "other chert" largely mimics that of NBC, suggesting that this category either represents currently unknown varieties of NBC or other

Table 11.5 Attributes of flakes tabulated by raw material class (itemized debitage only)

Raw Material Class	n	% of Total	Length (mm) average	Width (mm) average	Thick-ness (mm) average	Dorsal Scars average	Cortex none	lt 50%	gt 50%	Platform Characteristic Absent	Bifacial	Simple	Use Polish Absent	Present	Ground/Polished Present	Edge Wear Absent	Present	N/A
Unknown	340	7.3	19.4	16.7	3.9	4.1	287	43	10	29	41	270	258	81	1	177	53	110
N. Belizean Chert	3116	67.2	16.5	15.7	2.8	4.9	2826	225	65	239	597	2280	2147	953	16	2538	507	71
Chalcedony	608	13.1	23.4	20.9	5.7	4.2	392	162	54	42	21	545	545	56	7	354	137	117
Other Chert	557	12.0	20.8	20.1	4.1	5.3	451	77	29	41	117	399	355	191	11	446	84	27
Other Material	13	0.3	22.5	16.9	3.8	3.6	10	2	1	0	2	11	9	1	3	13	0	0
Total Count	**4634**						3966	509	159	351	778	3505	3314	1282	38	3528	781	325
% of Total		100.0					85.6	11.0	3.4	7.6	16.8	75.6	71.5	27.7	0.8	76.1	16.9	7.0

The categories of polish are parallel to those described above for tools, with the addition of a fourth category only observed on flakes or portions of flakes: a ground and polished dorsal face indicating the removal of a flake from a ground and polished celt. The observation of use-polish further diverged from that of formal tools in that the presence of a thick use-polish with visible striations was noted simply as present or absent. When flakes are sorted by raw material and polish collapsed into the three categories (absent, present as use-polish, and present as a ground and polished surface), then significant variation in the presence of both use-polish and a ground/polished surface is apparent (table 11.5). Among NBC and other chert materials, 30% and 34% of the flakes bear use-polish on their dorsal surface, respectively. In contrast, only 9% of the chalcedony and 8% of the other material display evidence of use-polish. Of the 284 flakes with striated polish, 94% were either NBC or other chert flakes. The pronounced presence of use-polish, thus, is another indicator (along with flake size and platform characteristics) that NBC and other chert flakes are likely the result of edge-refurbishing and recycling activities. Only thirty-eight flakes with ground and polished dorsal and platform faces were recorded, and twenty-seven (71%) had been removed from a celt made of either NBC or other chert (table 11.5). The remaining 29% came from chalcedony, other material, and a badly burned flake classified as unknown raw material. Given the lack of any evidence for the production of ground and polished celts at the production site of Colha, it is likely that the laborious task of grinding and polishing a chert celt was undertaken at K'axob. Since this type of surface finish prolongs the use life of a tool (Hayden 1987:40–41), it was likely worth the labor input for residents of K'axob, who had limited access to hard stone.

Marginal retouch, or edge-wear, evidence of the use of a flake or the fabrication of a tool from a flake or core was noted simply as present or absent. Within the sample of itemized flakes, the chalcedony flakes contain the highest percentage (23%) of marginal retouch and edge wear (table 11.5). In contrast, NBC and other chert flakes exhibit much lower percentages of utilized flakes: 16% and 11%, respectively. This contrast can be explained by the fact that the chalcedony flakes, on average, are larger and were often produced specifically to be used as tools. Nonetheless, 507 NBC flakes and eighty-four flakes of other chert bore clear evidence of marginal retouch and/or use-wear.

One of the most distinctive types of marginal retouch consisted of the fashioning of the distal end of a flake into a long drill tip that could be used, among other purposes, to drill holes in shell (figure 11.15). Many of the twenty-two drill fragments are found within Chaakk'ax and Early K'atabche'k'ax midden layers of operation 1 (specifically in zones 57, 59, 63, and 111) and within the underlying artifact-rich paleosol (zones 70 and 220). Perhaps not coincidentally, Harrigan (chapter 18) also reports higher than average frequencies of freshwater shell, specifically *Nephronaias* spp., from many of these zones. Commonly called mother-of-pearl, *Nephronaias* spp. belongs in the Unionidae family and, as Isaza (chapter 14) indicates, this bivalve was a popular material for the fabrication of shell beads. Taken together, the drill fragments and freshwater shell provide evidence of local crafting of beads during Chaakk'ax times.

SPATIAL AND TEMPORAL PATTERNS IN ACQUISITION AND USE

The relative frequency of tool types across the seven excavation units appears largely to be a function of the size of the excavation unit (table 11.6). As discussed in chapter 3, operation 1, by far, was the largest and deepest unit to be excavated, and it yielded 49.4% of the tools. Next in size were operations 11, 7, 12, and 10, from which were recovered 17.6%, 10.4%, 12.7%, and 3.5% of the tools, respectively. Operations 8 and 13 rank among the smallest excavations and also produced only 4.6% and 1.8% of the tools. As expected, the highest diversity of tool types was recovered from the largest excavation unit—operation 1—which produced examples of sixteen of the nineteen tool types. Oval bifaces and nondiagnostic bifaces, two of the most ubiquitous types, were found in every single excavation, regardless of size, while reworked bifaces as well as stemmed and unstemmed macroblades were found in all but one unit. Hammerstones were absent only at operations 10 and 13.

Pure, stratified Chaakk'ax complex deposits were only found within the basal layers of operation 1, and this fact must be kept in mind while interpreting table 11.7, an array of tool types across ceramic complexes. Surprisingly, Early Nohalk'ax deposits yielded the highest frequencies of tools (24.7% of the total) followed by Late K'atabche'k'ax layers (19.6%) and Early Chaakk'ax deposits (18.2%). Thirty-seven percent (n = 27) of all oval bifaces were discovered in Early Nohalk'ax deposits, as were over 40% of each of the following tool types: chunky bifaces, reworked bifaces, stemmed macroblades, and hammerstones. Oval bifaces, in particular, are more common in K'atabche'k'ax and Nohalk'ax deposits than in the underlying Chaakk'ax levels. The earliest Chaakk'ax deposits were distinctive in yielding the highest percentage (56% combining early and late facets) of unstemmed macroblades and 100% of the T-shaped unifaces (n = 4), the latter known to be a Middle Formative tool type. Stemmed macroblades, considered a hallmark of Late Formative tool production at Colha, are found primarily in K'atabche'k'ax and Nohalk'ax deposits. As anticipated, the small, side-notched projectile points were recovered only from

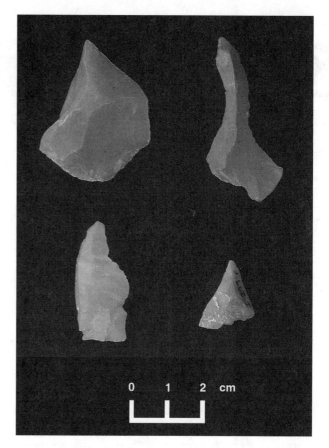

Figure 11.15 Drill tips from Early Chaakk'ax midden in operation 1, zone 59

the surface of excavation units (table 11.7). In other respects, however, most tool types are distributed across all time periods, albeit in varying frequencies. If surface collections are excluded, the seven most frequent tool types are found to be distributed throughout the temporal spectrum (table 11.7), indicating some measure of stability in the types of tools utilized at K'axob.

In an attempt to monitor temporal changes in the incidence of use-polish on oval bifaces, the sample of seventy-three oval bifaces was arrayed across the ceramic complexes. When all of the subcategories of polish were grouped together, this analysis revealed a slight increase in the percentage of use-polish through time (table 11.8). Sample size varies considerably through time (as do the percentages with polish), but it may be significant that nearly 89% of the Early Nohalk'ax oval bifaces showed evidence of use-polish (as opposed to 84% from Late K'atabche'k'ax times). In summary, during Early Nohalk'ax times oval bifaces were not only more frequent but they were also more frequently coated with observable use-polish.

Table 11.6 Frequency of each tool type across excavation units

Type of Tool	Operation (Excavation Unit) 1	7	8	10	11	12	13	Total	% of Total
Nondiagnostic	14	–	–	1	5	–	1	21	4.8
Preform	–	–	–	–	–	1	–	1	0.2
Oval Biface	25	11	5	2	16	13	1	73	16.9
Chunky Biface	6	3	–	1	4	3	–	17	3.9
Nondiagnostic Biface	67	13	1	5	26	16	2	130	30.0
Reworked Biface	10	2	1	2	3	4	–	22	5.1
Blade	8	–	1	–	5	2	1	17	3.9
Stemmed Macroblade	15	11	4	1	–	1	1	33	7.6
Nondiagnostic Blade	5	–	–	1	–	–	–	6	1.4
Reworked Blade	1	–	–	–	2	–	–	3	0.7
Tranchet-bit	1	–	–	1	1	1	–	4	0.9
Hammerstone	5	2	1	–	4	1	–	13	3.0
Sidescraper	–	–	1	–	–	–	–	1	0.2
Projectile Point	2	–	5	–	–	–	1	8	1.8
Unstemmed Macroblade	48	2	1	1	10	13	–	75	17.3
Triangular Biface	1	–	–	–	–	–	–	1	0.2
End Scraper	–	1	–	–	–	–	–	1	0.2
T-shaped Uniface	4	–	–	–	–	–	–	4	0.9
Uniface	2	–	–	–	–	–	1	3	0.7
Total	**214**	**45**	**20**	**15**	**76**	**55**	**8**	**433**	
% of Total	**49.4**	**10.4**	**4.6**	**3.5**	**18**	**13**	**1.8**		**100**

With regard to temporal trends in the debitage that underwent an itemized analysis, the most sensitive debitage type appears to be flakes. In table 11.9, the raw frequencies of flakes from each ceramic complex and facet are arrayed against raw material, cortex, and polish. Of the 4,634 flakes, 33% (n = 1527) were recovered from Early Chaakk'ax deposits, thus skewing the sample toward this early time period. In contrast, Early Nohalk'ax deposits yielded only 6% (n = 291) of the flake sample, providing a clear contrast with the large sample of tools from this Early Classic time period. Among the categories of raw material, there appear to be two patterns, one that prevailed from Early Chaakk'ax through Early K'atabche'k'ax times, and another that prevailed from Late K'atabche'k'ax times onward. During the earlier time, other chert material was relatively common (almost 90% of the total for this material class), as was chalcedony (80% of total chalcedony), and there were relatively lower proportions of NBC (53% of total NBC). This pattern

Table 11.7 Frequency of tool types within each ceramic complex and facet

| Type of Tool | CERAMIC COMPLEX AND FACET | | | | | | | |
| | Chaakk'ax | | K'atabche'k'ax | | | Nohalk'ax | | |
	Early	Late	Early	Late	Terminal	Early	Surface	Total
Nondiagnostic	6	1	7	3	1	3	–	21
Preform	–	–	–	1	–	–	–	1
Oval Biface	6	2	4	19	7	27	8	73
Chunky Biface	1	1	2	2	2	8	1	17
Nondiagnostic Biface	23	12	15	32	11	28	9	130
Reworked Biface	1	2	2	6	1	9	1	22
Blade	2	2	6	1	–	3	3	17
Stemmed Macroblade	1	1	5	6	5	14	1	33
Nondiagnostic Blade	4	1	–	–	–	1	–	6
Reworked Blade	1	–	2	–	–	–	–	3
Tranchet-bit	–	–	1	–	2	1	–	4
Hammerstone	1	1	–	3	1	6	1	13
Sidescraper	–	–	–	1	–	–	–	1
Projectile Point	–	–	–	–	–	–	8	8
Unstemmed Macroblade	30	12	9	11	7	4	2	75
Triangular Biface	–	–	–	–	–	1	–	1
End Scraper	–	–	–	–	–	1	–	1
T-shaped Uniface	2	2	–	–	–	–	–	4
Uniface	1	1	–	–	–	1	–	3
Total	79	38	53	85	37	107	34	433
% of Total	18.2	8.8	12.2	19.6	8.5	24.7	7.9	100.0

reversed itself beginning in Late K'atabche'k'ax times and continuing through Early Nohalk'ax times, when other chert all but vanished (just 10% of total other chert) and the combined proportion of chalcedony diminished to 20% while that of NBC increased to 45%. This disjuncture appears to indicate a shift in patterns of acquisition that occurred around 200 BC, when chalcedony and other chert became relatively less accessible and NBC more accessible. This trend coincides with observed changes in the intensity of tool production at Colha (Shafer and Hester 1991:82).

Diminished access to or acquisition of other chert and chalcedony may explain the pronounced reduction in cortex-bearing flakes over time (table 11.9). Both chalcedony and other chert flakes, on average, are larger and retain more cortex, indicating that they entered the residences of K'axob in a state that was less processed than NBC material. Regarding polish, the large sample of

Table 11.8 Frequency of use-polish on oval bifaces by ceramic complex and facet

Presence of Use Polish	Chaakk'ax		K'atabche'k'ax			Nohalk'ax			% of Total
	Early	Late	Early	Late	Terminal	Early	Surface	Total	
Absent	–	1	1	3	2	3	3	13	17.8
Present	6	1	3	16	5	24	5	60	82.2
Total	6	2	4	19	7	27	8	73	
% of Total	8.2	2.7	5.5	26.0	9.6	37.0	11.0		100.0

Table 11.9 Frequency of flake characteristics by ceramic complex

Ceramic Complex and Facet	CLASSES OF RAW MATERIAL					CORTEX				USE POLISH				G & P*		Total Count
	Un-known	N. Belize Chert	Chal-cedony	Other Chert	Other Mat.	Absent		Present		Absent		Present		Present		
						n	Row %	n.	Row %	n	Col. %	n	Col. %	n	Col. %	
E. Chaakk'ax	107	921	229	264	6	1233	80.7	294	19.3	1085	32.7	424	33.1	18	47.4	1527
L. Chaakk'ax	70	339	143	132	6	569	82.5	121	17.5	519	15.7	158	12.3	13	34.2	690
E. K'atabche'k'ax	63	395	115	103	1	572	84.4	105	15.6	507	15.3	167	13.0	3	7.9	677
L. K'atabche'k'ax	30	765	66	41	–	831	92.1	71	7.9	625	18.8	276	21.6	1	2.6	902
T. K'atabche'k'ax	34	392	19	9	–	420	92.5	34	7.5	321	9.7	132	10.3	1	2.6	454
E. Nohalk'ax	27	229	28	7	–	264	90.7	27	9.3	193	5.8	97	7.6	1	2.6	291
Surface	13	71	8	1	–	78	83.9	15	16.1	66	2.0	26	2.0	1	2.6	93
Total	344	3112	608	557	13	3967		667		3316	100.0	1280	100.0	38	100.0	4634

* G & P, Ground & Polished surface

Chaakk'ax flakes skews the column percentages for both the presence and absence of polish (table 11.9). Even the large sample of Chaakk'ax flakes, however, cannot hide the fact that almost 82% of the flakes removed from ground and polished celts were discarded in Chaakk'ax layers. Although ground and polished celts are present throughout the temporal spectrum (see chapter 13), only one has been recovered from Chaakk'ax layers. Nevertheless, the strong signature of flakes with ground and polished platform and dorsal facets indicates that they were a much more common Chaakk'ax tool type than is indicated by the single broken fragment. Moreover, this diagnostic debitage is concentrated in the earliest occupation levels, when land clearance would have been an important activity.

Although the column percentages of table 11.9 seem to indicate that use-polish diminished through time, an examination of the relative percentage of polish within each ceramic complex and phase actually indicates that flakes from Early Nohalk'ax levels contain the largest proportion of use-polish (33%). This fact corroborates the finding noted above regarding the increased frequency of oval bifaces with use-polish during Early Nohalk'ax times.

In summary, no obvious differences in tool assemblages can be observed among excavation units since broken fragments of most major tool forms were recovered from every excavation, and artifact diversity within each excavation appears to be largely a function of the size of the excavation unit. Temporal trends are

Table 11.10 K'axob tool types arrayed by archaeological context

| Type of Tool | CONTEXT OF DEPOSITION | | | | | | | | | | |
	Burial	Cache	Construction Fill	Fire Feature	Floor	Midden	Pit	Surface	Wall Tumble	Wall	Total
Nondiagnostic	3	–	2	–	2	10	2	2	–	–	21
Preform	–	–	–	–	–	1	–	–	–	–	1
Oval Biface	7	2	22	–	6	11	11	12	2	–	73
Chunky Biface	–	–	8	–	2	1	1	4	1	–	17
Nondiagnostic Biface	10	1	39	1	9	42	10	10	3	5	130
Reworked Biface	2	1	7	–	1	4	3	3	1	–	22
Blade	2	–	3	–	1	6	–	5	–	–	17
Stemmed Macroblade	4	3	12	–	2	6	4	1	1	–	33
Nondiagnostic Blade	–	–	1	–	–	5	–	–	–	–	6
Reworked Blade	–	–	–	–	–	2	1	–	–	–	3
Tranchet-bit	1	–	1	–	–	1	–	1	–	–	4
Hammerstone	–	–	4	–	3	3	–	1	2	–	13
Sidescraper	–	–	–	–	–	1	–	–	–	–	1
Projectile Point	–	–	–	–	4	–	–	2	2	–	8
Unstemmed Macroblade	7	–	5	2	4	38	13	6	–	–	75
Triangular Biface	–	–	–	–	–	–	–	–	1	–	1
End Scraper	–	–	1	–	–	–	–	–	–	–	1
T-shaped Uniface	–	–	–	–	–	4	–	–	–	–	4
Uniface	–	–	1	–	–	1	–	–	1	–	3
Total	36	7	106	3	34	136	45	47	14	5	433
% of Total	8.3	1.6	24.5	0.7	7.9	31.4	10.4	10.9	3.2	1.2	100.0

another matter, however. Oval bifaces and stemmed macroblades increase in frequency through time at the expense of unstemmed macroblades, which are most common during Chaakk'ax times. Similarly, oval bifaces bearing use-polish are more common during Nohalk'ax times. The few temporally restricted tool types include the T-shaped uniface (found only in Chaakk'ax layers) and the side-notched projectile points (found only near the surface). Gradational trends in the proportional representation of raw material classes is a strong feature of the K'axob debitage. High proportions of other chert and chalcedony dominate earlier time periods, but by Late K'atabche'k'ax times NBC begins to rule the debitage assemblage. Patterns of cortex also conform to this temporal hinge point. Flakes from ground and polished celts are nearly restricted to Chaakk'ax levels, while the proportion of flakes with use-polish increases through time.

Table 11.11 K'axob debitage types arrayed by archaeological context

Type of Debitage	CONTEXT OF DEPOSITION													
	Burial	Cache	Construc-tion Fill	Fire Feature	Floor	Midden	Misc	Paleosol	Pit	Posthole	Surface	Wall Tumble	Wall	Total
Quarry Blank	–	–	1	–	–	–	–	–	–	–	–	–	–	1
Core	14	–	37	2	30	28	–	4	1	2	2	2	–	122
Core Tool	2	–	4	–	4	3	–	1	1	–	–	1	–	16
Flake	1075	199	640	47	390	1691	6	253	115	84	72	42	21	4635
Flake Fragment	604	170	352	29	232	851	1	138	89	45	67	31	19	2628
Fire Shatter	280	13	289	33	128	518	2	50	56	35	33	26	4	1467
Angular Debris	34	17	49	2	26	123	–	2	10	6	22	5	–	296
Tranchet Flake	–	–	1	–	–	–	–	–	–	–	–	1	–	2
Cobble	–	–	–	–	–	2	–	–	–	–	–	–	–	2
Total	2009	399	1373	113	810	3216	9	448	272	172	196	108	44	9169
% of Total	21.9	4.4	15.0	1.2	8.8	35.1	0.1	4.9	3.0	1.9	2.1	1.2	0.5	100

CONTEXT OF CHIPPED STONE TOOLS AND DEBITAGE

The immediate archaeological context of chipped stone can be informative of activities as well as of patterns of discard and reuse. The clear stratigraphy and many intrusive features encountered in excavations at K'axob render feasible a contextual analysis of deposits grouped by context or type of deposit. First, contextual patterns in the distribution of formal tools are explored, and then contextual patterns in debitage are analyzed. The latter includes the reduction of golden NBC oval bifaces in scattering rituals over cache deposits and burial interments (never before described for K'axob).

The archaeological contexts documented during excavations at K'axob represent, in many cases, the context of chipped stone deposition rather than use. The nineteen types of tools were recovered from ten different contexts (table 11.10). In the interest of clarifying broad patterns of deposition, some of the contexts listed in table 11.10 (and table 11.11) represent combinations of contextual categories. For instance, the categories of surface, plowzone, and topzone have been merged, as have those of pit and sherd-lined pit. Midden deposits reused as construction fill were initially coded separately, but their

content so closely matched that of primary midden deposits that these two categories have been merged. Similarly, several variations on construction fill were noted in the field, but here all have been collapsed into a single category (see tables 11.10 and 11.11). Below, each tool-bearing context is discussed in descending order of tool frequency.

As might be expected, midden deposits yielded over 30% of all tools, but this context was closely followed by construction fill, within which almost 25% of tools had been deposited. Both contexts enjoyed the highest diversity of tool types, although oval bifaces tended to be more common in construction fill while nondiagnostic tools and unstemmed macroblade fragments were more frequently retrieved from midden contexts. Intrusive pit features and surface materials each yielded over 10% of the tool sample. Oval bifaces and nondiagnostic bifaces were frequent in both contexts, but intrusive pits also yielded a significant proportion of unstemmed macroblades. A high proportion (over 8%) of total tools were retrieved from burial fill, which is not surprising considering the fact that the material used to refill burial pits often consisted of nearby midden material. A closer examination of the tools from burial fill revealed that only one of the thirty-six tools was complete, and that was a reworked biface. Only one stone tool was ever noted by excavators to have been clearly associated with a burial interment, and that tool was a ground and polished jade celt (see chapter 13). Floor contexts yielded a total of thirty-four tools (nearly 8% of the total), and seven of these were complete. This hopeful sign of in situ floor deposits is dashed, however, by the fact that the majority of tools were recovered from the matrix of floors and were likely deposited as floor ballast. Ironically, a more optimistic context for in situ artifacts is presented by wall tumble, which contributed 3.2% (n = 14) of the tool total, including two of the small, Postclassic projectile points. Heavily weighted toward bifaces, hammerstones, and projectile points, this context may reflect activities undertaken amid the collapsed debris of abandoned or derelict structures. Often found close to the surface, contexts of wall tumble show the least amount of site maintenance and thus may reflect actual activity sets as opposed to ultimate discard locations. A similar situation may prevail for the five nondiagnostic bifaces retrieved from retaining or free-standing walls (1.2% of the total). Conceivably these bifaces were part of the construction material, but it is also possible that they were stashed within a wall for later use and never retrieved. Fire features constitute the context least likely to be one of tool deposition as only one nondiagnostic biface and two unstemmed macroblade fragments (0.7% of the total) were recovered from it.

The final context, containing slightly more tools than either fire features or walls, consists of caches that yielded a total of seven tools (1.6%). Although small in number, these tools were purposefully deposited and thus do represent in situ artifacts from five cache deposits. The largest cache of stone tools was encountered within an Early Nohalk'ax construction unit at operation 7 (see chapter 4), which contained an offering of two complete stemmed macroblades and one partial biface (figure 11.16). Another complete stemmed macroblade was retrieved from the base of a large flat-bottomed bowl in a Late K'atabche'k'ax context at operation 12 (see chapter 14). Associated with skeletal material, this cache contained the secondary remains of a child and an adult male (see chapter 4). The four remaining biface fragments were found in less obvious K'atabche'k'ax-complex caches within operation 1. Zone 85 contained the proximal end of an oval biface and a small, reworked biface fragment, while zone 97 contained a 26 mm long, proximal fragment of an oval biface that was loosely associated with three jade beads and snake vertebrae. Finally, a cache from zone 121, principally an upright Laguna Verde

Incised vessel, also contained a 45 mm long distal fragment of a thin biface with a tapered bit. Stone tools were not the only kind of chipped stone to have been associated with caches, as we shall see shortly.

The high density of debitage in the K'axob chipped stone sample was recovered from a higher diversity of archaeological contexts than those within which stone tools were found (table 11.11). In addition to the ten contexts described above, debitage was encountered in postholes, in paleosol at the base of operation 1, and in low densities from several contexts grouped here as miscellaneous (table 11.11). Midden contexts, once again, top the list, containing 35.1% of the total debitage and some of the highest overall diversity (only quarry blanks and tranchet flakes were absent). In a departure from tool contexts, however, burials contain the second highest amounts of debitage (almost 22%, primarily flakes and flake fragments), thus displacing construction fill contexts to third place. The frequent occurrence of flakes in burial fill is partly the result of the practice of using midden material to back fill interments (as mentioned above), but other more purposeful behaviors, discussed below, also contributed to the high proportion. Cobbles are the only debitage type missing from construction fill that yielded 15% of the total debitage. The lack of cobbles may be an indicator of the high value placed on raw material at K'axob. Once again, a respectable percentage of chipped stone (8%) was excavated from floor contexts or, more properly stated, floor ballast, representing a large diversity of types (absent are quarry blanks, tranchet flakes, and cobbles). Paleosol is next in relative proportion, garnering almost 5% of the debitage. But diversity is sharply reduced within this context as 87% of the debitage consisted of flakes and flake fragments. The same can be said of debitage from cache contexts that contributed 4.4% to the total (more on this context below). The significance of the low diversity of debitage types in paleosol and cache contexts is heightened by the fact that the contexts of pit, surface, and posthole—each contributing the lower proportions of 3%, 2.1%, and 1.9%, respectively—exhibit a greater diversity of debitage types (table 11.11). The final four contexts—fire feature, wall tumble, intact wall, and miscellaneous—each contributed less than 2% of the total debitage tally.

The distribution of debitage types across the thirteen contexts appears primarily to be a function of sample size; that is, the three most frequent types—flakes, flake fragments, and fire shatter—were found in

Figure 11.16 Cached offering of two complete stemmed macroblades and a biface fragment from an Early Nohalk'ax construction unit within operation 7, zone 6a, square B

every single context. The next two most frequent types—angular debris and cores—were absent only from miscellaneous contexts and wall contexts (cores were also missing from cache contexts). Frequencies vary by context, however, and this variation could be explored in further detail. The prevailing impression of the contextual analysis of the debitage, however, is that much of it reflects the final contexts of discard or deposition within an actively maintained and continually rebuilt environment. A subset of the debitage from K'atabche'k'ax burials and caches provides a very important exception to this generalization.

RITUAL SCATTERING OF FLAKES

In the course of excavating operation 1, excavators noted that several burials and one cache yielded high densities of microdebitage. These contexts included the two focal Terminal K'atabche'k'ax multiple interments (burials 1-1 and 1-2) along with a Late K'atabche'k'ax flexed burial, 1-13 (see chapter 6). The Late K'atabche'k'ax cache, which has been dubbed the "quad cache" due to the cruciform arrangement of four small bowls, provides the fourth and final case of a ritual deposit with large amounts of associated microdebitage. Some of the more striking characteristics of this microdebitage are summarized in table 11.12. First of all, flakes and flake fragments dominate these contexts (98% of the total). Among the four contexts, debitage dimensions range, on average, between 7 and 15 mm in length, 7 and 13 mm in width, and 1 and 3 mm in thickness, significantly smaller than the flake dimensions for the entire itemized sample (see table 11.4). The preferred raw material, clearly, is NBC (99% of the flakes). Contrary to the prevalence of burning in the flake assemblage as a whole, a meager 7% of this debitage was burned. This fact indicates that the physical context into which the debitage was deposited was not exposed to environmental influences but, rather, was quickly sealed. Almost 20% of the flakes from these special deposits contained bifacial platforms, indicating that the core under reduction was bifacial. In three out of four contexts, incidence of use-polish on the dorsal face of flakes and flake fragments was greater than 40%, indicating that the bifaces under reduction were well-used tools, most likely oval bifaces.

Visually, the most striking quality of the reduction debris is the color of the microdebitage. All of the reduction events were undertaken with golden northern Belizean chert. The color yellow, *k'an* in Yucatec Mayan, is the color of ripe maize, so, metaphorically, the scattering of golden microdebitage may have been akin to a scattering of "durable" maize kernels or pollen. At this time, such reduction events at K'axob are known from a very limited time period, being restricted to Late and Terminal K'atabche'k'ax times, the time during which northern Belizean chert begins to dominate the K'axob chipped stone assemblage. In all cases, the scattering of golden chert micodebitage occurred in conjunction with rituals that featured the quadripartite motif. Within the three burial contexts, the cross motif had been painted on the base of bowls interred with burials 1-1, 1-2, and 1-13. For the cache context, four small bowls had been arranged to form a quadripartite pattern (see chapter 4). In chapter 16, Headrick argues persuasively that the cross motif indicates the centrality of a place and the authority of those who are marked by it. The scattering of golden debitage that took place during the sealing of these ritual contexts is a further indication of the singular importance of the cache and the three burials to residents of K'axob during K'atabche'k'ax times.

CONCLUDING THOUGHTS

The foregoing presentation of the chipped chert and chalcedony tools and debitage of K'axob has produced information relevant to some of the issues outlined in the opening of this chapter. First of all, do the K'axob lithics answer questions regarding wetland reclamation? That is, are there pronounced temporal patterns in the incidence of polish or the presence of the oval biface? The analysis has shown that oval bifaces are present at K'axob from Early Chaakk'ax times but that they do increase in frequency through time, peaking in this sample during the Early Classic period. The

incidence of use-polish, present throughout the sequence, also increases proportionally through time. But there is no dramatic introduction of a new tool or a sudden appearance of use-polish on oval bifaces. The constancy of the pattern suggests that, if use-polish and oval bifaces are truly associated with wetland farming, then this type of agriculture was practiced from the first settlement of K'axob. Limited support is provided for the notion that wetland farming became more intensive through time.

Although there is no sudden introduction of new tool forms, there is a fairly abrupt cessation of flakes removed from ground and polished celts as well as T-shaped unifaces. To the extent that polished celts may have been land-clearance tools, the presence of these flakes in Chaakk'ax layers, as well as their absence from upper layers, suggests that the first settlers of K'axob did not move into a cleared environment; rather, Chaakk'ax farmers were involved in forest-clearance activities that required the use of large ground stone celts. Apparently, whoever used the land prior to the founding of the village of K'axob did not affect the forest in a manner that precluded the need for forest-clearance tools. Judging from the paucity of these diagnostic flakes in upper levels, maintenance of a domesticated agricultural landscape around K'axob was achieved with lower-mass cutting tools, perhaps the oval biface.

K'axob chipped stone, particularly debitage, has yielded information relevant to understanding changes in household provisioning. The identification of a chert, other than NBC, in the lowest levels of operation 1 indicates that patterns of household provisioning during the Middle Formative period were qualitatively different from those of the Late Formative and Classic periods. The exact provenience of "other chert" is not known, but it occurs at K'axob as flakes that are slightly larger and contain more cortex than NBC flakes, suggesting that this material was acquired in a less processed state. "Other chert" flakes also exhibit high percentages of bifacial platforms and use-polish, indicating that this material was not used in the expedient fashion in which chalcedony was utilized. All in all, the presence and characteristics of non-NBC chert suggest that it was used to produce tools at K'axob during Chaakk'ax times.

Trends in raw material classes indicate an increased presence of NBC starting with Late K'atabche'k'ax times, around 200 BC. As this date coincides with the earliest documented concentrated debitage deposits at

Table 11.12 Debitage from lithic reduction events at four ritual contexts, operation 1

Zone No.	Context	n	Av. Dimensions (mm)			Debitage Type					Raw Material			Condition		Type of Platform			Polish	
			L	W	Th	Flake	Flake Fragment	Fire Shatter	Angular Debris	Unknown	NBC	Chalcedony	Other Chert	Not Burned	Burned	Absent	Bifacial	Simple	Absent	Present
15	Burial	12	14.8	13	3.2	7	2	1	2	1	10	–	1	10	2	4	2	6	9	3
18	Burial	142	10.8	11.4	1.2	92	50	–	–	1	141	–	–	136	6	50	29	63	84	58
78	Burial	19	6.8	7	1	10	9	–	–	–	19	–	–	19	–	9	4	6	9	10
77	Cache	198	7.1	7	1.1	111	83	4	–	–	197	1	–	179	19	92	38	68	109	89
Total		371				220	144	5	2	2	367	1	1	344	27	155	73	143	211	160
%						59.3	38.8	1.3	0.5	0.5	98.9	0.3	0.3	92.7	7.3	41.8	19.7	38.5	56.9	43.1

Colha, could the shift in raw material proportions (decreased other chert along with decreased chalcedony and increased NBC) documented at K'axob represent the inception of the Colha stone tool trading network? Quite probably this is the case as the shift in raw materials is accompanied by a lack of what Rovner and Lewenstein (1997:11) refer to as "intermediate products—items terminated before reaching end-product status owing to error, breakage, flaw, or simple failure to complete the process."

Regardless of the true meaning of the shift in raw material classes, the chipped stone provides strong evidence that the Middle Formative period was qualitatively different from later times. Greater access to raw materials is not only reflected in the chipped stone but also in the ground stone (see chapter 13) and in pottery pastes (see chapter 7). The first settlers of K'axob may have been colonizing new lands, but they did so while maintaining a network of supply zones, the scale of which was never duplicated during later times.

While K'atabche'k'ax times appear to have ushered in a narrowing and a formalization of supply lines, certain tool forms (such as the stemmed macroblade) appear, for the first time, in ritual contexts. A putative spear tip, the stemmed macroblade may have been linked to distinctions in status and power that were formalized during this time. This tool type was distributed to the west as far as the Upper Grijalva basin (Clark 1988:63) and, on average, 90 km from its point of production at Colha (Santone 1997:77). K'axob was just one of the many far-flung recipients of this elegant fabrication. K'atabche'k'ax times witnessed internal elaboration and the formalization of authority structures within K'axob. The reduction of golden bifaces of northern Belizean chert in elaborate mortuary and cache rituals represents just one aspect of this process, albeit one that provides a glimpse into the multivalent qualities of the tools of the trade.

ENDNOTES

1. In Highland New Guinea, Steensberg (1980:14) notes that hafted axes were placed within ditches "so that the hafting can absorb moisture and tighten up again." The wooden haft and organic binding would absorb water, swell, and tighten around the stone blade.

2. This finding lends support to an autochthonous model of Maya settlement growth (as opposed to rapid colonization) in the eastern lowlands.

Chapter 12
Related CD Resources

Obsidian

OBSIDIAN BLADES AND SOURCE AREAS[1]

PATRICIA A. MCANANY

Volcanic glass from the southern highlands serves as an indicator of the macroregional connectivity of a Lowland Maya locale. Along with greenstone, obsidian was a valued material that could be acquired only through the establishment and maintenance of multinodal trading networks. Like greenstone, obsidian appears to have been valued for its surface qualities; that is, its smoky gray translucence. The optical characteristics of this material complemented the superior cutting ability of volcanic glass, rendering it a desirable implement for both domestic and ritual activities. In southern Mesoamerica, obsidian extraction was formalized into polyhedral core and prismatic blade production by the Middle Formative period; Clark (1987:278–281) has suggested that this formalization indicated a consolidation of political power at focal points on the landscape. In other words, obsidian came to possess status-enhancing properties that engendered very efficient modes of packaging and distribution. The special status of obsidian within the Maya Lowlands is germane to K'axob, a village founded in the Middle

Formative and that appears to have been well supplied with high-quality and locally traded chert (a thin flake of which was only marginally less sharp than an obsidian blade). However, as we shall see, K'axob was rather poorly supplied with highland volcanic glass.

This finding is paradoxical since K'axob is located astride a wetland that drains into the New River and, thus, was well positioned to take advantage of a New River trade corridor. Despite this fortuitous location, the Formative to Early Classic deposits of K'axob (which span nearly 1,000 years) contained only 143 small pieces of obsidian that weigh a total of 143 g (see *Obsidian Database*). While the seven excavation units reported here admittedly derive from only a fraction of the total universe of construction and occupational deposits at K'axob, nevertheless the conclusion that importation of massive amounts of obsidian was not a high priority, or perhaps not a possibility at Formative K'axob, is inescapable.

OBSIDIAN TYPES AND TEMPORALITY

As might be predicted, prismatic blades comprise 88% of the 143 pieces of K'axob obsidian, while flakes (debris lacking straight, parallel dorsal ridges as well as the overall dimensions of a blade) are a distant second (9%); the final 3% is comprised of four polyhedral core fragments (table 12.1 and figure 12.1). Spatially, the obsidian is distributed throughout the seven excavation units in a manner that is not proportionate to the size of the excavation units (table 12.1). For instance, the largest excavation unit, operation 1, yielded only 18% (n = 25) of the obsidian while operation 13, the smallest unit, comprises nearly 5% of the sample. The frequency of obsidian, therefore, is not simply a function of the volume of excavated deposits. On the other hand, when obsidian is cross-tabulated with a temporally sensitive variable such as ceramic complex, clear trends emerge (table 12.1).

Stratified Chaakk'ax (Middle Formative period) deposits are known only from operation 1, and it is clear that obsidian is quite infrequent in layers of this time period and that it exists only as blade fragments (figure 12.2). During the Late Formative, the frequency of obsidian increases at K'axob. During the early facet of the K'atabche'k'ax complex, obsidian is present in all operations (1, 10, and 11) at which construction has been documented. Moreover, one polyhedral core fragment was recovered from a midden in operation 11 (zone 92). Late K'atabche'k'ax times see only a marginal increase in obsidian despite the pronounced upsurge in construction activity at K'axob. Once again, obsidian was recovered from all excavation locales yielding Late K'atabche'k'ax construction phases. Sixteen of the eighteen pieces of Late K'atabche'k'ax obsidian are prismatic blade fragments; the remaining two are flakes. Yet another modest increase in obsidian is observed during Terminal K'atabche'k'ax times (n = 23), during which blades again dominate the collection with only four pieces classified as flakes.

To summarize the Late Formative pattern, obsidian frequencies plateau at a very low level during the K'atabche'k'ax complex, a time of dramatic population growth and village consolidation. Several excavation units contained little or no evidence of construction activity after K'atabche'k'ax times (see chapter 3). The ensuing early facet of the Nohalk'ax complex (Early Classic period) is represented by only a single construction phase at operations 1, 10, 11, and 12. Peak construction activity during this time occurred at

Figure 12.1 Two fragments of exhausted polyhedral obsidian cores (top row) and two possible core-rejuvenation flakes (bottom row). Note, photo taken after obsidian was sectioned for INAA. *All photos by K'axob Project*

Figure 12.2 Six obsidian prismatic-blade fragments from Chaakk'ax-complex deposits (three were sourced to San Martín Jilotepeque). Note: photo taken after obsidian sectioned for INAA.

Table 12.1 K'axob obsidian frequencies tabulated by type, ceramic complex, and operation

| | TYPE OF OBSIDIAN | | | | | CERAMIC COMPLEX | | | | | | |
| | | | | | | CHAAKK'AX | | K'ATABCHE'K'AX | | | NOHALK'AX | |
Operation no.	Prismatic Blade	Poly-hedral Core	Flake	Total	%	Early	Late	Early	Late	Terminal	Early	Surface
1	24	1	0	25	21	3	3	9	1	1	3	5
7	22	0	1	23	19	–*	–	–	1	7	14	1
8	8	0	1	9	7	–	–	–	3	2	–	4
10	22**	2	0	2	2	–	–	3	3	0	9	9
11	31	1	6	38	31	–	–	3	6	11	14	4
12	12	0	5	17	14	–	–	–	4	2	4	7
13	7	0	0	7	6	–	–	–	–	–	6	1
Total	126	4	13	143	100	3	3	15	18	23	50	31
% of Total	88	3	9	100								

* indicates no deposits dating to that ceramic complex.
** includes 1 blade reworked into a side-notched projectile point.

operations 7 and 13 and yielded evidence of five and three construction phases, respectively. Nevertheless, fifty pieces of obsidian (including three flakes and two polyhedral core fragments) were recovered from these Early Classic deposits, which indicates an indubitable supply increase at K'axob. Interestingly, while 28% of the Early Nohalk'ax obsidian (n = 14) came from operation 7 and 12% (n = 6) from operation 13, both polyhedral cores of this time period were found in the construction fill of operation 10 (zone 3a). Second in frequency only to the Early Nohalk'ax deposits, the surfaces of the seven excavation units yielded a total of thirty-one pieces of obsidian, including four flakes and one polyhedral core. As discussed below, the single piece of obsidian that was not sourced to Guatemala also came from the surface. The surface obsidian could date to any time period between the Late Classic and the start of the Colonial period. The presence of Late Postclassic-style projectile points from the surfaces of operations 1 and 8 (see chapter 11) as well as a large assemblage of net sinkers in the surficial layer of operation 10 (see chapter 10) suggests that the raised platforms of K'axob were utilized long after they ceased to be actively constructed and maintained domiciles.

SOURCE OF K'AXOB OBSIDIAN

The longitudinal nature of the K'axob obsidian sample renders it a prime candidate for independent evaluation of the thesis of sequential supply. This model suggests that highland Guatemalan obsidian trade commenced with supply from the San Martín Jilotepeque source during the Middle Formative, transferred to El Chayal during the Late Formative and through the Classic period, and culminated with a further shift to the eastern source of Ixtepeque (Nelson 1989:Fig. 2; Dreiss and Brown 1989:Fig. 3). Thirty-seven percent (n = 53) of the obsidian was submitted for source determination by instrumental neutron activation analysis at the University of Missouri Research Reactor. The sample was selected based on temporal, contextual, and technological considerations and should not be considered random. All four polyhedral core fragments were sourced, 33% of the flakes (n = 4) and 36% of the prismatic blades (n = 45). Given the predictable chemical signature of Guatemalan obsidian (Glascock et al. 1994), the majority of the samples were sourced using the abbreviated NAA procedure (Glascock, personal communication, 18 August 1994).

Table 12.2 Obsidian frequencies tabulated by source areas, method of platform preparation, and type of fragment

Ceramic Complex	OBSIDIAN SOURCE					METHOD OF PLATFORM PREPARATION		TYPE OF OBSIDIAN FRAGMENT			
	San Martín Jilotepeque	El Chayal	Ixtepeque	Pico de Orizaba	Total	Grinding	Striations	Proximal	Medial	Distal	Total
E. Chaakk'ax	1	0	0	0	1	0	0	1	2	0	3
L. Chaakk'ax	2	0	0	0	2	0	0	0	2	1	3
E. K'atabche'k'ax	5	1	1	0	7	2	1	5	7	3	15
L. K'atabche'k'ax	3	6	1	0	10	0	0	0	17	1	18
T. K'atabche'k'ax	2	5	2	0	9	3	1	5	16	2	23
E. Nohalk'ax	0	14	2	0	16	4	3	13	33	4	50
Surface	0	4	3	1	8	2	3	8	20	3	31
Total	13	30	9	1	53	11	8	32	97	14	143
% of Total	24%	57%	17%	2%	100%			22%	68%	10%	100%

Results provide modified support for the Nelson, Dreiss, and Brown model of sequential obsidian suppliers. Specifically, when the fifty-three pieces of sourced obsidian are arrayed against the temporal indicator of ceramic complex, a gradual shift over time in the three highland Guatemalan source areas can be detected (table 12.2). For instance, the three sourced blade fragments from Chaakk'ax deposits are indeed found to have originated at San Martín Jilotepeque. This Formative period source continues to provide K'axob with modest amounts of obsidian through K'atabche'k'ax times, including one polyhedral core fragment from an Early K'atabche'k'ax midden in operation 11 (zone 92). No sourced flakes derived from the San Martín source. In conformance to the Nelson, Dreiss, and Brown model, K'axob does not acquire any obsidian from the El Chayal source until the beginning of the K'atabche'k'ax complex. Importation peaked during Early Nohalk'ax times, when fourteen of the sixteen pieces of sourced obsidian were chemically linked to El Chayal. The remaining three polyhedral cores as well as three of the four sourced flakes were also fabricated of El Chayal obsidian. One of the polyhedral cores was collected from the surficial layer of operation 1 and thus cannot be associated with a specific time period, but the other two were retrieved from Early Nohalk'ax construction fill in operation 10 (zone 3a).

Increased access to El Chayal obsidian and possible on-site reduction during the Early Classic period is indicated by the sourcing results. Given the fact that the excavations reported in this volume contained no later Classic period deposits, a very low frequency of Ixtepeque obsidian is to be expected. Nevertheless, nine of the fifty-three samples were sourced to Ixtepeque (table 12.2), although one-third of the Ixtepeque obsidian derived from surficial layers of the excavations, including a flake from the top zone of operation 8. As with obsidian from the El Chayal source, Ixtepeque obsidian is absent from K'axob before Late Formative times (table 12.2). Unlike the El Chayal material, however, the Ixtepeque source is represented by continued low frequencies throughout K'atabche'k'ax and Early Nohalk'ax times and does not exhibit much of an increase even in the surficial layers.

In the future, source analysis of K'axob obsidian from stratified deposits of Late Nohalk'ax and Witsk'ax complexes will no doubt clarify the role of the Ixtepeque source in later patterns of obsidian acquisition. A "ringer" in the obsidian source determinations is represented by a 16 mm long prismatic blade fragment that had been reworked into a side-notched projectile point and ultimately discarded in the top zone of operation 10. Sourced to the Veracruz, Mexico, obsidian outcrop at Pico de

Orizaba, this small projectile was transported over 900 km and is the most exotic import yet found at K'axob. Its form and depositional context suggest that it, along with the seven other sourced pieces of surficial obsidian, likely refers to Epiclassic and Postclassic utilization of platform surfaces. Overall, the El Chayal source dominates the sample; over 57% (n = 30) of the sourced pieces match this quarry source. Second in frequency is San Martín Jilotepeque, which comprises 24% (n = 13) of the sample, and third is Ixtepeque, which comprises 17% (n = 9) of the sample. Unlike sites such as Tikal, where Mexican imports represent a significant percentage of obsidian (Moholy Nagy 1999:Table 2), no highland Mexican obsidian sources are represented in this sample. This absence provides another indicator of the local nature of K'axob procurement networks.

OBSIDIAN DIMENSIONS AND TECHNOLOGY OF BLADE PRODUCTION

In an effort to determine whether techniques of platform preparation were temporally sensitive or restricted to certain source areas, the presence of either a ground or striated surface on the platform of both blades and flakes was recorded (no proximal core fragments were recovered). Observations were based on examination with a 5X hand lens. A total of eleven platform-bearing pieces (nine blades and two flakes) showed evidence of grinding, while eight platform surfaces (all of blades) were roughened by abrasion, which produced a pattern of striations. Temporal trends are weak but do indicate that platforms were more frequently ground than striated during K'atabche'k'ax times (table 12.2). Of the two flakes that exhibited a ground platform, one was recovered from the top zone of operation 8 while the other was retrieved from a stratified Early Nohalk'ax deposit from operation 12 (zone 2a). Because six of the eight blades with striated platforms hail from upper stratigraphic units (either surface layers or Early Nohalk'ax deposits), one might suspect that platforms prepared via striations would be positively correlated with the latest Ixtepeque source. In fact, the pattern is just the opposite. Of the obsidian sourced to Ixtepeque, all three platform-bearing artifacts were ground while only one of the three El Chayal platform-bearing blades was ground (the other two bore evidence of striations). Ground platforms are often associated with highland Mexican Postclassic polyhedral core-reduction techniques, but the K'axob

Figure 12.3 Two unusually long prismatic blades from K'axob: left, a proximal fragment from an Early K'atabche'k'ax midden in operation 10 (zone 11a). Blade exhibits a ground platform and was sourced to Ixtepeque; right, distal fragment from Late K'atabche'k'ax burial in operation 11 (zone 16a) sourced to El Chayal. Note: photo taken after obsidian sectioned for INAA.

data indicate that the platforms of Ixtepeque prismatic blades were ground as early as the Early Classic period.

The lack of unequivocal trends in platform preparation could be linked to the extremely fragmentary nature of the K'axob obsidian sample; 22% are proximal fragments (n = 32), 68% are medial portions (n = 97), and the remaining 10% (n = 14) are classified as distal fragments (table 12.2). In short, there are no complete specimens of prismatic blades, polyhedral cores, or even flakes, and less than one-fifth of the sample contains a remnant of a platform. During all time periods, medial fragments, by far, are the most common (table 12.2). Their higher frequency relative to proximal and distal fragments probably relates to the fact that prismatic blades, in particular, may break transversely at more than one place, creating multiple medial fragments but always only one proximal and one distal fragment.

Dimensional characteristics of the K'axob obsidian further illustrate the small, fragmentary state of this material class and also the standardization in the width and thickness of the prismatic blades that were

Table 12.3 Summary statistics for dimensional variables of K'axob obsidian

Type	n	LENGTH (mm)				WIDTH (mm)				THICKNESS (mm)			
		mean	median	SD*	CV**	mean	median	SD	CV	mean	median	SD	CV
Prismatic Blade	126	20.6	19	10.7	0.519	11	11	2.9	0.264	2.4	2	0.7	0.292
Polyhedral Core	4	21.8	23.5	11.7	0.537	10.3	9.8	3.5	0.34	6.9	7.35	3.7	0.536
Flake	13	18.8	12	12.6	0.67	14.2	12	7.3	0.514	2.9	3	1.3	0.448

*SD for Standard Deviation.
**CV for Coefficiant of Variation

possibly produced at K'axob but were more likely imported from elsewhere (table 12.3). Average length of a blade was just under 21 mm, while average width was 11 mm and average thickness 2.4 mm. These dimensions compare favorably with the obsidian of nearby Cuello (Johnson 1991:Tables 8.7, 8.10). As might be predicted, the length dimension of K'axob blade fragments exhibited the greatest variability, with a coefficient of variation (CV) of 0.519 (CV = standard deviation/mean) indicating only that the point of breakage along a blade was more variable than its width or thickness. In fact, most blade fragments ranged in length from 5 mm to 43 mm; two exceptionally long blades measured 69 and 71 mm (see figure 12.3). In contrast, blade width and thickness, controlled in the production rather than in the breakage stage, exhibited much lower CV values of 0.264 and 0.292, respectively. Standardization in the production of blades is further clarified by comparison with the coefficients of variation for polyhedral core and flake dimensions, most of which exhibit a CV that is twice the size of blade width and thickness (table 12.3). One might expect the dimensions of polyhedral core and flake fragments that are closely linked with the production process to greatly exceed those of blade fragments; however, the average dimensions of the four core fragments exceed those of blades by only 1 mm in length and 4.5 mm in thickness. On average, flake fragments are about 2 mm shorter than blades, 3 mm wider, and less than 1 mm thicker (table 12.3). Core fragments found at K'axob resemble the "exhausted polyhedral core" illustrated as the endpoint of a core-reduction sequence by Clark and Bryant (1997:Fig. 3). The simple presence of four

exhausted polyhedral core fragments might indicate that limited blade production took place at K'axob. Conversely, due to the limited access to volcanic glass, small polyhedral core fragments, in and of themselves, could conceivably have been exchange items. Overall, dimensional data for K'axob obsidian suggest that prismatic blades, in particular, were not discarded until their size diminished to the point at which they were no longer useable; in short, at K'axob, volcanic glass was a highly curated resource.

OBSIDIAN IN CONTEXT

Further insight into obsidian use at K'axob can be gleaned from a consideration of contextual patterning in the distribution of obsidian. The sample of K'axob obsidian can be said to derive from six different types of deposits. The first—"surface"—includes all obsidian found within 10 cm of the modern ground surface while the other five include the following stratified contexts: midden, construction fill, burial, cache, and intrusive pits (such as postholes, sherd-lined pits, and fire features). When arrayed against the seven operations, significant trends can be detected (table 12.4). All twenty-five pieces of obsidian from operation 1 were recovered from either a midden or a unit of construction fill. No obsidian was found in the surface zone, nor was obsidian included in any of the many burials and cache deposits of operation 1. While midden and construction fill also formed the primary matrices of obsidian discard within operation 7, volcanic glass was also found on the surface, within domestic intrusive pit features, and within a cache (operation 7, zone 58, see figure 12.4).

Table 12.4 Obsidian frequencies tabulated by type of context

	FREQUENCY PER TYPE OF CONTEXT						
Operation no.	Surface	Midden	Construction Fill	Burial	Cache	Intrusive Pit or Posthole	Total
1	0	10	15	0	0	0	25
7	1	3	14	0	1	4	23
8	4	2	1	2	0	0	9
10	9	3	12	0	0	0	24
11	4	3	28	1	0	2	38
12	7	8	2	0	0	0	17
13	1	1	5	0	0	0	7
Total	26	30	77	3	1	6	143
% of Total	18%	21%	54%	2%	1%	4%	100%

The use of obsidian in ritual contexts is also apparent in operation 8, where blade fragments were placed in burial contexts (figure 12.5). Specifically, a medial fragment of an El Chayal obsidian blade and a greenstone bead were placed in the mouth of an old adult male who was then buried in a flexed posture. He held a mammiform tetrapodal pottery vessel (vessel 101) that had been carved with a mat design (burial 8-5, operation 8, zone 13; for additional information see chapters 6, 9, and 15). Stratigraphically above this Late K'atabche'k'ax interment, two males (a young and a middle-aged adult) were placed in a secondary interment (burials 8-3a and 8-3b). Around them, greenstone fragments were scattered along with large sherds from three mammiform tetrapods (vessels 096, 097, and 098), a carved shell bead, and a proximal fragment of an Ixtepeque obsidian blade (again, see chapters 6, 9, and 15 for detailed information).

Three additional pieces of obsidian were found in midden and construction fill contexts of operation 8, and four were recovered from the surface. Operations 10, 12, and 13 yielded obsidian from a restricted set of deposits that did not include any overtly ritual contexts or domestic pit deposits; rather, obsidian was found only within the surface layer and in stratified midden deposits and units of construction fill. Finally, the deposit types from which obsidian was recovered within operation 11 were as diverse as were those of operation 7. In addition to the contexts of surface, midden, and construction

fill, two intrusive pit features contained obsidian, and one burial may have been associated with a blade fragment. The association is unclear because the context in question (a young adult male, burial 11-3, zone 16) was placed upside down in a wrapped and seated position at the base of a chultun. Although several burial accoutrements were placed alongside him (a pottery vessel, a shell pendant, and a fragment of coral), the distal fragment of the El Chayal obsidian blade in question could have been associated with the general refuse in the pit rather than with the burial itself.

Overall, the context of construction fill yielded the largest fraction (54%, n = 77) of recovered obsidian, with midden contexts providing another 21% (n = 30) and the surface providing 18% (n = 26). Thus, 93% of the obsidian came from discard contexts that are not overtly ritual. The remaining 7% come from a combination of domestic pit features (4%), burials (2%), and a cache (1%). The conclusion seems to be that obsidian did not play an important role in the formation of the many ritual deposits of K'axob. Since volcanic glass was not readily available to the residents of K'axob, they apparently did not incorporate it into their ritual practices in the same manner as they did golden-colored northern Belizean chert (see chapter 11). Since 99% of the sourced obsidian from the contexts described above derived from three southern highland sources, it is possible that volcanic glass from one or more of the sources was incorporated preferentially into ritual deposits. While

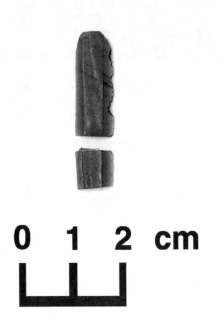

Figure 12.4 Medial fragment of Ixtepeque prismatic blade found with a small, inverted Sierra Red bowl in a Terminal K'atabche'k'ax cache from operation 7 (zone 58).

it is true that obsidian from San Martín Jilotepeque was found only in construction and midden deposits, it is also true that this obsidian comes only from operation 1 (and specifically from its lower levels), where obsidian was not incorporated into ritual deposits. Over 63% (n = 19) of the sourced El Chayal obsidian was found in construction fill; only two pieces were associated with mortuary deposits. While Ixtepeque obsidian was more evenly distributed among the contexts of surface, midden, and construction fill, only two samples were linked with ritual deposits (a burial and a cache). The equal and low-level representation of both El Chayal and Ixtepeque obsidian in ritual deposits indicates that neither was used preferentially in overtly ritual contexts.

FINAL THOUGHTS ON SMOKY GRAY VOLCANIC GLASS

In conclusion, the proximity of K'axob to the New River transportation corridor did not translate into a strategic positioning for the acquisition of obsidian during the Formative period. Slightly higher rates of importation can be detected for the Early Classic period, but during both time periods obsidian appears to have been curated and utilized until it reached a highly fragmentary state. From the inception of its importation to K'axob during the Middle Formative period, obsidian arrived as prismatic blades; this pattern was also observed at Cuello (Johnson 1991:Table 8.6). In contrast, the earliest Formative period obsidian importation at Cahal Pech consisted of flakes rather than blades (Awe 1992:Fig. 93). A reduction technology based predominantly on flake production has also been noted for the Formative deposits of Copan (Aoyama 1999:53–78, 2001:Table 2). The majority of obsidian from K'axob consisted of small fragments of prismatic blades that exhibited a low coefficient of variation along the dimensions of width and thickness, suggesting some measure of standardization in blade production. Given the small number of polyhedral core fragments, it is doubtful that prismatic blade production actually took place at K'axob rather than at a larger nearby center. Sourcing of obsidian through INAA confirms published reports that Middle Formative contexts tend to yield obsidian that originated at the San Martín Jilotepeque source, with a shift to El Chayal during the latter

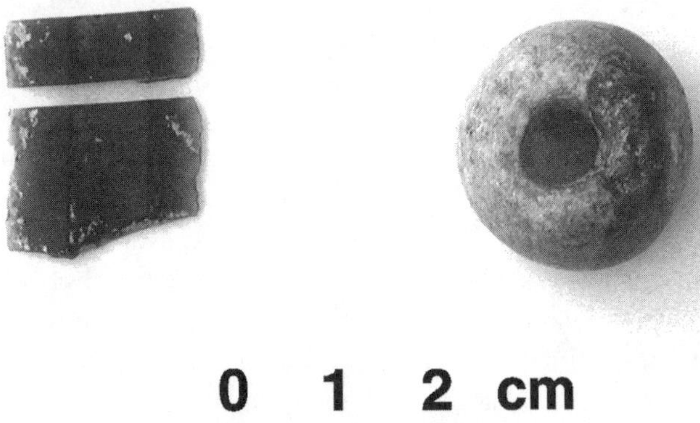

Figure 12.5 Medial fragment of El Chayal prismatic blade and greenstone bead found inside skull of burial 8-5 (operation 8, zone 13), a Late K'atabche'k'ax flexed interment. Note: photo taken after obsidian sectioned for INAA.

part of the Formative period and through the Classic period. The Ixtepeque source appears in low frequencies throughout the Late-to-Terminal Formative and Early Classic periods. The low proportion of Ixtepeque obsidian contrasts with Cuello, where a higher percentage of this source was detected (based on PIXE source analysis) within coeval deposits (see Hammond 1991d:198). The dearth of Late-to-Terminal Classic deposits in the excavation units reported on in this volume render it impossible to evaluate whether or not there was a later switch to Ixtepeque, as would be predicted. Perhaps as a result of the low volume of supply, obsidian from the highlands was seldom used in ritual deposits. Over 75% of the sample was recovered from either midden or construction fill, with only 3% coming from burials and caches.

The low frequency of obsidian is mirrored by a similar paucity of greenstone (n = 35; see chapter 15), another highly exotic material the acquisition of which required complex chains of negotiations. On the other hand, Caribbean seashells as well as high-quality chert from the vicinity of Colha are well represented in the earliest deposits of K'axob (see chapters 14 and 11, respectively). In short, villagers of K'axob seem to have maintained highly active single-nodal or short-distance exchange networks but less active long-distance networks. As a consequence, the array of cosmologically charged materials that was included in the ritual deposits of K'axob was drawn from a more locally defined universe.

ENDNOTE

1. The obsidian data set was coded originally by Victoria L. Bobo and revised by Justin P. Ebersole and Patricia A. McAnany. Source areas were determined by instrumental neutron activation analysis at the University of Missouri Nuclear Reactor Facility in 1994. INAA was supervised by Michael D. Glascock (Michael Glascock, personal communication, August 18, 1994, in a letter written to the author detailing the methods of INAA and the results).

Chapter 13
Related CD Resources

Ground & Polished Tools

CHAPTER 13

GROUND AND POLISHED STONE TOOLS

PATRICIA A. MCANANY AND JUSTIN P. EBERSOLE

The wetland and riverine landscape surrounding K'axob provided a wealth of plant and animal resources but little in the way of hard stone for the fabrication of tools. In chapters 11 and 12, the importation of chert, chalcedony, and obsidian was discussed; the former two were well represented at K'axob while the latter—a long-distance import—appeared in much lower frequencies. In this chapter, evidence pertaining to the acquisition and use of hard stone for the manufacture of ground and polished stone tools is presented and discussed. The substrate beneath K'axob is a soft, chalky limestone, locally called *sascab*, that was mined for construction material but that is not of sufficient hardness to create a ground stone tool such as a mano or metate. Although hard limestone was available less than 20 km to the west of K'axob at the Albion Island quarry, we shall see that limestone was not the preferred material for manos and metates; rather, a more desirable raw material—silcrete—was the most highly utilized raw material in the production of ground stone. Thus, the need to acquire suitable stone for ground

tools engendered yet another set of exchange relationships negotiated by the ancient inhabitants of K'axob.

TYPES OF GROUND AND POLISHED TOOLS

Because all hard stone had to be imported to K'axob, significant conservation efforts were expended to prolong the use life of stone tools, including the use of broken tool fragments for new purposes. This trend is apparent in both the chipped and ground stone assemblages. Keying into this ancient practice, excavators saved nearly all pieces of hard stone. Justin Ebersole, who analyzed the ground stone for his senior thesis (Ebersole 2001), found that many pieces displayed either remnants of a ground or polished surface or were geologically composed of an exotic material such as quartzite, which strongly suggested that the small, broken piece of stone must have once been a part of a valued mano or metate. The following typology of tools, therefore, includes both formally shaped tools as well as stone fragments. In total, excavations yielded 124 artifacts that

317

Table 13.1 Summary statistics for K'axob ground and polished stone tools

TOOL TYPE	n	% of Total	Length (mm) mean	SD*	CV**	Width (mm) mean	SD	CV	Thickness (mm) mean	SD	CV
Barkbeater	2	1.6	52.3	–	–	57.1	–	–	41.9	–	–
Celt	9	7.3	55.4	25.45	0.459	46.9	15.04	0.321	27.99	8.77	0.313
Large Stone Fragment	17	13.7	73.1	14.22	0.195	54.96	6.44	0.117	37.04	13.41	0.362
Mano	12	9.7	65.9	30.09	0.457	62.5	17.55	0.281	43.4	11.03	0.254
Metate	28	22.6	83.1	29.66	0.357	57.6	22.93	0.398	43.3	15.5	0.358
Percussion Tool	7	5.6	64.4	36.96	0.574	51	20.5	0.402	35.4	15.05	0.425
Rubbing Tool	5	4.0	43.7	21.99	0.503	31.8	13.37	0.42	20.34	11.11	0.546
Small Stone	3	2.4	41.2	–	–	35.3	–	–	26.5	–	–
Small Stone Fragment	32	25.8	39.8	10.4	0.261	31.1	8.84	0.284	20.1	7.99	0.398
Yuntun	9	7.3	54.6	10.25	0.188	51.2	6.7	0.131	–	–	–
Total	**124**	**100.0**									

* SD (Standard Deviation)
** CV (Coefficient of Variation)

had once been shaped by grinding and polishing (see *Ground and Polished Tools Database*). Tools were classified into the following nine types: bark beater, celt, large stone fragment, mano, metate, percussion tool, rubbing tool, small stones (and small stone fragments), and *yuntun*. Whenever possible, subtypes, based on morphology or assumed function, were also created. Frequencies and dimensional statistics (mean, standard deviation, and coefficient of variation), presented in table 13.1, reveal both the uneven spread of artifacts across the type categories as well as the highly fragmentary state of the ground stone from K'axob. For instance, the average value for metate length is 83.1 mm.

Fragments of two separate *bark beaters* were retrieved from an Early Chaakk'ax midden at K'axob (figure 13.1). These implements were used to pound the bark of *Ficus* spp. trees into paper. The largest fragment features a series of parallel grooves of two distinct widths running lengthwise on both broad surfaces. Additionally, there is a wide shallow groove that runs along the tool's equatorial circumference. This groove provides a means of hafting the tool to enable better leverage during pounding. While subtypes have been recognized, the presence of only three fragmentary pieces (two of which fit together) renders subtypes a futile exercise. In a recent survey of Mesoamerican ground stone, Garber (2001:301) reports that bark beaters generally appear at the end of the Preclassic period and persist through the Postclassic period. Nevertheless, from the nearby site of Cuello as well as the distant site of La Libertad in the Upper Grijalva Region, Hammond (1991c:189) and Clark (1988:138), respectively, report two bark beaters apiece from Middle Formative contexts. The discovery of such fragmentary pieces in a well-stratified Middle Formative midden from K'axob, along with other reports, pushes back the antiquity of paper-making technology in the Maya Lowlands.

Nine fragments of ground and polished *celts* were recovered from excavations. Generally, these tools are thought to have been used for tree felling and woodworking. No subtypes were designated in light of the fact that the celts were fragmentary and that there is little extant literature on morphological variation in celt form. Specimens were manufactured either from chert or chalcedony or a semiprecious stone such as

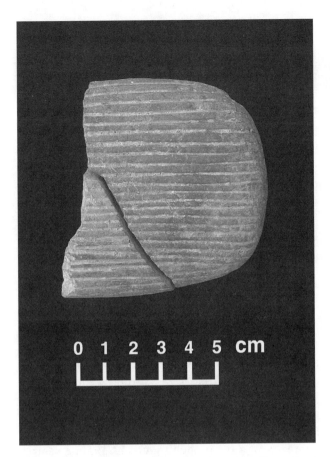

Figure 13.1 Bark beater from Early Chaakk'ax midden of operation 1 (zone 219). *All photos by K'axob Project staff*

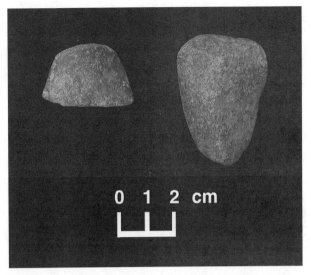

Figure 13.2 Two fragments of ground and polished celts: (left) jade celt from Terminal K'atabche'k'ax burial 1-45 in operation 1 (zone 236); (right) serpentinite celt fragment from paleosol of operation 1 (zone 70).

Figure 13.3 Drill support found in Early Nohalk'ax construction fill of operation 7, zone 4.

jade, serpentinite, or basalt (figure 13.2). Debitage from refurbishing the edges of celts has also been identified at K'axob and is discussed in chapter 11.

Unlike celts, which were carefully shaped, the next category, *large stone fragments* (as well as *small stone fragments*) represents a residual category of nonformal tools that nevertheless display evidence of a ground or polished surface or are the fragmentary remains of a ground tool fabricated from nonlocal material. The simple attribute of size differentiates the small from the large stone fragments (the latter displaying a length greater than 5.5 cm). Subtypes for these expedient tools follow a functional and morphological classificatory scheme (see *Ground and Polished Tools Database*). The seventeen large stone fragments represent a diverse group. Some appear to have been parts of once complete manos, metates, and other implements but were reused for various secondary purposes. For instance, one fragment has been subtyped as a *drill support*; it is a flat, tabular piece showing obvious burning and marring and surface pitting, seemingly from a drill device (figure 13.3). Thus, morphological characteristics

enabled its firm designation. A few other pieces, aside from the drill support, appear to be *smoothing* tools. A subtype labeled *vessel support* is also recognized. Within many traditional Maya houses, it is a common practice to support cooking vessels with cobble-sized fragments set in hearths. These hearthstones are likely to fracture due to heat stress, resulting in smaller fragments. Here, the subtype *vessel support* is employed for blocky stone fragments that are fire-fractured. A final subtype classification includes *lid* or possible *beehive plug*. This designation is based upon two artifacts exhibiting a flat,

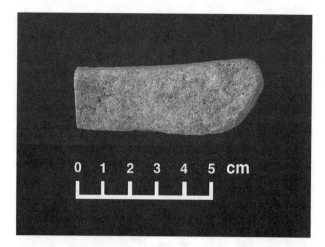

Figure 13.4 Turtleback metate fragment from operation 11, zone 20a, square A.

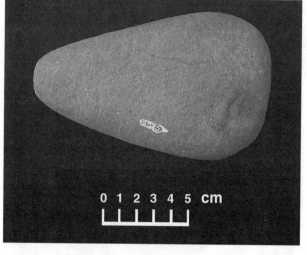

Figure 13.5 Percussion tool for pounding retrieved from Late Chaakk'ax redeposited midden in operation 1 (zone 160).

discoidal shape suggestive of a device used for capping a ceramic vessel or a hollow log beehive (ethnographic documentation of both is described by Sidrys 1983:298–299).

The twelve manos recovered from K'axob encompass a broad range of subtype designations. A mano itself is the hand-held counterpart to a metate and is used to abrade the substance placed on the quern's grinding surface. Known mano subtypes are based on morphological variation, which may or may not reflect functional variation. The classification proposed by Willey, Bullard, Glass, and Gifford (1965:457–462) for Barton Ramie is followed here. Subtypes include the following varieties: *square, rectangular thick, rectangular thin, round flat, circular, oval,* and *plano-convex* (see *Ground and Polished Tools Database*). Variations on each subtype appear in the K'axob sample of manos, but some of these subtypes are dubious as discrete categories since they likely represent the functional consequences of use-wear on a morphological shape. For example, over time a square mano will be worn down to a rectangular-thick and then rectangular-thin form (provided it does not break in the meantime). Similarly, circular forms may be worn into oval forms. The shape of a mano upon its archaeological deposition, therefore, depends on the grinding behavior of the individual using the tool as well as on the wear mechanics of the stone.

The most recognizable category is that of the *metate,* of which twenty-eight fragments were collected. This type classification reflects the well-known grinding quern, and there is no ambiguity surrounding its

functional attributes. Coe (1965b:599) identifies three subtypes that are common to most sites: *turtleback, rectangular block,* and *tripodal* (for listing of subtypes, see *Ground and Polished Tools Database*). The turtleback subtype (79% of the sample) was manufactured with a smoothed dorsal surface that broadly resembles the convexity of a turtle shell (figure 13.4). The ventral surface of these forms exhibits a trough of greater length than width and considerable depth (usually owing to extensive use-wear). The *rectangular block* form, of which there is only one example from K'axob, is a much more crudely shaped quern. It has a rough-hewn exterior and a dorsal surface that was modified into a blocky form. The ventral surface is demarcated by the presence of the basin or trough, which again is longer than it is wide. The final subtype is that of the *tripodal metate,* the most complex to manufacture. It is recognizable by its three conical legs and often by the fact that its grinding surface (ventral face) exhibits no trough as the entire ventral side is utilized evenly during grinding. One possible *tripodal metate fragment* was identified in the collection; four other metate pieces were too fragmentary to assign subtype.

Percussion tools, as the name implies, are those objects used for pounding, pecking, or otherwise striking another object. Seven such tools were noted in the ground stone sample, and they can be further subdivided (on the basis of impact scars on the exterior surface) into the following three subtypes: *pounder* (a large, hand-held ground stone tool; figure 13.5); *hammer* (smaller size and weight, likely to have been hafted); and *pecking tools* (small, usually cobble-sized implements that would have been hand-held for percussion work). All exhibit use-wear in the form of pitting and contusions on pointed and convex surfaces.

A category dubbed *rubbing tools* is represented by five artifacts. Some of these tools may have been used to smooth stucco, plaster, or to pack marl floors. Such *smoothers* are generally cobble-sized or larger pieces and exhibit one or more facets that were used to smooth surfaces. Such tools are modest versions of the more extensive mason's tool kit discovered at Dzibilchaltun (Rovner and Lewenstein 1997:Fig. 34). Frequently, they are recognizable by conspicuous amounts of plaster adhering to their ground surfaces. Smaller rubbing tools may have functioned as *polishing stones* (for lapidary work) or as *burnishers* in pottery production or any of a number of other artisan activities. Again, the size of the implement as well as the location of ground surfaces is taken to be indicative of its function.

The *small stones* (and *fragments*) are a motley mix of stone pieces; further subtyping is questionable due to the lack of satisfactory identifications. Many of the thirty-two fragments appear to be pieces of larger ground stone artifacts. Most do exhibit a plausible worked surface, but the main reason for their retention in the database is derived from the sheer scarcity of hard stone material in the immediate vicinity of K'axob. They are thus evidence of human transport and highly suggestive of curation and recycling activities. Some of the fragmentary as well as the three complete small stones may have been rubbing tools, one fragment resembles a pendant, while others may have been vessel supports. Note that, despite the fact that small stones represent the most ubiquitous category of ground stone (28% of the total), few subtypes have been established and most of the small stone pieces remain unclassified as to subtype.

A final type, *yuntun*, is represented by nine artifacts. All yuntunob are spheroid balls of limestone about 52 mm in diameter that may have been used as projectiles in a manner similar to a *bola* sling (figure 13.6). They are called yuntun in deference to the landowner of K'axob, Concepción Campos, who identified them as identical to the stone balls he launched with his slingshot when, as a child, he was dispatched to scare birds away from the corn fields. In a Yucatec Mayan dictionary (Barrera Vasquez 1995:983), "yuntunah" is defined as "hondear" or "tirar con honda, usar de aldo como de honda." In other words, it is an implement that today would be called a slingshot but that in ancient times may have been closer to a bola. Only one yuntun was

Figure 13.6 Yuntun found buried with a twelve- to thirteen-year-old adolescent (burial 1-32) who had been interred beneath the floor of an Early K'atabche'k'ax structure within operation 1 (zone 159).

found in a nonritual context; seven were placed around a cache and another was interred in a burial with an adolescent (shown in figure 13.6). This distribution suggests that the stones themselves may have been thought to offer protection.

RAW MATERIALS AND SOURCE AREAS

The sample of ground stone, while numerically small, nevertheless contains a wide variety of rock and mineral types, some of which remain obscure with regard to mineralogical content and geological provenience. The identification of raw materials was undertaken in consultation with petrographer Dr. Drew Coleman who, in 2001, was a member of the Earth Sciences Department at Boston University. He examined a representative subset of the ground stone as selected by Justin Ebersole. Coleman observed the physical properties of the hand specimens and conducted basic HCL and hardness tests when necessary. Most specimens could be identified accurately using these methods. Those that defied classification were thin-sectioned and observed under a spectrographic microscope by both Dr. Coleman and

Dr. Paul Goldberg (a geoarchaeologist in the Department of Archaeology at Boston University). The identified subset was then used to classify the geology of the remaining sample, which resulted in the following list of fourteen geological source materials.

Arkose

A type of sandstone in which the particles are held together by calcite cement, arkose is identifiable due to the presence of feldspar. "The mineral composition of arkose indicates that the grains were derived from granitic source rocks" (Tarbuck and Lutgens 1999:147). This statement is further confirmed by the presence of granitic outcrops in the Maya Mountains of southern Belize. A potential source could be found in any of the rivers and creeks draining the Maya Mountains. In the past, such acquisition would require traveling a linear distance of at least 60 to 70 km to reach potential riverbeds in order to procure raw material for the single percussion tool made of arkose.

Basalt

Usually encountered as an extrusive volcanic, basalt is a dense, fine-grained material often containing hornblende and chlorite. In southern Mesoamerica, the material is well known from the highlands of Guatemala and related regions, where outcrops of basaltic lava have long been exploited by the Maya.

Calcite marble

Metamorphic in origin, marble is usually a fine-grained rock comprised of either calcite, as in this case, or dolomite (Chesterman 1978:742). Owing to its softness, it remains a prime stone for easy shaping into artifacts; one of the metate fragments had been produced from this material. Calcite marble forms from metamorphic processes and, in this case, the sole region containing exposed metamorphic rock types exists in the Maya Mountains and the adjacent mountains of Guatemala. Few geological reports mention marble per se, so it must be a fairly restricted source.

Chert and chalcedony

Similar materials, both chert and chalcedony are fine-grained sedimentary rocks of "microcrystalline silica" (Tarbuck and Lutgens 1999:151). They are dense and produce conchoidal fractures when struck, making them desirable flint-knapping materials. Commonly found in Belize as nodules locked in limestone beds, chert and chalcedony can be produced by both chemical alteration and through the process of compaction and subsequent recrystallization of the crystal lattice of parent sediments (a somewhat metamorphic process according to Chesterman 1978:723). Although not immediately available in the environs of K'axob, chalcedony nodules are found a few kilometers to the east of K'axob on the interfluve between the New River and Freshwater Creek (McAnany 1989). The famed golden-to-gray chert nodules of northern Belizean chert were quarried around Colha, about 30 km to the south of K'axob (see chapter 11). Lewenstein (1987:78) notes another source of chert around Saltillo, Belize.

Granite and two-mica porphyritic granite

Granite is an intrusive volcanic rock that is termed phaneric because of the large size of its component crystals (Tarbuck and Lutgens 1999:72). Two pieces of granitic ground stone were recovered from K'axob. The first, listed simply as granite, could not be further identified with a hand lens. The second, a metate fragment, carries the name "two-mica" granite because it is composed partly of biotite and muscovite. The sample also contains alkali feldspar. The term porphyritic in its title relates to the presence of large crystals. According to Coleman, this particular piece underwent two stages of development: a slow cooling period deep inside a magma chamber that enabled the formation of large crystals followed by shallow-level emplacement that promoted rapid cooling which resulted in the formation of smaller crystals. Coleman also terms this piece an S-type granite because it was derived from the melting of sedimentary rocks that contained high amounts of aluminum (common to weathered sediments).

The mountainous regions of southern Belize and nearby Guatemala provided the only source area for this intrusive rock. The Maya Mountains contain three known granite sources: the Mountain Pine granite, the Cockscomb-Sapote granite, and the Hummingbird-Mullins River granite (Bateson and Hall 1976:14). Based on Bateson and Hall's work, Coleman concludes that the granite metate fragment could not have been quarried from any of the three known batholiths; rather, it most likely came from outcrops of granite porphyry just northwest of Baldy Beacon in the Maya

Mountains. As for the other granite artifact, given present geological data no specific source could be asserted other than the Maya Mountains.

Jade

Chesterman (1978:549) characterizes jade, or more correctly jadeite, as a "sodium aluminum silicate, often with some calcium and iron [as additional constituents]." It is fine-grained and metamorphic in origin, with such diverse color grades as green (most common) and white. Among the ancient Maya it was highly prized for its color and beauty. However, owing to its hardness, it requires extensive effort to shape; however, it is capable of taking on a high polish, thereby adding to its value as adornment. The only confirmed source of this semi-precious metamorphic material is located in the Motagua River Valley of eastern Guatemala, where it can be retrieved as cobbles and boulders within the river-bed. This chapter discusses the single tool, a celt, that was fashioned from jade (see chapter 15 for a description of additional greenstone ornaments).

Limestone

Undeniably, the most abundant rock across the Yucatan Peninsula and within northern Belize is limestone. In fact, the entire region is a giant geological shelf of the material. Interestingly, it comprises a whole spectrum of grades and degrees of hardness, color, and matrix particle size, all of which are largely composed of calcite. Limestone is sedimentary and can form from organically derived shell (such as ocean bivalves, foraminifera, and even coral reefs) or organically derived precipitates and other such chemically altered forms of calcite (Tarbuck and Lutgens 1999:150–151). Forty-five percent of the ground stone sample was fashioned from either pure limestone or a variant with calcite cement or travertine concretions. Although no limestone exists in the immediate neighborhood of K'axob, there are several sources of hard limestone within 20 to 30 km of the site. For instance, a modern limestone quarry on Albion Island is located less than 20 km to the west.

Quartz (vein)

Quartz is a very common mineral that is composed of silicon dioxide. Fairly hard (about seven on Mohs scale), it can be transparent to opaque white in color as well as many other shades. Quartz acts as a constitu-

ent mineral in many varieties of rock (Chesterman 1978:502–503). It also appears as pure quartz in the form of veins passing through rock matrices. The seven quartz artifacts are essentially pure quartz and may have been retrieved from a larger vein of the same material, perhaps as far away as the Maya Mountains.

Quartzite

Formed metamorphically, quartzite's parent material is usually sandstone, particularly quartz sandstone (Tarbuck and Lutgens 1999:179). As such, it is generally grainy in appearance and rather dense. It often takes on a variety of colors, as attested by the pink hues of the K'axob metate fragments. The digital database lists several variants of quartzite; however, all should be considered the same material. One artifact was identified as a river cobble, which suggests that it was taken from the riverbed of a drainage located in the Maya Mountains of Belize. Metamorphic in origin, quartzite could not be acquired locally. Today, a known source is Baldy Beacon, a peak found near the headwaters of the Sibun watershed on the northern flanks of the Maya Mountains (Sidrys and Andresen 1976:184). Shipley and Graham (1987:379) also note that the Santa Rosa Group of the Mountain Pine Ridge exposure contains a variety of quartzite.

Sandstone

The aforementioned arkose sandstone already provided an essential description of this rock type; briefly, sandstone is a sedimentary rock composed of weathered particles of rocks and minerals (most often quartz) held together by some form of cement. Depending on the degree of natural sorting, sandstone can be very fine-grained to incredibly coarse-grained with interspersed fine-grained particles. It is a commonly encountered rock, although not known to exist within 30 km of K'axob.

Schist

A metamorphic rock formed from sedimentary, igneous, or even other metamorphic rocks, schist is named after its foliation pattern—"schistose-foliation"—which reflects the flattened and lens-like crystal particles of which it is composed (Chesterman 1978:733). Three main constituents of this rock are muscovite, calcite, and biotite. Depending on the degree of metamorphism, the component crystals can be stretched, compressed, and otherwise distorted into a "parallel alignment" of varying grades. Yet another metamorphosed material, schist has not been provenienced as to its exact location within the Maya Mountains.

Serpentinite

Although some confusion may arise as to the designation of serpentinite versus serpentine, the term "serpentinite" encompasses the latter. Serpentinite is metamorphically derived and displays a fine-grained and dense mineralogical composition, primarily of "antigorite and chrysotile" (Chesterman 1978:748–749). It may show some banding. Moreover, it takes on many shades of color across spectra of white, yellow, black, and green (748). The ancient Maya considered it a semiprecious stone, and it was used extensively, probably due to its resemblance to certain grades of dark green jade. Unlike jade, it is relatively easy to shape. This material is not local to northern Belize and can only be found within metamorphic regions. We can posit that its source locale is similar to that of jade; namely, the Motagua Valley and adjacent areas. However, some speculation has been offered concerning the possibility of another source in the Maya Mountains (Hammond 1991c).

Silcrete

The term "silcrete" refers to a diverse class of material that is essentially a precipitate, forming in silica-rich regions. Silcrete ranges from chert to quartzite-affiliated materials and, according to Dapple (1979:113), is "a precipitate from chert, forming at low temperatures in soils and arguably requiring semiarid environments." Silcrete is similar to caliche in that it forms as a type of natural concrete exhibiting the physical properties of a dense, siliceous, and often rather brittle material. With respect to its geographical origin, it is fair to conclude that silcrete was locally acquired as the region south of K'axob is well known for its chert and limestone. In fact, the prevailing geology of northern Belize is that of siliceous rocks, and the abundance of silcrete artifacts at K'axob argues favorably for its availability within a local sphere.

Volcanic glass (altered)

Identified by Coleman after thin-section analysis, in this case altered volcanic glass is a devitrified form of extrusive volcanic glass. This identification suggests that the material came from the highlands of Guatemala, where a better known form of volcanic glass—obsidian—can be encountered in restricted locations.

PROCUREMENT ZONES

The fourteen raw materials composing the ground and polished tools of K'axob can be classified into three different groupings based on the distance from their point of geological origin to K'axob as the crow flies (table 13.2). Zone 1 includes geological materials available within approximately 30 km of K'axob: chert, chalcedony, limestone, and silcrete. Zone 2 is composed of geological materials accessible from the Maya Mountains, the northern flank of which is about 120 km south of K'axob: arkose, calcite marble, granite, vein quartz, quartzite, sandstone, and schist. Of the zone 3 materials only basalt and jade have been solidly provenienced, but it is likely that serpentinite and altered volcanic glass also belong in this group. Collectively, they have a geological origin that is in excess of 200 km from K'axob.

Composing over three-fourths of the ground stone (76.6%), zone 1 materials may have been directly procured, although evidence suggests that many of the chert tools came by way of an exchange network that linked K'axob with tool producers at Colha, located only 30 km to the south (see chapter 11). The same could also be said for the silcrete material, which was likely indirectly procured via local contacts. The distance separating K'axob from the geological sources of both zones 2 and 3, however, necessitated some form of indirect acquisition or multinodal trading network. The rich geological provenance of the Maya Mountains (zone 2) represents 18.5% of the ground stone sample. Imports from distant zone 3, comprising 4.8% of the total, are not very common. They represent the semiprecious materials, analogous to obsidian in their distance from K'axob, that do not seem to have been acquired with great frequency.

RAW MATERIAL PREFERENCES

Considering the paucity of hard stone, it is easy to imagine that ultrafunctional ground and polished stone tools might be fabricated from whichever locally available sources to which the residents of K'axob enjoyed access. On the contrary, an examination of ground stone tool types tabulated against the three ac-

Table 13.2 Raw materials and procurement zones for K'axob ground/polished stone tools

| | PROCUREMENT ZONE | | | | |
RAW MATERIAL	Zone 1	Zone 2	Zone 3	Total	% of Total
Arkose	-	1	-	1	0.8
Basalt		-	1	1	0.8
Calcite Marble	-	1	-	1	0.8
Chert & Chalcedony	8	-	-	8	6.5
Granite	-	2	-	2	1.6
Jade	-	-	1	1	0.8
Limestone	55	-	-	55	44.4
Vein Quartz	-	7	-	7	5.6
Quartzite	-	8	-	8	6.5
Sandstone	-	3	-	3	2.4
Schist	-	1	-	1	0.8
Serpentinite	-	-	2	2	1.6
Silcrete	32	-	-	32	25.8
Volcanic Glass (Altered)	-	-	2	2	1.6
Total	**95**	**23**	**6**	**124**	**1**
% of Total	**76.6**	**18.5**	**4.8**		**100**

quisition zones reveals clear raw material preferences (table 13.3). Tools fabricated from the proximate zone 1 materials include two of the most distinctive tools in the set—bark beaters and yuntunob—both of which are made exclusively of limestone. Just over half of the celts (five out of nine) were made from zone 1 chert and chalcedony, and a large percentage of manos (66.7%) and metates (78.6%) were fabricated from zone 1 materials, with an emphasis on silcrete. As expected, a large percentage of the more expedient and nonformal tools were made from zone 1 materials: 76.5% of the large stone fragments, 71.4% of the percussion tools, and 78.1% of the small stone fragments.

The many types of hard stone available in the Maya Mountains (zone 2) seem to have been desired for metates (21.4% of the metate total) and manos (33.3% of the mano total). Fragments from breakage of zone 2 tools compose 23.5% of the large stone

category and 15.6% of the small stone fragments. Significantly, the only tools fabricated from zone 3 materials were four celts (although the two small stone fragments of altered volcanic glass are also included in this category). All told, the distribution of tool types across the three zones suggests that the residents of K'axob maintained networks for the acquisition of ground and polished stone tools that ranged in scale from proximate to K'axob to over 120 km distant.

TEMPORAL VARIATION IN TOOL TYPES AND RAW MATERIALS

The ground and polished stone tools recovered from excavations at K'axob can be examined for temporal trends in the importation of tools and raw materials. Employing the temporally sensitive ceramic complex

Table 13.3 Frequency of ground/polished stone tools by procurement zone

TOOL TYPE	PROCUREMENT ZONE						
	Zone 1	Row %	Zone 2	Row %	Zone 3	Row %	Total
Barkbeater	2	100.0	–	–	–	–	2
Celt	5	55.6	–	–	4	44.4	9
Large Stone Fragment	13	76.5	4	23.5	–	–	17
Mano	8	66.7	4	33.3	–	–	12
Metate	22	78.6	6	21.4	–	–	28
Percussion Tool	5	71.4	2	28.6	–	–	7
Rubbing Tool	3	60.0	2	40.0	–	–	5
Small Stone	3	100.0	–	–	–	–	3
Small Stone Fragment	25	78.1	5	15.6	2	6.3	32
Yuntun	9	100.0	–	–	–	–	9
Total	95		23		6		124

Table 13.4 Frequency of ground/polished stone tools by ceramic complex

TOOL TYPE	CERAMIC COMPLEX AND FACET							
	Chaakk'ax		K'atabche'k'ax			Nohalk'ax		
	Early	Late	Early	Late	Terminal	Early	Surface	Total
Barkbeater	2	–	–	–	–	–	–	2
Celt	1	–	1	2	1	2	2	9
Large Stone Fragment	2	–	2	5	1	6	1	17
Mano	5	–	–	2	2	1	2	12
Metate	10	2	1	7	2	5	1	28
Percussion Tool	3	1	–	–	1	2	–	7
Rubbing Tool	–	1	2	1	–	1	–	5
Small Stone	–	1	1	1	–	–	–	3
Small Stone Fragment	2	4	6	11	3	2	4	32
Yuntun	–	–	2	–	7	–	–	9
Total	25	9	15	29	17	19	10	124
% of Total	20.2	7.3	12.1	23.4	13.7	15.3	8.1	100.0

Table 13.5 Frequency of stone from procurement zones through time

| Ceramic Complex | Facet | PROCUREMENT ZONE | | | |
		Zone 1	Zone 2	Zone 3	Total
Chaakk'ax	Early	19	5	1	25
	Late	7	1	1	9
K'atabche'k'ax	Early	11	4	–	15
	Late	26	3	–	29
	Terminal	12	2	2	16
Nohalk'ax	Early	13	5	1	19
Surface		7	3	1	11
Total		**95**	**23**	**6**	**124**

designation (see chapters 3 and 8 for more on ceramic complexes) for each provenience, the tool types can be arrayed against the six time periods (plus surface material; see table 13.4). Discretion must be used in interpreting these data, however, since the cubic meters of excavated material is not constant across the ceramic complexes. Nevertheless, several striking trends emerge. First, two artifact types display noticeable clumping into a few time periods. Bark beaters are restricted to Early Chaakk'ax times, while the small limestone spheres (yuntunob) are present only in Early and Terminal K'atabche'k'ax deposits. The remainder of the tool types are spread more or less across all time periods, with some gaps that could be attributable to the vagaries of sampling, especially in light of the fact that ground and polished tools never occur in very high frequencies.

This configuration of the ground stone data permits examination of temporal trends in the frequency of mano and metates. If these types of ground stone were used primarily to process maize, then, all things being equal, their increased presence should be an indicator of an increase in the contribution of maize to the overall diet. These data do not provide any indication that maize processing increased through time. In fact, within Early Chaakk'ax times, manos and metates collectively compose 60% of total ground stone from that ceramic complex—a percentage that is not equaled in later times, when these types of ground stone never exceed 31%. An interesting fact about the Early Chaakk'ax manos and metates is that

a significant percentage of them were made of zone 1 silcrete (table 13.5). Examining the distribution of raw material types across the time periods, it becomes clear that Early Chaakk'ax layers contained a high frequency not only of silcrete but also of other zone 1 materials—a fact that is not altogether surprising. Despite this dominance of zone 1 material, there is a relatively high percentage of materials from the zone 2 Maya Mountain region (20% of all Early Chaakk'ax ground stone). Within Late Chaakk'ax layers, the percentage of local zone 1 material increases slightly to around 78% relative to the percentage of zone 2 materials. During Late K'atabche'k'ax, use of zone 1 materials peaks at nearly 90%.

SPATIAL AND CONTEXTUAL TRENDS IN GROUND AND POLISHED TOOLS

Identification of temporal trends in the acquisition of ground stone that was fabricated from distant source material leads us indirectly to a consideration of spatial patterns in the ground stone data. As noted in chapter 3, operation 1 is the only excavation locale at which stratified Chaakk'ax material was encountered. In fact, any temporal trends identified for the earliest three time periods are, for the most part, a function of artifact retrieval from operation 1. Although operation 1 was only one of seven excavation units, geometrically more cubic meters were excavated there than at any other unit. This fact explains why the sample size from operation 1 swamps that from all other units (57.3%

Table 13.6 Ground/polished stone tools by excavation unit

TOOL TYPE	FREQUENCY PER OPERATION (EXCAVATION UNIT)							
	1	7	8	10	11	12	13	Total
Barkbeater	2	–	–	–	–	–	–	2
Celt	6	–	–	1	2	–	–	9
Large Stone Fragment	7	1	–	–	2	5	2	17
Mano	8	1	–	–	–	2	1	12
Metate	14	1	1	–	7	2	3	28
Percussion Tool	4	–	1	–	2	–	–	7
Rubbing Tool	4	–	–	–	–	1	–	5
Small Stone	2	–	–	1	–	–	–	3
Small Stone Fragment	15	–	5	2	4	5	1	32
Yuntun	9	–	–	–	–	–	–	9
Total	71	3	7	4	17	15	7	124
% of Total	57.3	2.4	5.6	3.2	13.7	12.1	5.6	100.0

of the total; table 13.6). Operations 11 and 12, the next largest in size and the most similar to operation 1 in terms of yielding a mixture of construction and midden deposits, account for 13.7% and 12.1% of the ground stone, respectively. The remaining four excavations (operations 7, 8, 10, and 13) probed sequences of construction fill and yielded only limited amounts of ground and polished stone.

Given these circumstances, only limited conclusions can be drawn from an examination of the representation of ground stone by excavation unit. First, both bark beaters and yuntunob are restricted to operation 1. Celts, while heavily weighted to operation 1 (6 out of 9), also appear in operations 10 and 11. Considering the disparities in unit size and the low counts for some of the types, the remaining ground stone types appear to be distributed fairly evenly across the operations, although no single type occurs in all excavation units. The two most commonly occurring types, small stone fragments and metates, are absent only from operations 7 and 10, respectively.

To examine patterning in the distribution of ground stone in a more refined fashion, the presence of each type of ground stone can be cross tabulated with context type (table 13.7), regardless of excavation unit or time period. Given the size of the sample, this grouping is necessary. In this table, nine different types of context are differentiated: burial (includes burial fill as well as burial accoutrements), cache, construction fill, midden (includes midden redeposited as construction fill), paleosol (found primarily at the base of operation 1), pits and enigmatic features, plaster floors, surface finds, and wall tumble. As might be predicted, the highest frequency (23.4%) of ground stone was recovered from midden contexts, including 33% of the manos, 25% of the metates, 57% of the percussion tools, and 28% of the small stone fragments. Celts and yuntunob, on the other hand, are conspicuously absent from midden areas. The context to yield the second highest percentage of ground stone was construction fill. With nearly 18% of the total, this context contained low frequencies of every type of ground and polished stone except bark beaters. The fact that 29% of the large stone fragments and 14% of the metates hail from construction fill probably indicates the tendency for pieces of hard stone to be incorporated into the structural fill of platforms after wear and breakage had rendered them unsuitable for further use.

Table 13.7 Ground/polished stone tools by excavation context

	FREQUENCY OF TOOLS BY CONTEXT									
TOOL TYPE	Burial	Cache	Construc-tion Fill	Midden	Paleosol	Pits & Misc. Features	Plaster Floor	Surface	Wall Tumble	Total
Barkbeater	–	–	–	2	–	–	–	–	–	2
Celt	1	–	2	–	1	2	–	1	2	9
Large Stone Fragment	1	–	5	2	–	2	5	1	1	17
Mano	–	–	2	4	1	1	1	2	1	12
Metate	2	–	4	7	–	6	7	2	–	28
Percussion Tool	–	–	1	4	–	–	2	–	–	7
Rubbing Tool	2	–	2	1	–	–	–	–	–	5
Small Stone	–	–	2	–	–	–	1	–	–	3
Small Stone Fragment	5	–	3	9	1	7	2	4	1	32
Yuntun	1	7	1	–	–	–	–	–	–	9
Total	12	7	22	29	3	18	18	10	5	124
% of Total	9.7	5.6	17.7	23.4	2.4	14.5	14.5	8.1	4.0	100.0

Pits and miscellaneous features yielded the third highest percentage of ground stone (almost 15%), with one-third of the total tally (six out of eighteen) represented by metate fragments. Moreover, four of the six metates were found in a large, Late K'atabche'k'ax storage pit that was reused for refuse disposal (operation 11, zone 20). Over 14% of the ground stone was recovered from plaster floor contexts; however, the plaster floors of K'axob (really packed marl) can be up to 20 cm thick and often contain hefty ballast. Thus, it is not surprising that twelve out of eighteen artifacts from this context are either metates or large stone fragments. In situ floor artifacts were seldom encountered at K'axob. A similar overlap between construction and in situ deposits exists in relation to burial deposits. While a total of twelve pieces of ground and polished stone (approaching 10% of the total) were associated with burials, the ancient practice of refilling burial pits with locally available midden material brings this association into question. If an artifact is broken, badly burned, or was not positioned adjacent to the corpse, the association is probably spurious. Such is the case for the single large stone fragment, the two metate

fragments (both of which are less than 10 cm in length), and the five small stone fragments.

The case is not so clear for the two pebble-sized rubbing tools that exhibit smoothed surfaces. Both smoothing stones were found in the burials of single, older adults—one a secondary interment of a male (burial 1-26) and the other a flexed interment of indeterminate sex (burial 12-11). Given the size of the artifacts and the lack of field identification of the items as burial accoutrements, it is likely that they constitute part of the burial fill. In contrast, the single jade celt and limestone yuntun were identified in the field as part of the burial accoutrements. The celt fragment was buried with a flexed adult male (burial 1-45) who was placed at the bottom of a complex series of multiple interments (burial 1-2) in a Terminal K'atabche'k'ax shrine in operation 1. During Early K'atabche'k'ax times, a twelve- to thirteen-year-old adolescent (burial 1-32) had been buried in an extended position with a single yuntun and three *Pomacea* spp. shells placed near the head.

In contrast to the ambiguity surrounding ground stone artifacts in burials, there is a clear and singular association between a single cache deposit and seven yuntunob. This Terminal K'atabche'k'ax cache (operation 1, zone 17) has been dubbed the triadic cache because of the numerical symbolism of its triadic groupings of objects, which were placed inside a barrel-shaped pottery vessel and capped with a lid and an upright flanged polychrome bowl. (See chapters 4, 9, 14, and 15 for in-depth descriptions of the context, the pottery vessels, and the shell and stone ornaments, respectively.) Arranged in a rough circle around the pottery containers, the yuntunob seem to provide a sort of protective frame for this cache of precious items. This overtly ritual context provides a strong reminder that even ancient bola stones cannot be assumed to have carried only utilitarian significance.

The final context of interest is that of construction tumble from which two celts and a mano were recovered. Found amid collapsed wall debris, these artifacts may have been stashed in the cracks between wall courses and never retrieved.

CONCLUDING THOUGHTS

The window into the daily life of Formative and Early Classic residents of K'axob has opened a little wider as a result of the analysis of ground and polished stone tools. This most mundane artifact class has yielded profound insights into ritual practices and trading spheres as well as into patterns of discard and recycling. The inhabitants of K'axob always grappled with the lack of hard stone in their immediate environment. The small size of the ground stone fragments plus the evidence of their recycled use as hearth stones, polishing tools, and a drill base provide ample evidence of the conservation ethic at work. On the procurement side, this analysis indicates that, from Early Chaakk'ax times, arrangements for acquiring hard stone for manos and metates (either as blocks or finished implements) existed thanks to the mineralogically rich Maya Mountain region. For nearby Cuello, Hammond (1991c:187) reports a similar pattern in his description of roseate metamorphosed sandstone that was acquired from the Maya Mountains. In reference to K'axob pottery types and their constituent paste materials, both Bartlett (chapter 7; see also Angelini 1998) and López Varela (chapter 8; see also López Varela 1996; McAnany and López Varela 1999) comment on the rich diversity of Early Chaakk'ax pottery and suggest the existence of far-flung trading networks among the founding inhab-

itants of K'axob. The presence of ground stone from distant zone 2 origins provides further support for this thesis. On the other hand, links with the more distant Guatemalan Highlands appear to have been tenuous, at best. The low incidence of Guatemalan imports among ground and polished stone artifacts mirrors the low incidence of obsidian at K'axob.

The highest percentage of material found in Early Chaakk'ax deposits is locally procured silcrete and limestone. Not available within the immediate environs of K'axob, these raw materials could have been directly procured or acquired through an exchange network such as the one that existed for chert tools. The lack of an exact geological provenience for silcrete (as well as sandstone) constrains inferences regarding the acquisition of this material and indicates that more resource inventories need to be completed in the Maya region. In this respect, archaeology is greatly indebted to geology as some of our most fundamental inferences regarding the regional scope of exchange processes are dependent upon the geochemical identification of raw materials and source areas.

The external connectivity of K'axob is but one part of the picture. Through the ground stone analysis, the early incidence of paper making has become apparent. This discovery leads to the obvious question of why paper was being produced at K'axob during Middle Formative times. Were the paper makers preparing a medium for writing or record keeping or for sacrificial offering? Was the paper produced actually a kind of cloth that was worn, much like tapa cloth in Polynesia? Without additional evidence, it is difficult to select one option over another. The limestone spheres (yuntunob) and the jade celt provide evidence of the inclusion of ground and polished stone tools in ritual deposits; namely, burials and caches. Both items held utilitarian and symbolic significance and provide the clearest examples of the bivalent nature of artifacts. In summary, the ground stone of K'axob has informed us not only of the procurement and use of hard stone for daily maize-grinding activities but also of items selected to accompany the burials of a youth and an adult male. It also served to frame, and possibly to protect, a cache of symbolically charged artifacts. Through ground stone we have glimpsed fundamental concepts of Maya cosmology as well as external strategies employed to acquire hard stone from distant lands.

PART V

PERSONAL ADORNMENT AND COSMOLOGICAL EXPRESSION

Mortuary interments often contain artifacts that project a very strong sense of personal identity or group identity. Part V considers these objects and their potential range of meanings, both to the individuals who claimed them during their lives and to the kin groups who decided to place them with their deceased. In chapter 14, Ilean Isaza turns to the worked shell of K'axob. She examines not only shell ornaments placed in mortuary contexts but also those recovered from fill and midden contexts, the latter being suggestive of on-site bead production, especially during Chaakk'ax times. Isaza demonstrates that there are strong temporal trends in the types of shell interred with the dead, and she chronicles the transition from discoidal shell bead adornment to the more elaborate carved pendants and *Oliva* spp. tinklers of the Terminal K'atabche'k'ax and Early Nohalk'ax interments. Through a close analysis of context, Isaza is able to identify a new aspect of early K'axob mortuary ritual: the scattering of unfinished beads over the bodies of deceased adults. The use of worked shell to mark personal identity is strongly indicated in the 2,000+ shell beads interred with one of the "founder" burials at K'axob (burial 1-43) and is more poignantly expressed in the placement of shell adornment on the bodies of deceased children.

In chapter 15, Mary Lee Bartlett examines artifacts made of bone and semiprecious stone. Found primarily but not exclusively in burial contexts, the bone artifacts include needles and handles as well as hollow, elaborately carved tubes fashioned from the long bones of large mammals, some identifiable as human. Similarly, semiprecious stone, including thirty-five pieces of greenstone, is restricted primarily to distinctive burial contexts. But Bartlett finds that greenstone is distributed in low frequencies throughout all but one of the excavation units. Present primarily as single beads, the greenstone of K'axob appears to have been but one element that defined the social identity of a deceased individual.

The meanings of the cross, or quadripartite, motif, found on mortuary vessels of K'atabche'k'ax manufacture, are explored by Annabeth Headrick in chapter 16. Characterizing the cross as a fundamental symbol in a deeply rooted Mesoamerican visual vocabulary, Headrick traces the association between the bowl form and the cross symbol back to Olmec times. Through a contextual and art-historical comparative analysis, she suggests that the bowls painted with a cross may have been used for divinatory purposes, for sacrificial blood-letting, or as more generalized markers of the centralized authority of K'axob elites. Regardless of the specific use of the cross vessels, their restricted distribution in the heart of the old village of K'axob, underneath plaza B, indicates that they signified authority.

GUIDE TO ACCOMPANYING DIGITAL MATERIALS.

The shell beads, tinklers, pendants, and other types of worked shell are presented with photos of selected artifacts in the digital *Worked Shell Database*. Because of the singular nature of burial 1-43, who was covered with thousands of shell beads, the worked shell from this interment is presented in a separate database called *Burial 1-43 Worked Shell*. Two data sets accompany chapter 15, a *Carved Bone Database* and a *Greenstone Database*. Although vessels adorned with the quadripartite motif are available for viewing in the general *Pottery Vessels Database*, they are also presented in a separate database entitled *Cross Motif Vessels*. Additional information regarding the individuals with whom these vessels were interred can be gleaned by viewing the *Burials Database*.

Chapter 14
Related CD Resources

Worked Shell
Burial 1–43 Worked Shell
Burials

THE ART OF SHELL WORKING AND THE SOCIAL USES OF SHELL ORNAMENTS

ILEAN ISEL ISAZA AIZPURÚA

In prehispanic Mesoamerica shells were perceived as symbolic of water, life, and fertility (Andrews IV 1969; Fearer and Gill 1982; Novella 1995). The exploitation of marine and freshwater resources for the making of personal ornaments seems to have paralleled the development of plant domestication in Archaic Mesoamerica. The earliest archaeological evidence of worked-shell ornaments comes from Coxcatlan Cave, Tehuacan Valley, where MacNeish reported evidence of shell ornaments in mortuary features dating to the second half of the Riego phase (6500–4800 BC; MacNeish et al. 1967:147). It was not until the Formative period, however, that shell working fully developed among Mesoamerican cultures, particularly in settlements along the seacoast and freshwater areas where rich food resources and easy access to transportation were available.

Given the ease with which shell could be cut, shaped, drilled, and incised, mollusca were a common raw material for the making of personal adornment. Within the Maya area the art of shell crafting endured from the Middle Formative until the sixteenth century. Friar Diego de Landa documented that the Maya used shells for the crafting of personal ornaments, musical instruments, and tools as well as for subsistence (Tozzer 1941). Young Maya girls wore bivalve shells covering their pelvic area as a sign of eligibility for marriage (Suárez-Díez 1989:25). Because of their symbolic connotations, shells could be used to portray images of gods or divine individuals. In the pages of the Madrid and Dresden codices, for example, images of shells identified as *Spondylus* and *Strombus* species represent deified personages such as the elderly God N who is also known as Mam, the earth god (Fearer and McLaughlin 1982). Shells were also associated with specific ceremonies and/or temples and were often used as grave goods in burial contexts (Novella 1995:3; see also chapter 18).

Despite the longevity of shell craftsmanship, as well as the abundance and importance of shell artifacts among Mesoamerican cultures, general studies of shell craft production and technology are scarce. The most distinguished works are those of Suárez-Díez (1989)

Table 14.1 Frequency of K'axob worked shell tabulated by ceramic complex and excavation unit

Ceramic Complex	Facet	OPERATION 1	7	8	10	11	12	13	Total
Unknown		2	—	2	—	—	3	—	7
Nohalk' ax	Early	—	5	—	—	1	2	1	9
K' atabche' k' ax	Terminal	70	3	1	—	1	7	—	82
K' atabche' k' ax	Late	19	—	2	1	5	29	—	56
K' atabche' k' ax	Early	129	—	—	—	2	—	—	131
Chaakk' ax	Late	66	—	—	—	—	—	—	66
Chaakk' ax	Early	2,203	—	—	—	—	—	—	2,203
Total		2,489	8	5	1	9	41	1	2,554
Percentages		97.45	0.31	0.2	0.04	0.35	1.61	0.04	100

and Novella (1995), which focuses on materials from Western Mexico, and Velázquez Castro (1999), which focuses on the shell artifacts from the Templo Mayor of Tenochtitlan. Research on Maya shell production and technology has concentrated on site-specific studies. Regarding the Maya Lowlands, the publication of *Archaeological Use and Distribution of Mollusk in the Maya Lowlands* (Andrews IV 1969) was the first work to provide a thorough discussion of shell craft occurrences, modern distribution of shell species, prehispanic trade systems, and the social significance of shell ornaments. Following this publication, researchers involved with worked-shell analyses obtained greater awareness of the potential of worked shell to contribute to the study of regional customs. Among site-specific reports that have contributed greatly to the understanding of shell craftsmanship and social uses of worked shells are those of Moholy-Nagy (1994) on Tikal; Cobos (1991, 1994) on Chichen Itza and Caracol; Buttles (1992), Dreiss (1994), and Potter (1982) on Colha; Garber (1989) on Cerros; and Taschek (1994) on Dzibilchaltun.

The analysis of worked shell from K'axob complements the technological studies mentioned above and permits understanding of the initial development of shell craftsmanship and the social connotations of shell adornment within a Formative Maya village. During three seasons of field research at K'axob, a total of 2,554 worked-shell ornaments were excavated from seven excavation locales in the southern part of K'axob (figure 2.2). The sample is dominated by 2,019 shell artifacts excavated from a single Early Chaakk'ax interment, burial 1-43. The other 535 crafted artifacts were distributed within ninety-eight ritual and domestic contexts within the different excavation units. The frequency of K'axob's worked shells was directly related to the size of the excavated areas and their proximity to the ancestral core of the site (table 14.1). Excavation units located near the large aguada west of plaza B, operations 1, 11, and 12, for example, contained the largest and most diverse types of crafted shell artifacts.

The analysis of worked shell involved meticulous examination of the physical characteristics of each object and descriptions of the associated archaeological context. The information was tabulated in two separate data files, and both can be viewed in the accompanying digital materials. One database contains descriptions of the 2,019 worked-shell ornaments and is identified as *Burial 1-43 Worked Shell*, while the other file contains recorded information from the remaining 535 ornaments encountered in ninety-eight different features (*Worked Shell Database*). This study defines not only general trends in shell crafting but also chronological changes in the presence, frequency, and type of worked shell across different contexts.

THE ART OF SHELL WORKING AMONG THE K'AXOB MAYA

The physical examination of K'axob's worked-shell assemblage allowed identification of production

Table 14.2 Classification of K'axob worked shell by type and subtype

Type	Subtype	Counts	Relevant Image
Bead	Unfinished	319	Figure 14.1 left end
	Unevenly shaped	30	Figure 14.1 bottom, 2nd from left
	Finely shaped	61	Figure 14.1 right half
	Carved	8	Digital photo ID. 0072 c & Digital photo ID 0006 a,b
Pendant	Unmodified (gastropod)	13	Digital photo ID 0243
	Unmodified (bivalve)	6	Digital photo ID 0004 a-e
	Regular	3	Figure 14.2 & Digital photo ID 0005 b,g
	Carved	5	Figure 14.3 & Digital photo ID 0005
Blank/ Figurine	Non-drilled worked shell	9	Digital photo ID 0251
Disk	Regular	4	Digital photo ID 0012
	Carved	2	
Tinkler	Miniature	11	Figure 14.4
	Medium	48	Digital photo ID 0013
	Large	4	Digital photo ID 0007 left
	Carved	1	Digital photo ID 0007 right
Culturally reshaped shell pieces	Miscellaneous	13	Figure 14.5
Total		537	

techniques and, in some cases, of the shell species chosen to craft personal ornaments. The assemblage includes beads; disks; pendants; tinklers; carved figurines of anthropomorphic, zoomorphic, phytomorphic, and geometric shapes; blanks; and culturally reshaped fragments of shells crafted from both marine and freshwater species (table 14.2). These ornaments were discovered in features associated with the Early Chaakk'ax through the Early Nohalk'ax ceramic complexes.

Overall, these worked shells are complete and well preserved. Some objects, primarily those found within burials and cache deposits, present crystallized or corroded surfaces, a condition known as Byne's disease (Davis 1989). The disease resulted from the extremely acidic environment to which the artifacts were exposed when buried. Such conditions caused the gradual surface disintegration of the shells and, hence, their powdery surface appearance. To prevent the continuation of the disease, we avoided washing the artifacts with distilled water and stored them inside plastic bags and metal cabinets.

The majority of the objects are heavily worked, rendering the identification of the shell species used to craft them nearly impossible. Because of this situation taxonomic classification of the worked shell is limited to the order and/or family level. Only the specimens that received slight modification to the shell structure, such as the unmodified gastropod and bivalve pendants and tinklers, were possible to identify at the genus level.

Although K'axob is situated near a freshwater environment (along the southern arm of Pulltrouser Swamp) it is also only 20 km from the Caribbean coastline; 87% of the identifiable worked-shell adornments are marine, while 13% are freshwater. Interestingly, the data described herein differ greatly from the unworked-shell identifications provided by Harrigan (chapter 18). The only freshwater specimens identified as being used by the K'axob Maya to craft personal adornments belong to the Unionidae family, specifically *Nephronaias* sp.

Thoroughly worked artifacts such as beads, disks, figurines, and pendants were crafted from marine

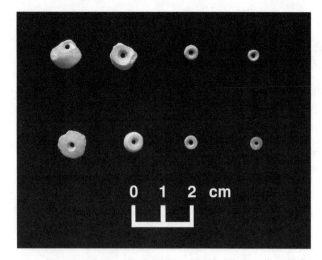

Figure 14.1 Sample of beads from midden deposit at operation 1, zone 63, identified by Worked Shell ID no. from left to right, top to bottom: top row, WS 03, WS 168, WS 186, and WS 145; bottom row, WS 142, WS 148, WS 162, and WS 524. *All photos by K'axob Project staff*

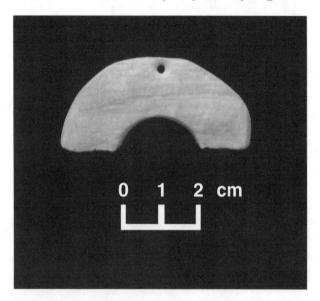

Figure 14.2 Shell pendant (WS 091) from midden deposit in operation 1, zone 63.

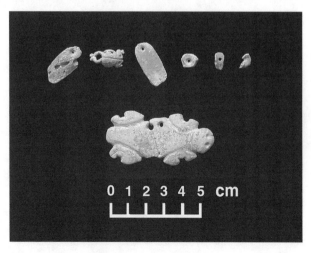

Figure 14.3 Carved shell pendants, shaped pendants, and beads. Upper row depicts grouped artifacts from burial 1-41, operation 1, zone 80a, identified by Worked Shell ID no. from left to right: WS 630, WS 631, WS 629, WS 015, WS 020, and WS 140. Lower row contains carved pendant (WS 455) found in floor context at operation 7, zone 46.

gastropods and freshwater bivalves. The physical analysis of the least modified shells and unfinished ornament types indicates that Strombidae, Dentaliidae, and Unionidae families were the shells primarily used to craft such types of objects. Tinklers, on the other hand, were exclusively crafted from the *Oliva* genus, with few modifications to the physical structure of the shell.

The methods of shell craft production are reconstructed based on the overall structure of unfinished ornaments, particularly beads and tinklers. Marine shell beads seemed to have been cut from the body whorl of the Strombidae shell as most of the unfinished specimens conserved the natural blunt nodes of the shell (figure 14.1). The overall characteristics of the assemblage suggest that the bead sections were first cut, then drilled and edge ground. The fact that 63% of the beads present irregular ground edges suggest that this was the last step in the crafting of shell beads (table 14.3). Stringing holes were bifacially or unifacially drilled at the center of the beads, with major emphasis on the internal section of the shell. Finished marine beads present a discoidal shape and were finely ground along the edges as well as on both shell surfaces. Once ground, selected pieces were grooved around the edges in order to produce a flower-shaped bead (see WS 099, in *Worked Shell Database*). Freshwater shell beads, on the other hand, were cut from different parts of the Unionidae bivalve and left with unground edges.

Pendants are relatively large ornaments pierced near the edge of the artifact for suspension, sometimes with more than two orifices (figures 14.2 and 14.3). Unmodified gastropods and bivalve pendant subtypes included pierced or punctured shells with no evidence of edge grinding. Bivalve pendants generally contain two suspension holes at the dorsal margin drilled along the edges of the shell's umbo (see WS 023, WS 238, WS 364, WS 376, and WS 632 in *Worked Shell Database*). The majority of the gastropod pendants, primarily those found in the Terminal K'atabche'k'ax cache at operation 1, were simply punctured at the shoulder or body whorl level (see figure 15.9). Other pendants were carved from marine shells into elaborate geometric and zoomorphic shapes, such as those retrieved from Late K'atabche'k'ax deposits in burial 1-41 and a floor in operation 7 (figure 14.3).

The physical structure and density of disks, figurines, and blanks indicate that they were carved from the whorl of marine gastropods; few specimens were carved from freshwater bivalves. All disks, figurines, and blanks were finely finished and their edges well

Table 14.3 Type of edge grinding on beads

Type of edge grinding	Counts	%
Fine	80	19
Irregular	261	63
Cut	5	1
Not ground	71	17
Total	**417**	**100**

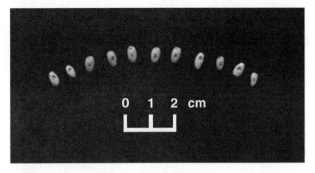

Figure 14.4 Miniature tinklers from burial 1-35, zone 211: WS 195–204 and WS 243.

Figure 14.5 Culturally shaped fragments of marine gastropods from different archaeological contexts, identified by Worked Shell ID no. clockwise from left: WS 453, WS 454, and WS 316.

ground. Of particular interest is the incised carving on pendants and figurines. In addition to the frogs shown in figure 14.3, representations include a fishhook, or comma, shape and anthropomorphic figurines (see WS 015, WS 020, WS 140, and WS 629–631 in *Worked Shell Database*).

Tinklers are bell-shaped adornments made from *Oliva* shells. The majority of K'axob's tinklers are medium sized, sometimes pierced more than once. The suspension holes were either cut or drilled from the outer surface of the shell. The number of pierced holes, however, depended upon the type of perforation. Tinklers with cut holes tend to present a single perforation along the shell's shoulder, while drilled tinklers presented two to four suspension holes through any part of the shell surface (see WS 460–494 in *Worked Shell Database*). Most tinklers were cut and ground at the base to create a flat bottom and thereby standardize the size of the ornaments. Differences in the perforation styles could be related to the type of knot used to intertwine the tinklers. Large tinklers contained a single suspension hole and were cut and ground at the base (see WS 040 in *Worked Shell Database*). A distinctive specimen identified in burial 1-14 was carved and perforated six times along the body whorl in order to re-create an anthropomorphic image that resembles the copper death heads dredged from the sacred Cenote of Sacrifice at Chichen Itza (see WS 319 in *Worked Shell Database*; Coggins and Shane 1984:Fig. 139). Similar carved tinklers were documented from Classic period deposits at Chiapa de Corzo (Lee 1969:Fig. 135) and a late Terminal Classic midden at Colha (Dreiss 1994:Fig. 2g).

A unique Chaakk'ax assemblage found in burial 1-35 yielded evidence of miniature *Oliva* shells, less than 8 mm in length, with unground edges and pierced holes along the upper section of the shell (figure 14.4). The *Oliva* shells were used as a necklace associated with a child's skull. These particular adornments were classified as miniature tinklers because of the shell species.

In addition to the shell adornments recovered from burials and caches, there were the miscellaneous fragments of worked shell from domestic features. Some fragments resemble tool-shaped artifacts (figure 14.5, lower right), while others are residual columella fragments from marine gastropods (figure 14.5, left and top right). One particular columella fragment (figure 14.5, top right) closely resembles that illustrated by Dreiss (1994:Figs. 10c and 10e) for the site of Colha and identified as a *Strombus* sp.

Eighty-seven percent of K'axob's identifiable worked shells were crafted from marine specimens. The high frequencies of marine shell artifacts depart from the chronological identification of miscellaneous fragments of worked marine shell as well as from Harrigan's counts of unworked shell. The fact that the site is located near a swamp, where the available freshwater species possessed shells too fragile for the crafting of personal ornamentation, perhaps encouraged the K'axob Maya to import marine specimens through the most likely route, the New River. The contextual association of worked marine shells at different stages of manufacture with fragmented drill tips suitable for shell working supports the idea of small-scale local production of shell ornaments (see chapter 11).

CULTURAL TRENDS IN THE USE OF WORKED SHELLS

This section focuses on the contexts of worked-shell deposits, their frequencies, and cultural trends in the use of shell ornamentation at K'axob. The temporal descriptions are based upon López Varela's ceramic chronology and the contextual patterns as described by field excavators.

The highest frequency of worked shell at K'axob was recovered from Early and Late Chaakk'ax deposits at the operation 1 locale (table 14.1). The shell artifact assemblages from this period are represented by a high frequency of marine shell beads and, to a lesser extent, disks, pendants, and miniature tinklers crafted from marine gastropods. The ornaments were found within twenty-five cultural deposits, including burials, midden, construction fill, pits, and the earliest level of the "kitchen" floor of structure 4 (see chapter 3). The most spectacular Chaakk'ax deposit of worked shell, burial 1-43, contained the remains of a male adult interred with two inverted vessels above the skull, a jade bead, 2,017 shell beads scattered throughout different parts of its anatomy, and two shell disks within the burial's fill (see figures 3.1 and 6.1). Rebecca Storey's analysis (chapter 6) of the skeletal remains determined that the individual was placed in a prone position; this discovery modifies Isaza and McAnany's (1999) published descriptions of the frequency and anatomical distribution of the shell beads, which were based on the assumption that the individual was supine rather than prone. Finely worked discoidal beads were associated with the individual's carpi, head, torso, and pelvic area, while semi-tubular beads cut from Dentaliidae shells were restricted to the upper humeri (table 14.4). The beads along the carpi and humeri were arranged in series of five to six layers as remnants of armbands and bracelets (see figure 6.1). The other arrangements provide evidence of a headband, necklace, and belt. It is possible that some beads were

Figure 14.6 Marine and freshwater irregular beads from burial 1-28, operation 1, zone 137, including WS 042, WS 070, WS 377, and WS 377–408.

sewn to a garment. Irregular-shaped or unfinished beads were found dispersed near the carpi and humeri. No other Formative deposit at K'axob approaches burial 1-43 in abundance of bead ornamentation or clear anatomical association of worked shell.

Burial 1-43 was placed under the paleosol surface (zone 220) of operation 1, considered the initial living surface of the plaza B complex. The paleosol averaged 20 cm in depth throughout the excavation perimeter. It contained large quantities of lithic debitage, four drill tips, and eleven shell beads at different stages of manufacture, crafted exclusively from marine gastropods. East of burial 1-43 a second interment, burial 1-46, contained the remains of a female adult in an extended supine position with a single shell bead scattered within the burial's fill. Differences in the quality and quantity of burial goods associated with these ritual deposits clearly demonstrate that established social identities were present during the Early Chaakk'ax complex. Burial 1-43 most likely represents one of K'axob's high-ranking villagers, perhaps a founding ancestors of the site (Isaza and McAnany 1999). Coeval associations were retrieved from two terminal Bladen phase interments (burials 114 and 123) at the neighboring Maya village of Cuello (Hammond 1991a; Hammond et al. 1991).

Additional evidence of Early Chaakk'ax distinct social identities was collected from a secondary interment, burial 1-35. This particular interment yielded the first occurrence of *Oliva* shells used to craft a miniature tinkler necklace associated with the skull of a child (figure 14.4). The *Oliva* shells were simply modified with punctured holes along the upper section of the shell. Three irregular beads were also found scattered throughout the burial fill.

Of particular relevance to the re-creation of Chaakk'ax mortuary ritual is the discovery of unfinished beads scattered throughout the fill of primary extended

Table 14.4 Anatomical distribution of worked shell from burial 1-43

Anatomical association	Worked shell subtype	Number of Specimens
Skull	Uneven discoidal beads	50
Torso	Fine discoidal beads Unevenly shaped discoidal beads	3 31
Humerus (R)	Uneven tubular beads	143
Humerus (L)	Fine discoidal beads Uneven tubular beads Unfinished beads	3 436 1
Humerus Distal section (L)	Fine discoidal beads Unevenly shaped discoidal beads Unfinished beads	2 2 2
Carpus (R)	Fine discoidal beads Unevenly shaped discoidal beads Unfinished beads	97 487 2
Carpus (L)	Fine discoidal beads Unevenly shaped discoidal beads Unfinished beads	1 114 8
Radius (L)	Fine discoidal beads Unevenly shaped discoidal beads	82 54
Pelvis (L)	Fine discoidal beads Unevenly shaped discoidal beads	7 25
Body (R)	Fine discoidal beads	7
Exterior of Carpus (R)	Unfinished beads	3
Exterior of Radius (R)	Unfinished beads	19
From flotation	Fine discoidal beads Unevenly shaped discoidal beads Unfinished beads Disks	88 305 45 2
Total		**2,019**

adult interments in a manner similar to burial 1-43 (table 14.5). Burial 1-28, for example, contained two inverted vessels and a bivalve shell above the cranium of the female adult occupant and thirty-two unfinished beads, crafted from marine and freshwater shells, scattered throughout the fill (figure 14.6). Burial 1-30a also contained an extended individual with two inverted vessels placed above the cranium and a scattering of fourteen unfinished beads. The disposal of irregular-shaped beads throughout adult burial fill appears to have continued until the Late K'atabche'k'ax complex, at which time fewer than five beads were scattered in adult interments (burials 1-23, 1-24, 1-25, 1-29, and 1-34a).

Other major occurrences of Chaakk'ax worked shell come from the midden deposits adjacent to the primary and frequently renovated structure 1 of operation 1 (see chapter 3). The high incidence of crafted shell objects in these deposits corresponds to the high counts of the freshwater *Nephronaias* sp. (see chapter 18) and the presence of drill fragments identified by McAnany and Peterson (see table 14.6: zones 59, 61, 63, 160, 219, and 57). The assemblages in midden deposits included beads at different stages of manufacture, carved pendants, disks, and a few miscellaneous fragments of worked shell crafted primarily from marine shells and, to a lesser extent, from freshwater species. Interestingly, the majority

Table 14.5 Worked shell encountered in K'axob burials tabulated by ceramic complex and operation locale. (*Continued on next page*)

Ceramic complex	Op.	Zone	Burial	Burial type	Age/ sex	Type and number of worked shell	Location of shell
Early Chaakk' ax	1	250	1-46	Single extended	Adult female	1 bead	Scattered
Early Chaakk' ax	1	233	1-43	Single extended	Adult male	2,017 beads 2 disks	Anatomically distributed
Early Chaakk' ax	1	229	1-42	Single secondary	Adult male	2 beads	Scattered
Early Chaakk' ax	1	176	1-38	Multiple secondary	Adult male	1 bead	Scattered
Early Chaakk' ax	1	203	1-37a	Multiple extended	Child	2 beads	Right hand
Early Chaakk' ax	1	211	1-35	Single secondary	Child	11 tinklers 3 beads	Associated with the skull
Late Chaakk' ax	1	143	1-30a	Single extended	?	14 beads	Scattered
Late Chaakk' ax	1	137/166	1-28	Single extended	Adult	32 beads	Scattered
Early K' atabche' k' ax	1	235	1-44	Single secondary	Child	2 beads	Scattered
Early K' atabche' k' ax	1	152a	1-34a	Multiple extended	Adult female	4 beads	Scattered
Early K' atabche' k' ax	1	159	1-32	Single extended	Adolescent	1bead	Scattered
Early K' atabche' k' ax	1	152	1-31	Multiple secondary	Adult male	1 bead	Scattered
Early K' atabche' k' ax	1	115a	1-29	Single extended	Adult male	2 beads	Scattered
Early K' atabche' k' ax	1	135	1-27	Single extended	Child	1 bivalve pendant	Over pelvis
Early K' atabche' k' ax	1	87a	1-26	Single secondary	Adult	1 bead 1 worked shell frag.	Scattered
Early K' atabche' k' ax	1	99/115	1-25	Single extended	Adult male	4 beads	Scattered
Early K' atabche' k' ax	1	113b	1-24	Single extended	Adult female	2 beads	Scattered
Early K' atabche' k' ax	1	103	1-18	Multiple secondary	Child	5 beads	Associated with cranium
Early K' atabche' k' ax	11	60	11-7	Multiple seated	Child	1 blank 1 bivalve pendant	Scattered

Table 14.5 (*Continued from previous page*)

Ceramic complex	Op.	Zone	Burial	Burial type	Age/ sex	Type and number of worked shell	Location of shell
Late K' atabche' k' ax	1	80a	1-41	Multiple secondary	Adult	3 beads 3 pendants	Beneath the mandible
Late K' atabche' k' ax	1	107	1-23	Single extended	Adult	3 beads unworked Pomacea	Scattered
Late K' atabche' k' ax	1	81a	1-15a	Multiple seated	Adult male	1 bead	Scattered
Late K' atabche' k' ax	1	81	1-15b	Multiple secondary	Child	2 beads	Scattered
Late K' atabche' k' ax	1	83	1-14	Single extended	Child	1 carved tinkler 2 beads	Child's knee, east side
Late K' atabche' k' ax	1	30a	1-3	Single flexed	Adult	1 bead	Scattered
Late K' atabche' k' ax	8	6	8-1	Single secondary	Adult female	2 beads	Scattered
Late K' atabche' k' ax	11	16b & c	11-3	Single seated	Adult male	1 bead 1 bivalve pendant	Scattered
Late K' atabche' k' ax	12	52	12-13	Multiple seated	Adult female	3 beads	Scattered
Late K' atabche' k' ax	12	42e	12-11	Single flexed	Adult	3 beads 1 worked shell frag.	Scattered
Late K' atabche' k' ax	12	40 & 40b	12-9	Single seated	Adult	3 beads	Scattered
Late K' atabche' k' ax	12	42a	12-10	Single seated	Adult	2 beads	Scattered
Terminal K' atabche' k' ax	1	18	1-2	Multiple, various positions	Adolescent Adult	2 beads 1 bivalve pendant 1 cowry shell 39 tinklers	Scattered
Terminal K' atabche' k' ax	1	15a	1-1a	Multiple seated	Adult male	4 tinklers	Scattered
Terminal K' atabche' k' ax	1	15c	1-1c	Multiple secondary	Adult	1 tinkler	Scattered
Terminal K' atabche' k' ax	8	5	8-3a	Multiple secondary	Adult male	1 large carved bead	Scattered
Terminal K' atabche' k' ax	12	30	12-3	Single extended	Adult	3 beads	Scattered
Early Nohalk' ax	7	27	7-1	Single secondary	Child	2 beads	Scattered
Early Nohalk' ax	12	32	12-2	Single flexed	Adult male	1 bead 1 tinkler	Scattered

Table 14.6 Worked shell identified in K'axob midden deposits tabulated by ceramic complex and provenience

Ceramic complex	Op.	Zone	Associated Structure	Worked shell	Associated materials	Incidence of Nephronaias sp.
Early Chaakk' ax	1	220	Paleosol	11 beads	Lithic debitage, 4 drill tips	———
Early Chaakk' ax	1	63	Above Structure 4	58 beads, 1 blank, 1 pendant	Lithics, mano frag., jadeite frag., 3 drill tips	30
Early Chaakk' ax	1	219a	Above zone 63	12 beads, 2 disks, 1 carved pendant	Chert fragments, projectile point, butterfly net weight	———
Early Chaakk' ax	1	162	Structure 1	1 bead	———	———
Early Chaakk' ax	1	87b	Structure 1	1 bead	———	———
Early Chaakk' ax	1	59	Structure 4	60 beads, 1 pendant, 1 blank, 1 worked shell frag.	Lithic debitage, animal bones, *Pomacea* shells, carved deer antler, prismatic obsidian, macroblade flake, mano frag., 1 jade bead, 5 drill tips	49
Early Chaakk' ax	1	61	Structure 1	10 beads	———	———
Late Chaakk' ax	1	160	Above Structure 1, zone 161	3 beads 1 worked shell frag.	Daub frags., sherds, lithics, mano, bone	———
Late Chaakk' ax	1	57	Structure 4	12 beads	Lithics, obsidian frag., animal tooth, *Pomacea* shells, 1 possible drill	———
Early K' atabche' k' ax	1	141	Structure 3	9 beads 1 blank	Sherds, debitage, shell debris	———
Early K' atabche' k' ax	1	51	Above plaza floor, zone 53	24 beads	Sherds, lithic debitage, obsidian flakes, shell debris	———
Early K' atabche' k' ax	1	111	North of Structure 1	11 beads, 1 bivalve pendant, 1 worked shell frag.	Sherds, Lithics, fragmented drill tip	46
Early K' atabche' k' ax	1	87	North of Structure 1	11 beads, 1 carved pendant	———	48
Early K' atabche' k' ax	11	72	Structure 5	1 worked shell frag.	Lithic debitage, animal bones, *Pomacea* shells	———
Late K' atabche' k' ax	12	48	Outside Structure 2	1 bead	Lithics, shell debris	25
Late K' atabche' k' ax	12	42	Eastern edge of Structure 2	5 beads	———	21
Late K' atabche' k' ax	12	10a	Structure 2	4 beads	Lithics, mano and metate fragments, shell debris	20

of K'axob's finely finished shell beads (60%), such as those illustrated in figure 14.1 right half, were found in the midden deposits. The association of shell beads at different stages of manufacture with lithic tools suitable for shell working alludes to the crafting of personal adornment at locales proximate to the family residence. In the case of this particular Maya village, both marine and freshwater resources were used not only for human consumption but also for the crafting of specialized jewelry that helped define personal identities.

Few unfinished or irregularly shaped worked shells were retrieved from architectural features such as construction fill, floors, walls, and pit features (table 14.7). The incidence of worked shell inside wall structures, floors, and postholes is most likely the product of unintentional deposition from domestic tasks such as sweeping. On the other hand, the specimens encountered in units of construction fill may be the result of the cultural distortion and deposit transport that occurred during resurfacing and construction activities.

The Chaakk'ax patterns of shell bead production continued into the early part of the K'atabche'k'ax complex. Subtle changes had occurred and were seen primarily at operation 1. A high number of interments included scattered beads, albeit in fewer quantities. On occasion these interments contained at least one finely finished discoidal bead. Burial 1-18, for example, contained a child's cranium with five carved beads and an inverted Sierra Red bowl covering the head. The beads were carved into flower shapes similar to those found in the Cenote at Chichen Itza (Coggins 1992:Fig. 5.29a). Also introduced at the time were unmodified gastropod and bivalve pendants present primarily within child interments such as burials 1-27 and 11-7. The former contained an unmodified bivalve pendant placed over the child's pelvis and possibly serving as a pubic shield. The seated child placed in burial 11-7 was buried with a shell blank and an unmodified *Pelecypod* pendant; however, field notes failed to describe the position of the artifacts. Nonetheless, data from these deposits suggest that worked shells were used as markers of identity for children as well as adults since the Middle Formative (Isaza and McAnany 1999:124).

Shells from the Late K'atabche'k'ax complex deposits reveal coeval developments among shell crafting and architectural and ritual elaboration. During this facet, structure 1 at operation 1 was rebuilt into a rectangular platform, and low structures were erected at satellite locales. Concurrently, the frequency of beads in mortuary contexts decreased and, when found, were associated with seated or flexed individuals (burials 1-3, 11-3, 12-9, 12-10, 12-11, and 12-13) or with secondary interments placed within a multiple burial facility (burials 1-41, 1-15b, 8-1). Pendants and *Oliva* tinklers began to assume importance within a limited number of K'axob burials. Late K'atabche'k'ax child interment—burial 1-14, for example—contained an intricately carved effigy tinkler (see WS 319 in *Worked Shell Database*) and two irregular beads placed along the east section of the child's knees (figure 14.7). The adult buried in burial 1-41, on the other hand, contained a carved frog pendant framed by two rectangular shell pendants, three shell beads, and a stone pendant placed underneath the individual's mandible (figure 14.3).

Coupled with the changes in shell crafting was the advent of clustered arrangements of unworked freshwater gastropods, primarily *Pomacea flagellata*, in burial and cache deposit such as burial 1-32 (figure 14.8). Such arrays simulated a carpet deposit, as if the K'axob Maya conceived of placing the individuals in a watery environment (Isaza and McAnany 1999).

During the Terminal K'atabche'k'ax complex, the crafting of beads seems to have ceased at the operation 1 locale. New locations for the crafting of shell artifacts apparently emerged within the southern structures, particularly in the excavated areas of operations 7 and 10, where scattered shell debris were encountered, albeit lacking the density of unfinished worked shell found in earlier deposits at operation 1. Coeval with these changes is the introduction of new shell species used to craft personal adornments. Medium-sized *Oliva* tinklers, for example, become particularly ubiquitous in Terminal K'atabche'k'ax multiple interments, such as burials 1-1 and 1-2, where they are found in groups of five associated with select individuals (see figure 14.9). Large-size tinklers, on the other hand, were found alone and were most likely worn as pendants. Occurrences of large tinklers include the one retrieved from the Early Nohalk'ax male adult interment, burial 12-2, and the fragmented large tinklers unearthed from a Late K'atabche'k'ax floor and an Early Nohalk'ax pit feature at operations 10 and 7, respectively.

A cache deposit (zone 17) placed in the uppermost floor of structure 1, operation 1, marked the increased formalization and ritualization of shell use at K'axob. The deposit included a triadic coded arrangement of artifacts inside an upright barrel-shaped vessel cylinder (see chapters 4 and 15). The cache contained

Table 14.7 Worked shell from architectural features at K'axob tabulated by ceramic complex and provenience. (*Continued on next page*)

Ceramic complex	Op.	Zone	Feature	Associated Structure	Worked shell	Associated Materials
Early Chaakk'ax	1	230	Fire feature	Above zone 219	1 bead	*Pomacea* shells, fish bone fragments
Early Chaakk'ax	1	228	Sherd-lined pit	Cut into midden, zone 63	1 bead	Lithics
Early Chaakk'ax	1	224	Sherd-lined pit	North of Structure 1	1 bead	———
Early Chaakk'ax	1	214	Wall	Structure 1	2 beads	———
Early Chaakk'ax	1	200	Construction fill	NW edge of Structure 1 floor, zone 161	1 bead	———
Early Chaakk'ax	1	175	Pit	Cut into the SW corner of Structure 1 floor, zone 161	3 beads	———
Early Chaakk'ax	1	58	Kitchen Floor	Structure 4	4 beads	———
Late Chaakk'ax	1	56	Construction fill	Above middens zones 57 and 58	2 beads	Sherds and lithics
Late Chaakk'ax	1	156	Post hole	Cut into Structure 1 floor, zone 142	1 bead 1 blank	Sherds, shell debris
Early K'atabche'k'ax	1	114	Sherd-lined pit	Cut into midden, zone 141	6 beads	Sherds, debitage, shell debris
Early K'atabche'k'ax	1	131	Pit	Cut into midden, zone 141	1 bead	Sherds, shell debris
Early K'atabche'k'ax	1	133	Pit	Cut into midden, zone 141	4 beads	———
Early K'atabche'k'ax	1	53	Construction fill	Above plaza and Structure3	2 beads	Sherds, lithics, shell debris
Early K'atabche'k'ax	1	52	Plaster Floor	Covered zone 53	1 bead	———
Early K'atabche'k'ax	1	136	Sherd-lined pit	Cut into NW of Structure 1 floor, zone 134	1 bead	*Pomacea* shells, 1 macroblade, 1 lithic flake
Early K'atabche'k'ax	1	128	Construction fill	Above Structure 1 floor, zone 134	3 beads 1 carved disk	Sherds, lithics, shell debris
Early K'atabche'k'ax	1	122	Plaster floor	Structure 1, 4th floor level	13 beads	Sherds, bone, lithics, charcoal fragment, *Pomacea* shells
Early K'atabche'k'ax	1	98	Pit	Cut into Structure 1 floor, zone 104	2 beads	Sherds, lithic debitage, 1 *Pomacea* shell
Early K'atabche'k'ax	11	69	surface	Above patio and Structure 5	1 bead	Sherds, animal bones, shell debris

Table 14.7 (*Continued from previous page*)

Ceramic complex	Op.	Zone	Feature	Associated Structure	Worked shell	Associated materials
Late K' atabche' k' ax	1	89	Construction fill	Above Structure 1 floor, zone 47	1 bead	_____
Late K' atabche' k' ax	1	32	Clay floor	Above Structure 1 floor, zone 33	1 tinkler	_____
Late K' atabche' k' ax	7	57	Construction fill	Structure 9	1 worked shell frag.	_____
Late K' atabche' k' ax	7	46	Floor	Structure 8	1 pendant	_____
Late K' atabche' k' ax	7	45	Construction fill	Structure 8	1 worked shell frag.	_____
Late K' atabche' k' ax	11	25a	Pit	Cut into Structure 3	1 bead	Human mandible
Late K' atabche' k' ax	12	49	Pit	Cut into Structure 1 floor, zone 24	1 bead	Chert debitage, burin, sherds, animal bones, freshwater shell debris
Late K' atabche' k' ax	12	45	Wall	Structure 3	2 beads	_____
Late K' atabche' k' ax	12	44	Sherd-lined pit	Cut into Structure 3 floor, zone 43	1 bead	_____
Late K' atabche' k' ax	12	43	Floor	East of Structure 3	1 bead	_____
Late K' atabche' k' ax	12	45c	Post hole	Cut into Structure 3 wall, zone 45	3 beads	_____
Late K' atabche' k' ax	12	37	Sherd-lined pit	Cut into patio adjacent to Structure 1	2 beads	_____
Late K' atabche' k' ax	12	35	Sherd-lined pit	Cut into patio adjacent to Structure 1	1 bead	_____
Late K' atabche' k' ax	1	89	Construction fill	Structure1	1 bead	_____
Late K' atabche' k' ax	1	32	Floor	Structure 1	1 tinkler	_____
Late K' atabche' k' ax	1	22	Floor	Structure 1	1 tinkler	Lithic debitage, shell debris
Terminal K' atabche' k' ax	10	4	Floor	Second patio	1 tinkler	Lithics, shell debris
Terminal K' atabche' k' ax	11	10	Construction fill	Structure 3	1 pendant	_____
Terminal K' atabche' k' ax	12	6	Construction fill	Structure 1	1 worked shell frag.	Lithics, shell debris
Early Nohalk' ax	7	23	Pit	Structure 5	1 tinkler	_____
Early Nohalk' ax	7	2	Construction fill	Structure 1	2 worked shell frag.	_____
Early Nohalk' ax	11	2	Floor	Uppermost patio	1 worked shell frag.	_____

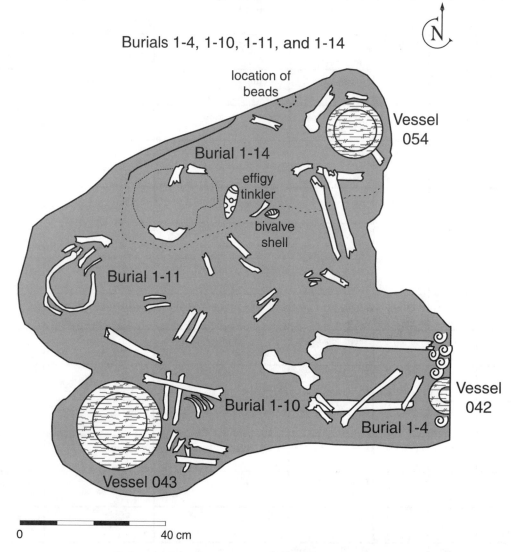

Figure 14.7 Plan view drawing of burial 1-14, zone 83, showing intricately carved effigy tinkler placed along east section of child's knees. *Illustration by K'axob Project staff*

Burial 1-32

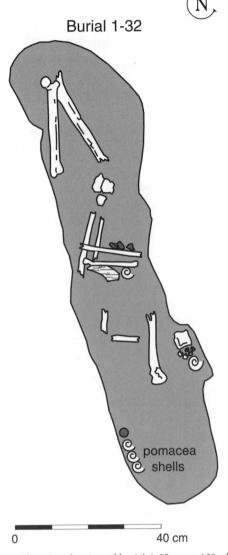

0   40 cm

Figure 14.8 Plan view drawing of burial 1-32, zone 159, showing *Pomacea* shells (drawn as spirals) distributed around cranial area. *Illustration by K'axob Project staff*

0   5 cm

Figure 14.9 Composition of medium-sizes tinklers and other crafted artifacts associated with burial 1-2, operation 1, zone 18.

twenty-two worked shell items that included beads, blanks, figurines, tinklers, and pendants crafted from Unionidae, *Oliva, Marginella* sp., Neritidae, and *Polinices* shells (see figure 15.9 and *Triadic Cache Contents Database*). Given that our most recent analysis failed to confirm the taxonomic identification of *Spondylus* shells used for the crafting of the cache's figurines, beads, and banks, we reject our previous speculations (Isaza and McAnany 1999:123–125) until structural studies of the shell are performed. Although the offering was not spatially patterned, the triadic structure of the cache is defined by the tripartite groupings of the shaped artifacts. This cache deposit marks a new trend in shell crafting and in the ritual use of shells. Of particular interest is the associated occurrence of anthropomorphic and geometric figurines crafted in jade, hematite, and shell. During this time period, shell seems to acquire a more symbolic importance among the K'axob Maya. A K'atabche'k'ax deposit, identified as burial 8-3, contained a sizable jadeite bead associated with a large carved marine shell bead, suggesting a trend toward the manufacture of larger, finely carved items of worked shell.

The incidence of worked shell in architectural features related to construction events increased. Beads, the most common shell ornament in construction fills and middens, tend to co-occur with lithics and shell debris (as indicated in tables 14.6 and 14.7). Continuing through the K'atabche'k'ax and Nohalk'ax complexes, the domestic deposits that contained the most diverse types of worked shell were those associated with the frequently renovated structure 1 at operation 1, and structure 2 at operation 12. This association provides additional support for the presence of small-scale craft production of marine and freshwater shell adornments, particularly at the operation 1 locale, where McAnany and Peterson identified a variety of broken drill tips.

CONCLUDING REMARKS

The analysis of K'axob's worked shell suggest that the art of shell crafting and shell ornamentation corresponds to patterns reported from neighboring Maya settlements. The high frequency of marine shell artifacts identified in burial interments and architectural deposits argues that the K'axob Maya oriented part of their marine shell resources toward the crafting of personal ornaments. From the Early Chaakk'ax until the Late K'atabche'k'ax complexes, marine shells were used for the crafting of beads and, to a lesser extent, disks and pendants. Freshwater specimens were used, but in fewer quantities, probably due to the fragile structure of the shells. The only unequivocally identified freshwater specimen used for crafting ornaments was the nacreous bivalve shell belonging to the Unionidae family, the *Nephronaias* sp. The contexts in which Harrigan (chapter 18) reports a high incidence of unworked *Nephronaias* also tend to contain large amounts of marine and freshwater shell beads at different stages of manufacture as well as fragmented drills suitable for shell working (see also chapter 11). The excavators did not identify shell workshops; however, the association of processed worked shells and drills in midden deposits suggest the K'axob Maya crafted personal adornment at locales proximate to the family residence.

The methods of shell crafting were standardized according to the type and subtype of ornaments. The examination of unfinished beads permits us to conclude that the majority of the marine specimens were cut from the body whorl of Strombidae shells, as is evidenced by the presence of the natural blunt nodes of the shell. Once a bead section was cut, the artisan drilled a single hole at the center of the artifact and finally edge ground the bead. The edge grinding was most likely performed through the rubbing of the bead against a hard surface or an abrasive agent such as sand. The freshwater beads crafted from Unionidae shells, however, were left unground. Pendants, disks, and figurines were carved from the whorl of marine gastropods or freshwater bivalves. They were all finely finished with well-ground edges. Tinklers, on the other hand, were crafted exclusively from *Oliva* shells, with only slight modifications to the shell structure. Suspension holes were either cut along the upper section of the body whorl or drilled in multiple areas of the shell's outer surface, depending on the size of the tinkler. Miniature and large tinklers contain a single perforation, while the medium-sized tinklers present either a single suspension cut hole or multiple drilled holes. The differences in perforation style and number could have been related to the type of knot used to intertwine the tinklers and the adornment's function. The tinklers were cut and ground at the base of the shell in order to create a flat bottom and to standardize their size.

The art of shell crafting at K'axob seems to have been oriented toward the marking of personal identities

(Isaza and McAnany 1999), which appears to have been linked to the number of adornments with which an individual was buried (particularly with regard to shell beads). Eighty-seven percent of the shell beads were retrieved from burial interments, 2,017 of which were accompanying a single Early Chaakk'ax interment, burial 1-43. The overwhelming number and uniformity of shell beads used by the individual in burial 1-43 as bracelets, armbands, headband, and necklace denote the presence of an important personage, perhaps one of K'axob's founding ancestors. Of particular relevance to the re-creation of Formative mortuary ritual is the discovery of low quantities of scattered unfinished beads throughout the fill of adult interments such as burial 1-43.

The Early Chaakk'ax child interment, burial 1-35, associated with a necklace composed of miniature *Oliva* tinklers, marked the beginning of a long tradition of unique votive offerings placed with selected children and/or adolescent burials. Burial 1-18, an Early K'atabche'k'ax child interment, for example, contained five finely carved beads associated with the individual's skull. Two other Early K'atabche'k'ax child interments, burials 1-27 and 11-7, contained bivalve pendants, one of which was anatomically placed above the individual's pelvis, probably serving as a pubic shield. In a Late K'atabche'k'ax child interment, burial 1-14, two irregular beads and a spectacular effigy tinkler were placed beside the individual's knees. The evidence retrieved from K'axob's child and adolescent burials connotes the existence of early initiation practices similar to those documented by Landa (Tozzer 1941) for the sixteenth-century Yucatec Maya. Only a single Late K'atabche'k'ax adult interment (burial 1-41), placed in a unique stone-lined pit deposit that cut into the plaza area of operation 1, contained an equally distinctive arrangement of shell adornment placed beneath the individual's mandible. The arrangement included a frog-effigy pendant flanked by two rectangular shell pendants and a single black stone pendant.

Variation in quantities of shell beads and unique shell adornments included in the Formative burials attests to the diversity of identities of varying status that existed during the Chaakk'ax and K'atabche'k'ax complexes. Changes in the crafting and ritual use of worked shell during the Terminal K'atabche'k'ax and Early Nohalk'ax complexes correspond with the architectural transformations of the site. Worked shell continued to support expressions of identity in burials 1-1, 1-2, and 8-3a, where prodigious amounts of shell beads are replaced by the introduction of tinklers, bivalve pendants, large carved beads, and ritually pierced gastropod shells. The Terminal K'atabche'k'ax cache in zone 17, operation 1—with its tripartite groupings of beads; blanks; anthropomorphic and comma-shaped figurines; tinklers; and pendants crafted from shells, hematite, and jade—seems to mark the formalization of shell use at operation 1. The evidence indicates that trends in shell crafting and its ritual use tracked the architectural transformation of the site.

Chapter 15
Related CD Resources

Greenstone
Carved Bone
Burials

CHAPTER 15

ORNAMENTS OF BONE AND SEMIPRECIOUS STONE

MARY LEE BARTLETT

Carved bone and exotic imported stone attest to the participation of K'axob villagers in the larger Maya world. The position of the site along the New River provided the avenues for communication with larger centers in Belize and perhaps the rest of Mesoamerica. The carved objects uncovered at K'axob attest to the craftsmanship of artisans at the site with regard to working bone and stone for both utilitarian and ritual use. On the pragmatic side, there are bone awls and needles that were probably used for working cloth or leather. In one instance, bone was fabricated as the handle for a tool. Ornamentally carved bone, probably used for display, was placed with a notable burial interment (burial 1-2).

Greenstone, or jadeite, used primarily for personal adornment, provides evidence that K'axob was linked, even if somewhat tenuously, to the far-flung trading networks of the Maya world. The similarity of carved bone and semiprecious stone objects at K'axob to objects from other Maya sites indicates the universality of personal adornment, technology, and ritual activities within Maya society.

ORNAMENTS OF STONE

Although not plentiful at K'axob, greenstone, frequently referred to as jadeite (Thomson 1987; Hammond 1991b; Buttles 1992), is found in a variety of contexts and in all but one of the residential complexes excavated. Greenstone objects were recovered from Early Chaakk'ax midden features, attesting to access to long-distance trade networks from the time of first settlement. The total number of greenstone objects recovered from K'axob is thirty-five (see *Greenstone Database*). Such a small total sample, representative of the entire Formative period, suggests that K'axob was only a peripheral participant in the trade or gift-giving present at larger sites along the New River.

Although most of the jadeite was excavated from operation 1, which was the largest and only excavation containing stratified Chaakk'ax deposits, the most richly adorned burial in terms of the size and craftsmanship of the jadeite beads was excavated from a single housemound (operation 8). The paucity of the

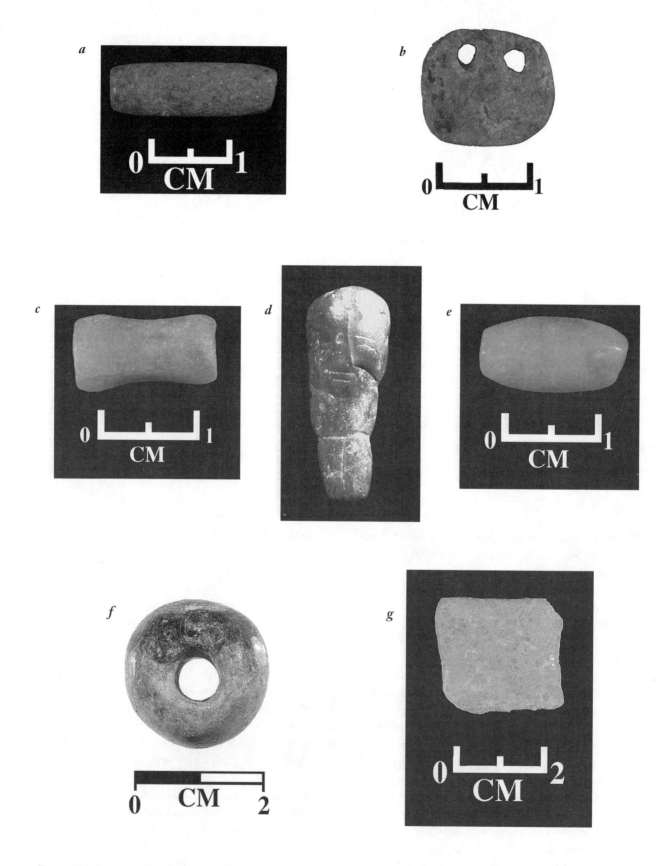

Figure 15.1 Examples of greenstone artifacts excavated at K'axob: (a) tubular bead made of fuchsite; (b) carved face made from dark green jadeite; (c) apple-green jadeite tubular bead; (d) small carved figurine of apple-green jadeite; (e) apple-green jadeite tubular bead; (f) large round bead made of dark green jadeite with white banding; and (g) square object made of white jadeite with green patches. *All photos by Mary Lee Bartlett*

material overall suggests that greenstone was a rare and probably highly valued item, but simple evidence of differential access by residential unit is not present at K'axob. This finding suggests that either ranking was not clearly defined at small villages during the Formative period or, more likely, this material can only be used as a status marker when considered in conjunction with other types of artifacts and contextual information.

Types of greenstone raw material

Five different types of greenstone were uncovered at K'axob, suggesting different resource networks (figure 15.1). The most common material is a muscovite granite, or "muscovy glass," called fuchsite, a mid-tone green colored stone with large micaceous flecks (figure 15.1a). This type of material can be found in the Maya Mountains well to the south of K'axob (Graham 1987). Dark greenstone, probably serpentinite, is also present at K'axob and would have been imported from areas beyond northern Belize. This material was used for celts as well as for the manufacture of beads (see chapter 13). One of the more unusual dark greenstone objects found at K'axob is a disk with an incised face. This object was excavated from an Early K'atabche'k'ax burial in operation 1 (figure 15.1b). The disk is oval shaped (1.2 cm x 1.43 cm; 0.35 cm thick), flat and unpolished on the back side, and polished and slightly outcurved on the front. Two holes were drilled to represent eyes, and an upturned, crooked mouth was incised (figure 15.1b).

Greenstone is also present in a translucent apple green color, which was highly polished and lustrous. The two examples are tubular beads, one from a midden dating to the Early Chaakk'ax period and the second from a Late K'atabche'k'ax cache in operation 7 (figures 15.1c and 15.1e). The small central figurine (figure 15.1d), discussed below, is an example of a dark apple colored stone with slight mottling.

Other jadeite pieces are slightly different in appearance. The largest round bead excavated from K'axob is a dark greenstone with a band of white (figure 15.1f). Other pieces are mottled with patches of light and dark green or contain white banding. One unique piece of greenstone has a white base with light green flecks (figure 15.1g). This artifact was carved and smoothed into a square but had no perforations, indicating that it was never suspended. The object was excavated from a burial dating to the Terminal K'atabche'k'ax complex

(operation 8) and was associated with four other pieces of finished and unfinished greenstone.

The presence of finished and unfinished pieces of greenstone in secondary burials 8-3a and 8-3b of operation 8 is unusual. The partial completion of some of the pieces, along with the tiny broken fragments, suggests three possibilities: (1) the pieces were broken during use; (2) the young and middle-aged adults with whom the greenstone was deposited were artisans buried with works in progress; or (3) this is a ritual termination event involving the breakage and scattering of the stone. If indeed greenstone ornaments were fabricated here, then this would represent an activity rarely documented at other Maya sites. At Cuello (Hammond 1991b: 199), Cerros (Garber 1983a, 1983b, 1989), and Colha (Buttles 1992), the investigators have interpreted broken fragments as the result of wear or ritual deposition. Shattered pieces, in particular, are reported in dedicatory contexts at Cerros (Garber 1983a). In the K'axob example, the smoothed and polished greenstone excavated from operation 8 appears to be unfinished rather than broken. The intentional breakage of greenstone does not appear in any other deposits at K'axob.

Types of greenstone beads

The semiprecious worked stone of K'axob occurs primarily as beads, either round (subspherical), disk, or tubular shaped (table 15.1). Perforated holes in the tubular pieces were drilled from both ends of the pieces. The tubular beads are beautifully made and polished, suggesting the work of a skilled artisan and the expenditure of effort and time in production. Some of the smaller rounded beads, particularly those with incurving ends, are less finished, suggesting the work of a less skilled artisan or, at the least, less effort involved in the production.

Rounded beads are either (1) finished, smoothed, and polished with rounded edges (figures 15.2a and 15.2c) or (2) flat with incurving ends with no rounding on the edges (figure 15.2b). As stated above, these latter beads tend to be more crudely made, with the perforations frequently off-center. There is a total of fourteen round beads, and their size varies greatly. The smallest bead is 0.2 cm in length, with a diameter of 0.3 cm, while the largest bead measures 1.75 cm in length, with a diameter of 2.3 cm. The majority of beads range between 0.2 and 0.28 cm in length, with a diameter of 0.3 cm to 0.5 cm. Round beads are present throughout the

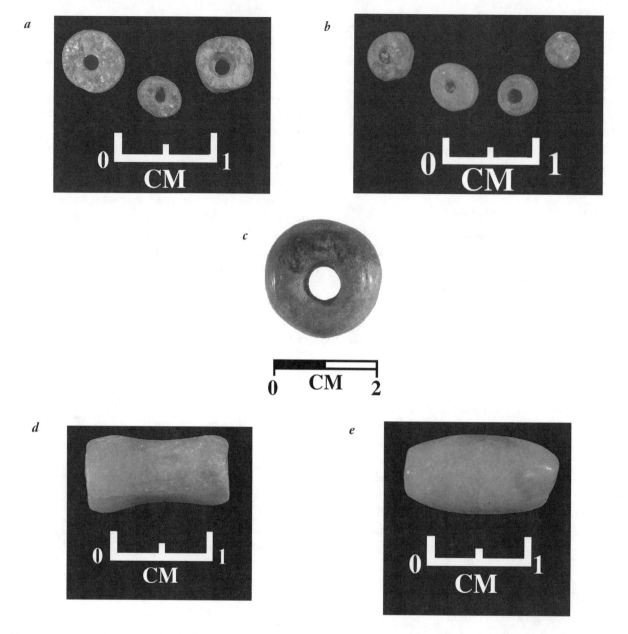

Figure 15.2 Types of greenstone beads excavated from K'axob: (a and c) finished, smoothed, and polished beads; (b) unfinished bead; (d and e) tubular beads drilled biconically.

Preclassic period and are made from a variety of jadeite material (table 15.1).

Tubular beads are elongated rods with holes drilled from both ends. The sides can be either straight, incurved, or outcurved (figures 15.2d and 15.2e). The nine tubular beads uncovered were made from all three types of greenstone material discussed above. The diameter of these examples varies from 0.5 to 0.9 cm. Only five of the beads are whole, and these five vary in length from 1 to 2 cm.

SLATE/SOAPSTONE ORNAMENT

Greenstone is not the only type of stone used to fashion ornamental objects at K'axob. Very dark grey slate, or soapstone, was also carved and worn as part of a necklace (figure 15.3). This carved piece resembles a bird or perhaps a leaping fish and was excavated from a burial dating to the late facet of the K'atabche'k'ax complex, operation 1. The object would have hung vertically from a hole perforated in the area where eyes would have appeared. The pendant was smoothed and

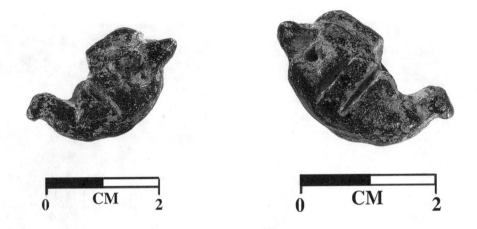

Figure 15.3 Two views of slate pendant excavated at K'axob.

deeply incised along both sides. These grooves are less apparent on one side, which was perhaps worn smooth during the object's use life (figure 15.3, left image). An appendage extends on the top of the piece and may be meant to represent bird plumage or a fin. Two rounded knobs extend from the front of the rounded body, and an extension resembling a tail or possibly human legs and feet extend downward from the back.

The significance of this part-anthropomorphic and part-zoomorphic figure is unknown. The object is obviously the work of an artisan. Similar to the greenstone, the stone was imported from beyond the alluvial plain of northern Belize. The object was probably brought to K'axob as a finished piece and was either traded or (more likely) given as a gift, possibly to the individual with whom it was interred.

The variability in the types of green and black stone excavated from K'axob indicate that this small village did participate (albeit to a limited extent) in the widespread trade networks, or gifting, reported at other, larger sites in the Maya Lowlands. The presence of greenstone in both the larger ceremonial precinct and in a single housemound suggests that this material cannot be used as the only evidence marking status. In addition, the unfinished appearance of the greenstone recovered from burials in the single housemound suggests possible fabrication or finishing at the site, but the evidence is inconclusive.

In addition to greenstone, ornamental and utilitarian uses of bone are evident at K'axob. The pieces of carved and shaped bone at K'axob are similar to those found at most other Maya sites (Hammond 1991a;

Figure 15.1 Greenstone object types and raw materials

Type of object	Fuchsite	Dark greenstone	Apple–green stone	Mottled green stone	Totals
Tubular beads	5	1	3		9
Polished blanks, no discernible shape	1	1		1 white with green patches	3
Disk with face		1			1
Cache items (not beads)			3		3
Round bead	8	3 (includes one with white bands)	2	1	14
Fragments	2		3 (1 very light color)		5
Totals	**16**	**6**	**11**	**2**	**35**

a

b

c

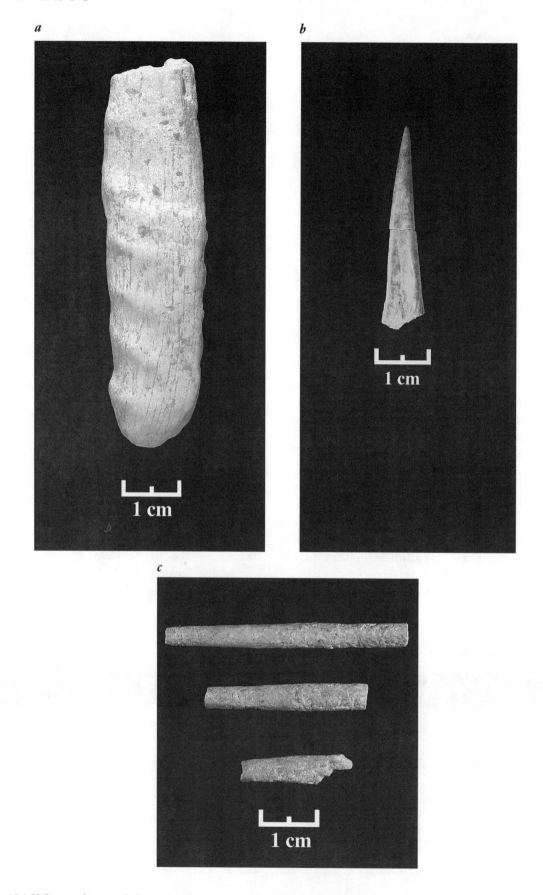

Figure 15.4 Utilitarian objects made from carved bone: (a) carved bone knife handle, (b) bone awl, and (c) bone needles or pins.

Buttles 1992; Shaw 1991; Garber 1989; Willey 1972; Lee 1969 et al.), attesting to the participation of the people of K'axob in the ritual and economic life of larger centers in the Maya world.

ORNAMENTAL BONE

At K'axob, carved bone was either created to fulfill some ornamental purpose or it had a utilitarian and economic use (see *Carved Bone Database* for detailed descriptions). Carved and polished bones were recovered from three types of contexts: burials, middens, and the plowzone. Utilitarian objects such as awls and needles were found in both burial contexts and middens. Carved bone tubes, probably used as fan handles, were excavated from burial 1-2, which was the only burial that also contained greenstone. The only other context to contain both worked bone and greenstone was an Early Chaakk'ax midden in operation 1. This Chaakk'ax midden context contained one broken apple-green jadeite fragment and a round fuchsite bead in addition to four pieces of worked bone. Identification of species for bone is made where possible, but in most cases the fragmentary condition and the size of the pieces of bone made accurate identification difficult.

Utilitarian bone objects

Utilitarian bone objects include a carved and polished fragment that is grooved on one side and polished on the other (figure 15.4a). This object is from the Early Chaakk'ax midden context discussed above. The bone is thick and dense, with a width of 1.7 cm, a length of 6.25 cm, and a thickness of 1 cm. One end is smoothed and rounded while the other is broken. Five grooves were carved and smoothed into the piece. The grooves, or smoothed indentations, are approximately 0.65 cm apart and are separated by a rounded smoothed protuberance approximately 0.25 cm wide. This piece fits comfortably into the right hand, with the widest indentation, near the broken end, providing a perfect resting place for the thumb. There is little doubt that this object was part of a hand-held tool, probably the handle of a knife. The bone is from a large mammal but is too altered to identify as to species.

A bone awl (figure 15.4b), which was smoothed to a sharp point on one end, was also uncovered from the same midden context. A possibly natural, rounded groove on the interior surface and a lack of denseness suggests that this is a bird bone. Bone awls are reported for Colha (Buttles 1992) and Cuello (Hammond 1991b:182), although the example at Cuello is much larger than the specimen from K'axob. Awls were probably used for puncturing holes in leather or other soft material. Buttles (1992) reports this usage among modern villagers in the Guatemala Highlands.

Other utilitarian bone objects include three broken fragments of bone needles or pins that were excavated from Late K'atabche'k'ax burial 11-6 (figure 15.4c). Willey (1978) suggests that this type of object may have been worn in the hair or used for fastening clothing. Since none of the pieces is complete, it is impossible to determine if these fragments were adornment or were used for sewing. Their presence in a burial context suggests adornment. Bone needles and pins are reported at Colha (Shaw 1991; Buttles 1992), Seibal (Willey 1978), and Altar de Sacrificios (Willey 1972), among other Maya Lowland sites. At Cuello, one artifact features a perforated hole, indicating that it was probably used for sewing, while a second example, which has no perforation, may be a bone pin (Hammond 1991b:182).

Ornamental bone objects

Carved bone was also produced by the Formative Maya for decorative or ornamental purposes. The type of objects present at K'axob include the bone pins discussed above, bone beads, and bone tubes that were possibly used as fan handles or as hair adornment.

The *bone tubes* recovered from K'axob were excavated from multiple burial 1-2 of operation 1 (McAnany and López Varela 1999:162; chapter 6). These tubes were found in association with two jadeite beads. The first bead was fashioned from fuchsite and is the largest of the tubular beads excavated at K'axob (figure 15.1a). The second greenstone bead is one of the smallest of the round beads. Fragments of at least eleven bone tubes were found in this large burial context (figure 15.5). Several smaller fragments of worked bone, probably broken from the more intact tubes, were also excavated (figure 15.5 shows the larger examples of these broken fragments). In addition to the bone tubes, several fragments of modified human bone were found. A hole had been drilled in one large fragment of a human femur. This bone also has multiple cut marks (figure 15.6). Other smaller fragments also had evidence of observable cut marks (figure 15.6).

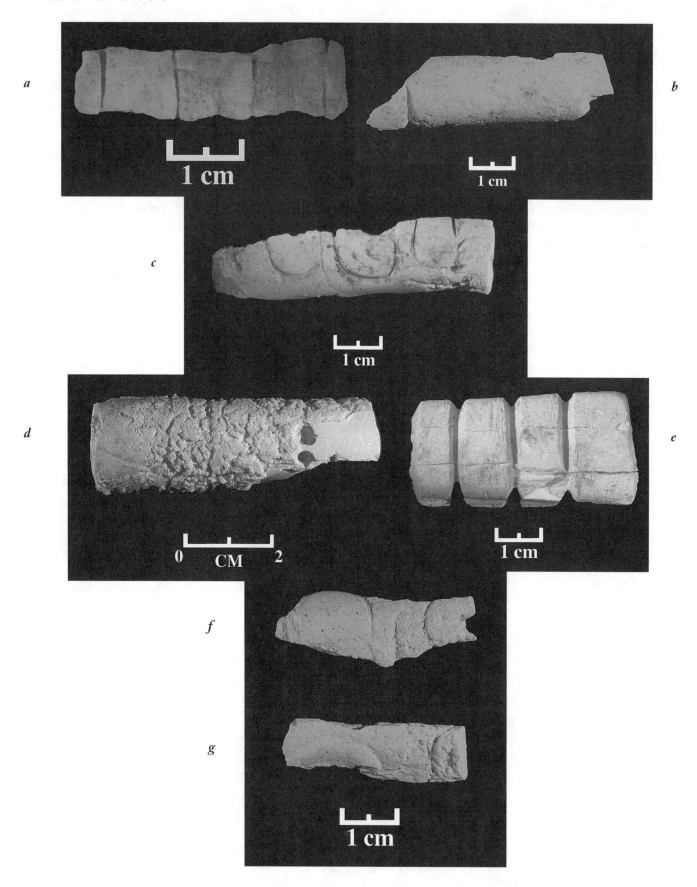

Figure 15.5 Carved bone tubes excavated from multiple burial 1-2, operation 1.

Figure 15.6 Possible human bone with a perforation and cut marks (the latter marked by arrows), burial 1-2.

Two long bones, both incurving, appear to be a matching set. These two bones are from a medium to large mammal, probably a deer or peccary. Two concentric rings were incised on either end of the tube (figure 15.7). The incising is irregular with some overlapping. The bones were sawed and smoothed on each end. At Chiapa de Corzo, Lee (1969:211–212) notes that several carved bones appeared to have been incised or sawn to a depth of 3 to 5 mm. The resulting groove was probably then snapped and the edges smoothed. This same process was apparent at Colha (Shaw 1991; Buttles 1992) and appears to be the process used at K'axob. Although the purpose of these tubes is not known, their large size suggests that they were used as handles for feather fans (Schele and Miller 1986:143, 152, 166, Plate 50) or as hair ornaments (Schele and Miller 1986:186, 197, Plate 61). The two tubes (figure 15.7) are the least ornate of the bone tubes excavated from this context.

The remainder of the bone tubes are shorter in length and more finely decorated (figure 15.5). These may have been used as pendants or necklaces. Willey (1972) suggested that some incurved bone may have been used as ear spools, although the tubes from K'axob appear to be too long for that purpose. Decorative patterning includes concentric rings, deep wide angular grooves, circles or ovals, and partially

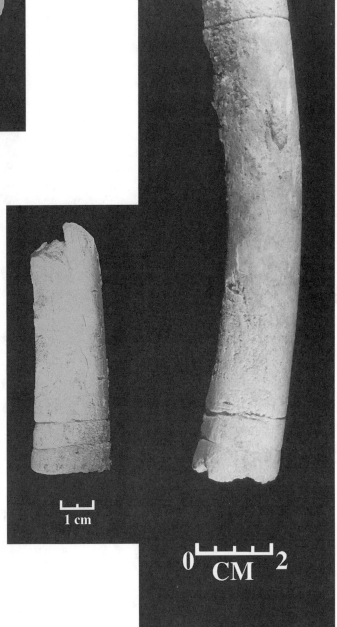

Figure 15.7 Two long tubes of matching bones possibly used as fan handles or hair ornaments, burial 1-2.

a

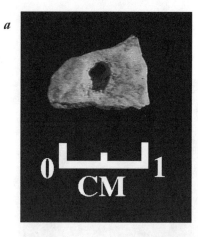

b

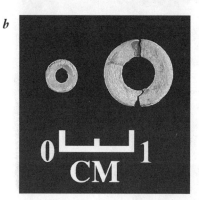

Figure 15.8 Beads made from bone: (a) unfinished bead excavated from an Early Chaakk'ax midden, and (b) two beads made from fish vertebrae.

perforated holes. The bone with the deepest angular grooves (figure 15.5e) has also been shaped to form a square. Each of the examples has been grooved and snapped at either end, and the resulting breaks were then smoothed. Some of the bones appear to have been polished. Similar examples are reported for Cuello (Hammond 1991a: 180–183), Colha (Shaw 1991; Buttles 1992), Cerros (Garber 1989), Altar de Sacrificios (Willey 1972), and Chiapa de Corzo (Lee 1969).

Bone was also shaped to form *beads* (figure 15.8). At K'axob, these beads occur in three different forms: unsmoothed and unrounded, modified fish vertebra, and tubular.

The first bone bead is the most crudely manufactured of the three (figure 15.8a). Three of the edges are rough with no evidence of rounding or smoothing. These edges may be the result of either incomplete production or postdepositional breakage. Bone thickness measures 0.3 cm. The fragment is too small to identify as to species other than to state that it is mammalian. This piece was excavated from an Early Chaakk'ax burial (1–42).

The next example is a small round tube that is 0.8 cm in length and 0.45 cm in diameter, with a center hole diameter of 0.15 cm. (figure 15.8b illustrates an outer and inner fragment of the bead). The bead is finely wrought, round, and probably made from a fish vertebra. The exterior edge is perfectly round and the sides are incurving. The small fragment shown to the left in figure 15.8b is the middle section of the larger bead. The exterior edge of the larger bead is round and the flat sides are incurving. These two pieces were

excavated from an Early Chaakk'ax midden. Shaw (1991) reports fish vertebrae beads from Colha that appear similar to the example from K'axob. The final possible bead has a cylinder shape but with no perforation. The object was excavated from the plowzone in operation 12 (not shown). This piece was either in the process of manufacture or is a broken fragment of a bone pin.

The final bone ornament excavated from K'axob is a carved and polished *ear spool* excavated from a Terminal K'atabche'k'ax burial in operation 8. Only half of the

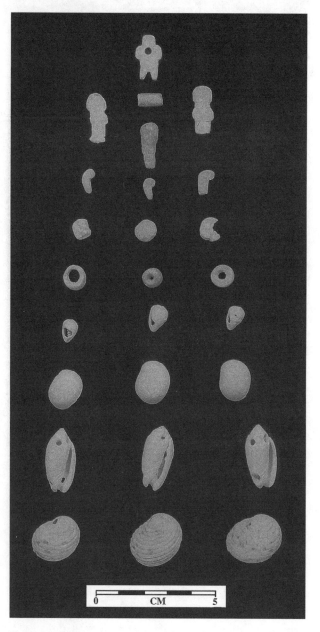

Figure 15.9 Cache elements arranged according to triadic and color-coded structure.

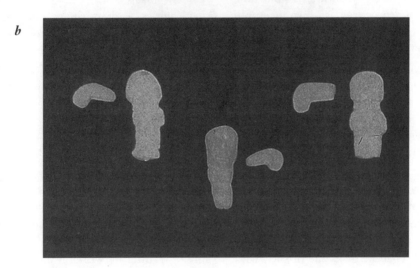

Figure 15.10 Selected elements of triadic cache: (a) four central figures from triadic cache; and (b) three central figures with color-coded, comma-shaped elements arranged as speech scrolls.

spool was recovered. The width of the ornament is 1.4 cm, with a thickness of .15 cm and a diameter of 2 cm. The sides are slightly incurving, and rounded ridges were carved on either end. The piece resembles the clay spool discussed in chapter 10 and is possibly a large fish vertebra. Willey (1972) refers to this type of ear spool as a napkin ring. Buttles (1992) reports a similar example excavated from a Terminal Preclassic burial at Colha. The material at Colha was a shark vertebra and possibly the example from K'axob is also. Masson (chapter 17) discusses the presence of shark vertebrae at K'axob. Garber (1989) reports similar examples from Cerros but does not identify the bone type. Use of fish vertebrae

for ear spools is also reported for Preclassic Altamira (Green and Lowe 1967), so this seems to be a widespread practice.

TRIADIC CACHE

Jadeite in combination with shell is found in a very distinctive cache context at K'axob. Due to the singularity of this deposit, its contents are described as a unit. The small greenstone figure discussed in the beginning of this chapter is a part of the cache. This deposit was excavated from a Terminal K'atabche'k'ax structure that was built about the same time as the burial shrine complex of burials 1-1 and 1-2, operation 1 (chapter 4; McAnany and López Varela 1999:162). These objects had been placed inside a dedicatory vessel capped by a plate or lid. Although the offering contained no discernable spatial patterning, it was laden with color and numerical symbolism.

This cache consists of twenty-nine objects. The total count includes two small irregular pieces of hematite, two small snail shells possibly naturally occurring, and a broken red stone bead (see *Triadic Cache Database*). With the exception of these objects, one greenstone bead, and four central figures of the cache, the remainder of the excavated material can be grouped into sets of three (figure 15.9).

The cache is dominated by four central human figures (figure 15.10a). One figure, with a round hole perforated through the chest area, was manufactured from mother-of-pearl. McAnany and López Varela (1999:162) note that this figure may be associated with the one tubular greenstone bead found in the assemblage. Three additional figures, two of a pale orange iridescent shell and one of greenstone with incised features, complete the assemblage of human figures. The color coding extends to three associated comma-shaped objects (figure 15.10b). One comma is greenstone and the other two are made from shell. These commas are reminiscent of the symbols for speech present in the murals of Teotihuacan (Berrin 1988:Plates 15–18). Figure 15.10b shows the possible scrolls so arranged.

The triadic scheme continues with three disks: a completely round greenstone disk, one of shell with a more irregular shape, and the last a "half moon" also made of shell. The next row contains three beads: again one is manufactured from jadeite and the other two from shell. At this point, the color symbolism ends, but the triadic structure continues with three small perforated snail shells followed by three larger perforated snail shells. The next to the last row contains three uncut tinklers, each with one perforation at the top and at the bottom. The final row contains three snail shells with black and white banding. This particular type of tree snail is quite common in the high bush adjacent to the river.

The colors of red, green, and white; the materials jadeite, mother-of-pearl, and freshwater and marine shell; and the shape of the objects all strongly suggest a ritual significance to this cache. McAnany and López Varela (1991:162) note that the colors and triadic nature of the cache suggest primordial fertility and possibly sacrifice. Certainly the perforation of the one figure through the chest suggests heart sacrifice. At Palenque, Gods I, II, and III occur together and are called the Palenque triad (Miller and Taube 1993:129–130). These three gods appear to be the patron deities of Palenque, although individually their glyphic names are found at other sites. According to ancient Maya texts, they were born in 2360 BC over a three-week period. Miller and Taube (1993:129–130) suggest that they could be considered triplets. By the seventh century AD, the lords of Palenque, including the famous K'inich Janaab' Pakal I the Great, make reference to these deities. Perhaps the trinity figures and symbolism at K'axob are an earlier manifestation of this belief. Obviously, placement within the southwestern corner of a focal structure at K'axob attests to the symbolic value of this cache for the inhabitants of K'axob.

SUMMARY

Greenstone was present at K'axob from the time of earliest settlement. It was used as an ornament, and in the Terminal Preclassic was used as an important element in the unique triadic cache. The paucity of exotic stone material at K'axob does suggest that these villagers were only marginal participants in widespread trading networks found at larger sites. This scarcity could imply that access to exotic stone objects was through gifting mechanisms rather than trade networks. The presence of possible unfinished greenstone in burials within the single residential complex suggests possible manufacturing. Placement in burials of carved exotic stone, both broken and complete, and incised bone presents a pattern similar to that found at larger Maya sites, and it reflects the connection of the people of K'axob to the belief systems and rituals of the wider Maya world. The similarity in utilitarian objects of bone also suggests consistency in technical development, use of resources, and craft technology throughout the Maya area, from small villages to major centers.

Chapter 16
Related CD Resources

Cross Motif Vessels
Burials

CHAPTER 16

THE QUADRIPARTITE MOTIF AND THE CENTRALIZATION OF POWER

ANNABETH HEADRICK

When a person dies in the small Mexican town of Huaquechula, Puebla, there is a tradition of first making a cross-shaped design of sand and lime on the floor (Carmichael and Sayer 1991:95). After tracing the design on the floor, the mourners then place the body of the deceased over the cross. This funeral rite is a seemingly simple one, and the dominance of Catholicism in the area would suggest a decisive Christian meaning for the cross under the corpse; however, in Mexico, as in all modern areas of what was once Mesoamerica, such quick conclusions are not always as solid as they might seem. As archaeologists we know that by taking a brush and moving away the layers of soil below that floor, we will find that evidence of the past is quite close to those living in the present. Yet it is often with surprise that we realize how persistent pre-Columbian traditions are among those who inherited the soils that were Mesoamerica.

The impetus for the crosses underneath the dead of Huaquechula could stem from many sources. Certainly, the motive for placing the crosses could be purely Roman Catholic, linking the death of the present with that of Christ two millennia ago. Alternatively, as I suggest below, it is possible that the tradition has its foundation in pre-Columbian rituals performed at an even earlier time than the Christian catalyst. There is certainly room for the more likely explanation of syncretism, in which the act pulls from both great traditions and seamlessly blends them into a potent concoction that defiantly resists our attempts to pry apart its divergent origins. In truth, even with all of our scientific tools, we will never know just how indebted these Huaquechula crosses are to either tradition; that is, we will never be able to assign a percentage to how Christian or pre-Columbian an act of the present might be.

While acknowledging the critical role Roman Catholicism plays in shaping the ritual lives of modern-day Mesoamericans, this volume concerns the past, specifically the Middle Formative to Early Classic peoples who lived and died at K'axob; therefore, this chapter considers the possible pre-Columbian contribution to the Huaquechula crosses. Although no direct

367

link to this particular Pueblan town is made, the cross emerges as a decidedly Mesoamerican symbol that appeared in the earliest Mesoamerican symbol system—a system that the residents of K'axob helped develop through their early participation in it. In Mesoamerica the cross was elaborated, modified, and historically manipulated; further, it crossed geographical and cultural boundaries. Nonetheless, it persisted throughout the entire temporal period of Mesoamerica and functioned as one of the most fundamental symbols in

Figure 16.1 Two Early K'atabche'k'ax complex Sierra Red shallow dishes interred with burial of two adults (burials 1-25 and 1-29). *Photo from K'axob Project archives*

the Mesoamerican visual vocabulary. A discussion of the Mesoamerican cross could begin in many places, but a particular set of vessels from K'axob serve as the perfect vehicle with which to begin an exploration of the complex ideology of this simply formed visual design.

CROSS VESSELS OF K'AXOB

The seven vessels in question fit into a rather tightly circumscribed set of characteristics (see *Cross Motif Database*). Each of them is from the K'atabche'k'ax ceramic complex: two fall into the early facet (400–200 BC) Sierra Red variety (figure 16.1; see also vessels 013 and 014 in *Cross Motif Database*), and the other five belong to the late to terminal facet (200 BC–AD 150/250) Society Hall Red variety (figure 16.2; see vessels 021, 023, 033, 034, and 046; McAnany and López Varela 1999; McAnany, Storey, and Lockard 1999). As for their form, the bowls are either low and shallow with outflaring rims, or they are deep with straight, vertical sides and flaring rims. In all but one case, the bowls are covered with red slip in their interior and exterior surfaces, except for the exterior base which is largely unslipped aside from a simple cross made by two streaky and rapid brushstrokes. The crossing of the brushstrokes ranges from almost right angles to a less structured and more uneven crossing. The only exception to this pattern is a particularly large, straight-sided terminal-facet bowl (figure 16.2) that reverses the decoration. Instead of painting the cross on the exterior

base, the ceramicist applied a thin slip to the interior bottom and sides and painted a cross across the bottom and sides of the bowl. In the center of this cross a circle marks the crossing of the two lines. This distinctive cross decoration has led to the project moniker for the vessels—the quadripartite motif.

Not only are these K'axob vessels fairly uniform in their appearance but they also share a decidedly similar context, for each of them came from one of five different burials (McAnany, Storey, and Lockard 1999). Of these, burials 1-25 and 1-29 represent the earliest individuals at K'axob to be interred with a cross-decorated vessel. These two individuals were interred in twinlike fashion. Each adult male was placed in an extended position accompanied by one of the Sierra Red cross vessels (figure 6.3). In burial 1-25 the cross vessel was found inverted near the skull, suggesting that it was originally positioned over the face of the deceased, while the vessel in burial 1-29 was near the individual's right arm. A cross vessel was positioned over the head of a flexed adult in burial 1-13 (figure 3.8), and this individual was also accompanied by a unique effigy vessel depicting a plump face that may represent a "fat god" (Taube in McAnany, Storey, and Lockard 1999:138). Burial 1-1a consisted of a young to middle-aged adult, probably male, in a seated position with one large cross vessel inverted over the head and another sitting upright at his side (figure 6.8). Around this individual were the secondary remains of six other individuals. Similarly, burial 1-2e included a bundled young adult, probably male, with a particularly large cross vessel inverted over the head, and two other vessels, one of which bears the cross motif. In addition, the grave included shell pendants and tinklers, hematite, and the secondary remains of eight other individuals (figure 6.9).

From these burials certain patterns emerge (McAnany, Storey, and Lockard 1999). First, except for burial 1-29, at least one of the cross vessels was inverted over the head of the deceased in each of the burials. Second, all of the cross-decorated bowls came from excavations in operation 1, which was placed on the eastern side of structure 18, a pyramidal structure on the west side of plaza B, and it seems clear that these were some of the richest Formative period burials at the site. Finally, the cross vessels were exclusively associated with adults, which may indicate that they were reserved for individuals with accumulated status. Another indication of status may be that two of the individuals in these burials were either seated or flexed, probably wrapped in the form of mortuary bundles. McAnany, Storey, and Lockard (1999) argue that flexed burials may be a marker of status and authority. They compare the shift from early facet K'atabche'k'ax extended burials to late facet K'atabche'k'ax flexed burials with similar changes in burial patterns in Oaxaca, suggesting that flexed burials may indicate the emergence of a more institutionalized power (Marcus 1999; Marcus and Flannery 1996). Another pattern of note is the inclusion of numerous secondary burials with the principal individuals in burials 1-1 and 1-2. Because the Terminal K'atabche'k'ax period seems to be one of increased centralization of authority, the secondary burials may represent an attempt to gather ancestral remains in order to increase the concentration of kingroup identity in the location of operation 1 (McAnany and López Varela 1999; McAnany, Storey, and Lockard 1999).

Figure 16.2 Interior and profile drawing of vessel 034 found inverted over head of principal individual in burial 1-2. *Photo and illustration from K'axob Project archives*

Taken as a whole, the evidence suggests that individuals buried with cross vessels held some degree of elevated status among the people of K'axob. Because in subsequent periods the pyramidal structure 18 rose over these burials, it is likely that the ancestors interred in this location during the Middle to Late Formative evolved into a base of power for those who dominated the political structure of the site. As noted by McAnany, Storey, and Lockard (1999) the location of operation 1 seems to function as the hub of the site, with other satellite structures clustering around it. They further emphasize the fact that many of the burials in operation 1 are multiple, secondary interments, which indicates curation of bones. Such curation could signal a growing interest in ancestors and reckoning kin groups, a practice that clearly accompanied power in the Classic period (McAnany 1995a). All in all, the unique circumstances surrounding the cross vessels of K'axob provide an exciting window onto the formulation of power in a small Formative site; yet to comprehend the full import of these vessels, it is necessary to step outside of K'axob. By putting these bowls into the context of the greater Mesoamerican symbol system, we can better understand how the residents of this site shared the strategies of power that were used elsewhere in Mesoamerica.

THE CROSS AND THE BOWL IN MESOAMERICA

Because the K'axob cross vessels are simple in form and motif, it would be helpful to compare them to other Mesoamerican artistic traditions that tend to elaborate upon their subjects. Through comparison and patterning we can trace a motif as it transforms due to the forces of historical and cultural manipulation. In keeping with the temporal focus of the K'axob project, it seems only fitting to first look to the art of the Middle Formative Olmec. While the Olmec comparative materials may be geographically distant from K'axob, we may still entertain the idea that K'axob participated in the emerging ideological complex and its symbol system, which developed in the Middle Formative. Recent scholars have argued against the old concept of the Gulf Coast Olmec heartland as the single source of a new iconographic symbol system, suggesting instead that diverse geographical regions contributed to the symbol set (Clark 1997; Coe 1968). In particular, Kent Reilly has coined the term "Middle Formative Ceremonial Complex" to refer to the highland-lowland interaction that resulted in the development of an ideologically based rationale of governance, of which art is but one material manifestation (Reilly 1990, 1995). Following Reilly's model, people throughout Mesoamerica devised and manipulated the symbols representing this new ideology, thus it was a fluid system involving long-distance trade and interaction. This evidence for pan-Mesoamerican interaction justifies comparisons of the K'axob materials to objects traditionally referred to as "Olmec." Within the art of the Middle Formative Olmec, one particular object stands out in its ability to explain the meaning of the K'axob cross vessels.

That object is the well known Humboldt Celt (figure 16.3), which unfortunately was looted but is thought to have originated in Central Mexico.[1] Over-

bowl in cross section

Figure 16.3 Humboldt Celt (after Joralemon 1971:Fig. 32).

all, the celt depicts a ruler wearing cosmological symbols on his body. Although the top is broken, his arms appear at the top. Below this are three clouds surrounding an eye, which is a common Mesoamerican symbol for stars. The eye indicates that the three circles below are stars, specifically the three hearthstones that many textual and ethnographic sources indicate are in the constellation Orion (Freidel, Schele, and Parker 1993). Below this are a set of symbols arranged in a cruciform shape that extend from a circle marked by a cross. As Kent Reilly (1994) has argued, this cruciform assemblage may represent a Middle Formative attempt to depict a cosmological image of the world. The cross in the center would represent just that—the center of the universe—while the four clusters of symbols surrounding the cross may be very early glyphs for the four cardinal directions. Specifically, Reilly suggests that the uppermost glyph compound, which prominently features the crossed-bands, is the direction "north." Conceptually, north is up, or celestial, in Mesoamerica, which would explain the stars above the north symbol. Near the bottom of the celt is a U-shape with outflaring rims that precisely describes the shape of a bisected bowl in profile. This bowl, I would argue, is conceptually the same as the quadripartite bowls found at K'axob (figures 16.1 and 16.2).

In order to best understand this, it is important to acknowledge that Olmec stylistic conventions for depicting space differ from Western conventions (Reilly 1994, 1995). While Western artists prefer to depict their images from one viewpoint, Olmec artists felt free to combine multiple points of view in order to offer the viewer the greatest amount of information. On the Humboldt Celt a masterful artist did just that by providing his audience with both a profile and bird's-eye view of the universe. The bowl at the bottom and the arms of the ruler at the top appear in profile, thus the viewer can read the bowl as down and the torso as up. However, the cardinal directions at the center of the celt are arranged as though the viewer were looking from above as the four directions spread out from the center, all the while remembering that north is also up.

Keeping all of this in mind, then, just how is it possible to relate this iconography to the K'axob bowls? In fact, the symbolism of the K'axob bowls appears in several versions on the greenstone celt. First, the profile bowl obviously functions as the bowl itself, and above, as part of the north glyph, the crossed-bands serve as the cross. Despite all of the extra "static" of the additional iconography, the Humboldt Celt still pairs the bowl with the cross. Second, the artist offered a view of the bowl from above, for in the center of the directional glyphs is a circle with a cross. This symbol for center could also be read as the round shape of a bowl with the cross in the middle; that is, the viewer looks down into the bowl at the decoration painted on the bottom (figure 16.2).

Concerning this interpretation, it is critical to recognize that the cross in the north glyph and the cross in the center of the directional glyphs are different. In iconographic terms the cross in the north glyph is dubbed the "crossed-bands," which are generally interpreted as symbolizing the sky or, more specifically, the path of the Milky Way as it crosses the ecliptic (Schele, Freidel, and Parker 1993). The other cross with its arms at right angles is the Kan-cross, which represents the concepts of blue-green, center, and preciousness. It is quite clear that the Olmec and the Classic Maya made distinctions between these two symbols; however, because the intersection of the Milky Way and the ecliptic was also considered to be the center of the sky, there is a degree of conceptual overlap between these two symbols. Furthermore, the present discussion concerns the K'axob bowls, and the design of the bowls would suggest that the crosses on these vessels were meant to encompass both symbols. Of particular note is the fact that the K'axob artists were not particularly precise when painting the crosses on the vessels. Some crosses are at right angles while others vary slightly from this pattern. Rather than a sign of disregard, the variations could simply indicate that the point was to paint a cross (a symbol that communicated the entirety of both the Kan cross and the crossed-bands)—a strategy that was both powerful and comprehensive. The crosses in the K'axob bowls, then, simultaneously referred to the idea of the center of the earth, the heart of the sky, the arch of the sun and the Milky Way, preciousness, and even the blue-green bowl of water, which was a metaphor for the empty ocean at the beginning of time. The most poetic expression of this concept comes from the opening words of the *Popol Vuh*, which offer a description of the universe before creation:

> Heart of the Lake, Heart of the Sea
> Maker of the Blue-Green Plate,
> Maker of the Blue-Green Bowl (Tedlock 1985:71)

Just as these words attempt to express the incomprehensible, the multiple meanings of the cross lent enormous power to this simple symbol.

Thus, the artist of the Humboldt Celt offers multiple points of view in order to convey both horizontal and vertical space, and the two-dimensional plane of the celt succeeds in expressing three-dimensional space as well. The import of this observation is all the more clear when we recognize what these symbols, as a whole, are meant to convey. The arms at the top of

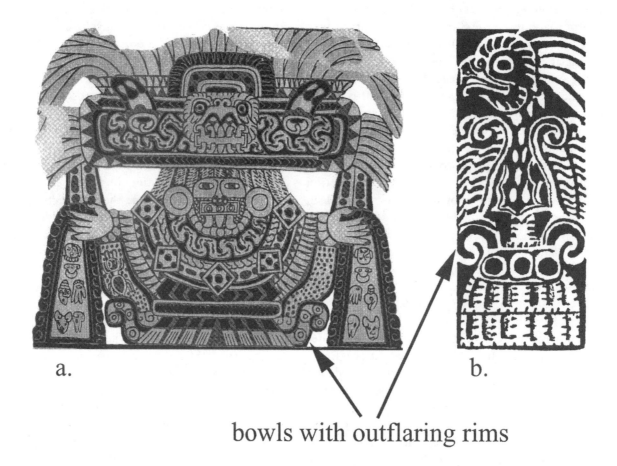

a.   b.

bowls with outflaring rims

Figure 16.4 Teotihuacan images of divining bowls: (a) Great Goddess rising from divining bowl in mural from Tetitla, Teotihuacan (after Villagra Caleti 1971:Fig. 14); and (b) sculpture of partially defleshed bird rising from bowl, Palace of Quetzalpapalotl, Teotihuacan (after von Winning 1987:175).

the stone indicate that, fundamentally, the Humboldt Celt is a depiction of an Olmec ruler. He wears bracelets on his arms and further decorates his body with the symbols of the cosmos. As is so often the case in Olmec art, the ruler applies the cosmological symbols to his body to assert that he is the center of the universe and that all things revolve around him. On the Humboldt Celt the four cardinal directions literally spread from the core of the king's body; therefore, he is symbolically the center of the world.

Powerful as that may be, the Humboldt artist took this concept even further by suggesting that the ruler not only commanded horizontal space but also controlled vertical space. To fully explore this aspect, we must turn to the use of bowls in Mesoamerican ritual. In an influential paper on the iconography of mirrors, Karl Taube (1992) showed that bowls served as divining vessels in

Mesoamerica. Shamans could look into bowls and conjure objects, including supernaturals, and cause them to rise up into the world of humans. The Humboldt Celt may depict such an image, but in this case it is the ruler himself who rises up from the bowl, thus conveying his ability to contact the supernatural realm.

Especially clear images of divining bowls come from Classic period Teotihuacan. In a mural from the apartment compound of Tetitla, the Great Goddess rises up from the center of a divining bowl (figure 16.4a). As she enters the human realm, she sprinkles gifts of jade and preciousness. Similarly, in the sculpture decorating the patio of the Palace of Quetzalpapalotl, partially defleshed birds emerge from divining bowls (figure 16.4b). Such bowls served as openings to the supernatural world, and there were a number of ways shamans could turn them into

sun-marked bowl

Figure 16.5 Tablet of the Cross, Palenque (drawing courtesy of Linda Schele).

portals. As Taube (1992) argues, shamans could throw sastun stones into water-filled bowls in order to divine the sacred. In light of this, I would suggest that the three obsidian insets on the bowls of the Palace of Quetzalpapalotl represent three sastun stones. The large size of some of the K'axob cross bowls may indicate that these were feasting vessels used by K'axob's elite, yet the cosmological symbolism of their decoration might attest to their possible use as divining vessels. This, in turn, would suggest that the individuals buried with a cross vessel may have held a shamanic role in K'axob society.

Another means of transforming a bowl into a portal to the supernatural world involved sacrifice, as is shown in the Late Classic period carved panel from the Temple of the Cross at Palenque (figure 16.5). Pakal and his son, Kan Balam, stand on either side of the quadripartite badge, which consists of a defleshed head surmounted by a sun-marked bowl shown in profile. Sitting in the bowl are offerings, including a stingray spine, bundle, and a shell. The stingray spine indicates that bloodletting was performed and that an offering of the blood was put into the bowl. As a result of this sacrifice, the world tree rises up from the bowl.

The world tree is of critical importance for the present discussion because of its decided cruciform shape and the fact that it emerges from a bowl. Though much more elaborate than the K'axob bowls, the Palenque panel nonetheless expresses a similar concept, for the central motif is a bowl associated with a cross, the essential components of the quadripartite motif (figures 16.1, 16.2, and 16.3). The presence of bloodletting iconography on the Palenque panel offers another possibility for the original function of the

Figure 16.6 Stela 25, Izapa (drawing courtesy of Linda Schele).

trees, one supernatural and one ritual. On the left we see a depiction of the supernatural world tree, which takes the form of a downturned caiman with leaves sprouting from its tail and a bird sitting in the branches. To the side an individual, probably an actor dressed as the culture hero Hunahpu, holds a ritual representation of the tree. This earthly version consists of a pole inserted into a bowl with a snake wrapped around the shaft and a bird perched in the branches of the pole. Together the bowl and the pole, with its horizontal extensions, compose another version of the bowl with the cross.

Such examples demonstrate that the concept of bowls with trees emerging from them was a widespread Mesoamerican idea—one that arguably traveled to K'axob. Because K'axob absorbed the bowl and cross combination and incorporated it into its symbol system, there is no reason to believe that it did not share the Olmec artistic tradition of using flat surfaces to suggest three-dimensional concepts. In other words, I would argue that the people of K'axob not only saw the painted crosses on their vessels as representative of the four cardinal and horizontal directions but that they also thought of these crosses as emerging from these bowls to symbolize the world tree and its three cosmological levels. Indeed, the bowls are simple in design but complex in concept.

Like the Humboldt Celt, the cruciform branches of the Palenque cross represent the four horizontal directions, while the verticality of the image suggests the three cosmological zones of the lower, middle, and celestial realms. The zones are easily seen on the Tablet of the Cross, with the skull representing the underworld realm of death, the trunk of the tree signaling the plane of human existence, and the bird sitting in the branches of the tree symbolizing the heavenly realm. Furthermore, as with the Humboldt Celt, the individuals deemed worthy of close association with these cosmological forces are two kings. In both the Middle Formative and the Late Classic images, kings proclaim their status by associating themselves with the center, the four cardinal directions, and the three vertical regions. Of critical importance is the recognition that the bowl and the cross functioned as one of the fundamental symbol sets by which kings proclaimed themselves the center. The context of the K'axob cross vessels would suggest that here too elites (probably those with the most political power at the site) chose to emphasize their power through associating with these symbols. The crosses on the bowls spoke not only

K'axob bowls; perhaps the cross vessels were bloodletting bowls used in public ceremonies by K'axob's elites.

The arrangement of the image from the Temple of the Cross makes it worthwhile to return to the Humboldt Celt (figure 16.3) and reassess the iconography. I have already suggested two contenders for the cross—the Kan-cross and the crossed-bands. However, on the Palenque sculpture the cross emerges from the bowl, and a second look at the Humboldt Celt reveals that here too a cross rises up from the bowl at the bottom of the celt. If we consider the assemblage of the four directional glyphs and observe their cruciform arrangement, then we see that the glyphs themselves comprise a world tree with branches. This insight also demonstrates that the Olmec king depicted on the celt associates himself with the world tree (as he substitutes his own body for that of the tree). A third example from the formative site of Izapa (figure 16.6) offers additional evidence of this pattern. Stela 25 depicts two world

of the centrality of the location where they were buried but also of the central political power of those with whom they were buried.

To fully grasp how important the bowl and cross combination was to Formative period rulership, it is necessary to understand the K'axob bowls in their simplest form. Certainly we must think of the bowls as vessels and containers meant as receptacles for other objects, but we must also conceptually reduce them to their most fundamental visual forms. Essentially, a bowl can be viewed from two main angles: (1) from above, which reveals a circular form, as in the central motif of the Humboldt Celt that depicts a cross circumscribed by a circle; and (2) from the side, as at the bottom of the Humboldt Celt, which results in a U-shaped form. For the moment, the latter is critical to understanding the meaning behind the K'axob bowls because U-shapes, especially when paired with X-shapes like the crosses painted on the K'axob bowls, served as one of the most fundamental symbols of Olmec iconography. This in turn reveals that, during Epi-Olmec times, the residents of K'axob fully participated in a symbol system that was found throughout Mesoamerica.

OLMEC VERSIONS OF THE QUADRIPARTITE MOTIF

A Middle Formative sculpture of a were-jaguar mask provides an ideal place to begin a comparison of the bowl and cross motif of K'axob with a version found in Olmec iconography (figure 16.7a). Its diagnostic features—the large downturned upper lip and fangs—are quite clear; however, for present purposes the markings on the eyes are more important. Two motifs mark the eyes. A simple X covers the right eye, while an equally simple U with a dot in its center marks the left eye. From the perspective of K'axob iconography, this were-jaguar incorporates the fundamental forms of the bowls under discussion. The U serves as a bowl in profile, and the X functions as the painted crosses on the K'axob bowls. Although, in isolation, this comparison seems stretched, when the prevalence of this pairing is clear the connection is much stronger.

The combination of the X and the U on this were-jaguar is far from unique. In fact, the pairing is extremely common—so much so that Joralemon (1971:14) included it in his compendium of standard Olmec motifs.[2] Several other examples of the paired X and U in Olmec iconography illustrate the standard-

ization of this pairing. On a ceremonial ax (figure 16.7b) of unknown provenience the same motifs once again appear on the forehead of another Olmec werejaguar. Likewise, a jade perforator (figure 16.7c) presents a highly abstract version of the motifs. In this version the downturned lip of the werejaguar becomes a simplified upside down U. The eyes of the creature each have a cleft in the top, and one eye has the X, while the other has a U with a dot in the center.

Another example (figures 16.7d and e) is a bit different, but there are still similarities. Once again the subject is a werejaguar, but this time the body is attached to the head. The body shows that the werejaguar is indeed a human, albeit a human with remarkable acrobatic skills. He crosses his arms in front of him and bends his legs over his back until his feet touch his head. It is this and other such imagery that have led Peter Furst (1968, 1995) and Kent Reilly (1989) to argue that werejaguars are human rulers involved in trancing activities—be they hallucinogenic or, as in this case, acrobatic. Through these trancing activities, they transform into their animal companion, the jaguar. Returning to the motifs under consideration, this time the X and the U appear on the bottom of the figure's feet (figure 16.7e). However, the continuity is not lost, for the figure places his feet on his head, resulting in an X and U that once again mark its forehead.

All of the above examples of the X and U pairing appear on objects depicting werejaguars, and, apart from the acrobatic figure, the ruler himself is seemingly absent. Unlike the Humboldt Celt, the hacha, perforator, and mask depict the supernatural entity without direct evidence of the human who might have transformed into this creature. However, through both medium and function, the presence of the ruler is surely implied. The jade or greenstone objects were rare commodities, most often found in elite contexts. When held in the hand of a ruler, the depersonalized aspects of the image decreased due to his/her possessing and displaying the object in a public context. For example, if a ruler held up the ceremonial ax to a crowd, then the imagery would proclaim his/her ability to transform into a jaguar nagual (spirit co-essence or companion) and to control the bowl-like portal and the four quadrants of the world. In another Olmec example the depersonalization is lessened by the presence of the ruler's portrait.

On a Middle Formative celt (figure 16.8) we see, from bottom to top, the ruler's hand and then the

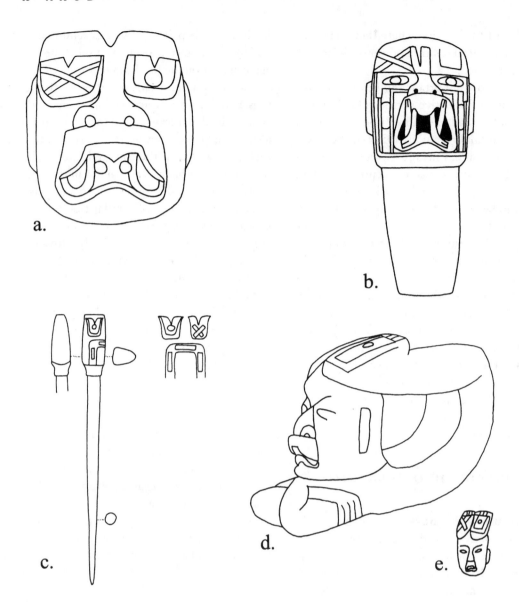

Figure 16.7 Olmec images of were-jaguars with X and U pairing (after Joralemon 1971:Figs. 153, 167, 124, 23).

ruler's head, wearing a buccal mask with a sharp hooked tooth. Above the L-shaped eye we see the paired motifs, except this time they are conflated. The U sits right above the eye, and the X appears inside the U. The dot that frequently marks the center of the U now marks the center of the X. The reason for the conflation of the motifs is that we are receiving a profile rather than frontal view of the supernatural. By combining the motifs into one, we can see both objects still on the forehead above the eyes.

This last example most closely approximates the quadripartite vessels of K'axob because the U actually contains the X in the same manner as the K'axob ves-

sels contain their crosses. Even though it appears in an extremely abstracted form on the Olmec celt, the special unity of the bowl and the cross emerges as a fundamental symbol of rulership. Furthermore, the dot at the center of the cross explains why the artist of K'axob vessel 034 (figure 16.2) painted a circle at the center of the cross. Though isolated at K'axob, when seen within the context of Olmec iconography, the dotted cross fits within the pattern of Mesoamerican iconography. An additional similarity between the Olmec examples and the K'axob bowls stems from the position of the motif. Repeatedly, the X and U pairing appears on the forehead of the werejaguar or ruler—

the same place where Mesoamerican rulers wore their royal headbands. At K'axob we have no extant evidence of royal diadems; however, by placing the cross-marked bowls over the heads of the deceased, the people of K'axob could claim to control the same forces as did Olmec rulers in larger sites.

THE K'AXOB BOWLS IN PERSPECTIVE

In sum, the cross vessels of K'axob offer a glimpse into the strategies of an emerging elite in a small, rural village. It appears that, during the K'atabche'k'ax complex, a kin group secured enough power to begin creating an ancestral shrine, where the bones themselves served as a claim to power (McAnany and López Varela 1999; McAnany, Storey, and Lockard 1999). These burials included grave goods that were probably the possessions of the deceased, and the cross vessels seemed not only worthy of inclusion but also emblematic of power. Whether their original function was as feasting vessels, divining bowls, or as receptacles for sacred blood offerings, the decoration and vessel form conveyed multiple messages concerning the individual's role in society. The crosses initially marked the owner of the vessel as capable of tapping into the forces of the universe through his/her ability to connect the three cosmological levels, for the cross symbolized that most fundamental of Mesoamerican concepts—the world tree. In a similar fashion the quadripartite motif represented the four cardinal directions and positioned the vessel owner as the center of the horizontal axis and the human realm.

Eventually, the repeated burials in one concentrated location resulted in the location itself transforming and absorbing all of this symbolism. Thus, when structure 18 was built over these burials, the structure and the human actors within it both functioned as the heart of K'axob. What we see at K'axob is the genesis of power in a small site; however, because K'axob shared a symbol system with the rest of Mesoamerica, we can assume that similar plays for power, using symbols in comparable arrangements, were being enacted throughout Mesoamerica.

Were it not for their archaeological context, the simplicity of the K'axob cross bowls might result in their being overlooked as a source of inspiration for a discussion of iconography. The power of these bowls comes from our knowing that, even though stylistically rudimentary and simplistic, they came from K'axob burials all of which were more elaborate than the many

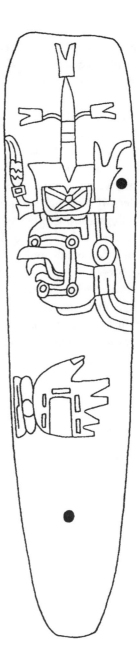

Figure 16.8 Jade celt with Olmec ruler wearing X and U over eye (after Benson and de la Fuente 1996:267).

simple interments at K'axob. Yet their simplicity is deceiving, for the concepts that they convey are complex. Through the cross, these vessels manage to express the core ideology of the Mesoamerican belief system. Rather than label them as crude, we might admire the artists's ability to convey all of this with such brevity.

Both the Olmec art discussed above and the sculpture of Palenque are far more elaborate than any art found at the smaller and more provincial site of K'axob. Yet to equate style and quality with the ability to fully comprehend the import of symbols would be to miss the function of these symbols in smaller, rural sites in Mesoamerica. Indeed, K'axob enables us to understand how such symbols were used in smaller sites and to better grasp how fully the Mesoamerican symbol system permeated all the corners of the region. In short, we can safely say that the elites of K'axob were not agrarian outsiders who mimicked the art of larger cities without understanding their symbols. On the contrary, the quadripartite bowls of K'axob indicate that the elites of this site fully understood the symbols that they used, for they used them in the same manner as did the elites of grander sites. Furthermore, one might presume that the non-elites of K'axob were also fluent in the visual vocabulary of Mesoamerica as the manipulation of these symbols could not have been effective if it were not understood by an audience. Thus, the appearance and context of the quadripartite bowls demonstrate that both the elites and the non-elites of K'axob had a sophisticated understanding of the Mesoamerican symbol system and that they adapted and manipulated it to create their own truly Mesoamerican society.

ENDNOTES

1. Much of this interpretation of the Humbolt Celt is based on the excellent iconographic analysis of Kent Reilly (1994).

2. Joralemon (1971) referred to this pairing as the "Dotted Bracket-Crossed Bands," which puts more emphasis on the dot within the U than the present paper. Because a star often substitutes for the dot, there may be some attempt by the Olmec artists to indicate that the image has a celestial referent.

PART VI

BIOLOGICAL RESOURCES

In Part VI we return to the physical landscape of K'axob to examine the role of wetland and terrestrial fauna in the diet and ritual practices of the denizens of K'axob. Collectively, the two chapters that form Part VI complement chapter 5, in which Victoria Bobo discusses sherd-lined pits as facilities for the preparation of cuisine based on maize and wetland fauna. In chapter 17 Marilyn Masson shows that the major proportion of K'axob fauna derived from the wetlands, with small fish and turtle being particularly persistent menu items in the cuisine of the village. Masson finds that, through time, the genera of fauna exploited remain remarkably stable except for a relatively higher proportion of terrestrial mammal species during Late K'atabche'k'ax times. This spike coincides with the construction of a raised rectangular platform within operation 1 and represents the final time period during which domestic facilities and debris are well represented at this locale. The emphasis on high-status fauna such as deer during this time provides yet another indicator of increasing differentiation and hierarchy. Masson notes that certain types of fauna—such as snake, deer, and frog—were placed in cache contexts, and she emphasizes the seasonality and thus the calendrical significance of fetal deer bones found in the cache of four vessels arranged in a cross pattern.

In chapter 18 Ryan Harrigan examines the mollusca of K'axob. Harrigan finds ample evidence that the apple snail, or *Pomacea* spp., was an important dietary component. But the uses of *Pomacea* shell extended beyond consumption for supper, and Harrigan documents the many burial contexts in which a layer of *Pomacea* was placed—a practice also discussed by Isaza in chapter 14. Thus, the symbolic import of shell, known throughout the Mesoamerican world as indicative of the fertility of the primordium and, for that reason, a substance that was often placed in burials, is expressed at K'axob through this locally available freshwater species.

GUIDE TO ACCOMPANYING DIGITAL MATERIALS.

Two data sets accompany the chapters of Part VI: the *Fauna Database* and the *Mollusca Database*.

Chapter 17
Related CD Resources

Fauna

CHAPTER 17

CONTRIBUTION OF FISHING AND HUNTING TO SUBSISTENCE AND SYMBOLIC EXPRESSION

MARILYN A. MASSON

This chapter examines the use of vertebrate animal resources at the archaeological community of K'axob. It assesses trends over time from contexts that have been dated to the Middle Formative through the Early Classic periods. It also examines spatial patterns within each temporal interval through evaluating the distribution of taxa in a variety of contexts. These contexts include floors, primary and redeposited middens, paleosols, burial, fill, pits, sherd-lined pits, and fire features from domestic units. This contextual analysis of K'axob faunas provides clues to the use of animals in ritual as well as for sustenance at this site.

Patterns of animal exploitation throughout all periods reveal that a variety of aquatic and terrestrial resources were utilized in human harvests of this rich wetland and agrarian environment. Previous analyses of faunal use in northern Belize indicate considerable variation among different communities with regard to the staple and preferred taxa that were exploited (Masson 2004). Northern Belize is made up of a mosaic of ecotones, and Maya archaeological communities

are found in zones of fertile clays and along cultivable wetland swamps, rivers, and freshwater inland lagoons (Wright et al. 1959). Pockets of sandy pine ridge also dot the northern Belize landscape, and these ecological zones hosted additional faunal communities. The impacts of agrarian activities on ancient environments affected the types of game available for exploitation (Masson 2004), though foraging species such as deer, peccary, and rodents thrive in fallow agricultural fields. Some sites, like Laguna de On, exhibit a paucity of animal resources during the Classic period and an abundance of high forest species during the Postclassic period, a trend that suggests environmental depletion followed by rejuvenation (Scott 1980, 1982; Shaw and Mangan 1994; Masson 1997).

Previous studies of Formative period Maya faunal use have been performed for the sites of Cerros (Carr 1989), Cuello (Wing and Scudder 1991), and Colha (Shaw 1991; Masson 2004). All three of these studies emphasize the significance of mammals in the diet, especially dogs and deer, and Shaw's analysis of Colha fauna indicates the importance of dogs in feasting activities sponsored by the site's emergent elites. Dogs, deer, and, to a lesser extent, turtles are the primary taxa of significance in Cuello Formative assemblages (Wing and Scudder 1991:85). The coastal site of Cerros had greater proportions of marine species than did these inland sites (Wing and Scudder 1991:87) and the K'axob assemblages described below.

A previous analysis of animal bone recovered from K'axob and other Pulltrouser Swamp communities—including Tibaat, Pech Titon, and Los Cocos—indicates that medium and large game mammals were available to the occupants of these sites throughout all time periods, though their relative abundance is difficult to measure due to differences in sampling methodology (Masson 2004). The analysis presented here builds upon the former by taking a closer look at materials collected solely from the 1990–1993 seasons, including those collected primarily through flotation. Materials collected from former seasons are not directly considered here, thus the samples from various temporal and spatial contexts analyzed here are directly comparable. Updated contextual and chronological assignments have been added to the faunal database, and proportions of NISP (Number of Identified Specimens) have been recalculated with this new information. This chapter also considers spatial trends in the element distribution of particular species from selected contexts in order to assess the evidence for animal processing and/or taphonomic factors that may have affected the faunal content of deposits.

METHODS

Samples analyzed in this study represent one-quarter-inch screen collections from all contexts and flotation samples from selected features. The samples are quantified according to the relative frequencies of counts of bone fragments (NISP) that have been identified according to taxa and element (see *Fauna Database* for full listing). Due to the small sample size of most contexts MNI (Minimum Number of Individuals), a common zooarchaeological quantification tool, has not been utilized. This measurement is highly appropriate for large sample sizes from a small number of contexts (Masson and Holderby 1994), and these circumstances are not found in the K'axob assemblage. For most contexts, MNI = 1 (*Fauna Database*), and this renders its calculation of little use for this analysis. Many taxa are represented solely by diaphyseal long bone fragments,

from which it is not possible to calculate MNI. A close relationship between NISP and MNI has been shown in statistical calculations, and some scholars consider NISP to be a superior measurement (Grayson 1984:29–31, 92). Identification of the K'axob specimens was facilitated through comparisons to collections of modern fauna housed at the Vertebrate Paleontology Lab and the Texas Archeological Research Lab of the University of Texas at Austin, and the collections of David Huelsbeck at Pacific Lutheran University. Osteology manuals published by Olsen (1982) facilitated further identifications.

The quantification of this assemblage according to NISP has one primary drawback. NISP can exaggerate the dietary contribution of small taxa, taxa with large numbers of bones, or taxa with bones that are prone to fragmentation due to cultural practices or their fragile natural properties (Reitz and Scarry 1985; Wing and Scudder 1991; Masson and Holderby 1994). As some of the K'axob samples have large quantities of small fish bones in them, the relative abundance of these tiny taxa compared to larger taxa (such as deer or dog) is inflated. This problem was similarly encountered in the faunal analysis of Preclassic contexts from the Cuello site (Wing and Scudder 1991:85). However, as long as this disproportionate representation is acknowledged, the significance of fish in the K'axob diet can be assessed in proper perspective.

RESULTS

The sample analyzed here was collected during the 1990–1993 seasons, and it consists of a total of 4,508 bone fragments (table 17.1). Forty percent (1,832) of these fragments were small crumbs of bone that were not identifiable to taxonomic class. Sixty percent (2,776) of the sample was identified (table 17.1), including 1,174 fragments from the Early Chaakk'ax complex (Early Middle Formative period), 98 fragments from the Late Chaakk'ax complex (Late Middle Formative period), 737 fragments from the Early K'atabche'k'ax complex (Early Late Formative period), 311 fragments from the Late K'atabche'k'ax complex (late Late Formative period), 202 fragments from the Terminal K'atabche'k'ax complex (terminal Late Formative period/Protoclassic), 141 fragments from the Nohalk'ax complex (Early Classic), and 13 fragments from surface lots of uncertain date. The eroded nature of ceramics from the surface lots prevents their chronological assignment and inhibits their interpretation.

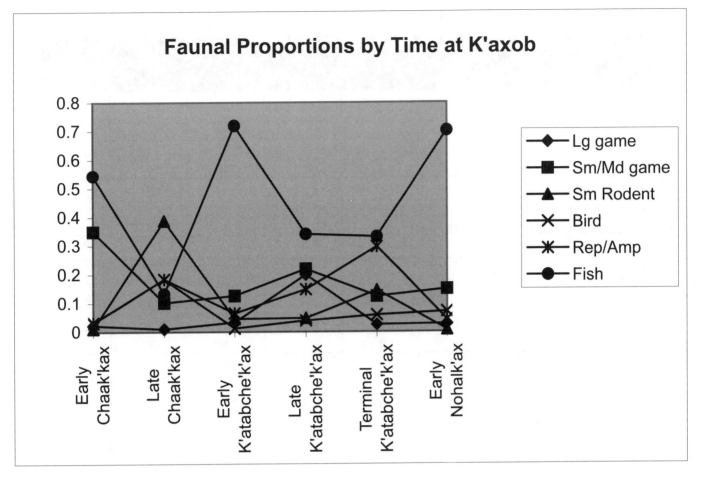

Figure 17.1 Faunal proportions by time at K'axob. *All illustrations by Marilyn Masson*

The results of temporal and spatial analysis of faunal use patterns at K'axob are presented below. The raw data that form the basis for all calculations are provided in the *Fauna Database*. First, a consideration of the percentage of NISP of various categories of animals, including large mammals, small mammals, small rodents, birds, reptiles/amphibians, and fish, is offered for composite assemblages of each ceramic complex (table 17.1, figure 17.1). These comparisons illustrate the fluctuation in use of different species over time, and percentages shown are calculated as a percentage of identified taxa.

This assessment is followed by a look at the distribution of these categories of taxa throughout selected contexts within each time period. Contexts selected for analysis included all of those that represented primary deposits. Contexts eliminated from spatial analysis (but included in temporal data summarized in table 17.1 and figure 17.1) include redeposited midden, construction fill/sascab, postholes, tumble, walls, and surface soils. The ritual use of fauna is evident in at least one cache from K'axob (operation 1, zone 77) that dates to the Late K'atabche'k'ax complex. The meaning of this cache is explored through determining whether it is analogous to rituals recorded in early Colonial Maya history.

Contextual analysis also includes a consideration of the distribution of cranial and postcranial elements for large and medium-sized mammals, small rodents, and fish. These taxa were chosen for different reasons. According to previous analyses of the distribution of elements within Maya communities, large and medium-sized mammals and fish are the most likely taxa to have been processed and consumed in different spatial locations (Masson 1999; Masson and Holderby 1994). Small rodent elements are examined to see whether they are likely to represent intrusive, commensal taxa in various features at the site or whether they were consumed in some way.

Table 17.1 K'axob fauna by complex. (*Continued on next page*)

Taxa	Early Chaakk'ax		Late Chaakk'ax		Early K'atabche'k'ax		Late K'atabche'k'ax		Terminal K'atabche'k'ax		Early Nohalk'ax		Surface	
	N	%	N	%	N	%	N	%	N	%	N	%	N	%
Odocoileus (white-tailed deer)	16	1.4	1	1.0	14	1.9	61	19.6	3	1.5	1	0.7		-
Mazama (brocket deer)	1	0.1		-		-		-		-		-		-
peccary		-		-	3	0.4		-		-		-	1	7.7
large mammal	9	0.8		-	7	0.9	1	0.3	2	1.0	3	2.1		-
TOTAL LARGE MAMMAL	**26**	**2.2**	**1**	**1.0**	**24**	**3.3**	**62**	**19.9**	**5**	**2.5**	**4**	**2.8**	**1**	**7.7**
canid	9	0.8	2	2.0	7	0.9	5	1.6	3	1.5	1	0.7		-
carnivore		-	1	1.0	2	0.3	1	0.3		-		-		-
large rodent	2	0.2		-		-		-		-		-		-
agouti	2	0.2		-		-		-		-	1	0.7		-
armadillo	295	25.1	2	2.0	5	0.7	2	0.6		-	6	4.3		-
medium mammal	1	0.1		-		-		-		-		-		-
small mammal	13	1.1	1	1.0	1	0.1		-		-		-		-
mammal	89	7.6	4	4.1	78	10.6	60	19.3	22	10.9	13	9.2	3	23.1
TOTAL SMALL/ MEDIUM MAMMAL	**411**	**35.0**	**10**	**10.2**	**93**	**12.6**	**68**	**21.9**	**25**	**12.4**	**21**	**14.9**	**3**	**23.1**
small rodent	13	1.1	38	38.8	32	4.3	15	4.8	29	14.4	1	0.7		-
rabbit		-		-	1	0.1		-		-		-		-
TOTAL SMALL RODENT	**13**	**1.1**	**38**	**38.8**	**33**	**4.5**	**15**	**4.8**	**29**	**14.4**	**1**	**0.7**	**0**	**-**
bird	36	3.1	18	18.4	9	1.2	12	3.9	12	5.9	10	7.1	1	7.7
TOTAL BIRD	**36**	**3.1**	**18**	**18.4**	**9**	**1.2**	**12**	**3.9**	**12**	**5.9**	**10**	**7.1**	**1**	**7.7**

TRENDS IN ANIMAL USE THROUGH TIME

Fish

Taxonomic frequencies of each ceramic complex at K'axob are provided in table 17.1, where the percentage of identified taxa is calculated for each taxon and for subgroups of related taxa. This information is presented visually in figure 17.1, which illustrates the fluctuating percentages of each taxa group over time.

This graph illustrates that fish are the most numerically abundant group and that their highest percentages are observed in Early Chaakk'ax (54.5%), Early K'atabche'k'ax (71.9%), and Nohalk'ax (70.2%). They remain common in the Late and Terminal K'atabche'k'ax complexes (34.1% and 33.2%, respectively). Their decreased proportions in the Late Chaakk'ax assemblage (13.3%) may be related to the smaller sample size of this assemblage. It is puzzling,

Table 17.1 (*Continued from previous page*)

Taxa	Early Chaakk'ax N	%	Late Chaakk'ax N	%	Early K'atabche'k'ax N	%	Late K'atabche'k'ax N	%	Terminal K'atabche'k'ax N	%	Early Nohalk'ax N	%	Surface N	%
turtle	30	2.6	17	17.3	34	4.6	40	12.9	55	27.2	5	3.5	7	53.8
mud turtle (Kinosternidae)	2	0.2		-	3	0.4		-		-		-		-
snake	2	0.2		-	3	0.4	1	0.3		-		-		-
reptile		-		-	2	0.3		-	1	0.5		-		-
lizard	1	0.1		-	4	0.5		-		-		-		-
iguana	1	0.1		-		-		-		-	1	0.7		-
crocodile		-		-		-		-		-		-	1	7.7
amphibian	1	0.1		-		-	1	0.3		-		-		-
frog		-	1	1.0	2	0.3	4	1.3	4	2.0		-		-
TOTAL REPTILE & AMPHIB.	**37**	**3.2**	**18**	**18.4**	**48**	**6.5**	**46**	**14.8**	**60**	**29.7**	**6**	**4.3**	**8**	**61.5**
catfish	9	0.8		-	7	0.9		-	5	2.5	2	1.4		-
Osteichthyes (bony fish)	630	53.7	13	13.3	523	71.0	100	32.2	62	30.7	97	68.8		-
shark		-		-		-	6	1.9		-		-		-
TOTAL FISH	**639**	**54.4**	**13**	**13.3**	**530**	**71.9**	**106**	**34.1**	**67**	**33.2**	**99**	**70.2**	**0**	**-**
crab	1	0.1		-		-	2	0.6		-		-		-
marine shell	11	0.9		-		-		-	4	2.0		-		-
TOTAL MARINE	**12**	**1.0**	**0**	**-**	**0**	**-**	**2**	**0.6**	**4**	**2.0**	**0**	**-**	**0**	**-**
GRAND TOTAL ALL IDENTIFIED BONE	**1174**	**100**	**98**	**100**	**737**	**100**	**311**	**100**	**202**	**100**	**141**	**100**	**13**	**100**
Unidentified	951		27		546		111		186		7		4	

however, to note that small rodents are most abundant in the Late Chaakk'ax assemblage (38.8%, compared to under 14.4% for all other periods), though perhaps sampling bias has affected these proportions.

As noted previously, the proportions of fish relative to other faunal categories is not a direct reflection of their significance in the diet as larger animals provided a greater amount of food. The count frequencies are valid, however, as a reflection of fluctuating abundance of fish in the assemblages compared to other taxonomic groups. These data indicate that fish formed between 33% and 71% of the assemblages of five out of six ceramic complexes and that these taxa were a regular component of the subsistence strategy at K'axob. This fact is not surprising considering the proximity of this settlement to the wetlands of Pulltrouser Swamp and the New River. Catfish was the most common species identified, and all others were freshwater (primarily from the Cichlidae family). Marine fish were not identified in the K'axob assemblages, although they were present in low numbers at Cuello (Wing and Scudder 1991:87). Although K'axob may have traded with the coastal center of Cerros during the Formative period, marine fish were apparently not an important commodity for this site.

Small rodents

Small rodents are present in all assemblages in variable proportions. In the Early Chaakk'ax, Early and Late K'atabche'k'ax, and Nohalk'ax samples, they form small percentages (1.1%, 4.5%, 4.8%, and .7% respectively, table 17.1). In two samples, they form greater percentages, including Late Chaakk'ax (38.8%) and Terminal K'atabche'k'ax (14.4%). Rabbits are rare at K'axob (n = 1, Early K'atabche'k'ax), and rodent bones are primarily those of small rats or mice. Such taxa are commonly attracted to human habitations and debris. It is not known whether they were consumed or whether they simply inhabited domestic areas in a commensal relationship with humans. These issues are examined in greater detail below, where I discuss contextual patterns. Sample size may affect the anomalous large proportion of these creatures in Late Chaakk'ax deposits.

Birds

Birds are also present in low numbers throughout all of the assemblages compared in table 17.1. They form between 1.2% and 7.1% of all samples except for those of the anomalous Late Chaakk'ax assemblage, where they represent 18.4%. Birds identified from K'axob assemblages are small, and turkey, surprisingly, is absent. Small birds and turkeys were also present in very low numbers at Cuello (Wing and Scudder 1991:Tables 4.9–4.11).

Reptiles and amphibians

Few amphibians were identified at K'axob. Frogs were found in low numbers in four out of six samples (table 17.1). Snakes and lizards were rare; and turtles represent the primary form of identified reptile. Turtles were present in low percentages in Early Chaakk'ax (2.8%), Early K'atabche'k'ax (5.0%), and Nohalk'ax (3.5%),

and they were more common in intervening periods, including Late Chaakk'ax (17.3%), Late K'atabche'k'ax (12.9%), and Terminal K'atabche'k'ax (27.2%). Most turtles at K'axob were of the pond turtle family (Emydidae), although mud turtles were also identified in two assemblages (Early Chaakk'ax and Early K'atabche'k'ax). It is difficult to know whether their fluctuating abundance over time is the result of human predation or changing environmental conditions. Mud turtles are generally much smaller than pond turtles, and their presence during two out of three periods of low overall turtle frequencies may suggest a diversification of harvesting strategies related to shortages of pond turtles. Fluctuating proportions of species can occur from overexploitation, especially for a potentially preferred food such as turtle. This species is a popular food source in the region today. A comparison of northern Belize faunal assemblages through all periods indicates that this taxa was an important dietary component at many communities (Masson 2004). Depletion of turtle resources has been inferred from similar cyclical alternations in the abundance of these species at southern Everglades wetlands sites in Florida (Masson and Hale 1989).

An interesting lack of crocodilian remains is observed in the K'axob faunal assemblage, despite the probability that this species was locally available throughout the time periods examined. Crocodiles thrive in swamp and riverine environments of northern Belize today and likely did so in the past. Only one bone fragment from this large and meaty taxon was recovered, and this was in the Nohalk'ax assemblage (table 17.1).

Medium and small mammals

Medium/small mammals are present in substantial proportions throughout all of the K'axob assemblages (table 17.1). They are in greatest abundance in Early Chaakk'ax (35%), though this percentage is inflated by the presence of 295 armadillo scutes in the sample. Without the armadillo bones, medium/small mammals make up 13.2% of the Early Chaakk'ax assemblage. They are present in similar proportions for almost all of the other samples, including Late Chaakk'ax (10.2%), Early K'atabche'k'ax (12.6%), Terminal K'atabche'k'ax (12.4%), and Nohalk'ax (14.9%). Due to a large number of bone fragments in this sample that were not identified to species (classified as mammal only), greater proportions of medium/small mammals are observed in Late K'atabche'k'ax (21.9%). Common species identified in the medium/small mammal category include canids (dogs or foxes, all samples) and armadillo (five out of six samples, with agouti present in only two of six samples).

Large mammals

Large mammal bone fragments represent a small proportion of the faunal counts in table 17.1, ranging from 1.0% to 3.3% in five out of six samples. They form a greater percentage in only one sample, Late K'atabche'k'ax (19.9%). Although the proportions are low, these taxa, including white-tailed deer, brocket deer, and peccary, would have contributed much more to the diet than smaller avian or aquatic taxa. The Late K'atabche'k'ax surge in large mammal proportions is accompanied by large quantities of medium/small taxa (discussed above) and a decline in fish relative to Early K'atabche'k'ax times (table 17.1). These trends may indicate an intensified focus on terrestrial resources at this time, although this pattern did not endure into Terminal K'atabche'k'ax times.

Marine shell and crab

Marine shell and crab remains recovered in these assemblages represents debris that may be related to food and, in the case of marine shell, to ornament production. Other shell artifacts are reported elsewhere in this volume, and marine shell debris, present in low numbers in all faunal samples examined here, is more appropriately considered along with those artifacts. Crab was present in two of six contexts examined (Early Chaakk'ax and Late K'atabche'k'ax). Crab shell was not identified to species. Marine shell fragments included those of conch and bivalves.

CONTEXTUAL COMPARISONS OF TAXA FREQUENCIES BY TIME PERIOD

The proportions of taxa in selected contexts at K'axob are illustrated in figures 17.2a to 17.2f. Percentages shown are those of all identified taxa within each group of feature types. During the Early Chaakk'ax complex, middens and pits had noticeably higher proportions of medium/small game (figure 17.2a). Pits also differed from other types of features in having greater proportions of turtle and no fish. Perhaps these features were used for cooking of game and turtle resources. Large

game, small rodents, birds, and reptiles/amphibians showed no clear patterns that associated them with specific types of features. Fish were more variably distributed, occurring in greatest proportions in sherd-lined pits (100%), fire features (79.2%), and burials (figure 17.2a). They also form a major portion of midden/paleosol features (49.8%). This generalized distribution suggests that fish frequencies within burials parallel patterns observed in areas where food refuse was also discarded and that fish likely were deposited into burial fill in the form of secondary debris. Sample sizes are low for all types of features except for middens in the Early Chaakk'ax assemblage, and these low numbers may be affecting the distribution patterns. It is notable that few bones are found in fire features, sherd-lined pits, and other pits. The use of these features may have entailed rigorous cleaning, or the faunal bone may have little relation to the features' functions.

In the Late Chaakk'ax assemblages only two types of features had faunal bone and can be examined: floors and burials (figure 17.2b). Small game and fish were the only types of taxa associated with floors, and burials had greater proportions of small rodents (61.4%) and birds (21.1%) than other types of taxa, which were present at levels of 7% or lower (figure 17.2b). The Early Chaakk'ax association of fish with burials is absent in Late Chaakk'ax deposits.

Fish are abundant (82.8%) in burials once again in Early K'atabche'k'ax deposits (figure 17.2c). They are also abundant in midden (66.8%) and floor (79.2%) deposits. Fish comprised 27.1% of sherd-lined pits and were absent in cache and floor contexts. Small game was most common in middens (a trend shared with Early Chaakk'ax) and in sherd-lined pits (figure 17.2c). One snake vertebra was found in an Early K'atabche'k'ax cache (see chapter 4 for additional information). Turtles were most abundant in pit contexts (figure 17.2c).

The distribution of faunal bone in Late K'atabche'k'ax contexts is difficult to interpret (figure 17.2d). Large game is most common in cache contexts, although this bone represents the teeth and crania of a single deer skull from one cache (operation 1, zone 77). Small game is quite common in pit contexts, as it was in Early Chaakk'ax and Early K'atabche'k'ax pits (figures 17.2a, 17.2c). Mammal bone is also common in burial contexts, though this consists of fragments not identified to species and may be part of secondary fill material. Bird bone is most common in floor contexts (figure 17.2d), although this trend is unimpressive as

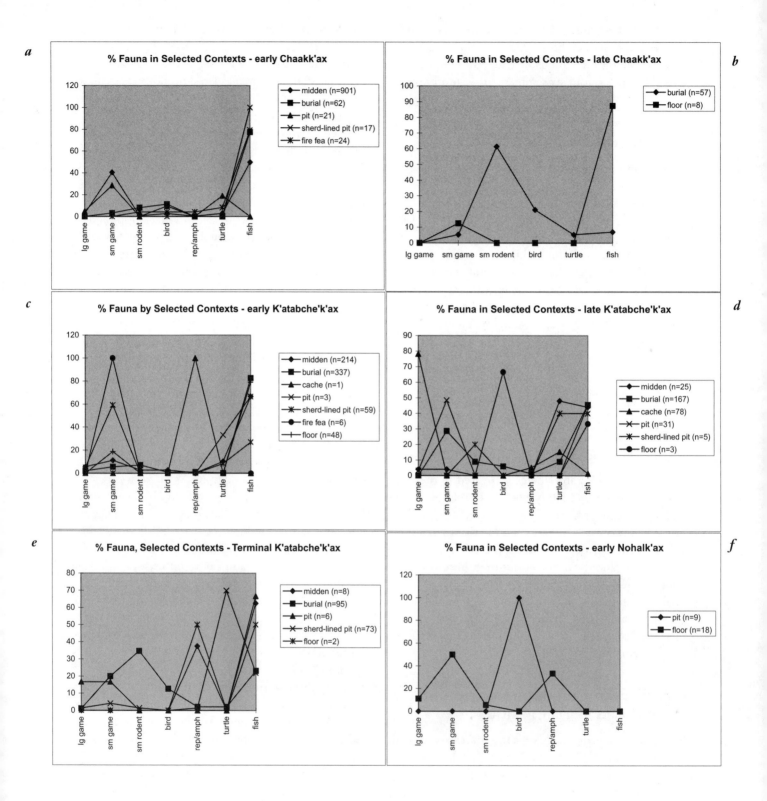

Figure 17.2 Faunal proportions by archaeological context and ceramic complex.

only two bird bone fragments were recovered, and these compose two-thirds of the sample of three bones from floors for this period. Turtle is common in middens and sherd-lined pits. Fish, as observed in Early Chaakk'ax and Early K'atabche'k'ax deposits, are quite common in burials in Late K'atabche'k'ax deposits (45.5%, figure 17.2d), although this taxon is also common in middens (44%), pits (45.2%), sherd-lined pits (40%), and floors (33%) during this period. Given this generalized distribution, it is not likely that fish proportions in burial samples are meaningful.

In Terminal K'atabche'k'ax deposits, large game (16.7%), small game (16.7%), and fish (66.7%) form the greatest proportion of pit fauna, although this sample size is very small (n = 6, figure 17.2e). Fauna recovered from sherd-lined pits constituted primarily turtles (69.9%) and fish (21.9%). Burials in these deposits show a greater proportion of small rodent bones (34.7%) for this time period than for earlier periods (figure 17.2e), though this trend is difficult to explain. Unlike most previous temporal intervals, burials in Terminal K'atabche'k'ax deposits do not contain high proportions of fish bones (23.2%). Fish bones are most common in pits (66.7%, n = 6), middens (62.5%, n = 8), and floors (50%, n = 2). As the sample sizes are so small for pits, middens, and floors, these trends should be assessed with caution. The paucity of bone in these features is notable and indicates that these contexts were seldom the final locales of faunal discard.

Only two contexts were examined from Early Nohalk'ax deposits (figure 17.2f). Sample sizes are low for these as well (pit, n = 9; floor, n = 18). The pit assemblage consists entirely of bird, and the floor assemblage is dominated by medium/small mammals (50%) and turtle bone (27.8%).

FAUNAL USE IN K'AXOB CACHES

The amount of faunal material in caches at K'axob is minimal. One snake vertebra in association with jadeite beads was recovered from an Early K'atabche'k'ax cache (operation 1, zone 97). The primary case of faunal use is represented by the inclusion of late-term fetal or newborn deer skulls, fish bones, turtle bones, and frog bones in a quadripartite cross arrangement of four small vertical-walled bowls. These date to the Late K'atabche'k'ax complex (operation 1, zone 77; see chapter 4; McAnany 1995a:Fig. 3.14). Rows of newborn deer teeth were identified in the west vessel and were found in less intact form in

the other vessels. Frog bones were also found in the vessels (east, west, and north). These bones were not well preserved and were recovered in many small fragments. Small lithic flakes were found in the fill above and below the cache and in the east vessel. The cache vessels were located directly north of a small shrine (McAnany 1995a:Fig. 2.18), albeit in a stratigraphically earlier construction phase.

At K'axob, this fauna may have formed part of an agricultural ceremony marking the onset of the rainy season, perhaps not unlike modern Ch'a-Chak ceremonies. Deer were sacrificed for many sorts of fertility rituals during protohistoric times (Pohl 1981, 1983:62–73, 74, 80), and this practice continues for Ch'a-Chak events today (Freidel et al. 1993:2). Frogs, in groups of four, are also directly impersonated in these ceremonies (Freidel et al. 1993:2). Frog and Chaks share associations with quadripartite calendrical partitions (Taube 1988b:207), and similar earlier associations may be symbolized in the inclusion of frog bones in the vessels of this cache. The identification of newborn deer dentition in the K'axob cache suggests that these animals were sacrificed during the birthing season of May/June, before or at the beginning of the rainy season. Deer skulls were also part of two Late Formative period caches at Cuello (Robin and Hammond 1991:226), and twenty-five of thirty-five individuals were juveniles (Wing and Scudder 1991:85, 87, table 4.15). Deer were sacrificed for many calendrical occasions during the Postclassic and Colonial periods, as is indicated in the Maya codices and in Landa's (1941) account. Season of death was not established for the deer skulls at Cuello (Wing and Scudder 1991).

CONTEXTUAL COMPARISONS OF ELEMENT PROPORTIONS OF SELECTED TAXA

Tables 17.2 and 17.3 consider the element proportions of large/medium mammals, small rodents, and fish. Element proportions can be examined for evidence of processing or postdepositional disturbance of bone assemblages (Masson 2004; Masson and Holderby 1994). Midden assemblages represent primary contexts in which the proportions of cranial to postcranial elements may reflect the normal activities of butchering, processing, and consumption of animal products. If specialized processing activities were associated with different areas at the household level, within the community, or outside of it, then middens would primarily reflect the consumptive end of the trajectory of animal

Table 17.2 Element proportion comparisons for selected mammals (large/medium mammals include deer, canid, peccary, and agouti). (*Continued on next page*)

			cranial	limb	foot	rib, vertebral, scapular, and pelvic	crania: postcrania ratio
Early Chaakk' ax							
	middens & paleosol						
		large/medium mammals	24	53	2	1	0.4
		small rodents	1	5			0.2
	pits						
		large/medium mammals	1				n/a
	fire features						
		small rodents				1	n/a
	burials						
		large/medium mammals	2				n/a
		small rodents		4	1		0.0
	TOTAL		**28**	**62**	**3**	**2**	**0.4**
Late Chaakk' ax							
	burials						
		large/medium mammals	1				n/a
		small rodents		35			n/a
	TOTAL		**1**	**35**			**0.03**
Early K'atabche'k' ax							
	middens						
		large/medium mammals	7	17	1	1	0.4
		small rodents	1	4	1		0.2
	sherd-lined pits						
		large/medium mammals	4	11	1		0.3
	fire features						
		large/medium mammals		2			n/a
	pits						
		large/medium mammals		3			n/a
	plaster floors						
		large/medium mammals		9			n/a
		small rodents		1			n/a
	burials						
		large/medium mammals	8	10		2	0.7
		small rodents	1	23			0.04
	TOTAL		**21**	**80**	**3**	**3**	**0.2**

Table 17.2 (*Continued from previous page*)

			cranial	limb	foot	rib, vertebral, scapular, and pelvic	crania: postcrania ratio
Late K'atabche'k' ax							
	middens						
		large/medium mammals	1	1			1.0
	sherd-lined pits						
		small rodents	1				n/a
	pits						
		large/medium mammals	8	5	1	1	1.1
	caches						
		large/medium mammals	61				n/a
	burials						
		large/medium mammals	5	22			0.2
		small rodents	2	10		3	0.2
	TOTAL		**78**	**38**	**1**	**4**	**1.8**
Terminal K'atabche'k' ax							
	sherd-lined pits						
		large/medium mammals		4			n/a
		small rodents		1			n/a
	pits						
		large/medium mammals			1		n/a
	burials						
		large/medium mammals	3	2			1.5
		small rodents	9	23		1	0.4
	TOTAL		**12**	**30**	**1**	**1**	**0.4**
Early Nohalk' ax							
	plaster floors						
		large/medium mammals	2	6	1		0.3
		small rodents		1			n/a
	TOTAL		**2**	**7**	**1**		**0.3**

Table 17.3 Element proportion comparisons for catfish and other bony fish.

			cranial	vertebral	spines	crania: postcrania ratio
Early Chaakk' ax						
	middens & paleosol					
		catfish	1		5	0.2
		other bony fish	53	72	315	0.1
	sherd-lined pits					
		other bony fish	5		12	0.4
	fire features					
		catfish		1	18	0.0
	burials					
		catfish			2	0.0
		other bony fish	6	5	35	0.2
	TOTAL		**65**	**78**	**387**	**0.1**
Late Chaakk' ax						
	plaster floors					
		other bony fish	4		3	1.3
	burials					
		other bony fish	1		3	0.3
	TOTAL		**5**		**6**	**0.8**
Early K'atabche'k' ax						
	middens					
		catfish			3	n/a
		other bony fish	16	14	92	0.2
	sherd-lined pits					
		other bony fish			16	n/a
	pits					
		other bony fish	1		1	
	plaster floors					
		other bony fish	38			n/a
	burials					
		catfish			3	n/a
		other bony fish	17	37	216	0.1
	TOTAL		**72**	**51**	**331**	**0.2**

			cranial	vertebral	spines	crania: postcrania ratio
Late K'atabche'k' ax						
	middens					
		other bony fish	1	4	6	0.1
	sherd-lined pits					
		other bony fish			2	n/a
	pits					
		other bony fish	3	2	9	0.3
	caches					
		other bony fish	1			n/a
	burials					
		other bony fish	7	6	57	0.1
	TOTAL		**12**	**12**	**74**	**0.1**
Terminal K'atabche'k' ax						
	middens					
		other bony fish		1	3	0.0
	sherd-lined pits					
		other bony fish		7	9	0.0
	pits					
		other bony fish	1		2	0.5
	plaster floors					
		other bony fish		1		n/a
	burials					
		other bony fish	1	15	6	0.05
	TOTAL		**2**	**24**	**20**	**0.05**
EarlyNohalk' ax						
	sherd-lined pits					
		other bony fish			1	n/a
	TOTAL				**1**	**n/a**

use. Among hunter-gatherer societies of the North American Plains, bone assemblages have been identified as "kill" versus "processing" activity areas based on the presence or absence of bones of least utility, such as cranial or foot elements which are often discarded at kill locations (Todd 1987; Brink and Dawe 1990; Davis and Fisher 1990). Processing of catfish at Maya archaeological sites has been identified through the comparison of cranial to postcranial element ratios at Northern River Lagoon in northern Belize (Mock 1994; Masson 2004) and for other fish species at the northern Yucatecan site of Isla Cerritos (Carr 1989).

Due to patterns of differential fragmentation of skeletal elements caused by factors of preservation, cultural processing, or varying numbers of skeletal elements for mammalian and nonmammalian species, a uniform measure of expected numbers of cranial versus postcranial fragments in species is difficult to project. In cases where differential cranial-to-postcranial preservation problems are not suspected, such indices may be calculated for individual species according to bone weight (Masson and Holderby 1994). As bone weight by element is not available for the samples examined here, and as secondary deposition of animal bones in floors, fill, or burial contexts is likely to have affected preservation, crania:postcrania ratios are considered below solely as relative measures with which to compare samples from different temporal components.

Comparisons of crania:postcrania ratios for large/medium mammals and small rodents in K'axob features are made difficult by the small sample sizes for each set of contexts (table 17.2). Midden samples for large/medium mammals for the Early Chaakk'ax and Early K'atabche'k'ax deposits exhibit a crania:postcrania ratio of 0.4. Many features possessed only cranial or only postcranial remains, but low numbers of bone make the interpretations of these trends inadvisable. In Early K'atabche'k'ax sherd-lined pits, the ratio of crania:postcrania is slightly lower (0.3) for large/medium mammals than it is in middens (table 17.2). Burials have a slightly higher ratio of 0.7, though this difference is not substantial. Rodent ratios are lower than those of large/medium mammals for middens (0.2) and burials (0.04). The recovery of (predominantly) limbs among the rodent bones in burials of this period suggests that these bones were disturbed and are present in burial fill in secondary or tertiary contexts. All of these ratios are very low, suggesting that either disturbed contexts have affected preservation or that full carcass processing did not occur in this general vicinity.

This trend is paralleled for rodent remains in Late K'atabche'k'ax deposits, where crania:postcranial ratios are 0.2 (table 17.2). The same ratio is observed for large/medium mammals in burials of this period. In pits of Late K'atabche'k'ax, more large/medium mammal cranial fragments were recovered than postcranial, with a ratio of 1.1 (table 17.2).

Burial fauna of Terminal K'atabche'k'ax deposits exhibits a much greater proportion of large/medium mammal crania compared to postcrania (ratio 1.5, table 17.2). Rodent crania fragments are also present in higher proportions than they are in Late K'atabche'k'ax deposits, and it is possible that some of these rodents burrowed intrusively into the burials. The plaster floors of Nohalk'ax deposits indicate a ratio of large/medium mammal crania:postcrania of 0.3 (table 17.2). What do these trends of mammal element ratios suggest? Deposits with ratios of .04 to 0.7 crania:postcrania elements are common in table 17.2, with only a few anomalies present, notably the greater proportions of large/medium mammal crania in Late and Terminal K'atabche'k'ax burials and Late K'atabche'k'ax pits. These distributions may suggest a greater association of cranial elements with these features or their associated deposits. Cranial elements may have been included as grave offerings for these intervals, or the deposits used for grave fill may simply have had more cranial elements that might reflect butchering of more complete carcasses in the vicinity. Similar whole-carcass butchering activities in the vicinity of Late K'atabche'k'ax pits could also be responsible for greater cranial element representation in pit fill. However, due to small sample sizes, these interpretations must remain tentative.

Evidence for fish processing is also plagued by many samples with low numbers of bone (table 17.3). Ratios of 0.2 should indicate a lack of differential processing as fish that were not processed at the Northern River Lagoon site were represented by 23% cranial bones (Masson 2004). Early Chaakk'ax deposits reveal this ratio for catfish in middens and other types of fish in burials. Fish heads are represented in greater proportions than expected in sherd-lined pits and in lesser proportions in middens of this period (table 17.3). This trend may loosely imply some processing trends associated with fish crania and sherd-lined pits during this period. For all of the features of Early Chaakk'ax considered together, the number of cranial fragments compared to postcranial fragments is low (0.1, table 17.3).

This trend is not observed in Late Chaakk'ax times, when fish heads are present at greater proportions than expected (with ratios of 1.3 for plaster floors and 0.3 for burials). Fish in Early K'atabche'k'ax middens exhibit expected crania:postcrania ratios (0.2), and calculations for the total sample of features in table 17.3 reveals the same ratio. Pits have equivalent proportions (n = 2), plaster floors yielded only cranial fragments (n = 38), and sherd-lined pits contained only spines (n = 16). In burials, ratios of crania:postcrania are low for this period (0.1). Occasionally, dorsal spines were culturally modified (see *Fauna Database*, especially the operation 1, zone 59 midden) and were probably used as perforation devices. Higher proportions of dorsal spines in some features (such as burial 1-43 from operation 1, zone 233) may, in certain contexts, indicate a use-related bias in element representation.

Similar variation is observed in Late K'atabche'k'ax times, but a lower overall ratio of crania:postcrania is observed (0.1), a trend that is paralleled in middens and burials (table 17.3). Cranial fragments are more frequent in pits, with a ratio of 0.3. Terminal K'atabche'k'ax features yielded few cranial fragments; only two were recovered from a sample of forty-six pieces of fish bone. The overall ratio for these deposits was .05. No cranial fragments were found in the small sample size from Nohalk'ax deposits (n = 1).

SUMMARY

Early Chaakk'ax animal use is marked by higher proportions of fish and lower proportions of mammals and turtles, though these latter taxa probably contributed more protein to the diet than did the small-sized fish. Some fish processing may be implied by greater proportions of cranial fragments near sherd-lined pits as compared to other areas.

Late Chaakk'ax patterns indicate greater proportions of rodents and fewer fish, and turtles are also present in greater abundance than they were in Early Chaakk'ax patterns. More fish crania are present in the assemblage than expected, a trend that may imply processing.

Early K'atabche'k'ax deposits exhibit a resurgence in fish proportions and a corresponding decline in turtle bone. Pits and sherd-lined pits are associated with greater proportions of aquatic resources (turtles and fish, respectively). Cranial:postcranial fish ratios look normal and do not imply particular processing activities. Rodent bones in burials are primarily limbs, suggesting that these creatures arrived in burial lots with the fill in which they were originally deposited.

The Late K'atabche'k'ax complex is anomalous in relation to other complexes in that it features greater proportions of mammals (large and small). A high crania:postcrania ratio is observed in mammal elements, perhaps indicating on-site butchering. Birds are also far more common in this assemblage than in others at the site. Turtle is more common in middens and pits, and pits have more fish crania than other types of features.

The Terminal K'atabche'k'ax deposits exhibit greater proportions of turtles, and moderate quantities of fish and other taxa are observed. Burials of this complex have greater amounts of rodent bones, and increased ratios of rodent crania imply that the mice and rats may have died near the burials and may perhaps have intruded into them. Turtle bone is common in the sherd-lined pits of this complex.

Early Nohalk'ax faunal patterns are similar to those of earlier periods in that abundant quantities of fish are noted, and moderate quantities of mammals are present. Turtles are lower in number, perhaps due to their depletion during the Terminal K'atabche'k'ax occupation. The single piece of crocodile bone was identified in the Nohalk'ax assemblage. Features dating to this complex yielded very little bone, and this fact probably relates to the lack of excavated Early Nohalk'ax middens in this collection—a trend also noted by Harrigan (chapter 18) in reference to molluscan fauna.

DISCUSSION

Animal use at K'axob entailed the exploitation of a diverse array of wetland and terrestrial species. While variation in the proportions of different species is observed over time, the list of species exploited in each temporal interval is similar. These patterns indicate a complex and intimate knowledge of local resources and probably reflect a diversified, flexible, and opportunistic set of procurement strategies that adjusted to fluctuating availability of local game. The mammals common in the K'axob assemblage are those that easily adjust to agrarian conditions, including deer, peccary, armadillo, agouti, small rodents, and canids. High forest species such as tapir are lacking in the assemblage, and a puzzling lack of crocodile bone is noted for all complexes prior to Nohalk'ax. The rarer brocket deer (*Mazama americana*) is scarce at K'axob, and lizards, snakes, and frogs were occasionally exploited. Turtles were a regular component in the diet of all periods, and their exploitation appears to fluctuate in a cyclical pattern that may be due to environmental factors or human predation. The most anomalous interval is that of Late K'atabche'k'ax times, when the exploitation of terrestrial mammals and birds is far greater than it is in other periods. The freshwater fish of Pulltrouser Swamp and the New River were also a regular component of the diet during all periods. Fish and turtles were probably collected in nets of the type that continues to be useful in northern Belize today. Net weights, the durable component of that technology, are well represented at K'axob (see chapter 10).

Animal use also extended to realms beyond that of subsistence. A snake vertebra was included in an Early K'atabche'k'ax cache, and newborn deer skulls and frogs were used in a cache event that occurred during the Late K'atabche'k'ax complex. One Terminal K'atabche'k'ax burial (operation 1, zone 15, burial 1-1) was interred with fifteen pieces of carved bone (including several carved bone tubes; see chapter 15). The use of fauna in ritual is not limited to K'axob but is also recorded for the nearby site of Cuello (Robin and Hammond 1991; Wing and Scudder 1991). The manipulation of animal resources in feasting was also integral in the emergence of power hierarchies in northern Belize, particularly during the Late Formative period (Shaw 1991). The increased use of mammals and birds during the Late K'atabche'k'ax interval parallels patterns that Shaw observed at Colha for the same period. She suggests that the emergence of a distinct elite class at this time was aided by raising animals (dogs in particular) for use in feasting. Such animal resource manipulation may also be reflected during this period at K'axob. Clearly, animal use profoundly penetrated aspects of subsistence, ritual, and political life in northern Belize of the past.

Chapter 18
Related CD Resources

Mollusca

MOLLUSCA OF K'AXOB: FOR SUPPER AND SOUL

RYAN HARRIGAN

Shell remains, seen as the remnants of once living organisms, can be analyzed as evidence not only of the invertebrates that inhabited K'axob but also as indicators of temporal change and spatial variation in the use of aquatic resources by ancient Maya residents. Comparison of the various amounts and types of species found in the varied deposits around K'axob allows for an understanding of how the Maya incorporated mollusca into subsistence, ritual, and architecture. Shell remains have been collected and identified for time periods as early as 800 BC and as late as AD 250; nearly 1,000 years of shell use at K'axob can be documented. In terms of shells and shelled organisms, analyses can decipher the level of Maya dependence on these gifts from the freshwater, the sea, and the surrounding territory. Shell counts and identifications tell us what species the Maya of K'axob were using as well as their relative abundance. Spatial affiliations can associate particular species of shell with their respective utility at K'axob, while analysis of temporal trends reveal how shell use may have changed in relation to the dynamics of subsistence, ritual, and construction techniques.

Freshwater mollusca must have been considered a great gift of the earth by the Maya people. Now, the unimpressive remnants of these long-dead organisms can once again be valued by the informed archaeologist not as a source of sustenance or spirit but, rather, as a source of information. One of the most subtle pieces of evidence from K'axob can lead to a clear understanding of how the Maya in this area exploited an integral group of organisms and how these organisms contributed to their spiritual, physical, and economic well-being.

IDENTIFICATION

In order to facilitate identification, species first had to be separated and grouped by similar appearance. From these groupings, eight genera stood out as completely distinct and unique; these eight types represented the full complement of shells found at K'axob. Each type

Table 18.1 Six species identified at K'axob and total counts of each

Species	Count
Pomacea flagellata	1722
Nephronaias sp.	1127
Pectinidae sp.	684
Euglandina cylindracea	67
Orthalicus princeps	116
Marginella sp.	3
Total	**3719**

was given an arbitrary number and was sent to be identified by Dr. Fred G. Thompson, head of the Department of Malacology at the Florida Museum of Natural History, University of Florida, who compared the genera of K'axob with the vast mollusca collection in the Museum of Natural History. After observing and comparing the shells, Thompson identified six of the eight genera sent to him as unique. The additional two types were discovered to be different life stages of already identified genera. Thus, the 3,719 specimens from K'axob are identified by genus and sometimes by species (table 18.1). For a full listing of specimens by provenience, see *Mollusca Database*.

It should be noted that minuscule fragments of unknown shells were occasionally recovered from the operations at K'axob. These fragments cannot be identified without microscopic comparative analysis, and their rarity in the record led to the assumption that they did not play a significant role in the mollusca use patterns at K'axob.

All genera were counted using an MNI approach. Pieces were matched and counted only if they could be positively identified as belonging to a single individual. In the case of bivalves, halves of shells were matched and counted as one individual. When halves could not be matched they were counted as one individual, assuming that the matching half was not found in the archaeological record. In order to understand how these genera relate to the archaeological record, it is necessary to review their characteristics, life cycles, and habitats.

The most prevalent shelled organism found in the archaeological record has been positively identified as *Pomacea flagellata* (Thompson personal communication

1998).[1] This species is a freshwater gastropod with a shell that averages between 4.5 cm and 5.5 cm in length (figure 18.1). Adult *Pomacea* have a rosy, durable shell that is relatively round. The surface of the shell is glossy in this adult form, and some yellow can be seen near the spiral apex, which is a remnant of the juvenile shell coloration. This spiral apex was useful in MNI counts as each *Pomacea* has only one such feature. The shells of juvenile *Pomacea* are completely beige and do not display the glossy hue characteristic of adults (see *Mollusca Database*).

Due to its coloration in adult form and its overall shape, *Pomacea* is often referred to as an apple snail. The genus *Pomacea* is a tropical American group that is distributed from Argentina to Mexico. It is also found in the Caribbean Islands and Florida. With over 150 brightly colored species, *Pomacea* is valued as an aquarium inhabitant but not as an archaeological specimen. For this reason, little research has been conducted on its significance in Central and South American sites (F. King 1996). A worthy exception is the work of Covich, which identified *Pomacea* at Pulltrouser Swamp in Belize (Turner and Harrison 1983).

Pomacea flagellata, the species that has been identified at K'axob, is most closely related to *Pomacea paludosa*, a native Florida species. Using this information, and other clues about the *Pomacea* genus, some ideas about its life cycle and mobility have been ascertained. According to Thompson, *Pomacea* is an annual genus, which means that its life cycle lasts only one year. Each year, a new group of *Pomacea* will inhabit an area only to be replaced the following year. This life cycle has been documented for *Pomacea paludosa*, and Thompson believes that it also characterizes *Pomacea flagellata*.

As far as mobility is concerned, *Pomacea flagellata* is limited as a species. It has been suggested that a few dozen meters may represent the range this species can expect to travel in a lifetime. Research by Thompson indicates that the one exception to this movement may be seen in *Pomacea* males, which may move upstream hundreds of meters when tracking a sexually active female. These aspects of the life of *Pomacea flagellata* are vital for our understanding of its inclusion in the residential deposits of K'axob.

A prevalent species found at K'axob, rivaling *Pomacea flagellata*, is *Nephronaias* sp. This genus, which contains several similar species, cannot be reliably separated further for taxonomic purposes based on shell alone. *Nephronaias* sp. is a freshwater pelecypod, or bivalve (figure 18.1). With an elongate shell, these

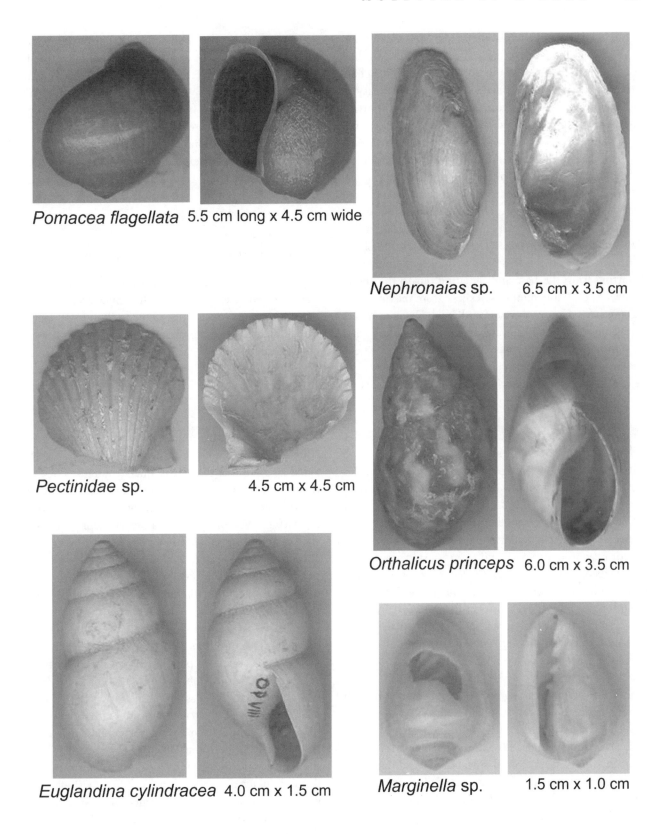

Figure 18.1 Six identified species of freshwater, terrestrial, and marine shell found at K'axob. *Photos by Ryan Harrigan*

individuals are approximately 6.5 cm long and 3.5 cm wide. Characteristic of this genus is a pearlescent hue on the inside of each of the bivalve halves. This characteristic color not only makes *Nephronaias* sp. easy to locate in the archaeological record but it also contributed to its being valued by the Maya for personal adornment and for its use as beads (see chapter 14).

Another common shell found in the archaeological deposits of K'axob belongs to the genus *Pectinidae*. *Pectinidae* sp. is a marine pelecypod that can be collected from shoreline locations. This genus measures, on average, 4.5 cm in both length and width and is characterized by a typical "seashell" pattern and shape (figure 18.1). *Pectinidae* is lined with deep, defined ribs, starting from the base and radiating out to the shell's extremities. Large numbers of shells from the *Pectinidae* genus have been recovered from K'axob. Their numbers are enigmatic for a freshwater site, yet the condition and location in which they were found may support a geological explanation of their presence.

The species *Orthalicus princeps* has been positively identified at K'axob (figure 18.1). This species has a characteristic spiraled, swirling shell with neatly arranged orange stripes running lengthwise. Juveniles possess the same shell shape but have bright blue stripes rather than orange ones. In addition, juveniles are much whiter than their yellowish adult counterparts (see *Mollusca Database*). Thompson notes that *Orthalicus princeps* has been identified as an arboreal species and may spend a good portion of its lifetime in or near trees in South and Central America. It may be inferred that, where *Orthalicus princeps* was gathered, high bush or trees would have dominated the landscape. Individual adults collected measured, on average, 6.0 cm in length and 3.5 cm in width. It should be noted that extremes on both ends of this average were seen in a few cases (as long as 10 cm, as short as 1 cm, with corresponding widths).

Relatively rare among the shells collected at K'axob were those positively identified by Thompson as *Euglandina cylindracea*. This mollusc possesses a tubular shell and averages 4.0 cm in length and 1.5 cm in width (figure 18.1). Shell surfaces are dull and frequently damaged, making fragments often impossible to count under MNI considerations. Confounding this problem is the fact that such an extremely fragile shell often incurs damage even when being transported from the site. *Euglandina cylindracea* is a freshwater, terrestrial species of Central and South America, yet little is known about its overall life cycle or mobility patterns.

Rarest among the shells collected were the small, glossy remnants of the genus *Marginella*. This marine genus must have been imported to K'axob. Measuring an average of 1.5 cm in length by 1.0 cm in width, this genus ranges in color from bright yellow to light blue and has an inner corkscrew morphology (figure 18.1). The relatively few shells found, coupled with their smaller size, probably exclude them as a valuable source of sustenance for the Maya at K'axob. However, a more ornamental or ritual association may have been assigned to this particular genus.

ANALYSES OF SHELLS IN THE K'AXOB RECORD

Shells from the six species that were positively identified were counted in each of the zones and in seven excavation units (operations). Due to the size of operation 1, that is were the majority of the analyses were concentrated. Operations 7, 8, 10, 11, 12, and 13 were also included in the analyses.

Operation 1

From operation 1, the numbers of shells identified and counted among zones or individual contexts were divided up according to three frequency ranges. The first range was represented by shells numbering less than 10; the second was represented by shells numbering from 10 to 99; and the third range was represented by shells numbering greater than 100. These ranges were chosen for comparative analysis only and do not represent distinctions in the archaeological record. They do allow for accurate distinctions to be made between the numbers of shells found in each zone and, therefore, provide some insight into the relationship between these numbers and their associated zones.

Of the six zones in operation 1 with shell counts exceeding 100, five are defined as middens or sherd-lined pits, and one is defined as a construction fill (tables 18.3, 18.4, and 18.5). This would indicate that large quantities of shell at operation 1 were purposely deposited or thrown away in specific areas or pits. The role that these shells played prior to their deposition can be ascertained through analyses of the ratios of different shell types within distinct contexts. For instance, in construction fill zones, proportionately fewer *Pomacea* shells are found relative to shell totals than is the case in many of the midden or sherd-lined pit zones. Of the 125 shells found in zone 114, which defines a sherd-lined pit, 120 have been identified as *Pomacea* shells (table 18.4). In contrast,

Table 18.2 Mollusca counts in burial and cache contexts at K'axob

Op.	Zone	Pomacea flagellata	Nephronaias sp.	Pectinidae sp.	Euglandina cylindracea	Orthalicus princeps	Marginella sp.	Total
1	30	2	13	2				17
1	38	1	2	1				4
1	41	6		1				7
1	78	16	7	1				24
1	80	5	8	5				18
1	81	4	10	3				17
1	83		2					2
1	88	6	8	3				17
1	97		3	1				4
1	99			1				1
1	100	1	5	2				8
1	103		1					1
1	107		7	1				8
1	113	7	15	2				24
1	115	4	18	5				27
1	135		1					1
1	137		8	2	1			11
1	143		5					5
1	145	5	2					7
1	152	25	19	2				46
1	157		3	2				5
1	159	10	3					13
1	166			2				2
1	182	1	3			1		5
1	229	3						3
1	236	8	4					12
1	250	4	1			2		7
7	17		3	2				5
7	30			1				1
8	5	13	10	25	9	2		59
8	6	1	2					3
8	8			2				2
8	13	4		1	1			6
10	22		1					1
10	24	1	4	2				7
11	7					2		2
11	13		1	1				2
11	16	97	4	6	1			108
11	19	70	18	2	4	20		114
11	36	1						1
11	52	1		2				3
11	53	28	3	1		2		34
11	60		1	1				2
11	93	5						5
12	4		2	1				3
12	30	5	1	7				13
12	31	14		2	1	2		19
12	32	6	1	2	1	1		11
12	40		2	1				3
12	52	33	18	4	1	1		57
13	9			1				1

Table 18.3 Mollusca counts in midden contexts at K'axob

Op.	Zone	Pomacea flagellata	Nephronaias sp.	Pectinidae sp.	Euglandina cylindracea	Orthalicus princeps	Marginella sp.	Total
1	59	89	49	6		11		155
1	63	89	30	6	2	7		134
1	87	156	50	12	2	2		222
1	90			9				9
1	111	21	46	7				74
1	141	3	12	2				17
1	162	6	3		1			10
1	219	68	29	2	5	13		117
8	9		1					1
8	15		38	13				51
10	11		9	5				14
10	17		6					6
11	38	1	1	6	1			9
11	64	27						27
11	72	18						18
12	10	62	20	5	7	2		96
12	42	5	21	3	1	1	1	32
12	48		25			1		26
13	8		4					4

of the 100 shells recovered from the redeposited fill seen in zone 57, only thirty-one are *Pomacea* sp. This may indicate that the residents of K'axob were throwing out more remnants of *Pomacea* sp. than other shells in zone 114, suggesting a possible subsistence use (see chapter 5). *Pomacea* sp. has been determined to be a high source of protein, one that may have been exploited by the Maya people. The evidence that masses of *Pomacea* shells were purposely deposited in distinct areas may lend support to their use as a valuable food item at K'axob.

Zones with shells numbering between ten and ninety-nine also lend support to this idea. Twenty-two zones were found to fall within this range in operation 1; of these, eleven were characterized by burial practices, while the rest were defined as construction fill, midden, or plaster floor zones. With 50% of these sites representing burials, it may be that a small number of shells, at least in operation 1, were deposited in graves at K'axob rather than simply forming part of the fill material. With at least forty-six shells in one burial context, there is reason to believe that the shells placed in burial zones may be higher in number than would be expected if one were looking at chance alone (table 18.2). Small numbers of perhaps deliberately placed shells, especially *Pomacea*, allow for some tentative conclusions. First, assuming that *Pomacea flagellata* did

provide at least some part of the food regimen of the Maya at K'axob, it may also have served as an important component in burial practices. This would indicate that *Pomacea* was more than a protein source, as the Maya used shells to symbolize fertility and regeneration (Isaza and McAnany 1999). The inclusion of a small number of these shells in burial sites indicates that *Pomacea* may have been used as some kind of ideological symbol rather than as a mass sacrifice of foodstuffs. Large quantities of *Pomacea* certainly do not appear to have been allocated to burials. And it is not known whether these shells were whole organisms or simply what was left over from once living organisms when they were deposited in burial contexts. Resolving this uncertainty may prove essential to understanding the exact role of *Pomacea* in the symbolic realm of the Maya.

Large quantities of *Nephronaias* sp. are seen among the burials and midden zones of operation 1. Of the sixteen zones that contain ten or more *Nephronaias* shells, eleven are associated with midden or burial features (tables 18.2 and 18.3). This parallel between counts of *Pomacea* and *Nephronaias* may suggest that they were used at similar locations. It is more difficult to prove that they were used for similar purposes. The association of *Nephronaias* with burial and midden sites

Table 18.4 Mollusca counts in pit contexts at K'axob

Op.	Zone	Pomacea flagellata	Nephronaias sp.	Pectinidae sp.	Euglandina cylindracea	Orthalicus princeps	Marginella sp.	Total
1	39	1	1					2
1	93		1	2				3
1	98	1						1
1	125		2					2
1	132		4					4
1	133		1					1
1	112		4					4
1	114	120	4	1				125
1	118		1					1
1	136	8						8
1	151		2					2
1	175	7	1	2	2			12
1	208	2	1	1				4
1	228	4	1	1		1		7
1	231	1	1					2
7	11			1				1
7	41	4	13	2				19
7	53			4				4
7	62		1					1
8	21		2	1				3
11	6	2						2
11	20	162	10	5	2	3		182
11	25		1					1
11	35	6	2				1	9
11	42			1				1
11	55	1		1				2
12	26	3		18				21
12	28	26		2	4	9		41
12	29	7	4			2		13
12	35	3	1					4
12	37	7		2		1		10

would lead to the conclusion that this shell may have been used as (1) a protein source, (2) a raw material for shell beads (see chapter 14), and (3) a symbol of the fertile watery world. The relatively large size of this shell, coupled with the sheer numbers of the shells found, supports a protein source hypothesis. *Nephronaias* was also found at every fire feature zone in operation 1, indicating that it may have been cooked before consumption. To date, no evidence on the palatability of this type of mollusc has been gathered.

Evidence of vast numbers of specimens may not necessarily indicate a subsistence use. *Pectinidae*, a prolific genus seen at K'axob, originally was thought to play a role in subsistence patterns at this site. After this genus was identified as a marine invertebrate,

suspicion grew as to the validity of this idea. First, K'axob is not proximate to any seashore. Upon observing the condition of the *Pectinidae* shells, further doubts came about. Shells often appeared flattened or fossilized, and were often clumped together with pieces of limestone or other rock. This led to the conclusion that this shell may actually compose part of the geological layers found in the site of K'axob and may not have been purposely deposited. No extremely large numbers (n > 50) of *Pectinidae* were found in any one zone, and its remains were well distributed over all contexts. This would support the idea that *Pectinidae* remains were geological in nature and a constituent of the marine limestone from which building material was derived.

Table 18.5 Mollusca counts in fill contexts at K'axob

Op.	Zone	Pomacea flagellata	Nephronaias sp.	Pectinidae sp.	Euglandina cylindracea	Orthalicus princeps	Marginella sp.	Total
1	46		5	1				6
1	53		8					8
1	56		21					21
1	86	32	13	2	1			48
1	120	34						34
1	123		1	1				2
1	124		10	1	1			12
1	127		3					3
1	128		9	7				16
1	129		1	2				3
1	130	10	3	8				21
1	139		10					10
1	210	2		3	2			7
1	219	68	29	2	5	13		117
7	16		1					1
7	34		1	1				2
10	3		1	20				21
11	4	2						2
11	10			3				3
11	18	6	4					10
12	6	3	2	5	1			11
12	54	1	2					3
13	5		1		1	1		3

The species *Euglandina cylindracea* is seen in limited numbers in various types of zones. These zones range from burials, to middens, to sherd-lined pits, to construction fills. Goodrich and van der Schalie (1937) have examined distributions of mollusca in Petén and north Alta Verapaz, Guatemala, and have found *Euglandina cylindracea* in close association with *Pomacea flagellata*. Although sometimes occupying different habitats or niches, these two species can, in some cases, be located within meters of each other. There are two explanations for their presence at K'axob: (1) *Euglandina* was not highly sought after as a protein source or for ritual purposes, and its limited presence at K'axob is a byproduct of the collection process for *Pomacea*; (2) *Euglandina* was purposefully collected along with *Pomacea* on a limited basis and for unknown reasons. With such small numbers appearing in the record (n = 18 for all contexts in operation 1), it may be difficult to ascertain the true contribution of this genus. Personal adornment or ritual use may be possible functions, but the extreme fragility of *Euglandina* shells would tend to discredit these ideas. Although a subsistence use

cannot be ruled out, *Euglandina* sp. is most often recognized as an environmental indicator rather than as a valuable protein source (Hammond 1991f).

Appearing in slightly higher numbers in operation 1 is the species *Orthalicus princeps*. This arboreal species has been found in small numbers, primarily in two types of zones: middens and burials (tables 18.2 and 18.3). Their numbers in midden contexts appear to be too small to warrant hypothesizing that they served as a significant contribution to either type of zone. Even a single shell in a zone, however, may represent a significant piece of the archaeological record. *Pomacea* shells have already been associated with burial zones, and it has been suggested that small quantities of shells may have been placed in burials for ritual purposes. Evidence of *Orthalicus* individuals in this type of context may support this suggestion. The shell of this genus is durable, colorful, and intricately shaped; these characteristics are often seen in shells used for adornment or symbolic purposes. *Spondylus* shells seen in some Moche burials are a good example of this type of symbolism. While a symbolic use cannot be ruled out, in other studies *Orthalicus* has been considered a noneconomic shell (Hammond 1991f).

Rarest, and most enigmatic, of the shells collected were those from the genus *Marginella*. In Operation 1, no evidence of these shells in any of the zones was discovered. Later operations did yield small quantities of these shells.

Operation 7

Freshwater shells from operation 7 provide further support for earlier findings. Although little *Pomacea* was found within this operation, four individuals were found in a zone defined as a subfloor. This may indicate subsistence use for *Pomacea*—as foodstuffs domestically stored. *Nephronaias* (n = 13) was also found within subfloor zones at these operations, indicating possible domesticate use. Both *Euglandina* and *Orthalicus* were extremely rare in these operations, possibly as a result of sample size. The ratios of these genera to total numbers of shells collected in operation 7 were comparable to ratios seen in operation 1. By far the most dominant genus recovered in operation 7 was the bivalve *Pectinidae* (n = 73). This fact corresponds to the idea that *Pectinidae* is geological in origin rather than archaeological. Operation 7 is dominated by construction fill and plaster floor zones. Only two midden concentrations and two burial features were excavated in this operation. Therefore, we would expect inflated *Pectinidae* numbers as they contribute a greater proportion of the fill material at K'axob than does, say, *Pomacea* or *Orthalicus*. Again, no *Marginella* was seen within this operation.

Operation 8

Operation 8 contradicts some of the findings of earlier analyses. Contexts with the largest numbers of shells (> 50) correspond to either middens or burials, yet almost no *Pomacea* is found within these zones (tables 18.2 and 18.3); rather, the midden of zone 15 is dominated by *Nephronaias* shells, whereas the burial of zone 5 is dominated by *Pectinidae* shells. *Nephronaias* makes sense in a midden zone if it is seen as a protein source, yet the presence of *Pectinidae* in a burial zone is puzzling. Further examination of these shells in the burial zones reveals little sign of geological deposition; the shells are free of rock debris and appear to be in good condition. These individual shells do not appear to have been geological in origin; rather, it may be that, like their *Spondylus* counterparts, these marine bivalves were acquired as burial accoutrements. Within the

same burial, an unusually high number of *Euglandina* shells were also found (n = 9), indicating a similar function for them. This burial is unique at K'axob as the secondary remains of two male adults surrounded by jade and smashed mammiform tetrapodal pottery vessels were found here. It is likely these other features of the burial explain why some otherwise enigmatic shell types are found here.

Operation 10

Only a single zone from operation 10 yielded a shell count greater than 100. This zone, a plaster floor deposit, was dominated by *Pectinidae* shells and appeared geological in nature. It is likely that these shells were embedded within the material used to construct the floor itself. As in operation 7, *Pectinidae* sp. contributes a disproportionate amount to the total shell count from operation 10, particularly in fill and floor contexts (table 18.5). This finding, combined with the limestone-covered condition of these shells, reiterates *Pectinidae*'s geological role in the archaeological record.

No zones in operation 10 yielded more than a single *Pomacea* individual, and any suggestions as to the reasons behind its presence would be speculation. However, its absence from this operation does provide some information; namely, it is unlikely that *Pomacea* was being deposited after subsistence use at operation 10. *Nephronaias* sp. is found in relatively large quantities in midden contexts (n = 15, table 18.3). This may be a consequence of natural deposits, or it may represent a small contribution of *Nephronaias* to subsistence patterns at operation 10. *Euglandina* and *Orthalicus* shells were again seen in limited numbers at operation 10 (n = 3 for each), and it is unlikely that they were used in large quantities at this operation. *Marginella* sp. is not found in operation 10.

Operation 11

Operation 11 yielded large amounts of shells in several different zones, supporting earlier findings and revealing new patterns. Three zones with shells numbering greater than 100 were observed. All three of these zones correspond to burials or pits in the operation (tables 18.2 and 18.4). In addition, these zones were dominated by *Pomacea* shells and often contained few other types of shell. A notable exception is zone 19, corresponding to a burial, which contained seventy *Pomacea* shells and twenty *Orthalicus* shells. This type of disproportionate representation of *Orthalicus* within a burial indicates strong support for the idea that it had a ritual or symbolic use (table 18.2).

Similar trends to those in operation 1 are seen within the other zones of operation 11. Midden zones and sherd-lined pits are dominated by *Pomacea* shells, while *Nephronaias* shells turn up in smaller numbers. *Pectinidae* is seen consistently within plaster floor and construction fill zones, supporting its geological origins. The rare genus *Marginella* makes an appearance within this operation in a zone identified as a pit (table 18.4). With only one *Marginella* shell found in this zone, an explanation for the presence of this shell must be delayed until further associations can be made.

The dominance of *Pomacea* within operation 11 again supports the protein source hypothesis. This operation, unlike operation 7, is made up of many midden and burial zones where *Pomacea* is abundant and dominant relative to other types of shell (tables 18.2 and 18.3).

Operation 12

The shell ratios seen at operation 12 reveal new trends in the analysis of shell use and function at K'axob. *Pomacea* again dominates the record, with high numbers seen in midden and burial zones. For example, over 60% of the shells recovered from zone 10, a midden zone, were identified as *Pomacea*. Within this same zone, over 20% were identified as *Nephronaias* (table 18.3). Composing over 80% of the total shells from this midden, these shells were clearly thrown away in large quantities, presumably after their primary benefits had already been extracted. The remaining four genera are represented in a limited fashion in midden zones of operation 12. Similar trends are also seen in the burial zones of operation 12 (zones 31 and 52). *Pomacea* and *Nephronaias* are seen in large numbers relative to the other four genera (table 18.2).[2]

Evidence of terrestrial *Euglandina* and *Orthalicus* shells is seen within the zones of operation 12 in patterns that remain consistent with operations discussed above. Zone 2, defined as an earthen layer close to the surface, contained surprisingly large amounts of each of these shells. Their presence probably indicates natural processes involved in the abandonment of this area and its subsequent reforestation. *Euglandina* is a known terrestrial genus, and although *Orthalicus* is arboreal in nature, some terrestrial deposition may occur.

The presence of *Marginella* shells in this operation allows, finally, for some conclusions to be made about this genus. One of these specimens was associated with the earthen layer, zone 2, while the other was found within a midden (table 18.3). The notion that *Marginella* was being used as a source of protein is unlikely. Measuring only 1.5 cm x 1.0 cm, such small individuals are unlikely to have been utilized as a food source as it would have required a great deal of energy expenditure to gather enough of them to provide sufficient nourishment. It is possible that this *Marginella* was treated as a delicacy, much as is escargot today, but the presence of two individuals does not support this idea. More likely is the hypothesis that *Marginella*, like several of its marine counterparts, was valued for its appearance rather than for its protein composition. With a corkscrew spiraling up the center, and a durable, glossy exterior, *Marginella* would make an appealing addition to necklaces, headpieces, or other forms of adornment. For this reason, it is believed that *Marginella* was used exclusively for ornamentation purposes; with no evidence of its being associated with burials, it cannot be assumed that *Marginella* reflected a ritual significance other than that imparted by the jewelry into which it may have been incorporated (see chapter 14).

Operation 13

With a total of sixteen shells collected, little can be decisively concluded about shell ratios in operation 13. No *Pomacea* was collected from any of the zones excavated, while *Nephronaias* and *Pectinidae* compose a fair portion of the total shells collected. *Pectinidae* is found within zones that represent wall and floor features, again supporting a fill material hypothesis. In the one midden zone in operation 13, only *Nephronaias* shells are present, further supporting the idea that subsistence patterns may have included this type of shell (table 18.3). Although these data tend to support earlier findings, further speculation using this limited sample may be unwarranted.

TRANSITIONS THROUGH TIME IN FRESHWATER SHELL USE

Determining particular uses of mollusca provides only one aspect of their overall contribution to the archaeological record. How these uses have changed throughout the history of K'axob adds a key component to the overall understanding of the role of mollusca in this Maya community. Through such analysis, it becomes apparent that the use of mollusca was far from temporally static; depending on availability, necessity, and value, a particular shell species may take on a variety of roles through time.

From the very beginnings of the K'axob community, during the Early Chaakk'ax period, *Pomacea flagellata* seems to have played a significant role. Composing nearly 60% of the total shells recovered from this time period, *Pomacea* is likely to have played an important sustenance role at early K'axob (figure 18.2). The majority of the *Pomacea* from this time period was found within midden contexts, further supporting the idea that this genus contributed to an early subsistence strategy. While never reaching the percent contribution seen within the Early Chaakk'ax complex, *Pomacea flagellata* remains an important component of the total mollusca counts in later time periods. Throughout the Chaakk'ax and K'atabche'k'ax periods, *Pomacea* composes no less than 30% of the total shell recovered, indicating an important role for this species even during changing times at K'axob.

A significant role for *Pomacea flagellata* during an extended time period at K'axob should not be mistaken for a static use for this species. A change in the cultural aspects of a community, resulting in the discovery of a new function for an already-used mollusc species, may lead to similar counts within the archaeological record; these similar numbers can represent very different uses by the K'axob people from these time periods. It is necessary to garner additional support from other analyses in order to be assured that a mollusc species did indeed maintain a constant use throughout time.

Pomacea flagellata, throughout all time periods, is associated with very similar context types. Regardless of time, the presence of *Pomacea* within middens and burials is constant. This fact, combined with its relatively high proportions of total shell counts during all time periods (figure 18.2), gives strong support to the idea that the role of *Pomacea* was stable for a long period of time. It appears likely that *Pomacea* was used at least as a supplementary protein source throughout the history of mollusca use at K'axob; in some early time periods, it may have taken on a more primary role. The importance of *Pomacea* during these early times may actually be underestimated in the archaeological record. The earliest time periods show the highest ratios of *Pomacea flagellata* when compared to other species. Considering how fragile the shell of this species is, it is likely that many individual shells from earlier periods may have been crushed to the point where MNI collection procedures cannot recognize them as individuals. Taking this fact into consideration,

Pomacea must have indeed played a vital role in the subsistence strategies at early K'axob.

Nephronaias sp. also contribute a significant proportion to total shell counts in all time periods in which shells were collected. This overall trend for *Nephronaias* is exemplified in the Late Chaakk'ax, where this shell composes nearly 60% of the total shells collected (figure 18.2). This may have represented a peak in the use of this genus, either for subsistence or as a raw material for adornment items (see chapter 14). Considering the large numbers of *Nephronaias* found in middens during this period at K'axob, it is likely that this species was used early on as a protein source. It is unclear why the relative abundance of this shell declines steadily after this period; by the Early Nohalk'ax, *Nephronaias* composes less than 20% of the total shells collected. It may be that environmental conditions caused the decline of the habitat for this shell in the area around K'axob; it is equally likely that the K'axob community began to exhaust it as a readily available resource. It is also possible that, in later time periods, the community at K'axob no longer valued *Nephronaias* to the same extent as did their ancestors. Later finds of this genus are located in earthen layer and construction fill contexts, indicating that subsistence or adornment value for *Nephronaias* may have decreased.

The temporal transition of *Pectinidae* sp. counts reveals a shift in construction material composition at K'axob. The relative contribution of *Pectinidae* sp. increases dramatically through time, from less than 5% in the Early Chaakk'ax to a culmination of nearly 50% in the Early Nohalk'ax (figure 18.2). If it is assumed, due to its depositional contexts, that *Pectinidae* had no practical use for the Maya at K'axob, then how can this temporal fluctuation in relative contribution be explained?

The most likely explanation is that a shift in the type of material used in construction, or simply more massive constructions, led to increased counts of this genus. Later communities at K'axob may have valued a fill or floor medium unlike that of earlier communities; this new construction material may have been richer in *Pectinidae* than earlier materials used. It is unlikely, however, that this increase in *Pectinidae* represents a new use for this genus, or its shell, alone. In this case, the Maya may have had an additional use for mollusca as integrated parts of construction material. The fact that *Pectinidae* individuals are most often found in geological deposits, regardless of time period, does not support an increase in its use as an economic or social resource.

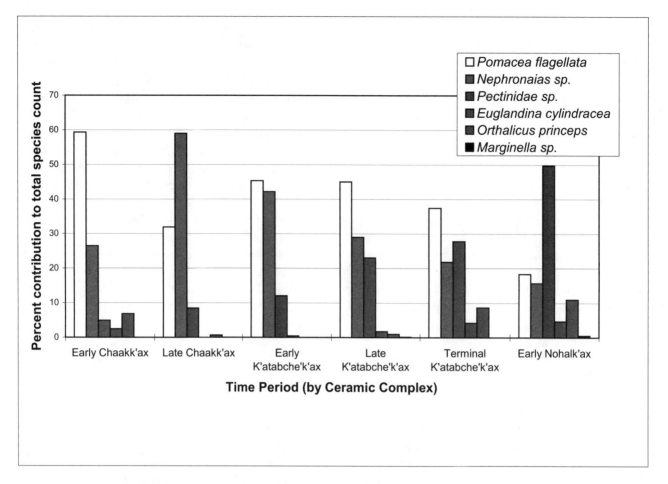

Figure 18.2 Contribution of each species to total mollusca counts in each time period at K'axob

Orthalicus princeps increases in relative abundance in later time periods at K'axob, and is also relatively abundant in the earliest deposits. Due to the sheer variety of contexts in which *Orthalicus* is found, conclusions about the role of this genus through time are difficult to justify. If the shells of *Orthalicus* were ever used symbolically, as they are found in relatively large quantities in burials, it may be that this symbolism fluctuated over time. Early communities at K'axob show little sign of using this species symbolically; only a single *Orthalicus* shell is found during Early Chaakk'ax times and it is associated with a burial context. In contrast, in later time periods, *Orthalicus* is found in higher numbers in burial contexts (table 18.2, figure 18.2).

Both *Euglandina cylindracea* and *Marginella* sp. represent a relatively small proportion of the total shells collected at K'axob. *Marginella* sp., during any time period, represents no more than 0.5% of the total shell count. For this reason, it is impossible to suggest changes in the use of *Marginella* through time (only

three *Marginella* shells were recovered for all time periods). *Euglandina* is seen in similarly low numbers, with a relative percentage that is never more than 5% in any time period. This genus is associated with middens and burials in a variety of time periods, which would indicate a similar function (if any) regardless of time period. The small component of *Euglandina* in any given time period makes temporal transitions in use patterns difficult to ascertain.

From this analysis, it becomes clear that changes in time can lead to changes in mollusca use patterns. Too often in the literature mollusca are tied only to their location; in the past archaeologists have been content merely to identify and count the mollusca found at a site. Only with a temporal consideration of how mollusca populations change, or are differently exploited, can the archaeologist hope to understand the complete role of these shelled organisms at the site in question. Even an analysis that points to a constant use through time for a particular species, such as that of

Pomacea flagellata at K'axob, provides new information concerning the mollusca within the record. It is clear that *Pomacea* was present at K'axob and was used as a source of protein. Now it can be concluded that *Pomacea flagellata* had subsistence value for hundreds of years and was used in a way that has left behind consistent and reliable evidence for the conscientious archaeologist to uncover.

THE ROLE OF SHELLS IN THE LIVES OF THE K'AXOB MAYA

When analyzing shells separate from other components of the archaeological record, several unique aspects of this type of evidence must be considered. Each shell collected was once a dynamic, evolutionarily efficient organism carrying out a life cycle. Whether that cycle was completed or interrupted by a human hand, the biology of these invertebrates must nonetheless be integrated into any cultural conclusions regarding shell. The life of *Pomacea flagellata* is just now being explained by malacologists and biologists alike. This species is thought to move relatively little; however, even small migrations may be misunderstood by archaeologists who remain unaware of such activity patterns. For instance, *Pomacea* shells found even a few hundred meters from wetlands may be considered naturally deposited unless one considers their extremely limited mobility. Although often seen as static in nature, shells found in the archaeological record must always be analyzed in relation to the mobile organisms from which they arose.

From the data gathered at K'axob, Belize, shell counts have been analyzed both within and among zones from seven different operations. Comparing across operations in terms of ratios, as well as defining the significance of total shell counts within a zone, several hypotheses have been purported.

In most cases, *Pomacea flagellata* is the dominant species in the archaeological record, both in terms of number and total biomass. It becomes apparent from operation 1 that large numbers of *Pomacea* occur in midden zones, while more moderate numbers appear in burials. This has led to the belief that *Pomacea* was used primarily as a source of protein for the people of K'axob, while also serving in burials as a symbol of regeneration. Rarely are burial zones found at K'axob without some inclusion of *Pomacea* shell. Additionally, because of its prevalence throughout the site of K'axob, *Pomacea* may have been unintentionally incorporated into fill zones, postholes, or floor structures (see

accompanying digital *Mollusca Database* for a complete list of unworked shell recovered from K'axob).

Caution must be taken when approaching zones containing fewer than ten shell specimens. Single shells found in zones are unreliable indicators of patterns because redistribution or misassignment between shell and zone may have occurred. Drawing conclusions concerning whole layers based on a few shells in that zone can be uninformative and/or misleading; yet in some cases it may be appropriate. Zones that contain ten or fewer shells are seen in burial sites, indicating support for earlier arguments. Other small shell numbers are seen in zones representing postholes or construction fill, which may indicate that these shells were accidentally mixed in while constructions were under way. No definitive proof that these shells were purposely deposited was found in low-density deposits.

Research at Cuello, an early Maya community, indicates that *Pomacea* were consumed in large quantities. Additionally, the tight size distribution of *Pomacea* in the archaeological record may indicate that a particular size range was selected for consumption by the residents of Cuello (Miksicek 1991). *Pomacea flagellata* is likely to have been a part of the Maya subsistence strategy, based on its protein value and relative abundance in particular zones. Is it possible, then, to determine subsistence significance of additional species based on their presence or absence in similar zones at K'axob?

Second in sheer numbers collected, *Nephronaias* sp. is also thought to have played a role in subsistence as well as personal adornment at K'axob. Present in midden zones and burials, *Nephronaias* sp. most likely shared uses with *Pomacea flagellata*. One aspect of the record that is worthy of note is the fact that there is no way to tell whether these shells were deposited in burial sites alive or dead. If *Nephronaias* and *Pomacea* were buried as organisms, then they may represent grave goods in the form of common foodstuffs. If, on the other hand, they were placed in burials as shells rather than organisms, then they had transcended their function as a mere source of protein and had become symbolic of something more.

The genus *Pectinidae* was found throughout the deposits of K'axob in relatively high numbers. The fossilized condition of most of these remains, coupled with their prevalence in construction fill or plaster floor zones, leads to the hypothesis that this shell is more geological than archaeological in nature. Evidence of *Pectinidae* in relatively good condition in burial zones imparts a second function for it: ritual symbol.

The terrestrial *Euglandina* and the arboreal *Orthalicus* are represented relatively equally across the operations at K'axob. Evidence of these genera in limited numbers throughout many different types of zones makes determining their role difficult. The fragile nature of the *Euglandina* shell, as well as its mundane appearance, may eliminate it as a device of ornamentation; rather, it is thought that this genus may have been used as a supplementary protein source or perhaps as a symbol. Most are found in either burial or midden zones. Previous studies have labeled *Euglandina* an environmental indicator (Hammond 1991f). In contrast, *Orthalicus* has a durable shell as well as a beautiful juvenile and adult form, and it may have had an ornamentation function. It is possible that these species may have been consumed on a limited basis; however, it is just as likely that their presence within deposits is the unintentional consequence of collecting more valuable protein sources, such as *Pomacea*.

The genus *Marginella* is seen in extremely rare cases in the archaeological record at K'axob. Research at Colha, Belize, supports the idea that *Marginella* was used for some anthropogenic purpose; what this purpose was remains unclear (Feldman 1994). While numbers of this genus are limited at K'axob, it is hypothesized that, due to its aesthetically pleasing shape and color, small size, and durability, *Marginella* may have been used for jewelry or other types of adornment.

K'axob Maya must have been truly thankful that they could gather a plentiful bounty from the watery world in the form of the mollusca. Like no other resource, the mollusca at K'axob served myriad purposes. *Pomacea* may have been collected as a side dish for supper, *Nephronaias* carefully drilled as a sparkling social symbol to adorn the neck, while any mollusca valued in life may have been placed with a loved one in death.

This variety in use ensured that the freshwater and marine mollusca of K'axob became a vital component of the economic, social, and spiritual well-being of the Maya who resided there. Now, after serving hundreds of years simply as space-fillers, the remnants of these organisms once again have some use. At K'axob, these mollusca now serve not for supper or soul but, rather, for knowledge—a piece of information to be gleaned by archaeologists.

ACKNOWLEDGMENTS

I would first like to thank Patricia McAnany for providing me the opportunity to work on such a fulfilling project and for her constant support and advice. I would also like to thank everyone who worked during the 1998 field season at K'axob for helping me become personally attached to the K'axob experience (special thanks go to Vildo, Amir, and Julian for killing many large snakes and keeping me alive so I could finish this chapter). Thanks to Lora Harrigan for inspiration and editing help at desperate times. Finally, thanks to the Maya, past and present, of Belize; may the wonders of your world never be lost to the soils of the earth.

ENDNOTES

1. A telephone conversation between Thompson and Harrigan in February of 1998 resulted in additional information from Thompson regarding the identification and biology of the K'axob mollusca that has been incorporated into this chapter.

2. Unfortunately, the mollusca from operation 12, zone 57 (a ritual burial/cache feature) was not available for study at the time of this analysis.

PART VII

DENOUEMENT

DENOUEMENT

PATRICIA A. MCANANY

The reader who has made her or his way through the chapters of this book now comes to a final synthetic and reflexive chapter. As a reader, perhaps you are thinking that you have learned a lot about the material remains of these Formative period villagers and a bit about their cuisine and ritual practices. But you wonder about the fact that hundreds of pages have been devoted to a "text-free" site that never became a seat of expansive political power. Can a village that persisted for a millennium and witnessed the political upheaval that likely accompanied the rise of governance by divine rulers—while revealing only subtle changes—possibly have anything to tell us about the big picture of Maya society? The definitive answer is yes: K'axob has everything to tell us about the self-conscious construction of life, identity, and meaning and the manner in which materiality was manipulated in response to larger political dictates. Below, I answer the questions of "how" and "why" this assertion is true, drawing heavily upon the information presented in the previous chapters.

LIFE, IDENTITY, AND MEANING AT FORMATIVE K'AXOB

Adopting a self-referential perspective, Prechtel (1999:5) provides an image of the highland Guatemalan Tzutujil village of Santiago Atitlán as a center of the universe, a protean hub of a network of work and ritual. Nonetheless, villagers are acutely aware of the larger external world and are realistic about their position within it. Here, I suggest that a similar perspective is appropriate for the ancient village of K'axob, where archaeological deposits reveal a conscious chronology of place making with few haphazards or weakly structured remains. The foundation burials at the base of operations 1 and 8; the close timing of mortuary ritual with construction activity; and the structured and highly symbolic content of the quadripartite, triadic, and lip-to-lip caches indicate the extent to which materiality showcased ideology. The intentionality of these highly structured deposits suggests that a self-conscious history was under construction, in a literal sense, and that stability of tradition (in everything from pottery technology to tool use) helped to forge meaning and identity.

A perception of the centrality of the village within a larger cosmos was clearly articulated in the crosses that were painted on pottery vessels and formed by the cruciform arrangement of cached pottery vessels. Not coincidentally, this motif first appeared after 200 BC, a time of marked regional political change and related economic adjustments. At this time, the physical geometry of the Lowland Maya landscape began to radically change. New peaks in the topography of rolling hills, wetlands, and valleys were created by the construction of towering pyramids—places for the storage and display of great spiritual and political power. While excavations have revealed that domicile construction greatly accelerated at K'axob during this time, no pyramids were built. Nearby, ambitious construction projects at Nohmul, San Estevan, and Cerros—as well as the raising of a massive (33 m tall) pyramid only 50 km upriver at the long-term capital of Lamanai—indicate that the spiritual and political landscape of northern Belize had altered dramatically and had assumed a more hierarchical form.

Within K'axob, the onset of nearby monumental constructions was reflected in profound changes that are apparent in mortuary patterns, in the diminished scale of exchange spheres, and in an assertion of village identity and centrality that was materialized in ritual contexts. By 100 BC the mortuary pattern of K'axob shifted from an emphasis on adults and children to young males who were accorded burial in the ancestral heartland of the village. Often interred as secondary remains, the age and sex of these burials is consonant with that of warriors and suggests that young men were either actively involved in homeland defense in the sense of resistance to emergent overlords or were drawn into the inevitable conflicts between competing seats of power. For residents of K'axob, the emergence of a political economy with centralized nodes of power resulted in the elimination of the far-flung procurement networks of earlier times. Procurement zones become highly localized and entrenched. Petrographic and neutron activation analysis of pottery pastes indicate that many vessels were fabricated from clays available within 10 km of K'axob. Gone also were the exotic cherts that may have come from the Maya Mountains; instead, chert tools increasingly bore the production mark of Colha—a massive tool-producing site located only 30 km to the south—

and there is little debitage to indicate anything but the refurbishing and recycling of imported, finished tools. In short, procurement efforts within the immediate catchment of K'axob were intensified, while acquisition of goods from distances greater than 10 km seems to have become highly controlled.

Within this context, residents of K'axob manipulated their material culture to express their own identity and centrality within a changing world. Pottery represents a very plastic medium of expression, and although the monochromatic Sierra Red tradition of the Late Formative period has often been characterized as a homogeneous horizon, closer inspection reveals that the artisans of K'axob crafted ceramic forms and decorative motifs distinct from those produced by surrounding communities. Furthermore, seven vessels associated with centrally positioned burial features dating from Late to Terminal Formative times (specifically 200 BC to circa AD 250) were painted with a cross motif and inverted over the head or body of a deceased male. The use-context of these vessels prior to interment is not clear; however, it is clear that the quadripartite motif is a Maya symbol of centrality and is used to mark an axis mundi. This assertion of centrality was carried one step further with the circa 100 BC dedication of a new plaza floor in the center of the ancestral village. This construction was marked by the placement of four small red bowls arranged in a cross pattern. The bones of fetal deer and frog were placed inside the bowls, and a scattering of golden chert microdebitage was sprinkled over the entire offering. Ironically, the burial and cache deposits featuring a cross motif—seemingly a materialization of the protean centrality of K'axob—were created at a time when larger political forces were marginalizing the village and restricting access to resources. Identity, it appears, became vested in a very localized existence that was given meaning and graphically illustrated by a cycle of ritual keyed to the nuances of an immediate landscape. In this manner, external political and economic forces hardened the outlines of identity consciousness, and those outlines can be perceived in the ritual deposits of Late and Terminal Formative K'axob.

If the latter part of the Formative period was a time of political centralization, then what of the Middle Formative period? Did an ethos of political segmentation, egalitarianism, and open trading networks prevail at that time? The earliest known domicile (built before 600 BC) is a large, 64 m^2, solidly built apsidal structure with a white packed-marl floor, wattle-and-daub walls, and an appended kitchen structure. Shortly before this domicile was constructed, two individuals were buried in the midden-rich soil under its future location. A male, adorned with over 2,000 shell beads and two distinctive pottery vessels, may have been one of the village founders. His interment contained two of the three artifact types characterized by Joyce (2000b:69) as the earliest recognizable products of "high culture" in Mesoamerica—well-made pottery and marine shell costume ornaments. This burial contrasted sharply with that of an accompanying female who was interred with no adornment or pottery.

The basis on which such gender inequality was constituted is not clear; however, these basal interments accent the fact that, at K'axob, Formative village social life was not structured around an ethos of egalitarianism. One of the pottery vessels interred with the putative apical ancestor—a Timax Incised bowl—was decorated with a faux resist technique; both the technique and the paste are foreign to K'axob. In fact, during this early settlement phase, much of the pottery, chipped stone tools and debitage, as well as ground stone, were procured or traded from distances of up to 100 km. The scale of this expansive and integrated network of procurement was never again achieved at K'axob. This pattern stands in great contrast to the post-200 BC period, during which procurement zones became tightly circumscribed. Even during the earlier time period, however, two prestige-linked valuables from the more distant southern highlands—jade and obsidian—were scarce items at K'axob, indicating the spatial and social limits of the procurement net. Macrobotanical remains from the basal levels of K'axob point toward a fully agricultural village that subsisted on maize and cultivated several orchards species, including cacao, avocado, and *mamey zapote* (Miksicek n.d.; Turner and Miksicek 1984:Table 1). Additionally, the plenitude of fish and turtle remains in the basal levels indicates that the faunal resources of adjacent wetlands provided a valuable source of protein that was not always present in the Mesoamerican diet. The cuisine of this Middle and Late Formative village seems to have been composed of local agrarian harvest complemented by the harvesting of aquatic resources. Such a well-rounded diet, no doubt, contributed to the low incidence of nutritionally related paleopathologies. Differences in accoutrements of Middle Formative mortuary remains, plus the unusually large size of the earliest known structure, suggest the early presence of leadership positions.

However, architectural remains are those of domiciles rather than palaces, indicating kinship or seniority-based leadership. Active maintenance of networks of procurement that extended well beyond the limits of the village intimates that Middle Formative village leaders enjoyed the authority to initiate and participate in trading relationships without meddling from overlords.

Regardless of the changing scale of the networks that linked K'axob to a larger region, a sense of local identity pervades the material remains—more so in upper levels. The village was constructed and expanded using the hard woods, thatch, and soft marl that were locally available. Carved marl blocks retained the apsidal and rectangular house plinths and platforms; often these well-built structures were buried in toto by later construction projects. But hard limestone construction blocks were rarely imported. Plenty of pottery was fashioned by skilled artisans who utilized locally available clays. In short, if a resource could be locally acquired, then it was plentiful and skillfully utilized. If it could only be acquired through multinodal trade linkages, then it tended to be rare at K'axob, another indicator of the local framework of the village. Small jadeite beads, for instance, were recovered as single occurrences, primarily from distinctive burial interments. Moreover, K'axob residents consistently conserved and recycled materials, whether locally available or imported from far distances. Pieces of broken pottery vessels formed mosaic linings for pits utilized in food preparation or were shaped and notched to serve as weights for fishing nets. Exhausted metates were broken into large cubes and used as hearthstone supports for cooking vessels. Fragments of broken chert bifaces and macroblades were recycled into cores. The small sample and short individual lengths of obsidian blades, moreover, suggest that the use life of volcanic glass was extended as long as possible. Had we the opportunity to experience it directly, much of daily life at K'axob would seem completely alien, but the ethos of conservation and recycling would ring true to many self-styled twenty-first-century environmentalists.

Imports, as a rule, appear to have been highly valued, curated, and used selectively. For instance, several golden yellow chert bifaces—likely imported from the workshops of Colha—were selectively reduced to microdebitage over a quadripartite arrangement of cache vessels and several burials. The latter also contained pottery vessels painted with a cross. The color yellow—*k'an* in Mayan (Barrera Vasquez 1995:374)—refers to ripened maize. The symbolism of earthly fertility is rendered all the more intriguing when one realizes that the materials under reduction were oval bifaces bearing traces of use-polish from earth penetration. Value, in this context, may have derived from several factors: importation status, color, and association with earth and cultivation. This example illustrates two points. First, notions of value are cosmologically complex and cannot, in a facile manner, simply be equated with some quintessential quality of long-distance exotics (contra Helms 1998:164–173). Second, the entangling of ritual practice and agricultural practice provides support for Monaghan's (1998:48) suggestion that archaeologists should not treat ritual as a discrete category but, rather, as part of a contextualized, local theory of production. Under most archaeological classification schemes, the reduction of a stone tool would be dubbed utilitarian, but in these examples the reduction activity serves to emphasize the inseparability of work and ritual. The seamless manner in which these two realms co-existed stands in stark contrast to the manner in which they are segregated in Western society. K'axob house floor plans provide yet another powerful reminder of this holism as subfloor burial interments of ancestors existed side-by-side with culinary features, particularly sherd-lined pits.

The close correspondence of work and ritual created an enduring cosmological totality—one that facilitated social reproduction (often with remarkable replication). Manifest in a long-term stability that is unimaginable by twenty-first-century standards, traditions were long-lived at K'axob. Pottery technology, shell working, use of specific tool types (particularly the oval biface), and a cuisine of wetland fauna mixed with maize show remarkable stability over a period of a thousand years. A knowledge base that included techniques of working clay and shell, cultivating the soil, and harvesting the wetlands—not to mention ritual performance—was transmitted to over forty generations, with variation in only selected realms of knowledge. From artisan to apprentice, from father to son, from mother to daughter, the meaning of life and the means of livelihood in this village world were reproduced through the generations.

FINAL REFLECTIONS

If we could time travel back to the first millennium BC, would the reanimation of the past world (à la Thomas 2001:181) of K'axob that is offered in this book resemble—in any way—the shape and form of daily practice in this village? As the editor of this volume and director of the K'axob Project, of course I hope that we have reached some approximation. But the past is created in the present, and one cannot travel back to check interpretive precision. Because of the nonreplicable nature of the historical science of archaeology, one cannot help but wonder about the impact of choices made along the way regarding the location and size of excavation units, sieve size, and specimens to be radiocarbon dated. As the construction phase plans show, many deposits that have been crucial to the narrative of K'axob were discovered on the very margins of excavation units. Many factors contributed to the interpretations presented herein, including the alertness of field workers and analysts, the seminal interpretations offered on field forms, and the choice of variables monitored during artifact analysis. If we had followed a different trajectory, would the final interpretation have been radically different? Without following those other tracks, one can never know. The long-term stability of K'axob bolsters the notion that alternative tracks may eventually have converged, although intrasite contextual distinctions obviously would have been altered.

Regardless, not all of the contexts and trends documented for Formative K'axob lend themselves to ready interpretation. For instance, is the diminishing frequency of sherd-lined pits referable to changes in cuisine, the scale of food-processing, or some other factor? Are the cyclic dips in the relative frequency of turtle remains a result of periodic overharvesting or an artifact of sampling? What type of thing was cooked, roasted, or fired in the gigantic pit at the base of operation 10? Does the cessation of construction in the operation 1 area indicate a loss of power, a conscious "entombing" of the past, or just a Classic period shift in the locus of monumental construction? In contrast to these ambiguities, our studies have provided some compelling glimpses into a past dominated by concerns with family, work, ritual, and survival in a changing political world. Family members who lived and died in that world take pride of place in this re-creation. These contexts include the secondary remains of young males who were interred in two focal plaza burials of operation 1; the individuals who formed the foundation burials at the base of several structures; the old seated male who was buried with the spouted duck effigy vessel in operation

11; the young male buried with a yuntun, or bola stone; the adult female buried with a neonate in her pelvic region; the many dual-generational burial contexts in which parents and children were seemingly reunited in death; and the children adorned with shell ornaments who died far before their time.

The work of gaining a livelihood from the stone-free soils of K'axob was imprinted indelibly on the oval bifaces and edge-refurbishing flakes that are coated with a dull earth polish. The fragments of bark beaters from the earliest midden at K'axob conjure images of paper-making activities, likely for ritual purposes. The encircling of the vessel containing the small jadeite and shell figurines of the triadic cache with a border guard of seven yuntunob provides a dramatic and highly structured example of ritual performance. Although highly patterned, the remains of Formative K'axob do not refer to a static world but to ontogenetic processes. The Maya metaphor of "flowering earth," a state of becoming, is a highly durable concept that figures prominently in cosmologies both past and present. A multivalent metaphor, flowering can refer to the cultivation and maturation of a person or place as well as plant life. This metaphor is highly relevant to K'axob, a village that was founded, prospered, stayed the course, and negotiated a continued existence through the first millennium BC, a time that can justly be described as one of great transformations.

BIBLIOGRAPHY

Adams, A. E., W. S. MacKenzie, and C. Guilford
1984   *Atlas of Sedimentary Rocks under the Microscope.*
        New York: John Wiley and Sons.

Adams, R. E. W.
1971   *The Ceramics of Altar de Sacrificious, Guatemala.*
        Peabody Museum of Archaeology and Ethnol-
        ogy Papers, Harvard University, 63(1).
        Cambridge: Harvard University Press.

Adams, R. E. W., and F. Valdez, Jr.
1979   The Ceramics of Colha, Belize, Report on the
        First Season. *Ceramica de Cultura Maya* 10:72-
        79.

Adams, R. E. W., and N. Hammond
1982   Maya Archaeology, 1976-1980: a Review of
        Major Publications. *Journal of Field Archaeology*
        9:487-512.

Aliphat, M. M.
1994   *Classic Maya Landscape in the Upper Usumacinta
        River Valley.* Ph.D. dissertation, University of
        Calgary. Ann Arbor: University Microfilms
        Intl.

Allison, P. M.
1999   *The Archaeology of Household Activities.*
        Routledge: London and New York.

Andrefsky, W., Jr.
1998   *Lithics: Macroscopic Approaches to Analysis.* Cam-
        bridge: Cambridge University Press.

Andrews IV, E. W.
1969   *The Archaeological use and distribution of mollusk
        in the Maya Lowlands.* Middle American Re-
        search Institute. New Orleans: Tulane
        University.

Andrews IV, E. W., and E. W. Andrews V
1980   *Excavations at Dzibilchaltun, Yucatan, Mexico.*
        Middle American Research Institute Publication
        48. New Orleans: Tulane University.

Andrews V, E. W.
1990   The Early Ceramic History of the Lowland
        Maya. In *Vision and Revision in Maya Studies,*
        edited by F. S. Clancy and P. D. Harrison, 1-
        19. Albuquerque: University of New Mexico
        Press.

Andrews V, E. W., and N. Hammond
1990   Redefinition of the Swasey Phase at Cuello, Belize. *American Antiquity* 55(3):570-584.

Andrews V, E. W., W. M. Ringle, P. Barnes, A. Barrera R., and T. Gallareta N.
1984   Komchen, an Ancient Maya Community in Northwest Yucatan. In *Investigaciones Recientes en el área Maya*. XVII Mesa Redonda, Sociedad Mexicana de Antropología, San Cristobal de las Casas, Chiapas, June 21-27, 191, Mexico.

Angelini, M. L.
1998   *The Potter's Craft: A Study of Formative Maya Ceramic Technology at K'axob Belize*. Ph.D. Dissertation, Boston University. Ann Arbor: University Microfilms, Intl.

Anthony, D. S.
1987   An Analysis of the Preclassic Households Beneath the Main Plaza at Colha, Belize. Master's thesis, University of Texas, Austin.

Aoyama, K.
1999   *Ancient Maya State, Urbanism, Exchange, and Craft Specialization: Chipped Stone Evidence from the Copán Valley and the La Entrada Region*. University of Pittsburgh Memoirs in Latin American Archaeology, Vol. 12. Pittsburgh: University of Pittsburgh.
2001   Classic Maya state, urbanism, and exchange: chipped stone evidence of the Copan Valley and its hinterland. *American Anthropologist* 103(2):346-360.

Arnold, D.
1989   *Ceramic Theory and Cultural Process*. New York: Cambridge University Press.
1992   Comments on Section II. In *Chemical Characterization of Ceramic Pastes in Archaeology*, edited by Hector Neff, 159-166. Wisconsin: Prehistory Press.

Arnold, D., H. Neff, and R. Bishop
1991   Compositional Analysis and "Sources" of Pottery; An Ethnoarchaeological Approach. *American Anthropologist* 93: 70-90.

Arnold, P. P.
2001   *Eating landscape: Aztec and European occupation of Tlalocan*. Boulder: University Press of Colorado.

Ashmore, W.
1989   Construction and Cosmology: Politics and Ideology in Lowland Maya Settlement Patterns. In *Word and Image in Maya Culture, Explorations in Language, Writing, and Representation*, edited by W. F. Hanks and D. S. Rice, 272-286. Salt Lake City University of Utah Press.
1991   Site-planning principles and concepts of directionality among the ancient Maya. *Latin American Antiquity* 2:199-226.

Ashmore, W., and B. Knapp, eds.
1999   *Archaeologies of Landscape: Contemporary Perspectives*. Malden, MA: Blackwell Publishers.

Aveni, A. F.
1980   *Skywatchers of Ancient Mexico*. Austin: University of Texas Press.
1989   *Empires of Time: Calendars, Clocks, and Cultures*. New York: Basic Books, Inc.
1992   Pre-columbian Images of Time. In *Ancient Americas: Art from Sacred Landscapes*, 48-59. Chicago and Munich: Art Institute of Chicago/Prestel-Verlag.

Awe, J. J.
1992   Dawn in the Land Between the Rivers: Formative Occupation at Cahal Pech, Belize and its Implications for Preclassic Development in the Maya Lowlands. Ph.D. dissertation, University of London, Institute of Archaeology.

Ball, J. W.
1972   Ceramic Sequence at Becan, Campeche, Mexico. Second (Final) preliminary report: 1972. *Ceramica de Cultura Maya* 8:34-41.
1977   *The Archaeological Ceramics of Becan, Campeche*. Middle American Research Institute Publication 43. New Orleans: Tulane University.
1983   Notes on the Distribution of Established Ceramic Types in the Corozal District, Belize. In *Archaeological Excavations in Northern Belize, Central America*, Monograph 17, edited by R. Sidrys, 203-220. Los Angeles: UCLA Institute of Archaeology.

Barrera Vasquez, A. D. (director)
1995   *Diccionario Maya*. Editorial Porrúa, S. A., México, D. F.

Barrett, John C.
2001   Agency, the Duality of Structure, and the Problem of the Archaeological Record. In *Archaeological Theory Today*, edited by I. Hodder, 141-164. Cambridge: Polity Press.

Bartlett, M. L., and P. A. McAnany
2000a   "Crafting" Communities: The Materialization of Formative Maya Identities. In *The Archaeology of Communities: a New World Perspective*, edited by M. A. Canuto and J. Yaeger, 102-122. Routledge Ltd.: London.
2000b   The Orange Walk Town Bypass Project: Summary Report of Archaeological Mitigation.

Ms on file, Department of Archaeology, Belize, and Department of Archaeology, Boston University

Bartlett, M. L., H. Neff, and P. A. McAnany

2000   Differentiation of Clay Resources on a Limestone Plain: The Analysis of Clay Utilization during the Maya Formative at K'axob Belize. *Geoarchaeology* 15 (2): 95-133.

Bassie-Sweet, K.

1996   *At the Edge of the World: Caves and Late Classic World View*. Norman: University of Oklahoma Press.

Bateson, J. H., and H. S. Hall

1976   *Geological Map of the Maya Mountains, Belize.* Institute of Geological Sciences Memoir 3. London: Overseas Division.

Becker, M. J.

1992   Burials as Caches; Caches as Burials: A New Interpretation of the Meaning of Ritual Deposits among the Classic Period Lowland Maya. In *New Theories on the Ancient Maya*, edited by E. C. Danien and R. J. Sharer, 185-196. Philadelphia: The University Museum, University of Pennsylvania.

Bender, B.

1993   *Landscape: Politics and Perspectives*. Berg: Oxford.

1998   *Stonehenge: Making Space*. Berg: Oxford.

Bender, B., S. Hamilton, and C. Tilley

1997   Leskernick: Stone Worlds; Alternative Narratives; Nested Landscapes. *Proceedings of the Prehistoric Society* 63:147-78.

Benson, E. P., and B. de la Fuente, eds.

1996   *Olmec Art of Ancient Mexico.* Washington, DC: National Gallery of Art.

Berrin, K., ed.

1988   *Feathered Serpents and Flowering Trees: Reconstructing the Murals of Teotihuacan.* San Francisco: Fine Arts Museum of San Francisco.

Berry, Kimberly A.

forthcoming   Farming the Scales of the Crocodile: Cultural and Geoarchaeological Evidence for Ancient Maya Wetland Reclamation at K'axob, Belize. Ph.D. dissertation, Boston University, Department of Archaeology.

Berry, K., and P. A. McAnany

1998   Bogged Down in Wetland Controversy: Current Investigations at K'axob, Belize. *Context* 13(3-4):1-4.

2000   Feeding and Clothing K'axob: Evidence for Wetland Cultivation at a Maya Settlement.

Paper presented at the Annual Meeting of the Society for American Archaeology, Philadelphia, April 9.

Binford, L. R.

1979   Organization and formation processes: looking at curated technologies. *Journal of Anthropological Research* 35(3):255-273.

Bishop, R.

1992   Comments on Section II: Variation. In *Chemical Characterization of Ceramic Pastes in Archaeology*, edited by Hector Neff, 167-170. Wisconsin: Prehistory Press.

Blake, M., J. E. Clark, B. Voorhies, G. Michaels, M. W. Love, M. E. Pye, A. A. Demarest, and B. Arroyo

1995   Radiocarbon Chronology for the Late Archaic and Formative Periods on the Pacific Coast of Southeastern Mesoamerica. *Ancient Mesoamerica* 6:161-183.

Blanton, R. E.

1994   *Houses and Households: A Comparative Study*. Plenum Press: New York and London.

Blatt, H.

1992   *Sedimentary Petrology.* New York: W.H. Freeman and Co.

Bobo, M. R.

1995   Operation I Excavation Report. In *K'axob Project, Interim Report, 1993 Field Season*, edited by P. A. McAnany, 33 pp. Submitted to the Department of Archaeology, Belmopan, Belize, On file, Department of Archaeology, Boston University.

Brady, J. E., and W. Ashmore

1999   Mountains, Caves, Water: Ideational Landscapes of Ancient Maya. In *Archaeologies of Landscape: Contemporary Perspectives*, edited by W. Ashmore and B. Knapp, 124-145. Malden, MA: Blackwell Publishers.

Brady, J. E., J. W. Ball, R. L. Bishop, D. C. Pring, and N. Hammond

1998   The Lowland Maya "Protoclassic": a Reconsideration of its Nature and Significance. *Ancient Mesoamerica* 9: 17-38.

Brink, J., and B. Dawe

1990   *Final Report of the 1985 and 1986 Field Season at Head-Smashed-In Buffalo Jump*, Alberta. Archaeological Survey of Alberta Manuscript Series 16. Edmonton : Archaeological Survey of Alberta.

Bryant, D., and J. E. Clark,

1983   Los primeros Mazas precolombinos de la

cuenca Superior del Rio Grijalva. In *Homenaje a Frans Blom: Antropología e Historia de los Mixe-Zoques y Mayas*, edited by L. Ochoa and T. A. Lee, Jr., 223-239. México: Centro de Estudios Mayas, Universidad Nacional Autónoma del México.

Buikstra, J. E., and D. H. Ubelaker
1994   *Standards for Data Collection from Human Skeletal Remains.* Arkansas Archeological Survey Research Series 44. Fayetteville: Arkansas Archeological Survey.

Bullard, W. R., Jr.
1965   *Stratigraphic Excavations at San Estevan, Northern British Honduras.* Occasional Paper 9. Toronto: Royal Ontario Museum.

Burger, R. L.
1992   *Chavin and the Origins of Andean Civilization.* London: Thames and Hudson Ltd.

Buttles, P. J.
1992   Small Finds in Context: The Preclassic Artifacts of Colha, Belize. Master's thesis, University of Texas, Austin.

1994   Ceramic and Stone Artifacts from the Northern River Lagoon Site. In *Continuing Archaeology at Colha, Belize*, edited by Thomas Hester, Harry Shafer, and Jack Eaton, 285-292. Studies in Archaeology 16. Austin: Texas Archeological Research Laboratory, University of Texas.

Cackler, P. R., M. D. Glascock, H. Neff, H. Iceland, K. A. Pyburn, D. Hudler, T. R. Hester, B. M. Chiarulli
1999   Chipped Stone Artefacts, Source Areas, and Provenance Studies of the Northern Belize Chert-bearing Zone. *Journal of Archaeological Science* 26:389-397.

Carmichael, E., and C. Sayer
1991   *The Skeleton at the Feast: The Day of the Dead in Mexico.* Austin: University of Texas Press.

Carr, C.
1990   Radiography and analysis: applications and potentials. *Journal of Archaeological Science* 17: 13-34.

Carr, H. S.
1989   Patterns of Exploitation and Exchange of Subsistence Goods in the Late Classic-Early Postclassic Yucatan: A Zooarchaeological Perspective. Paper presented at the 54th Annual Meeting of the Society for American Archaeology, April 5-9.

Carsten, J., and S. Hugh-Jones, eds.
1995   *About the House: Lévi-Strauss and Beyond.* Cambridge University Press, Cambridge.

Chase, A.
1991   Cycles of Time: Caracol in the Maya Realm. In *Sixth Palenque Round Table, 1986*, edited by M. G. Robertson, 32-38. Norman: University of Oklahoma Press.

Chase, D.
1985a   Between Earth and Sky: Idols, Images, and Postclassic Cosmology. In *Fifth Palenque Round Table, 1983*, edited by M. G. Robertson and V. M. Fields, 223-233. San Francisco: Pre-Columbian Art Research Institute.

1985b   Lifeline to the Gods: Ritual Bloodletting at Santa Rita Corozal. In *Fourth Palenque Round Table, Volume 6*, edited by E. Benson, 89-96. San Francisco: Pre-Columbian Art Research Institute.

1988   Caches and Cvenserwares: Meaning from Maya Pottery. In *A Pot for all Reasons: Ceramic Ecology Revisited*, edited by C. C. Kolb and L. M. Lackey, 81-104. Philadelphia: Laboratory of Anthropology, Temple University.

Cheetham, D.
1990   Interregional Interaction, Symbolic Exchange and the Emergence of Socio-political Inequality in the Maya Lowlands. Master's Thesis, Department of Anthropology and Sociology, University of British Columbia, Vancouver.

Chesterman, C. W.
1978   *The Audubon Society Field Guide to North American Rocks and Minerals.* New York: Alfred A. Knopf, Inc..

Clark, J. E.
1987   Politics, Prismatic Blades, and Mesoamerican Civilization. In *The Organization of Core Technology*, edited by J. K. Johnson and C. A. Morrow, 259-284. Boulder: Westview Press.

1988   *The Lithic Artifacts of La Libertad, Chiapas, Mexico: An Economic Perspective.* Papers of the New World Archaeological Foundation No. 52. Provo, Utah: Brigham Young University.

1997   The Arts of Government in Early Mesoamerica. *Annual Review of Anthropology* 26:211-234.

Clark, J. E., and M. Blake
1994   The Power of Prestige: Competitive Generosity and the Emergence of Rank Societies in Lowland Mesoamerica. In *Factional Competition and Political Development in the New World*, edited by E. M. Brumfiel and J. W. Fox, 17-30. Cambridge: Cambridge University Press.

Clark, J. E., and D. D. Bryant
1997   A Technological Typology of Prismatic Blades
        and Debitage from Ojo de Agua, Chiapas,
        Mexico. *Ancient Mesoamerica* 8(1):111-136.

Clark, J. E., and D. Gosser
1995   Reinventing Mesoamerica's First Pottery. In
        *The Emergence of Pottery: Technology and Innova-
        tion in Ancient Societies*, edited by W. K. Barnett
        and J. W. Hoopes, 209-221. Washington, D.C.:
        Smithsonian Institution Press.

Clark, J. E., and R. D. Hansen
2001   The Architecture of Early Kingship: Compara-
        tive Perspectives on the Origins of the Maya
        Royal Court. In *Royal Courts of the Ancient Maya*,
        Vol. 2, edited by T. Inomata and S. D. Hous-
        ton, 1-45. Boulder: Westview Press.

Clark, J. E., R. D. Hansen, and T. Perez S.
2000   La Zona Maya en el Preclasico. In *Historia de
        Mexico: Vol. 1: El Mexico Antiguo, sus Areas
        Culturales, los Origines y el Horizonte Preclasico*,
        edited by L. Manzanilla and L. Lopez Lujan,
        437-510. Mexico City: INAH.

Clark, J. E., and M. E. Pye
2000   The Pacific Coast and the Olmec Question. In
        Olmec Art and Archaeology in Mesoamerica, edited
        by J. E. Clark and M. E. Pye, 217-251. Studies
        in the History of Art 58, Center for Advanced
        Study in the Visual Arts, Symposium Papers
        XXXV. Washington, D.C.: National Gallery of
        Art and New Haven: Yale University Press.

Cliff, M.
1988   Domestic Architecture and Origins of Complex
        Society at Cerros. In *Household and Community
        in the Mesoamerican Past*, edited by R. R. Wilk
        and W. Ashmore,199-225. Albuquerque: Uni-
        versity of Texas Press.

Cliff, M. B., and C. J. Crane
1989   Changing Subsistence Economy at a Late
        Preclassic Maya Community. In *Prehistoric Maya
        Economies of Belize*, edited by P. A. McAnany and
        B. L. Isaac, 295-324. Research in Economic
        Anthropology, Supplement 4. Greenwich, CT:
        JAI Press.

Cobos, R.
1991   Craft Specialization during Prehispanic Times:
        An Example from Chichen Itza, Yucatan. Pa-
        per presented to the 47th International
        Congress of Americanists, New Orleans.

1994   Preliminary Report on the Archaeological Mol-
        lusca and Shell Ornaments of Caracol, Belize.

In *Studies in the Archaeology of Caracol, Belize*, ed-
        ited by Diane Z. Chase and Arlen F. Chase,
        1-11. Monograph 7. San Francisco: Pre-
        Columbian Art Research Institute.

Coe, M.
1968   *America's First Civilization*. New York: Ameri-
        can Heritage.

Coe, W. R.
1959   *Piedras Negras Archaeology: Artifacts, Caches, and
        Burials*. Philadelphia: University of Pennsylva-
        nia Museum.

1965a   Caches and Offertory Practices of the Maya
        Lowlands. In *Handbook of Middle American In-
        dians, Volume 2; Archaeology of Southern
        Mesoamerica, Part 1*, edited by G. R. Willey,
        462-468. Austin: University of Texas Press.

1965b   Archaeology of Southern Mesoamerica, Part 2.
        In *Handbook of Middle American Indians, Vol. 3*,
        edited by G. R. Willey. University of Texas
        Press, Austin.

1990   *Excavations in the Great Plaza, North Terrace and
        North Acropolis of Tikal*. Monograph 61 (Tikal
        Report 14). Philadelphia: The University Mu-
        seum, University of Pennsylvania.

Coggins, C.
1980   The Shape of Time: Some Political Implications
        of a Four-Part Figure. *American Antiquity*
        45:727-739.

1992   *Artifacts from the Cenote of Sacrifice*. Memoirs of
        the Peabody Museum of Archaeology and Eth-
        nology Harvard University Vol. 10, No. 3.
        Cambridge: Harvard University Press.

Coggins, C. C., and O. C. Shane, III
1984   *Cenote of sacrifice Maya treasures from the sacred
        well at Chichen Itza*. Austin: The University of
        Texas Press.

Culbert, T. P.
1963   Ceramic Research at Tikal, Guatemala.
        Ceramica de Cultura Maya 1(2-3): 34-42.

1993   *The Ceramics of Tikal: Vessels from the Burials,
        Caches and Problematical Deposits*. Monograph
        81 (Tikal Report 25 Part A). Philadelphia:
        The University Museum, University of Penn-
        sylvania.

Dapple, E. C.
1979   Silica as an Agent in Diagenesis. In *Diagenesis
        in Sediments and Sedimentary Rocks*, Volume 1,
        edited by Gunnar Larsen and George
        Chilingar, 99-141. Amsterdam: Elsevier Scien-
        tific Publishing Co.

Darch, J. P.
1983   The Soils of Pulltrouser Swamp: Classification and Characteristics. In *Pulltrouser Swamp: Ancient Maya Habitat, Agriculture, and Settlement in Northern Belize*, edited by B. L. Turner II and P. D. Harrison, 52-90. Austin: University of Texas Press.

Darch, J., and P. A. Furley
1983   Observations on the Nature of Sascab and Associated Soils in Cayo and Orange Walk Districts, Belize and in El Peten, Guatemala. In *Resources and Development in Belize*, edited by F. M. Robinson and P. A. Furley, 179-221. Edinburgh: Department of Geography, University of Edinburgh.

Daszkiewicz, M., G. Schneider and E. Bobryk
1999   Report on Laboratory Analysis of Maya Pottery from K'axob. Ms. on file at the Department of Archaeology, Boston University, Boston.

Davis, L. B., and J. W. Fisher
1990   A Late Prehistoric Model for Communal Utilization of Pronghorn Antelope in the Northwestern Plains Region, North America. In *Hunters of the Recent Past*, edited by L. B. Davis and B. O. K. Reeves, 241-276. London: Unwin Hyman, Ltd.

Davis, N.
1989   Conservation of Archaeological Shell Artifacts. In *Proceedings of the 1986 Shell Bead Conference: Selected Papers*, edited by Hayes Charles F. III and Lynn Cecci, 13-16. Rochester, NY: Rochester Museum and Science Center Research Division.

Deevey, E. S., D. S. Rice, P. M. Rice, H. H. Vaughn, M. Brenner and M. S. Flannery
1979   Maya Urbanism: Impact on a Tropical Karst Environment. *Science* 206:298-306.

Demarest, A. A.
1986   *The Archaeology of Santa Leticia and the Rise of Maya Civilization*. Middle American Research Institute Publication 52. New Orleans: Tulane University.

Demarest, A. A., and R. Sharer
1982   The Origins and Evolution of Usulutan Ceramics. *American Antiquity* 47:810-822.

Demarest, A. A., R. Switsur, and R. Berger
1982   The Dating and Cultural Associations of the "Potbellied" Sculptural Style: New Evidence from Western El Salvador. *American Antiquity* 47(3):557-571.

Dixon K. A.
1959   *Ceramics from Two Preclassic Periods at Chiapa de Corzo, Chiapas Mexico*. Papers of the New World Archaeological Foundation 5, Publication 4. Provo: New World Archaeological Foundation, Brigham Young University.

Dobres, M. A., and J. E. Robb
2000   Agency in Archaeology: Paradigm or Platitude? In *Agency in Archaeology*, edited by M. A. Dobres and J. E. Robb, 3-17. London: Routledge.

Dockall, J. E., and H. J. Shafer
1993   Testing the Producer-Consumer Model for Santa Rita Corozal, Belize. *Latin American Antiquity* 4(2):158-179.

Dominguez Carrasco, M. del R.
1994   *Calakmul, Campeche: Un Análisis de la Cerámica*. Campeche: Universidad Autónoma de Campeche.

Dreiss, M. L.
1994   The Shell Artifacts of Colha: The 1983 Season. In *Continuing Archaeology at Colha, Belize*, edited by Thomas Hester, Harry J. Shafer, and Jack D. Eaton, 177-199. Studies in Archaeology 16. Austin: Texas Archaeological Research Laboratory, The University of Texas at Austin.

Dreiss, M. L., and D. O. Brown
1989   Obsidian Exchange Patterns in Belize. In *Prehistoric Maya Economies of Belize*, edited by P. A. McAnany and B. L. Isaac, 57-90. Research in Economic Anthropology, Supplement 4. Greenwich, CT: JAI Press.

Durán, Fray Diego
1964   *History of the Indies of New Spain*, translated by Doris Heyden. Norman: University of Oklahoma Press.

1971   *Book of Gods and Rites and the Ancient Calendar*, translated and edited by F. Horcasitas and D. Heyden, with foreward by M. Leon-Portilla. Norman: University of Oklahoma Press.

Ebersole, J. P.
2001   The Ground and Polished Stone Artifacts of K'axob, Belize, Central America. Senior Work for Distinction. Boston University, Department of Archaeology.

Edmonson, M. S.
1971   *The Book of Counsel: The Popol Vuh of the Quiche Maya of Guatemala*, Middle American Research Institute, Publication 35. New Orleans: Tulane University.

Estrada Belli, F.
1993   Operation VIIA Report. In *K'axob Project: Interim Report, 1992 Field Season*, edited by P. A. McAnany, 41 pp. Submitted to the Department of Archaeology, Belmopan, Belize, Central America. On file, Department of Archaeology, Boston University.

Fearer Safer, J., and F. McLaughlin Gill
1982   *Spirals from the Sea, an Anthropological Look at Shells*. New York: Potter Inc. Publishers.

Feeley-Harnik, G.
1985   Issues in Divine Kingship. *Annual Review of Anthropology* 14:273-313.

Feldman, L. H.
1994   A Second Preliminary Report on Archeological Molluscan Remains from Colha, Belize. In *Continuing Archaeology at Colha, Belize*. Edited by T. R. Hester, H. J. Shafer, and J. D. Eaton, 201-207. Studies in Archaeology 16. Austin: Texas Archaeological Research Laboratory, University of Texas.

Firth, R.
1967   *Primitive Polynesian Economy*. London: Routledge and Paul Kegan.

Flannery, K. V.
1976   The Early Formative Household Cluster on the Guatemalan Pacific Coast. In *The Early Mesoamerican Village*, edited by K. V. Flannery, 31-34. Academic Press: New York.

Flannery, K. V., and J. Marcus
1994   *Early Formative Pottery of the Valley of Oaxaca, Mexico, with Technical Ceramic Analysis by William O. Payne*. Prehistory and Human Ecology of the Valley of Oaxaca, Vol. 10, Memoirs of the Museum of Anthropology 27. Ann Arbor: University of Michigan.

Flores, G.
1952   Geology of Northern British Honduras. *American Association of Petroleum Geologists Bulletin* 36: 404-409.

Foias, A. E.
1996   Changing Ceramic Production and Exchange Systems and the Classic Maya Collapse in the Petexbatun Region, Vols. 1-2. Ph.D. Dissertation, Vanderbilt University, Nashville, Tennessee.

Forsyth, D. W.
1989   *The Ceramics of El Mirador, Peten, Guatemala*. El Mirador Series, Part 4. Papers of the New World Archaeological Foundation 63. Provo, Utah: Brigham Young University.

Freidel, D. A.
1979   Culture Areas and Interaction Spheres: Contrasting Approaches to the Emergence of Civilization in the Maya Lowlands. *American Antiquity* 44:36-54.

Freidel, D. A., and L. Schele
1988   Kingship in the Late Preclassic Maya Lowlands. *American Anthropologist* 90(3):547-567.

1989   Dead Kings and Living Temples: Dedication and Termination Rituals Among the Ancient Maya. In *Word and Image in Maya Culture: Explorations in Language, Writing, and Representation*, edited by W. F. Hanks and D. S. Rice, 233-243. Salt Lake City: University of Utah Press.

Freidel, D. A., L. Schele, and J. Parker
1993   *Maya Cosmos: Three Thousand Years on the Shaman's Path*. New York: William Morrow.

Fry, R. E.
1983   The Ceramics of the Pulltrouser Area: Settlements and Fields. In *Pulltrouser Swamp: Ancient Maya Habitat, Agriculture, and Settlement in Northern Belize*, edited by B. L. Turner II, and P. D. Harrison, 194-211. Austin: University of Texas Press.

Furst, P. T.
1968   The Olmec Were-Jaguar Motif in the Light of Ethnographic Reality. In *Dumbarton Oaks Conference on the Olmec*, edited by E. P. Benson, 143-174. Washington, D.C.: Dumbarton Oaks Research Library and Collection.

1995   Shamanism, Transformation, and Olmec Art. In *The Olmec World: Ritual and Rulership*, 69-81. Princeton: The Art Museum, Princeton University.

Garber, J. F.
1983   Patterns of Jade Consumption and Disposal at Cerros, Northern Belize. *American Antiquity* 48: 800-807.

1986   The Artifacts. In *Archaeology at Cerros, Belize, Central America, An Interim Report, Volume 1*, edited by R. Robertson and D.A. Freidel, 117-126. Dallas: Southern Methodist University.

1988   The Notched Ceramic Pieces from Cerros, Belize. *Ceramica de Cultura Maya* 15:35-40.

1989   *Archaeology at Cerros, Belize, Central America, Volume II, the Artifacts*. Texas: Southern Methodist University Press.

2001   Ground Stone Tools. In *Archaeology of Ancient Mexico and Central America: An Encyclopedia*, edited by S. T. Evans and D. L. Webster, 300-303. New York: Garland Publishing Inc.

Garber, J. F., W. D. Driver, L. A. Sullivan, and D. M. Glass

1998   Bloody Bowls and Broken Pots: The Life, Death, and Rebirth of a Maya House. In *The Sowing and the Dawning: Termination, Dedication, Transformation in the Archaeological and Ethnographic Record of Mesoamerica*, edited by S. B. Mock, 125-133. Albuquerque: University of New Mexico Press.

Gerhardt, J. C.

1988   *Preclassic Architecture at Cuello, Belize*. BAR International Series 464. Oxford: BAR Publications.

Gibson, E. C.

1989   The Organization of Late Preclassic Maya Lithic Economy in the Eastern Lowlands. In *Prehistoric Maya Economies of Belize*, edited by P. A. McAnany and B. L. Isaac, 115-138. Research in Economic Anthropology, Supplement 4. Greenwich, CT: JAI Press.

Gifford, J. C.

1965   Ceramics. In *Prehistoric Maya Settlement Patterns in the Belize Valley*, edited by G. R. Willey, W. R. Bullard, Jr., J. B. Glass, and J. E. Gifford. Peabody Museum of Archaeology and Ethnology Papers 54. Cambridge, MA: Harvard University Press.

1976   Prehistoric Pottery Analysis and the Ceramics of Barton Ramie in the Belize Valley. *Memoirs of the Peabody Museum of Archaeology and Ethnology* 18. Cambridge: Harvard University Press.

Gillespie, S. D.

2000   Maya "Nested Houses": The Ritual Construction of Place. In *Beyond Kinship: Social and Material Reproduction in House Societies*, edited by R.A. Joyce and S.D. Gillespie, 135-160. Philadelphia: University of Pennsylvania Press.

2001   Personhood, Agency, and Mortuary Ritual: A Case Study. *Journal of Anthropological Archaeology* 20(1):73-112.

Gillis, J.

1982   Analysis of Miscellaneous Ceramic Artifacts from Colha, Belize: 1979-1981. In *Archaeology at Colha, Belize: The 1981 Interim Report*, edited by Thomas Hester, Harry Shafer and Jack Eaton, 229-236. San Antonio: Center for Archaeological Research, University of Texas.

Glascock, M.

1992   Characterization of Archaeological Ceramics at MURR by Neutron Activation Analysis and Multivariate Statistics. In *Chemical Characterization of Ceramic Pastes in Archaeology*, edited by Hector Neff, 11-26. Wisconsin: Prehistory Press.

Glascock, M. D., H. Neff, K. S. Stryker and T. N. Johnson

1994   Sourcing Archaeological Obsidian by an Abbreviated NAA Procedure. *Journal of Radioanalytical and Nuclear Chemistry* 180(1):29-35.

Goodrich, C., and H. van der Schalie

1937   *Mollusca of Petén and North Alta Vera Paz, Guatemala*. Ann Arbor: University of Michigan Press.

Gossen, G. H.

1999   *Telling Maya Tales: Tzotzil Identities in Modern Mexico*. New York: Routledge.

Graham, E. A.

1985   Facets of Terminal to Postclassic Activity in the Stann Creek District, Belize. In *The Lowland Maya Postclassic*, edited by A. F. Chase and P. Rice, 215-229. Austin: University of Texas Press.

1987   Resource Diversity in Belize and its Implications for Models of Lowland Trade. *American Antiquity* 52: 753-767.

1994   *The Highlands of the Lowlands: Environment and Archaeology in the Stann Creek District, Belize, Central America*. Monographs in World Archaeology 19. Madison, Wisconsin: Prehistory Press.

Grayson, D. K.

1984   *Quantitative Zooarchaeology: Topics in the Analysis of Archaeological Faunas*. New York: Academic Press.

Green, D. F., and Gareth Lowe

1967   *Altamira and Padre Piedra: Early Preclassic sites in Chiapas, Mexico*. Papers of the New World Archaeological Foundation 20. Provo, Utah: Brigham Young University.

Grube, N., and S. Martin

1998   Política Clásica Maya dentro de una Tradición Mesoamericana: un Modelo Epigráfico de Organización Política Hegemónica. In *Modelos de entidades políticas mayas, primer seminario de mesas redondas de Palenque*, edited by S. Trejo, 131-146. México: Consejo Nacional para la Cultura y las Artes, Instituto Nacional de Antropología e Historia.

Hammond, N.

1977   The Earliest Maya. *Scientific American* 23:116-133.

1984   Holmul and Nohmul: a Comparison and Assessment of two Maya Lowland Protoclassic sites. *Ceramica de Cultura Maya* 13:1-17.

Hammond, N., ed.

1991a   *Cuello: an Early Maya Community in Belize*. Cambridge: Cambridge University Press.

Hammond, N.

1991b   The Maya and their Civilization. In *Cuello: an Early Maya Community in Belize*, edited by N. Hammond, 1-7. Cambridge: Cambridge University Press.

1991c   Ceramic, Bone, Shell and Groundstone Artifacts. In *Cuello: an Early Maya Community in Belize*, edited by Norman Hammond, 176-191.Cambridge: Cambridge University Press.

1991d   Obsidian Trade. In *Cuello: an Early Maya Community in Belize*, edited by N. Hammond, 197-198. Cambridge: Cambidge University Press.

1991e   Jade and Greenstone Trade. In *Cuello: an Early Maya Community in Belize*, 199-203, edited by Norman Hammond. Cambridge: Cambridge University Press.

1991f   Archaeological Investigations at Cuello, 1975-1987. In *Cuello: an Early Maya Community in Belize*, edited by Normon Hammond, 8-22. Cambridge: Cambridge University Press.

Hammond, N., and J. R. Bauer

2001   A Preclassic Maya sweatbath at Cuello, Belize. *Antiquity* 75:683-4.

Hammond, N., A. Clarke, and C. Robin

1991   Middle Preclassic buildings and burials at Cuello, Belize: 1990 Investigations. *Latin American Antiquity*, 2(4): 352-363.

Hammond, N., A. Clarke, and S. Donaghey

1995   The long goodbye: Middle Preclassic Maya archaeology at Cuello, Belize. *Latin American Antiquity* 6:120-128.

Hammond, N., A. Clarke, and F. Estrada Belli

1992   Middle Preclassic Maya buildings and burials at Cuello, Belize. *Antiquity* 66:955-964.

Hammond, N., and J. C. Gerhardt

1990   Early Maya Architectural Innovation at Cuello, Belize. *World Archaeology* 21 (3): 466-476.

Hammond, N., and L. J. Kosakowsky

1991   Ceramics. In *Cuello: an Early Maya Community in Belize*, edited by N. Hammond, 173-176. Cambridge: Cambridge University Press.

Hammond, N., L. J. Kosakowsky, K. A. Pyburn, J. R. Rose, J. C. Staneko, S. Donaghey, C. M. Clark, M. Horton, C. Gleason, D. Muyskens and T. Addyman

1988   The Evolution of an Ancient Maya City: Nohmul. *National Geographic Research* 4(4):474-495.

Hammond, N., D. Pring, R. Berger, R. Switsur, and A. P. Ward

1976   Radiocarbon Chronology for Early Maya Occupation at Cuello, Belize. *Nature* 260:579-581.

Hansen, R. D.

1998   Continuity and Disjunction: The Pre-Classic Antecedents of Classic Architecture. In *Form and Meaning in Classic Maya Architecture*, edited by S. D. Houston, 49-122. Washington, D.C.: Dumbarton Oaks Research Library and Collection.

Harrison, E.

2001   Nourishing the Animus of Lived Space: Caching Ritual at K'axob. Master's Research Paper, Boston University, Department of Archaeology.

Harrison, P. D.

1983   The Pulltrouser Settlement Survey and Mapping of Kokeal. In *Pulltrouser Swamp: Ancient Maya Habitat, Agriculture, and Settlement in Northern Belize*, edited by B.L. Turner II, and P. D. Harrison, 140-157. Austin: University of Texas Press.

1989   Functional Influences on Settlement Pattern in the Communities of Pulltrouser Swamp, Northern Belize. *Household and Communities: Proceedings of the Twenty First Annual Conference of the Archaeological Association of the University of Calgary*, 460-465. Calgary: The University of Calgary Archaeological Association.

1996   Settlement and Land Use in the Pulltrouser Swamp Archaeological Zone, Northern Belize. In *The Managed Mosaic: Ancient Maya Agriculture and Resource Use*, edited by S. L. Fedick, 177-190. Salt Lake City: University of Utah Press.

Harrison, P. D., and R. E. Fry

2000   *Pulltrouser Swamp: A Lowland Maya Community Cluster in Northern Belize. The Settlement Maps.* Salt Lake City: University of Utah Press.

Haviland, W. A.

1997   The Rise and Fall of Sexual Inequality: Death and Gender at Tikal, Guatemala. *Ancient Mesoamerica* 8:1-12.

Hayden, B.

1987   From Chopper to Celt: The Evolution of Resharpening Technologies. *Lithic Technology* 16(2-3):33-43.

Hedges, R. E. M., R. A. Housely, C. R. Bronk, and G. J. van Klinken

1992   Radiocarbon Dates from the Oxford AMS System: Archaeometry Datelist 15, *Archaeometry* 34:337-338.

Helms, M. W.

1998   *Access to Origins: Affines, Ancestors, and Aristocrats.* Austin: University of Texas Press.

Henderson, H. H.

1993   Interim Report on Operation 10. In *K'axob Project: Interim Report, 1992 Field Season*, edited by P. A. McAnany, 31 pp. Submitted to the Department of Archaeology, Belmopan, Belize, Central America. On file, Department of Archaeology, Boston University.

1995   Operation XII Excavation Report. In *K'axob Project: Interim Report, 1993 Field Season*, edited by P. A. McAnany, 55 pp. Submitted to the Department of Archaeology, Belmopan, Belize, Central America. On file, Department of Archaeology, Boston University.

1998   The Organization of Staple Crop Production in Middle Formative, Late Formative, and Classic Period Farming Households at K'axob, Belize. Ph.D. dissertation, University of Pittsburgh.

Hertz, R.

1960   *Death and the Right Hand.* Translated by R. and C. Needham. Glencoe: The Free Press.

Hester, T. R., J. D. Eaton, and H. J. Shafer, eds.

1981   *The Colha Project: Second Season, 1980 Interim Report.* Second printing. San Antonio: Center for Archaeological Research, University of Texas.

Hester, T. R., and N. Hammond

1979   Preface. In *Maya Lithic Studies: Papers from the 1976 Belize Field Symposium*, edited by T. R. Hester and N. Hammond. Special Report No. 4, Second Printing. San Antonio: Center for Archaeological Research, The University of Texas.

Hester, T. R., and H. J. Shafer

1984   Exploitation of Chert Resources by the Ancient Maya of Northern Belize, Central America. *World Archaeology* 16(2):157-173.

1987   Observations on Ancient Maya Core Technology at Colha, Belize. In *The Organization of Core Technology*, edited by J. K. Johnson and C. A. Morrow, 239-257. Boulder: Westview Press.

1992   Lithic Workshops Revisited: Comments on Moholy-Nagy. *Latin American Antiquity* 3(3):243-248.

Hester, T. R., H. J. Shafer and T. D. Berry

1991   Technological and Comparative Analysis of the Chipped Stone Artifacts from El Pozito, Belize. In *Maya Stone Tools: Selected Papers from the Second Maya Lithic Conference*, edited by T. R. Hester and H. J. Shafer, 67-84. Monographs in World Archaeology No. 1. Madison: Prehistory Press.

Hodder, I.

2000   *Towards a Reflexive Method in Archaeology: the Example of Catal Hoyuk.* Cambridge: McDonald Institute for Archaeological Research.

Hohmann, B., and T. Powis

1996   The 1995 Excavations at Pacbitun, Belize: Investigation of the Middle Formative Occupation in Plaza B. In *Belize Valley Preclassic Maya Project: Report on the 1995 Field Season*, edited by P. F. Healy and J. J. Awe, 98-127. Department of Anthropology, Occasional Papers in Anthropology No. 12. Peterborough, Ontario: Trent University.

Houston, S., ed.

1998   *Function and Meaning in Classic Maya Architecture.* Washington, D.C: Dumbarton Oaks Research Library and Collection.

Houston, S., and P. A. McAnany

2003   Bodies and Blood: Critiquing Social Construction in Maya Archaeology. *Journal of Anthropological Archaeology* 22:26-41.

Iceland, H. B.

1997   The Preceramic Origins of the Maya: Results of the Colha Preceramic Project in Northern Belize. Ph.D. dissertation, University of Texas, Austin.

Isaza A., I. I.

1997   Shell Working and Social Differentiation at the Formative Maya Village of K'axob. Unpublished Master's Research Paper, Boston University, Department of Archaeology.

Isaza A., I. I. and P. A. McAnany

1999   Adornment and Identity: Shell Ornaments from Formative K'axob. *Ancient Mesoamerica* 10: 117-127.

Jackson, L.

1993   Excavations at Operation I. In *K'axob Project: Interim Report, 1992 Field Season*, edited by P. A. McAnany, 76 pp. Submitted to the Department of Archaeology, Belmopan, Belize, Central America. On file, Department of Archaeology, Boston University.

Johnson, J. K.

1991   Obsidian: a Technological Analysis. In *Cuello: an Early Maya Community in Belize*, edited by N. Hammond, 169-173. Cambidge: Cambridge University Press.

Johnson, W.
1983   The Physical Setting: Northern Belize and Pulltrouser Swamp. In *Pulltrouser Swamp: Ancient Maya Habitat, Agriculture, and Settlement in Northern Belize*, edited by B. L. Turner and P. D. Harrison, 8-29. Austin: University of Texas Press.

Jones, J. G.
1999   Analysis of Pollen from K'axob, Belize. In *Where the Water Meets the Land: 1998 Excavations in Wetland Fields and along Transects at K'axob, Belize*, edited by P. A. McAnany and K. Berry,125-137. Submitted to the Department of Archaeology, Belmopan, Belize.

Jones, L. D.
1986   *Lowland Maya Pottery, the Place of Petrological Analysis*. Oxford: BAR International Series 288.

Joralemon, P. D.
1971   A Study of Olmec Iconography. In *Studies in Pre-Columbian Art and Archaeology* 7, edited by E. P. Benson. Washington, D. C.: Dumbarton Oaks Research Library and Collection.

Joyce, A., and M. Winter
1996   Ideology, Power, and Urban Society in Pre-Hispanic Oaxaca. *Current Anthropology* 37:33-46.

Joyce, R. A.
1992   Ideology in Action: Classic Maya Ritual Practice. In *Ancient Images, Ancient Thought: The Archaeology of Ideology, Proceedings of the 23rd Annual Chacmool Conference*, edited by A. S. Goldsmith, S. Garvie, D. Selin, and J. Smith, 497-505. Calgary: Department of Archaeology, University of Calgary.
2000a   Heirlooms and houses: materiality and social memory. In *Beyond Kinship: Social and Material Reproduction in House Societies*, edited by R.A. Joyce and S.D. Gillespie, 189-212. Philadelphia: University of Pennsylvania Press.
2000b   High Culture, Mesoamerican Civilization, and the Classic Maya Tradition. In *Order, Legitimacy, and Wealth in Ancient States*, edited by J. Richards and M. van Buren, 64-76. Cambridge: Cambridge University Press.

Joyce, R. A., and S. D. Gillespie, eds.
2000   *Beyond Kinship: Social and Material Reproduction in House Societies*. Philadelphia: University of Pennsylvania Press.

Joyce, R. A., and J. S. Henderson
2001   Beginnings of Village Life in Eastern Mesoamerica. *Latin American Antiquity* 12(1):5-23.

Kent, K. P., and S. Nelson
1976   Net Sinkers or Weft Weights? *Current Anthropology* 174(1):152.

King, D.
1996   Cretaceous-Tertiary Boundary Stratigraphy near San Antonio, Orange Walk District, Belize, Central America. *Transactions of the Gulf Coast Association of Geological Societies* 46:213-217.

King, F. W.
1996   Freshwater snails of Florida identification manual. Internet site, http://www.flmnh.ufl.edu/natscu/malacology/fl-snail/snails1.htm.

King, R. B., I. C. Basillie, T. M. B. Abell, J. R. Dunsmore, D. A. Gray, J. H. Pratt, H. R. Versey, A. C. S. Wright, and S. A. Zisman
1992   *Land Resource Assessment of Northern Belize*. Volume 1, Bulletin 43. United Kingdom: Natural Resources Institute.

Kobza, V. L.
1994   A Study of the Form, Constitution, and Function of Sherd-lined Facilities from K'axob, Belize. Senior Work for Distinction, Boston University, Department of Archaeology.

Kosakowsky, L. J.
1983   *Intrasite Variability of the Formative Ceramics from Cuello, Belize: an Analysis of Form and Function*. Ph.D. dissertation, University of Arizona. Ann Arbor: University Microfilms, Intl.
1987   *Preclassic Maya Pottery at Cuello, Belize*. Anthropological Papers of the University of Arizona 47. Tucson: University of Arizona Press.

Kosakowsky, L. J., and N. Hammond
1991   Ceramics. In *Cuello: an Early Maya Community in Belize*, edited by Norman Hammond, 173-176. Cambridge: Cambridge University Press.

Kosakowksy, L. J., and D. C. Pring
1998   The Ceramics of Cuello, Belize, a new Evaluation. *Ancient Mesoamerica* 9:55-66.

Laporte, J. P.
1995   Despoblamiento o Problema Analítico? El Clásico Temprano en el sureste del Peten. In *VIII Simposio de Investigaciones Arqueológicas en Guatemala, 1994*, edited by J. P. Laporte and H. Escobedo, 729-761. Guatemala: Ministerio de Cultura y Deportes, IDAEH, Asociación Tikal.

Laporte, J. P., and V. Fialko C.
1990   New Perspectives on Old Problems: Dynastic References for the Early Classic at Tikal. In *Vision and Revision in Maya Studies*, edited by F. S.

Clancy and P. D. Harrison, 33-66. Albuquerque: University of New Mexico Press.

Lawrence, D. L., and S. M. Low

1990   The Built Environment and Spatial Form. *Annual Review of Anthropology* 19:453-505.

Lee, D. F. H.

1996   Nohoch Na (The Big House): The 1995 Excavations at the Cas Pek Group, Cahal Pech, Belize. In *Belize Valley Preclassic Maya Project: Report on the 1995 Field Season*, edited by P. F. Healy and J. J. Awe, 77-97. Department of Anthropology, Occasional Papers in Anthropology No. 12. Peterborough, Ontario: Trent University.

Lee, T. A., Jr.

1969   *The Artifacts of Chiapa de Corzo, Chiapas Mexico.* Papers of the New World Archaeological Foundation 26. Provo, Utah: Brigham Young University.

Lemmonier, P.

1986   The Study of Material Culture Today: Toward an Anthropology of Technical Systems. *Journal of Anthropological Archaeology* 5(1): 147-186.

1993   *Technological Choices: Transformation in Material Cultures since the Neolithic.* London: Routledge.

Levi, L.

1993   *Prehispanic Residence and Community at San Estevan, Belize.* Ph.D. dissertation, University of Arizona. Ann Arbor: University Microfilms, Intl.

Lévi-Strauss, C.

1982   *The Way of the Masks.* Translated from French by Sylvia Modelski. Seattle: University of Washington Press.

Lewenstein, S. M.

1987   *Stone Tool Use at Cerros: The Ethnoarchaeological and Use-Wear Evidence.* Austin: University of Texas Press.

1991   Woodworking Tools at Cerros. In *Maya Stone Tools: Selected Papers from the Second Maya Lithic Conference*, edited by T. R. Hester and H. J. Shafer, 239-250. Monographs in World Archaeology No. 1. Madison: Prehistory Press.

Lincoln, C. E.

1985   Ceramics and Ceramic Chronology. In *A Consideration of the Early Classic Period in the Maya Lowlands*, edited by G. R. Willey and P. Mathews, 55-94. Albany: SUNY Institute of Mesoamerican Studies Publication 10.

Lonardo, C.

1996   The Architectural Development of Maya Ritual Space at Formative K'axob, Belize. Senior Work

for Distinction, Boston University, Department of Archaeology.

Longyear, J. M.

1952   *Copan Ceramics: a Study of Southeastern Maya Pottery.* Publication 597. Washington: Carnegie Institution of Washington.

López Varela, S. L.

1989   *Análisis y Clasificación de la Cerámica de un Sitio Maya del Clásico: Yaxchilán, Chiapas.* BAR International Series 535. Oxford: British Archaeological Reports.

1995   El análisis de la cerámica de Pomoná y Yaxchilán: una nueva problemática en las Tierras Bajas Noroccidentales. In *Memorias del Segundo Congreso Internacional de Mayistas*, 611-623. México: Instituto de Investigaciones Filológicas, Centro de Estudios Mayas, UNAM.

1996   *The K'axob Formative Ceramics: The Search for Regional Integration through a Reappraisal of Ceramic Analysis and Classification in Northern Belize.* Ph.D. dissertation, University of London. Ann Arbor: University Microfilms, Intl.

1997   Pottery Classification Procedures and Documentation of Partially and Wholly Restorable Vessels. In *K'axob Project: Interim Report of the 1995 Field Season*, edited by P. A. McAnany, 203-270. Submitted to the Department of Archaeology, Belmopan, Belize, On file, Department of Archaeology, Boston University.

1998   El Análisis cerámico de Yaxchilán y Pomoná un ejemplo para entender la estructura económica y política en la zona del Usumacinta. In *Modelos de Entidades Políticas Mayas, Primer Seminario de Mesas Redondas de Palenque*, edited by Silvia Trejo, 183-207. México: Consejo Nacional para la Cultura y las Artes, Instituto Nacional de Antropología e Historia.

Lowe, G. W.

1962   *Mound 5 and Minor Excavations, Chiapa de Corzo, Chiapas Mexico.* Papers of the New World Archaeological Foundation 12. Provo: Brigham Young University.

1977   The Mixe-Zoque as Competing Neighbors of the Early Lowland Maya. In *The Origins of Maya Civilization*, edited by R. E. W. Adams, 197-248. Albuquerque: University of New Mexico Press.

1978   Eastern Mesoamerica. In *Chronologies in New World Archaeology*, edited by R.E. Taylor and C.W. Meighan, 331-393. New York: Academic Press.

Lowe, G. W., and P. Agrinier
1960   *Mound 1, Chiapa de Corzo, Chiapas, Mexico.* Papers of the New World Archaeological Foundation 7. Provo: Brigham Young University.

MacNeish, R., A. Nelken-Terner and I. W. Johnson
1967   *The Prehistory of the Tehuacan Valley Vol. 2 Nonceramic Artifacts.* Published for the Robert S. Peabody Foundation Phillips Academy, Andover. Austin and London: University of Texas Press.

Mallory, J. K.
1986   "Workshops" and "Specialized Production" in the Production of Maya Stone Tools: A Response to Shafer and Hester. *American Antiquity* 51:152-58.

Marcus, J.
1984   Reply to Hammond and Andrews. *American Antiquity* 49(4):829-833.

1999   Men's and Women's Ritual in Formative Oaxaca. In *Social Patterns in Pre-Classic Mesoamerica*, edited by D. C. Grove and R. A. Joyce, 67-96. Washington, D. C.: Dumbarton Oaks Research Library and Collection.

Marcus, J., and K. V. Flannery
1996   *Zapotec Civilization: How Urban Society Evolved in Mexico's Oaxaca Valley.* London and New York: Thames and Hudson.

Martonova, I.
1993   Excavation Report for Operation XIII. In *K'axob Project: Interim Report, 1992 Field Season*, edited by P. A. McAnany, 34 pp. Submitted to the Department of Archaeology, Belmopan, Belize, Central America. On file, Department of Archaeology, Boston University.

Masson, M. A.
1993   K'axob Caches and Community Integration: Preclassic Manifestations of a Pervasive Maya Pattern. Paper presented at the 58th Annual Meeting of the Society for American Archaeology, St. Louis.

1997   Cultural Transformation at the Maya Postclassic Community of Laguna de On, Belize. *Latin American Antiquity* 8(4):1-26.

1999   The Manipulation of "Staple" and "Status" Faunas at Postclassic Maya Communities. *World Archaeology* 31:93-120.

2001   The Economic Organization of Late and Terminal Classic Period Maya Stone Tool Craft Specialist Workshops at Colha, Belize. *Lithic Technology* 26(1):29-49.

2004   Fauna Exploitation from the Preclassic to the Postclassic Periods at Four Maya Settlements in Northern Belize. In *Maya Zooarchaeology: New Directions in Method and Theory*, Monograph 51, edited by Kitty Emery. Los Angeles: Cotsen institute of Archaeology at UCLA.

Masson, M. A., and H. S. Hale
1989   *Faunal Remains from the Honey Hill Site (8BD411): Strategies of an Everglades Wetland Foraging Economy.* Report on file with the Archaeological and Historical Conservancy, Miami, FL, and the State of Florida Division of Archives, History, and Records Management.

Masson, M. A., and M. W. Holderby
1994   Subsistence Patterns at 41HY209 and 41HY202: An Analysis of Vertebrate Faunal Remains. In *Archaic and Late Prehistoric Human Ecology in the Middle Onion Creek Valley, Hays County, Texas*, edited by R. A. Ricklis and M. B. Collins, vol. 2, 403-489. Studies in Archaeology 19. Austin: Texas Archeological Research Laboratory, University of Texas.

Matheny, R. T.
1986   Investigations at El Mirador, Petén, Guatemala. *National Geographic Research* 2:332-353.

McAnany, P. A.
1986   *Lithic Technology and Exchange Among Wetland Farmers of the Eastern Maya Lowlands.* Ph.D. dissertation, University of New Mexico, Albuquerque. Ann Arbor: University Microfilms, Intl.

1988   The Effects of Lithic Procurement Strategies on Tool Curation and Recycling. *Lithic Technology* 17(1):3-11.

1989   Stone Tool Production and Exchange in the Eastern Maya Lowlands: the Consumer Perspective from Pulltrouser Swamp, Belize. *American Antiquity* 54(2):332-346.

1991   Structure and Dynamics of Intercommunity Exchange. In *Maya Stone Tools: Selected Papers from the Second Maya Lithic Conference*, edited by T. R. Hester and H. J. Shafer, 271-293. Monographs in World Archaeology No. 1. Madison: Prehistory Press.

1992   Agricultural Tasks and Tools: Patterns of Stone Tool Discard near Prehistoric Maya Residences Bordering Pulltrouser Swamp, Belize. In *Gardens of Prehistory: The Archaeology of Settlement Agriculture in Greater Mesoamerica*, edited by T. W. Killion, 184-213. Tuscaloosa: University of Alabama Press.

1993a   Resources, Specialization, and Exchange in the Maya Lowlands. In *The American Southwest and Mesoamerica: Systems of Prehistoric Exchange*, edited by J. E. Ericson and T. G. Baugh, 213-245. New York: Plenum Press.

1995a   *Living with the Ancestors: Kinship and Kingship in Ancient Maya Society.* Austin: University of Texas Press.

1998b   Ancestors and the Classic Built Environment. In *Function and Meaning in Classic Maya Architecture*, edited by S. D. Houston, 271-298. Washington, D.C: Dumbarton Oaks Research Library and Collection.

McAnany, P. A., ed.

1993b   *K'axob Project: Interim Report, 1992 Field Season.* Submitted to the Department of Archaeology, Belmopan, Belize, Central America. On file, Department of Archaeology, Boston University.

1995b   *K'axob Project: Interim Report, 1993 Field Season.* Submitted to the Department of Archaeology, Belmopan, Belize, Central America. On file, Department of Archaeology, Boston University.

1997   *K'axob Project: Interim Report of the 1995 Field Season.* Submitted to the Department of Archaeology, Belmopan, Belize, On file, Department of Archaeology, Boston University.

1998a   *Where the Water Meets the Land: 1997 Excavations in Maya Residences and Wetland Fields, K'axob, Belize.* Submitted to the Department of Archaeology, Belmopan, Belize, On file, Department of Archaeology, Boston University.

McAnany, P. A., and K. Berry, eds.

1999   *Where the Water Meets the Land: 1998 Excavations in Wetland Fields and along Transects at K'axob, Belize.* Submitted to the Department of Archaeology, Belmopan, Belize, On file, Department of Archaeology, Boston University.

McAnany, P. A., and S. L. López Varela

1999   Re-Creating the Formative Maya Village of K'axob: Chronology, Ceramic Complexes, and Ancestors in Architectural Context. *Ancient Mesoamerica* 10:147-168.

McAnany, P. A., R. Storey and A. K. Lockard

1999   Mortuary Ritual and Family Politics at Formative and Early Classic K'axob, Belize. *Ancient Mesoamerica* 10:129-146.

McCormack, V.

1993   Operation VIII Field Report. In *K'axob Project: Interim Report, 1992 Field Season*, edited by P. A. McAnany, 31 pp. Submitted to the Department of Archaeology, Belmopan, Belize, Central America. On file, Department of Archaeology, Boston University.

1995   Excavations at Operation XI. In *K'axob Project: Interim Report, 1993 Field Season*, edited by P. A. McAnany, 60 pp. Submitted to the Department of Archaeology, Belmopan, Belize, Central America. On file, Department of Archaeology, Boston University.

McDermott, M.

1991   *Excavations at Operation VII, The 1990 Season of the K'axob Project*, 36 pp. ms. on file, Department of Archaeology, Boston University.

McDonald, R. C., and N. Hammond

1985   The Environment of Northern Belize. In *Nohmul: A Prehistoric Maya Community in Belize, Excavations 1973-1983*, edited by N. Hammond. BAR International Series 250 (I), 13-42. Oxford: British Archaeological Reports.

McGee, R. J.

1998   The Lacandon Incense Burner Renewal Ceremony: Termination and Dedication Ritual among the Contemporary Maya. In *The Sowing and the Dawning: Termination, Dedication, Transformation in the Archaeological and Ethnographic Record of Mesoamerica*, edited by S. B. Mock, 41-46. Albuquerque: University of New Mexico Press.

McGregor, R.

1994   Analysis of Miscellaneous Ceramic Artifacts from Colha, Belize: 1983 Season. In *Continuing Archaeology at Colha, Belize*, edited by T. R. Hester, H. J. Shafer, and J. D. Eaton, 245-255. Studies in Archaeology 16. Austin: Texas Archeological Research Laboratory, University of Texas.

McKinnon, S.

2000   The Tanimbarese *Tavu*: The Ideology of Growth and the Material Configuration of Houses and Hierarchy in an Indonesian Society. In *Beyond Kinship: Social and Material Reproduction in House Societies*, edited by R. A. Joyce and S. D. Gillespie, 161-176. Philadelphia: University of Pennsylvania Press.

McSwain, R. A.

1989   Production and Exchange of Stone Tools Among Preclassic Maya Communities: Evidence from Colha, Belize. Ph.D. dissertation, University of Arizona, Tucson.

1991   A Comparative Evaluation of the Producer-Consumer Model for Lithic Exchange in Northern Belize, Central America. *Latin American Antiquity* 2(4):337-351.

Meskill, F. K.

1992   Ceramics and Context: a Protoclassic Perspective from the Sites of Kichpanha and Colha, Northern Belize. Master's Thesis, the University of Texas at San Antonio, San Antonio.

Miksicek, C. H.

1991   The Ecology and Economy of Cuello. In *Cuello: an Early Maya Community in Belize*, edited by Normon Hammond, 70-97. Cambridge: Cambridge University Press.

n.d.   Paleoecology and Subsistence at Pulltrouser Swamp: The View from the Float Tank: Manuscript in possession of author.

Miller, M. E.

1988   The Boys in the Bonampak Band. In *Maya Iconography*, edited by E.P. Benson and G.G. Griffin, 318-330. Princeton: Princeton University Press.

Miller, M., and K. Taube

1993   *The Gods and Symbols of Ancient Mexico and the Maya*. New York: Thames and Hudson.

Mitchum, B. P.

1994   Lithic Artifacts from Cerros, Belize: Production, Consumption, and Trade. Ph.D. dissertation, Southern Methodist University, Dallas.

Mock, S. B.

1994   The Northern River Lagoon Site (NRL): Late to Terminal Classic Maya Settlement, Saltmaking, and Survival on the Northern Belize Coast. Ph.D. dissertation, Department of Anthropology, University of Texas at Austin.

Mock, S. B., ed.

1998   *The Sowing and the Dawning: Termination, Dedication, and Transformation in the Archaeological and Ethnographic Record of Mesoamerica*. Albuquerque: University of New Mexico Press.

Moholy Nagy, H.

1990   Misidentification of Mesoamerican Lithic Workshops. *Latin American Antiquity* 1:268-279.

1994   Tikal material culture: Artifacts and social structure at a Classic Lowland Maya City. Ph.D. dissertation, University of Michigan.

1999   Mexican Obsidian at Tikal, Guatemala. *Latin American Antiquity* 10(3):300-3313.

Monaghan, J.

1998   Dedication: Ritual or Production? In *The Sowing and the Dawning: Termination, Dedication, and Transformation in the Archaeological and Ethnographic Record of Mesoamerica*, edited by S. B. Mock, 47-52. Albuquerque: University of New Mexico Press.

Morley, S., G. Brainerd, and R. Sharer

1983   *The Ancient Maya*. California: Stanford University Press.

Neff, H.

1992   Ceramics and Evolution. In *Archaeological Method and Theory*, Volume 4, edited by Michael B. Schiffer, 141-193. Tucson: University of Arizona Press.

Neff, H., R. Bishop, and D. E. Arnold

1988   Reconstruction of Ceramic Production from Paste Compositional Data: An Example from Guatemala. *Journal of Field Archaeology* 15:239-348.

Nelson, F. W.

1989   Rutas de Intercambio de Obsidiana en el Norte de la Peninsula de Yucatán. In *La Obsidiana en Mesoamérica*, edited by M. Gaxiola G. and J. E. Clark, 363-368. México, D. F.: Instituto Nacional de Antropologia e Historia.

Netting, R. M., R. R. Wilk, and E. J. Arnould, eds.

1984   *Households: Comparative and Historical Studies of the Domestic Group*. Berkeley: University of California Press.

Novella, R. A.

1995   *Classification and Interpretation of Marine Shell Artifacts from Western Mexico*. BAR International Series 622. Oxford: British Archaeological Reports.

Olsen, S. J.

1978   Special Problems of Faunal Analysis in the Maya Area. Paper presented at the 43rd Annual Meeting of the Society for American Archaeology, Tucson.

1982   *An Osteology of Some Maya Mammals*. Peabody Museum of Archaeology and Ethnology Papers 73. Cambridge: Harvard University.

Pearson, M. P., and C. Richards, eds.

1994   *Architecture and Order: Approaches to Social Space*. New York: Routledge.

Pendergast, D. M.

1979   *Excavations at Altun Ha, Belize, 1964-1970 Volume 1*. Toronto: Royal Ontario Museum.

1981   Lamanai, Belize: Summary of Excavation Results, 1974-1980. *Journal of Field Archaeology* 8(1):29-53.

1982a   *Excavations at Altun Ha, Belize, 1964-1970 Volume 2.* Toronto: Royal Ontario Museum.

1982b   *Excavations at Altun Ha, Belize 1964-1970 Volume 3 .* Toronto: Royal Ontario Museum.

1998   Intercessions with the Gods: Caches and Their Significance at Altun Ha and Lamanai, Belize. In *The Sowing and the Dawning: Termination, Dedication, and Transformation in the Archaeological and Ethnographic Record of Mesoamerica*, edited by S. B. Mock, 55-64. Albuquerque: University of New Mexico Press.

Peterson, F. A.

1963   *Some Ceramics from Mirador, Chiapas, Mexico.* Papers of the New World Archaeological Foundation 15, Publication 11. Provo: Brigham Young University.

Peterson, P. A.

2001   Testing the Producer-Consumer Model for Lithic Exchange: a View from K'axob, Belize. Masters Thesis, Department of Archaeology, Boston University.

Phillips, D. A., Jr.

1979   *Material Culture and Trade of the Postclassic Maya.* Ph.D. dissertation. Ann Arbor: University Microfilms Intl.

Plunket, P., editor

2002   *Domestic Ritual in Ancient Mesoamerica*, Monograph 46. Los Angeles: Cotsen Institute of Archaeology at UCLA.

Pohl, M.

1981   Ritual Continuity and Transformation in Mesoamerica: Reconstruction of the Ancient Maya *Cuch* Ritual. *American Antiquity* 46:513-529.

1983   Maya Ritual Faunas: Vertebrate Remains from Burials, Caches, Caves, and Cenotes in the Maya Lowlands. In *Civilization in the Ancient Americas Essays in Honor of Gordon R. Willey*, edited by R. Leventhal and A. L. Kolata, 55-103. Albuquerque: University of New Mexico Press.

Pohl, M., and P. Bloom

1996   Prehistoric Maya Farming in the Wetlands in Northern Belize: More Data from Albion Island and Beyond. In *The Managed Mosaic: Ancient Maya Agriculture and Resource Use*, edited by S. Fedick,145-164. Salt Lake City: University of Utah Press.

Pohl, M. D., P. R. Bloom and K. O. Pope

1990   Interpretation of Wetland Farming in Northern Belize: Excavations at San Antonio Río Hondo. In *Ancient Maya Wetland Agriculture: Excavations on Albion Island, Northern Belize*, edited by M. D. Pohl,187-254. Boulder: Westview Press.

Pohl, M. D., K. O. Pope, J. G. Jones, J. S. Jacob, D. R. Piperno, S. D. deFrance, D. L. Lentz, J. A. Gifford, M. E. Danforth and J. K. Josserand

1996   Early Agriculture in the Maya Lowlands. *Latin American Antiquity* 7(4):355-372.

Pope, K. O., and B. H. Dahlin

1989   Ancient Maya Wetland Agriculture: New Insights from Ecological and Remote Sensing Research. *Journal of Field Archaeology* 16:87-106.

Pope, K. O., M. D. Pohl and J. S. Jacob

1996   Formation of Ancient Wetland Fields: Natural and Anthropogenic Processes. In *The Managed Mosaic: Ancient Maya Agriculture and Resource Use*, edited by S. L. Fedick,165-176. Salt Lake City: University of Utah Press.

Potter, D. R.

1982   Some results of the second year of excavations at operation 2012. In *Archaeology at Colha, Belize: The 1981 interim report*, edited by T.R. Hester, H. J. Shafer, and J. P. Eaton, 98-122. San Antonio: Center for Archaeological Research, University of Texas and Venice: Centro Studi e Ricerche Ligabue.

1991   A Descriptive Taxonomy of Middle Preclassic Chert Tools at Colha, Belize. In *Maya Stone Tools: Selected Papers From the Second Maya Lithic Conference*, edited by T. R. Hester and H. J. Shafer, 21-29. Monographs in World Archaeology No. 1. Madison: Prehistory Press.

Potter, D. R., T. R. Hester, S. L. Black and F. J. Valdez

1984   Relationships between Early Preclassic and Early Middle Preclassic Phases in Northern Belize: a Comment on "Lowland Maya Archaeology at the Crossroads". *American Antiquity* 49:628-631.

Prechtel, M.

1999   *Long Life, Honey in the Heart: a Story of Initiation and Eloquence from the Shores of a Mayan Lake.* New York: Penguin Putnam Inc.

Pring, D.

1977a   The Preclassic Ceramics of Northern Belize. Ph.D. dissertation, Institute of Archaeology, University of London. Ann Arbor: University Microfilms, Intl.

1977b   Influence or Intrusion? The Protoclassic in the Maya Lowlands. In *Social Process in Maya Prehistory*, edited by Norman Hammond, 135-156. New York: Academic Press.

Proskouriakoff, T.

1962   The Artifacts of Mayapan. In *Mayapan, Yucatan, Mexico*, edited by H.E.D. Pollock, R. Roys, T. Proskouriakoff, and A. Ledyard Smith, 322-423. Publication 619. Washington D.C.: Carnegie Institute of Washington.

Pyburn, K. A.

1989a   *Prehistoric Maya Community and Settlement at Nohmul, Belize*. Oxford: British Archaeological Reports International Series 509.

1989b   Maya Cuisine: Hearths and Lowland Economy. In *Research in Economic Anthropology: Prehistoric Maya Economies of Belize*, Supplement 4, edited by P. A. McAnany and B. L. Isaac, 325-346. Greenwich, CT: JAI Press, Inc..

Reents-Budet, D., ed.

1994   *Painting the Maya Universe: Royal Ceramics of the Classic Period*. Durham: Duke University Press.

Reents-Budet, D., R. L. Bishop and B. MacLeod

1994   Painting Styles, Workshop Locations and Pottery Production. In *Painting the Maya Universe: Royal Ceramics of the Classic Period*, edited by D. Reents-Budet, 164-233. Durham: Duke University Press.

Reese, K., and F. Valdez, Jr.,

1987   The Ceramic Sequence of Kichpanha: 1979-1985 Seasons. In *Maya Ceramics Papers from the 1985 Maya Ceramic Conference*, edited by P. Rice, and R. Sharer, 37-45. BAR International Series 345 (i). Oxford: British Archaeological Reports.

Reilly, F. K., III

1989   The Shaman in Transformation Pose: A Study of the Theme of Rulership in Olmec Art. *Record of the Art Museum* (Princeton University) 48(2):4-21.

1990   Cosmos and Rulership: The Function of Olmec Style Symbols in Formative Period Mesoamerica. *Visible Language* 24(1):12-37.

1994   Visions to Another World: Art, Shamanism, and Political Power in Middle Formative Mesoamerica. Ph.D. dissertation, University of Texas, Austin.

1995   Art, Ritual, and Rulership in the Olmec World. In *The Olmec World: Ritual and Rulership*, 27-45. Princeton: Princeton University Press.

Reina, R. E., and R. M. Hill II

1978   *The Traditional Pottery of Guatemala*. Austin: University of Texas.

Reitz, E. J., and C. M. Scarry

1985   *Reconstructing Historic Subsistence with an Example from Sixteenth Century Spanish Florida*. Society for Historical Archaeology, Special Publication Series, Number 3.

Rice, P. M.

1979   Ceramic and Nonceramic Artifacts of Lakes Yaxha-Sacnab, El Peten, Guatemala. Part I, The Ceramics. Section A, Introduction and the Middle Preclassic Ceramics of Yaxha-Sacnab, Guatemala. *Ceramica de Cultura Maya* 10:1-62.

1987a   *Pottery Analysis; A Sourcebook*. Chicago: University of Chicago Press.

1987b   Lowland Maya Pottery Production in the Late Classic Period. In *Maya Ceramics: Papers from the 1985 Maya Ceramics Conference*, edited by P. M. Rice and R. J. Sharer, 525-543. BAR International Series 384 (ii). Oxford: British Archaeological Reports.

1991   Specialization, Standardization, and Diversity: a Retrospective. In *The Ceramic Legacy of Anna O. Shepard*, edited by R. L. Bishop and F. Lange, 257-279. Boulder: University Press of Colorado.

Ricketson, O. G., Jr.

1937   *Uaxactun, Guatemala Group E—1926-1931. Part I: the Excavations*. Publication 477, Washington, D.C.: Carnegie Institution of Washington.

Ricketson, O. G., Jr. and E. B. Ricketson

1937   *Uaxactun, Guatemala: Group E—1926-1931*. Publication 477. Washington D. C.: Carnegie Institute of Washington.

Ringle, W. M., and E. W. Andrews V

1988   Formative Residences at Komchen, Yucatan, Mexico. In *Household and Community in the Mesoamerican Past*, edited by R. R. Wilk and W. Ashmore, 171-197. Albuquerque: University of New Mexico Press.

Robertson, R. A.

1983   Functional Analysis and Social Process in Ceramics: The Pottery from Cerros, Belize. In *Civilization in the Ancient Americas: Essays in Honor of Gordon R. Willey*, edited by R. Leventhal and A. L. Kolata, 105-142. Albuquerque: University of New Mexico Press.

1986   The Ceramics. In *Archaeology at Cerros, Belize, Central America: an Interim Report vol. 1*, edited by Robin A. Robertson, and D. A. Freidel, 89-103. Texas: Southern Methodist University Press.

Robertson-Freidel, R. A.

1980   The Ceramics from Cerros: A Late Preclassic Site in Northern Belize. Ph.D. dissertation. Harvard University, Cambridge, MA.

Robin, C.

1989   *Preclassic Maya burials at Cuello, Belize.* BAR International Series 480. Oxford: British Archaeological Reports.

1997   Rural Household and Community Flux at Classic Maya Xunantunich. Paper presented at the 62nd Annual Meeting of the Society for American

Robin, C., and N. Hammond

1991   Burial Practices. In *Cuello: an Early Maya Community in Belize,* edited by N. Hammond, 204-225. Cambridge: Cambridge University Press.

Robin, C., N. Hammond, and J. C. Gerhardt

1991   Ritual and Ideology. In *Cuello: an Early Maya Community in Belize,* edited by N. Hammond, 204-234. Cambridge: Cambridge University Press.

Rovner, I., and S. M. Lewenstein

1997   *Maya Stone Tools of Dzibilchaltún, Yucatán, and Becán and Chicanná, Campeche.* Middle American Research Institute, Publication 65. New Orleans: Tulane University.

Rye, O.

1981   *Pottery Technology: Principles and Reconstruction.* Washington, D.C.: Taraxacum Press.

Sabloff, J. A.

1975   Ceramics. In *Excavations at Seibal, Department of Peten, Guatemala,* edited by G. R. Willey. Memoirs of the Peabody Museum of Archaeology and Ethnology, Volume 13, Number 2. Cambridge: Harvard University Press.

Santone, L.

1997   Transport Costs, Consumer Demand, and Patterns of Intraregional Exchange: a Perspective on Commodity Production and Distribution from Northern Belize. *Latin American Antiquity* 8(1):71-88.

Saul, F. P., and J. M. Saul

1991   The Preclassic Population of Cuello. In *Cuello: an Early Maya Community in Belize,* edited by N. Hammond, 134-158. Cambridge: Cambridge University Press.

Saul, J. M., and F. P. Saul

1997   The Preclassic Skeletons from Cuello. In *Bones of the Maya: Studies of Ancient Skeletons,* edited by S. L. Whittington and D. M. Reed, 28-50. Washington, DC: Smithsonian Institution Press.

Schele, L., and D. A. Freidel

1990   *A Forest of Kings: The Untold Story of the Ancient Maya.* New York: William Morrow.

Schele, L., and M. Miller

1986   *Blood of Kings.* New York: George Braziller, Inc.

Schiffer, M. B.

1987   *Formation Processes of the Archaeological Record.* Albuquerque: University of New Mexico Press.

Schiffer, M. B., and J. M. Skibo

1989   A Provisional Theory of Ceramic Abrasion. *American Anthropologist* 91:102-116.

Schulz, J.

1997   Operation 14: Excavations at Structure 54. In *K'axob Project: Interim Report, 1993 Field Season,* edited by P. McAnany, 17-42. Submitted to the Department of Archaeology, Belmopan, Belize, Central America. On file, Department of Archaeology, Boston University.

Scott, R. F., IV

1980   Further Comments on Faunal Analysis and Ancient Subsistence Activities at Colha. In *The Colha Project, Second Season, 1980 Interim Report,* edited by T.R. Hester, J.D. Eaton, and H.J. Shafer, 281-288. San Antonio: University of Texas, Center for Archaeological Research and Venezia: Centro Studi e Ricerche Ligabue.

1982   Notes on Continuing Faunal Analysis for the Site of Colha, Belize. In *Archaeology at Colha, Belize: The 1981 Interim Report,* edited by Thomas R. Hester, Harry J. Shafer, and Jack D. Eaton, 203-207. San Antonio: University of Texas, Center for Archaeological Research and Venezia: Centro Studi e Ricerche Ligabue.

Sellet, F.

1993   Chaîne Opératoire: the Concept and its Applications. *Lithic Technology* 18(1/2):106-112.

Shafer, H. J.

1976   Belize Lithics: "Orange Peel" Flakes and Adze Manufacture. In *Maya Lithic Studies: Papers from the 1976 Belize Field Symposium,* edited by T. R. Hester and N. Hammond, 21-34. San Antonio: Center for Archaeological Research, University of Texas.

1983a   Lithic Artifacts of the Pulltrouser Area: Settlement and Fields. In *Pulltrouser Swamp: Ancient Maya Habitat, Agriculture, and Settlement in Northern Belize,* edited by B. L. Turner and P. D. Harrison, 212-245. Austin: University of Texas Press.

1983b   The Tranchet Technique in Lowland Maya Lithic Tool Production. *Lithic Technology* 12(3):57-68.

1985   A Technological Study of Two Maya Lithic Workshops at Colha, Belize. In *Stone Tool*

Analysis: Essays in Honor of Don E. Crabtree, edited by M. G. Plew, J. C. Woods and M. G. Pavesic, 277-315. Albuquerque: University of New Mexico Press.

1994   Community-wide Lithic Craft Specialization in the Late Preclassic Lowland Maya: A Case for Northern Belize. In *Continuing Archaeology at Colha, Belize*, edited by T. Hester, H. Shafer, and J. Eaton, 25-30. Austin: University of Texas.

Shafer, H. J., and T. R. Hester

1983   Ancient Maya Chert Workshops in Northern Belize, Central America. *American Antiquity* 48(3):519-543.

1986a   *An Ancient Maya Hafted Stone Tool from Northern Belize*. Working Papers in Archaeology, No. 3. San Antonio: Center for Archaeological Research, University of Texas.

1986b   Maya Stone-Tool Craft Specialization and Production at Colha, Belize: Reply to Mallory. *American Antiquity* 51(1):158-165.

1991   Lithic Craft Specialization and Product Distribution at the Maya site of Colha, Belize. *World Archaeology* 23(1):79-97.

Sharer, R. J., ed.

1978   *The Prehistory of Chalchuapa, El Salvador. Pottery and Conclusions*, Vol. 3. Philadelphia: University of Pennsylvania Press.

Sharer, R. J.

1983   *The Ancient Maya*. Fourth revised edition. Stanford: Stanford University Press.

1992   The Preclassic Origins of Lowland Maya States. In *New Theories on the Ancient Maya*, edited by E. C. Danien and R. J. Sharer, 131-136. Philadelphia: The University Museum, University of Pennsylvania.

Sharer, R. J., and J. C. Gifford

1970   Preclassic Ceramics from Chalchuapa, El Salvador, and Their Relationships with the Maya Lowlands. *American Antiquity* 35(4):441-462.

Sharer, R. J., and D. W. Sedat

1987   *Archaeological Investigations in the Northern Maya Highlands, Guatemala: Interaction and the Development of Maya Civilization*. Philadelphia: The University Museum, University of Pennsylvania.

Shaw, L. C.

1991   *The Articulation of Social Inequality and Faunal Resource Use in the Preclassic Community of Colha, Northern Belize*. Ph.D. dissertation, University of Massachusetts, Amherst. Ann Arbor: University Microfilms, Intl.

Shaw, L. C., and P. H. Mangan

1994   Faunal Analysis of an Early Postclassic Midden, Operation 2032, Colha, Belize. In *Continuing Archaeology at Colha, Belize*, edited by T. Hester, H. Shafer, and J. Eaton. Studies in Archaeology No. 16. Austin: Texas Archaeological Research Lab, University of Texas.

Shepard, A.

1939   Technological Notes on the Pottery of San Jose. In *Excavations at San Jose, British Honduras*, edited by J. E. Thompson, 251-277. Washington: Carnegie Institute of Washington.

Shipley, W. E., III and E. A. Graham

1987   Petrographic Analysis and Preliminary Source Identification of Selected Stone Artifacts from the Maya Sites of Seibal and Uaxactun, Guatemala. *Journal of Archaeological Science* 14:367-383.

Sidrys, R., editor

1983   *Archaeological Excavations in Northern Belize, Central America*. Monograph XVII. Los Angeles: UCLA Institute of Archaeology.

Sidrys, R., and J. Andresen

1976   Metate Import in Northern Belize. In *Maya Lithic Studies: Papers from the 1976 Belize Field Symposium*, edited by T. Hester and N. Hammond, 177-190. Special Report No. 4. San Antonio: Center for Archaeological Research, University of Texas.

Sinopoli, C. M.

1991   *Approaches to Archaeological Ceramics*. Plenum Press, New York.

Smith, A. L.

1950   *Uaxactun, Guatemala: Excavations of 1931-1937*. Carnegie Institution of Washington Publication 588. Washington, D.C: Carnegie Institution of Washington.

1972   *Excavations at Altar de Sacrificios: Architecture, Settlement, Burials, and Caches*. Peabody Museum of Archaeology and Ethnology Papers 26(2). Cambridge, MA: Harvard University.

1982   *Excavations at Seibal: Major Architecture and Caches*. Memoirs of the Peabody Museum of Archaeology and Ethnology 15(1). Cambridge, MA: Harvard University.

Smith, R. E.

1955   *Ceramic Sequence at Uaxactun, Guatemala*. Middle American Research Institute Publication No. 20. New Orleans: Tulane University.

1971   *The Pottery of Mayapan*. Peabody Museum of Archaeology and Ethnology Paper 66. Cambridge, MA: Harvard University.

Smith, R. E., and J.C. Gifford

1966   *Maya Ceramic Varieties, Types and Wares at Uaxactun: A Supplement to Ceramic Sequence at Uaxactun, Guatemala*. Middle American Research Institute Publication 28:125-174. New Orleans: Tulane University.

St. Laurent, R. A.

1993   The Excavation of Operation XII. In *K'axob Project: Interim Report, 1992 Field Season*, edited by P. A. McAnany, 28 pp. Submitted to the Department of Archaeology, Belmopan, Belize, Central America. On file, Department of Archaeology, Boston University.

Steensberg, A.

1980   *New Guinea Gardens: A Study of Husbandry with Parallels in Prehistoric Europe*. London: Academic Press.

Sterner, J.

1989   Who is Signaling Whom? Ceramic Style, Ethnicity and Taphonomy among the Sirak Bulahay. *Antiquity* 63: 451-459.

Stone, D.

1957   *The Archaeology of Central and Southern Honduras*. Peabody Museum of Archaeology and Ethnology Paper 49(3). Cambridge: Harvard University.

Stuart, D.

1987   *Ten Phonetic Syllables. Research Reports on Ancient Maya Writing 14*. Washington, D.C: Center for Maya Research.

1996   Kings of Stone: A Consideration of Stelae in Ancient Maya Ritual and Representation. *Res* 29-30:148-171.

1998   "The Fire Enters His House": Architecture and Ritual in Classic Maya Texts. In *Function and Meaning in Classic Maya Architecture*, edited by S. D. Houston, 373-425. Washington, D.C: Dumbarton Oaks Research Library and Collection.

Stuart, G. S.

1992   The Arts. In *Lost Kingdoms of the Maya*, edited by Gene S. Stuart and George E. Stuart, 96-111. Washington D C: National Geographic Society.

Suárez-Díez, L.

1989   *Conchas Prehispánicas en México.* BAR International Series 514. Oxford: British Archaeological Reports.

Sullivan, L. A.

1991   Preclassic Domestic Architecture at Colha, Belize. Master's thesis, University of Texas, Austin.

Tarbuck, E., and F. K. Lutgens

1999   *Earth: An Introduction to Physical Geology*. 6th Edition. Upper Saddle River, New Jersey: Princeton Hall.

Taschek, J. T.

1994   *The Artifacts of Dzibilchaltun, Yucatan, Mexico: Shell, Polished Stone, Bone, Wood and Ceramics*. Middle American Research Institute Publication 50. New Orleans: Tulane University.

Taschek, J. T., and J. W. Ball

1999   Las Ruinas de Arenal: Preliminary report on a subregional major center in the western Belize Valley (1991-1992 excavations). *Ancient Mesoamerica* 10:215-235.

Taube, K.

1988a   A Prehispanic Maya Katun Wheel. *Journal of Anthropological Research* 44:183-203.

1988b   The Ancient Yucatec New Year Festival: The Liminal Period in Maya Ritual and Cosmology. Ph.D. dissertation, Department of Anthropology, Yale University.

1992   The Iconography of Mirrors at Teotihuacan. In *Art, Ideology, and the City of Teotihuacan*, edited by J. C. Berlo, 169-204. Washington, DC: Dumbarton Oaks Research Library and Collection.

Tedlock, D.

1985   *Popol Vuh: The Definitive Edition of the Mayan Book of the Dawn of Life and Glories of Gods and Kings*. New York: Simon and Schuster.

Thomas, J.

2001   Archaeologies of Place and Landscape. In *Archaeological Theory Today*, edited by I. Hodder, 165-186. Cambridge: Polity Press.

Thompson, J. E. S.

1939   *Excavations at San Jose, British Honduras*. Carnegie Institution of Washington Publication No. 506. Washington, D. C.: Carnegie Institution.

1940   *Late Ceramic Horizons at Benque Viejo, British Honduras*. Carnegie Institution of Washington Publication No. 528, 1-35. Washington, D. C.: Carnegie Institution.

1954   *The Rise and Fall of Maya Civilization*. Norman: University of Oklahoma Press.

1970   *Maya History and Religion*. Norman: University of Oklahoma Press.

Thompson, R.H.

1958   Modern Yucatecan Maya pottery making.

Memoirs of the Society of American Archaeology, no. 15. American Antiquity 23, no.4, part 2.

Thomson, C. W.

1987   Chalcatzingo Jade and Fine Stone Objects. In *Ancient Chalcatzingo*, edited by David C. Grove, 295-304. Austin: University of Texas Press.

Tobey, Mark H.

1986   *Trace Element Investigations of Maya Chert from Belize*. Papers of the Colha Project, Vol. 1. San Antonio: Center for Archaeological Resarch, The University of Texas.

Todd, L. C.

1987   Taphonomy of the Horner II Bone Bed. In *The Horner Site: Type Site of the Cody Cultural Complex*, edited by G. C. Frison and L. C. Todd, 107-198. New York: Academic Press.

Tourtellot, G.

1988   *Excavations at Seibal, Department of Peten, Guatemala: Peripheral Survey and Excavation, Settlement and Community Patterns*. Memoirs of the Peabody Museum of Archaeology and Ethnology 16. Cambridge, MA: Harvard University Press.

Tozzer, A. M., translator

1941   *Landa's Relación de las cosas de Yucatán*. Peabody Museum of Archaeology and Ethnology Papers Papers 18. Cambridge, MA: Harvard University.

Turner II, B. L., and P. D. Harrison

1981   Prehistoric Raised Field Agriculture in the Maya Lowlands. *Science* 213:399-405.

Turner II, B. L., and P. D. Harrison, eds.

1983   *Pulltrouser Swamp: Ancient Maya Habitat, Agriculture, and Settlement in Northern Belize*. Austin: University of Texas Press.

Turner II, B. L., and C. H. Miksicek

1984   Economic Plant Species Associated with Prehistoric Agriculture in the Maya Lowlands. *Economic Botany* 38(2):179-193.

Valdés, J. A.

1993   Arquitectura y Escultura en la Plaza Sur del Grupo H, Uaxactún. In *Tikal y Uaxactún en el Preclásico*, edited by J. P. Laporte and J. A. Valdés, 96-122. México, D. F.: Universidad Nacional Autónoma de México.

Valdez, F., Jr.

1987   The Prehistoric Ceramics of Colha Northern Belize. Ph.D. dissertation. Harvard University, Cambridge, MA.

Valdez, F., Jr. and J. A. Gillis

1980   A Preliminary Note on Miscellaneous Ceramic Artifacts from Colha, Belize. 1979-1980. In *The Colha Project, Second Season: 1980 Interim Report*, edited by T. Hester, J. Eaton, and H. Shafer, 327-329. San Antonio: Center for Archaeological Research, University of Texas and Venezia: Centro Studie Ricerche Ligabue.

Velázquez Castro, A.

1999   *Tipología de los Objetos de Concha del Templo Mayor de Tenochtitlan: Proyecto Templo Mayor*, 20 Aniversario. México, D.F.: Instituto Nacional de Antropología e Historia.

Viel, R.

1993   *Evolución de la Cerámica de Copan, Honduras*. Tegucigalpa: Instituto Hondureño de Antropología e Historia.

Villagra Caleti, A.

1971   Mural Painting in Central Mexico. In *Handbook of Middle American Indians*, vol. 10, 135-156. Austin: The University of Texas Press.

Vogt, E. Z.

1969   *Zinacantan: A Maya Community in the Highlands of Chiapas*. Cambridge: Harvard University Press.

1970   *The Zinacantecos of Mexico: A Modern Maya Way of Life*. New York: Holt, Rinehart and Winston.

1976   *Tortillas for the Gods: A Symbolic Analysis of Zinacanteco Rituals*. Cambridge: Harvard University Press.

1998   Zinacanteco Dedication and Termination Rituals. In *The Sowing and the Dawning: Termination, Dedication, and Transformation in the Archaeological and Ethnographic Record of Mesoamerica*, edited by S. B. Mock, 21-30. Albuquerque: University of New Mexico Press.

von Winning, H.

1987   *La Iconografía de Teotihuacan: los Dioses y los Signos*, vol. 1. Mexico: UNAM.

Walker, D. S.

1998   Smashed Pots and Shattered Dreams. In *The Sowing and the Dawning: Termination, Dedication, and Transformation in the Archaeological and Ethnographic Record of Mesoamerica*, edited by S. B. Mock, 81-99. Albuquerque: University of New Mexico Press.

Welsh, W. B. M.

1988   *An Analysis of Classic Lowland Maya Burials*. BAR International Series 409. Oxford: British Archaeological Reports.

West, R. C.

1964   Surface Configuration and Associated Geology

of Middle America. In *Handbook of Middle American Indians*, Volume 1, edited by R. C. West, 33-83. Austin: University of Texas Press.

White, J.

1990   Operation 1, 1990 Season, 12 pp. ms. on file, Department of Archaeology, Boston University.

Wilk, R. R., and H. L Wilhite, Jr,

1991   The Community of Cuello: Patterns of Household and Settlement Change. In *Cuello: an Early Maya Community in Belize*, edited by N. Hammond, 118-133. Cambridge: Cambridge University Press.

Willey, G. R.

1970   Type Descriptions of the Ceramics of the Real Xe Complex, Seibal, Peten, Guatemala. In *Monographs and Papers in Maya Archaeology*, edited by W. R. Bullard, 313-355. Peabody Museum of Archaeology and Ethnology Papers 61. Cambridge: Harvard University Press.

1977   The Rise of Maya Civilization: a Summary View. In *The Origins of Maya Civilization*, edited by R. E. W. Adams, 383-423. Albuquerque: University of New Mexico Press.

1972   The Artifacts of Altar de Sacrificios. *Papers of the Peabody Museum of Archaeology and Ethnology* 64(1). Cambridge: Harvard University Press.

1978   Excavations at Seibal: Artifacts. *Memoirs of the Peabody Museum of Archaeology and Ethnology*, Vol. 14(1), Cambridge: Harvard University Press.

Willey, G. R., W. R. Bullard, Jr., J. B. Glass and J. C. Gifford

1965   *Prehistoric Maya Settlements in the Belize Valley*. Peabody Museum of Archaeology and Ethnology Papers 54. Cambridge: Harvard University Press.

Willey, G. R., and J. C. Gifford

1961   Pottery of the Holmul I style from Barton Ramie. In *Essays in Precolumbian Art and Archaeology*, edited by S. K. Lothrop, 152-170. Cambridge: Harvard University Press.

Wing, E. S., and S. J. Scudder

1991   The Exploitation of Animals. In *Cuello: an Early Maya Community in Belize*, edited by Norman Hammond, 84-97. Cambridge: Cambridge University Press.

Wright, A. C. S., D. H. Romney, R. H. Arbuckle, and V. E. Vial

1959   *Land in British Honduras: Report of the British Honduras Land Use Survey Team*. London: Her Majesty's Stationery Office.

AUTHOR BIOGRAPHIES

MARY LEE BARTLETT, PhD, is a free-lance archae-ologist and museum consultant residing in Texas. In addition to Mesoamerican Archaeology, her research interests include Historical Archaeology, the settlement and decline of the American frontier, the evolution of complex societies, and the development of craft specialization. She is the author of several articles relating to the development of community identity during the Maya Formative and to the evolution of ceramic technology. Bartlett is a research fellow at Boston University and Texas Tech University.

KIMBERLY A. BERRY, a PhD candidate in Archaeology at Boston University, has worked as an excavation director and field director on the K'axob project since 1995. She has also served as a surveyor and lab director on the Xibun Archaeological Research Project. In addition to work in the Maya area, Kim has conducted fieldwork in Ohio and New England. Her dissertation research focuses on Maya agricultural use of wetland habitats and is entitled "Farming the Scales of the Crocodile:

Cultural and Geoarchaeological Evidence for Ancient Maya Wetland Reclamation at K'axob, Belize."

VICTORIA L. BOBO is a cultural resource specialist and education program coordinator for Geo InSight International, Inc. She specializes in the integration of archaeological studies with pre-collegiate education. She has taught archaeology to young students through Geo InSight's educational programs and through the Center for Talented Youth administered by Johns Hopkins University. Her research interests include household archaeology in Mesoamerica and the application of geographic information systems and other technologies to archaeology.

JUSTIN P. EBERSOLE, a PhD student in Anthropology at Vanderbilt University, received a B.A. in Archaeology from Boston University in 2001. His senior thesis, entitled "The Ground and Polished Stone Artifacts of K'axob, Belize, Central America," is an in-depth study of the ground stone of K'axob. He has conducted archaeological fieldwork in the Sibun River Valley of Belize; at Holmul, Guatemala; and in the Eastern Woodlands of the United States.

RYAN HARRIGAN, a PhD candidate in Biology at Boston University, is researching the genetics, systematics, and phylogeography of the American Black Duck and Mallard complex. He previously completed graduate work on the reproductive behaviors and success rates of Ovenbirds in Massachusetts and the feeding behaviors of cichlids of the Lake Victoria region. In addition to fieldwork at K'axob, Ryan has extensive field experience in the forests of New England as well as in the prairie potholes of Canada. Ryan intends to pursue a career in biology, perhaps with a concentration on a species slightly more mobile than the mollusca of K'axob.

ELEANOR HARRISON-BUCK is a PhD candidate in Archaeology at Boston University. Her research interests include Mesoamerican ritual and cosmology as well as trade networks and interregional exchange. Her research in the Sibun River Valley of Belize is focused on a series of Epiclassic period sites, which seem to reflect shifts in political, economic, and religious systems that occurred in the wake of the Classic Maya collapse. Beyond her academic research, Eleanor served as curator of an international exhibit on contemporary Maya religion, which opened in November 2001 at the Museum of World Religions in Taipei, Taiwan.

ANNABETH HEADRICK is an Assistant Professor of Art History and Anthropology at Vanderbilt University. She received her PhD from the University of Texas at Austin and specializes in the cultures of Mesoamerica, primarily concentrating on the city of Teotihuacan. Her publications include "The Street of the Dead . . . It Really Was: Mortuary Bundles at Teotihuacan" (published in the journal *Ancient Mesoamerica*, 1999) and "Merging Myth and Politics: The Three Temple Complex at Teotihuacan" (in a book co-edited by Annabeth and entitled *Landscape and Power in Ancient Mesoamerica*, Westview Press, 2001). She has served as lab director on several archaeological projects in Belize, including excavations organized by Boston University, the University of Texas, and Pacific Lutheran University.

ILEAN ISEL ISAZA AIZPURÚA is a PhD candidate in Archaeology at Boston University. Her doctoral work in the United States was sponsored by the Panamanian National Bureau of Science Technology and Innovation, SENACYT. Her research interests include the study of New World pre-Columbian cultures from Mesoamerica and Lower Central America, evolution of social inequality, chiefdoms, metallurgy, and the application of remote sensing techniques to archaeological research.

SANDRA L. LÓPEZ VARELA is research associate professor in the anthropology department of the Universidad Autónoma del Estado de Morelos, Cuernavaca, México. Her research interests include ceramic analysis and commercial networks in the Maya area and the structure and spatial organization of human activities. She has participated in field research at Teotihuacan, Yaxchilán and Pomoná, Sayil, K'axob, and the Sibun River Valley, and she is principal investigator of an ethnoarchaeological project in Morelos. Her research publications have appeared in Academic Press, Cambridge University Press, University of Utah Press, Middle American Research Institute, MoVince Verlag, Tübingen, British Archaeological Reports, Bonner Amerikanistische Studien, Fondo de Cultura Económica, Instituto Nacional de Antropología e Historia, and Universidad Nacional Autónoma de México.

TAMARRA MARTZ received a B.A. in archaeology from Boston University. While at Boston University she worked in the K'axob lab analyzing the pottery vessels. Employed by the UCLA Digital Archaeology Lab, Tamarra served as the West Coast project manager for the digital portion of the K'axob publication. She has contributed to the interim reports of the K'axob Project. After serving a term as a Peace Corps volunteer, Tamarra intends to pursue graduate education in primatology.

MARILYN MASSON is associate professor in the Department of Anthropology at the University at Albany, SUNY. She has worked in northern Belize since 1983. Since 1991 her research has focused specifically on Postclassic Maya social transformations. She is the principal investigator of the Belize Postclassic Project, the results of which are presented in her publication *In the Realm of Nachan Kan* (University Press of Colorado Press, 2000). In collaboration with Carlos Peraza Lope, she is conducting field research at the Postclassic Maya city of Mayapán, which will facilitate comparisons of economic patterns of the Belize region with northwest Yucatán.

PATRICIA A. MCANANY is a professor of archaeology at Boston University. She has directed archaeological projects in the Maya Lowlands since 1990, primarily at K'axob and in the Sibun River Valley of Belize. She is the author of *Living with the Ancestors* (University of Texas Press, 1995) and of numerous journal articles and book chapters. Her research interests include ritual practice (particularly ancestor veneration and cave rituals), landscape archaeology, and lithic technology.

POLLY A. PETERSON is a PhD candidate in Archaeology at Boston University. Primarily interested in Mesoamerican cosmology, lithics, and trade and ex-change, her doctoral dissertation examines the use of caves by the ancient Maya in the Sibun River valley of Belize, Central America. Her MA research is incorporated into chapter 11 of this volume.

REBECCA STOREY is an associate professor in the Department of Anthropology at the University of Houston. Her research interests include bioarchaeology and the pre-Columbian peoples of Mesoamerica, particularly those of the Teotihuacan and Maya civilizations. She is the author of *Life and Death in the Ancient City of Teotihuacan* (University of Alabama Press, 1992).

GLOSSARY

Bladen ceramic complex is an early component of the Middle Formative period at the site of Cuello.

Ceramic complex. A cluster of co-occurring ceramic types (as defined by the type-variety system) that are present within a set of stratigraphic units; together they form a site-specific relative chronology.

Chaakk'ax complex. A ceramic complex present at K'axob that is coeval with the Middle Formative period and is subdivided into an early and late facet.

Chicanel ceramic complex and sphere is characterized by a group of Late Preclassic ceramic types that were found to co-occur at Uaxactun, Guatemala. Now known to be widely distributed across the Maya Lowlands, Chicanel is recognized as a ceramic sphere with local variants. The type Sierra Red is the most prevalent among the Chicanel types.

Contruction phase and **subphase**. A group of archaeological deposits that relate to an integrated construction or use event; here, each construction phase is represented by a separate plan-view drawing. Construction phases are numbered from the base of an excavation to the top, that is, construction phase 1 defines the earliest construction at an operation. Minor renovations or additions to a construction are labeled with lowercase letters and called subphases.

Debitage. Chipped stone debris from the reduction of core material as well as production and refurbishing of a stone tool. Here, debitage includes cores that demonstrably are not recycled biface fragments and flakes that may or may not exhibit use-wear and marginal retouch or shaping.

Extended burial. A human interment that is positioned in an extended pose (with legs extended and arms by the sides), either prone or prostrate.

Facet. A subdivision within a ceramic complex that is established on the basis of differences in proportional frequencies of ceramic types or presence/absence of certain types.

Fireclouding. The result of differential firing on the surface of a slipped pottery vessel; fireclouding generally appears as blotches of dark gray amidst the desired slip color.

Flexed burial. A human interment that is placed in a "fetal" position with legs tightly flexed. The body is usually positioned on its side.

K'atabche'k'ax complex. A ceramic complex present at K'axob that is coeval with the Late Formative or Late Preclassic period and is subdivided into an early, late, and terminal facet.

K'axob. Site name established by Peter D. Harrison in 1981to reflect the fact that the land was in various stages of milpa fallow (*k'ax* means fallow field in Yucatec Mayan).

Kimilk'ax complex. A ceramic complex present at K'axob that is coeval with the Postclassic period.

Mammiform tetrapod. A ceramic dish, bowl, or cylinder with four hollow supports that assume mammary shapes and often include an interior small, circular pellet, presumably for acoustical effect.

Mamom ceramic complex and sphere is characterized by a group of Middle Preclassic ceramic types that were found to co-occur at Uaxactun, Guatemala (see Chapter 1 for further discussion). Now known to be widely distributed across the Maya Lowlands, Mamom is recognized as a ceramic sphere with local variants. The type Joventud Red is the most prevalent among the Mamom types.

Nohalk'ax complex. A ceramic complex present at K'axob that is coeval with the Early Classic period. In this volume, only the early facet is discussed.

Operation. The physical location of an excavation unit identified by a unique number.

Paleosol. A buried humic soil sometimes encountered at the base of a construction sequence within the excavation units of K'axob.

Provenience. The key to the location of an artifact within an excavation. At K'axob, a provenience is a combination of the operation, zone (sometimes with a subzone letter), and a square designation.

Seated burial. A human interment that is placed in a seated position with legs crossed and arms generally resting on the upper leg bones.

Subzone. An arbitrary level assigned to a very thick zone.

Swasey ceramic complex of Cuello, Belize, is controversial as to chronological position and ceramic uniqueness. It belongs either to the latest facet of the Early Formative period or the earliest facet of the Middle Formative period.

Witsk'ax complex. A ceramic complex present at K'axob that is coeval with the Late Classic period.

Xe and Real ceramic complexes define an early facet of the Middle Formative period at Altar de Sacrificios and Seibal, respectively.

Zone. The smallest discrete unit of physical remains that is identifiable as having a uniform cultural significance or function. A unique number is assigned to each zone within each operation, generally commencing with the top (surface) zone which receives the number "1".

INDEX

Abelino Red ceramics
    classification of, 175–176
    forms of, 173f
    frequency of, 172t
    imported, 173–174
Abell, T. M. B., 149, 157
Actuncan ceramics
    findings of, 252, *253*, 256–259
    frequency of, 190t
adornments
    bone, 359–363
    digital resources for, 333
    fired clay, 265–267
    semiprecious stone, 353–359
    shell, 335–351
age, burials determining, 110, 135t
agouti, frequency of, 386t
agricultural strategies, 8
Aguacate Orange ceramics, 78
    findings of, 238, 239f, 248–251, 254–255
    frequency of, 186t, 190t
    popularity of, 171t
    stylistic attributes of, 185
Aguila ceramics
    characteristics of, 171t
    disks made of, 271, 272f, 273

findings of, 252, *253*, 258, 259f
    frequency of, 186t, 190t
    stylistic attributes of, 189
Ainu, ceramics used by, 271
Allison, P. M., 23
alluvium, 144
Altar de Sacrificios
    ceramic sequence of, 194t
    clay beads of, 266
    Xe ceramics of, 177
amphibians, frequency of, 387t, 388
ancestors
    burials for gathering, 132
    redepositing, 84
anemia, iron-deficiency, 138
angular debris, 292
    deposition context of, 301t
    dimensions of, 291t
    scattering, 305t
animal motifs
    butterfly symbolism as, 267
    deer symbolism as, 71–72
    frog symbolism as, 71, 72
    monkey symbolism as, 188, 268, 269f
    serpent symbolism as, 70
animal resources. *See* fauna

anthropomorphism, 264, 357
aplastic minerals
    petrographic groups of, 153–155
    in soil, 145, 147, 149
apple-green stone, 354f, 355, 357t
apsidal platform structures, 72–74, 73f
Arbuckle, R. H., 149
*Archaeological Use and Distribution of Mollusk in the Maya
    Lowlands* (Andrews IV), 336
architecture. *See also* residential structures
    apsidal platform, 72–74, 73f
    differentiation in, 6
    monumental, 3
arkose
    procurement of, 325t
    properties of, 322
armadillo, frequency of, 386t, 388
Arnold, Philip, 7
artisans
    adornment, 265–267
    cloth production of, 265
    greenstone bead, 355–356
    ocarina, 264–265
    Olmec, 370–375
    ritual practices and, 7
    shell, 335
    skill of, 273
Ashmore, W., 68
authority
    emergence of, 5–6
    flexed burials and, 135t, 369
    gender inequality and, 82, 417
    were-jaguars and, 375–377, 376f, 377f
Aveni, A. F., 67
Awe, J. J., 265
awls, bone, 358f, 359
axe hafts, tightening, 305n1
axis mundi (centralized ritual space), 67

Balanza Black ceramics
    findings of, 260, 261f
    frequency of, 186t, 190t
Baldy Beacon, raw materials from, 322, 323
Ball, J. W., 75–76
barium, in clay, 158–159
barkbeaters
    dimensions of, 318t, 319f
    frequency of, 326t, 328t, 329t
    operations of, 328t
    purpose of, 318
Bartlett, Mary Lee, 6, 7, 140, 170, 332
Barton Ramie ceramics, 187, 194t
basalt
    procurement of, 325t
    properties of, 322
Basillie, I. C., 149, 157
Bateson, J. H., 322
beads
    carved bone, 362, 362f

fired clay, 265–266, 266f
    greenstone, 354f, 355–356, 356f
    irregular shaped, 340f, 341
    shell, 337t, 339f
Becker, M. J., 68, 72
beehive plugs, 319–320
Belize
    caches in, 75
    ceramic complexes of, 175–176
    ceramic technology in, 176
    chert of, 281–282, 281t
    clay sampling in, 144, 146f, 166n1
    geological resources in, 144–145
    landscapes of, 11–13, 383–384
    projects in, 3–4
    rock sampling in, 150f, 151
    site map of 2f, 11–13, 383–384
    soil matrix types in, 149t
    wetland farming in, 280
Berry, Kimberly, 7, 140
bifaces
    chunky, 285
    cortex of, 289
    deposition context of, 300t
    dimensions of, 286t
    examples of, 283f
    frequency of, 284t, 297t, 298t
    nondiagnostic, 285
    oval, 284–285
    polish found on, 280
    reworked, 285, 285f
    triangular, 288
bimodality, of sherd-lined pits, 95–96
birds
    deposition context of, 389, 390f, 391
    frequency of, 386t, 388
Bishop, R., 188
Black Rock Red ceramics, 181t
Blackman Eddy, caches of, 80
black-slipped ceramics, 163, 188
Bladen
    burials, 114
    ceramics, 175–176
blades. *See also* obsidian
    deposition context of, 300t
    frequency of, 284t, 297t, 298t
    types of, 285–286
Blake, M., 82
Blanton, R. E., 23, 24
blood letting, 77
Bobo, Victoria, 20, 315n1, 380
Bobryk, E., 170, 188
body sherds, 97–98
bone. *See* carved bone; skeletal bones
bony fish
    bone proportions of, 394t
    frequency of, 387t
bowls
    appearance of, 180

cross motif on, 368, 370–375
divining, 372–373, 372f
frequency of, 174
Humboldt Celt, 370–371, 370f
stylistic changes in, 182
sun-marked, 373f
tree symbolism on, 373–374, 373f, 374f
types and forms of, 173f, 179f, 184f
breakage patterns, in ceramics, 161
Brown, D. O., 309–310
Bullard, William, 3
burials. *See also* vessels
    "1-1," 127–128, 127f, 240, 368
    "1-2," 128–130, 129f, 242–247, 329, 368–369
    "1-3," 123, 210
    "1-4," 122, 210
    "1-6," 123, 212
    "1-10," 121, 122, 210
    "1-11," 121, 122
    "1-12," 122f, 123, 216
    "1-13," 122, 216, 368
    "1-14," 220, 339, 348f
    "1-15," 123, 218
    "1-17," 121–122, 220
    "1-18," 117, 118f, 120, 202, 345
    "1-19," 117, 118f, 120, 202
    "1-23," 121, 220
    "1-24," 115, 120, 202
    "1-25," 116–117, 117f, 120, 204, 368
    "1-26," 117, 329
    "1-27," 115, 206, 345
    "1-28," 113, 200, *201*, 341
    "1-29," 116–117, 117f, 120, 204, 368
    "1-30," 115
    "1-30a," 113
    "1-31," 115–116, 116f
    "1-32," 115, 329, 349f
    "1-33," 113
    "1-34," 115–116, 116f, 206
    "1-35," 112, 339, 340
    "1-37," 112–113
    "1-38," 112
    "1-39," 112–113
    "1-40," 112
    "1-41," 122–123, 122f
    "1-42," 112
    "1-43," 110–112, 111f, 120, 198, 199f, 340, 341t
    "1-44," 120
    "1-45," 128, 129f, 246, 329
    "1-46," 110
    "7-1," 133
    "7-2," 133, 256
    "8-1," 222
    "8-2," 222
    "8-2 through 8-6," 124–125, 131f, 185, 238, 355
    "10-1," 125
    "10-2," 125, 230
    "10-3," 258
    "11-1," 130–131, 232

    "11-2," 131, 252
    "11-3 through 11-6," 124, 232, 234, 238, 359
    "11-7 through 11-10," 119, 208, 345
    "11-12a," 208
    "12-1," 130, 254
    "12-2," 133, 258
    "12-3," 130, 254
    "12-4," 133
    "12-6," 130, 254
    "12-9," 125, 126f, 236
    "12-10," 236
    "12-11," 329
    "12-12," 236
    "12-16," 125, 126f, 236
    "13-2," 133, 258
    "13-3," 133–134, 133f, 260
    "13-4," 133
    adornments found in, 332
    age determination from, 110, 135t
    for ancestor gathering, 132
    Bladen, 114
    body position in, 135t
    Chaakk'ax, 61t, 110–115, 132
    of children, 112–113, 115, 117, 119, 120, 121–123
    cross motifs in, 116–117, 122, 127, 368–370
    Cuello, 76, 84, 114–115, 132
    debitage types in, 301t
    dedicatory rituals and, 133–134
    family, 114, 117, 120–121
    fauna frequency in, 390f, 392–394t, 395–396
    flexed, 369
    frog pendant in, 123
    greenstone in, 355
    individual, 126
    inherited status denoted by, 110, 112, 120, 121
    K'atabche'k'ax, 61t, 115–132
    Mamom, 114
    mass, 76, 84, 132
    Nohalk'ax, 61t, 132–134
    obsidian frequency in, 313t
    of Operation 1, 27, 56, 61t, 115, 121–124, 127–131
    of Operation 7, 57, 61t, 133
    of Operation 8, 57, 61t, 124–125
    of Operation 10, 57–58, 61t, 125
    of Operation 11, 58, 61t, 115, 117–118, 124, 130–131
    of Operation 12, 58–59, 61t, 125, 126f, 130, 133
    of Operation 13, 59, 61t, 133–134, 133f
    seated, 135t
    secondary, 110, 112, 126, 128, 133–134
    sex determination from, 110, 134, 135t
    shells in, 341, 342–343t, 345, 348–349f
    skeletal bones in, 134–138
    Swasey, 114
    termination rituals and, 130, 133–134
    Tikal, 68, 72
    tool types in, 329t
    types of, 109–110
    wealth denoted by, 120, 130
burnishers, 321

butterflies, symbolism of, 267
Buttles, P. J., 363
Byne's disease, 337

caches
    architectural context of, 81t
    Cerros, 67, 83, 84
    color-coding, 74–75, 74f, 362f, 364
    cosmology of, 66–67
    cross motif in, 71–72, 71f
    debitage types in, 301t, 302
    description of, 69t
    earliest, 68, 70, 76
    ethnography of, 82–85
    faunal use in, 391, 392–394t
    functions of, 65, 81t
    lip-to-lip, 58, 69t, 79
    as memory and identity markers, 67–68
    obsidian frequency in, 313t
    Operation 1, 66, 68–76
    Operation 7, 76–78
    Operation 8, 78
    Operation 10, 78–79
    Operation 11, 79–80
    Operation 12, 80–81
    patterns of, 66–67, 81t
    shell, 345, 350
    of stemmed macroblades, 302, 303f
    terms, 85n1
    as time and space markers, 67
    tool types in, 329t
    triadic, 72–75, 73f, 74f
    utilitarian, 79–80
Cahal Pech, ocarinas of, 265
calcite
    in clay, 145, 147, 147t, 157
    distribution of, 155f
    examples of, 152
    firing, 165
    with fossils, 152, 154
    frequency of, 154
    limestone with, 323
    marble, 322, 325t
    in rocks, 163
    silt-sized, 149, 149t
    in soils, 151
    tempering with, 160
calcium, barium v., 158–159
calcium carbonate. See limestone
Campos, Concepción, 13, 321
Campos, Rafael, 12
canals, evidence of, 280
canonical communication, 24, 62
canonical discriminant analysis, 156, 156f, 159
capitalism, 23
carved bone
    awls, 358f, 359
    beads, 362, 362f
    fan handles, 359, 361, 361f

patterning, 361–362
    tubes, 359, 360f
Castro, Velázquez, 336
catfish
    bone proportions of, 394t, 395
    frequency of, 387t
Catholicism, cross motif and, 367–368
Cauac, 83
celts
    dimensions of, 318t, 319f
    frequency of, 326t, 328t, 329t
    ground and polished, 318–319
    hard stone, 285
    Humboldt, 370–375, 370f
    purpose of, 318–319
    raw materials for, 325
ceramic complexes
    Belize, 175–176
    Bladen, 175
    Chaakk'ax, early facet of, 172–174, 194t, 196–199
    Chaakk'ax, first villagers of, 170
    Chaakk'ax, late facet of, 174–175, 194t, 200–201
    Chaakk'ax, origins of, 176–179
    characteristics of, 171t
    classification schemes for, 175–176
    Colha, 176, 178–179, 194t
    Cuello, 175–176, 194t
    fauna by, 386–387t
    flake frequency by, 299t
    forms of, 173f
    K'atabche'k'ax, advent of, 179–180
    K'atabche'k'ax, early facet of, 202–209
    K'atabche'k'ax, late facet of, 181–185, 194t, 210–239
    K'atabche'k'ax, terminal facet of, 185–189, 194t, 238–255
    Nohalk'ax, early facet of, 189–191, 194t, 256–261
    obsidian frequencies by, 310t
    ritualistic practices and, 183, 185
    sedentism and, 176–177
    shell frequency by, 342–343t
    spatial analysis of, 173–174
    Swasey, 175
    tool frequency by, 298t, 326t
    types of, 172t
    use-polish frequency by, 299t
    varieties of, 172t, 173f
ceramic production, 102, 104. See also clay
    analytical techniques for, 143
    breakage patterns in, 161
    burnishers for, 321
    changes in, 143, 157–159
    clay minerals used in, 145
    formation techniques for, 160–161
    independent lines of, 177
    limestone for, 144
    paste preparation for, 159–160
    pastes for, 151
    resource procurement for, 157
    stylistic attributes of, 162–165, 164f

technological changes in, 176, 180–184
temper techniques for, 160
void patterns in, 161
ceramics. *See also* vessels; *specific types of ceramics*
black-slipped, 163, 188
breakage patterns of, 161
chemical composition of, 173–174
chronology based on, 13–16
clay samples compared to, 144
codification of, 3, 195
coiling, 160–161
coloration of, 153
construction phases by, 26t
digital resources for, 141, 195
geological resources for, 144–145
grog in, 145, 153–154
imported, 173–174
INAA groups of, 155–157, 156f
lining types of, 88–89
polychrome, 133, 188, 191
porosity of, 98–99
sampling methods for, 144
"secondary use" of, 97
of sherd-lined pits, 88, 90, 97–98
stylistic influences of, 140
tempering, 154–155, 160, 166
thermal conductivity of, 97, 98–99
xeroradiography of, 161–162
Cerros
caches of, 67, 83, 84
greenstone of, 355
tool production at, 282
Chaakk'ax (Middle Formative period), 13
burial features of, 61t, 110–114, 132
carved bone of, 359
ceramic classification schemes for, 175–176
ceramic complexes of, early facet, 172–174, 194t, 196–199
ceramic complexes of first villagers of, 170
ceramic complexes of, late facet, 174–175, 194t, 200–201
ceramic origins of, 176–179
faunal proportions of, 385f, 386–387t, 390f
greenstone of, 353, 355
obsidian from, 308f, 310t
shell frequency of, 336t, 342f, 342t, 344t
skeletal bones of, 134t
tool deposits of, 296
tool frequency of, 327t
unifaces of, 287, 289f
vessel appliqué of, 268, 269f
Ch'a-Chak ceremony, 72
chalcedony, 322
attributes of, 295t
availability of, 281t, 282
in clay, 147, *152*
flakes, 294
frequency of, 284t
Chalchuapa, ceramic sequence of, 194t
"Charlie Chaplin" offerings, 75–76

Chase, Diane, 67, 77
chemicals
in ceramics, 173–174
in soils, 151
Chen Mul-style incensarios, 56, 266f, 267
chert, 322. *See also* Northern Belizean Chert
attributes of, 295t
in clay, 147, 147t
examples of, *154*
formation of, 147
frequency of, 153
golden, 72, 80, 304
procurement of, 298–299, 299t, 325t
ritual importance of, 80
silcrete and, 324
in Type 1 groundmass, 149, 149t
Chesterman, C. W., 322, 323
Chiapa de Corzo, ceramic sequence of, 194t
Chicago Orange ceramics, 81, 90, 97
discontinuation of, 171t
findings of, 218, *219*
firing temperature of, 165
forms of, 173f
frequency of, 172t, 174–175, 181t, 183t, 186t, 190t
technological changes in, 182
Chicanel ceramics
appearance of, 179
codification of, 3
stylistic attributes of, 180
varieties of, 181t, 183t, 186t, 190t
children
burials of, 112–113, 115, 117, 119, 120, 121–123
infection in, 138
chipped stone tools
debitage and, 283
deposition context of, 301–303, 301t
types of, 281t
chi-square tests, 94–95, 166n9
Christianity, cross motif and, 367
chronology, 13–16, 16t
ch'ul ajaw (divine lord), 1
Chunhinta Black ceramics
forms of, 173f
frequency of, 172t
chunky bifaces, 285
Clark, J. E., 82, 189, 307, 318
Classic period. *See also* *Nohalk'ax*
dedicatory caches of, 67
defining, 5
naming, 13
time frame of, 3
clay
aplastic minerals in, 145, 147, 149
chemical characterization of, 151
groundmass groups of, 153
mineral content of, 145
rock sampling for tempering, 151
sampling, 144–145, 146f, 148f, 162f
shells in, 147t, 149, *154*
smectite, 145

technological changes in, 182
vitrification of, 165
clay, fired
    adornments, 265–267
    as beads, 265–266, 266f
    as disks, 271–273, 272f, 273f
    as earflares, 266–267, 267f
    as net sinkers, 267–268, 268f, 269–271, 270f
    as ocarinas, 264–265, 264f
    purposes of, 263–264, 273
    residential use of, 263
    reworked, 269–273
    as roller stamps, 265, 265f
    as spindle whorls, 265, 265f
    for subsistence, 273
    unclassified objects of, 268–269
clothing. *See also* adornments
    beads for, 265–266
    carved bone for, 359
    net weights for, 271
    roller stamps for, 265, 265f
    spindle whorls for, 265, 265f
cobble debitage, 291t, 301t
Cockscomb-Sapote granite, 322
Coe, W. R., 320
Coggins, C., 67
coiling, 160–161
Coleman, Drew, 321–322
Colha
    carved bone of, 359, 363
    ceramic complexes of, 176, 178–179, 194t
    debitage of, 293
    net sinkers of, 268
    sherd-lined pits of, 89t
    spindle whorls of, 265
    tools of, 280, 282, 289, 324
colors
    cache coding by, 74–75, 74f, 362f, 364
    ceramic, 153
    debitage, 304
    greenstone, 355
    shell, 74, 364
    symbolism of, 364
columella fragments, 339
"competitive feasting," 82
Consejo Red ceramics, classification of, 175–176
construction fills
    debitage types by, 301t
    obsidian frequency by, 313t
    shell frequency by, 346–347t
    tool types by, 329t
construction phases, 26–27, 26t
    caches of, 69t
    mortuary rituals *v.*, 60–62, 61t
    of Operation 1, 27, 28–37f, 56–57
    of Operation 7, 38–41f, 57
    of Operation 8, 42–45f, 57
    of Operation 10, 46–47f, 57–58
    of Operation 11, 48–51f, 58
    of Operation 12, 52–54f, 58–59

of Operation 13, 55f, 59
sherd-lined pits and, 89t
cooking
    lids, 319–320
    sherd-lined pits for, 98–100
    technological changes in, 180, 181–182
    vessels, 97, 179f, 319–320
cores
    deposition context of, 301t
    dimensions of, 291t
    examples of, 292f, 293f
    obsidian, 312t
cortex
    categories of, 289
    frequency of, 299t
    presence of, 289–290
cosmology
    of caching, 66–67
    cross motif and, 371–375
    figurines denoting, 75–76
    of settlement, 67
    twins and, 56
crabs, frequency of, 387t, 389
crocodiles, frequency of, 387t, 388
cross motif, 27, 56
    on bowls, 368, 370–375
    in burials, 116–117, 122, 127, 368–370
    in caches, 71–72, 71f
    cosmology and, 371–375
    inverted vessel with, 369
    Kan, 131, 132
    Olmec art and, 370–377
    Palenque, 373–374, 373f
    religious source of, 367–368
    scattering rituals using, 304
    symbolism of, 71, 72
    on vessels, 164f, 185, 368–378
    were-jaguar and, 375–377, 376f, 377f
    wooden, 83
cryptocrystalline, 174
crystals
    in granite, 322
    in schist, 323–324
cuch ceremony, 70, 71–72
Cuello
    burials of, 76, 84, 114–115, 132
    carved bone of, 359, 362
    ceramic complexes of, 175–176, 194t
    fauna of, 383–384
    health indicators at, 138
    net sinkers of, 268
    obsidian of, 312
    residential structures of, 3–4
    sherd-lined pits of, 89t, 102
    tools of, 289
Cunil ceramics, importation of, 176
cylinder stamps, 265

Dapple, E. C., 324
Darch, J., 147, 153, 166n4

Daszkiewicz, M., 170, 188
debitage
    categorization of, 293–294
    chipped stone tools and, 283
    color of, 304
    cortex of, 289
    deposition context of, 301–303, 301t
    dimensions of, 291t
    flint-knapping, 291
    golden chert, 72, 80
    of K'axob, 283, 291–296
    scattering, 80, 303–304, 305t
    temporal patterns of, 297–298
dedicatory caches
    burials and, 133–134
    of Classic period, 67
    definition of, 66
    function of, 67
    symbolism of, 70
deer
    in caches, 391
    deposition context of, 389, 390f
    frequency of, 386t, 389
    symbolism of, 71–72
Dentaliidae shells, 340
deposition context
    of chipped stone tools, 301–303, 301t
    of fauna, 389–391, 390f
    of ground and polished tools, 327–330, 329t
    of obsidian, 312–314, 313t
diet. See fauna
digital materials
    for adornments, 333
    for biological resources, 381
    for built environment, 21
    for ceramics, 141, 195
    for mortuary ritual, 107
    for stone tools, 277
dishes
    cross motif on, 368f
    types and forms of, 173f, 184f
disks
    greenstone, 364
    reworked clay, 271–273, 272f, 273f
    shell, 337t
divining bowls, 372–373, 372f
dogs, 383–384, 386t, 389
dolomite, in clay, 153, *158*, 160
Dos Arroyos Orange ceramics
    findings of, 258, 259f, 260, 261f
    frequency of, 190t
Dreiss, M. L., 309–310
drills
    supports for, 319, 319f
    tips for, 296f
drinking vessels, 97
Dunsmore, J. R., 149, 157

ear flares, 266–267, 267f

ear spools, 362–363
Early Classic period. *See Nohalk'ax*
"earth polish," 280, 290
Ebersole, Justin P., 315n1, 317, 321
edge grinding, 339t
Edmonson, M. S., 71
effigy disks, 272, 273f
effigy jars, 185
egalitarianism, 417
El Chayal, obsidian from, 310, 310t, 313–314
El Mirador, ceramic sequence of, 194t
El Salvador
    ceramics from, 185
    map of, 2f
epigraphy, 84
ethnography
    of caches, 82–85
    of weft weights, 271
Euglandina cylindracea
    frequency of, 400t, 403–406t
    identification of, 401f, 402
    of Operation 1, 406
    of Operation 10, 407
    of Operation 12, 408
    purpose of, 410, 412

family. *See* kinship
fans, bone handles for, 359, 361, 361f
farming, wetland, 280
fauna
    bone proportions of, 391–396, 392–394t
    in caches, 391
    deposition context of, 389–391, 390f
    frequency of, 386–387t
    mollusca as, 412
    sampling methods, 384
    spatial analysis of, 384–385, 385f
fertility
    cross motifs and, 71, 72
    jade and shells for, 74, 364
figurines
    color-coded, 75
    fragments of, 268, 269f
    greenstone, 354f
    shell, 337t
fire features, fauna in, 390f, 392–394t
fire shatter, 292, 293f
    deposition context of, 301t
    dimensions of, 291t
    scattering, 305t
fired clay. *See* clay, fired
firing
    coloration and, 153
    sherd-lined pits and, 88, 89t, 102, 104
    successful, ensuring, 145
    temperatures, 163, 165
Firth, R., 7
fish
    bone proportions from, 394t, 395–396

deposition context of, 389, 390f, 391
net sinkers for, 267–271
spatial analysis of, 385f
trends in, 386–388, 387t
flakes
    attributes of, 295t
    deposition context of, 301t
    dimensions of, 291t, 293–294
    frequency of, 299t
    obsidian, 312t
    polish on, 295, 295t
    scar patterns on, 294
    scattering of, 80, 303–304, 305t
    types of, 291–294
Flannery, K. V., 100
flexed burials, 135t, 369
flint-knapping
    chert used for, 80
    debitage, 291
    procurement zones for, 282
floors
    debitage frequency in, 301t, 302
    fauna frequency in, 390f, 392–394t
    shell frequency in, 345, 346–347t
    tool frequency in, 329t
Flor Cream ceramics, 181t, 183t, 186t, 190t
formal tools, codification of, 283
Formative period. See also Chaakk'ax; K'atabche'k'ax
    authority during, 5–6
    key issues of, 1, 4
    naming, 13
    sites of, 2f, 3–4
    time frame of, 3
fossils, in calcite, 152
fragments. See flakes; stone fragments
Freidel, D. A., 67
freshwater shells, 295–296, 341. See also mollusca
frogs
    in caches, 391
    carved pendant of, 123
    frequency of, 387t
    symbolism of, 71, 72
fuchsite, 357t
Furley, P. A., 147, 166n4

Garber, J. F., 271, 318
gastropods, 338, 339f
gender inequality, 82, 417
geological history, 144–145
Gifford, J. C., 187
Glascock, Michael D., 309–310, 315n1
gods
    depiction of, 83
    location of, 84
Goldberg, Paul, 322
golden chert. See chert
Graham, E. A., 101, 323
granite
    muscovite, 355

procurement of, 325t
properties of, 322–323
grave goods
    absence of, 136
    phases associated with, 114
    wealth denoted by, 120, 130
Gray, D. A., 149, 157
greenstone, 76, 314f
    bead types of, 354f, 355–356, 356f, 357t
    in burials, 355, 363–364
    carved bone with, 359
    disks, 364
    figurines, 354f
    procurement of, 315, 353, 355
    raw material types of, 355, 357t
    in triadic caches, 363–364
    value of, 307
grog (crushed ceramics), 145, 153–154, 157, 158, 165
ground and polished stone tools
    classification of, 321–322
    composition of, 317
    deposition context of, 327–330, 329t
    frequency of, 326t, 327t, 328t, 329t
    procurement zones for, 324, 325t, 326t, 327t
    purpose of, 327
    raw materials for, 317, 321–325
    source areas of, 321–324
    temporal variation in, 325, 327
    types of, 317–321, 318t
groundmass. See also soils
    petrographic groups based on, 153
    types of, 149, 149t, 152
    usage changes in, 157–159
Guacamallo ceramics, 186t, 190t
Guatemala
    ceramics of, 181
    macroblades of, 77–78
    map of, 2f
    obsidian trade with, 309–310
    tool source materials of, 322–323
Guitara Incised ceramics
    findings of, 196, 197f, 200, 201
    forms of, 173f
    frequency of, 172t, 174, 181t, 183t
    stylistic attributes of, 180
gypsum
    in clay, 147t, 166n6
    examples of, 154
    formation of, 147

hafnium
    distribution of, 155f
    in soils, 151, 167n11
half-moon motifs, 188
Hall, S. H., 322
hammers, 320
hammerstones, 287
    deposition context of, 300t
    dimensions of, 286t

examples of, 288f
frequency of, 284t, 297t, 298t
Hammond, Norman, 4, 84
    ceramic classification by, 176
    clay bead dating by, 266
    landscape research by, 12–13
    sherd-lined pits research by, 102, 104n1
    tool materials research by, 281, 318, 330
Hansen, R. D., 189
Harrigan, Ryan, 5, 295, 337, 380
Harrison, Peter D., 12–13, 280
Harrison-Buck, Eleanor, 7, 20
Headrick, Anabeth, 5, 7, 332
health indicators, 134, 136–138
Hester, Thomas, 281
Hillbank Red ceramics
    chemical content of, 182
    disks made of, 271, 272f
    frequency of, 183t, 186t, 190t
"house society" model, 6
    components of, 23–24
    supportive evidence for, 62
Huaquechula crosses, 367–368
Huetche ceramics, location of, 177
Humboldt Celt, symbolism of, 370–375, 370f
Hummingbird-Mullins River granite, 322
hunting. *See* fauna
hyperostosis, porotic, 136t, 137t, 138
hypoplasias, 136t, 137t, 138

iconography. *See* symbolism
iguanas, frequency of, 387t
illite, in clay, 145
imports. *See* procurement zones
INAA (instrumental neutron activation analysis), 77
    ceramic groups determined by, 155–157, 156f
    for chemical characterization of soils, 151
    obsidian sources determined by, 309–310, 315n1
    procedure for, 166–167n10
    reliability of, 155
incensarios, 266f, 267
Incense Burner Renewal ceremony, 83
incised ceramics, 180. *See also specific types of incised ceramics*
infections, bone, 136t, 137t, 138
inhumation, 110, 112–113
instrumental neutron activation analysis. *See* INAA
iron deficiency, 138
iron oxides
    in clay, 147t, 167n13
    coloration by, 153
    examples of, *154*
    frequency of, 153
    silt-sized, 149, 166n8
Isaza, Ilean, 7, 295–296, 332
Ixcanrio Orange ceramics
    findings of, 238, 242, 250
    frequency of, 186t, 190t
Ixtepeque, obsidian from, 310, 310t, 311f, 314f
Izapa cross, 374, 374f

Jacob, J. S., 280
jade. *See also* greenstone
    offerings, 70, 74
    procurement of, 325t
    properties of, 323
jars
    absence of, 172
    appearance of, 174–175, 180
    changes in, 180, 181–182
    characteristics of, 171t
    effigy, 185
    forms of, 179f
    rims of, 173f
jewelry. *See* adornments
Jocote Brown ceramics, 177–178
Johnson, I. W., 335
Johnson, W., 157
Joralemon, P. D., 375
Joventud Red ceramics, 97
    disks made of, 273
    findings of, 196, 197f, 200, *201*
    forms of, 173f
    frequency of, 172t, 174, 181t, 183t, 190t
    imported, 173–174
    replacement of, 171t
Joyce, R. A., 417

Kan Balam, 373, 373f
Kan cross, 131, 132, 371
kaolinite, in clay, 145
K'atabche'k'ax (Late Formative period), 13
    burials, early facet, 61t, 115–121
    burials, late facet, 121–126
    burials, terminal facet, 126–132
    caches of, 70–71
    carved bone of, 362–363
    ceramics, advent of, 179–180
    ceramics, early facet, 202–209
    ceramics, late facet, 181–185, 194t, 210–239
    ceramics, terminal facet, 185–189, 194t, 238–255
    construction phases of, 56–59
    faunal proportions of, 385f, 386–387t, 390f
    musical instruments from, 264, 264f
    obsidian from, 308, 310t
    roller stamps from, 265, 265f
    shell frequency of, 336t, 342–343t, 344t
    skeletal bones of, 134t
    tool deposits of, 296
    tool frequency of, 327t
K'axob
    caches of, 68, 69t, 81–82, 81t
    ceramic characteristics of, 171t
    ceramic sequence, 194t
    ceramic styles of, 162–165, 164f
    chipped stone tools of, 283
    chronology of, 13–16, 16t
    cross vessels of, 377–378
    debitage of, 283, 291–296
    dimensions of, 25–26, 25t

geology of, 144–145
greenstone of, 353–356, 357t
mapping, 12–13
mortuary patterns of, 110–138
obsidian in, 307
shell ornaments of, 336
sherd-lined pits of, 89t, 90–95
site map of, 2f
slate of, 356–357, 357f, 359
soil sampling in, 148f
stone tools of, 276
tools of, 283–291
Kekchi Maya hearths, 79
Kent, K. P., 271
K'iche' language, ceramics named in, 3
Killion, Thomas W., 13
kilns, sherd-lined pits as, 102, 104
Kimilk'ax (Postclassic period), 13, 194t
King, R. B., 149, 157
kinship, 6
    burials based on, 114, 117, 120–121
    succession based on, 84–85
Knapp, B., 68
Kosakowsky, L. J., 175
kuum (softened maize), 101

Lagartos Punctated ceramics, 181t
Laguna Verde Incised ceramics, 70
    findings of, 206, *207*, 246, *247*
    forms of, 184f
    frequency of, 181t, 183t, 186t, 190t
Lamanai, 6, 12, 160
Landa, Diego de, 335
landscape features, 11–13, 383–384
Laporte, Juan Pedro, 3
Las Ruinas de Arenal, Belize, caches of, 75, 75f
Late Formative period. *See K'atabche'k'ax*
leaching, 154
Lee, T. A., Jr., 361
Lévi-Strauss, C., 6, 23–24
Lewenstein, S. M., 305
limestone
    ceramic production using, 144
    locations of, 144–145
    procurement of, 317, 325t
    properties of, 323
    in sherd-lined pits, 100–102
    variability of, 153
lip-to-lip caches, 58, 69t, 79, 183
Living with the Ancestors (McAnany), 13
lizards, frequency of, 387t
Lockard, A. K., 369
López Varela, Sandra L., 7, 13, 15, 74, 140
Lowe, G. W., 178
Lucha Incised ceramics, 186t, 190t

MacNeish, R., 335
macroblades
    deposition context of, 300t

dimensions of, 286t
frequency of, 284t, 297t, 298t
purpose of, 285–286
stemmed, 286
from Taysal cache, 77–78
macroflakes, 291–292, 291t, 292f
magnesium, in ceramics, 182
Mahalanobis distance calculation, 159
maize
    evidence of farming, 8
    flake scattering and, 304
    soaking, 100–102
    tools for producing, 327
males, authority of, 82
mammals
    bone proportions of, 392–393t
    deposition context of, 389, 390f, 391
    frequency of, 386t, 388–389
mammiform vessels, 188, 238, 239f, 250, 251f
Mamom ceramics
    burials and, 114
    characteristics of, 171t
    codification of, 3
    frequency of, 172t, 181t, 183t, 186t, 190t
    location of, 177
    shell in, 149
manos
    definition of, 320
    dimensions of, 318t
    frequency of, 326t, 328t, 329t
    raw materials for, 325
    subtypes of, 320
marble, calcite, 322, 325t
Marginella sp.
    frequency of, 400t, 403–406t, 407–408
    identification of, 401f, 402
    purpose of, 410, 412
marine shells. *See also* mollusca
    for adornment, 339–340
    frequency of, 387t, 389
mariposas, 269–271, 270f
marl. *See* sascab
masks
    on ceramics, 185
    on ocarinas, 264, 264f
    were-jaguar, 375–376, 376f
mass burials, 76, 84, 132
Masson, Marilyn, 5, 13, 71–72, 380
Matamore Dichrome ceramics
    appearance of, 175
    findings of, 200, *201*
mazamas, frequency of, 386t
McAnany, Patricia A.
    cache research by, 72, 74
    cross motif research by, 369
    formal tool codification by, 283
    landscape research by, 12–13
    obsidian codification by, 315n1
McSwain, R. A., 289

memory, caches marking, 67–68
metamorphic materials, 322–324
metates
    dimensions of, 318t
    frequency of, 326t, 328t, 329t
    granite, 322–323
    raw materials for, 325
    subtypes of, 320
micrite, in clay, 147t, *152*, 154
microcrystalline silica, 322
microdebitage. *See* flakes
microprobe analysis, of ceramics, 188
middens
    debitage frequency in, 301t
    fauna frequency in, 390f, 391–395
    obsidian frequency in, 313t
    shell frequency in, 344t, 345
    tool frequency in, 329t
Middle Formative period. *See Chaakk'ax*
Miksicek, Charles, 8
Milky Way, symbolism of, 371
Miller, M., 364
minerals
    aplastic, 145, 147, 149, 153–155
    clay, in soils, 145
    petrographic groupings of, 153–155
Mixtec, 82
Mock, S. B., 66
mollusca
    identification of, 399–402
    Operation 1, 402–407
    purpose of, 411–412
    spatial analysis of, 408–411
    species of, 400t
    temporal analysis of, 408–411
Monaghan, J., 71, 418
Monkey Falls ceramics, 97, 163
    frequency of, 183t, 186t, 190t
    technological changes in, 182
monkey motifs, 188, 268, 269f
monocrystalline quartz, in clay, *152*
mortuary rituals. *See also* burials
    Chaakk'ax patterns of, 110–115
    construction phases and, 60–62, 61t
    digital resources for, 107
    health indicators and, 134, 136, 136t, 137t, 138
    K'atabche'k'ax patterns of, 115–132
    Nohalk'ax patterns of, 132–134
Mountain Pine granite, 322
mudstone, in clay, *154*
Munsell coloration, 144
muscovite granite, 355
musical instruments, fired clay, 264–265
Muxanal Red-on-Cream
    forms of, 173f
    frequency of, 172t, 174, 181t, 183t
mythology. *See* symbolism

National Science Foundation (NSF), funding by, 13

NBC. *See* Northern Belizean Chert
needles, bone, 358f, 359
Negras, Piedras, 80
Nelken-Terner, A., 335
Nelson, F. W., 309–310
Nelson, S., 271
Nephronaias sp.
    frequency of, 400t, 403–406t
    identification of, 400–402, 401f
    of Operation 1, 404–405
    of Operation 7, 407
    of Operation 13, 408
    ornaments, 295–296, 341
    purpose of, 409, 411–412
net sinkers, 267–268, 268f
    reworked, 269–271, 270f
neutron activation. *See* INAA
New River Valley, landscape of, 12
NISP. *See* Number of Identified Specimens
Nohalk'ax (Early Classic period), 13
    burials of, 61t, 132–134
    ceramic complexes of, early facet, 189–191, 194t, 256–261
    construction phases of, 57–59
    disks of, 273f
    earflares of, 267f
    faunal proportions of, 385f, 386–387t, 390f
    obsidian from, 308–309, 310t
    shell frequency of, 336t, 343t
    skeletal bones of, 134t
    tool deposits of, 296
    tool frequency of, 327t
Nohmul, 6, 12, 94
noncalcareous matrix, 182
nondiagnostic bifaces, 285
Northern Belizean Chert (NBC)
    attributes of, 295t
    availability of, 281–282, 281t
    flakes, 294
    frequency of, 284t
    scattering of, 303–304, 305t
Novella, R. A., 336
NSF. *See* National Science Foundation
Number of Identified Specimens (NISP), 384

obsidian
    characteristics of, 307
    codification of, 315n1
    cores, 312t
    deposition context of, 312–314, 313t
    dimensional variables of, 311–312, 312t
    extraction of, 307
    flakes, 312t
    frequency of, 309t, 310t, 313t, 314–315
    INAA of, 309–310, 315n1
    K'axob findings of, 307
    by operation and construction phase, 308–309
    platform preparation for, 310t, 311
    polyhedral, 312t

prismatic, 312t
procurement of, 77, 309–311, 313–314
ritual deposits of, 276
sources of, 309–311, 315n1
technology for production of, 311–312
temporality of, 308–309, 308f
types of, 308–309, 309t, 310t
ocarinas, 264–265, 264f
offerings
    ceramic styles for, 183, 185
    "Charlie Chaplin," 75–76
    color-coded, 74–75, 74f
    deer, 71–72
    placement of, 67
    symbolism of, 66
    of Yucatec Maya, 71
    of Zinacantan Maya, 67
Oliva shells, 338f, 339, 340, 345
Olmec
    authority derived from, 5
    symbolic bowl art of, 370–375
    were-jaguar art of, 375–377, 376f, 377f
Operation 1
    burials of, 27, 56, 61t, 115, 121–124, 127–130
    caches of, 66, 68–71
    ceramics of, 56, 195t, 268
    chert of, 282
    chipped stone tools of, 283
    construction trends of, 27, 56–57
    cross motif in, 369–370
    dimension patterns of, 60t
    disks found in, 271–272, 272f
    incensario fragments of, 266f, 267
    mollusca analysis of, 402–407
    musical instruments from, 264, 264f
    obsidian of, 308, 313t
    phase 1a of, 28f
    phase 1b of, 29f
    phase 2d of, 30f
    phase 4 of, 31f
    phase 6a of, 32f
    phase 6b of, 33f
    phase 7 of, 34f
    phase 8a of, 70–71
    phase 8c of, 35f, 56, 71
    phase 9 of, 36f, 72, 76
    phase 12 of, 37f, 56–57
    shell frequency of, 336t, 342–343t, 346–347t, 402–407
    sherd-lined pits of, 27, 91–92, 92t, 93f, 101f
    tool frequency at, 297t, 328t
    zone 9 of, 240
    zone 15 of, 240
    zone 17 of, 242
    zone 18 of, 242–245
    zone 30a of, 210
    zone 38 of, 210
    zone 41 of, 212
    zone 42 of, 212
    zone 77 of, 214

    zone 78 of, 216
    zone 80 of, 216
    zone 81 of, 218
    zone 83 of, 220
    zone 88 of, 220
    zone 100 of, 202
    zone 103 of, 202
    zone 107 of, 220
    zone 113b of, 202
    zone 115 of, 204
    zone 118 of, 204
    zone 121a of, 206
    zone 135 of, 206
    zone 137 of, 200
    zone 143 of, 200
    zone 152a of, 206
    zone 208 of, 196–197
    zone 233 of, 198
    zone 236b of, 246
Operation 7
    burials of, 57, 61t, 133
    caches of, 76–77
    ceramics of, 56, 189, 191, 195t
    chipped stone tools of, 283, 283f
    construction trends of, 57
    dimension patterns of, 60t
    disks found in, 271, 273f
    fired clay pieces of, 268–269, 269f
    mollusca analysis of, 403–406t
    obsidian of, 309, 313t
    phase 1 of, 38f
    phase 3a of, 39f
    phase 5 of, 40f
    phase 7 of, 41f
    shell frequency of, 336t, 343t, 347t, 403–406t
    sherd-lined pits of, 92t, 93
    tool frequency at, 297t, 328t
    zone 3 of, 248
    zone 58 of, 248
    zone 59 of, 248
    zone 63 of, 256
    zone 69 of, 256
Operation 8
    burials of, 57, 61t, 124–125
    caches of, 78
    ceramics of, 57, 195t
    chipped stone tools of, 283
    construction trends of, 57
    dimension patterns of, 60t
    disks found in, 272, 272f
    mollusca analysis of, 403–406t
    phase 1a of, 42f
    phase 1c of, 43f
    phase 2a of, 44f
    phase 2b of, 45f
    shell frequency of, 336t, 343t, 403–406t
    sherd-lined pits of, 57, 92t, 93
    Structure 102 of, 78
    tool frequency at, 297t, 328t

zone 6 of, 222
zone 8 of, 222
zone 10 of, 224
zone 13 of, 238
zone 22 of, 224
zone 25 of, 226
Operation 10
    burials of, 57–58, 61t, 125
    caches of, 78–79
    ceramics of, 58, 195t
    construction trends of, 57–58
    dimension patterns of, 60t
    disks found in, 271–272, 272f, 273
    mollusca analysis of, 403–406t
    net sinkers of, 267–268, 268f
    obsidian of, 311f, 313t
    phase 1a of, 46f
    phase 3 of, 46f
    phase 4 of, 47f
    shell frequency of, 336t, 347t, 403–406t
    tool frequency at, 297t, 328t
    zone 9 of, 228
    zone 10 of, 230
    zone 23 of, 258
    zone 25 of, 230
Operation 11
    burials of, 58, 61t, 115, 117–118, 124, 130–131
    caches of, 79–80
    ceramics of, 58, 189, 191, 195t
    chipped stone tools of, 283
    construction trends of, 58
    debitage of, 291
    dimension patterns of, 60t
    disks found in, 271–272, 272f
    mollusca analysis of, 403–406t
    obsidian of, 308, 311f, 313t
    phase 1a of, 48f
    phase 4a of, 49f
    phase 5 of, 50f
    phase 6 of, 51f
    shell frequency of, 336t, 342–343t, 346–347t, 403–406t
    sherd-lined pits of, 58, 92t, 93–94
    tool frequency at, 297t, 328t
    zone 7 of, 232
    zone 8 of, 234
    zone 16c of, 232
    zone 17 of, 232
    zone 19 of, 252
    zone 20c of, 234
    zone 53 of, 234
    zone 90a of, 208
    zone 93c of, 208
Operation 12
    burials of, 58–59, 61t, 125, 126f, 130, 133
    caches of, 80–81
    ceramics of, 58–59, 195t
    chipped stone tools of, 283
    construction trends of, 58–59
    debitage of, 291

    dimension patterns of, 60t
    disks found in, 271–272, 272f
    mollusca analysis of, 403–406t
    obsidian of, 313t
    phase 2 of, 52f
    phase 3 of, 53f
    phase 5 of, 54f
    shell frequency of, 336t, 343t, 347t, 403–406t
    sherd-lined pits of, 92–93, 92t, 99f
    tool frequency at, 297t, 328t
    zone 4 of, 254
    zone 30b of, 254
    zone 31 of, 254
    zone 33 of, 254
    zone 40 of, 236
    zone 42 of, 236
    zone 57 of, 236
Operation 13
    burials of, 59, 61t, 133–134, 133f
    ceramics of, 59, 189, 191, 195t
    chipped stone tools of, 283
    construction trends of, 59
    dimension patterns of, 60t
    mollusca analysis of, 403–406t
    obsidian of, 308, 309, 313t
    phases 2 and 3 of, 55f
    shell frequency of, 336t, 403–406t
    tool frequency at, 297t, 328t
    zone 27 of, 260
"orange peel" flakes, 292–293
orange slips
    emergence of, 171t
    varieties of, 187
Orange Walk, 162f, 166n4
ornaments. *See* adornments
Orthalicus princeps
    frequency of, 400t, 403–406t
    identification of, 401f, 402
    of Operation 1, 406–407
    of Operation 11 and 12, 407–408
    purpose of, 410, 412
oval bifaces, 284–285
    cortex of, 289
    deposition context of, 300t
    dimensions of, 286t
    frequency of, 284t, 297t, 298t
    polish on, 296, 299t

paintings, musical instruments in, 264–265
Palenque cross, 373–374, 373f
paleosol
    debitage frequency in, 301t
    fauna frequency in, 392–394t
    shell frequency in, 344t
    tool frequency in, 329t
paper production, 318
pastes, ceramic, 151
    changes in, 182
    preparation of, 159–160

pecking tools, 320–321
Pectinidae sp.
  frequency of, 400t, 403–406t
  identification of, 401f, 402
  of Operation 1, 405
  of Operation 7, 407
  purpose of, 409, 411
pectorals, 267
pendants
  shell, 337t, 338f
  slate, 356–357, 357f
percussion tools
  dimensions of, 318t, 320f
  frequency of, 326t, 328t, 329t
  subtypes of, 320–321
Perez, T., 189
personal adornments. *See* adornments
Peterson, Polly Ann, 72, 283
petrographic analysis
  aplastic or mineral grains grouped by, 153–155
  digital resources for, 141
  groundmass grouped by, 153
  of paste preparation, 159–160
  of soil differences, 145, 149
Phillips, D. A., Jr., 265, 268
phi-square tests, 94
Pico de Orizaba, obsidian from, 310–311, 310t
Pita Incised ceramics, 186t, 190t
Pital Cream ceramics, 172t, 173f
pits. *See also* sherd-lined pits
  debitage frequency in, 301t
  fauna frequency in, 390f, 392–394t
  obsidian frequency in, 313t
  shell frequency in, 345, 346–347t
  tool frequency in, 329t
plaster floors. *See* floors
platforms
  apsidal, 72–74, 73t
  obsidian preparation using, 310t, 311
  shape patterns of, 60t
Pleistocene, warming during, 144–145
plinths, shape patterns of, 59, 60t
Pohl, M., 70, 71, 72, 280
polish
  on flakes, 295, 295t
  frequency of, 296, 299t
  on tools, 280, 290
polished stone tools. *See* ground and polished stone tools
Polvero Black ceramics
  found sherds of, 268, 269f
  frequency of, 186t
polychrome ceramics, 133, 188, 191
polycrystalline quartz, in clay, 147, 147t, *152*
polyhedral obsidian cores, 312t
Pomacea flagellata
  in burials, 112, 115, 117–118, 345
  frequency of, 400t, 403–406t
  identification of, 400, 401f
  of Operation 1, 402, 403

of Operation 7-13, 407–408
  purpose of, 409, 411–412
  in sherd-lined pits, 95, 99–100
Pope, K. O., 280
Popol Vuh, 79, 371
porcelain production, 145
porosity, ceramic, 98–99
porotic hyperostosis, 136t, 137t, 138
porphyritic granite, 322–323
postholes
  debitage types by, 301t
  obsidian frequency by, 313t
  shell frequency by, 345, 346–347t
potbellied sculptures, 185
pottery. *See* ceramics
pounders, 320
Pratt, J. H., 149, 157
Prechtel, M., 415
preforms, 284, 297t, 298t, 300t
principal components analysis, of ceramics, 158–159
Pring, D. C., 175, 185, 187
prismatic obsidian blades, 312t
procurement zones
  for ceramics, 173–174
  for chert, 298–299, 299t, 325t
  for greenstone, 315, 353, 355
  for ground stone tools, 324, 325t 326t, 327t
  for hard stone tools, 7–8, 276–277, 282
  for obsidian, 77, 309–311, 313–314
  for slate, 357
projectile points, 288, 289f
  deposition context of, 300t
  dimensions of, 286t
  frequency of, 284t, 297t, 298t
protoclassic ceramics, 188
public rituals, 78–79, 82
Pucte Brown ceramics, 186t, 190t
Puleston, Dennis, 280
Puletan Red ceramics, 181t
Pulltrouser Swamp
  clay mineral content in, 145
  farming at, 280
  project, 12–13
  soil composition in, 151, 157
  topography of, 145
pyramids
  identification of, 3
  location of, 14f, 15f
  social structure and, 6
  "Structure 18," 76

quadripartite motif. *See* cross motif
quarry blanks, 291–292, 292f
  deposition context of, 301t
  dimensions of, 291t
quarry sites, 150f, 151
quartz
  in clay, 147, 147t
  examples of, *152, 154*

firing, 165
frequency of, 153
procurement of, 325t
properties of, 323
silt-sized, 149, 149t
veins, 323, 325t
quartzite, 323, 325t

rabbits, frequency of, 386t
radiocarbon dating, 178
raw materials
for greenstone, 355
for ground stone tools, 317, 321–325
for hard stone tools, 281–282, 281t, 304–305
for shell working, 335, 344t
Real ceramics
characteristics of, 177
varieties of, 172t
reclamation, wetland, 280
rectangular block metate, 320
recycling, tool, 289, 290
red-ware ceramics. *See also specific types of red-ware ceramics*
coloration of, 153
sites of, 3
Reilly, Kent, 371
renewal ceremonies, 188
Repollo Impressed ceramics, 183t
reptiles
deposition context of, 390f
frequency of, 387t, 388
residential structures
building materials of, 24, 82
characteristics of, 4
construction phases of, 26–59
dimensions of, 25–26, 25t, 59–60, 60t
distinctions of, 62
excavation recording for, 24–25
fabrication of fired clay artifacts at, 263
house society model of, 23–24
mortuary rituals at, 60–62, 61t
projects uncovering, 3–4
shape patterns of, 59–60, 60t
trends in, 23, 27, 56–59
resist-technique ceramics, 178
reworked bifaces and blades, 285, 285f
deposition context of, 300t
dimensions of, 286t
frequency of, 284t, 297t, 298t
reworked clay, 269–273
Rice, P. M., 97
rituals. *See also* mortuary rituals; offerings
artisan production and, 7
axis mundi of, 67
caching and, 65–85
ceramic styles and, 183, 185
changes in, 7
debitage scattering, 303–304, 305t
dedicatory, 66
epigraphic understanding of, 84

flake scattering for, 80, 303–304, 305t
ideologies of, 7
incensarios for, 267
memory and identity markers of, 67–68
musical instruments in, 264–265
obsidian deposits for, 276
public, 78–79, 82
purpose of, 83
space and time markers of, 67
termination offerings for, 66
Robertson-Freidel, R. A., 160
Robin, C., 112
rocks
metamorphic, 322–324
sampling, 150f, 151
rodents
bone proportions of, 392–393t
deposition context of, 389, 390f, 391
frequency of, 386t, 388
roller stamps, 265, 265f
Romney, D. H., 149
rope, twisted, 267
Rovner, I., 305
rubbing tools
dimensions of, 318t
frequency of, 326t, 328t, 329t
purpose of, 321
rulership. *See* authority
Rye, O., 102, 160, 161

sampling
fauna, 384
rock, 150f, 151
soil, 144–145, 146f, 148f
San Martin Brown ceramics, 57, 76
findings of, 256, *257*
frequency of, 186t, 190t
San Martín Jilotepeque obsidian, 310–311, 310t
San Pablo Ridge, 145
sandstone
arkose, 322
procurement of, 325t
properties of, 323
quartz, 323
Santa Teresa ceramics, 186t, 190t
Sapote Striated ceramics, 183t, 190t
sascab. *See also* limestone
composition of, 145
pits lined by, 89t
use of, 26
Saul, F. P., 138
Saul, J. M., 138
Savana Orange ceramics, 178
scar patterns
on flakes, 294
on tools, 290
scattering
of flakes, 80, 303–304, 305t
of skeletal remains, 128

Schele, L., 67
Schiffer, M. B., 97
schist
    procurement of, 325t
    properties of, 323–324
Schneider, G., 170, 188
scrapers, 288f
    deposition context of, 300t
    dimensions of, 286t
    frequency of, 284t, 297t, 298t
sculptures
    boulder, 185
    Palenque, 373–374, 373f
    potbellied, 185
seated burials, 135t
sedentism, technology and, 176–177
Seibal
    caches of, 83
    ceramic sequence of, 194t
    Real ceramics of, 177, 185
semiprecious stones. *See* stone ornaments
serpentinite
    procurement of, 325t
    properties of, 324
serpents
    deposition context of, 389, 390f
    frequency of, 387t
    symbolism of, 70
settlement
    cosmology of, 67
    growth theories of, 305n1
    hierarchies, 9
    pre-K'axob, 4
sex
    burials determinative of, 110
    ratio, 134, 135t
Shafer, Harry J., 280, 281, 290
Sharer, R. J., 6, 177–178, 187
sharks, frequency of, 387t
shell working
    architectural features and, 346–347t
    artisans, 335
    burial "1-14," 348f
    burial "1-28," 341
    burial "1-32," 349f
    burial "1-35," 112, 339, 340
    burial "1-43," 340, 341t
    by ceramic complex, 342–343t
    Chaakk'ax, 336t, 342f, 342t, 344t
    classification of, 337t
    cultural trends in, 340–341, 345, 350
    development of, 335
    edge grinding types for, 339t
    frequency of, 336t, 340, 342–343f, 345
    K'atabche'k'ax, 336t, 342–343t, 344t
    methods of, 338, 350
    Nohalk'ax, 336t, 343t
    by operation, 342–343t
    purpose of, 335

raw materials for, 335, 344t
    studies of, 335–336
shells. *See also* mollusca; *specific species of shells*
    beads made from, 266, 266f, 337t
    in clay, 147t, 149, *154*
    color-coding, 74, 364
    families of, 338
    freshwater, 295–296, 341
    irregular shaped, 340f, 341
    of K'axob, 336
    marine, 339–340
    preservation of, 337
    reshaped, 337t
    in sherd-lined pits, 95, 99–100, 346–347t
    snail, 364
    symbolism of, 335, 350
    types of, 337t
Shepard, Anna, 160, 161
sherd-lined pits
    bimodality of, 95–96
    building, 90
    for ceramic manufacturing, 102, 104
    ceramic types for, 88, 90, 97–98
    ceramic vessels found in, 196, 204
    characteristics of, 96–97
    chronology of, 90
    comparative data on, 88, 89t
    construction phases and, 89t
    for cooking, 98–100
    dimensions of, 90, 91f, 95–96, 95f
    distribution of, 96t, 97f
    durability of, 97
    excavation areas of, 91–93
    facilities of, 87–88
    fauna frequency in, 390f, 392–394t
    firing indicators for, 88, 89t, 102, 104
    functions of, 20, 94, 98–104, 103t
    lime deposits in, 100–102
    linings other than, 88
    for maize soaking, 100–102
    morphology of, 95–104
    of Operation 1, 27, 91–92, 92t, 93f, 101f
    of Operation 7, 92t, 93
    of Operation 8, 57, 92t, 93
    of Operation 11, 58, 92, 92t, 93–94
    of Operation 12, 92–93, 92t, 99f
    shells in, 95, 99–100, 346–347t
    spatial analysis of, 91–95
    stratigraphy of, 100
    termination of, 98
    vessel fragments of, 88, 90, 96–97
    in workspaces, 94
sherds
    body, 97–98
    reworked, 269–273
Shipley, W. E., III, 323
sidescrapers, 288f
    deposition context of, 300t
    dimensions of, 286t

frequency of, 284t, 297t, 298t
Sierra Red ceramics, 77, 78, 90
    appearance of, 175
    characteristics of, 171t
    classification of, 175–176
    cross motif on, 368, 368f
    findings of, 200–237, 242–249
    forms of, 184f
    frequency of, 181t, 183t, 186t, 190t
    technological changes in, 182
silcrete
    importance of, 317
    procurement of, 325t
    properties of, 324
silica
    microcrystalline, 322
    polish, 280, 290
sinkers, net, 267–271
Sinopoli, C. M., 102
skeletal bones
    animal proportions of, 391–396
    demography of, 134, 134t, 138
    health indicators in, 134, 136, 136t, 137t, 138
    position of, 135t
    shell working and, 340, 341t
slate ornaments, 356–357, 357f, 359
slingshot stones. *See yuntunob*
slips, ceramic
    black, 163, 188
    examples of, 154, *158*
    orange, 171t
    paste preparation for, 160
    red, 174
    stylistic attributes of, 163
smectite clays, 145
Smith, Robert E., 3
smoothing tools, 319, 321
snail shells, 364
snakes. *See* serpents
soapstone ornaments, 356–357, 357f, 359
social structure, 6
Society Hall Red ceramics, 71, 76
    findings of, 214–216, 222–225, 228–229, 240–247
    frequency of, 181t, 183t, 190t
    stylistic attributes of, 163, 171t
    uses for, 182
soils
    aplastic mineral composition of, 145, 147
    chemical characterization of, 151
    clay mineral content of, 145
    matrices of, 149, 149t
    petrographic analysis of, 145, 149
    sampling, 144–145, 146f, 148f
    zones of, 150f
spalling, of clay, 165
sparitic calcite
    in clay, 147t
    examples of, *152*
    in rocks, *163*

silt-sized, 149, 149t
spatial analysis
    of ceramic complexes, 173–174
    of fauna, 384–385, 385f
    of mollusca, 408–411
    of sherd-lined pits, 91–95
specialization. *See* artisans
spindle whorls, 265, 265f
spirits, objects housing, 83
Spondylus sp., 350
stamps, roller, 265, 265f
steaming. *See* cooking
Steensburg, A., 305n1
stelae
    cross, 374, 374f
    placement of, 83–84
stemmed macroblades, 286
    caches of, 302, 303f
    deposition context of, 300t
    dimensions of, 286t
    examples of, 287f
    frequency of, 284t, 297t, 298t
stone fragments
    dimensions of, 318t, 319
    frequency of, 326t, 328t, 329t
    large, 319
    raw materials for, 325
    small, 321
    subtypes of, 319–320
stone ornaments
    greenstone as, 353–356, 357t
    slate as, 356–357, 357f, 359
stone tools. *See also* chipped stone tools; ground and
        polished stone tools
    acquisition of, 296–300
    burned, 291t, 292
    by ceramic complex, 298t
    chert for making, 147, 281
    codification of, 283
    cortex of, 289
    debitage of, 291–296, 291t
    deposition context of, 300t
    digital resources for, 277
    dimensions of, 286t, 291t
    frequency of, 284t, 297t, 298t
    household use of, 280–282
    identification of, 283–284
    of K'axob, 283–291
    polish found on, 280, 290, 299t
    preforms for, 284
    procurement zones for, 7–8, 276–277, 282
    raw materials for, 281–282, 281t, 304–305
    recycling, 289, 290
    scar patterns on, 290
    standardization of, 281
    temporal changes in use of, 296–300
    use-wear of, 290–291
    for wetland reclamation, 280
stone-lined pits. *See* sherd-lined pits

storage vessels, 179f
Storey, Rebecca, 5, 80, 106, 369
Stowe, Leanne, 283
stratigraphy, of sherd-lined pits, 100
Strombidae shells, assemblage of, 338, 338f
Stuart, D., 77, 83
surfaces
    debitage frequency on, 301t
    obsidian frequency on, 313t
    shell frequency on, 346t
    tool frequency on, 329t
Swasey
    burials, 114
    ceramics, 175–176
symbolism
    anthropomorphic, 264, 357
    butterfly, 267
    color, 364
    creation, 79
    cross motif, 71, 72
    deer, 71–72
    fertility, 71, 72, 74, 364
    flake scattering, 304
    frog, 71, 72
    Humboldt Celt, 370–375, 370f
    Kan cross, 371
    Milky Way, 371
    monkey, 188, 268, 269f
    ocarina, 264–265
    offering, 66
    Olmec system of, 370–375
    rope, 267
    serpent, 70
    shell, 335, 350
    tree, 83–84, 373–374, 373f, 374f
    were-jaguar, 375–377, 376f

Tablet of the Cross, 373–374, 373f
Taschek, J. T., 75–76
Taube, Karl, 364, 372–373
technology
    ceramic, 176–177
    obsidian production, 311–312
    paper-making, 318
tecomate
    replacement of, 171t, 174, 180
    types and forms of, 173f
tectonic activity, 151
teeth, health indicated by, 137t, 138
tempering ceramics, 154–155, 160, 166
Temple of the Cross, 373–374, 373f
temporal analysis
    of debitage, 297–298
    of ground and polished stone tools, 325, 327
    of hard stone tools, 296–300
    of mollusca, 408–411
    of obsidian, 308–309, 308f
Teotihuacan, divining bowls of, 372–373, 372f
termination rituals

burials and, 130, 133–134
    caches from, 66
    greenstone from, 355
thermal conductivity, 97, 98–99
Thompson, Fred G., 400, 402
Thompson, J. Eric, 3, 67, 71
Tierra Mojada ceramics
    classification of, 178
    forms of, 173f
    imported, 174
Tikal
    caches of, 68, 72
    ceramic sequence of, 194t
    obsidian from, 311
Timax ceramics
    findings of, 198, *199*
    frequency of, 172t
    imported, 174
time and space. *See also* spatial analysis; temporal analysis
    caches marking, 67
    figurines denoting, 75–76
tinklers
    characteristics of, 339
    composition of, 349f
    subtypes of, 337t
Tlaloc, 75
Tohil, legend of, 71
tools. *See* chipped stone tools; ground and polished stone tools; stone tools
Toribio ceramics
    findings of, 198, *199*
    frequency of, 172t
trade. *See* procurement zones
tranchet-bit tools, 286–287
    deposition context of, 300t
    dimensions of, 286t
    examples of, 287f
    flakes from, 291t, 292–293, 294f, 301t
    frequency of, 284t, 297t, 298t
tree symbolism, 83–84, 373–374, 373f, 374f
triadic caches, 72–75, 73f, 74f
    greenstone in, 363–364
triangular bifaces, 288
    deposition context of, 300t
    dimensions of, 286t
    frequency of, 284t, 297t, 298t
tripodal metate, 320
Triunfo ceramics, 186t, 190t
T-shaped unifaces, 287
    dimensions of, 286t
    examples of, 289f
    frequency of, 284t, 297t, 298t
tubes, carved bone, 359, 360f
Turner, B. L., II, 12, 280
turtleback metate, 320, 320f
turtles
    deposition context of, 390f
    frequency of, 387t, 388
twins, cosmology and, 56

two-mica porphyritic granite, 322–323
type-variety classification
    benefits of, 169
    for middle formative period, 175–176
Tzakol ceramics, 186t, 190t

Uaxactun Project, 3, 194t
Uayeb ceremonies, 79
unifaces, 287
    deposition context of, 300t
    dimensions of, 286t
    examples of, 288f
    frequency of, 284t, 297t, 298t
Union Appliqué ceramics, 181t, 183t, 186t, 190t
Unionidae shells, 338, 338f, 350
use-wear, 290–291
Usulutan ceramics, 185
utilitarian
    caches, 79–80
    carved bones, 358f, 359

Valdés, Juan Antonio, 3
Valdez, F., Jr., 176
veins, quartz, 323, 325t
Versey, H. R., 149, 157
vessels
    "001," 198, *199*
    "002," 198, *199*
    "003," 200, *201*
    "004," 200, *201*
    "005," 204, 205f
    "006," 196, 197f
    "007," 196, 197f
    "008," 202, 203f
    "009," 202, *203*
    "010," 202, *203*
    "011," 220, *221*
    "012," 202, *203*
    "013," 204, 205f
    "014," 204, 205f
    "015," 206, *207*
    "016," 206, 207f
    "017," 200, *201*
    "018," 200, *201*
    "019," 206, *207*
    "020," 240, *241*
    "021," 240, *241*
    "022," 240, 241f
    "023," 240, *241*
    "024," 242, 243f
    "025," 242, 243f
    "028," 242, 243f
    "029," 214, 215f
    "030," 214, *215*
    "031," 242, 243f
    "032," 214, *215*
    "033," 244, 245f
    "034," 244, *245*, 369f
    "035," 214
    "036," 244, 245f
    "037," 244, *245*
    "038," 246
    "039," 210, *211*
    "040," 210, 211f
    "042," 210, *211*, 348f
    "043," 210, *211*
    "044," 212, *213*
    "045," 212, *213*
    "046," 216, *217*
    "047," 216, *217*
    "048," 216, *217*
    "049," 218, *219*
    "050," 218, *219*
    "051," 218, *219*
    "052," 220, *221*
    "053," 220, 221f
    "054," 220, *221*, 348f
    "055," 206, *207*
    "056," 246, 247f
    "057," 246, *247*
    "059," 248, *249*
    "060," 248, 249f
    "061," 222
    "062," 222
    "063," 222, *223*
    "064," 222
    "065," 222
    "066," 224, *225*
    "067," 224
    "068," 224
    "069," 226, *227*
    "070," 226, *227*
    "072," 226, *227*
    "073," 230, *231*
    "074," 230, 231f
    "075," 227, 228f
    "076," 227, 228f
    "077," 230, 231f
    "078," 230, 231f
    "079," 232
    "080," 232, 233f
    "081," 232, *233*
    "082," 232, *233*
    "083," 234, 235f
    "084," 234, *235*
    "085," 234, *235*
    "086," 208, 209f
    "087," 208, *209*
    "088," 234, *235*
    "090," 236, 237f
    "091," 236, 237f
    "092," 236, 237f
    "093," 236, 237f
    "095," 248, 249f
    "096," 250, 251f
    "097," 250, 251f
    "098," 250, 251f
    "100," 238, 239f

"101," 238, 239f
"102," 252, *253*
"103," 252, *253*
"104," 252, *253*
"106," 238, *239*
"107," 254, 255f
"108," 254, 255f
"109," 256, *257*
"110," 256, *257*
"111," 256, *257*
"112," 238, 239f
"113," 258, *259*
"114," 254, 255f
"115," 260, 261f
"116," 260, 261f
"117," 258, 259f
"118," 254, 255f
"121," 196, 197f
"122," 208, *209*
"124," 258, 259f
"125," 227, 228f
"126," 227, 228f
appliqué for, 268, 269f
categories of, 97–98
classification of, 195–196
cooking, 97, 179f, 319–320
cross, 164f, 185, 368–378
head covered by, 136
inverted, 66, 76, 78
lip-to-lip, 58, 69t, 79
mammiform, 188, 238, 239f, 250, 251f
Operation 1, 196–201
polychrome, 133, 188, 191
serving, 184f
for sherd-lined pits, 88, 90, 96–97
smashed, 66, 76
storage, 179f
supports for, 319–320
upright, 70
Vial, V. E., 149
vitrification, of clay, 165
Vogt, E. Z., 67, 82, 83
void patterns, in ceramics, 161
volcanic glass, altered. *See also* obsidian

procurement of, 325t
properties of, 324

wall tumble deposits
debitage types by, 301t, 302
shell frequency by, 345, 346–347t
tool types by, 329t
wedge-shaped unifaces. *See* T-shaped unifaces
were-jaguars, 375–377, 376f, 377f
wetlands
landscape features of, 11–12
reclamation of, 280
whistles. *See* ocarinas
Willey, Gordon, 3, 359, 361, 363
wits (mountains/pyramids), 84
Witsk'ax (Late Classic period), 13, 194t, 310t
wooden crosses, 83
"world trees," 83–84, 373–374, 373f, 374f
Wright, A. C. S., 149

Xe ceramics
characteristics of, 177–179
varieties of, 172t
xeroradiography
clay mineral content by, 145
process of, 161–162

Yaloche Cream ceramics, 252, *253*
Yucatec Maya, 71, 321
yuntunob (limestone slingshot stones)
in burials, 56
in caches, 72
dimensions of, 318t, 321f
frequency of, 326t, 328t, 329t
origin of, 321

Zinacantan Maya
house rituals of, 83
offering placement by, 67
residential construction by, 82
stelae of, 83–84
zirconium, in soils, 151
Zisman, S. A., 149, 157